P9-DMU-390

A Writer's Grammar

A Writer's Grammar

C. Beth Burch
Binghamton University, SUNY

New York   San Francisco   Boston
London   Toronto   Sydney   Tokyo   Singapore   Madrid
Mexico City   Munich   Paris   Cape Town   Hong Kong   Montreal

Vice President/Publisher: Eben W. Ludlow
Senior Supplement Editor: Donna Campion
Executive Marketing Manager: Ann Stypuloski
Production Manager: Eric Jorgensen
Project Coordination, Text Design,
    and Electronic Page Makeup: WestWords, Inc.
Cover Design Manager: John Callahan
Cover Illustration: Courtesy of PhotoDisc
Manufacturing Buyer: Al Dorsey
Printer and Binder: Courier Corporation—Stoughton
Cover Printer: Coral Graphic Services, Inc.

For permission to use copyrighted material, grateful acknowledgment is
made to the copyright holders on pp. 4, 12, 63, 69, 91, 106, 121, 125, 127,
131, 135 which are hereby made part of this copyright page.

Library of Congress Cataloging-in-Publication

Burch, C. Beth.
    A writer's grammar / C. Beth Burch.
        p. cm.
    ISBN 0-205-31804-5
        1. English language—Grammar. 2. English language—Rhetoric.
    3. English language— Style. I. Title.

    PE1112.B746 2002
    428.2—dc21

                                                                2002073178

Copyright © 2003 by Pearson Education, Inc.

All rights reserved. No part of this publication may be reproduced, stored
in a retrieval system, or transmitted, in any form or by any means, electronic, mechanical, photocopying, recording, or otherwise, without the pri-
or written permission of the publisher. Printed in the United States.

Please visit our Web site at http://www.ablongman.com

ISBN 0-205-31804-5

1 2 3 4 5 6 7 8 9 10—CRS—05 04 03 02

For Paul-William and Nathan,
whose love and silliness sustain me

Contents

Preface xiii
Acknowledgments xiv

Chapter 1

The Shape of Things: Sentence Patterns   1

Transitive Patterns   2
    Direct Object Pattern   3
    Figure 1.1 Direct Object Pattern   4
    About Prepositional Phrases   5
    Compound Elements in Patterns   7
    Indirect Object Pattern   8
    Objective Complement Pattern   11
    Figure 1.2 Objective Complement Pattern   12
    Possible Confusions: Appositives   14

Linking Patterns   15
    Predicate Noun Pattern   16
    Predicate Adjective Pattern   16

The Intransitive Pattern   19

The Big Picture: Looking at All the Patterns   21

Chapter 2

Naming the Parts, I: Form Classes,
Noun Clusters   25

Form Classes   26
    Nouns and Nounness, Nominals and Naming   26
    Adjectives and Noun Clusters   30
    Adjectives   30
    Other Parts of the Noun Cluster: The Determiner   33
    Other Parts of the Noun Cluster: Noun Adjuncts   33
    Other Parts of the Noun Cluster: Prepositional Phrases   34

Summing Up: Noun Clusters   37

Chapter **3**

Naming the Parts, 2: Form Classes, Verb Clusters, Structure Words 39

Verbs: The Heart of the Sentence **39**
  Verbs and Agreement   41

Conjugation of Open, Perfect Tenses   **43**

Conjugation of Open, Progressive Tenses   **44**
  Verb Clusters   48
  Auxiliaries and Verbs   48
  Adverbs   49
  Other Parts of the Verb Cluster: Intensifiers   50
  Other Parts of the Verb Cluster: Prepositional Phrases   51

Structure Words   **53**
  Determiners   53
  Pronouns   54
  Conjunctions   55
  Auxiliaries   57
  Intensifiers   58
  Interrogatives   58

Nominal Versus Verbal: A Rhetorical Observation   **59**

Summing Up: Verb Clusters   **60**

Chapter **4**

Patterns Transformed 61

Negative Transformations   **61**
  Figure 4.1 Negative Transformation   63

Question Transformations   **64**
  Creating Yes/No Question Transformations   65
  Creating Interrogative Question Transformations   65
  Questions by Intonation   66

Passive Transformations   **67**
  Figure 4.2 Passive Transformation   69

Expletive Transformation   **73**

Emphatic Transformations   **75**
  Shifting Emphasis with Inversion   75
  Creating Emphasis with the Cleft Sentence   77
  Creating Emphasis by Varying Diction or Word Choice   79

Mixing and Shifting Levels of Usage   81
Creating Emphasis by Formatting   82

Summing Up   84

Chapter **5**

Clustering, Compounding, Verbals, and Nominative Absolutes   *87*

Compound Sentence Elements   87

Verbals   89
Infinitives   90
Figure 5.1 Split Infinitive in Conversation Bubble; Gerund in Caption   91
Gerunds   94
Participles   98
Reviewing All Verbals   100

Nominative Absolutes   104
Figure 5.2 Nominative Absolute and Gerund   106
Rhetorical Impact of Absolutes   106
Distinguishing Nominative Absolutes from Verbals   110

Looking at Passages for Style   111

Putting it All Together   112

Chapter **6**

Joining and Combining Patterns and Other Elements   *113*

Distinguishing Phrases and Clauses   113

Distinguishing Independent Clauses and Dependent Clauses   116

Creating Compound Sentences   116
Creating Compound Sentences with a Semicolon Joining
Patterns   119
Creating Compound Sentences with Semicolon and
Conjunctive Adverb Joining Patterns   119
Creating Compound Sentences with a Colon Joining Patterns   120
Figure 6.1 Compound Sentence with Three Independent Clauses   121

Creating Complex Sentences   123
Creating Complex Sentences: The Adjective Clause   123
Restrictive and Nonrestrictive/Essential and Nonessential
Adjective Clauses   124
Figure 6.2 Adjective Clause, Participles, and Infinitive   125

Figure 6.3 Adjective Clause, Subordinator Ellipted   127
Adjective Clauses and Participial Phrases: Rhetorical Choices   127
Creating Complex Sentences: The Adverb Clause   129
Figure 6.4 Adverb Clause   131
Creating Complex Sentences: The Noun Clause   133
Figure 6.5 Noun Clauses   135
Clauses and Comparison   137

Creating Combination or Compound-Complex Sentences   138
Reviewing Patterns and Combinations   140
Looking Ahead   141

Chapter **7**

From Grammar to Style: Rhetorical Strategies and Figures   143

Parallelism   144

Antithesis   145

Anastrophe   146

Apposition   147

Parenthesis   148

Ellipsis   150

Asyndeton   151

Polysyndeton   152

Assonance   153

Alliteration   153

Anaphora   154

Epistrophe   155

Epanalepsis   156

Anadiplosis   156

Antimetabole   157

Onomatopoeia   158

Virtual Sentence   159

Chapter **8**

A Dozen Prose Passages: Reading for Grammatical Understanding   161

Gerald Early on Muhammad Ali   161

x

Oliver Sacks—from "A Leg to Stand On"   162

Rhonda White's Autobiography   163

Mary Roach and the Common Cold   164

Charles McGrath: Thinking about Internet Time   165

Thomas Paine's "The Crisis": Enjoining Patriots   166

Molly Ivins on America   166

Kim Hendon on Learning to Read in a Private Religious School   167

Wilbert Rideau: Why Prisons Don't Work   168

John Irving's Personal History: "Slipped Away"   168

George Orwell, "Marrakech"   169

Anne Bradstreet, a Seventeenth Century "Meditation, Divine and Moral"   169

Chapter **9**

A Punctuation Gallery   *171*

External Punctuation   171

     Period   171

     Question Mark   175

     Exclamation Point   177

     Passages to Punctuate: Terminal Marks   179

Internal Punctuation   180

     Comma   180

     Semicolon   190

     Colon   193

     Passages to Punctuate: Internal Marks   195

     Em Dash   196

     Hyphen   197

     Apostrophe   199

     Quotation Marks   200

     Parentheses   202

     Brackets   203

     Slash or Virgule   204

     Passages to Punctuate   207

Glossary   207

Index   221

Preface

A *Writer's Grammar* is designed in a sequence to help you learn grammar most efficiently. It begins with the basic patterns that underlie sentences and verbals, then goes on to break down those patterns into the building blocks of sentences—form classes and structure words. Then you learn to expand and combine the patterns. When you have acquired quite a bit of expertise at crafting grammatical structures, you might turn to the chapters on figures and see how they can help you improve your style. You will find a chapter of passages to analyze and a special chapter on punctuation. If you need the definition of a term, refer to the glossary at the end of the book. An Instructor's Manual is available for this book.

A *Writer's Grammar* does not assume that you know such concepts as *subject, object, tense*; rather it explains and demonstrates such concepts. This book does not attempt to mimic the learning of grammar and language as native speakers acquire it. Rather it presents a formal and hierarchical study of grammar, where concepts build logically, one upon the other. This is a writing-intensive study of grammar, where you are asked to construct the kinds of grammatical structures you are studying—in effect, to apply your knowledge. If you are working with nominative absolutes, for instance, you will be asked to write perhaps 30 sentences demonstrating nominative absolutes. Writing your own examples of the structures requires you to internalize them, thereby creating linguistic traces in your conscious mind that you can revisit when a rhetorical or writing situation so demands.

The grammar in *A Writer's Grammar* is linked to matters of rhetorical effect and style as such connections are appropriate. When, for instance, adverbial clauses are introduced, you will also read about the emphasis that adverbial clauses demand. Does it matter where the adverbial clause comes in the sentence—at the beginning, at the end, or sandwiched in the middle? The text addresses not only these considerations but also those of punctuation: how are introductory adverbial clauses typically punctuated? And concluding adverbial clauses—how are they punctuated? If you violate these conventions of punctuation, what rhetorical "message" do you send? In addition, you will learn about specific rhetorical figures so that you can consider the effects of strategies of balance, repetition, and coordination. In short, you will think about grammatical knowledge as relevant to writing. And you will become a writer more aware and more sensitive to the nuances of language.

I would like to hear about your experience with this book. Please write to me at Binghamton University, Division of Education, Box 6000, Binghamton NY 13902-6000 or post an e-mail message to me at bburch@ binghamton.edu.

Acknowledgments

A good part of this project was completed while I was on sabbatical leave from my position as associate professor at Binghamton University, SUNY. I am grateful to Dean Ernest Rose, Provost Mary Ann Swain, and President Lois DeFleur for making the leave possible and for making Binghamton University a fine place to be a professor.

I thank Eben Ludlow, vice president of Longman, who has encouraged and supported this project from its inception and who has been patient with me besides. And thanks go to Bill Russo at Longman, for his always efficient assistance. I have also been helped greatly by the reviewers of the manuscript for this book: to William J. Carpenter, Lafayette College; Ed Eleazer, Francis Marion University; and Robert Funk, Eastern Illinois University. I owe appreciation for lessons learned and sound advice. The students in my graduate Rhetorical Grammar course have also helped me to think about grammar and writing more clearly, and I am grateful to all for their questions and fine work.

I am grateful for the love, support, and interest in my work that is always forthcoming from my parents, Harmon Saulmon and Ellagwyn Saulmon: thank you. And to Vivian Burch, I thank you for all your love and support and bless the memory of Jacob. For my oldest boys and their families—Paul and Meg and Zachary, Nena, Emma Beth, and Ami Sue— I love you and thank you for your affection. It is to my husband Paul William and to our youngest son Nathan, though, that I owe most: I love you and thank you for all the ways you sustain and love me every day. I am the luckiest woman in the world.

1

The Shape of Things: Sentence Patterns

Grammar is a way of organizing what we know about language so that we can talk about and manipulate this knowledge. Much of our adult knowledge of grammar is intuitive and unconscious, acquired as we learned language as children. By trial and error and by imitation of the adults around us, we learned grammatical structures and how to organize speech to communicate our needs, to ask questions, and to name the world. But there is also a conscious aspect to grammar, a reservoir of linguistic understanding that we can access when we speak and write. When we access this conscious information, make conscious choices about sentence form and organization, and when we arrange words to create specific effects, we apply grammatical knowledge to create a rhetoric of the sentence. The study of rhetoric concerns the choices writers make and the effects of these choices upon their readers. Using rhetoric means choosing what to write, how to express our thinking, how to order this expression, and what to emphasize—all within an ethical context. As writers and users of rhetoric, we consciously decide what to write; we determine how to order, arrange, and punctuate our words and sentences so that we can create a response in our audience. Thus, this book addresses not only grammar but grammar within a framework of rhetoric. You will be asked to learn about grammar and also to consider the rhetorical implications of your grammatical choices.

Just as there is more than one way to think about the English language, so there is more than one grammar to describe its structures and its functions. Think of it this way: a grammar is like a supermarket. Go to any supermarket, and you will find certain products in fairly predictable places: the Ben and Jerry's ice cream and the frozen spinach are going to be in the refrigerated cases; the fresh bagels are going to be near the Italian bread; most of the Coca-Cola and Pepsi will be down one aisle; and the pet food and supplies will be down another. Similar grocery products cluster together. That doesn't mean that you won't find a kind of product in more than one place in the store (you might find fresh bagels one place, frozen ones another), but it does mean that you can predict with some certainty that fresh green beans will be in the produce section—not with the soda and not with cleaning supplies. You also might find green beans in other parts of the store, according to how they are prepared: canned ones in one place and frozen ones in yet another.

Grammars are like this. Not every grammar is alike (just as every grocery store is slightly different from others), but there are some grammatical principles that operate consistently and predictably, regardless of the kind of grammar we may be discussing. Thus talking about grammar becomes a matter of understanding what things go together, under what circumstances they go together, and why. A **grammar** is a way of describing what a language does. **Rhetoric** considers the way that grammatical elements (or parts of sentences) work together to create certain effects. If you place a clause at the beginning of a sentence instead of at its end, for instance, you send readers a particular message and you emphasize a specific aspect of your message. In this chapter, you'll find a description of the basic ways that English sentences fit together—the **patterns** of English— and you'll think about the effects of using each one.

An important concept underpinning most English grammars is this: patterns exist in the ways that we speak and write. Over and over the same structures occur, with regularity. One major feature of all English patterns is that English is a **verb-medial language**. This means that verbs typically occur in the medial or middle position in the sentence. This makes English, in terms of the world's languages, a minority language. Many languages (like Japanese) are **verb-frontal languages**—where the verb is the first word in the sentence. In English, as in many languages, the verb is the key player in the sentence: the verb determines the pattern of the sentence. So we will pay special attention to verbs as we consider patterns. English has **transitive verbs, linking verbs,** and **intransitive verbs**—and a number of patterns for each kind. Let's look at some basic examples of patterns for each kind of verb.

Transitive Patterns

Look at the following bare-bones sentences. What structural similarities do you see? How are the sentences similarly built? What elements or major parts do they have in common? Use the language of nouns and verbs, adjectives and adverbs, that you may recall from high school to describe the pattern you see here. (We'll look more closely at nouns, verbs, adjectives, and adverbs soon. But for now you may experience a curious and somewhat maddening phenomenon: to explain a grammatical structure, I have to use grammatical language, which may not be clear to you until the grammatical concept is clear. This means that all the concepts may become clear all at once and that sometimes you may be working with imperfect understanding of what is being discussed. Be patient and be willing to be confused temporarily. Eventually the concept will become clear.) If high school grammar is not coming back to you, try to explain what each word seems to be *doing* in these sentences.

> Nothing surprises me.
>
> We have your book.
>
> The killers hit the bishop.
>
> Frost wrote a letter.
>
> My best friend Sarah likes the indispensable black travel dress.

To begin, each sentence has at its front a noun, noun substitute or pronoun, or **noun cluster** (a noun plus its attendants, the words that pattern with it, modify it, or describe it). Nouns are naming words, words that we use to label objects, people, and ideas. This front or initial noun or noun cluster tells what the sentence is to be about, its **subject**: *Nothing, We, The killers, Frost, My best friend Sarah*. Then, each subject is associated with a **verb**: *surprises, have, hit, wrote, likes*. Verbs express or refer to action in a sentence, to what is happening. Each verb asks a question—*Who*? *Whom*? or *What*?—and needs something more to complete it. Finally, each verb doesn't sound quite finished without the answer to the question *Whom*? or *What*? Nothing surprises *whom*? We have *what*? The killers hit *whom*? Frost wrote *what*? My best friend Sarah likes *what*? Finally, note that each sentence has a noun or pronoun to answer that "Who?" or "What?" question: Nothing surprises *me*; We have *your book*; The killers hit the *bishop*; and Sarah likes the *dress*. The nouns that follow the verb and complete its meaning by answering the question *Whom*? or *What*? are called **direct objects**, which are part of a larger group of words called **complements** or completers. Complements, including direct objects, work with subjects and verbs to impart information and to create complete grammatical structures or *sentences*. Notice that direct objects, like all **objects** when we speak in the language of grammar, are always nouns or noun substitutes that follow verbs or verbals and complete them. Thus the word *objects* is a clue here to the kind of word that fits the pattern: a noun.

Direct Object Pattern

So we call this pattern **S-V-O: subject-verb-object**. In an S-V-O sentence, a subject does something to or acts upon an object. In this pattern, some kind of action (either physical, emotional, psychological, or intellectual) is transferred from the subject through the verb to the object. We call these verbs **transitive** verbs, verbs that *take* an object and that *transfer* some kind of action from subject to object. The subject of each of these direct object sentences is also an **agent**. *Agent* is a cognate of the Latin verb *ago, agere*, which means *to do*. Thus an agent is a do-er, and typically the subject also does something, acts. The object, on the other hand, is acted upon: somebody does something to the subject. S-V-O is the most common pattern in English: readers are accustomed to reading about the subject first, then the verb, then the object. Any time you interrupt or subvert or rearrange this basic arrangement, you draw the reader's attention and emphasize the idea that is being interrupted, subverted, or rearranged.

When you choose an S-V-O pattern, then, you are presenting events directly, showing an actor and describing what the actor did to something or to someone. The rhetorical effect is directness and, usually, clarity. It is obvious what was done and who did it.

Sentence patterns manifest themselves in all kinds of places. Look at the sentences in the cartoon caption in Figure 1.1 to see two examples of S-V-O patterns: *You / will like / Mr. Woofard* and *He / has / disorder.* The repetition of this sentence pattern is very directive (one student tells the other what to do) and at the same time reminiscent of the language of elementary reading books, which often repeat patterns for emphasis and

"You will like Mr. Woofard. He has an attention-deficit disorder."

Figure 1.1
Direct Object Pattern.
© The New Yorker Collection 1991 George Booth from cartoonbank.com. All Rights Reserved.

improved comprehension. The use and repetition of the direct object pattern helps to create the humor of the caption.

About Prepositional Phrases

Let's interrupt the discussion of patterns a moment to consider **prepositional phrases**. Prepositional phrases remain outside the S-V-O structure (or the structure of any pattern) and are not considered elements or constituents of the pattern (those things that constitute the pattern or compose it). Prepositional phrases enhance the pattern, elaborate the pattern, make the pattern more interesting. But they are not part of the pattern, nor do they change the pattern. So here's a tip: when you sort out the pattern of a sentence, **ignore prepositional phrases entirely.** Prepositional phrases are added to basic patterns to expand, develop, or modify them. Pattern elements or main parts (the S, V, or O) are **not** found within prepositional phrases. This is an important concept to grasp as you work to understand how sentences fall into various patterns.

Take a few minutes to review prepositional phrases because you need to recognize them as you identify patterns. A prepositional phrase is built of a preposition plus its object, which is a noun or a noun cluster: *for + low-income housing, of + daily therapeutic care, during + the past five years, at + the eleventh hour, in + the injected knee, off + the roof.* Some of the most common prepositions are these:

around	*down*	*through*
at	*during*	*to*
beneath	*for*	*toward*
beside	*in*	*with*
between	*of*	*within*
by	*on*	*without*

If the object has modifying words clustered around it, the cluster or string is part of the prepositional phrase.

Sometimes prepositions themselves occur in phrases, thus creating **phrasal prepositions**. Prepositions can pattern together and act as a unit to create variations on the original meaning of the preposition. Consider this partial list of phrasal prepositions: *according to, along with, as for, because of, except for, instead of, next to, thanks to, by means of, in back of, in charge of, in spite of, on behalf of.* Phrasal prepositions make possible subtle variations of meaning and delicate levels of explanation and understanding; when you use a phrasal preposition, you express a complex grammatical relationship.

Each phrasal preposition functions or acts just like a single-word preposition and when patterned with a noun or noun cluster of its own, creates a prepositional phrase: *in spite of/my friend's best efforts, according to /the rules of the game, instead of/vegetable lasagna.* It is important to understand that in English several words can—and frequently do—function as a unit expressing one idea. We are accustomed to hearing these clusters or units in English and making perfect sense of them. But when we see them in print, on the page, we tend not to see the units but rather to think of individual words. As you build grammatical understanding, you may find it helpful to think of concepts as residing in phrases rather than in individual words.

Remember that as valuable as prepositional phrases are to the development and even the subtlety of a sentence, they are *not* part of the sentence pattern. When you are trying to determine the pattern of a given sentence, consider striking out the prepositional phrases so you can see the skeletal pattern elements better exposed.

For Discussion

In your study group, talk about the following S-V-O sentences, identifying what words function as subjects, verbs, and direct objects. Be prepared to explain fully any of the sentences to the class after the small-group discussions. Your group should discuss the relationships among the words, how the subject is related to the object—and vice versa. You should also explain how each subject is an agent—what it does. The elements of the pattern (that is, the S, the V, and the O) are frequently headwords of larger clusters that include determiners, possessives, adjectives, adverbs, intensifiers, and even prepositional phrases. Observe also how the sentences are punctuated, or in this case, often not punctuated except for end punctuation. These sentences are correct without internal punctuation because *we do not separate the simple elements of a pattern with punctuation.* Don't break up a simple pattern with punctuation between any of the basic elements. No punctuation goes between subject and verb or between verb and object, for instance.

Here are some sentences to prepare for class discussion:

1. In the sometimes rancorous discussion, Frost didn't raise his voice.
2. These books explain Hitchcock's creative processes to the layman.
3. Jones savored the victory.
4. Old friends celebrated their memories with joy.
5. The Cirrus delivers power.
6. Full resort amenities include golf for amateurs and professionals, tennis, a fitness center, and a spa.
7. PaineWebber crunched the numbers.
8. The bull market was drawing con artists.
9. By Web or by phone, scamsters can tell lies.
10. The Wyandottes would not desecrate graves.

(continued)

11. Police in Bavaria find 5.6 grams of superpure plutonium-239 in the garage of a money counterfeiter.
12. I believe the songs.
13. He ends his posthospital tour with an outdoor show in Kansas City, Missouri.
14. He's muffed his share of big moments.
15. Many movies put their heroes through life-changing experiences.
16. Survivors Hopkins and Baldwin confront a hungry bear.
17. Ehrlich includes some enticing recipes here.
18. Try a Day-Timer personal organizer for 90 days. [The subject in this sentence is understood, thus not stated. Imagine a *You* at the beginning of the sentence.]
19. I need more hours in the day.
20. We've packaged a unique set of tools.
21. An eloquent ad campaign can turn around troubled Apple Computer within months.
22. Ted Turner announced his $1 billion gift to the United Nations.
23. You can engage your prospects in a relevant, one-to-one conversation.
24. Rosemary Warren makes hats for children.
25. Ancient Tibetan mandalas symbolize wholeness.

Compound Elements in Patterns

All parts of the pattern can be compounded. You can, for instance, create a compound subject:

Stan
and   } will hide the valuables in a paper bag.
Ollie

Here you have two subjects that are attached to one verb phrase. Stan will hide the valuables—and so will Ollie. In the next sentence, you will see a compound verb, where one subject patterns with two separate verb phrases:

Sammy {
washed the dishes
and
pressed his white shirt.

Here Sammy completes two actions, washing dishes and pressing a shirt. In this sentence, each verb phrase happens to have the same pattern, a transitive verb plus a direct object, but it is possible to have compound verbs that have different patterns. You'll read more about those later. You may also write or read sentences with all sorts of **compound elements**. Here's an example of a sentence with compound direct objects:

All evening Nathan drew $\left\{\begin{array}{l}\text{the posters}\\\text{and}\\\text{the charts.}\end{array}\right.$

As long as only some elements of a pattern are compounded, you still have one pattern.

FOR WRITING

Now it's time for you to practice writing the S-V-O pattern. In your writer's notebook (either paper or electronic), compose 30 S-V-O sentences. To make the task interesting, include the name of a person from history, either living or dead, in each sentence, either as subject or direct object. Example: *Napoleon loves eclairs* or *Many presidents have admired George Washington*. In at least 3 of the 30 sentences, include a compound sentence element. When you finish your sentences, check to see that each verb is transitive, that is, that it takes an object, that the subject acts or is an agent. Then review them with your writers' group. Your sentences don't have to be historically correct.

Indirect Object Pattern

The S-V-O pattern is not the only transitive pattern. There are others. Take a look at the following skeleton sentences with an eye toward detecting similar structures in the sentences. What sentence features do you see?

> We'll send you a Day-Timer personal organizer.
>
> My aunt gave us girls a Vignelli dinner plate.
>
> Gram made us some chocolate chip cookies.
>
> The Jaguar XJR shows true fans its stuff.
>
> The lieutenant is giving Mike the bad news.

In these sentences you can probably make out the subject clusters (*We, My aunt, Gram, The Jaguar XJR, the lieutenant*), the verbs (*send, gave, made, shows, is giving*), and the direct object noun clusters that answer the question *What?* or *Whom?* (*a Day-Timer personal organizer, a Vignelli dinner plate, some chocolate chip cookies, its stuff, the bad news*). And you probably also detected the presence of another noun or noun substitute located between the verb and the direct object: *you, us girls, us, true fans, Mike*. These elements intervening between the verb and direct object are **indirect objects**. They answer the questions *To whom was something done or given?* or *For whom was something done or given?*

We write the indirect object pattern **S-V-IO-DO**. Note the location of the indirect object: between the verb and the direct object. This is its required place. There is no other place in the sentence where it can exist and still remain an indirect object. If, for instance, you revise the indirect object sentence

The lieutenant is giving **Mike** the bad news

to read

The lieutenant is giving the bad news to **Mike**,

an indirect object does not exist in the revised sentence. The revision changed the pattern to S-V-O, and the indirect object becomes the object of a preposition and part of a prepositional phrase modifier, *to Mike*. (Some grammarians disagree with this analysis; they maintain that it is only not the position of the noun but its function or the task it performs in the sentence that makes it an indirect object. Nevertheless, the form changes dramatically.) In the revised sentence, the grammatical importance of the original object *bad news* decreases because it has moved to midsentence, a place of little emphasis. The importance of the indirect object **Mike** increases when the indirect object is moved to the prepositional phrase because it falls at the end of the sentence, a place of natural emphasis. *Giving Mike the bad news* buries *Mike*, the receiver of the bad news, in midsentence. As a writer, you choose where the emphasis should be. This is a **rhetorical** choice. A note: observe that three separate **noun clusters** (also called **N-groups** by some grammarians) exist in this pattern: *lieutenant, news,* and *Mike* all have modifiers clustering around them. Each noun refers to a separate entity. In *Gerry gave her friends a cookie,* the nouns *Gerry, friends,* and *cookie* refer to three separate entities. We say that these nouns have separate **referents**.

FOR DISCUSSION

Analyze the following S-V-IO-DO sentences in your writers' group. Identify what words function as subjects, verbs, indirect objects, and direct objects. Discuss the relationships among the words, how the subjects are related to the objects and the indirect objects—and vice versa. Observe that, as in an S-V-O sentence, each subject is still an agent, that it still performs an action—in this pattern, the subject performs an action to or for someone. The elements of the pattern (that is, the S, the V, the IO, and the DO) are frequently headwords for larger clusters that also include determiners, possessives, adjectives, adverbs, intensifiers, and even prepositional phrases. Remember: when you sort out the pattern of a sentence, **ignore prepositional phrases**

(continued)

entirely. Prepositional phrases are added to a basic pattern to expand, develop, or modify it. Pattern elements (the S, V, IO, or DO) are **not** found in prepositional phrases. Here, then, are some indirect object sentences for your group to prepare for the whole-group discussion:

1. Aunt Jean taught the brat a lesson.
2. Your kiss gave me shivers.
3. The waiter poured me coffee in a flashy silver mug.
4. You can save me time and stress.
5. Our psychology professor assigned us a paper and a project.
6. Nixon forwarded his secretary the message.
7. I gave Emily a blue notebook with a denim cover.
8. The florist sold him a yellow rose.
9. Paul bought me a gold Claddaugh ring in Galway.
10. With glee, John gave Drew a black eye.
11. The real estate agent showed Joe the big brick house.
12. Ralph handed her the pencil.
13. In legal documents, Engelbert granted me his power-of-attorney.
14. The grocer sold the customer a fruit basket of lemons, limes, grapes, and apricots.
15. Goldie built her puppy a doghouse.
16. I wrote my friend Adam a letter on expensive stationery.
17. An anonymous donor sent the school a new computer and printer.
18. I purchased Mel a scented candle for her birthday.
19. The tourists sent them pictures of azure oceans and purple mountains.
20. The nurse handed Brad a milky concoction.
21. The Jolly Green Giant handed the shopper a can of beans.
22. Jimi Hendrix played his fans "Purple Haze" with gusto.
23. The soldier wrote his love a syrupy letter.
24. The inventive witch sent the warlock a poisoned letter in the U.S. mail.
25. The veterinarian prescribed the poodle some medicine for her headaches.

Verbs for the Indirect Object Pattern. Did you notice that the verbs in the indirect object pattern have similar meanings? These verbs are a rather small class of verbs like *give*. We call them **give verbs**. There are considerably fewer verbs that fit in this class, so your options for composing indirect object sentences are slimmer than with the direct object pattern. Here are some of the most common *give verbs:*

award	make	send
buy	play	serve
give	pour	show
grant	purchase	teach
hand	sell	write

For Writing

Now it's time for you to practice writing this pattern. In your writer's notebook (either paper or electronic), compose 30 S-V-IO-DO sentences. To make the task interesting, include a noun that begins with the letter **G** somewhere in each sentence; you'll want to include the noun in any one of the noun slots (subjects, indirect objects, and direct objects can all have clusters). Example with three **G** words: *The goonies handed the grandma a shiny guilder.* Remember: as you write these sentences, you will find that you are choosing verbs from a considerably smaller pool than with S-V-O sentences. Do not be alarmed if you seem to use the same or similar verbs over and over.

Objective Complement Pattern

Besides their patterning with direct and indirect objects, transitive verbs can pattern in English sentences in still another way. Study the following examples to see the relationships among elements in these sentences:

> My child believes me ridiculous.
>
> The class found the professor intolerable.
>
> Everyone considered the event successful.
>
> Question 6 left me puzzled.
>
> She probably thinks me rude.

and these:

> The boss called me her colleague.
>
> His friends nicknamed him Oscar.
>
> The workers elected Hoffa president of the union.
>
> The Green Party considered Ralph Nader an ally.
>
> The sportswriters named the successful quarterback most valuable player.

Once again, you see the familiar S-V-O structure. In this pattern, though, the direct objects tend to answer the question *Whom?* more than *What?:* The class found *whom?* Everyone considered *what?* The boss called *whom?* The workers elected *whom?* Even though there is a direct object, the pattern remains incomplete until the final complement is added after the direct object. This final complement completes the relationship founded upon the subject-verb relationship. This kind of complement (or completer) of the direct object is called the **objective complement** or the completer of the object.

We write this pattern **S-V-DO-OC** for subject-verb-direct object-objective complement. Notice how in the first group of examples the objective complements are adjectives that refer to, describe, or modify the direct objects: *ridiculous me, intolerable professor, successful event, puzzled me, rude students.* In the second group of examples, the objective complements are nouns that refer to or rename the direct object: *her = colleague, him = Oscar, Hoffa = president, Ralph Nader = ally, quarterback = player.* In both these cases, we say that the direct object and the objective complement have the same **referent**, that is, they refer to the same person or the same thing. The subjects have totally different referents than the direct objects or their objective complements. In *The workers elected Hoffa president of the union,* the subject *workers* refers to one group of people, and the direct object *Hoffa* and its complement *president* refer to another person totally separate from the first: thus they have different referents.

Look at Figure 1.2 to see an example of the objective complement pattern: *you / won't find / Miss Miriam Hirschman / nut.* In this caption,

"*You won't find Miss Miriam Hirschman an easy nut to crack, Mr. Leno.*"

Figure 1.2
Objective Complement Pattern.
© *The New Yorker Collection 1991 Danny Shanahan from cartoonbank.com. All Rights Reserved.*

Mr. Leno is a noun of direct address; Miss Hirschman is addressing her remarks to him (even though he's only on the television!). Miss Hirschman compares herself to a *tough nut;* *Miss Hirschman* and *nut* have the same referent.

FOR DISCUSSION

In your writers' group, prepare to present an analysis of any of the following S-V-DO-OC sentences to the class as a whole. Identify what words function as subjects, verbs, direct objects, and objective complements. Discuss the relationships among the words, how the subjects are related to the objects and how the direct objects and the objective complements are related, whether the objective complements are nouns or adjectives. As in all kinds of transitive sentences, each subject is an agent: it does something. The elements of the pattern (that is, the S, the V, the DO, and the OC) are frequently part of larger clusters that include determiners, possessives, adjectives, adverbs, intensifiers, and even prepositional phrases. Remember: when you sort out the pattern of a sentence, **ignore prepositional phrases entirely.** Prepositional phrases are added to a basic pattern to expand, develop, or modify it. Pattern elements (the S, V, DO, and OC) are *not* found in prepositional phrases. Here are some objective complement sentences to talk about:

1. The Marilyn Manson groupie painted his lips black.
2. First-year college students and older students too called the cafeteria food garbage.
3. Betsy believed the book about Princess Diana scandalous.
4. In 1963, Bob Dylan's political anthems made him the voice of the Movement.
5. Critics may proclaim this performance the best.
6. This album might make him hip again.
7. The reviewer called Caleb Carr clever.
8. The board named my daughter a National Science Scholar.
9. The magazine *Fortune* will vote one company Most Generous Company in America.
10. The ICD-70 makes commute time and downtime productive time!
11. Together we can make the planet better for everyone.
12. *Vanity Fair* called Monica a minor-league Marilyn Monroe.
13. My friends consider the reform ideas ludicrous.
14. At one time Texas voters considered Bush a political lightweight.

(continued)

15. Most of us believe statistics unreliable and unbelievable.
16. His habits make me uneasy.
17. That class left me clueless.
18. The inspector and the engineer deemed the bridge safe.
19. You made your Democratic friends proud with this issue.
20. The police called the suspect a liar.
21. Sue dyed her shirt red.
22. The height and the angle of descent made me dizzy.
23. Nikolai called the officers imperious.
24. Diners at Number 5 find the Cobb salad delicious.
25. I consider this sentence the end.

FOR WRITING

Now it's time for you to practice writing this pattern. In your writer's notebook (either paper or electronic), compose 30 S-V-DO-OC sentences. As you write these sentences, you will find that you are choosing verbs from an even smaller verb pool than with S-V-IO-DO sentences. If you believe you are using the same verbs repeatedly, you probably are—but you haven't much latitude. After you write the sentences, check to see that in each sentence, your direct object and objective complement have the same referent. Here is a list of the most common verbs in objective complement sentences:

believe	consider	make
call	deem	name
choose	elect	paint
color	find	proclaim

Possible Confusions: Appositives

Sometimes appositives look like objective complements, and it's easy to confuse the two. **Appositives** are nouns patterning with and renaming other nouns. Generally, appositives are in apposition with the nouns they relate to—this means that they are literally in position with their nouns, side by side. Here are some examples of transitive sentences with appositives:

Our friend, the new chef at Le Jardin, makes wonderful cherry tarts.

Friend and *the new chef at Le Jardin* are in apposition; *the new chef at Le Jardin* renames *friend*. This is still an S-V-O sentence, and the pattern has not changed; the subject just has an appositive.

The panel of chefs awarded our friend, *the new chef at Le Jardin,* the prize for best cherry tarts.

Friend and *the new chef at Le Jardin* are still in apposition; now they are functioning as the indirect object and appositive in an S-V-IO-DO sentence. Note that their relationship is still the same, even though the pattern of the sentence changes.

It's easy to confuse appositives with other sentence elements that are nouns. It is particularly easy to confuse appositives with objective complements as in a sentence like this:

We congratulated our friend, the new chef at Le Jardin.

In this sentence, *friend* and *the new chef at Le Jardin* are direct objects in an appositional relationship. *The new chef at Le Jardin* is an appositive to the noun *friend*—and *friend* serves as the direct object of the verb. The relationship is fundamentally different than that between direct object and objective complement, where the object and its complement still have the same referent but where the action and power of the verb extend across the entire sentence. In this S-V-O sentence, the verb's power ends with *friend,* its object. The verb has no impact on *the new chef at Le Jardin,* the appositive that merely renames the direct object.

But in an S-V-DO-OC sentence like

The panel of chefs named our friend winner!

The action of the verb is not completed when we get to *our new friend* in the sentence; the panels named *our new friend* something—*winner*—and until that information is presented, the verb is not complete and the reader doesn't have the whole idea of the sentence. In other words, you can omit an appositive but not an objective complement without changing the meaning of the sentence. Understanding the concept behind the objective complement will help you to sort out the differences between appositives after direct objects and objective complements.

L inking Patterns

The transitive patterns present scenarios where subjects act upon or do something to objects—to something or someone else—and variations on this pattern—giving something to someone else, doing something for someone else, calling or naming somebody something. The linking patterns present an entirely different concept. Take a look at the sentences that follow and see if you can explain the relationships you see between the subjects, the verbs, and the complements.

Tom Savage is a Delaware builder.

His departure from Sportscenter is an obvious career move.

Judith Exner was Sam Giancana's girlfriend.

Isuzu means adventure.

El Niño was a freakish, destructive disruption in worldwide weather.

Predicate Noun Pattern

The complements following the linking verbs in these sentences are nouns; we call them **predicate nouns** (nouns that rename the subject and occur in the predicate, after the verb). We name the pattern **S-LV-PN**: subject-linking verb-predicate noun. The purpose of predicate noun sentences is to identify and name; the complements rename the subjects (they are often called **subjective complements** or completers of the subject). **Linking verbs** join or link the subject to the complement. In these sentences, the subjects and complements have the same referents: *Tom Savage* and *the Delaware builder* are one and the same person; *Exner* was the *girlfriend,* and *El Nino* was the *disruption.* Compare, for instance these sentences:

Judith Exner criticized Sam Giancana's girlfriend

The transitive verb *criticized* takes the direct object, *girlfriend. Exner* and *girlfriend* refer to two different people

and

Judith Exner was Sam Giancana's girlfriend

(the linking verb *was* takes the complement or predicate noun, *girlfriend. Exner* and *girlfriend* now refer to the same person).

Now take a look at the following sentences and determine how they are like the first set of linking sentences given—and how they are different as well:

Her skin is clear.

Her joints feel fine.

Olbermann is glib.

School has been easy for Matthew Teague.

And Bob Dylan is newly famous as the father of the Wallflowers' Jakob Dylan.

Predicate Adjective Pattern

How are these subjective complements different from the ones in the first group of sentences? These complements are **predicate adjectives** that describe or modify the subject: skin = clear, joints = fine, Olbermann = glib, School = easy, he = famous. Like predicate nouns, predicate adjectives and subjects have the same referent. Like predicate nouns, predicate adjectives are joined to their subjects via linking verbs.

You may find it useful simply to memorize the major linking verbs so you can recognize them more easily. They are:

- **forms of the verb** *be: is, am are, was, were, be, being, been* (including *has been, have been, had been, is being, will be,* etc.);
- **the verbs naming the senses:** *looks, sounds, smells, feels, tastes;*
- **and an odd assortment of verbs** like *seem, appear, become, remain,* and *grow.*

As you memorize these verbs, remember that these verbs **may** be linking but they are not necessarily **always** linking. In

> The shrimp gumbo tastes spicy

the linking verb *tastes* links *gumbo* and *spicy. Spicy* and *gumbo* have the same referent and refer to the same entity. But in

> Bubba tastes the gumbo

tastes is a transitive verb. *Bubba* and *gumbo* are clearly different entities with different referents, and *Bubba* acts upon the *gumbo,* does something to the *gumbo*—he tastes it.

Not all adjectives that occur in the predicate are predicate adjectives; only adjectives that modify or pattern with the subject are predicate adjectives. The sentence *The students are diligent* contains a predicate adjective, *diligent,* that patterns with and describes the subject, *students.* But the sentence *They are diligent students* does not contain a predicate adjective because *diligent* (an adjective occurring in the predicate part of the sentence) modifies or describes or patterns with the predicate noun *students,* not with the subject *They.*

For Discussion

Analyze the S-LV-PN and S-LV-PA sentences that follow for presentation in a class discussion, identifying what words function as subjects, verbs, predicate nouns, and predicate adjectives. Discuss relationships among words, how subjects are related to complements, whether complements are nouns or adjectives. In this pattern, subjects are no longer agents; rather in these sentences subjects are being described, renamed, amplified—completed—through and by means of the complement. Notice also that the elements of the pattern (that is, the S, the LV, the PN or PA) are frequently headwords of larger clusters that include determiners, possessives, adjectives, adverbs, intensifiers, and even prepositional phrases. Observe how the sentences are punctuated. Remember: we do not use punctuation to separate the main parts of a sentence pattern. Also remember that when you are sorting out the pattern of a sentence or even

(continued)

first composing a sentence of a certain pattern, **ignore prepositional phrases entirely**. Prepositional phrases are added to a basic pattern to expand, develop, or modify it. Pattern elements (the S, LV, PN, and PA) are **not** found in prepositional phrases. Here are some linking pattern sentences to discuss:

1. "Time out of Mind" is a spare, spooky-sounding album.
2. I feel afraid.
3. The movie is preposterous—and hugely entertaining. [Do you see the compound complements?]
4. Their issues are Social Security and the cost of prescription drugs. [More compound elements]
5. The gentlest things for your skin are aloe vera, cocoa butter, and pure merino wool. [Look for compound complements.]
6. White House aides are aghast.
7. He's an intellectual heavyweight.
8. I was awake before dawn on April 8, 1998.
9. The saga of Monica Lewinsky, Ken Starr, and Bill and Hillary Clinton was great entertainment.
10. Education is the most important issue for all citizens.
11. These marvelous glasses are heavy.
12. You're a daring Italian pilot with a handsome mustache.
13. This flower is a gardenia.
14. He was a clairvoyant.
15. Sam Adams is famous for a few things.
16. Life will be a little easier with a Sierra by GMC.
17. Lewis was a clear winner in the poll.
18. Your comments are an exaggeration.
19. Herta was graceful and gentle and articulate. [Notice the compound elements.]
20. The poodles were sleek and dainty.
21. We are hip!
22. Kubrick may be unique among directors.
23. This is not a question of screen violence.
24. These private scenes became commonplace for most of his old fans.
25. DiMaggio was the classic player of our century.

For Writing

Now it's time for you to practice writing these patterns. In your writer's notebook (either paper or electronic), first compose 30 S-LV-PN sentences and then write 30 S-LV-PA sentences. To make

(continued)

things interesting, use only predicate adjectives beginning with the letter *M* in the S-LV-PA sentences. As you write these sentences, remember to use linking verbs and remember that your complements—the predicate noun and the predicate adjective—must refer to (or have the same referent as) the subject. After you write the sentences, check to see that in each sentence your subject and subjective complement (predicate noun or predicate adjective) have the same referent.

T *he Intransitive Pattern*

A third kind of sentence pattern centers on the **intransitive verb**, the verb with no complement whatsoever. This means that it has no complement or object, that the verb is complete in itself. Check out these sentences.

> Negotiations came to a halt.
> You should stroll in Central Park.
> Over the last several years, crime in New York City has dropped.
> I'm speaking out now.
> Around here, time doesn't stand still.
> It laughs, smiles, and plays in the sun.

The elements in these sentences are simply subjects and verbs. Yes, there are sometimes prepositional phrases used adverbially (*to a halt, in the sun*) or **adverbial** words (*now*), but you will recall that adjectives, adverbs, and prepositional phrases can constitute part of a cluster around a noun or verb but (except for the predicate adjective) do not constitute elements of the sentence pattern. Rather they are modifiers that add to what is known about the elements, words that expand, develop, enhance, limit, or modify them. All the verbs in these sentences are **intransitive complete**—that is, verbs not taking or requiring an object or complement, verbs complete in themselves: *came, should stroll, has dropped, am speaking, does stand, laughs, smiles, plays.*

We write this pattern **S-V** or **S-V (adv)** to show that an adverbial element is an option.

Many verbs can be both transitive and intransitive. For instance, consider the verb *walk*. In this sentence, *walk* is intransitive: *All the players walked casually onto the field.* The verb has no complement, only an adverbial modifier (*casually*) and a prepositional phrase (*onto the field*). But in this sentence, *walk* is transitive because it takes compound objects, *poodles* and *collies: Sister Ellen walked the poodles and the collies together.*

For Discussion

In your writers' group, discuss the following S-V sentences in preparation for a presentation to the class as a whole. Identify what words function as subjects and verbs. If there are adverbials, point them out. The elements of the pattern (that is, the S and the V) may frequently be part of larger clusters that include determiners, possessives, adjectives, adverbs, intensifiers, and even prepositional phrases. Remember: when you sort out the pattern of a sentence, **ignore prepositional phrases entirely**. Prepositional phrases are added to a basic pattern to expand, develop, or modify it. Pattern elements (the S and V) are **not** found in prepositional phrases. As you talk about the sentences, don't forget to observe how they are punctuated. Here are some intransitive sentences to talk about:

1. Residential streets blend with the world's most fashionable drives.
2. Bits and bytes and ones and zeroes fly around the planet. [Observe the compound subjects.]
3. We should meet at one o'clock at Lutece.
4. Tennessee Williams moved into the literary world with a collection of stories.
5. This offer will expire soon.
6. Then the phone beside him rang.
7. Letters arrived at Clairol headquarters.
8. She never wavered in her belief in the dream.
9. Mary Cassatt left for Parma with her friend Emily Sartain.
10. Love dies hard.
11. The black poodle stretched out languidly on the snow-white carpet.
12. Fifi Brown screamed at the mouse.
13. He played in center field.
14. Many of us are waiting.
15. California congressman Leo Ryan and a group of journalists flew to Guyana.
16. Trent Lott was aiming in the right direction.
17. These moments pass so quickly!
18. She frets about her husband's decision.
19. Everyone will retire for the night in a camp of authentic-looking tepees.
20. Gingrich rises with his knapsack.
21. The Brontosauruses in his imagination never died.
22. During World War II, a group of Americans parachuted into the war zone.

(continued)

23. Many French generals and ministers came to Dien Bien Phu.
24. One thinks of Aeschylus, the great poet and tragedian of ancient Greece.
25. I had arrived in Vietnam eight weeks earlier as a private.

For Writing

Now it's time for you to practice writing this pattern. In your writer's notebook (either paper or electronic), compose 30 S-V sentences. As you write, remember to use intransitive complete verbs and remember that your sentences will not have complements—but they may have adverbials. To make it interesting, add one prepositional phrase to each sentence and make one of the nouns in each sentence begin with the letter **T**.

The Big Picture: Looking at All the Patterns

Now let's summarize the sentence patterns. Here's a list presenting each pattern and a key example for each pattern:

S-V-O	The United States inculcated democracy in postwar Germany.
S-V-IO-DO	Tom's of Maine can give you a better fluoride toothpaste.
S-V-DO-OC	Mario Cuomo called the New York prison boom stupid.
S-LV-PN	You are the expert witness for this case.
S-LV-PA	Language is very complex.
S-V	The correctional facility sits near the town.

For Discussion

Working with your writers' group, read the following sentences and identify the pattern of each. Talk about how the parts of the sentences fit together. Be prepared to discuss your findings with the class as a whole.

1. Mr. Carlton became my most important mentor in high school.
2. She had better control of her temper tantrums after therapy.

(continued)

3. I lift my microscope down from the shelf.
4. A huge gap appeared in the fabric of time.
5. In the South, cicadas have a breeding cycle of 13 years.
6. Sean wrote poems about the sea.
7. The wedding party drove idly into the city.
8. The railroad made the Industrial Revolution an accomplished fact.—Peter Drucker
9. Read these prospectuses carefully.
10. Holy Cross Monument shone atop a nearby mountain.
11. Memory is sometimes mythical.
12. My favorite salad features asparagus, raspberry vinaigrette, and walnuts.
13. The Church has become more conscious of its role in the key events of the century.
14. Dogs can think.
15. It's the face of an angel.
16. The technology committee faces another issue.
17. The collapsed buildings were shoddy.
18. The educational environment was hostile to reform.
19. This is a poignant story.
20. Accidents happen.
21. New Yorkers once elected Guiliani mayor.
22. The desert glistened with water.
23. I shut my eyes tightly.
24. Gary followed the other passengers through the golden arches.
25. Savor the aroma of our fine tea.

You should know that not all grammarians agree that these six patterns best describe how English happens on the page. Some grammarians describe more patterns; some, fewer. Some use other designators: for instance N-V-N rather than S-V-O. I have found, though, that the **functional labels** like S-V-O, labels that describe the *function* or *job* of each sentence component, serve the purpose of describing sentences well. I have also found that these six patterns are all we need to characterize whatever sentences we may find or create. It is important, though, that you realize that other grammars, other texts, other grammarians may describe or label these ideas in other ways—and that the differences don't mean that some of us are wrong.

Something else to consider is the reiterative nature of these patterns, which occur again and again in different ways. For instance, in future chapters you'll see how the patterns manifest themselves in verbal phrases (such as infinitive, gerund, and participial phrases) and in clauses. In grammar, everything is tied to everything else; thus you'll find that you revisit this idea of patterns (as well as the important notion of clusters, about which you will read in future chapters) throughout this book. If the concepts remain a bit fuzzy now, you'll encounter them again later. If you believe you are seriously confused, though, now is the time to reread the chapter, try the assignments again, and talk to your professor.

What you have been working with so far are simple sentences, fairly unadorned except for prepositional phrases and occasional adjective and adverb modifiers. Chapters that come after this will explore how we expand or amplify these patterns by adding other structures and how we combine patterns to create compound and complex sentences, structures to fit and display the complexity of our thinking and the relationships we observe in the world. In short, we'll explore how your rhetorical choices multiply as your understanding of grammatical structures deepens.

Soon, in fact, we will look at ways to expand these patterns—not only with single-word modifiers like adjectives and adverbs but also with verbals and verbal phrases. Coming up: two chapters on form classes—and more about prepositional phrases.

2

Naming the Parts, I: Form Classes, Noun Clusters

*E*nglish is a binary language. That means that its **syntax** or structured word order can be rather neatly divided into halves, chunks of two, dual parts; into subject and verb; then into verb and complement; into adjective and noun; into **determiner** and noun; and into preposition and noun—and so forth. This also means that utterances tend to organize themselves into clusters around the parts of the binary. Certain kinds of words and structures cluster around nouns, and certain kinds of words and structures cluster around verbs. Together, noun clusters and verb clusters make up sentences, whole units of discourse and communication. Each kind of cluster, noun and verb, has an important linguistic function. This chapter explores those functions and examines how simple noun clusters and verb clusters are built. Our ears and brains are accustomed to these clusters and to this binary structure of English, and you will want to be mindful of this notion—the twoness of English—as you work to understand sentences.

Your knowledge of the patterns will entwine here with your increasingly sophisticated understanding of clusters. Clusters make up patterns. Patterns are composed of clusters. Understanding clusters helps you identify patterns, and knowing patterns helps you understand clusters. So much grammatical knowledge is interdependent. We have examined the patterns carefully; now let's look at the components of the patterns, clusters, and their components—form classes and structure words.

This chapter and the next are about the **form classes**, which are the major sentence building blocks, and the **structure words**, which constitute the cement that joins the form class words and makes their relationships clear. This chapter explores how form class words and structure words

25

create noun clusters, which combine with **verb clusters** to create patterns. A noun cluster is a noun plus all the words that pattern with it or modify it. A verb cluster is a verb plus all the words that pattern with it or modify it. The next chapter explains how form classes and structure words create verb clusters and describes the kinds of structure words.

F orm Classes

The building blocks of **syntax** or sentence structure are the form classes and structure words. In traditional grammar, both form classes and function words are called the **parts of speech** (and there are traditionally eight parts of speech—noun, verb, adjective, adverb, preposition, conjunction, pronoun, and interjection). In reality, however, form classes and structure words are two very different kinds of word classes, two different kinds of sentence building material: bricks and mortar. The bricks—or form classes—give the structured sentence its essential character—its tone, shape, color, and primary meaning. The mortar—the structure words—pattern with the form class words to show the relationships among the form class words and to hold the ideas in place. Of course, structure words also have meaning. In this chapter, we'll look at two of the form classes that comprise noun clusters—*nouns and adjectives*—and see what other kinds of words congregate to form noun clusters. In the next chapter, we'll continue our look at the form classes of *verb* and *adverb* and review the structure words.

Nouns and Nounness, Nominals and Naming

Nouns name. Naming the world is the purpose of nouns. In traditional grammar you may have heard words like *nominal* and *nominative*—words that have as a root the Latin *nominalis,* meaning *name.* Nouns are naming words, words that designate objects, people, places, feelings, phenomena, theories. How do we understand the quality of being a noun—or nounness? How do we recognize nouns? There are several ways that we identify nouns, besides simply memorizing them.

Position of Nouns in the Sentence. One major way we recognize any word is by its position in a sentence. Nouns regularly occur at certain places in a pattern:

- before a verb (as the subject of a sentence);
- after a verb (as the direct object or predicate noun), answering the question "What?" or "Whom?" raised by a verb;
- after a preposition (as the object of the preposition), as in *at <u>school</u>* or *in my <u>sandwich</u>;*
- after a determiner such as *a, an, the, first,* as in *a <u>kitten</u>, an <u>orange</u>, first <u>try</u>.*

Look at the positions of the underscored words in these sentences adapted from John McPhee's "Heirs of General Practice":

"**Nellie Burns** has a fast-growing **tumor** in her **stomach**."

"The **Conklings** now live in a **cabin** up a **trail** in a **forest** far from **town**."

"**Asians** do it."

"A **woman** takes her **husband** to an **internist** because he's been having **pain** in his **chest**."

"Duodenal **ulcer**, for example, is not a surgical **problem** unless you bleed, perforate, obstruct."

Many of these nouns occur at the very beginning of sentences (*ulcer, woman, Asians, Conklings, Nellie Burns*) in the subject position. Other nouns come after verbs and seem to complete them (*tumor, husband, problem*)—in the complement positions as direct objects, indirect objects, predicate nouns. Some nouns follow prepositions to create prepositional phrases: *in his chest, from town.* Still others tend to come close on the heels of determiners, what we used to call articles or article adjectives: *a problem, her husband, an internist, a cabin, a tumor, a trail.* Our ears and brains are accustomed to these patterns or structures in sentences. We look for nouns in certain places within patterns, particularly in the subject position, the complement position, and the object-of-the-preposition position.

Nouns' Plural Potential. Many nouns name specific, countable things and as such may have **number**; that is, they may refer to one item or to more than one item. If a noun refers to more than one specific item, it is plural and ends in *-s* or *-es,* for the most part. Some words (like *deer, woman*) have irregular plurals. In the McPhee sentences, we see these already plural nouns: *Conklings, Asians.* And we see other words that could be made plural: *tumor, stomach, cabin, trail, woman, husband, internist, pain, chest, ulcer, problem.* These are a class of nouns called **count nouns**, or nouns that name things that can be counted. Not all nouns can be made plural, you understand, but the possibility of plurality is one feature of many nouns.

Proper Nouns and Capital Letters. You'll also note that some nouns, names of specific families or countries or places (*Conklings, Asians*), begin with capital letters; these are proper nouns, nouns that refer to the name of a very specific or particular person, place, organization, or thing. But be careful: not all capitalized words are proper nouns; some aren't even nouns!

Nouns and the Possessive Possibility. Many other nouns, specifically those referring to people, may have a **possessive** form (this is also called

possessive case): my *sister's* coat, *Janet's* new briefcase. The possessive case, indicated by an apostrophe plus an *s*, doesn't always have to mean possession of a material object; it can simply describe—as in *a day's wages for a day's work*. In speech, possessive nouns sound just like plural nouns because they both have the *s* marker or *s* sound, but you can distinguish between them when you write. Just keep the notion of singular and plural distinct from the idea of possessive. That is, to make a singular noun possessive, add an apostrophe plus *s*. If the singular noun already ends in *s*, you may still add apostrophe *s*. To make a plural noun possessive, add an apostrophe after the final *s* at the end of the word. If the plural form does not end in *s*, add apostrophe plus *s* (as in *children's* toys or *men's* clothing). Consider, for instance, the plurals and possessive forms of *boy:*

Singular noun	boy	(the unadorned noun)
Singular possessive	boy's	(singular noun plus apostrophe and *s*)
Plural noun	boys	(singular noun plus *s*)
Plural possessive	boys'	(plural noun already ending in s, plus apostrophe)

Just plain singular nouns and just plain plurals don't require apostrophes. A common error in commercial signs is the unnecessary apostrophe: *Get your doughnut's here!* reads (incorrectly) a sign in a local shop.

Now take a look at the plural and possessive forms of the proper noun *Ross*, whose singular form ends in *s:*

Singular noun	Ross
Singular possessive	Ross's new boots
Plural noun	Rosses (a whole family of them!)
Plural possessive	the Rosses' summer home

Now put your understanding of possessives to work by filling in the following chart. This work will give you practice in using possessives correctly.

·· | WORK WITH POSSESSIVES | ·······································

Study the first few rows in this chart, then fill in the empty slots by determining the pattern of plurals and possessives.

Singular	Singular Possessive	Plural	Plural Possessive
boy	boy's	boys	boys'
family	family's	families	families'
student	student's	students	students'
evening	evening's	evenings	

(continued)

dog		dogs	dogs'
house		houses	
	mouse's		
bus			
			moments'
deer		deer	
			friends'
	horse's		

Being able to differentiate plural from possessive is key to choosing the appropriate form in writing, particularly when you revise. Remember: if the word you wish to make possessive is singular, simply add an apostrophe plus an *s*. If the word is already plural, add the apostrophe only if the word already ends in *s*. If it does not end in *s*, add apostrophe plus *s*.

For Writing

Choose one row from the previous chart and write four sentences, one using each form of the noun correctly. Be sure to include enough contextual clues in your sentences to make the nouns make sense.

Noun Suffixes. Another way we identify nouns, perhaps even subconsciously, is by certain suffixes that typically mark nouns:

- *-er*, meaning one who does a certain action or one who represents a certain quality. Added to a verb **base form**, *-er* produces *teacher, writer, dancer, lamplighter, joker, lover, fighter*. The base form is the verb form without any endings; the base form is the same as the present tense form for all verbs except *be*. A variation of this is the *–or* suffix: *favor, rumor, traitor*. Be careful: not every word ending in *-er* or *-or* is a noun: think of *slower*, for instance, or *freer*, which are not nouns.

- *-ness*, meaning *state, quality, condition,* or *degree of being*. Added to an adjective, *-ness* produces *happiness, greediness, emptiness, wariness, loveliness*.

- *-ity*, meaning *state* or *quality of being*, as in *probity, rarity, charity, alacrity*

- *-cy*, also meaning *state, condition,* or *quality* as in *bankruptcy, lunacy, idiocy, truancy, fluency*

- *-dom*, meaning *state, condition, domain,* or *a particular office or position*, as in *kingdom, freedom, boredom*

- *-ment*, designating an *action or process* or *the result of an action or process*, as in *excitement, embarrassment, judgment, accomplishment, embezzlement*

- *-tion,* meaning *a state, quality,* or *condition,* as in *abbreviation, accumulation, action, direction*

- *-ure,* meaning *act, process,* or *function,* as in *departure, aperture, closure, fissure*

Test Sentence for Nouns. In *Understanding English* (1958), linguist and grammarian Paul Roberts identified test sentences for all form classes. Once you think you have identified a noun, you can try it in Roberts's noun test sentence:

I lost my _____.

Almost every noun you can think of, concrete or abstract, count or non-count, will fit into this sentence:

I lost my **money.**
I lost my **joy.**
I lost my **happiness.**
I lost my **books.**
I lost my **card.**
I lost my **purse.**
I lost my **enthusiasm.**
I lost my **love.**
I lost my **England.** (Only metaphorically!)
I lost my **Smith** (if you owned one!).

Adjectives and Noun Clusters

Certain words—adjectives and determiners, specifically—tend to hang around nouns to create noun clusters. A noun cluster is a noun plus any modifiers or words that pattern with the noun or relate to it in some way, words that enhance or restrict or define or amplify the meaning of the noun.

Adjectives

The most common and important of these modifying words is the **adjective,** a form class most closely related to nouns and clustering with nouns. The function of adjectives is to describe and to limit, to tell us more about the noun in question. There are several ways you can identify adjectives:

Position of Adjectives in the Sentence. Most adjectives in English occur very near nouns, typically (but not always) **before** nouns: the *yellow* dress, her *dirty* hair, a *fresh* flower, a *weary* soldier, a *friendly* smile. Another position where you'll often find adjectives is following a *be* verb (*am, is, are, was, were, be, being, been*) or other verbs that function as linking verbs as part of an **S-LV-PA pattern**. Linking verbs link or join the subject and a sentence completer or complement:

> The child is *young*.
> The dog is *rabid*.
> We will be *late*.
> The food was *fresh*.
> Our fire will be *hot*.
> The journey seems *long*.
> Fred's voice sounded *raspy*.

Occasionally, adjectives may not be in their usual positions—they may be neither pre-noun (before the noun) nor postlinking verb (after a linking verb). Sometimes adjectives do follow nouns. In such cases, adjectives occurring in such unfamiliar sentence positions attract extra attention from readers and listeners alike. They are more rhetorically **emphatic**. When this is the case, the adjectives are frequently paired:

> The road, *hot* and *dusty* beneath our feet, stretched far into the horizon.
> We ate the peaches, *succulent* and *warm*, as quickly as we could.

The rhetorical effect of paired adjectives after the noun is two–fold: the adjectives slow down the sentence, creating a sentence-interrupting phrase; and they lend emphasis to the noun as the recipient of the attention from the set-off words. These adjectives also draw extra attention because they are not in their usual place in the sentence. If you want to be sure that your readers notice a particular idea or thing or phenomenon, use a pair of adjectives following it to draw more attention to it.

Adjectives and the Potential of Degree. In addition to its position in a sentence, an adjective can be identified by its ability to express degree or intensity. For instance, we can say "I am *rich;* but John is *richer;* and Frances is *richest* of us all." When you compare two items, use the *-er* degree or **comparative form** or the word *more* (with most words of more than three syllables). When you compare more than two items, use the *-est* degree or **superlative form** of the adjective or the word *most* (also with most words of more than three syllables). Sometimes we also use *more* and *most* with the basic form of the adjective because the sound is more euphonious or pleasing. Look at these series of adjectives:

ugly	uglier	ugliest
tall	taller	tallest
lonely	lonelier	loneliest
late	later	latest

cheap	cheaper	cheapest
friendly	friendlier	friendliest
weary	wearier	weariest
maudlin	more maudlin	most maudlin
sanitary	more sanitary	most sanitary

Adjective Suffixes. Like nouns, some adjectives have characteristic endings. We just looked at the adjectival suffixes that signal degree, *-er* and *-est*. Other suffixes typical of adjectives are in the following list. All of them add the meaning of "the quality of being" or "full of" or "characteristic of" or "concerning" to the base word.

-ly, as in *lovely, lonely, friendly*

-y, as in *blurry, teary, mopey, dirty, flirty*

-able, as in *comfortable, lovable, huggable*

-ful as in *playful, sorrowful, mournful*

-ish as in *bookish, waspish, greenish*

-ous as in *dangerous, virtuous, bounteous*

-ic as in *scientific, horrific, beatific*

-less as in *friendless, useless, worthless*

Test Sentence for Adjectives. We can also identify adjectives with a test sentence. To test whether a word is an adjective, try putting it in another of Roberts's test sentences. Here is his test sentence for adjectives:

A(n) _____ something is something that is _____.

An *old* something is something that is *old;* a *smelly* something is something that is *smelly;* a *red* something is something that is *red;* a *tall* something is something that is *tall.* Try a noun in the slot: a **chair** something is something that is **chair**—it doesn't make sense. Try a verb: a **run** something is something that is **run**. This option doesn't make sense either. But some forms of verbs, the ones called **participles**, the ones that end in *-ed,* *-en,* or *-ing,* can function or act as adjectives to pattern with nouns: A **running** something is something that is **running**. In most cases where participles pattern before nouns, the difference between the participle and an adjective that would occur in the same position is not clear—and is simply not significant. If it does the job of an adjective and fits in the test pattern, call it an adjective. This is one of the principles of structural grammar; although items can often be identified by form (their physical shape) as well as by their function (what they do or how they act) and although both form and function matter in ascertaining form class, function is somewhat more important than form in understanding and labeling words.

Other Parts of the Noun Cluster: The Determiner

Determiners are structure words that also signal nouns and are vital parts of the noun cluster. (You can read more about them in the next chapter in the discussion of structure words.) Determiners help to *determine* or specify nouns. Some determiners are these:

> *a, an, the* (called *articles* in traditional grammar)
>
> *her, his, my, our, their* (*personal possessive pronouns* in traditional grammar)
>
> *this, that, these, those* (*demonstrative pronouns* in traditional grammar)
>
> *some, any, many, few, most, least* (quantitative words)

Any time you see a determiner, look for a noun soon to follow.

FOR WRITING

Create a noun cluster for each noun by adding a determiner and at least one adjective to each noun. Use a variety of determiners and adjectives. You might also consider adding some prepositional phrases. Some examples are done for you:

1. plan=a bold plan
2. figurines=some breakable figurines from her collection
3. bears=many dirty brown bears with long mangy hair
4. turns=
5. director=
6. teacher=
7. waffles=
8. mall=
9. hearing=
10. room=

Other Parts of the Noun Cluster: Noun Adjuncts

In noun clusters, sometimes nouns pattern alongside other nouns: *the computer lab, a time machine, a dust cloth, a bicycle rack, a test case, a hat rack, skin diseases, bush pilots.* In these phrases, words ordinarily considered nouns (like *computer*) pattern with other nouns (like *lab*) to restrict and define the original nouns. The first noun in each pair functions adjectivally, even though it doesn't quite fulfill the criteria for a true adjective. We call these modifying nouns **noun adjuncts**, nouns functioning as adjunct to other nouns (or alongside them in a supporting role). These noun adjuncts function only **before** the noun, not in postnoun or postverb positions as complements. For instance, we can say *The patient has a skin disease* but not *The patient has a disease skin* or *The disease is skin*. Incidentally, many noun adjuncts eventually end up as parts of compound words: *fireplace, lamppost, thumbnail, bonfire* (originally *bone + fire*).

For Discussion

In your writers' group, discuss the following sentences, all of which contain a variety of adjectives, determiners, and noun adjuncts in their noun clusters. Be ready to explain the components of the noun clusters to the class as a whole.

1. Jerry broke the leg of the desk chair.
2. Our small investment group made a lot of money before the crash of tech stocks.
3. Do you know the way to the computer center?
4. In her will, Aunt Bea left her antique china cabinet to Opie.
5. Tanika's small clothes closet is stuffed with long coats.

For Writing

Create a noun cluster by adding a determiner plus a noun adjunct to each of the following nouns. Add prepositional phrases where they are appropriate. A few examples are done for you.

1. case=a camera case
2. agent=my insurance agent
3. worker=the iron worker from Pittsburgh
4. markers=
5. zone=
6. friend=
7. teeth=
8. inspector=
9. quality=
10. babies=

Other Parts of the Noun Cluster: Prepositional Phrases

Another common component of the noun cluster is the prepositional phrase. A prepositional phrase is built of a preposition and its object, a noun, and any words that may cluster around the noun object. If the noun object has modifiers of its own, all the modifiers are *constituent*—that is, they *constitute* part of the prepositional phrase and are thus considered part of the prepositional phrase. When prepositional phrases occur in noun clusters, they serve nouns. This is called *patterning with* or *modifying* the noun. It is possible to have prepositional phrases within prepositional phrases within prepositional phrases— and noun clusters within noun clusters within noun clusters.

There are many prepositions in English, and they are important in the scheme of the sentence, for they express relationships between words and ideas. Often these relationships are spatial (as signaled by *near, over, around*). Some common prepositions are

above	*down*	*through*
around	*during*	*to*
at	*for*	*toward*
below	*from*	*with*
beneath	*in*	*within*
beside	*near*	*without*
between	*of*	
by	*on*	

In English, we also have phrasal prepositions, several prepositions patterning together with a noun to create a prepositional phrase. Some phrasal prepositions are

according to	*by means of*	*instead of*
ahead of	*except for*	*next to*
along with	*in case of*	*on behalf of*
because of	*in front of*	*out of*
but for	*in spite of*	*thanks to*

Each phrasal preposition functions or acts just like a single-word preposition and when patterned with a noun or noun cluster, creates a prepositional phrase: *in spite of my friend's best efforts, according to the rules of the game, instead of vegetable lasagna*. It is important to understand that several words can—and frequently do—function as a unit in English. Remember to look for phrasal prepositions when you are analyzing sentences and remember to use them to show particular relationships within the sentence.

FOR DISCUSSION

For each noun cluster, discuss in your writers' group how the prepositional phrase functions or operates. Consider how the prepositional phrase changes or restricts or develops the idea presented by the noun headword. Some of the phrases have phrases within them. Make note of adjectives and noun adjuncts in the noun clusters in your discussion as well and be prepared to present some of your discussion to the class as a whole.

1. . . . an ordinary inspector **in a paper bag factory**
2. . . . a dirty plastic bottle **of about 200 plain white pills**
3. . . . something **about the whole village**
4. . . . a shrill sound **of pain**
5. . . . a fatal accident **in the gravel quarry**
6. . . . some nasty rumors **about deaths from sickness**

(continued)

7. . . . the greenhouse effect **of pollution**
8. . . . a report **from the commodities market**
9. . . . the soft sound **of waves on the shore**
10. . . . a wad **of cotton**
11. . . . a quart **of light beer**
12. . . . a new battery **in the radio**
13. . . . the carpets **in the sitting room**
14. . . . an electrified fence **outside the electrified fence around the perimeter**
15. . . . the light **over the shaving mirror**

For Writing

Make a list of 40 prepositional phrases using the prepositions mentioned earlier and others you can think of. Then think of a separate noun **headword** for each phrase to pattern with and pair that noun headword with a determiner. A headword is the word at the head or center of the cluster. Finally, link the headword and the phrase to create 40 noun clusters that include prepositional phrases. Here are three examples:

1. beneath the floor + treasure = the treasure beneath the floor
2. without stripes + awnings = those awnings without stripes
3. in time and money + cost = the cost in time and money

Remember to create the prepositional phrase first; it's easier that way.

For Writing

Look at the following simple noun clusters and see if you can first, point out the noun headword or word that all the other words tend to cluster or gather around; and second, identify the other kinds of words that make up each cluster:

1. the delta of a small stream
2. a demolished automobile
3. the rate change
4. the small, sleeping female bear
5. some yellow, curling sycamore leaves
6. too many boring chords
7. the famous Henry James
8. literary embarrassment
9. a bad mustache with sprinkles of gray hair
10. four towns in Kosovo

> ### FOR WRITING
>
> Now build noun clusters of great variety around any 10 of these nouns: *damage, freedom, crux, reader, philosopher, book, foundation, leg, magnetism, sheet, opera, pages, eternity, herring, universe, journey, mother, sculpture, beggar, objection, witness, flowers.*

> ### FOR WRITING
>
> Then work each of these nouns, adjectives, determiners, or noun adjuncts into separate noun clusters: *aggressive, development, last-second, two, this, tiny, brief, dusk, hitless, several.*

> ### FOR DISCUSSION
>
> In the following passage, choose two noun clusters you think are interesting. Copy out just the noun clusters. Then, working with your writers' group, analyze the structures of the clusters and report your findings to the class. Remember: you can find noun clusters within noun clusters, nested like Russian dolls.
>
> > This observation makes Mr. Krech laugh now, a soft, quick chuckle that wells up from his broad chest. He is a tall man with a slightly forward-leaning stance and sharp eyes that seem to spot every bird on the horizon, most of which he can identify. One can easily imagine him a formidable hunter, even in the deep snows of a forest that was alien to him.—Jeff Sharlet

S *umming Up: Noun Clusters*

Nouns and noun clusters most likely constitute our first contact with language; for babies learning to talk and navigate their environments, naming the world about them is the first step to becoming a being with verbal language. Thus nouns are usually the first words uttered: *mama, dog, dada, milk, bug.* Nouns are indeed a large part of our vocabularies; they are essential for communication, for they name what we are talking, thinking, and dreaming about. But noun clusters are only half of written and oral expression; verbs are the other half. Go to the next chapter now to learn about verbs and verb clusters as well as the structure words that help hold sentences together.

3

Naming the Parts, 2: Form Classes, Verb Clusters, Structure Words

We have just finished working with the form classes of nouns and adjectives and the structure words that compose noun clusters. Let us now turn to verb clusters, which typically contain the other two major form classes, verbs and adverbs, as well as structure words. We will then look more closely at the structure word classes.

Verbs: The Heart of the Sentence

Verbs are the other major building block of English syntax or sentence structure, the other half of the noun/verb binary. Together, nouns and verbs constitute most of the content or meaning in a sentence. Nouns are naming words, essentially static words expressing *what*. Verbs, however, are rooted in a concept of time; they express the *how*, frequently through action or the description or reflection or trace of action—action that may be physical, psychological, emotional, or social. Think of these verbs: *do, working, be, grabbed, remain, fretted, arguing, sign, will meditate*. Some of them (like *working*) evoke a physical action; others, a mental one (*meditate*, for example). But all imply that something is happening, occurring, in some variable state of energy. In short, verbs animate nouns. Verbs move ideas. Verbs make sentences go. Verbs differ greatly from nouns; verbs complement or complete nouns. Together these two binaries within the English sentence create complete ideas and utterances.

How can you identify verbs? In many of the same ways that you can identify nouns: by their positions in sentences, by their suffixes, and by their making sense in a test sentence. But verbs also differ from nouns in an important way—their ability to have tense. Let's begin our work with verbs here, with tense.

Verbs' Ability to Have Tense. One way to identify a verb is to realize that it can express an element of time and that all English verbs can express both present and past time. Past time is expressed in **past tense**. Many verbs form past tense simply by adding an *-ed* to the base of the verb: *added, worked, listened, imagined*. Sometimes you may see the verb base referred to as the **verb stem** or the **infinitive**; the base also looks like the present tense, singular, form. On the other hand, many verbs form past tense by adding *-t* or other endings, or by vowel changes inside the word: *teach-taught; buy-bought; see-saw; go-went; do-did*; and so on. Regardless of how past tense is formed, the fact that it *can* be formed means the word in question is a verb. To test whether a word is a verb, then, see if you can make it past tense.

Another identifying characteristic of verbs is the fact that they have principal parts with which to form various tenses. You may remember in elementary school rehearsing the **principal parts of verbs**. Some of these verb parts combine with auxiliaries to form the various tenses. The principal parts include (1) the base or infinitive or present tense form, (2) the past tense form (usually signaled by *-ed*), (3) the past participle form (usually ends with *-ed, -en, -n,* or *-t),* and the (4) present participle form (ends always in *-ing*). It may be useful to recall some principal parts of verbs by working through the next writing task. Here are the principal parts of the verb *choose:*

Base form	*choose,* as in *I choose what I want to eat.*
Past tense form	*chose,* as in *Jack chose Fred for his partner two years ago.*
Past participle	*chosen,* as in *The team has chosen to kneel.*
Present participle	*choosing,* as in *Annie is choosing her wedding gown now.*

For Writing—Principal Parts of Verbs. Fill in the following chart with the missing principal part of the verb. If you can't recall some of the forms of these verbs, you can look them up in a dictionary under the verb in question. The first few are completed as examples.

• •

Simple Present (1st Person)	Past Tense	Past Participle	Present Participle
1. (I) look	(I) looked	(I have) looked	(I am) looking
2. run	ran	run	running
3. emphasize	emphasized	emphasized	emphasizing
4. drive	___	driven	___
5. ___	___	___	sneaking

(continued)

6. treat	treated	____	____
7. go	____	gone	____
8. ____	____	____	roasting
9. dive	dived	____	____
10. ____	lay	lain	lying
11. lay	____	laid	laying
12. wear	wore	worn	____
13. ____	loved	____	____
14. grade	____	____	grading
15. abjure	____	____	____
16. ____	had	____	____
17. ____	____	believed	____
18. ____	____	____	frying
19. open	____	opened	____
20. ____	____	____	agitating

Verbs and Agreement

English verbs and their subjects have very close, even symbiotic, relationships. Thus, a verb must reflect (or match or agree with) the person of its subject; this means the form of a verb may change if your discourse changes from first person (*I, we*) to second person (*you*) or to third person (*he, she, it, they, the teacher, Sam*). To clarify: **first person** refers to the person speaking or doing the acting: *I*. **Second person** refers to a person being addressed or spoken to: *you*. **Third person** refers to a person spoken of or talked about, as if the person were not present: *he, she, it, miners, Tom Swift, Madeleine Albright, lambs, my piano teacher* (more about this later with conjugations).

A verb must also reflect or agree with the number of its subject. Number refers to how many people are embodied in the subject—but English distinguishes only two levels of number: one and more than one—or singular and plural. Thus we learn from childhood to say *Doug Flutie was* (not *Doug Flutie were*) and *The birds fly* (not *The birds flies*). English verbs change as their subjects change: if a subject is singular, the verb must reflect that singularity or *agree* with the number of its subject.

English verbs also have several other ways of presenting themselves. They have, for instance, mood (also called **mode**): **indicative**, **imperative**, and **subjunctive** (also called **conditional**). Don't let the language of these terms distract you. *Indicative* is the mood of the simple statement; you might think of its association with *indicate* (meaning *to point out*); verbs in the indicative mode simply point to some phenomenon, stating ideas or facts or presenting information. This is the usual (and most common) verb mode. A second mode is the *imperative* or command mode; here you can just remember an *imperious* person telling or commanding someone else what to do: *Take out the trash! Revise that poem!* Imperative mode verbs give orders. Finally, verbs may be cast in the *subjunctive* or *conditional* mood or mode; this mood expresses ideas contrary to fact, ideas in the realm of the imagined, ideas articulating something wishful or anticipatory: *If I were you, I'd cut my hair* or *Were this my boat, I would get a bigger motor.* Pay attention to the *If I were* structure: *be* has an important role in the subjunctive mode. The subjunctive mode is used less than it used to be. Fewer educated people know about and understand the subjunctive, and fewer people use it still. So you may indeed hear educated people say *If I **was** that lottery winner, I'd invest in Microsoft.*

You should also know that verbs have still another quality called aspect: **aspect** refers simply to whether the action of the verb is completed or ongoing. You'll read more about this when you work with perfect and progressive aspects, which are often also called perfect and progressive tenses. The perfect aspect is created with a form of *have* plus the past participle of the verb (*have shopped, had done, will have written*); the progressive aspect is created with a form of *be* plus the present participle of the verb (*is shopping, had been shopping, will have been shopping*). When you package all this information about person, number, mood, aspect, and tense, you have a verb conjugation. When you chart out these forms of a verb, you **conjugate** that verb. Let's put all these elements of verbs into a rubric, then, and look at some **conjugations**.

Here is an active voice, indicative mood conjugation of the regular verb *open*, with all the simple tenses laid out for you to see:

CONJUGATION OF *OPEN*, SIMPLE TENSES

Singular   Plural

PRESENT TENSE

I open	We open
You open	You open
She opens*	They open

*The third person singular form of the verb always ends in *-s* in English.

PAST TENSE

I opened	We opened
You opened	You opened
He opened	They opened

This regular verb forms its past tense by adding *-ed.*

FUTURE TENSE

I shall open	We shall open
You will open	You will open
She will open	They will open

Historically, *shall* is used with first person future tenses; *will*, with second and third persons—but rarely these days.

Conjugation of Open, Perfect Tenses

Perfect tenses (also *aspects*, you'll remember) are formed with the appropriate tense of **have** plus the past participle (ends in *-ed, -en,* or *-n*) of the verb being conjugated. In this case, the past participle is *opened*. The *perfect aspect* of the verb shows that the action of the verb was ongoing but is now completed. Don't forget that *aspect* simply refers to whether the verb's action is completed or ongoing.

PRESENT PERFECT

I have opened*	We have opened
You have opened	You have opened
He has opened	They have opened

*Note the *-ed* form of the verb or the past participle, paired with the present tense of *have*. The present perfect describes an action, here *opening*, that has taken place repeatedly in the past and continues into the present: He *has opened* that cellar door every day for the last 20 years.

PAST PERFECT

I had opened	We had opened
You had opened	You had opened
She had opened	They had opened

Derive the past perfect of *open* by pairing the past tense of *have* with the past participle of *open*. Past perfect refers to an action that was begun and completed in the past: The children *had opened* their presents by one o'clock.

FUTURE PERFECT

I shall have opened	We shall have opened
You will have opened	You will have opened
He will have opened	They will have opened

To form the future perfect tense of *open*, use the future tense of *have* plus the past participle of *open, opened*. The future perfect refers to a future time when something will be completed: By the time the next watchman makes a round, he *will have opened* the vault.

C onjugation of Open, Progressive Tenses

Progressive tenses are formed with the appropriate tense of **be** plus the present participle (ends in *-ing*) of the verb being conjugated—in this case, *opening*. Progressive tenses, which illustrate the *progressive aspect* of the verb, indicate an ongoing or continuing action.

PRESENT PROGRESSIVE

I am opening*	We are opening
You are opening	You are opening
She is opening	They are opening

*Present progressive is formed with the present tense of *be* (*am*) plus the present participle (ending in *-ing*). Present progressive describes an event in progress at the current time: We *are opening* the garage door right now.

PAST PROGRESSIVE

I was opening	We were opening
You were opening	You were opening
He was opening	They were opening

Past progressive refers to what was happening at a given point in the past: When the alarm went off, he *was opening* the vault. Use the past tense of *be* (*was*) with the present participle.

FUTURE PROGRESSIVE

I shall be opening	We shall be opening
You will be opening	You will be opening
She will be opening	They will be opening

Future progressive describes what will be going on at a given point in the future: By this time next year, we *will be opening* our new restaurant in Nashville. Form future progressive by combining the future tense of *be* (*will be*) plus the present participle, *opening*.

PRESENT PERFECT PROGRESSIVE

I have been opening	We have been opening
You have been opening	You have been opening
Thomas has been opening	They have been opening

Present perfect progressive describes an ongoing action begun in the past and continuing into the future: You *have been opening* that package for 10 minutes. Present perfect tense of *be* plus the present participle of *open, opening,* yields the perfect progressive.

PAST PERFECT PROGRESSIVE

I had been opening	We had been opening
You had been opening	You had been opening
Francine had been opening	The children had been opening

Past perfect progressive refers to an action entirely in the past; the action was at one time ongoing but then at one point stopped: The children *had been opening* their holiday gifts before the bomb hit. Note the past perfect tense of *be* plus the present participle.

FUTURE PERFECT PROGRESSIVE

I shall have been opening	We shall have been opening
You will have been opening	You will have been opening
She will have been opening	They will have been opening

The future perfect progressive refers to an action begun some time in the past and enduring to a definite point in the future: By tomorrow morning, the coroner's deputies *will have been opening* graves for 24 hours. Combine the future perfect tense of *be* plus the present participle of *open.*

Besides this simple conjugation in active voice, you can also make a conjugation to illustrate subjunctive or conditional mood (used to express an action that is contrary to fact, imagined, or hypothetical). You can also create a conjugation in passive voice (more about passive voice later). For now, though, here's a conjugation of *tell* in active voice with all the simple tenses, all in one chart.

·· CONJUGATION OF *TELL*, ACTIVE VOICE ······················

Tense	Singular Forms	Plural Forms
Simple Present Tense	I tell	We tell
	You tell	You tell
	James tells	They tell
Simple Past Tense	I told	We told
	You told	You told
	Eleanor told	All the boys told
Simple Future Tense	I shall tell	We shall tell
	You will tell	You will tell
	My sister will tell	They will tell
Present Perfect	I have told	We have told
	You have told	You have told
	She has told	They have told
Past Perfect	I had told	We had told
	You had told	You had told
	Sean had told	The whole class had told

(continued)

Future Perfect	I shall have told	We shall have told
	You will have told	You will have told
	The punk will have told	They will have told
Present Progressive	I am telling	We are telling
	You are telling	You are telling
	Sue is telling	The children are telling
Past Progressive	I was telling	We were telling
	You were telling	You were telling
	The general was telling	They were telling
Future Progressive	I shall be telling	We shall be telling
	You will be telling	You will be telling
	Francine will be telling	All of them will be telling
Present Perfect Progressive	I have been telling	We have been telling
	You have been telling	You have been telling
	The comedian has been telling	Our teachers have been telling
Past Perfect Progressive	I had been telling	We had been telling
	You had been telling	You had been telling
	He had been telling	They had been telling
Future Perfect Progressive	I shall have been telling	We shall have been telling
	You will have been telling	You will have been telling
	The first-grader will have been telling	All the children will have been telling

---

FOR WRITING

Conjugate three of these verbs through all the simple, perfect, and progressive tenses in indicative mood: *catch, comfort, continue, care, come, count, cause, confuse.* Then choose one of the verbs and write a sentence using each tense appropriately.

Not all grammarians think about verbs in the same way or describe verbs with similar language. Some grammarians argue that English actually has only two tenses, present and past, and that what we have in a conjugation and sometimes call a variety of tenses are actually variations in mood and aspect of the verb. If, for example, you want to indicate a future action in conjunction with your homework, you might combine the subjunctive or conditional form *will* with the present *do* and write *I will do my homework later.* Thinking about the tenses and the language in this way may simplify the concept of tense for you.

Verbs' Position in the Sentence. Verbs and verb clusters pair with and follow nouns in sentences. A typical English sentence (but don't forget: many sentences are not typical) begins with a noun cluster, which is then followed by a verb cluster; this is the case in the following sentences, where verb clusters (*bold*) follow the noun subjects.

- The coyotes **are howling**.
- The sky **opens up to reveal the sun**.
- Frederick **sighed loudly**.
- Two dogs **slept in the stream of sunlight**.

In other kinds of sentences, verbs or verb clusters occupy a middle slot between two nouns or noun clusters and express a relationship between the nouns:

- Janet **put** a log on the fire.
- Nathan **answered** the phone.
- The electrician **will clip** the wires.
- These teachers always **grade** many examinations.

Verb Suffixes. Another way to recognize verbs is by their characteristic suffixes. A few endings besides the *-ed*, *-en*, and *-ing* tense endings may affix themselves to verbs: *-ify*, as in *typify; -en*, as in *whiten* or *lighten; -ate*, as in *agitate;* and *-ize*, as in *womanize* and *legalize*. In fact, many nouns and adjectives are transformed into verbs in just this way. Add *-ize* to the noun *computer*, for instance, and you get *computerize: The consulting firm can computerize all the records for you.* Some language purists do not like these new word formations or **neologisms** (*neo* = new and *logos* = word). Most linguists recognize, however, that languages change and adapt to fit the needs of native speakers to express themselves. Linguists understand these new words and changes in word forms as natural and healthy in the life of a language.

Test Pattern for Verbs. Another way you can test a word to determine its "verbness" is to see if you can fit it into one of these test patterns for verbs by Paul Roberts:

Let's _____. (or) Let's _____ it. (Let's **eat**. Let's **finish** it.)
He might _____. (or) He might _____ it. (He might **succeed**. He might **forget** it.)

The Phrasal Verb. A verb may also be phrasal; it may combine a verb plus a particle, which is a preposition without its object—*up*, for example, or *out*. Prepositions have to have objects; particles don't. The meaning of the verb is subtly affected by the particle paired with it. Consider the verb *turn;* if you pair it with *up,* you have *turn up*—as in *turn up the thermostat.* This meaning of *turn* is quite different from *turn* + *around: That new coach will turn around the team's performance within a week.* And it also differs from *turn* + *down,* as in *turn down the stereo* and *turn* + *over,* as in *turn over a new leaf.* Each meaning of *turn* is unique because of a combination with a particle.

Some of the most common phrasal verbs are

break in	*made out*	*turn around*
break out	*made up*	*turn down*
break through	*make up with*	*turn over*
break up	*pass around*	*turn up*
come forward	*pass out*	*wear out*
give in	*pull through*	

Can you think of others?

Verb Clusters

Simple verb clusters are composed of verbs, their auxiliaries, their most common modifiers—adverbs—and the words that modify or pattern with them. Let's take a look at auxiliaries first and then adverbs, a very versatile class of words.

Auxiliaries and Verbs

Auxiliary means secondary, functioning alongside or patterning with the primary word—in this case, a verb. You have probably heard **auxiliary verbs** called *helping verbs.* This class of words is fairly small and composed largely of the forms of *do, be,* and *have: Do* you *remember* the answer? I *am* tired, We *had* completed the task, You *will be* bored. Although this class of words is small, it is important: *do* and *did* are critical for asking questions; the *be* verbs are essential for forming progressive tenses and passive voice; and *have* is necessary for perfect tenses. Also included in the class of auxiliary verbs are what are also called the modal verbs or modals. Modals, which express conditions applying to main verbs, are never used as main verbs, only as auxiliaries (except in some sentences where the verb is implied). Modals can help the main verb express these conditions: possibility, probability, obligation, necessity, anticipation. Here are examples to fit each condition:

> *can, could* (the condition of possibility)
> *may, might* (the condition of probability)
> *shall, should* (the condition of obligation)
> *must, have to* (the condition of necessity)
> *will, would* (the condition of intent or anticipation)

Did you see that the modals have only the two tenses (or the one aspect)? We can't create a present perfect tense with *can* or *shall,* for instance, because these words have no participle. We don't say *I have can* or *You are shalling.*

Auxiliaries, including modals, have two rhetorical purposes and effects. First, they allow you the writer to express different tenses or states of verbs and subtly to differentiate time and duration (take another look at the section on aspects of verbs if you are fuzzy on this). And second, auxiliaries make it possible to express conditionality, to hedge, to equivocate, to qualify. Consider these statements:

1. *We may buy a new car this spring.* (We're not sure and we're not committing ourselves!)
2. *Johnnie Fred could go to Paris.* (But we're not sure that he is going: he's simply capable of doing so.)
3. *Ellie should be going to the Rangers games this season.* (But there's no absolute certainty that she will.)

Adverbs

As a form class, adverbs pattern with verbs to express three main conditions of verbs: **where, how,** and **when.** The *where* class of adverbs specifying place or location can be represented by the typical adverb *there.* The *how* class of adverbs or the adverbs of manner are epitomized in *thus.* And the *when* adverbs or the *temporal* (related to time) adverbs can be recalled with the typical adverb *then.* It's easy to remember the **there/thus/then** trio of meanings. Incidentally, the largest of these adverb groups is the *thus* group—*angrily, beautifully, fully*—the adverbs formed by the addition of *-ly* to adjectives like *angry, beautiful,* and *full.* Regardless of what kind they are, however, adverbs work with verbs to limit, define, or extend the meaning of verbs. You might remember this by thinking of an *adverb* as a word that **ad**heres to **verbs.** We use adverbs rhetorically to expand verb clusters and to deepen the reader's understanding of the action of the sentence, regardless of the extent of that action (which may not be physical or overt, you will recall).

Understanding Adverbs: Movability. The most definable characteristic of an adverb or adverbial phrase or clause is movability: anything adverbial is more portable and flexible than any other form class. Think of the adverb *quickly,* for instance, and of all the places you can insert it in this sentence:

The students left the room.

Quickly the students left the room.

The students **quickly** left the room.

The students left the room **quickly.**

Try substituting the adverbial phrase *in a rush* in the same slots that quickly occupies: you'll find that the phrase works in exactly the same way as the word. The movability factor also applies to adverbial clauses; you'll find that *when the fire alarm rang* can also fit in the previous sentences exactly where *quickly* fits: introducing the sentence; before the verb; after the verb phrase.

Understanding Adverbs: Sentence Position. Finally, adverbs tend to pattern in the blank slots in sentences like the following: "She walked _____" or "She had _____done it" (again, Paul Roberts's suggested test sentences). You can check whether a word is an adverb because it is likely to pattern in one of these sentences: *She walked **slowly** or She had **always** done it.* These slots literally cluster around the verb, right before and right after it.

Other Parts of the Verb Cluster: Intensifiers

Intensifiers (also called **qualifiers** by some grammarians) do exactly what their name says they do: they intensify or change the degree of meaning of words with which they pattern. The rhetorical effect of words like *too, very, quite, almost, so,* and *extremely* is to mitigate, increase, or reduce the impact of the words they modify. Intensifiers frequently pattern with adverbs in verb clusters. Think about the difference between *The thugs strode smugly out of the pool hall* and *The thugs strode very smugly out of the pool hall; My sister smiled slyly* and *My sister smiled quite slyly.* In traditional grammar, you would call these words *very* and *quite* adverbs modifying adjectives and other adverbs. They are different from regular adverbs because they don't pattern with verbs; they pattern only with adverbs and adjectives. Let's differentiate them and call them intensifiers.

FOR WRITING

Extend these verb clusters by adding adverbs and intensifiers to these verbs, auxiliaries, and (sometimes) objects. Two are done for you as examples.

1. is reading—*is very quietly reading an ancient volume*
2. took breakfast—*leisurely took a very long breakfast*
3. swills ale
4. slept
5. peeks
6. has considered
7. had scrubbed the hall
8. will order too much merchandise
9. had prayed
10. charges

Other Parts of the Verb Cluster: Prepositional Phrases

A prepositional phrase is built of a preposition plus its object, which is a noun or a noun cluster. If the object has words patterning with it or modifiers of its own, the string of modifiers is considered part of the prepositional phrase.

Just as prepositional phrases may serve in noun clusters, they may also serve verbs. This is called *patterning with* or *modifying* verbs. Prepositional phrases that pattern with verbs are usually functioning as adverbs that tell *where, when,* or *how: The poodles ate the steak **in dainty bites*** (tells *how*); ***After sunset,** the playground is empty* (tells *when*); *Many squirrels live **in the woods*** (tells *where*). Remember from our discussion of prepositions in noun clusters that there are many prepositions in English and that they are very important in the scheme of the sentence, for they express relationships between words and ideas. In verb clusters, this relationship conveyed by the prepositional phrase is frequently physical or spatial. At other times the relationship is temporal (having to do with time) or causal or analytical (having to do with how or why). Some common prepositions, you will recall, are *around, at, beneath, beside, between, by, down, during, from, for, in, of, on, through, to, toward, with, within, without.*

Just as verbs sometimes occur in phrases, thus creating phrasal verbs, so too with prepositions. Many prepositions pattern together and act as a unit to create variations on the original meaning of the preposition. Consider this partial list of phrasal prepositions:

according to	*except for*	*instead of*
along with	*in back of*	*next to*
as for	*in charge of*	*on behalf of*
because of	*in spite of*	*thanks to*
by means of		

FOR DISCUSSION

In your writers' group, discuss how the underlined prepositional phrases function or work in the following verb clusters. In other words, tell how the prepositional phrase alters or develops the meaning of the verb itself. Be ready to report on one or two of the sentences to the class as a whole.

1. . . . were being passed **down the tables**
2. . . . were moving **in a flat-footed but stealthy way**
3. . . . danced **with a young woman**
4. . . . were vibrating **with the forceful sound waves**

(continued)

5. . . . held the accordion **over his head**
6. . . . tried the same trick **with some success**
7. . . . came back **to the ranch**
8. . . . had not seen **for five years**
9. . . . were leaning **against the wall**
10. . . . **in late summer** accepted a modest sum of money
11. . . . did not marry again **for four seasons**
12. . . . measured a capful **into her glass**
13. . . . came **into Danny's Diner**
14. . . . sat always **at the same corner table**
15. . . . landed **in Binghamton**

For Writing

Make a list of 20 verbs that begin with the letter **P**. Then, using the list of prepositions (both single and phrasal prepositions) provided and others you can find or recall, create a prepositional phrase to accompany each verb—thus creating a verb cluster that includes a prepositional phrase. You may also add objects for the verbs as well as adverbs and intensifiers. Here are a few examples:

pose coyly (for the camera)

has praised her pot roast (to the skies)

is pushing the cart (over the hill)

For Writing

Now build a full and interesting verb cluster around 10 of these verbs: *see, improvise, try, tune, loosen, answer, begin, continue, gather, flicker, hear, yearn, point, rock, get, power, carry, last, affect, glow, break, glitter.* You may use any tense of these verbs.

For Writing

Now work 10 of these words or phrases, all different components of verb clusters, into separate verb clusters: *had, again, at last, in the middle of the room, not, quite, frequently, flinging, from the ceiling, perhaps, always, obligingly, apparently, swiveled.*

For Discussion

In the following passage, choose two verb clusters you think are interesting. Copy out just the verb clusters. Then, working with your writers' group, analyze the structures of the clusters and report your findings back to the class. Remember: you can find clusters within clusters.

> During the days that followed, Sholem Waldman went downhill. His face yellowed, his beard turned greyish, the tip of his nose was ugly with veins and old age overtook him all at once. A bad patient, he longed for spices and greasy foods and fought the super's wife when she came with his drops. He would not budge from his bed, and on the few occasions when a neighbor entered, made believe he was asleep . . . . With medicines and drops and what the super's wife chiseled, the whole business was costing Goldfarb a nice few dollars. —Wallace Markfield

---

S *tructure Words*

We have studied the form classes and along with those, noun and verb clusters. In the discussion of verb clusters, we looked at a few structure words (like prepositions, for instance). Now let's examinine the structure words classes more carefully. These include determiners, pronouns, conjunctions, auxiliaries, intensifiers, and interrogatives. Some structure words have already been discussed extensively elsewhere in this book, so they are omitted here: preposition and particle. Structure words delineate relationships among form class words.

Determiners

You can find determiners before nouns. Their function is to determine or limit the noun, to help the reader or listener ferret out or specify some quality of the noun. Although determiners pattern in some places where you also can find adjectives, determiners are fundamentally different from adjectives. Determiners, unlike adjectives, cannot be headwords or accumulate modifiers; they are strictly words that serve adjectives. These are the most common determiners:

- *a, an, the* (in traditional grammar, called *article adjectives*)
- *no, few, some, several, many, most, all* (in traditional grammar, *indefinite pronominal adjectives*—or pronoun adjectives)
- *my, your, its, his, her, their* (in traditional grammar, the *personal pronominal adjectives*)

- *first, second, third,* and so on (in traditional grammar, *ordinal adjectives*)
- *this, that, these, those* (in traditional grammar, *demonstrative adjectives*)
- *each, every, either, neither*

The students ate many cookies means something totally different than *The students ate few cookies.* The difference lies in the determiner *few,* which limits our concept of *cookies* in this sentence. In the same way, *Dad gave me a dollar* is different from *Dad gave me the dollar. The dollar* refers to a specific dollar, one mentioned specifically in a previous utterance. *A dollar* is a nonspecific, indefinite dollar not referred to previously.

For Discussion

In your writers' group, read the following paragraph aloud, taking care to consider the bolded determiners. Then try substituting other determiners for the bolded ones: what is the effect? How would you explain the significance of determiners to the clear communication of the ideas in this passage from *The Bean Trees* by Barbara Kingsolver? Be prepared to explain your responses to the class as a whole.

> **A** fig grew by **the** back door, **an** old, stubborn tree that was slow to leaf out. **The** moon threw shadows of fig branches that curled like empty hands across Estevan's face and **his** chest. Something inside **this** man was turning inside out. (132)

Pronouns

Pronouns are noun substitutes, common function words whose duty is to stand in for nouns. Pronouns can assume any sentence role that nouns can assume; rhetorically, they help you vary the sound of a sentence and prevent redundancy and repetition. So if you are writing a paragraph about Izzy, the black poodle, and you would ordinarily refer to Izzy throughout eight sentences and 92 words, you can occasionally refer to Izzy as *she* or *her* instead of repeating her name. You can allude to *Izzy's special qualities* by writing *her special qualities* without having to bore your reader.

Pronouns that function in the subject position (typically before verbs and in subject slots) are *he, she, it, I, we, they.* Pronouns that function in the object position (typically after verbs or prepositions and in the object slots) are *him, her, it, me, us, them.* Many pronouns also have a determiner form:

her, his, its, my, our, their—as in *her* brown eyes, *his* faded t-shirt, *its* lovely melody, *my* favorite music, *our* neighbors, *their* weak hearts. The following chart may help you sort out the pronouns.

● ●

Subject Pronouns	Object Pronouns	Determiner Form
I	me	my
we	us	our
you	you	your
she	her	her
he	him	his
it	it	its
they	them	their

You probably saw that some words are on both the pronoun and the determiner list. These overlapping lists illustrate the principle of **multifunction words**: many English words can indeed have multiple functions. In the sentence *He lost his* , *his* is a determiner patterning with the noun *wallet*. In the sentence *He lost his*, *his* is a pronoun substituting for the noun (perhaps *wallet*, in this context) referred to earlier in the discourse.

Conjunctions

Conjunctions are joining words. They join words, phrases, and/or clauses to create meaning. The root *-junct* (as in *junction, juncture*) refers to the joining function of conjunctions, and the prefix *con-* means *together, with,* or *joint*. Different kinds of conjunctions signal different relationships among elements being joined. We'll explore these concepts further in the chapters that examine phrases and clauses. For now, though, here are the major categories of conjunctions and the most common conjunctions in each category:

■ **Coordinating conjunctions** or **coordinators** are conjunctions that join items of equal grammatical importance. *Co-* means *with* or *jointly,* and the Latin root *ordo* means *order;* thus *coordinate* means *to order with* or *to order together.* The coordinators are *and, or, but, for, nor, so, yet.* These words are small, compact, and light. Here are some sentences containing coordinators:

> Izzy and Lady raced across the yard and down the fence line.
> We were early, so the doors were still locked.
> It was Franny or Butch outside the door.

■ **Correlative conjunctions** are coordinating conjunctions that come in pairs, two coordinators that *correlate* or *relate with* one another: *either* and *or; neither* and *nor; both* and *and; not only* and *but also*. Correlative coordinators join compound elements. When you use correlative coordinators, you call special attention to the items they join. When you see the first coordinator of the pair, you automatically anticipate the second one to follow—and pay attention to the text immediately around it. Look at these sentences, identical except for the coordinators.

The homicide detectives checked for blood spatters **and** tissue flecks.

To see the parallelism, look at the sentence this way:

The homicide detectives checked for $\left\{ \begin{array}{l} \textit{blood spatters} \\ \textit{and} \\ \textit{tissue flecks} \end{array} \right.$

The compound objects of the preposition *for, blood spatters* and *tissue flecks,* are joined by the coordinator *and.* Here's another version of the sentence with correlative coordinators:

The homicide detectives checked for **not only** blood spatters **but also** tissue flecks.

Do you see how much more emphatic the *blood* and *tissue* become once they are linked by the correlatives? The correlatives emphasize the parallelism of the compound objects:

The homicide detectives checked for $\left\{ \begin{array}{ll} \textit{not only} & \textit{blood spatters} \\ \\ \textit{but also} & \textit{tissue flecks.} \end{array} \right.$

■ **Subordinating conjunctions** or **subordinators** are conjunctions that join items, particularly clauses, of unequal grammatical importance—these conjunctions typically signal the power in relationship between the elements. *Sub-* means *below, beneath,* or *under;* thus *subordinate* means *to order some things below others.* Some common subordinators are *while, if, though, although, because, before, when.* The subordinating conjunctions also include what traditional grammarians call the **relative pronouns:** *who, whom, what, that, which.* These pronoun-conjunctions introduce a particular kind of clause, a **relative** or **adjective clause.** They are called relative pronouns because they clearly *relate* the clause to the noun with which it patterns; the relationship between the noun and its relative pronoun (and relative clause) is clear. Here are a few sentences illustrating subordinators:

Although we were young, we knew what we wanted.

No one cashed the lottery ticket **because** it had been washed and dried in the laundry.

We were too tired to recognize the soldier **who** was approaching.

- **Conjunctive adverbs** (adverbs that literally *join* one item *with* another, that have a connecting quality—note their frequently compounded structure): *however, therefore, nevertheless, henceforth, moreover, consequently.* Conjunctive adverbs typically appear as conjunctions in compound sentences. Some examples appear in the following sentences:

> We were young; **nevertheless**, we knew what we wanted.
>
> It is too late to study for the exam; **moreover**, you haven't even done your homework yet!
>
> Paul took the keys; **consequently**, the rest of us could go nowhere.

Some conjunctions also appear on the list of prepositions. This is another example of the principle of multifunction words. When, for instance, *before* functions as a preposition, it patterns before a noun or noun cluster in a prepositional phrase, linking the object of the preposition to the rest of the sentence, as in version *A*:

> *Version A:* We will reach the finish line **before you**.

When *before* functions as a conjunction, though, it links a whole pattern or clause to the rest of the sentence, as in version *B:*

> *Version B:* **Before you even get started**, we will reach the finish line.

We decide how to label a word depending primarily on how that word functions in a given sentence. In version A, *before* is a preposition; in version B, *before* is a conjunction. (You will hear more about clauses later.) The rhetorical impact of a phrase differs from that of a clause. A clause, because it has a complete pattern including a subject and a verb, signals more grammatical importance. Thus if the idea is an important one worth emphasizing, put it in a clause.

Auxiliaries

In our study of verbs, we considered that **auxiliary** means secondary, functioning alongside or patterning with the primary verb form. Note, though, that some words that can function as auxiliaries can also function as regular verbs: words like *do* (*does, did*), *be* (*is, am, are, was, were, be, being, been*) and *have* (*have, has, had, having*). Other auxiliary verbs are the modals *may, might; can, could; will, would; shall, should.* These modals express only two tenses, present and past, but they pattern with main verbs to create varied layers of meaning and many tenses. Observe how all these sentences with the main verb *frustrate* create subtly different understandings:

1. Aunt Edna *frustrated* the robber's attempt to enter her apartment.
2. The students *have been frustrated* throughout the semester by poor teaching.
3. By refusing to practice, Christina *has been frustrating* her piano teacher.
4. Your teasing *might frustrate* Nancy Jean.
5. The child's inability to understand conditionality *can frustrate* the parent's attempt to communicate.

6. The postal strike *will frustrate* our attempt to pay our bills on time.
7. Inability to hear clearly *does frustrate* an appreciation of music.

Intensifiers

Intensifiers are a structure class whose members pattern with adjectives and adverbs to mitigate or affect the impact of the adjective or adverb. Thus you will find intensifiers in noun and verb clusters where adjectives and adverbs are present. Examples of intensifiers are *very* and *pretty* (as in *Maggie's coconut pie was **very** good and The women's team was **pretty** exhausted*)—as well as a host of other words like *extremely, remarkably, mostly, noticeably, generally*. Many intensifiers ending in -*ly* can be multifunction words: *fairly*, for instance, can function as either intensifier (*The price was **fairly** high for this neighborhood*) or adverb (*The judge dealt with both parties **fairly***).

For Discussion

Find the intensifiers in the following sentences and discuss how they work to alter the meaning of the sentence. What, for example, would the sentence mean without the intensifier?

1. The dancers were rather late to rehearsal.
2. The designer suits at Neiman Marcus are incredibly expensive.
3. There was absolutely no way to cross the flooded street.
4. Last weekend, Uncle Mark was really broke.
5. Lou Ann was noticeably embarrassed by Bobby's loud and obnoxious conversation.
6. Very few students have your success!
7. The witness was pretty sure about what she saw.
8. The jurors were mostly cordial to the prosecuting attorney.
9. Sammy's new car was way cool.
10. The apple pie was too hot to taste.

Interrogatives

Interrogatives are used to form questions in English. Words like *who, what, when, where, how,* and *why* begin utterances and signal questions: *Why* is the fireplace painted pink? *Who* knocks on my door? *How* am I supposed to do this problem? *Where* is the secret treasure? Generally these interrogatives are also multifunction words: that is, besides signaling a question, they also function or work within the sentence, frequently as adverbs. In *Why is the fireplace painted pink?*, Why is a *thus* adverb. In *How am I supposed to do this problem?*, *how* is also a *thus* adverb. But in *Who knocks on my door? who* functions as a pronoun **and** the subject of the question.

N ominal Versus Verbal: A Rhetorical Observation

You may write in a style predominantly nominal—or one dominated by nouns and noun clusters—or a style predominantly verbal—one dominated by verbs and verb clusters. This is a significant stylistic difference that can affect the pace and readability of your prose. Text heavy with nouns slogs more slowly along than text peppered with lively verbs. This is one reason why readers complain that long passages of description bore them: the reality is that the preponderance of noun clusters necessary for describing keeps the text from seeming to move. Text dominated by verb clusters, on the other hand, is tolerated better by restless readers. See for yourself. Look at the following two passages and discuss with your writers' group which one moves with more alacrity and ease. Which passage is more nominal than the other?

PASSAGE A

Birds make adaptations to changes in seasons through migration. Migration is the movement of some species from one location to another. Age, sex, weather, breeding habits, and the availability of food, water, and shelter seem to be the major influences in migratory behavior. Many birds will migrate to areas where the food supply is plentiful and the weather is not as severe.

PASSAGE B

Birds adapt to seasonal changes by migrating. When birds migrate, they move from one location to another. A bird's age, sex, and breeding habits as well as the weather where it lives all influence its inclination to move. Birds also migrate to search for more readily available food, water, and shelter, relocating for a season to areas where food is plentiful and weather temperate.
—Adapted from *Bird Tracks*

As you can see, Passage A is much more nominal than Passage B. Although the two passages are approximately the same length, Passage B uses more verbs (**migrating** rather than **migration**, for instance). Passage B moves more smoothly and seems to read more quickly, all because of the verbs.

Here are two ways to make your writing more verb-centered and lively:

■ Change the vague *verb + noun* combination to a verb (usually the verb form is buried in the noun): from

The trooper issued us a warning about black ice

to

The trooper warned us about black ice.

Change

Vespucci Amerigo made the discovery of America

to

Vespucci Amerigo discovered America.

■ Change the noun following an expletive construction *There are* to a verb (only if you have no rhetorical purpose for using the expletive): from

There was a mark on the edge of the page from the scribe's erasure

to

The scribe's erasure marked the edge of the page.

Instead of

There was a serious delay in going to the dentist on Jerry's part,

try this:

Jerry seriously delayed going to the dentist.

S *umming Up: Verb Clusters*

Let's review what this chapter and the last have been about. English has four large word classes called form classes—noun, verb, adjective, and adverb—that carry most of the meaning of the sentence. English has several smaller word classes called function words. So far, we've examined prepositions, particles, auxiliaries, determiners, pronouns, intensifiers, and interrogatives—words that make clear the relationships among the form classes and that pattern together to form noun clusters and verb clusters. What we call or label a word depends on its function in the sentence, and many words are capable of multiple functions. What makes it possible to glean meaning from a sentence are the cues we get from the structure of the sentence (the arrangement of its words or its syntax) and from the form of those words. What makes it possible to extract clear understanding from a sentence is also that English has many syntactical and structural signals to prevent *ambiguity* (something that is *ambiguous* can be read with more than one meaning). Let's now see how the patterns we have defined can be transformed and amplified by the principles of addition and rearrangement.

4

Patterns Transformed

So far, we've examined the basic patterns of English and the form classes and structure words composing the patterns. Let us now think about how those patterns frequently get transformed in everyday speech and writing. To **transform** something means to change its form or appearance: water can be transformed into ice with the application of cold; an actor can be transformed from a young woman into an aged crone with makeup, a wig, padding, and clothes; a junked car can be transformed into a street rod with time, labor, parts, and paint. Notice that the young woman doesn't really become a crone; rather, her external form changes so that she appears to be one. Also note that ice can return to its original form of water and that a restored car can become again a junked car. So too can basic sentence patterns be transformed; that is, they can take different shapes, but underneath the basic structure remains. Many of our most common English sentences and expressions are transformations of basic patterns. In this chapter we'll examine some of the most common changes you can make to the six basic patterns. We'll work with

- negative transformations
- question transformations
- passive transformations
- expletive transformations
- emphatic transformations

Remember that at the heart of each transformation lies one of the basic sentence patterns and clusters you worked with in earlier chapters. A transformation does not change the substance of the sentence; it changes only its form. And the transformations have different rhetorical purposes and effects from the original patterns. Let's see how they work.

Negative Transformations

Perhaps the first transformation every English-speaking child learns is the negative transformation: how to negate the meaning of a specific statement.

You did not give me a cookie.

The water is not hot.

I never saw the money.

She is not my mother.

No book is in this box.

All these statements controvert or turn over an original, positive statement: *You did give me a cookie, The water is hot, I saw the money, She is my mother, A book is in this box*. The rhetorical purpose of the negative transformation is to negate, deny, correct, or clarify an incorrect or previously held impression. We use it to counteract what is said or heard or expected, to call into question someone else's positive or affirming statement. Thus you may find quite a few negative transformations in argumentative or persuasive pieces. You can transform any of the sentence patterns to a negative meaning by adding one of these negative words: *not, no, none,* or *never,* which we will call the **absolute negatives**.

Other words that have negative implications or that question the verity or positive nature of a statement are words like

barely

hardly

rarely

scarcely

very

To say *The water is barely hot* casts doubt on the temperature of the water and in effect negates the statement that the water *is* hot. Look at the cartoon caption in Figure 4.1 and find the negative transformations (*You aren't* . . . in addition to *It doesn't mean* . . . plus *It hasn't got* . . . And *I'm not* . . .). All these transformations play on the real song titles (which have nonstandard verb usages): "You Ain't Nothin' but a Hound Dog," "It Don't Mean a Thing If It Ain't Got That Swing," and "I Ain't Misbehavin.'"

Strictly speaking, however, all you have to do to create a negative transformation is to add *no* or *not* to a pattern. But with many sentences, you must add a tense of the verb *do* to the sentence to make it sound natural. You must add *do* to transform a sentence whose verb is not *be* to its negative form. You must add the auxiliary verb *do* in the appropriate tense when you negate a sentence that does not already have an auxiliary verb. Thus, to transform the sentence *The snowstorm blew in from the West Coast* to its negative form, we first have to change the sentence to its equivalent with *do* in the past tense: *The snow storm did blow in from the West Coast*. Now that we have a verb with an auxiliary, we can make the sentence negative by adding *not: The snowstorm did not blow in from the West Coast*. Now consider the sentence

Fran's cat seems ill.

Figure 4.1
Negative Transformation.
© *The New Yorker Collection 1988 Roz Chast from cartoonbank.com. All Rights Reserved.*

To transform this sentence into its negative form, you can write *Fran's cat seems not ill*, but that sentence sounds like something out of a different time. Today speakers are more likely to say *Fran's cat does not seem ill* or—to use the contracted form of *does + not* or *doesn't*—*Fran's cat doesn't seem ill*.

Now you create some negative transformations.

For Writing and Discussion

For each of the following basic patterns, produce a negative transformation, either absolute or implied. Write out the full transformation. Then compare your sentences with the sentences produced by members of your writing group. Did you use more absolute or

(continued)

more implied negatives? What problems did you find in creating these negative transformations? In your discussion, consider these questions: What are the basic patterns of these sentences? Does the negative transformation change the meaning or the physical pattern of these sentences? Can you make a generalization about when you seem required to use *do* to make the transformation sound natural? What is the relationship between auxiliary verbs and the negative transformation?

1. She exposed her husband's adultery.
2. My poodles are lying on the rug beside me.
3. Eric's telephone rings 50 times a day.
4. Emily's sister sent her an electronic greeting card for her birthday.
5. Leather shoes stretch.
6. In New York, the sun shines often in the winter months.
7. Poetry is a powerful social force.
8. Hamburgers grow on trees.
9. The social climate at her university is hostile.
10. Textbook prices are high.
11. Alan Greenspan deems the economy stable.
12. Owls look wise.
13. Nathan answered the telephone crisply yet kindly.
14. *Butch Cassidy and the Sundance Kid* is one of the best movies of the last 25 years.
15. Elementary children love fountain pens.
16. Mrs. Antos finds *The Odyssey* irresistible.
17. Jack explained the directions to his house slowly.
18. The road meanders through the county and across the township.
19. Black ink rubs off the newspaper onto my damp hands.
20. Mr. Jacques considers French studies a natural accompaniment to English studies.
21. The pine logs burn hot.
22. Jobs are plentiful in this country.
23. Taxes are probably too high everywhere.
24. Friends fly free on certain airlines.
25. Caramel candy is good for your teeth.

Q *uestion Transformations*

So far in this book, we have examined only statements or indicative utterances, patterns, and sentences. Americans don't, however, speak and write in the indicative mode exclusively. American speakers and writers ask questions too. In fact, we ask a good many questions. Questioning is part of the American way of life! All questions are transformations of basic patterns. But not all questions are alike, nor are their rhetorical effects alike. You probably already know several ways to create questions from basic patterns. Let's take a formal look at these ways.

Creating Yes/No Question Transformations

One of the most common kinds of questions is the **yes/no question**, one that can be answered with *yes* or *no*. One of the easiest ways to effect the question transformation is simply to reverse the order of subject and verb. Notice that only the *be* verb reverses simply.

> You can easily transform the statement

> This rose is pink

to

> Is this rose pink?

by reversing the order of subject and verb. The same applies to sentences like *Oakes is a professor* (*Is Oakes a professor?*) and *Esther's cookies are delicious* (*Are Esther's cookies delicious?*)

With verbs other than *be*, the question transformation requires the addition of an auxiliary verb, usually **do** or a form of *do* appropriate to the tense of the sentence being transformed. Look at these question transformations:

- *George photographs lions* becomes *George does photograph lions* becomes *Does George photograph lions?*
- *Cats meow noisily* becomes *Cats do meow noisily* becomes *Do cats meow noisily?*
- *Janice painted the barn red* becomes *Janice did paint the barn red* becomes *Did Janice paint the barn red?*
- *Fran will buy us a soda* becomes *Will Fran buy us a soda?* Because the verb in this sentence includes an auxiliary form already, we do not need to add *do* to create a question.
- *The rain is coming down hard* becomes *Is the rain coming down hard?*

Notice that when you use an auxiliary to form a question, the auxiliary and the main verb split and the subject slips in between them, with the auxiliary verb beginning the sentence.

Creating Interrogative Question Transformations

To ask questions that demand answers of more content and substance, speakers and writers use interrogative words and phrases: *who, where, what, when, why, how,* and *how much.* These words and phrases allow you to pinpoint exactly the kind of information you need. Consider, for instance the sentence, *Cats meow noisily.* To transform that into a question demanding a substantive answer, you may focus on either the subject (*What meows noisily?*); the verb (*What do cats do noisily?*) or the adverb (*How do cats meow?*). You can also ask *why cats meow noisily, which cats meow noisily, when cats meow noisily,* and *where cats meow noisily.* The interrogatives generate considerably fuller responses than do the yes/no questions.

Questions by Intonation

There is of course one more way to create the question transformation, and that is simply to change the intonation of a declaration so that the voice rises at the end of the sentence. On the written page, this kind of question is signaled merely by using a question mark after the sentence. Thus the statement *You want cream cheese on your bagel* becomes the question *You want cream cheese on your bagel?* This transformation is used most frequently in conversation and very informal writing.

FOR WRITING AND DISCUSSION

Transform the following declarative sentences or statement patterns into questions. You may generate yes/no questions or substantive questions (by using interrogative words). Afterward, compare your questions with the ones your writing group members produced and discuss how the transformations occurred. Note that a single sentence may contain both a negative transformation and a question transformation.

1. You are not paying attention to me.
2. The groceries are still in the car.
3. The drummer's rhythmic sense is keen.
4. Natalie appears tense.
5. The assembly elected Professor Smugly chairperson.
6. Textbooks are quite expensive.
7. A dental checkup is an ordeal for some people.
8. The recruit polished dozens of shoes to a sparkling shine.
9. Fatigue and boredom set in.
10. There was a loud, sudden pop from outside.
11. No laundry has been done tonight.
12. A new computer is necessary.
13. The French tapestry in the museum is quite valuable.
14. Students will choose new courses this semester.
15. Many people like unusual fonts.
16. Lemons typically taste sour.

(continued)

17. Electricity is inexpensive in our town.
18. We are all attending the commencement ceremonies in the gym.
19. Ellen turned on the lamp for her brother.
20. The dinner at the club was delicious but cold.
21. State government is inefficient.
22. Her son is lighting a fire.
23. No one will admit wrongdoing.
24. This circus no longer has freaks.
25. The attic felt dusty, dark, and cold.

P assive Transformations

You have probably heard about passive voice. Perhaps you have even been warned not to write sentences in passive voice. Some writing specialists dislike passive voice and caution other writers against it. But as you will see as we think together about the passive transformation, certain rhetorical occasions call for passive voice—and the passive transformation is not a structure to be avoided, but rather one to be used wisely.

Exactly what is passive voice? Passive voice refers to the verb specifically although the passive transformation affects the structure of the entire sentence. Look at the following sentence:

The angry student slammed the door.

This is a transitive verb and an S-V-O sentence: the subject (also called the **agent**) did something to something or someone; the student slammed the door. When we transform the sentence into passive voice, the sentence becomes

The door was slammed by the angry student.

The nature of the sentence changes, particularly the nature of what is happening to whom and who caused it. Here are some other active/passive sentences alongside one another:

The poodle chased the nimble squirrel.—active

The nimble squirrel was chased by the poodle.—passive

Which sentence is longer? Which sentence emphasizes the poodle? Which sentence emphasizes the squirrel? What operations did the writer perform on the active, transitive verb to turn it into the passive sentence?

Three things happen when an active verb is transformed into a passive verb:

1.　First, the object of the active voice sentence moves to the subject position for the passive sentence.

2.　Second, the subject or agent of the active voice sentence moves into a "by" phrase at the end of the passive sentence. This agent phrase or "by" phrase is optional; a passive voice sentence may or may not have an agent, depending on the importance of the agent to the meaning of the sentence. Many passive sentences have no "by" phrase. More about this in a minute.

3.　Finally, an appropriate form and tense of *be* is added to the verb, which assumes its **past participial form**. Thus *chased* in the active voice sentence becomes *was chased* in the passive sentence. *Chased* is past tense in the active sentence; its past participle happens to look exactly the same, *chased*. So we simply add the appropriate tense of *be* to the past participle *chased*. Because the active sentence is past tense, we use the past tense of *be, was*. This verb form is always the hallmark of passive voice, whose tense is easily recognizable as a form of *be* **plus the past participle**. You may sometimes also see *get* substituted for *be* in the passive transformation (Chad *got passed over* for the nomination; The toddlers *got tired* from playing at Chuck E. Cheese; The dirty sweaters *got sent* to the cleaners). This kind of structure is called a **get passive**. Study these pairs of active sentences and their passive transformations to see the process (the passive verb forms are italicized):

1. Active:　Nathan dropped the spaghetti dramatically and purposefully.

1. Passive:　The spaghetti *was dropped* by Nathan dramatically and purposefully.

2. Active:　The wind overturned the flamingoes on the lawn.

2. Passive:　The flamingoes on the lawn *were overturned* by the wind.

3. Active:　You are eating the whole box of Cheezits!

3. Passive:　The whole box of Cheezits *is being eaten* by you!

4. Active:　The artist will draw sketches of suspects.

4. Passive:　Sketches of suspects *will be drawn* by the artist.

5. Active:　Paul walked the poodles.

5. Passive:　The poodles *were walked* by Paul.

In effect, the subjects and objects just switch places. The subject of the active sentence moves to the end of the passive sentence to an agent phrase; the object of the active sentence moves to the front of the passive sentence as its new subject.

Look at how transforming an active voice sentence into passive voice shifts the rhetorical emphasis. Putting a noun in the subject slot gives it the most importance, so if you want to emphasize what overturned the flamingoes on the lawn (sentence 2), make the agent—the

THE FAR SIDE® **By GARY LARSON**

Tomorrow, they would be mortal enemies. But on
the eve of the great hunt, feelings were put aside
for the traditional Mammoth Dance.

Figure 4.2
Passive Transformation.
Gary Larson

wind—the subject in an active voice sentence. If you want to emphasize
what was overturned, put the original direct object—flamingoes—in the
subject slot and use the passive transformation. Finally, notice that in
many cases, the passive sentences could make just as much sense without the agent phrase; if what overturned the flamingoes on the lawn is
not important, for instance, the passive version of sentence 2 could read
simply *The flamingoes on the lawn were overturned*. This agent phrase or
"by phrase" (in sentence 2, *by the wind*) is frequently omitted when the
agent is unimportant or irrelevant.

The cartoon caption in Figure 4.2 illustrates passive voice; notice the
verb, the key marker of passive voice, in the second sentence: *were put aside*.
This is a passive phrasal verb: a form of *be* (*were*) plus the past participle of
put aside, which looks the same as its present and its past tenses: *put aside*.
Did you see the noun adjunct *Mammoth*?

Now it's your turn to transform some active voice sentences into passive voice.

FOR WRITING AND DISCUSSION

Change the active voice sentences to passive voice ones. Be sure to use comparable tenses. Compare your results with those of your writing group partners; then observe whether there are negative transformations in any of these sentences and discuss any unusual modifying words (like noun adjuncts) or phrases. Be prepared to report to the class.

1. You should not push those buttons.
2. Three patrol cars circled the block.
3. The apartment house had a buzzer system for entry.
4. John saw the pimple on Harriet's chin.
5. That class asks too many questions.
6. I will change my mind before sundown.
7. No one liked the idea of a qualifying examination.
8. Mother is protecting Aaron.
9. Most guests drank coffee or tea.
10. The maids drew the curtains and turned on the lights.
11. The ship reached the equator before midsummer.
12. The wolves circled their prey.
13. After the wedding, Christy and Jack sent notes of appreciation to more than 200 guests.
14. The 10-year-olds happily gobbled up the pizza and ice cream.
15. The arborist trimmed the stately oak tree by the back porch.
16. Myra ripped the ransom note to shreds.
17. Every morning, the chickadee family raids the bird feeder.
18. Frank examined the hammer carefully.
19. We put the Buddy Holly CD in the CD player.
20. Aunt Frieda will clean your room thoroughly.
21. The workmen installed a second telephone line.
22. No one fears a rabbit.
23. The friends exchanged looks.
24. We turned off all the appliances quickly.
25. They were shredding the evidence in haste.

All the sentences you transformed in the previous writing exercise were S-V-O sentences, sentences with subjects, transitive verbs, and direct objects. Yet we know that there are other transitive patterns than those with simple direct objects: there are transitive patterns with indirect objects and objective complements as well. What happens when we transform those patterns into passive voice? Here's an example of an indirect object pattern, an S-V-IO-DO sentence:

The friendly retriever gave all the guests kisses.

When you transform this indirect object sentence into a passive voice sentence, you'll get one of these options:

All the guests were given kisses by the friendly retriever

or

Kisses were given all the guests by the friendly retriever.

The first example, *All the guests were given kisses,* contains a *retained object.* The direct object is retained or kept in the transformation. In the second option, *Kisses were given all the guests,* the former direct object becomes the subject. You have the rhetorical option of choosing what you want to emphasize by making it the subject of the passive sentence.

Now what happens when you transform an S-V-DO-OC pattern, one with an objective complement, into passive voice? Here's the original S-V-DO-OC sentence:

The scholarship committee considered Sarah deserving of the award.

And here's the transformation:

Sarah was considered deserving of the award by the scholarship committee.

Only the direct object can serve as the subject of the transformed sentence. The same is true when the objective complement is a noun:

Our neighbors call their horse Dusty.

And the transformation . . .

Their horse is called Dusty (by our neighbors).

Although these verbs resemble linking verbs because of the presence of *be,* you'll recognize that they have the trademark passive combination of *be* + past participle: *was considered* and *is called.* In addition, the subject and the retained object have the same referent.

FOR WRITING AND DISCUSSION

Now try transforming these transitive sentences with more than one object or with an objective complement and see what happens. Talk about the results with your writers' group. What kinds of problems emerged?

1. One student passed another the answers to the hardest questions.
2. No one considered the president blameless.
3. Anthony bought Jennifer a huge diamond.
4. The clerk did not give me enough change.

(continued)

5. In the morning, the mail carrier brings us our bills, catalogs, and renewal notices.
6. The fashion police thought Cher's outfit outrageous.
7. Tom Sawyer painted the tall fence white.
8. That teacher will give Kip a hard time about his tardies.
9. The residents of Hinman Hall have elected Stephanie floor monitor.
10. Film critics have always believed Ingrid Bergman beautiful.
11. A charitable spirit makes one a pleasant person.
12. Titus's great-uncle left him cash for college.
13. The local press considered the firefighters heroes of the first degree.
14. The partygoers took the host a bottle of fumé blanc.
15. Nancy named her mother guardian of her baby son.
16. Parenthood has brought us happiness.
17. The set designer made the backdrop bold and bright.
18. Frances has called me a liar too many times.
19. Bonnie Raitt gave Bruce Springsteen a kiss.
20. The groundhog determinedly made the hole bigger.
21. Paul wrote the family a poem in honor of his birthday.
22. We made the edges of the death announcement a ribbon of black.
23. The students think the dean important to their school.
24. Everyone considered Dede a fool.
25. My editor made the book deal irresistible.

Remember that, rhetorically speaking, the passive transformation is not an indicator of bad writing. In fact, there are many occasions when passive voice is appropriate and even more effective than active voice. Sometimes, for instance, it is not important for the reader to know who the agent is. In a sentence like *All of Binghamton's roads were resurfaced last summer*, the agent (that is, *who* paved the roads) is so unimportant that it is omitted entirely from the sentence. What is emphasized in this sentence is what got paved, the subject: *all of Binghamton's roads*. In many cases too, the agent wishes not to be known. If, for instance, you must write a letter of denial to an applicant for a loan or a student who applied for a scholarship, you may not want to take the responsibility or the heat of being the agent of that denial. You may prefer to write something like

Regrettably, your application for a loan has not been approved.

instead of

Regrettably, I did not approve your application for a loan.

It is also possible that you need passive voice for logistical purposes, simply because you need a certain word at the head of a sentence or phrase.

Perhaps you are writing about Sarah's new cashmere scarf woven with iridescent pearly threads. You write something like

> Yesterday Sarah wore a cashmere scarf woven with iridescent pearly threads.

You want to emphasize that the scarf was handmade by artisans in Kurdistan, so you follow the first sentence with something like

> Artisans in Kurdistan made the scarf by hand.

But notice how much smoother your text sounds like this: *Yesterday Sarah wore a cashmere scarf woven with iridescent pearly threads,* **which was handmade by artisans in Kurdistan.** Transforming the active voice sentence into a passive voice clause allows you to follow the base clause immediately with an adjective clause referring to *scarf.* The adjective clause is closer to the word with which it patterns. In this case, passive voice makes a liquid link between patterns.

E xpletive Transformation

An easily recognizable transformation of the intransitive S-V pattern looks like this:

> There were fantastic schemes.
>
> There is a babyishness to his speech.
>
> There is a good deal of anguish and angst in his music.
>
> There is never any minimum charge.
>
> Here are your rhinestone tap shoes.
>
> There's only one place big enough for Earth's biggest selection.
>
> There are no guns in Jonestown.

Each sentence begins with the word *there* or *here* and is then followed by a verb—*were, is,* and *are* in these sentences. All these verbs are, in fact, forms of the verb *be,* by far the most common verb in this pattern. It is possible but not typical for other verbs to function in this pattern. Following the verbs are nouns—*schemes, babyishness, deal, charge, tap shoes, place, guns*—that act as the subjects of the sentences. These subject nouns are what the sentences are *about.*

This transformation is so common that some grammarians consider it a pattern, which they write as **There-V-S**. The elements in this transformation are the word *there* (or sometimes *here*) and then verbs and subjects—a reversal of normal word order. Note also that, as in other intransitive patterns, there are sometimes prepositional phrases used adverbially (*to his speech, in his music, for Earth's biggest selection, in Jonestown*). In these sentences *there* is called an **expletive**, that is, a word that fills a space without contributing any meaning. Expletives are placeholders: they take up space that other words might occupy—and they give the writer a chance to delay using a word, perhaps to gain greater impact by using it later in the sentence. The *there* front-loaded in the sentence tells the reader that something emphatic and interesting is coming later, thereby lending more importance to the subject that is wrenched from its normal place in the sentence anyway. *There* isn't the only word that functions in this place: *here* is also common (notice the one *here* sentence). When you use this transformation, you can delay the reader's knowledge of the subject.

To review then, here's how you transform an S-V sentence like *A fly is in my soup* into its expletive counterpart:

1. invert the order of subject and verb: *is a fly in my soup*
2. add the expletive *there* or *here*: *There is a fly in my soup*.

For Discussion

In your writers' group, discuss the following expletive or There-V-S transformations. Identify what words function as subjects and verbs. Determine the original sentence before the transformation. If there are other interesting sentence features, point them out. The elements of the transformed pattern (that is, the S and the V) may frequently be part of larger clusters that include determiners, possessives, adjectives, adverbs, intensifiers, and even prepositional phrases. Remember: when you are sorting out the pattern of a sentence or even first composing a sentence of a certain pattern, **ignore prepositional phrases entirely**. Don't forget to observe how these sentences are punctuated—no punctuation separates a simple verb from its subject. And one more thing: the subject and verb still agree, even though the subject follows the verb. If a subject is singular, the verb form is singular. If a subject is plural, the verb form is also plural.

1. There is no end to her patience.
2. Here is the culprit.
3. There was the sheriff.
4. Here goes nothing.
5. There can't be any fun today.
6. There is a boy with a Coke and some Doritos.
7. There is a bug on the saucer.
8. There might be some cheese in the refrigerator.
9. There are clouds to the west of us.
10. Here is your change.
11. There is no cure for AIDS.
12. There might be time for lunch.
13. There was an explosion in the countryside.
14. There has been a big mistake.

(continued)

15. There are many commercial advertisements on television.
16. Here waits the chariot.
17. There are too many commercials on MTV.
18. There is plenty of information for your report in the library.
19. There is too much screaming on that program.
20. Here is the rescue boat.
21. There is a billion-dollar problem.
22. There are several coupons in my purse.
23. There was a feud between those prominent families.
24. There could be more room in this house.
25. There are extremely low temperatures in the northeast part of the state tonight.

For Writing

Now it's time for you to practice writing this transformation. In your writer's notebook (either paper or electronic), compose 25 expletive or There V-S transformations. When you finish, take a look at the verbs: what are the most common verbs you have written? Make a note of them for class discussion.

E *mphatic Transformations*

We have just been thinking together about how passive voice and the expletive *there* can change the emphasis in a sentence. Good writers need to know how to get readers to attend to the important ideas, and while passive voice and expletives are ways to shift the reader's attention, you can also use other rhetorical strategies.

Shifting Emphasis with Inversion

Creating emphasis is partly about knowing the usual, psychologically expected structures and then occasionally altering them in a way to alert the reader that, in a particular sentence, something different is happening. In fact, we saw how passive voice can create emphasis by inverting the subject and the object of a transitive sentence. Any time you shift word order significantly in a pattern, you almost certainly draw attention to the word, phrase, sentence, or idea affected by the shift. Consider the difference in, for example, these sentences: one, a typical S-LV-PA pattern; the other, an inversion of that pattern:

S-LV-PA: *She was pretty and shy at the same time.*

S-LV-PA inversion: *Pretty she was, and shy at the same time.*

See how *pretty* leaps to the fore of the inverted sentence and how important the idea becomes? It receives additional emphasis because of the unusual order of the sentence. It's just not what readers expect, so the ear perks up and pays attention. Here's another example:

> Next come density tests.

The usual order of this S-V (adv) sentence would be *Density tests come next*, but in this sentence the sequence of events, signaled by **next**, is emphasized. (The author, Janice Paskey, is writing about snowpacks and avalanches.) And here's another:

> Past Spithead and the Isle of Wight the *Titanic* steamed.

Here the geographical locations at the front of the sentence are emphasized. Hanson Baldwin in "R.M.S. Titanic" emphasizes that the ship had been at sea by noting places the *Titanic* passed. He inverted the usual word order of the sentence and put the prepositional phrase at the head of the sentence. Key points of emphasis in any rhetorical structure are first, the front of the sentence and then the end of the sentence. What the reader sees first and last are most memorable; what falls in the middle of the structure can be more easily forgotten. This is one reason why, for instance, business writers buffer "bad news" (you didn't get the job or your loan was not approved) with pleasantries at the beginning of a letter and a good will statement at its end. With this strategy of burying bad news in the middle, they hope to diminish its impact. When you want to emphasize a word or idea that is currently buried in a sentence, move the word or phrase to be emphasized to the beginning of the sentence—or alternately, to its end. You may be moving major sentence elements (shifting subjects, verbs, complements) or words or phrases (adjectives, adverbs, prepositional phrases, for instance) that pattern with these major elements.

FOR WRITING

Choose a word or phrase you want to emphasize in these sentences, then try inverting the word order to see what happens. Do not add any words to these sentences; just rearrange what's already here. There may be more than one appropriate inversion of each sentence, so discuss your transformations with the members of your writing group. Are there any particular sentence patterns that don't invert well? Did you notice there are no transitive sentences here?

1. The departmental staff is certainly not friendly.
2. The snow is blowing in hard from the west.
3. These moments are precious and few.
4. Birds sit in the trees at dusk.
5. Bats fly out of belfries about that time too.   *(continued)*

6. Sixteen cars are ahead of us at the tollbooth.
7. All those brooms whisk across the floor noiselessly.
8. The computer consultant is quitting his job.
9. Movies with subtitles can be exquisitely boring.
10. Many students are returning to class today.
11. Her books are open on the library table.
12. The poodle groans in her sleep.
13. Margaret's mother is an emergency room nurse.
14. The sky is green.
15. Planets revolve around the sun.
16. This northeast wind is oddly vicious.
17. The advertisement for the wedding dress appeared in the local newspaper.
18. All my pencils are sharp.
19. The study of particle physics is demanding.
20. All the bells in town are ringing.
21. This wizard is neither shrewd nor cunning.
22. The old zoot suits hang in the tiny, musty closet.
23. Books are fine companions for a stormy day.
24. Too many tapes are in that cabinet.
25. Francis went shopping alone, with $4.65 in his tattered wallet.

Creating Emphasis with the Cleft Sentence

Another way to create emphasis is the **cleft sentence**. Among the meanings of *to cleave* is the idea of *to cut*; thus a cleft sentence is one that is cut in two, then rearranged with expletives to create emphasis. Expletives, you will remember, are place-holding words; they have little meaning, and typically they have no function in a sentence other than to fill a spot so that you can shift the placement of other words. Typical expletives are *it, what, there, here*. Here are some examples of sentences transformed into cleft sentences:

Plain: The dripping water from the bathtub is making the noise.

Cleft: It is the dripping water from the bathtub that is making the noise.

The plain sentence is cut midway through, between the subject and predicate. Then the expletive *it* is added to the first part and the second part is made into a *that* clause or pattern. Here are some others:

Plain: We want Coca-Cola for the party.

Cleft: It is Coca-Cola that we want for the party. (Emphasizes the Coca-Cola we want.)

or

It is for the party that we want Coca-Cola. (Emphasizes why we want the Coca-Cola) or

>It is we who want the Coca-Cola for the party. (Emphasizes who wants the Coca-Cola).

Plain: The rain flooded the garden, drowning the vegetable seedlings.

Cleft: It was the rain that flooded the garden, drowning the vegetable seedlings.

>It was the vegetable seedlings that were drowned when the rain flooded the garden.

>It was the garden that the rain flooded, drowning the vegetable seedlings.

>What was flooded was the garden in the rain, and the vegetable seedlings were drowned.

>What were drowned were the vegetable seedlings in the garden, flooded by the rain.

Notice that the cleft need not always begin with the expletive *it*; the cleft frequently begins with a *what*, *how*, or *that* introducing a pattern. Note also that changing the nature of the cleft or creating it to emphasize different parts of the sentence can force you to rewrite the sentence significantly. The meaning of the sentence is not really changed by the rewriting, but its emphasis is altered considerably. So keep these rhetorical possibilities in mind as you revise and rewrite sentences.

FOR WRITING

Rewrite all the following sentences to create cleft sentences. Remember that you'll first cut the sentence, then insert an expletive structure or create an internal pattern where you want emphasis.

1. Maurice was sick.
2. I received my formal education in Spanish at the local market.
3. Gran had a round childlike face and big eyes.
4. The hotel lobby buzzes with Polish and Yiddish.
5. My mother came from Tucson.
6. For years, I was too busy for the kitchen.
7. My brother put up his dukes and started yelling.
8. The memory of those chocolate cream puffs always makes Miriam happy.
9. The corners of closets smelled of mothballs.
10. In this town soccer is a Saturday morning sport.
11. My father hoisted the baggage.
12. I took my paints to the Louvre each day and copied famous paintings.

(continued)

13. Rivke always lived with her in-laws after the war.
14. The bridegroom is asking for a story.
15. In restaurants, we ate the vegetarian fare.
16. Life was complex during the 1950s.
17. We sat at Aunt Frieda's dining room table in mahogany chairs with needlepoint cushions.
18. I remembered the kitchen in my grandmother's Illinois farmhouse.
19. We invited the family.
20. She has the right to die on her own bedroom floor.
21. Dorothea married Uncle George.
22. I grow zucchini, tomatoes, lettuce, and cilantro in my backyard garden.
23. We went out to dinner on Saturday night.
24. Rugs were rolled up and floors were polished every spring.
25. In our neighborhood, the immigrant population dwindled, then vanished.

Creating Emphasis by Varying Diction or Word Choice

You can also create emphasis by varying diction and levels of usage; that is, by shifting from more to less formal expressions or using what linguists call different *registers* of expression. Diction refers to the writer's word choices. Linguist Martin Joos, in the classic *The Five Clocks*, identifies kinds of style among native English speakers. Let's consider how you can use some of the styles Joos described to create a specific tone or effect.

The most common of these styles, perhaps the most centered or average or most used of them, is the **consultative style**.

Consultative Style. We use this style when we communicate with strangers who speak our language but whose personal contexts differ widely from ours. Consultative style is marked by the explicit giving of information, background, and explanation. Someone writing consultative style does not assume that she or he will be understood automatically and as a result offers context and definition for what might not be clearly comprehended. Indeed, consultative style presents information as fast as it is needed and sometimes anticipates the need for it. If two speakers are having a conversation and all the public information needed for their conversation has been exhausted, a consultative discussion will end. Presenting the information is the purpose for the conversation. An example of consultative style is a sentence like this:

> Because the bank closes at three, we should leave now to get there before closing.

Casual Style. We find casual style written and spoken among friends, acquaintances, insiders. In casual style, there is frequently an absence of background information; the writer assumes the reader/listener does not need the background and takes public knowledge and information for granted. If information is exhausted in a **casual** conversation, in contrast to a consultative conversation, the conversation shifts to silence or kidding. Two defining features of casual style are **ellipsis** (omission of words and phrases) and **slang** (in the strictest sense, a widely current but short-lived expression like the recent *way cool*, which is already passé). In casual speech and writing, words that are commonly understood by all the members of the group are frequently ellipted—or left out or omitted. Instead of writing *We are sure that we are going*, for instance, the casual writer might write *We're sure we're going*, leaving out the *that* that introduces the clause and using contractions with the pronouns. Speakers and writers also use slang to signal that they are among the minority of the population who knows these words. The use of slang is part of the jockeying for position and control in social situations. Casual style is also punctuated by contractions (I'll, you'd, they're) and by simple, straightforward words: *we'll stay at home tonight* versus *we shall remain at our abode this evening*. An example of casual style is a sentence like this:

Let's get to the bank.

Intimate Style. Intimate style, used between people who know one another extremely well—good friends, family, very close colleagues—is characterized by **extraction** and **jargon**. Jargon means that in a close or intimate relationship certain code words are permanent fixtures; that is, certain words or expressions function like shorthand to refer to a vast set of experiences. Jargon is not slang; slang is used in conversations between insiders and outsiders. Insiders use slang in casual style to confirm their credibility to the group, and outsiders may use it to try to get into the group, to demonstrate that they belong. Between intimates, however, there is no insider/outsider relationship—and therefore no need for slang.

Extraction means that the listener or reader extracts some pattern or meaning from a casual sentence spoken by someone very close to him or her. What the speaker says may not be intelligible to anyone else except the person with whom he or she is intimate. This is not ellipsis, where a portion of the sentence remains. Extraction means deriving some meaning from an expression or utterance that appears to have no relationship at all to ordinary words. Your brother says "Hmmph" as he reads the editorial page. He has found something that made him indignant. Your style of communicating requires very few words, no background or public information, because each of you knows so much about the other. This style you share requires few to no transitions because you share so much information that only a brief reference will set you to thinking along the same lines. Joos writes that "good intimate style fuses personalities." An example of intimate style along the lines of our earlier sentences about getting to the bank might be

> Hey. Time!

The speaker and the listener (most intimate language is spoken rather than written) already understand that the bank closes at three and that they have an obligation to get there before that time. All one speaker needs to do is to offer up a slight reminder of the earlier stored conversation.

Formal Style. This style is designed to inform and to maintain a distance between the writer/speaker and the reader/hearer (the opposite of intimate style). The speaker or writer typically absents her- or himself from the text itself (no first person, usually) and depends on a strict form or shape, logical links among ideas, and explicitness. Formal text, characterized by detachment and cohesion, inserts background information in depth and with ordered precision; it assumes a captive, nonresponsive audience. It refrains from using ellipsis and doesn't even stoop to contractions. Its sentences tend to be long and complex. It is usually characterized by third person and frequently by words of many syllables derived from Latin—here a formal stylist would say "Latinate polysyllabic diction." All these qualities make the careful planning and organizing of such text a necessity. A formal version of our bank sentence might be something like

> Waterford National Bank closes at three; we should leave now to arrive before closing time.

Mixing and Shifting Levels of Usage

So what's the point about all these levels or **registers of expression**? Simply that you can create emphasis by shifting from one register to the other and then back again simply by altering a word or two. This is particularly noticeable when you make a shift that the reader does not foresee. Of course, this strategy can be used to create humor too, so you have to be careful that you don't make your reader smile when you aren't intending to be funny. Another danger of shifts that are too radical or too unexpected is that you can sound as if you are writing with a thesaurus.

Look at these versions of the same sentence:

1. Nettie put on her Skechers and rushed out the door.
2. Nettie donned her Skechers and hastened out the portal.
3. Nettie slapped on her Skechers and mobiled it right on out the door.

You can readily see the differences among the sentences. You probably wouldn't write number three unless you were writing dialogue or a friendly letter or talking to a friend. Number two sounds really formal, almost as if the writer were trying too hard to impress the reader, perhaps even by using the thesaurus. Number one is the most ordinary-sounding of all the sentences.

But if you write *Nettie donned her Skechers and rushed out the door*, changing just the more casual verb *put on* to the more formal verb *donned*, then your reader is going to perk up and pay attention. *Donned* is an interesting verb that gives dimension to Nettie's act, making it seem more purposeful.

Most of the time you'll write in a mixture of styles: primarily consultative with a solid dollop of casual and a bit of formal stirred in. This text that you are reading now is just that—a blend of consultative and casual with an occasional formal characteristic for emphasis. I'm not assuming that you know a lot of detail about grammar, so I try to explain everything thoroughly. On the other hand, I want you to feel comfortable as you read and work in this book, so I use second-person *you* and an occasional first-person *I* to draw you into the web of my ideas. I also use quite a few contractions. My ideas about grammar and style are, however, highly structured and arranged, and that's where the formal aspect of my style is perhaps most prominent.

FOR WRITING

Try writing casual, consultative, and formal versions of each sentence here. You may have to add or delete words and change word order.

Casual Style	Consultative Style	Formal Style
		We regret that we are unable to attend the opening of the opera.
Want some ice cream?		
	Recent studies of Binghamton's recycling habits show that recycling has saved the city's waste management department over $600,000 in the last fiscal year alone.	
The kids got home from school late today.		

Creating Emphasis by Formatting

There is one additional way to create emphasis on a given part of your text: with formatting. Simply put, you can make the physical text itself stand out by underlining it, italicizing it, writing it in all capital letters, or combining these devices. This rhetorical strategy is particularly useful when you are writing dialogue. Here are some examples of how formatting can create emphasis. Discuss how the following examples use formatting to create emphasis, considering the effectiveness of the strategy.

1. We searched *everywhere* for your car keys!
2. **No one** was willing to join the protest against the administration.
3. Please throw your paper trash HERE.

You may also create emphasis by using different fonts or colors for selected text. And you can create text boxes, make lists, use bullets, and employ borders on the page. All this is relatively easy to do with almost all word processing programs. The important thing to remember about changing the font or the color of text or about making any formatting change is to exercise restraint. If you have fourteen examples of text colored red or changed into a different font in the same document, your reader will become accustomed to your attempts to create emphasis—and then there's no emphasis! The reader becomes used to the change and no longer notices your efforts to create difference. Keep in mind, too, that text changes created via your computer may translate differently on-line or when opened by a different program (from WordPerfect to Word) or across a different platform (from Mac to PC, for instance).

FOR WRITING

Copy each of the following sentences, formatting one word or phrase in each sentence to emphasize it.

1. Jon's piggy friends drank all the Pepsi.
2. Inside you'll find a special blend of the tastiest fruits under the sun.
3. There are 200 French travel agents staying at the hotel today.
4. Your own customized program keeps all your information in one convenient place.
5. The spirit of this product is very different.

FOR WRITING

Now put to work everything you have learned about creating emphasis to revise these sentences. Your job is to revise each sentence so you shift the existing emphasis to a different word or section of the

(continued)

sentence. Keep in mind that you'll have to do more than just rearrange words in many of these sentences. Be prepared to explain the effects of your changes to your class.

1. There's not another car on the planet like this one.
2. A gathering of tourists stood outside the iron gates.
3. I went to Hamilton Farm one afternoon to see the animals.
4. It was a big school of bass, swimming just beneath the water's surface.
5. The National Archives in Washington, D.C. now has about 5 billion documents in storage.
6. In 1972 my parents sold their shop and moved to Louisiana.
7. My uncle was depressed by his sinking financial situation.
8. It was not just symphonies my brother and I were compelled to listen to.
9. The woman did not want to appear confrontational at the news conference.
10. In the early days of my father's illness, he told stories.
11. She must understand something about what I was saying.
12. We are discussing our favorite topic, the stupidity of our family.
13. I find Annie, sitting in the windowsill.
14. All this happened at 10 o'clock at night.
15. My aunt died in our ancestral home in Kingston, Jamaica.
16. Synthetic compounds do affect the reproductive capabilities of nonhuman mammals.
17. At the Moose Hotel, we sat at the long bar, wearing our stiff new hunting jackets and clean hunting caps.
18. I can't explain why, but shopping became important to me.
19. In the hospital I was first introduced to psychiatric medications.
20. I am polite by default.
21. Caroline patches the hole where the squirrels got in.
22. The four-man CBS news team is also waiting by the door for Castro.
23. He was always mercurial, mysterious, and confidential.
24. Davey believes that for most people suicide is a rational decision, often carefully planned.
25. There is no mechanism here to unseal the tomb.

S *umming Up*

Part of the way that English sentences gain variety is through transformation of the six basic patterns. The most common transformations allow for changing the meaning of an indicative sentence from positive to negative, for asking questions to elicit a variety of information, and for emphasizing key or important ideas through expletives, passive voice, inversion of word order, cleft structures, changes in diction, and formatting. Native speakers create these transformations with such ease that the resulting sentences seem quite normal.

Next we're going to examine how we expand and combine patterns, how we add details to or refine elements of the basic patterns and the transformations. If you're not entirely clear about the basic patterns and transformations, this is a good time to return to the beginning of this book and refresh your understanding.

5

Clustering, Compounding, Verbals, and Nominative Absolutes

*I*n earlier chapters you read about how various kinds of words shape themselves into clusters around nouns and verbs and how patterns can be expanded and combined into compound and complex sentences. In this chapter you'll delve more deeply into the formation of noun and verb clusters. First we will briefly review compound sentence elements to accustom ourselves to thinking about larger groups of words; then we'll move on to verbals (infinitives, gerunds, and participles) and nominative absolutes. Although these terms may sound intimidating, eventually they'll become familiar. Let's begin with a look at compound sentence elements.

C ompound Sentence Elements

Compound sentence elements (like compound subjects, verbs, or objects of any kind) occur when two ideas share the same basic sentence patterns and are joined by coordinators or coordinating conjunctions (usually *and, or, but* within a clause). A sentence with a compound subject has at least two subjects, even though it may have just one verb; a sentence with compound objects of the preposition has at least two prepositional objects for a single preposition. Consider, for instance, how a compound subject happens. A writer wants to note, for instance, that he finished his engineering homework. In addition, he observes that Sarah has also finished her engineering homework. He could say

> I have finished my engineering homework.

and

> Sarah has finished her engineering homework.

Or, because the original grammatical pattern of the two sentences is identical except for the subjects, he could combine them and say

> Sarah and I have finished our engineering homework.

He writes Sarah's name first because that is the polite thing to do when you write about someone and about yourself in the same sentence: mention the other person first!

Sentences with the same basic patterns but with different direct objects would look something like this:

> The puppy chewed my dad's slippers.

and

> The puppy chewed my sister's yearbook.

And the sentence with the compound direct objects would read like this:

> The puppy chewed my dad's slippers and my sister's yearbook.

Note that the basic patterns of these sentences share many words. Creating the compound sentence is a matter of pairing the information that is not shared—if it is structurally the same, of course.

Even objects of prepositions can be compounded. Can you create a sentence containing a prepositional phrase with compound objects from these sentences with the same basic structure?

> All the world is tired of lame television commercials.

> All the world is tired of game shows.

> All the world is tired of reality television.

Combining these sentences would yield

> All the world is tired of lame television commercials, game shows, and reality television.

One preposition—*of*—has three objects: *lame television commercials, game shows*, and *reality television*.

FOR WRITING AND DISCUSSION

To each of the following sentences, add the element specified to create a sentence with compound elements. In at least three sentences, use correlative coordinators. The first few are done for you.

1. Their very footprints are preserved in stone. (Make the subject compound.)

(continued)

Possible response: Their very footprints and handprints are preserved in stone.

2. They are herding their cattle out of the pastures for the night. (Make the direct object compound.)
Possible response: They are herding their cattle and sheep out of the pastures for the night.
3. Lunch was red beans. (Make the predicate noun compound.)
Possible response: Lunch was red beans, rice, cornbread, and sweet potatoes.
4. The flavor industry is highly secretive. (Make the predicate adjective compound.)
5. In 2000, Americans ate an average of about 50 pounds of fresh potatoes. (object of preposition)
6. I smelled black olives. (direct object)
7. The insects are collected. (verb)
8. Smoke flavor is added to barbecue sauces. (subject)
9. Maybe I'll buy myself a beanstalk. (direct object)
10. Rachel could never keep her eyes off my papers. (prepositional phrase)
11. I didn't like his implications. (verb)
12. You went out for ice cream cones with Uncle Larry. (object of either preposition)
13. The kitchen was quiet. (subject)
14. There's salt in the North Sea. (subject)
15. After settling in to my hotel room, I called my wife. (direct object)
16. The team of archaeologists unearthed human figurines. (direct object)
17. In Russia, medical care is expensive. (subject)
18. Other people don't seem to notice the bitterness. (direct object)
19. Hutton has read his manuscripts. (subject)
20. I paid her a couple of dollars. (indirect object)

V *erbals*

A verbal is a verb form that doesn't act or function like a verb. All the physical characteristics of verbals are those of verbs, but verbals function in a way that is distinctively nonverblike. Grammarians talk about three kinds of verbals: **infinitives**, **gerunds**, and **participles**. All have different physical structures, and all have slightly different functions. But all share many of the verb's qualities: that is, they have verb endings (*-ed* and *-ing*); they can pattern with modifiers or complements (just as certain kinds of modifiers pattern with verbs). You will find verbals with objects. You will find verbals that have their own clusters (and even their own clauses). You will find verbals that fit all the six kinds of sentence patterns. Let us now begin with the easiest verbal to recognize: the infinitive.

Infinitives

The infinitive verbal is easy to recognize. It consists of *to* plus a base verb: *to eat, to sleep, to read, to think.* Of course, infinitives may have their own clusters. They may be accompanied by objects and modifiers that typically pattern with verbs: **to eat** *lots of jalapeno peppers early in the morning,* **to sleep** *soundly on a new mattress, always* **to read** *mystery stories, never* **to think** *of another's wishes.* Infinitives may function as nouns, adjectives, or adverbs, but they always have the same basic form and look the same way (the *to* is your clue); thus they are easy to identify. When *to* is followed by a noun, it's a preposition, and you have a prepositional phrase; when *to* is followed by a verb, you have an infinitive. *To* is a multifunction word.

Functions of Infinitives. Look at the following sentences to see how the same infinitive, **to play** *in the state tournament,* can function in a variety of ways, from any variety of noun slots to adjective and adverb positions.

SUBJECT	**To play in the state tennis tournament** was her dream.
DIRECT OBJECT	She hoped **to play in the state tennis tournament**.
PREDICATE NOUN	Her dream was **to play in the state tennis tournament**.
APPOSITIVE	Her dream, **to play in the state tennis tournament**, was a fine dream.
ADJECTIVE	Her time **to play in the state tennis tournament** has not come.
ADVERB	She was afraid **to play in the state tennis tournament**.

The infinitive in the conversation bubble in Figure 5.1, *to unceremoniously cast me adrift,* is an example of a split infinitive. This means that a word, here *unceremoniously,* comes between the *to* and its verb—*cast,* in this case—effectively splitting the infinitive in two. Some grammarians and teachers consider splitting infinitives a breach of good usage, but split infinitives are often used by mature writers. This now silly rule against splitting the infinitive was first articulated by Robert Lowth in *A Short Introduction to English Grammar* (1762) and is less and less frequently observed. Indeed, some quite famous sentences in English have split infinitives, the most popular of which is Captain Kirk's split infinitive, "to boldly go where no man has gone before." Nevertheless, if you know that your readers (or listeners) are overly particular, don't split infinitives—or do it for a good rhetorical reason!

The crew can no longer tolerate Captain Bligh's ruthless splitting of infinitives.

Figure 5.1
Split Infinitive in Conversation Bubble; Gerund in Caption.
© *The New Yorker Collection* 1989 J.B. Handelsman from cartoonbank.com. All Rights Reserved.

For Thinking

Quickly identify the infinitive or the infinitive phrase (the infinitive plus all its cluster, all those words that group themselves around the infinitive) in the following sentences. If you have time in your writing group, explain how each infinitive functions (as noun, adjective, adverb). Be prepared to discuss these in class.

1. It is not difficult to make a glass mirror.
2. Ethan had managed to carve a study out of the little space in the apartment.
3. I was compelled to continue my journey.
4. To appreciate good pastries is a skill pleasurable to learn.
5. It is exalting to search for the right word.
6. To love one's enemies is a Christian precept.
7. When you are an expert, it is hard to make a mistake.
8. I did not want to abandon my old misconceptions.
9. We learned to pay attention to our financial affairs during the downturn of the stock market.
10. Her clutching the handlebar convulsively made it hard to steer the bike.
11. The prisoner was forced to speak.
12. To follow these severe regulations was disheartening as well as time-consuming.
13. To solve the mystery, it was necessary to solve the equations left in the cryptic note.
14. We remain here to watch over our chickens.
15. They gave me a form to fill out.
16. The commandant promised to question all of us later.
17. This word is used to describe the worshiper of images.
18. After the earthquake, it was impossible to identify the ragged and ruined belongings.
19. In the shelter, there is barely enough light to read by.
20. It was easy to identify the infinitives in these sentences!

Infinitives and Patterns. Because verbals share the characteristics of verbs, the structure of verbals also follows all the sentence patterns. After all, sentence patterns depend on the kind of verb in the sentence. And since any verb can also be part of an infinitive or infinitive phrase, it makes sense that, as verbals, infinitives would also follow the patterns. The following infinitive phrases mimic the basic sentence patterns. Here is an example of the V-O or direct object pattern:

> to read this sentence quickly

A sentence with this infinitive in it might look like this:

> Sally is very proud of being able **to read this sentence quickly**.

Read is a verb form, and *sentence* is its object, answering the question, "What is read?" Here are examples of how infinitives can reproduce the other sentence patterns as well:

V-IO-DO	to get me the latest version of the software
V-DO-OC	to name my friend winner of the contest
LV-PA	to smell fresh and clean
LV-PN	to become a public health nurse
V (Adv.)	to labor long and hard for a day's pay

It is rarely necessary to identify how you are using infinitives, but it is useful to know that they can have many different functions and can occupy many different spaces within a sentence.

For Writing

Here you will find a list of infinitives or infinitive phrases. Build a sentence around each infinitive phrase, using the phrase in any way you choose. Of course, you may alter the phrase or add to it as you wish. Read your favorite finished sentences to your writing group or to the class. The first one is done for you as an example.

to make fritters   The baker tried to **make fritters.** (This is an V-O patterned infinitive.)

1. to dull every spark of talent
2. to use up much of their ammunition
3. to eat the smoked pork
4. to go and play billiards in the bar downstairs
5. to control myself
6. to be solid and new
7. to earn one's bread
8. to find anything better
9. to reconstruct the accident after all the terror subsided
10. to say with precision
11. to spit on the ground
12. to be afraid of
13. to carry out a sentence
14. to extract a rabbit from a tall silk hat
15. to understand what formulas they were referring to
16. to scrape
17. to protect against death by gassing
18. to speak like a sailor
19. to reach far enough to touch the items on the top shelf
20. to fill out

(continued)

21. to survive
22. to judge from the anonymous, neat handwriting
23. to sauté two slices of onion
24. to know as little as possible
25. to admit it

Gerunds

Gerunds, like infinitives, are also consistent in form or physical appearance. They always end in the verb suffix *-ing*: *eating, sleeping, reading, thinking*. One difficulty in recognizing gerunds is that other verbals (participles, which you'll read about next) may also end in *-ing*. You can separate gerunds from similar-looking participles, though, by remembering that gerunds function as nouns and only as nouns: almost anywhere a noun can go, a gerund can also fit. As verb forms, gerunds may also have objects and modifiers that pattern with them in verb clusters: ***eating** waffles at the corner restaurant, never **sleeping** past seven o'clock, **reading** all the Louis L'Amour mysteries, unfortunately **thinking** about a sex goddess*. So remember: gerunds are verb forms that end in *-ing* and function as nouns.

There's also one grammatical commonplace, a rule that some grammarians now consider outdated, about gerunds that you should know. Because gerunds function as nouns, pronouns that precede them should be in possessive case. For example, you would write

Mother was not aware of **Jim's** going to the dance.

rather than

Mother was not aware of **Jim** going to the dance.

And according to this rule, you would write

No one knew about **his** stealing all the money from the trust fund.

not

No one knew about **him** stealing all the money from the trust fund.

Functions of Gerunds. Gerunds always function or work as nouns. Therefore, you will find them in places where nouns are typically found: as subject, direct object, predicate noun, appositive, and object of the preposition. Here are some examples of gerunds in different noun slots:

SUBJECT	**Playing in the state tennis tournament** was her dream.
DIRECT OBJECT	She enjoyed **playing in the state tennis tournament**.
PREDICATE NOUN	Her dream became **playing in the state tennis tournament**.

| APPOSITIVE | Her dream, **playing in the state tennis tournament**, was never realized. |
| OBJECT OF PREPOSITION | She never realized her dream of **playing in the state tennis tournament**. |

Rhetorical Impact of Gerunds. Using gerunds pumps up the pace of your writing a notch or two. What you do when you use a gerund is insert a word that looks like a progressive tense verb—an *-ing* verb that connotes or suggests motion—in a noun slot. Because nouns tend to be stolid and somewhat implacable in sentences, you get to have your cake and eat it too when you use gerunds: you use nouns, but they don't look like nouns. Gerunds name actions, and they can help you maintain a healthy pace for your prose.

FOR THINKING

Quickly identify the gerund or gerund phrase (the gerund plus all its cluster, all those words that group around the gerund) in the following sentences. If you have time in your writing group, explain in what nominal capacity each gerund functions (or how each gerund functions as a noun).

1. Watching everyone read out loud made her heart skip a beat.
2. You will be in charge of getting clean water.
3. We finished our cleaning early.
4. Organizing the food pantry was hard but rewarding work.
5. Was Batsheva interested in remarrying?
6. She feared running into her old boyfriend.
7. Joel was personally responsible for instituting Teacher Appreciation Day.
8. Pretending innocence won't work this time.
9. Cheating at poker was her specialty.
10. The whining annoyed her greatly.
11. He woke Fred up with the clacking of his jaw.
12. Fence mending was not her idea of an enjoyable way to spend an afternoon.
13. The doctor warned Mandy about sitting up too soon after surgery.
14. Her efforts at changing her financial situation came to nothing. (*Nothing* ends in *-ing* and occupies a noun slot but is not a gerund: why?)
15. Mrs. Petrocelli likes preparing dinner for her family.
16. Sunbathing is terrible for your skin!
17. Driving the beltway at rush hour is dangerous.
18. Frowning did not become the little princess.

(continued)

19. Filling out the grant report became our morning's task.
20. Denis was adept at chilling the wine to exactly the right temperature.
21. For being alert and saving the toddler, you win an award.
22. There is the sound of buzzing in this office.
23. Making digital movies is not as hard as it sounds.
24. By the time he was 25, Freddie was already tired of earning his way.
25. Smoking cigarettes is definitely dangerous to your health.

Gerunds and Patterns. Like infinitives, gerunds can also assume the familiar patterns of verbs in sentences. The following gerund phrases mimic the basic sentence patterns. Here is an example of the V-O pattern within a gerund:

reading this sentence quickly

A sentence with this gerund in it might look like this:

Sally is very proud of **reading this sentence quickly**.

If we think of *reading* as the verb equivalent in the gerund phrase, then *sentence* is its object, answering the question, "What is read?" Here are examples of how gerunds can reproduce the other sentence patterns as well:

V-IO-DO	getting me the latest version of the software
V-DO-OC	naming my friend winner of the contest
LV-PA	smelling fresh and clean
LV-PN	becoming a public health nurse
V	laboring long and hard for a day's pay

Troubleshooting Gerunds. Be especially mindful that gerunds function as nouns. In a sentence like

The guards will be noting our arrival.

noting is not a gerund. In this sentence, *noting our arrival* functions as a part of the verb phrase or predicate of the sentence, *will be noting our arrival.* Gerunds (and infinitives and participles too) are **nonfinite verbs**: they are not complete enough to constitute the entire main (or finite) verb in a sentence. Thus we say they are incomplete or nonfinite verbs. If you pair them with an auxiliary, of course you can make them finite: then, however, they are transmuted from gerunds (or infinitives or participles) into main verbs.

Also, do not write as an example of a gerund a sentence like

Noting our arrival, the guard scribbled furiously on his clipboard.

Observe that in this sentence *noting our arrival* does not function as a noun. *Guard* is the subject of the sentence; *clipboard* is the object of a preposition. These are the only nouns in the sentence. *Noting our arrival* does not occupy a noun slot nor behave like a noun. (It's really a participle, functioning as an adjective. More about this later.) To use the phrase *noting our arrival* as a gerund, use it in a sentence something like this:

The guard was occupied with **noting our arrival.**

Noting our arrival functions as a noun, the object of the preposition *with*. The phrase, which includes the nonfinite progressive tense form, *noting*, thus functions as a noun.

FOR WRITING

Here you will find a list of gerunds or gerund phrases. Build a sentence around each gerund phrase, using the phrase in any way you choose as long as it functions as a noun. Of course, you may alter the phrase or add to it as you wish. Read your favorite finished sentences to your writing group or to the class. Observe the pattern of each gerund or gerund phrase as you go along. The first one is done for you as an example. Remember to use each phrase in a NOUN's position.

> making fritters   *Making fritters* was the baker's task for the morning. (This gerund is used as the subject of the sentence; it is an V-O-patterned gerund, with *fritters* as the object of the gerund *making*. *Morning* ends in -*ing* and occupies a noun slot; because it is not a verb form, though, it is not a gerund—just a regular noun.)

1. furnishing him with an address
2. arriving from the ends of the earth
3. rationing
4. writing poetry
5. entering air-raid shelters
6. losing myself in the music
7. leaping out of the water
8. healing
9. surprising all the kindergarteners at once
10. accepting all the reports
11. rowing
12. freeing the chained captives
13. sewing the ivory buttons on the sealskin coat
14. watering the delicate African violets
15. adjusting his stock portfolio to meet the market downturn
16. arguing with his girlfriend on the telephone
17. downloading data from the data warehouse
18. singing while you drive
19. monitoring the police channel
20. seeing the sea at Carmel

(continued)

21. checking your e-mail
22. receiving visitors from his hospital bed
23. noting our arrival
24. watering the livestock
25. stealing

Participles

Participles are sometimes the most difficult verbals to identify because they may have several different endings. But if you remember that they are formed from the past-participial and present-participial forms of verbs, you may find this task easier. Past participles (*eaten, slept, read, thought*) are the forms that pattern with the auxiliary *have* in the perfect tenses; and present participles (*eating, sleeping, reading,* and *thinking*) pattern with the auxiliary *be* in the progressive tenses.

Functions of Participles. How can you distinguish present participles from gerunds? Participles function as **adjectives**, patterning with nouns or sometimes with whole sentences as sentence modifiers. And, just like infinitives and gerunds, participles may, like verbs, have objects and modifiers: the *partially eaten* bananas, a bed *barely slept in*, a book *read by 50 million readers*, an idea *thought ridiculous by many*—these are past participial phrases because they are made with the past participial forms (*eaten, slept, read, thought*). They are also all derived from passive structures: the bananas *were partially eaten*, the bed *was barely slept in*, the book *was read by 50 million readers*, the idea *was thought ridiculous by many*. The children *eating **the bananas*** and the dog ***quietly moving his paws in his dreams*** use participial phrases with present participles (*eating* and *moving*) at the head or center of the phrases. Where do you find participles? They are part of noun clusters and are found near nouns. Sometimes they occur before a noun:

Her *billowing* skirts were lovely and graceful. (*Billowing* patterns before the noun it describes.)

Sometimes they occur after a noun, typically in phrases:

Her skirts, billowing in the gentle breeze, were lovely and graceful. (*Billowing in the gentle breeze* is a participial phrase coming after its noun, *skirts*.)

Participial phrases can also appear at the head of the sentence. In this position, they sometimes modify the entire idea of the sentence as much as one specific noun:

Billowing in the gentle breeze, her skirts were lovely and graceful. (Here the participial phrase adheres to its noun, *skirts*, strongly.)

Running frantically from the collapsing building, thousands of New Yorkers managed to survive. (This participial phrase relates to more than just the subject noun, *thousands*; many grammarians would call this one a sentence modifier. Did you see the other present participle, *collapsing*? And did you also see the infinitive, to *survive*?)

Participles frequently appear solo, with no clustering words, as in *She lay her head down on her **crossed** arms* and *He moved quickly to the **crying** baby*. And remember: don't confuse participles and predicates. A participle or participial phrase is NOT the verb or predicate of a sentence. Participles are part of noun clusters; although they resemble verbs in form, they function as adjectives.

For Discussion

See if you can spot the participles and participial phrases in the following sentences. Remember to look for present participles ending in *-ing* and past participles ending in *-ed*, *-en*, and *-t*; and remember that participles and their clusters function as adjectives and pattern near nouns. Also remember that sometimes you will find a single word; other times you will find an extensive phrase or cluster (the participle with its modifiers). Be prepared to present one or two sentences to your whole class.

1. He looked like a young eagle with plumage ruffled by a storm.
2. The sagging skin of her face was yellow.
3. He is a commander attached to the general staff.
4. A man racked with fever lay on the dirty cot.
5. Hastily throwing their cigarettes away, the students hurried into the building under the disapproving eye of the principal.
6. Glancing at the basket of fruit sitting on the table, she thought regretfully about last night.
7. Shaking hands with all the guests, my father made his way around the crowded room.
8. Framed by a little black beard, Samuel looked older than ever.
9. He pronounced a few sharp, cutting words.
10. His speech was like a flame, taking fire from itself and growing from its own fuel.
11. We ran down the lighted streets.
12. All the dwelling places of the elders have been torn down.
13. The Roman museums were inspiring edifices.
14. Daily he searched the crowded streets.
15. On the day after the crime, he had been home, celebrating the holiday with his family.
16. Recognized by NASA, our sleep technology is raved about worldwide!
17. Looking out the window, I can see my garden, covered in snow.
18. Returning from his job as a night watchman, Samuel saw the pogrom.

(continued)

19. Discover newly recorded works by Aaron Copland.
20. Take a hiking and walking trip in Europe.
21. She likes interesting dancers.
22. The small plastic doll baked inside *rosca de reyes* is a symbol of the infant Jesus.
23. Addressing the health concerns of women, this guide gives comprehensive advice on everything from fitness to drugs and alcohol.
24. Eventually, the waiter brought me a small white bowl filled with hot chocolate topped with whipped cream flavored with cinnamon.
25. The witnesses deposed before the tribunal gave false testimony, but no one knew it.

Rhetorical Impact of Participles. Participles quicken your text and, when substituted for or used alongside regular adjectives, provide variety. Like gerunds and infinitives, participles provide a verb presence in a sentence; that is, they suggest energy and movement.

Participles and Patterns. Like gerunds and infinitives, participles can also assume the familiar patterns of verbs in sentences. The participial phrases here mimic the basic sentence patterns. Here is an example of the V-O pattern within a participle:

reading this sentence quickly

A sentence with this participle in it might look like this:

Reading this sentence quickly, Sally felt very proud.

If we think of *reading* as the verb of the pattern, then *sentence* is its object, answering the question, "What is read?" Here are examples of how participles can reproduce the other sentence patterns as well:

V-IO-DO	getting me the latest version of the software
V-DO-OC	naming my friend winner of the contest
LV-PA	smelling fresh and clean
LV-PN	becoming a public health nurse
V	dressed in an organdy dress

For Writing

Here you will find a list of participles or participial phrases; some of these are identical to the gerunds and gerund phrases from the previous section. Build a sentence around each participial phrase, using the

(continued)

phrase in any way you choose. Of course, you may alter the phrase or add to it as you wish. Read your favorite finished sentences to your writing group or to the class. And notice the pattern of each participle or participial phrase as you go along. Remember: because gerunds and participial phrases derived from present participles may look exactly alike, the only difference between some gerunds ánd their participial doubles will be *how they are used, their functions*. Gerunds are used as nouns, exclusively; participles are used as adjectives, exclusively. You may have to memorize this difference at first.

The first one is done for you as an example. Remember to use each phrase in an *adjectival* position; participles pattern with nouns and act to describe or limit or enhance nouns and noun clusters.

1. furnishing an address: Furnishing an address, the driver of the other car in the accident cooperated with the police.
2. arriving from the ends of the earth
3. rationed
4. writing poetry
5. entering air-raid shelters
6. lost in the music
7. leaping out of the water
8. healed by the medicinal herbs
9. surprised by all the kindergarteners
10. accepting all the reports
11. rowing
12. freed from a life of abject poverty
13. sewn onto the sealskin coat
14. watering the delicate African violets
15. adjusted to meet the market downturn
16. arguing with his girlfriend on the telephone
17. downloaded from the data warehouse
18. singing while you drive
19. monitored on the police channel
20. seen for the first time at Carmel
21. checking your e-mail
22. receiving visitors from his hospital bed
23. noted in the ledger
24. watering the livestock
25. stolen

Reviewing All Verbals

Let's reconsider what you know about verbals now, how they are alike, and in what ways they differ. The following chart summarizes this information:

Verbals and their clusters remind us of verb clusters. A verbal may function singly, just one word by itself, or it may pattern in clusters like a verb—with adverbial modifiers, objects, prepositional phrase modifiers, and even clauses (more about this later) to reproduce the major sentence patterns.

Infinitives	Gerunds	Participles
are readily identifiable by form: *TO* + verb (*to snore, to tear, to sigh*). They pattern with nouns to function as adjectives or with adjectives to function as adverbs. And they can also function anywhere a noun or noun substitute can function: as subject, direct object, predicate noun, object of preposition, appositive.	are also readily identifiable by their form: base verb + *-ing* (*working, cheering, smoothing*). They function only as nouns and can appear where nouns do: in the subject slot, the direct object, the predicate noun slot. They can also function as objects of prepositions and as appositives.	are the most difficult to identify by form because they can have more than one form: **past participial** form (ends in *-en, -ed, -t* as in *written, frayed, burnt*) or **present participial** form (ends in *-ing* as in *tearing, weeping, snoozing*). They have, though, only one function: as adjectives and patterning with nouns.

For Writing

Use a verbal form (either infinitive, gerund, or participle) of each verb in sentences of your own creation. You may use the verbals solo or in phrases or clusters: it's your choice. Your goal is to use as many of these verbals as possible in artful sentences (make them beautiful and interesting!). Mark the verbals, identifying each as infinitive, gerund, or participle. When you finish, share your completed sentences with your colleagues in your writers' group.

1. discuss
2. stare
3. stoop
4. gurgle

(continued)

5. reconstruct
6. swarm
7. trap
8. coil
9. suspect
10. hustle
11. shake
12. work
13. flutter
14. spread
15. knock
16. bulge
17. sleep
18. peer
19. dangle
20. bewilder
21. introduce
22. stumble
23. puff
24. distinguish
25. neglect

For Thinking and Talking

Read the following sentences and find the verbals in them. Be prepared to identify each verbal and to explain how it functions or works within the sentence as a whole. Some sentences may have more than one verbal or verbal phrase.

1. Overnight, the aristocracy would have given anything for the privilege of milking a cow. —The J. Peterman Company
2. He remembered his father's telling of his town in Europe, a common barrel of water, a town idiot, a baron nearby. —Arthur Miller
3. In criminal cases, it is common practice to bring relatives of defendants before grand juries. —Jane Mayer
4. The marriage broker, a skeleton with haunted eyes, returned that very night. —Bernard Malamud
5. In order to miss its chilly shadow our neighbors walked three blocks east to buy a loaf of bread. —Grace Paley
6. The grain is his hoarded wealth, his greed, his covetousness. —Norman Mailer

(continued)

7. The mud, frozen into peaks, was melting. —Cynthia Ozick
8. I bought him a little bone teething ring and a little gilded hat. —Isaac Bashevis Singer
9. To ensure that blood pressure, sugar, and fat levels are kept under control, you should strike the right balance by counting both grams and calories. "Food for Thought: Ideas for Diabetes-Friendly Eating"
10. He's nervous from working in the factory all day and riding in the crowded El. —Kate Simon
11. He sometimes played five or six hands of poker in the druggist's back room, trying his luck before getting on the streetcar. —Saul Bellow
12. Twilight is also the mind's grazing time. —Alfred Kazin
13. Reaching toward the sugar bowl, she lifted out the tongs, carefully pinched a cube of sugar, and held it up before his eyes. —Henry Roth
14. HandMade films was a groundbreaking production company owned and run by George Harrison. Adapted from a sentence by Anthony DeCurtis
15. I didn't know quite how to begin on a thing like that. —Daniel Fuchs
16. At the place of farewells and greetings, of winds of coming and winds of going, they say their good-bys. —Tillie Olsen
17. Scattering hat and tissue paper to the floor, he returned downstairs. —Philip Roth
18. They surround Simha, crouched on her stool. —E.M. Broner
19. Joshua, sighing, leans back in his chair. —E.L. Doctorow
20. I begin to be afraid. —Max Apple
21. The band's approach is decidedly British, balancing fey shoegazer misery and sunny acoustic-guitar strumming. —Jenny Eliscu
22. At first, Ricardo wanted to dismiss the query. —Melvin Jules Bukiet
23. He finishes off the éclair under her disapproving eyes. —Allegra Goodman
24. At breakfast the landlady seemed not so menacing. —Ludwig Lewisohn
25. She spat like a poisoned cat. —Michael Gold

N *ominative Absolutes*

The **nominative absolute** is a curious fellow. It is a phrase, not a sentence, although it seems sentence-like—and it can convey an almost fully realized thought. It evokes the absolute essence of a sentence—and looks like a sentence except for one thing: it doesn't have a finite verb. It has a subject or a noun (or nominative) at its head; therefore the word *nominative* is in its title. So, then, a nominative absolute is a noun-headed phrase that conveys the notion of a sentence absolutely—yet without a finite verb. Absolutes are attached to sentences as **free modifiers**; that is, they do not affix themselves to any particular word but to the concept expressed in the sentence. Consider this sentence:

> Tires deflated, frame bent, the bike rested against the wall.

You can see two nominative absolutes in this sentence: *tires deflated* and *frame bent*. Each of these phrases is headed by a noun: *tires* and *frame*. Each also has a verb, but not a finite or complete verb. In both instances, the auxiliary, a key part of the complete verb phrase, is missing. In the original basic or deep structure of this sentence, there are actually three sentences:

> The bike rested against the wall.
>
> Its tires were deflated.
>
> Its frame was bent.

The sentence resulting when all these sentences are combined contains two nominative absolutes with headwords that are closely related to (but not the same as) the subject of the original or base sentence, *bike*. When we combine the sentences, we leave the base sentence as it is. We shrink the sentences that will become absolutes by removing the auxiliary verbs, *were* and *was*, so that we now have

> The bike rested against the wall.
>
> Its tires deflated.
>
> Its frame bent.

In the final compilation of the sentence, we can eliminate *its* because the link between the *bike* and its *tires* and *frame* is clear. Sometimes we leave determiners like *its* in for clarity; in this case we can omit them. See how each absolute clearly retains the meaning of its original sentence and observe how each is really almost a sentence—but not quite.

> The bike rested against the wall, tires deflated, frame bent.

Does it matter that we placed the absolutes at the end of this version of the sentence rather than at its beginning (our original version)? No. In this sentence, the link between the noun subjects is so clear that we can move the absolutes to the end of the finished sentence if we so choose. It is not always this clear or this easy, however, so you will have to place the absolutes carefully to maintain the integrity of the sentence.

Look at the following cartoon in Figure 5.2. Can you spot the nominative absolute in the caption? The nominative absolute, *their habitat destroyed,*

THE FAR SIDE® By GARY LARSON

Some wolves, their habitat destroyed and
overwhelmed by human pressures,
turn to snorting quack.

Figure 5.2
Nominative Absolute and Gerund.
Gary Larson

pairs with a participial phrase, *overwhelmed by human pressures*. These two modifying phrases prepare the reader for the result of the destroyed habitat and the pressures—*snorting quack*, which is a gerund phrase that functions as the object of the preposition *to*.

Rhetorical Impact of Absolutes

The nominative absolute is very powerful. You will find it especially useful when you want to add layers of description to a passage or to fill in a scene with detail. If your professor reminds you to develop your examples or to show details, try writing nominative absolutes. They have the power to magnify the effect of any description. With the absolute, you add absolutely the idea of a new sentence without all its grammatical heaviness because you are not adding complete patterns (because of course the verb is nonfinite). With the absolute, you fatten the images and enrich the depth of your writing.

For Thinking

See if you can find the nominative absolutes in the sentences that follow. Some sentences have more than one absolute. Underscore the absolute and be prepared to talk in class about what it adds to the sentence where it resides.

1. Carr sits calmly, his concentration fixed, his hands folded reassuringly across his lap, with the equable, impersonal kindness of a priest or a cop.—Melanie Thernstrom
2. Hips swaying, I sauntered down the street in my platform shoes.
3. Pencil sharpened and paper piled neatly before me, I began to write the exam.
4. The little girls ran through the meadow, hair ribbons cascading behind them.
5. Antlers erect, the deer crossed the creek, eyes focused on the men across the way.
6. Eyes wide open, the cow jumped over the moon.
7. Tail switching slowly back and forth in pleasure, the cat snuggled into the chair.
8. The vampire, fangs dripping with blood, searched for another meal.
9. My insecurities gone, I performed the sonata without hesitation or error.
10. Hands steady, the nurse expertly gave the screaming patient a shot.
11. Here comes Uncle Benny, gift held proudly before him, a full day late for the birthday celebration.
12. We talked very little during the drive, each of us peering intently into the descending dusk for glimpses of the familiar and the unknown.—Lynda Van Devanter
13. In a late-summer drizzle, I teeter atop a starting block, my arms swollen as sausages from lactic acid, my head pounding from tension, lack of food, and good old self-loathing.—Jim Thornton
14. The girl pulled away, the crew laughing, and Santiago looked across, his eyes meeting Dillon's.—Jack Higgins
15. On cue, LuLing entered, her petite frame contrasting with GaoLing's sturdier one.—Amy Tan
16. He sat up and put his legs over the side of the bed, his flesh still numb, shivers running up and down his back as if he'd caught an ague.—John Gardner
17. I sit on the bed at a crooked angle, one foot on the floor, my hip against the tent of Mom's legs, my elbows on the hospital table.—Michael Dorris

(continued)

18. She plodded along beside me solemnly, her rubber boots making deep prints in the snow.—Richard Bradford
19. He waited, head cocked and hat with it, to see what she might make of such assorted wisdom.—John Updike

Did you notice how the absolutes give the reader more information about the central event in the sentence? Did you observe how the noun at the head of the absolute is very closely related to, but not the same as, a noun in the base sentence? This close relationship is critical to the success of your sentences containing nominative absolutes.

FOR WRITING

Now you try creating some sentences with nominative absolutes from the clusters of sentence ingredients provided. In each group, you will find from two to four sentences. One will be the base sentence; it will be marked *base*.

1. You should leave the base sentence as it is.
2. Change all the other sentences into absolutes by removing the auxiliary or the *be* verb.
3. Then fold all the absolute phrases (the ones with nonfinite verbs) into the base sentences.
4. You'll have to decide where the absolutes should go. What are the rhetorical implications for their locations in the sentence? If the absolutes introduce the sentence, they are likely providing detail that either (a) helps create a scene for the base clause or (b) provides some information necessary for understanding what happens in the base clause. If the absolute is placed midsentence, it is probably there for clarity—because two noun headwords need to pattern near one another to make the sentence make sense. If the absolute(s) is placed at the end of the sentence, it is more likely to be perceived as a comment on what happened in the rest of the sentence or an afterthought. So be careful where you insert the absolute(s).

Now try writing some sentences with absolutes by combining these elements (the first one is done as an example):

1. *The boy was rushed to the doctor.* (base)

    His knees were bleeding profusely.

    His ankle was twisted grotesquely.

(continued)

Yields *Knees bleeding profusely and ankle twisted grotesquely, the boy was rushed to the doctor.*

OR

The boy, knees bleeding profusely, ankle twisted grotesquely, was rushed to the doctor.

What is the difference in putting the absolutes after *boy* rather than at the beginning of the finished sentence? Which version do you prefer?

2. Icarus splashed down into the cold and salty sea. (base)

   His wings were fluttering wildly.

   His face was wearing a look of desperation.

3. John clutched the teddy bear. (base)

   Worry lines were etched into his forehead.

   His palms were sweating profusely.

   His eyes were searching the crowded room.

4. The wedding cake looked perfect. (base)

   Each tier was balanced carefully atop a larger one.

   The frosting was color-coordinated with the bridesmaids' gowns.

   A plastic bride and groom were standing on the very top layer.

5. The little girl woke up from a nightmare. (base)

   Tears were ebbing at the corners of her eyes.

6. Vandals had totally spoiled the car. (base)

   Its windows were shattered.

   Its paint was gouged with a large sharp object.

7. Natalie picked the perfect pink rose from the garden prematurely. (base)

   Its petals were tinted in a soft and luminous pastel shade.

8. John's dog ran joyously around the yard. (base)

   Its tail was wagging furiously.

   Its bark was resounding throughout the neighborhood.

9. The professor walked into the pouring rain. (base)

   Her umbrella was in her hand.

   Her coat was buttoned up to her chin.

10. She sprawled on the couch with ice cream and a movie. (base)

    Her homework was finished.

    Her ironing was done.

    All her troubles were temporarily at bay.

Distinguishing Nominative Absolutes from Verbals

Confusing nominative absolutes and verbals is natural. But you *can* tell them apart. The easiest way to distinguish them is to remember that nominative absolutes have **noun headwords** (or they cluster around nouns) and verbal phrases have **verb headwords** (or they cluster around a verb form). Each also springs from a different kind of deep structure. Consider the base sentence

> The Corvette tore out of the parking lot.

Now let's add to this base sentence about the Corvette the ideas in these sentences:

> The Corvette's tires were spinning.
> The Corvette's radio was blaring "Born to be Wild."
> The Corvette was running at full throttle in first gear.

Look: in the first two sentences, the subject is not the Corvette itself but two aspects of the Corvette, two items closely related to it—its *tires* and its *radio*. In the third sentence, the subject *Corvette* is identical to the subject of the base sentence, *Corvette*. Because the subject of the third sentence is the same as that of the base sentence, we will fold this sentence into the base sentence as a verbal, retaining only the main form of the verb:

> Running at full throttle in first gear, the Corvette tore out of the parking lot.

Because the other two sentences to be incorporated into the base sentence have different subjects than *Corvette*, we must incorporate them into the sentence as nominative absolutes, *tires spinning* and *radio blaring "Born to be Wild."* Our finished sentence might look something like this:

> Running at full throttle in first gear, (introductory *participial phrase*)
> the Corvette tore out of the parking lot, (*base clause*)
> tires spinning and (*nominative absolute*)
> radio blaring "Born to be Wild." (*nominative absolute*)

or

> Running at full throttle in first gear, the Corvette tore out of the parking lot, tires spinning and radio blaring "Born to be Wild."

The verbal and the absolutes coexist nicely in the same sentence, providing a detailed look at just how that Corvette exited the parking lot. The main verb, *tore out of* (a phrasal verb) also contributes to the notion of speed and recklessness surrounding the car's leaving the parking lot.

For Writing

Now you try writing some absolutes. Compose 10 sentences that contain a nominative absolute. You may write 10 sentences from scratch OR you may begin with 10 sentences you have composed

(continued)

for another purpose and add at least one absolute to each of them. Remember that absolutes have nouns at their heads: this is opposite from verbal phrases, which have a verb form at the head of the phrase.

L ooking at Passages for Style

Study the following passages, looking specifically for verbals and nominatives absolutes. Be prepared to explain to the class or to your writers' group how the free modifiers work to build the effect of the passage.

PASSAGE 1

The bull, striking into the wood from side to side with his horns, made a great noise. Then I saw a dark muzzle and the shadow of horns, and then, with a clattering on the wood in the hollow box, the bull charged and came out into the corral, skidding with his forefeet in the straw as he stopped, his head up, the great hump of muscle on his neck swollen tight, his body muscles quivering as he looked up at the crowd on the stone walls. The two steers backed away against the wall, their heads sunken, their eyes watching the bull.
—Ernest Hemingway

PASSAGE 2

Over his lavender collar, crushed upon a purple necktie, held by a diamond hoop: over his ammunition belt of tooled leather worked in silver, buckled cruelly around his gasping middle: over the tops of his glossy shoes Braggioni swells with ominous ripeness, his mauve silk hose stretched taut, his ankles bound with the stout leather thongs of his shoes.
—Katherine Ann Porter

PASSAGE 3

The firemen drew near at 3 a.m., walking through the powdery light in their bunker gear, their Irish and Italian names sparkling in reflective tape at the bottom of their jackets. These were the walking angels of the city.
—Adapted from Devin Friedman

PASSAGE 4

Leaning over the balcony railing, I see the waiters, dressed in white jackets, already arranging chairs on the sidewalk. A boy, his face hidden by the ample hood of a burnoose, is bicycling with difficulty toward the grocery store next to the café. Hung over the bar handles are two straw baskets overloaded with fat loaves of bread. Bread is the gift of Allah.
—Anonymous student writer

P *utting It All Together*

Here are some quick tips for recalling the different verbals and absolutes:

INFINITIVES—consist of *to* plus a base verb; can be used in a noun slot, as an adjective, or an adverb. **To earn my professor's respect** *was hard work.*

GERUNDS—consist of base verb plus *-ing* suffix; is used only in a noun's position, as subject, direct object, predicate noun, appositive, object of the preposition. **Earning my professor's respect** *was hard work.*

PARTICIPLES—consist of the past participle (ends in *-ed, -en, -t*) or the present participle (ends in *-ing*); used only as an adjective. **Earning my professor's respect**, *I labored diligently over the homework assignment.*

NOMINATIVE ABSOLUTES—noun-headed phrases that consist minimally of a noun and a nonfinite verb; used as a free modifier that is absolutely a sentence (but not quite, owing to the nonfinite verb). **Her hair mussed by the wind and her skin tinted pink by the sun**, *she emerged from an afternoon at the beach, looking casually beautiful and relaxed.*

Now let's turn to putting patterns together to create compound, complex, and combination sentences. Chapter 6 will test your understanding of the concepts of patterns.

6

Joining and Combining Patterns and Other Elements

U p to now in this book, you have worked primarily with **simple sentences**. This doesn't mean that the sentences you've looked at have been *easy*. It does mean that most every sentence you have worked with in this book so far has consisted of one clause, one sentence pattern. We call a sentence with just one independent clause and no dependent clauses a **simple sentence**. It is important to shed any grammatical notion of *simple* as *easy*: many simple, one-pattern sentences are quite long and difficult, with phrase piled upon phrase and modifier upon modifier. With this chapter, you'll clarify your understanding of simple sentences and develop your notion of sentence architecture to include compound sentences, complex sentences, and compound-complex sentences. You'll look at the kinds of clauses in complex sentences (adjective, adverb, and noun clauses), and you'll marvel at the beauty of combination sentences. Let's begin, however, by clarifying terms and distinguishing between **phrases** and **clauses**. Then we'll go on to talk about the difference between independent and dependent clauses, then categorize the kinds of sentences, all the while thinking about the rhetorical differences among kinds of sentences.

D istinguishing Phrases and Clauses

A **phrase** is a group of related words, a cluster that does NOT include a complete sentence pattern. You will find prepositional phrases, verbal phrases, noun phrases, adjectival phrases. Some examples of phrases follow; there are no complete patterns. Frequently what is missing from a phrase that would make it a sentence is either a finite verb or a subject cluster:

of the four British vacationers (prepositional phrase)

our very favorite places (noun phrase or cluster around *places*, the noun headword)

too perfect to be believed (adjective phrase clustered around the headword *perfect*; the adjective phrase includes an infinitive phrase *to be believed*—a phrase within a phrase)

a brilliant orange robe (noun phrase or cluster around the headword *robe*)

holding up the bags of grass (participial phrase; the headword is *holding up*; the participial phrase also contains a noun phrase, bags of grass—a phrase within a phrase)

Just as a phrase is a group of words, so is a clause. The difference is that a clause contains a sentence pattern—or a subject and a finite verb—whereas a phrase does not. Some clauses are complete sentences, and some are not (more about this later). If you see a subject plus a finite verb, however, you have found a clause, regardless of whether it sounds like a complete sentence. Incidentally, many grammarians call phrases **p-groups** (for preposition groups) and clauses **s-groups** (for sentence groups).

For Discussion

In your writers' group, explain what kind of phrase each of the following phrases is, pointing out the headword of each phrase or the word that seems to be the center of the phrase. Several items contain more than one phrase or phrases within phrases. Prepare to present several of your explanations to the whole class.

1. too scantily presented
2. a personal, actual experience
3. their innocent childhood
4. a Star Trek pillow cover
5. smiling oddly at Leroy
6. was sitting on the crest of a hill
7. a professor of humanities at City College
8. to make love in Venice
9. like two pieces of old furniture
10. the faint light coming up the stairwell
11. a very unpleasant faintness
12. the loud groaning of the hydraulic valves
13. crossed the city
14. in the soft dusk
15. to have a large family
16. asleep during breakfast
17. before the monsoon rains

(continued)

18. hanging precariously from the edge of the precipice
19. all the pretty horses
20. connected by the most fragile understanding

For Writing

Now look at the following items. Determine which are phrases and which are clauses and mark each as phrase or clause. Don't forget that a clause has a complete pattern, a subject and a finite verb. A phrase lacks some element that would make it a complete pattern. These phrases and clauses have been adapted from Rebecca Goldstein's book *Mazel*; most capitalization and punctuation marks have been removed.

_____ 1. from early morning
_____ 2. that went untouched
_____ 3. children had died before
_____ 4. from accident
_____ 5. in their midst
_____ 6. when Leiba got up from the seven days of mourning
_____ 7. in lovingly rendered translations
_____ 8. while Gordin had lain on his death bed
_____ 9. to be so famous
_____10. in 1909
_____11. when she had told him
_____12. a worldly man, a journalist, and a reformer
_____13. having groaned to himself
_____14. since their hearts had already been broken
_____15. from scattered little places
_____16. there was so much to catch up on
_____17. engrossed in their intertwining fantasies
_____18. to lavish advantages
_____19. the tailor wrote down the measurements
_____20. at 16 years old
_____21. to reward you for your kindness
_____22. milk fresh from the udder
_____23. he scribbles, too
_____24. Aunt Frieda had lived here
_____25. I forget myself
_____26. where the girls were lively and beautiful
_____27. you had a good chance of overhearing something
_____28. in the middle of this dazzling day
_____29. the most atrocious time of year

(continued)

_____30. well over 6 feet
_____31. his mouth was rather thin
_____32. when she played the piano
_____33. they were clumsy things, words
_____34. of the condition
_____35. had left all that behind
_____36. it had been rather pleasant there in the café
_____37. the itch of gregariousness
_____38. from village to village
_____39. what talkers they were
_____40. as Sorel neared the entrance
_____41. that led to a pond
_____42. if one were a fish
_____43. a good feeling about this audition
_____44. they were a pack of geniuses
_____45. as if there were a fire under the skin
_____46. rocking on his seat, back and forth
_____47. which had sunk to the faintest whisper
_____48. for several long moments
_____49. not until this spring
_____50. in the mysterious process of creativity

D istinguishing Independent Clauses and Dependent Clauses

As you worked through the previous exercise on phrases and clauses, you probably identified some clauses that sounded just like (and indeed are) complete sentences: *they were a pack of geniuses* and *it had been rather pleasant there in the café*, for instance. These clauses or complete patterns that sound complete by themselves *are* in fact complete by themselves; they are also called **independent clauses** because they can stand on their own as sentences. You probably also noticed some clauses (complete patterns with finite verbs) that did not sound quite right or complete enough to be sentences. These are called **dependent clauses** or **subordinate clauses**. Examples of dependent clauses are *which had sunk to the faintest whisper* and *As Sorel made her way to the entrance*. In a few pages you'll read more about kinds of dependent clauses (adjective, adverb, and noun clauses).

C reating Compound Sentences

Now to compound sentences. Put two independent clauses together, and you have a compound sentence. A **compound sentence** is composed of two or more independent clauses. All the clauses must be independent; that is, each clause within the compound sentence can be removed and exist as a sentence all by itself. So if you have the independent clause

I listened to the organic chemistry lecture

and the related independent clause

I was enthralled

you can create a compound sentence

I listened to the organic chemistry lecture, and I was enthralled.

Each independent clause is a complete pattern that can exist on its own as a complete sentence.

FOR WRITING

Mark the clauses as independent or dependent, then compare your results with those of your writing group. There is no punctuation here to help you. Ask yourself, "Does this pattern sound complete as it is?"

1. even after you have asked for death
2. no one ever thanked him
3. people were telling each other stories
4. Sarah Sally Smith was born in 1910
5. which I could throw overboard
6. before he heard her
7. forget it (Did you notice the ellipted or shortened subject and imperative mode?)
8. she does not want to go with them
9. if I lose 10 minutes' sleep
10. when Greg came home
11. a woman is singing to me
12. I walk through the long schoolroom
13. who once before came to Thebes
14. whatever influence I had over Mama
15. when he realized the truth about her
16. the woman looked up the road
17. because she caught me smoking
18. I must have seen a rabbit
19. which Mrs. Kincaid prayed
20. a bird streaked across the gray sky

Use compound sentences to link closely related independent clauses that you consider of equal importance. Rhetorically, the compound sentence yokes grammatically equal ideas. It also lends itself to balancing clauses or ideas and to parallelism because the **coordinator** or **coordinating conjunction** acts like the equal sign in an equation, mediating the two sides that must balance yet are somewhat different in composition and sometimes even subtly different in value. You have several options for punctuating compound sentences: you can use a coordinator plus a comma; a semicolon alone; a semicolon plus a conjunctive adverb; and in some special cases where the clauses are very closely related, a colon. Let's take a look at the rhetorical implications of each punctuation choice.

Creating Compound Sentences with Coordinators and Commas. The coordinator-comma combination is the most common way independent clauses are put together in compound sentences. This combination sounds casual and comfortable, it moves quickly, and it allows you to express a great many shades of meaning with the most popular coordinators:

and (meaning *addition*)	*so* (meaning *therefore*)
but (meaning *contrast*)	*yet* (meaning *contrast*)
for (meaning *because*)	*or, nor* (meaning *alternative*).

The comma goes *after the first pattern* (and then after each pattern if there are more than two). The comma and the coordinator are of equal importance in this scheme; consider the two of them a unit linking one independent clause to the next. Some of you may have been taught to insert a comma routinely before each *and* in a sentence: this is not a good idea. If you have been taught this as a tenet of punctuation, work hard to disabuse yourself of this notion. What this practice can lead to is misplaced commas between elements of compound subjects, compound verbs, or other compounded sentence elements. Just because there's an *and* in the sentence doesn't mean there should be a comma. Here are some examples of the comma-coordinator combination:

1. It had been a long day at the clinic, but there were no inpatients.
   —Ursula LeGuin
2. He made no secret of this, yet people did not believe him.
   —Franz Kafka
3. The husband went out to smoke in the first interval, and she was left alone in her seat. —Anton Chekhov

Do you see each pattern? For sentence 1, the patterns are *it / had been / day* (S-LV-PN) plus *there / were / inpatients* (THERE V-S); observe the comma and the coordinator *but*, which expresses something contrary to expectation. Sentence 2 contains two S-V-O patterns, *he / made / secret* and *people / did believe / him*. These two patterns experience the negative transformation, then are linked by *yet*, which emphasizes contrast and difference. Now you analyze how sentence three functions as a compound sentence.

Creating Compound Sentences with a Semicolon
Joining Patterns

When you join two (or more) independent clauses with only a semicolon between them, you send a rhetorical message to the reader that the reader needs to slow down and read deliberately. Here are some examples of the compound sentence where independent clauses are joined with only semicolons:

1. It was true, too; she really did not have time. —Alice Munro
2. And the earth is shallow; there is not a great deal of it before you come to the rock. —William Faulkner
3. He was all out of breath with whispering; I could hear him pant slightly. —Joseph Conrad

Emphasis falls on *too*, *shallow*, and *whispering*, the pivotal words in the sentences, respectively. A complete pattern occupies the space before and after the semicolons in each sentence.

You'll see in all these sentences that a semicolon brings the reader up almost as short as a period does, yet it's not quite a full stop. Rather it's a good long healthy pause midsentence. This makes the last part of the first clause and the first part of the last clause particularly powerful because they come at a very important juncture. Imagine the reader's slowing down to attend to the semicolon; this reader will therefore be dwelling longer on the material nearest the semicolon. This makes this physical place in the compound sentence a place of great rhetorical importance that you may exploit as a writer. Because the semicolon brings the reader up a bit shorter than does the comma and creates a longer pause, it also has a more formal personality: it is hard to sound breezy when your page is peppered with semicolons.

Creating Compound Sentences with Semicolon
and Conjunctive Adverb Joining Patterns

If the semicolon joining two independent clauses is more formal than the comma plus coordinator method, then the semicolon and conjunctive adverb is more formal still. When you add a conjunctive adverb to a semicolon, you heighten the formality of the prose considerably. Conjunctive adverbs are, literally, adverbs that join. They are frequently heavy, compound words that are fairly easy to recognize: *moreover*, *furthermore*, *consequently*, *nevertheless*, *henceforth*, *therefore*, *rather*. Examine the sentences with conjunctive adverbs and explain how the conjunctive adverb works.

1. In spite of the prohibition, clandestine readings still took place for a time in some form or another; however, by 1870 they had virtually disappeared. —Alberto Manguel
2. Little emphasis was given to manufacturing and railroads at these meetings; rather, the stress was on marketing, banking, and credit reform in the South. —Harold Woodman

3. We missed the deadline for filing our income taxes; therefore, we had to pay a fine.

Conjunctive adverbs will accomplish two goals: first, they will ask your reader to slow down (they are usually set off with commas); second, they will demonstrate the relationship between clauses. For instance, *furthermore* has a meaning similar to *in addition. Consequently* is close in meaning to *because. Nevertheless* means *in spite of this. Rather* signals a contrast. And *henceforth* means *from that time forward.* So if you want to create the rhetorical effect of solemnity, if you want to emphasize one point greatly, if you want to slow the text so that you can govern it better, use a conjunctive adverb.

Creating Compound Sentences with a Colon Joining Patterns

On rare occasions when two clauses are extremely closely related, you may use a colon after the first clause to announce the second or to telegraph to the reader their interrelatedness. Remember that a compound sentence has a set of two complete patterns or independent clauses. You absolutely need a complete pattern before the colon and one after as well if you're crafting a compound sentence.

1. She explained the stir: Mr. Hubber was coming at seven to take their photograph for the Christmas card. —John Cheever
   (The first independent clause sets up the second one and prepares the reader for the information. Observe also how much more emphasis this information receives than if it had been tucked away without the first clause.)
2. The word "sweetness" denoted a reality commensurate with human desire: it stood for fulfillment. —Michael Pollan
3. And so it has come to this: the Bible, once believed to have been written by God, has now, at least in part, been "written by teens." —Mark Oppenheimer

Sometimes—and this is only sometimes—writers join two very short independent clauses with only a comma or only a coordinator. This is done to create a sense of rapid movement through the sentence and to insist on the rhetorical linkage between the clauses. Here are some examples of each:

With only *and* and no comma:

1. Marion's not well and she can't stand shocks. —F. Scott Fitzgerald
2. Then they all gathered around Sonny and Sonny played. —James Baldwin
3. The wine sparkled in his eyes and the bells jingled. —Edgar Allan Poe
4. A breeze was blowing toward them and the grass rippled gently in the wind. —Ernest Hemingway

With only the comma and no *and*:

1. His father never looked at it, he never once looked down at the rug. —William Faulkner

2. For a brief moment I hesitated, I trembled. —Edgar Allan Poe
3. Why, I don't even know the man's first name, that's how close I ever was to him. —Dorothy Parker
4. Her whim is justice, her word is my law. —John Updike

The caption of the cartoon in Figure 6.1 illustrates a compound sentence with three independent clauses. Each clause has its own pattern. Each is an S-V-O pattern, with the phrase *to eat the dog* functioning as the direct object in the last clause. Observe how commas are used to separate each clause. What is the rhetorical effect of having all three independent clauses together to constitute one sentence? They are united in effect, as in reality: the relationship among them is demonstrably clear as the characters from the **Wizard of Oz** lay claim to the spoils of their adventure.

"He gets her heart, you get her brain, and I get to eat the dog."

Figure 6.1
Compound Sentence with Three Independent Clauses.
© *The New Yorker Collection 1992 Lee Lorenz from cartoonbank.com. All Rights Reserved.*

For Writing

Now you try your hand at writing some compound sentences. Here you will find a cluster of independent clauses. From these clauses and from some independent clauses that you construct and add,

(continued)

create 10 compound sentences, joined and punctuated in a variety of ways. You have choices: take one independent clause, make up another, and join them together. OR choose two independent clauses from the list and combine them to create one compound sentence. You are welcome to change tense or pronoun person or whatever you need to create interesting compound sentences. Be prepared to analyze and discuss the sentences you have written. Here are the independent clauses, not punctuated or capitalized, upon which you may build your compound sentences:

1. I was conscripted into the army
2. we were surprised by this assumption
3. it's terribly unfair
4. everybody blames us
5. they are ready to defend their deep and famous interests
6. they scowled
7. at one point I asked him about his favorite writers
8. we watched our first rodeo
9. I had touched a sensitive nerve
10. the third volume collects statistics
11. our relationship ended with a joke
12. Vivian sent gifts
13. the tone was shrill
14. he has been right about liberalism
15. he has an affair with an unnamed woman
16. we met at an evangelists' camp meeting near Coeur d'Alene, Idaho
17. the noise ceases abruptly
18. I turned off the oven and opened the door.
19. she is not a doctor
20. we'll meet you at that address
21. I'm not ever going back to school
22. we can wait for the bus here
23. in late November it began to snow in earnest
24. he's a very lonely man
25. I spent my entire lunch hour in a phone booth, trying to reach Alfredo
26. Thirty or forty children clamored for food
27. he brandished the gun
28. her presence embarrassed him
29. the doctor in the film had camera fright
30. he had never killed a juvenile

Creating Complex Sentences

A complex sentence is not at all like a compound sentence. Where the compound sentence is balanced on the fulcrum of the coordinator/comma, the semicolon/conjunctive adverb, or the semicolon alone, there is no such balance in the complex sentence. A complex sentence expresses explicit and usually unequal relationships between two or more clauses or patterns. One of the clauses clearly expresses the dominant or main idea, and the other clause or clauses express related but subsidiary ideas or relationships. Thus a complex sentence has one main or base clause (an independent clause) plus one or more dependent or subordinate clauses. Complex sentences are also rhetorically complicated; in their structures as well as in their words, they demonstrate the ways that ideas relate to one another.

Within complex sentences, the dependent clauses may be of three types: **adjective clauses, adverbial clauses**, or **noun clauses**. In any complex sentence, you will find at least one of these kinds of dependent clauses yoked to a related independent clause. Use complex sentences to express relationships among ideas, to note cause and effect, to link events to time, to explain conditions contrary to fact, to express all manners of contingency.

Creating Complex Sentences: The Adjective Clause

Adjective clauses function as adjectives and cluster around nouns. You can recognize an adjective clause by its position near a noun or within a noun cluster and by the subordinator that introduces the clause. The subordinators most identified with adjective clauses are what traditional grammarians call the **relative pronouns** (perhaps because they articulate and define relationships):

that	whose
who	which
whom	

But you may also find these words used to introduce adjective clauses:

where

when (on rare occasions)

why (following the phrase *the reason*)

So when you see one of these words, be alert for the possibility of an adjective clause.

Here are some examples of sentences with adjective clauses:

1. My friend Adam, **who had some anxiety problems of his own and was a real pooh-pooher of "talk therapy,"** found me a behaviorist at McLean. —Lauren Slater
2. It is precisely this conception of movies **that must be defeated**. —Susan Sontag

3. Castro slaps a hand against his own midsection, **which is relatively flat**. —Gay Talese
4. For in reality this is a brutally impolite world **where bad intentions frequently prevail**. —Verlyn Klinkenborg
5. Our mythic prototype of a creature from another planet has round luminous eyes on a face **whose other features seem atrophied**. —Gordon Grice

Take a look at the clauses themselves. Each is a complete pattern, with subject and finite verb, but each clause is incomplete if it stands alone. In these adjective or relative clauses, the subordinator usually assumes the role of one of the pattern elements, frequently the subject. Indeed, the relative pronouns *who, which,* and *that* always play a grammatical role in the adjective clauses they introduce, and they always begin the clause no matter which function they perform. The possessive *whose* functions as a determiner in any relative clause it introduces. Consider sentence 1's relative clause:

> who had some anxiety problems of his own and was a real pooh-pooher of "talk therapy"

In this clause, *who* is the subject of the clause and also the relative pronoun acting as the subordinator, and the verbs are compound: *who had problems* (S-V) and *who was pooh-pooher* (S-LV-PN). In your writing group, identify the patterns of the other adjective clauses.

In some sentences, the subordinator introducing the adjective or relative clause is omitted, so it is more difficult to notice the clause itself. Nevertheless, a pattern is still identified as an adjective clause if it patterns with a noun or noun substitute and if it has a subject and finite verb. Here are a few examples:

1. Here are the apples **we picked yesterday**. (The *that* ordinarily introducing the clause is omitted or ellipted.)
2. All the movies **I saw last year** were nominated for an Academy Award.
3. Today is the day **you have been waiting for**!

Look at the caption in Figure 6.2. There is an adjective clause in this sentence, *All you really need in life is the love of a good cat,* but it may be difficult to find because the relative pronoun or subordinator has been withdrawn or ellipted; it is merely understood. The adjective clause is *you really need,* ellipted from *that you really need,* patterning after *all* and articulating and qualifying how much of *all* is under discussion. The skeletal base sentence is *All is love,* S-LV-PN.

Restrictive and Nonrestrictive / Essential and Nonessential Adjective Clauses

You should pay attention to one other feature of the sentences with adjective clauses: some of those adjective clauses are set off from the rest of the

"All you really need in life is the love of a good cat."

Figure 6.2
Adjective Clause, Subordinator Ellipted.
© The New Yorker Collection 1992 George Booth from cartoonbank.com. All Rights Reserved.

sentence with commas, and some are not. Why are some adjective clauses separated from their sentences and some not? Adjective clauses are of two kinds; they may be *essential* to the understanding of the noun with which they pattern, or they may be *nonessential* to the understanding of that noun. Consider Gay Talese's sentence about Castro:

Castro slaps a hand against his own midsection, **which is relatively flat**.

This adjective clause, set off from the main clause with a comma, is a nonessential or nonrestrictive clause. That it is separated from the main clause means that its information is not required for an understanding of *midsection* or what happens to the midsection in this sentence. In contrast, look at Grice's sentence about extraterrestrials:

Our mythic prototype of a creature from another planet has round luminous eyes on a face **whose other features seem atrophied**.

No comma exists between the adjective clause and its noun, *face*. The adjective clause is essential to our understanding of *face*, and the adjective clause necessarily restricts our understanding of *face*: this is a **restrictive** or **essential** adjective clause.

You can remember the differences in these kind of clauses this way: if the clause must be in the sentence, don't use the comma to keep it out. Leave the gate open to show that the clause is essential. If, however, the clause is not essential to understanding the noun or the sentence, indicate this with a comma to show some degree of separation.

For Writing

Now it's time for you to create sentences with adjective clauses. Here is a list of adjective clauses. Fold these clauses (or revised but recognizable versions of these clauses) into independent clauses that you create to make complex sentences with adjective or relative clauses. Be conscious of whether you are creating essential or nonessential adjective clauses and punctuate them correctly!

1. which have little defense
2. that were destined to be broken
3. whose name is blessed
4. who was pouring hot water into a teacup
5. which were covered with snow
6. who was dressed entirely in black
7. who had a fear of military service
8. which appeared ragged at the edges
9. that was incredibly exciting
10. which were trembling
11. who lived in the town
12. whose work was on display at the gallery
13. where two girls lived
14. who sees everything and hears everything
15. that were blinking in the moonlight
16. which were covered with heavy shutters
17. who yearns to hear the news from you
18. that will affect her entire life
19. that is covered with gigantic yellow plastic flowers
20. who is crazy in love with Fredrick
21. whose daughter was studying at the Sorbonne
22. who was lifting his umbrella and waving it wildly in the air
23. which was a boring, tedious lesson
24. that was made of the finest silk
25. who had been introduced as Janus Man

Examine the caption of the cartoon in Figure 6.3. Here the adjective clause *who was getting just a little too sociable for his own good* patterns with the noun *Shep* (or *collie*: *Shep* is an appositive for *collie*). *Who* functions both as relative pronoun or subordinator linking the adjective clause to the independent or base clause. *Who* is also the subject of the adjective clause. *Who was getting sociable* is the pattern S-LV-PA. The adjective clause provides the punch line at the very end of the caption.

THE FAR SIDE® **By GARY LARSON**

Everything was starting to come into focus
for Farmer MacDougal–his missing sheep,
his missing beer, and his collie, Shep,
who was getting just a little too
sociable for his own good.

Figure 6.3
Adjective Clause, Participles, and Infinitive.
Gary Larson

Adjective Clauses and Participial Phrases: Rhetorical Choices

Sometimes a clause is just what you need to convey the importance of an idea. But sometimes a clause is too much or too long, and a phrase is more appropriate. You can reduce an adjective clause to a participle or a participial phrase that may function even better than a clause. This assignment asks you first to change some adjectival clauses into participial phrases and next to create some participial phrases of your own to add to base sentences. Look at this sentence that contains an adjective clause:

> The frustrated commuters **who are rushing for the last train** must have stayed late at the office.

Who are rushing for the last train is an adjectival clause, part of a cluster of words patterning around the noun *commuters*. In this sentence, though, we have some rhetorical and stylistic options. We can, for instance, shrink the adjective clause to a participial phrase. To do this, we eliminate the subject of the clause because it is the same as the subject of the base sentence. Then we eliminate the auxiliary verb to leave only the participial form of the verb. We keep the participle with its cluster, and our transformed sentence reads

> The frustrated commuters **rushing for the last train** must have stayed late at the office.

Rushing for the last train is a participial phrase functioning as an adjective and patterning with the noun *commuters*.

Here are some other sentences with adjectival clauses transformed into participles and participial phrases:

> The setting of the novel is Sri Lanka, **which was ravaged by civil war**.

becomes

> The setting of the novel is Sri Lanka, ravaged by civil war.

> The commentator who was speaking for the U.S. was shouted down.

becomes

> The commentator speaking for the U.S. was shouted down.

> Spielman had explained the main mechanisms that regulate sleep.

becomes

> Spielman had explained the main mechanisms regulating sleep.

With the last sentence, the form of the verb changes to the present participle to make sense. The participial form of the verb is the form used with auxiliaries or helping verbs, as in *was torn, have worked, is running, had estimated*. Participles most commonly end in *-ed, -en, -n, -t,* or *-ing*.

Present participles (both one-word and phrasal versions), past participles (one-word and phrasals), infinitive phrases, and gerunds are, then, derived from embedded sentences—the remains of sentences buried within the structure of the base sentence. Rather than insert the entire sentence representing each separate idea and risk repeating words, structures, or ideas, the writer shrinks the sentence to create a verbal, which then functions as a noun, adjective, or adverb within a base sentence. Thus a sentence like

Strolling through the upscale mall, the students gawked at the luxurious items in the well-stocked windows

has within it the embedded sentences:

The students gawked at the items.

The items were luxurious.

The items were in the windows.

The windows were well-stocked.

The students were strolling through the mall.

The mall was upscale.

FOR WRITING

Now you rewrite the following sentences, changing adjective clauses into participial phrases:

1. Sandra, who is wearing large metal earrings and shiny lipstick, is actually quite beautiful as she emerges from the darkness of the other room.
2. Joe, who was refusing a ride, shook hands with me for the first time.
3. Nittler, who is putting his veterinary training to use on the family homestead, has stayed at home in Kansas.
4. The trail ascended through the leafless birch and mountain ash that was ragged, scraggly.
5. All the noise that was coming so persistently from the backyard was really annoying me and keeping the baby awake.

Can you find and underline the participles and participial phrases in this sentence?

The glistening balls mistaken for a snack by Nevada prospectors were later identified as pack rat middens—globs of crystallized pack-rat urine containing sticks, plant fragments, bones, and animal hair. —Leon Jaroff

What was the original base clause from which the participial phrases were derived?

Creating Complex Sentences: The Adverb Clause

Adverb clauses function as adverbs, and like adverbs, they cluster around verbs. That is, adverbs pattern near verbs; they develop ideas by explaining *where, how,* or *when.* You will perhaps remember from the section on adverb form classes that sometimes adverbs are classified as *there* adverbs (adverbs of place, like *where*); *thus* adverbs (adverbs of manner, like *how*);

and *then* adverbs (adverbs of time, like *when*). As with adjective clauses, there are certain subordinators that introduce adverbial clauses, most popularly these:

after	because	once
although	before	since
as	even though	until
as if	if	when

Rhetorically speaking, adverb clauses are perhaps the most flexible of all dependent or subordinate clauses. Not only can they convey information about where, when, how, or why something occurs or exists, but the clauses themselves are quite flexible: they may typically be moved to different sentence locations. For instance, adverbial clauses frequently introduce the sentence or come right at its beginning; in this role, they sometimes provide important information the reader needs to know so that the information in the base clause can be accurately understood. Or they sometimes conclude the sentence, providing information that is an afterthought to the information in the base clause or information that comments upon main-clause information. Adverbial clauses may also occur midsentence, as interrupters. In this guise, they can slow the pace of the sentence and can help you place information at strategic points for the reader's consumption.

Look at these sentences, all of which contain adverb clauses:

1. **When the cops arrived at the meeting place**, the gang was all there.

Observe the *when* that begins the clause, then the S-V structure (*cops arrived*). Note that this clause, which introduces the sentence and is set off by a comma, is called an **introductory clause**. The clause also points to a specific time and fulfills the function of telling *when*.

2. **As the trial began**, the talk around the courthouse intensified.

Here we have another introductory clause, also a *when* adverb. *As* is the subordinator introducing the clause, which is the S-V pattern (*trial began*).

3. The rebels continued to strafe the plane **until the king was clearly dead**.

Until begins the clause, which is an S-LV-PA pattern—*king was dead*. The adverbial clause concludes the sentence; no comma separates the clause from the sentence because the clause ends the sentence. Most of the time, this is the case. Use a comma to set off a subordinate clause following the main clause if the subordinate clause has no effect on the outcome of the main clause. If the idea in the main clause is so linked to the idea in the subordinate clause that the main clause will not be realized without the subordinate clause, use no comma. You will find that clauses beginning with *although, even though, since*, and *while* are subject to this consideration. So when the adverbial clause begins with *although* or *even though*, a comma is usually necessary:

We were late to the Sting concert, even though we left early.

Sometimes a comma is also necessary to prevent misreading.

4. It is impossible, **when you are lost in the rain in Juarez**, to find the Jack of Hearts.

Here the adverb clause interrupts the main clause, as adverbs often do. The adverb clause is set off by commas on both sides. The clause begins with the subordinator *when*, then assumes one of two patterns, depending on how you focus your interpretive lens. *You are lost* can be an S-V pattern if you perceive the verb to be passive, with the *be* (*are*) + past participle (*lost*) form. Most of you will probably, however, see this as an example of the S-LV-PA pattern, with *lost* functioning as a predicate adjective. Either interpretation offers a clear understanding of how the sentence works.

5. Mitch knew Norm **because Norm had auditioned for a part in a movie**.

The adverb clause concludes the sentence, and no comma precedes it here. The clause has an S-V pattern (*Norm had auditioned*) as well.

Can you find the adverb clause in the caption in Figure 6.4? This clause tells *when* the remote control will be returned. Because the clause concludes the sentence, no comma separates it from the base or main clause. The

"You'll get it back once you articulate a coherent viewing policy."

Figure 6.4
Adverb Clause.
© *The New Yorker Collection 1992 Robert Mankoff from cartoonbank.com. All Rights Reserved.*

clause is more effective at the end of the sentence because it contains the punch line and is therefore in a position of emphasis.

FOR WRITING

Now it's time for you to build some sentences with adverb clauses. Below is a list of 25 adverb clauses. To each adverb clause, add a main clause so that the result is a complex sentence with an adverbial clause. You may modify the clauses in any way, just as long as the item remains a clause. Punctuate correctly.

1. before we reached Mrs. Littlejohn's house
2. when she came in
3. while they all stood in the hallway exchanging pleasantries
4. when he was young
5. as though there were no subject to be avoided (notice the subjunctive form)
6. when you realize the truth about it all
7. if they chose to complain
8. until you are exactly at the corner
9. while two men looked at him in contempt
10. when she pressed her head to my cheek
11. since he came to live with us
12. while his dinner got cold
13. when she entered the room carrying the knife
14. while the children played, united in their fear of the mother
15. after they had put on their nightdresses
16. as they stumbled up the walk
17. when she had finished
18. if he were killed
19. because he's not even going to look at the essays until Monday
20. because the doctor would like to marry her
21. as they went back to their seats
22. as my aunt's condition worsened
23. because they always wanted to pinch our cheeks
24. when I stepped into the living room
25. when the horse skidded up to the fence

FOR WRITING

Now you create the adverbial clauses and insert them into the following independent or base clauses. You may insert the adverbial clause at the beginning of the sentence (introductory clause), at the

(continued)

end of the sentence (concluding clause), or in the middle of the sentence (interrupting clause). Be sure to punctuate correctly.

1. The men were squatting there, talking intently.
2. She was the fastest runner in the seventh grade.
3. Elaine takes you down to her place by the river.
4. I was happy.
5. They put arsenic in the king's meat.
6. We must stop seeing each other.
7. The young man smiled urbanely.
8. Miss Rainey was late.
9. The lark sings at heaven's gate.
10. I learned my lesson.
11. A dragon longer than two lances pursued her.
12. A woman is singing to me.
13. Ophelia had a Christian burial.
14. An artist finds reality and satisfaction in work.
15. Sailors have an extra sense that alerts them to danger.
16. I sang the baritone lead in *Pirates of Penzance*.
17. The large Great Dane sleeps curled up on the blanket.
18. In a refrigerator an apple will keep for weeks.
19. This is a bad map.
20. He dipped the bread into the grease from the meat.
21. He left his pants upon the chair.
22. We sing together.
23. My conscience is active and alert.
24. I had many fine tools.
25. I ask your mercy.

Creating Complex Sentences: The Noun Clause

Noun clauses function exactly as nouns do. You will find noun clauses wherever you find nouns: in the subject slot, the direct object slot, the predicate noun slot, the slots for appositives and objects of the preposition. Like other subordinate or dependent clauses, noun clauses cannot function on their own; rather, they must link to a base clause. One way you can identify a noun clause is that when you remove the entire noun clause from the sentence, the sentence loses a big chunk of its important information. This loss of information makes sense, though, if you think about it, because the sentence loses a noun when a noun clause is removed. And nouns carry much of the important weight of the sentence as subjects, direct objects, predicate nouns, objects of the preposition, and appositives. Why would you use a noun clause when a simple noun might do? The rhetorical effect of using a noun clause instead of a noun is to give the idea more space, more gravity, and more emphasis. Because a noun clause has its own pattern, it can embody an expanded idea. So use a noun clause if you want to lend more power to a noun or if you just want or need to say more.

Besides recognizing that a noun clause removed from the sentence leaves a large gap of information, another way you can identify a noun clause is by the subordinator that introduces it. The most common subordinators introducing noun clauses are *who, what, why, how, where,* and *that.* The *that* introducing noun clauses is different from the *that* introducing adjective clauses, however. The noun clause *that* functions as an expletive; it plays no grammatical role in the clause. Did you observe that other of these subordinators can also introduce adjective or relative clauses?

When you think about how to punctuate a noun clause, think about how you punctuate nouns in sentences. Like a noun, a noun clause functioning as a subject, direct object, or predicate noun won't be separated from its verb by a comma; like a noun, a noun clause functioning as the object of a preposition shouldn't be separated from its preposition by a comma either. You may find that you need to separate a noun clause used as an appositive from the rest of the sentence with commas or dashes. Most of the time, noun clauses require no punctuation. Let's take a look at some and see. Here are some sentences with noun clauses (the clauses are in bold type).

1. **What you want** is **what you get at McDonald's today**.

This famous slogan from McDonald's contains two noun clauses. The first functions as the subject of the sentence whose verb is the linking verb *is*. The second noun clause acts as the predicate noun following the linking verb. Together they suggest the absolute unity of the customer's desires and McDonald's products; in this sentence, form follows meaning completely. The subordinator *what* links each noun clause to the sentence and functions as a direct object within each clause. The pattern of each clause is S-V-O: *you see what* and *you get what*.

2. **Why you wore that dress with spaghetti straps in the middle of winter** puzzles me.

If you lifted the boldfaced portion of the sentence away, you would have this kind of structure: _____ puzzles *me*. What is missing from this sentence is a subject, and this is exactly the precise function of the noun clause in sentence two—as subject of the verb *puzzles*. The noun clause constitutes a pattern all by itself, with the subject-verb-direct object structure (*you wore dress*).

3. Jeff couldn't figure out **how he could steal the money from the safe**.

Here the noun clause functions as the direct object of the phrasal verb *figure out*. Observe the pattern within the clause, S-V-O (*he could steal money*).

4. He noticed **that the cars were white with frost**.

This noun clause also functions as a direct object of the verb *noticed*. Note the pattern of the clause: S-LV-PA (*cars were white*).

5. I don't think **she likes the idea**.

The bolded clause, with its S-V-O structure (*she likes idea*), functions as the direct object of the verb *do think*. It answers the *what?* question that the verb asks and completes the verb. But this noun clause differs from the other examples because it is not introduced by a subordinator; the subordinator *that* is implied here but not articulated. This happens quite frequently, especially when the clause is in the direct object slot. The absence of the subordinator can make it more difficult for you to spot the clause.

For Discussion

Find the noun clauses in the following sentences adapted from Allegra Goodman's *Paradise Park*. Be prepared to talk about how each clause functions and about the pattern or structure of the clauses.

1. He had forgotten who she was.
2. That is what a woman would do!
3. A little change is what she needs.
4. Frances says she does not want to go with them.
5. This is how it turned out.
6. I want you to know that we were proud of our heritage. [Determine the relationship of the clause to the infinitive *to know*.]
7. Let me explain what we will do.
8. We went to where the land meets the sea.
9. What you have in your apron is a flower.
10. Why he is late coming from the mines is a mystery.
11. We talked about why the sun comes up in the morning.
12. The main thing we discussed was how we should live to prepare for the future.
13. I could never believe that he was married.
14. This is how it happened.
15. I told the Karinskys I couldn't talk to him while I was in my decision-making process.

"I do what they tell me, I eat what they give me. How do I know they're not a cult?"

Figure 6.5
Noun Clauses.
© *The New Yorker Collection 1998 Charles Barsotti from cartoonbank.com. All Rights Reserved.*

The caption of the cartoon in Figure 6.5 contains three parallel noun clauses, each functioning as the direct object. *What they tell me* is the direct object of *do*; *what they give me* is the direct object of *eat*; *(that) they're not a cult* is the direct object of *know*. The first two sentences are exactly parallel, and the third sentence is a question transformation of a sentence parallel to the first two.

FOR WRITING

Now it's time to write some sentences of your own with noun clauses. Begin by substituting noun clauses within the following independent clauses or base sentences. Remember: you will have to take out a noun and put a noun clause in its place. Here is an example:

> We forgot the **words** to the song.

Now we're going to substitute a noun clause for the noun phrase *the words of the song*.

> We forgot **what the song said**.

The pattern of the clause is S-V-O: *song said what*. Now here's a second example:

> The principal gave prizes to the contest **winners**.

Now we'll substitute a noun clause for the object of the preposition *to*:

> The principal gave prizes to **whoever won the contests**.

Whoever won the contests is also the S-V-O pattern, with *whoever* functioning as both subordinator and subject of the noun clause. The entire clause functions as the object of the preposition *to*. When you create complex sentences with noun clauses from the base sentences that follow, consider substituting noun clauses for the italicized nouns, just to simplify things. And know that you will have to invent some details to create sensible-sounding clauses!

1. *Those events* clinched it. (Try a noun clause beginning with *what*: *What happened at the playoffs clinched it.*)
2. He told us a story about *his wife and her Israeli folk dancing*. (Try a noun clause beginning with *how*: *He told us a story about how his wife took up Israeli folk dancing.*)
3. He showed us *places in the neighborhood*. (Try a noun clause beginning with *where*.)
4. Nobody in the class knew *the solutions to those problems*.
5. That is not *the meaning of education*.
6. I wanted him to see *the truth*.
7. I didn't hear *a word*.
8. *All the participants* were invited to lunch.
9. We wanted to reach *everyone sitting around the seminar table*.

(continued)

10. He shook his head at *all of us.* (Try *whoever* as the subordinator.)
11. The thing that hurts most is *your words.*
12. Do you know *the answer to my question?*
13. I actually had to remind myself of *the opening date for "South Pacific."*
14. I told him *the truth he wanted to hear.*
15. *Her words* made as much sense as anything.
16. I couldn't help confessing to the rabbi *my doubts.*
17. I had forgotten *the living conditions of others.*
18. *It* was all magic to me.
19. From the back of the room I watched *all the events.*
20. We talked about knowledge and about *life.*

Clauses and Comparison

A familiar English construction is the comparative construction, which can be any kind of clause and which can pattern with any sentence element—except of course a verb. Let's look at some examples of sentences that contain comparisons and clauses:

1. *Freddy is more friendly today than he was yesterday.*

In this sentence, the pattern of the base clause is S-LV-PA (*Freddy-is-friendly*). The comparison centers around *friendly* (an adjective), so the clause functions adverbially. The words *more* and *than* signal the comparison and function as subordinating links. *Friendly* is ellipted from the second clause.

2. *The SUNY students have higher scores than students in other state schools [do have].*

The pattern of the base clause is S-V-O (*students-have-scores*). The ellipted clause, *students in other state schools do have scores,* modifies the direct object *scores*; thus the dependent clause functions adjectivally. The comparison is signaled by *higher* and *than,* which function as subordinators.

3. *More consumers shop at Target than (consumers shop) at any other discount department store.*

This S-V base sentence (*consumers-shop*) has an ellipted clause signaled by the conjunctive pair *more* and *than.*

FOR DISCUSSION

Work with your writing group to analyze the following sentences, all of which have comparative elements and clauses. Most of the clauses are ellipted. Prepare to present your findings to the class as a whole.

(continued)

1. Nena has ridden more winning horses than any other rider.
2. As many people enjoy murder mysteries as enjoy fantasy.
3. That test item has given the fifth-graders more trouble than any other one.
4. Lady is more peaceful than Izzy.
5. That job was more difficult than the last job.

C reating Combination or Compound-Complex Sentences

The compound-complex sentence is at once compound *and* complex. That is, it has at least two independent clauses (like a compound sentence) and at least one dependent clause (like a complex sentence). You will create compound-complex sentences when you wish to articulate details about a complicated subject because in this kind of sentence, you can show not only parallel or equal grammatical relationships (with compound clauses) but also unequal or hierarchical ones (with complex clauses). Here are some examples and a brief analysis of each example; please review them carefully.

1. I would never again enumerate all that had been taken from me, and I blamed no one for this recurring phenomenon. —William Kennedy

The dependent clause is an adjective clause in passive voice patterning with *all*: *that had been taken from me*. Remove the dependent clause from the sentence so you can more easily see the compounded patterns, which are joined by the coordinator *and*. These patterns are S-V-O, *I would enumerate all*, and S-V-O, *I blamed no one*. The sentence also has a prepositional phrase, *for this recurring phenomenon*, within which you can find a present participle, *recurring*.

2. He cried from the tension, he cried from grief, he cried from the cab ride, from his coke habit, from the piggy insult, from his mother's having to be cramped up in a temporary coffin and then shifted over to a real one when it was ready. —Bruce Jay Friedman

This sentence, which describes a man's breaking down at the end of his mother's funeral, has multiple independent clauses: *he cried from the tension* (S-V); *he cried from grief* (S-V); *he cried from the cab ride, from the piggy insult, from his mother's having to be cramped up in a temporary coffin and then shifted over to a real one when it was ready* (a third S-V). The first three independent clauses are almost identical, the S-V pattern with a concluding prepositional phrase. The last independent clause, though, is most interesting. It has multiple prepositional phrases, all beginning with *from*: *from the cab ride, from the piggy insult, from his mother's having to be cramped up in a temporary coffin and then shifted over to a real one when it was ready*. The dependent clause occurs at the very end of the last long independent clause: *when it was ready*, an adverbial clause that tells *when* the mother's body was shifted over. Observe also the noun adjunct: *cab* ride. Observe the gerund phrase that acts as the object of the last *from*: *his mother's having to be cramped up in a temporary coffin and then shifted over to a real one when it was ready*. Finally, note the compound phrasal verbs, *cramped up* and *shifted over*, which are parallel to one another. Fittingly, the sentence winds down with the longest clause; the most important and momentous information is reserved until the end.

3. When the gold-seekers in their thousands rushed to the north, a very few made great strikes, almost everyone else came up with little or nothing, and the merchants who sold them their pans, grub, and shovels made good solid incomes year after year. —John McPhee

First, let's remove the dependent clauses, which are easy to spot: *when the gold-seekers in their thousands rushed to the north* (an introductory adverbial S-V pattern with *when* as the subordinator); and *who sold them their pans, grub, and shovels* (an adjectival S-V-IO-DO clause patterning with *merchants*, where *who* functions not only as the relative pronoun subordinator but also the subject of the clause's pattern). Then we are left with the three remaining independent clauses: *few made strikes* (S-V-O); *everyone came up with nothing* (S-V-O, with phrasal verb *came up with*); and *merchants made incomes* (S-V-O). One thing that makes the sentence so pleasing is the repetition of this basic direct object or S-V-O structure in the repetition of the patterns.

4. The Jews are a remembering people; it is what their religion is about. —Harvey Shapiro

Here the two independent clauses are readily visible, separated by the semicolon alone. The dependent clause is a noun clause within the second independent clause; this noun clause functions as predicate noun for the verb *is* in the second half of the sentence: *what their religion is about*. This noun clause is introduced by the subordinator *what*, but the *what* also plays a role in the clause's pattern. Let's reorder the clause: *their religion is about what*. You may see two ways of understanding this pattern: first, *is* is an intransitive verb and *about* is a preposition with *what* as its object. But another way to look at the sentence is to consider the verb as phrasal, *to be about*: a person can *be about* his business, for instance. That would make the pattern S-V-O, with *religion* as subject, *is about* as transitive verb, and *what* as direct object. This is a more subtle understanding of the pattern, but the first reading is not incorrect, either.

For Discussion

Now you provide analyses of the following combination or compound-complex sentences. Point out the independent clauses and the dependent clauses and mark interesting features of the sentences: verbals, figures of speech, prepositional phrases, unusual diction or word choice. Discuss your analyses with the members of your writing group.

(continued)

1. The street had to be roped off, the policemen had to keep the crowds back, and children had to play hooky from school when there was a piano moving. —Betty Smith
2. Point it where you want to go, keep your weight on the pegs with the revs up, and this machine bounds over rough ground like a motorized gazelle. —Don Sherman
3. It takes about forty-five minutes for the movie [*The Lord of the Rings*] to emerge from Sir Ian McKellen's beard (he plays the garrulous wizard Gandalf), but once it does, this enormous hunk of quasi-medieval myth, based on the work of J.R.R. Tolkien, is consistently beautiful and exciting. —David Denby
4. He was never allowed into the mysterious warrens during the workday when he was younger, but at five p.m. he would carry a glass filled with amber fluid, push the swing door with his foot, and enter. —Michael Ondaatje
5. I was on the perpendicular part of the cliff, and unless I could get over it soon I would just peel off the wall. —James Dickey

For Writing

Try your hand now at writing some compound-complex sentences according to the specifications given. A word of advice: build the independent clauses first, then fold in the dependent clauses and the other required items.

1. Make one independent clause S-V and a second independent clause S-V-O. Let the dependent clause be an adjective clause. Include one prepositional phrase and one verbal somewhere in the sentence. Use the word *crevice*.
2. Write three independent clauses and two dependent clauses, one of which is an adverbial clause that begins with *because*. Include the word *power*.
3. Make one of the independent clauses S-V-DO-OC. Use a gerund somewhere and find a way to create alliteration.
4. Use a noun clause as one of the dependent clauses. Include three prepositional phrases. Write the word *foliage* someplace in the sentence.
5. Create a series of relative dependent clauses, each beginning with *who*.

Reviewing Patterns and Combinations

Now that you know how to expand individual patterns and how to combine patterns to create compound and complex sentences, you have enough in your grammar arsenal to understand and to create almost any kind of sentence. Try your hand at analyzing the following sentences. With your writing group, perhaps, discuss whether each of the following sentences is simple, compound, or complex. Look for the presence of verbals, nominative absolutes, and prepositional phrases. Look for compounded elements. Determine the patterns of clauses and verbals. Be on the lookout for figures of speech and unusually appropriate word choices. Be alert even to tenses of verbs and forms of nouns. In short, bring all your grammatical knowledge to bear on the following sentences.

1. Piano, who has a gray beard and never seems entirely comfortable in a business suit, speaks with a mellifluous Italian accent. —Paul Goldberger
2. Outside it was snowing and very cold, but the room was heated. —Primo Levi
3. For more than forty years, a bronze statue of Vladimir Vladimirovich Mayakovsky, the Russian Revolution's most celebrated poet, has towered over the square named after him: his massive torso triumphantly arched, an imaginary wind billowing the folds of his baggy pants, he incarnates Soviet man at his most optimistic and confident, striding toward the greatest future ever devised for humankind. —Francine du Plessix Gray
4. They both sat down on the window ledge, their eyes fixed upon the marching columns of soldiers below. —Shmerke Kaczerginski
5. Some went in the direction of *Weeperstraat*; others made for *Waterlooplein*. —Marga Minco
6. Choronzicki, well aware of the tortures that awaited him and the dangers of the whole conspiracy, swiftly swallowed a large dose of poison which the conspirators always carried on their person. —Stanislaw Kohn
7. All across the Earth, there are, of course, traces of climate history— buried in lake sediments, deposited in ancient beetle casings, piled up on the floor of the oceans. —Elizabeth Kolbert
8. Tall chestnut trees rustle in the night wind beside the church. —Isaiah Spiegel
9. According to the plan, the members of the organization had to mingle with the crowd: one group would identify the man and another would shoot him. —Hirsh Glick
10. The floor of what must have been the dining room was a mass of debris—broken utensils, bits of broken porcelain dishes, and crockery smashed as by the senseless fury of a madman. —Benjamin Ellis

Looking Ahead

Now that you have a solid understanding of the structure of sentences, it's time to examine some deliberate strategies for enhancing your style. The next chapter introduces you to figures and schemes and gives you a chance to practice writing them.

7

From Grammar to Style: Rhetorical Strategies and Figures

*I*f you lived in Shakespeare's day and were lucky enough to attend school, you would have naturally studied the art of rhetoric, then primarily an oral art. You would have learned how to organize your thoughts, your speech, and even your writing to produce certain effects in an audience—to sway them to your way of thinking, to impress them with your erudition or learning. And you would have learned, as a matter of course, to incorporate the **figures of speech** into your speech and writing to make your thoughts not only clear but lively. You would have been using the figures to study Latin because English grammar would not be invented until the eighteenth century. The figures are associated with an earlier time and originally with another language, but they survive in English in the present.

A **figure of speech**, says Edward P. J. Corbett, a historical linguist, is a generic term for "any artful deviation from the ordinary mode of speaking and writing." Tudor rhetoricians described over 200 different artful deviations or figures in Latin, and the figures were part of every Tudor schoolboy's education (then, most girls didn't receive formal schooling). Today the figures, adapted to English, are taught more rarely, partly because you need considerable background knowledge of grammar before you can use the figures well and purposefully—and grammar is not taught so routinely any more. (We have also come to rely less and less on figurative language in everyday discourse.) A sufficient well of grammatical knowledge makes creating the figures easier; indeed, figures are where many grammatical and rhetorical principles converge. Knowing how to produce them and understanding their patterns can make you not only a better writer but a better reader. Now that your grammatical background has deepened, you are ready to use that knowledge as you develop your personal style as a writer.

143

And so you will find in this chapter the most common figures for your study. Renaissance schoolboys learned the figures by copying and imitation, and that is how the figures are presented here: with examples for you to study and then to imitate. This means that the exercises will ask you first to copy a model passage exactly, noting its unique structure and punctuation. Then you will be asked to create your own sentence or passage, following exactly the form or shape of the model sentence but with **your** words and meaning, your content. Once the shape of the figure is ingrained in your consciousness, you should be able to reproduce it at the appropriate time and for the appropriate rhetorical occasion. It will become part of your automatic store of resources for writing. After all, despite the fact that the figures were first devised in Latin an awfully long time ago, they still offer us writers ways to make our writing (and speech) interesting and graceful. Even if we wish to effect primarily a plain style in our writing, the figures have much to teach us about balance and parallelism and order. To writers concerned with style, the figures, particularly the most common ones explained in this chapter, are well worth learning.

On, then, to the figures and a grammatical consideration of how they work and why they're effective. The general order here is that used by Corbett in his text *Classical Rhetoric for the Modern Student* (1971), but I have not included all the figures Corbett presents nor described them in the same manner. First Corbett describes the figures of balance: parallelism and antithesis. Thus these first two figures concern themselves with how we balance words along the fulcrum of the sentence and how we create meaningful patterns so that readers can easily follow our ideas. A note: the mostly Greek names of the figures may look exotic to you, so included in the discussion of each figure is a key to its pronunciation. Learn to pronounce these names: you'll enjoy rolling the names around in your mouth. After all, once you get used to them, you'll find them no more strange than other multisyllabic words like *Connecticut* and *Mississippi*.

P *arallelism*

Parallelism [PAR-∂-lel-iz-∂m] means that pairs or series of related words, phrases, or clauses have very similar structures. Think of parallel lines, notions of equidistance, and ideas that run in similar directions: parallel structures in sentences are similar in these ways. In a parallel construction, ideas that are equal are presented in equal grammatical structures: nouns balance nouns, prepositional phrases balance prepositional phrases, and introductory clauses balance introductory clauses. Parallel structures help readers organize and remember information. Whether you are writing a quarterly report, directions to the club for your corporation's holiday party, or a speech, you need to understand the notion of parallelism.

Parallelism: Some Model Passages

Here are some sentences with parallel elements for you to study. Choose one sentence, copy it, and think about its structure as you write. Then construct your own sentence, trying to imitate the model sentence word for word, phrase for phrase, and clause for clause.

1. *She didn't want to be saved; what she wanted was an American holiday, a fresh set of boyfriends, and a leather coat.* —Cynthia Ozick

Note the parallelism of articles (**a** or **an**), descriptors, and nouns as the complement of **was**:

an	American	holiday	
a	fresh	set	(of boyfriends)
a	leather	coat	

The holiday, fresh set of boyfriends, and leather coat are equally desired by the subject of this sentence. They are thus presented as grammatical equals with parallel structures.

2. *It is rather for us to be here dedicated to the great task remaining before us—that from those honored dead we take increased devotion to that cause for which they gave the last full measure of devotion; that we here highly resolve that these dead shall not have died in vain; that this nation, under God, shall have a new birth of freedom; and that government of the people, by the people, for the people, shall not perish from the earth.* —Abraham Lincoln

This very famous sentence from "The Gettysburg Address" is marked by more than one set of parallel structures. Notice the three parallel clauses beginning with *that*. This common beginning helps orient readers to a new idea and signals that the idea to be presented is on equal footing with the idea just discussed. So we have three equal aspects of the great task before us: *that* we take increased devotion to the cause; *that* we resolve the dead did not die in vain; and *that* this nation shall have a new birth of freedom. Then within the final *that* clause there is yet another example of parallel structure with the three parallel prepositional phrases *of the people, by the people* and *for the people*. Observe how the repetition of *the people* emphasizes the idea that a democracy does belong to its people. The extensive parallelism in this speech makes the message easy to listen to and easy to remember.

A ntithesis

Antithesis [an-TITH-i-sis] is the placing of contrasting ideas within physical proximity. These ideas are often (and most effectively) in parallel structure. Antithesis may exist in either the words or the ideas. If you manage antithesis capably, it can lend an air of wit to your prose.

Antithesis: Some Model Passages

Here are some passages with antithetical elements to consider. Choose one passage to work with. Copy the passage, thinking about its structure as you write. Then construct your own passage, trying to imitate the model passage word for word, phrase for phrase, and clause for clause.

1. *Illy also observed that what works in America may not work in Italy. "You like things big," he told me. "Big steaks, big cars, and a big cup of coffee. We use coffee not to drink but to sip. It's like eating a chocolate—a little burst of flavor. It's subtle. There is this overroasting culture in America," he continued. "It's by far too dark. This is why they feel the need to cover everything with milk and why they have all those syrups."* —Michael Specter

What works in America is echoed with what will not work in Italy, its opposite. The idea of bigness, repeated in big steaks, big cars, and a big cup of coffee, is contrasted with the little burst of flavor, its opposite. Dark is yoked with milk, its antithesis. Clearly, American and Italian ideas about coffee are very different.

2. *Airmobility, dig it, you weren't going anywhere. It made you feel safe, it made you feel Omni, but it was only a stunt, technology. . . . It was great if you could adapt, you had to try, but it wasn't the same as making a discipline, going into your own reserves and developing a real war metabolism, slow yourself down when your heart tried to punch its way through your chest, get swift when everything went to stop and all you could feel of your whole life was the entropy whipping through it. Unlovable terms.* —Michael Herr

Observe in this excerpt from **Dispatches** the contrast between the notions of mobility and stasis, the contrast between feeling safe and being safe, your metabolism's slowing down when your heart beats furiously and becoming swift when everything else stops, and entropy and whipping through it. Herr bluntly introduces the topic, airmobility, with the first word, then he uses second person *you* to make the passage immediate and personal.

3. *United there is little we cannot do in a host of cooperative ventures. Divided, there is little we can do—for we dare not meet a powerful challenge at odds and split asunder.* —John F. Kennedy

Antithesis occurs between *united* and *divided*, *little we cannot do* and *little we can do*. The dash that comes just after the antithesis emphatically separates—or splits in two—the ideas of possibility and impossibility from the reason why we must be united (we dare not meet a powerful challenge when we are weak and split in two).

Now for the schemes of unusual or inverted (turned around) word order, anastrophe and apposition, and unusual word order, parenthesis.

A *nastrophe*

Anastrophe [ə-NAS-trə-fe] is the inversion of the usual or natural word order. Because this inversion confounds the reader's expectations of how the sentence goes together, it is an especially effective attention-getting device and a strategy for emphasizing important ideas.

Anastrophe: Some Model Passages

Here are some sentences containing anastrophe. Study them all carefully, choose one sentence to work with, and copy the sentence, thinking about its structure as you write. Then construct your own sentence, trying to imitate the model sentence word for word, phrase for phrase, clause for clause.

1. *From America letters came.* —Nessa Rappoport

The normal word order of this sentence would be *Letters came from America.* By moving the prepositional phrase to the beginning of the sentence out of its usual place near the verb of the sentence, the writer forces readers to sit up and take notice. "This sentence is different" is clearly the rhetorical signal.

2. *"More bread!" somebody yells.* —Charles Simic

Somebody yells "More bread" would be the normal word order for this sentence: subject (somebody) plus verb (yells) plus complement ("More bread"—what someone yelled). Both the yells and the "More bread" receive more emphasis with this revision.

3. *Among the 562 vials are eighty different cap designs, possibly suggesting eighty different manufacturers, and each cap is usually produced in ten or twelve different colors.* —Paul Sheehan

This one is a bit harder to spot, but the typical word order for this sentence would be *Eighty different cap designs are among the 562 vials.* What do you think is the effect of revising the sentence to emphasize the number of vials being considered in this sentence?

4. *Inside was a gift shop that sold everything from rubber alligator jaws to t-shirts printed with a picture of a giant mosquito and the words "I gave blood in the Florida Everglades."* —Daisann McLane

The normal order for this sentence would go something like *A gift shop that sold everything from rubber alligator jaws to t-shirts printed with . . . was inside.* Beginning with the word *inside* helps readers picture where the shop is and emphasizes its location.

A *pposition*

Apposition [ap-∂-ZISH-∂n] occurs when you place two coordinate elements (that is, two elements that are grammatically equal) side by side. Typically, the second element (called the **appositive**) then explains or limits the first. We say the two elements are "in apposition." That means that they are positioned together in a special relationship. These appositioned elements are nouns or noun clusters. Apposition is quite common in writing but less frequent in speech. It does not wrench the sentence's natural order as does parenthesis—probably because it is grammatically *simpatico* with the element paired with it: both are typically nouns. Apposition is useful for defining or explain terms and for repeating key ideas.

Apposition: Some Model Passages

Here are some sentences illustrating apposition. Study them all carefully, choose one sentence to work with, and copy the sentence, thinking about its structure as you write. Then construct your own sentence, trying to imitate the model sentence word for word, phrase for phrase, clause for clause.

1. *Meet the first in-dash personal assistant, the Clarion AutoPC.*

The personal assistant equals the Clarion AutoPC; in this sentence they have the same referent. You point out the appositioned elements in the other sentences.

2. *BMW's new hybrid vehicle finally has a real name: X5.* —Georg Kacher

3. *Sly Stone, one of rock's most gifted artists and, sadly, one of its most famous burnouts, was destitute, incoherent, broke, out of hope.* —Jamie Kitman

4. *Wyoming's first-year coach, Steve McClain, an assistant at TCU from 1994–1998, brought Billy Tubbs's up-tempo style with him to Laramie.* —B. J. Schechter

5. *Lieberman's status as the conscience of the Senate made him an influential figure in the presidential impeachment saga, a calm voice that both sides listen to.* —Michelle Cottle

P *arenthesis*

Parenthesis [p∂-REN-th∂-sis] occurs when a cluster of words interrupts the normal word order of a sentence. A parenthesis diverts the reader's attention temporarily from the idea at hand; its purpose is sometimes to call attention to the parenthetical matter itself, to provide additional but not vital information, to suggest the writer's opinion or feeling, or to create a mood (often a conspiratorial one where the reader feels in cahoots with the writer). The parenthetical matter may also be a device for controlling the pace of the sentence. Stuck in the middle of a rather long clause, for instance, a parenthesis can dramatically alter the pace or break a monotonous stretch of words.

Because parenthetical material typically occurs midsentence, its boundaries need to be marked by punctuation. If the parenthetical material is plunked in the middle of a sentence with the regular sentence flowing before and after it, use the same marks on each side of the parenthetical material: either commas, dashes, or parentheses themselves. Each kind of punctuation creates a different rhetorical effect. Commas set the slightest boundaries and create the least resistance or interruption; dashes are far more dramatic and noticeable. Parentheses may suggest a conspiratorial or *by the way* effect that encourages the reader to draw the chair closer and listen harder.

Of course, if the parenthetical material begins midsentence then actually concludes the sentence, you'll put a period at the end of the interruption or at the end of the parenthetical material.

Parenthesis: Some Model Passages

Here are some sentences containing the scheme of parenthesis. Study them all carefully, choose one sentence to work with, and copy the sentence, thinking about its structure as you write. Then construct your own sentence, trying to imitate the model sentence word for word, phrase for phrase, clause for clause.

1. *The Park View Pharmacy—the drugstore my parents bought—stood on Colonial Avenue between Continental and Burr.* —Cynthia Ozick

Here the parenthetical material between the dashes, *the drugstore my parents bought,* is in apposition with and defines the Parkview Pharmacy. The dashes effectively keep the emphasis on the drugstore equal to the emphasis on Parkview Pharmacy; the reader can't miss that the two are the same entity. Notice also the repetition of the same idea in *drugstore* and *pharmacy.*

2. *One of the Dabney daughters was a fawn-faced creature of twelve named Edmonia; her fragile beauty (especially when contrasted with ill-favored brothers) and her precocious breasts and bottom had caused me—young as I was—a troubling, unresolved itch.* —William Styron

This sentence has two interrupting phrases, perhaps because it is a long sentence. Styron uses the parenthetical material to control the pace of the sentence. The first parenthetical material in parentheses has a kind of *sotto voce* or whispered effect; this material strengthens the notion of fragile beauty by contrasting Edmonia with her ordinary if not ugly brothers. The second parenthetical passage, *young as I was,* is set off by dashes to emphasize the writer's youth and provide context for this description.

3. *A nose ring, they might tell you, would be my last choice for a fashion accessory, way down on the list with a sag-enhancing specialty bra or a sign on my butt reading "Wide Load."* —Natalie Kusz

The clause *They might tell you* is here set off with commas; it functions as an aside, primarily to break up the length of the sentence.

4. *Ancient cultures (Greek, Egyptian, Chinese, Indian, and others) used color therapies of many sorts, prescribing colors for various distresses of the body and soul.* —Diane Ackerman

Here the material in parentheses defines or explains the noun just before it (*cultures*) by expanding it and naming its aspects. Because Ackerman uses parentheses around the added material rather than commas or dashes, we know that she wants us readers not too linger too long over the list.

Third are the schemes of omission, ellipsis and asyndeton. In each of these figures, something is left out. Also here is polysyndeton, the opposite of asyndeton, to round out this cluster.

E *llipsis*

Ellipsis [i-LIP-sis] is deliberate omission of a word or a cluster of words. If you use ellipsis, you can economize on sentence space—but you must be very careful to ensure that the omitted or understood words are grammatically compatible.

One kind of ellipsis, structural **ellipsis**, depends on the writer's knowing grammatical structure, usually knowing that a particular conjunction or preposition ordinarily belongs in a given structure. For instance, in the sentence "I think you are wrong," *that* is ellipted before *you are wrong*. And in a sentence like "We've waited for Godot two days already," *for* is ellipted before *two days already*.

Many headlines, titles, and advertising slogans are ellipted.

Ellipsis: Some Model Passages

Here are some sentences containing ellipsis, many of which are from advertisements. Study them all carefully, choose one sentence to work with, and copy the sentence, thinking about its structure as you write. Then construct your own sentence, trying to imitate the model sentence word for word, phrase for phrase, clause for clause.

1. *Introducing the world's smallest 35 mm zoom camera.*

Before ellipsis, this sentence was probably something like *We are introducing the world's smallest 35mm zoom camera;* the subject and the auxiliary verb have been ellipted. Removing the subject throws the emphasis on *introducing* and *camera*, the first and last words in the sentence. See if you can determine what the entire original sentence might have been for each of these ellipted sentences.

2. *Four questions you should ask about a vacuum.*
3. *Herbal Essences . . . a totally organic experience with style.*
4. *This doesn't mean missing your 3,000 mile oil change is okay.*
5. *Time for more milk.*
6. *We'll fix it right, guaranteed.*
7. *His eye was open to beauty, and his ear to music.* —Ralph Waldo Emerson
8. *She spoke of him with respect abroad, and with contempt in her closet.* —Royall Tyler

Verbatim Recoverability

Check the previous sentences for recoverability: that is, make sure the omitted or understood words are grammatically compatible with the part of the sentence actually on the page. For instance, saying that "the mother cat forgets her mittens, and her kittens their gloves" creates a nonstandard usage. Why? Because the ellipted verb *forget* is different than the articulated or written verb *forgets*. *Cat* is singular; *kittens*, plural. Consequently, different verbs are needed for each subject. The second verb cannot, therefore, be ellipted. This principle is called **verbatim recoverability** or the ability to recover the exact word.

A *syndeton*

Asyndeton [ə-SIN-di-ton] is a scheme of omission: it means that you leave out conjunctions between a series of related words, clauses, or phrases. Asyndeton speeds the pace of the sentence, creating either the impression of simultaneity (everything seems to happen at once) or else a sense of deliberateness and firmness. Remember: leave out the conjunctions; just let the punctuation do the work of separating the ideas.

Asyndeton: Some Model Passages

Here are some sentences containing asyndeton. Study them all carefully, choose one sentence to work with, and copy the sentence, thinking about its structure as you write. Then construct your own sentence, trying to imitate the model sentence word for word, phrase for phrase, clause for clause.

    1.   *Sexism, violence against women, and different, lowered expectations for girls cause them to lose touch of their interests, their confidence, their personhood.* —Carol Winkelman

    The items *interests, confidence, personhood* are much more emphatic because of the determination to push through them to the end of the sentence. There is no break for a conjunction, so the words appear to be part of a package, a group. The lack of a conjunction binds them closely. Also notice how emphatic *personhood*, as the last item in the list, becomes.

    2.   *In reality, taste buds are exceedingly small. Adults have about 10,000, grouped by theme (salt, sour, sweet, bitter), at various sites in the mouth.* —Diane Ackerman

    The parenthetical list is an example of asyndeton because there is no conjunction separating the taste "themes," especially between *sweet* and *bitter*, where we would expect an *and*. One of the effects of no conjunction in this list is that the list seems as if it could go on for quite a long time.

3.   *To outsiders, they look tough, scruffy, poor, wild.* —Donna Gaines, writing about high school students called "burnouts," students near the bottom academically, economically, and socially.

4.   *After Hegelstead left and the night was still, Jack tottered into the concrete-walled bathroom, pissed, rinsed his mouth with ice-cold iron-tasting water, drank a great draft, swallowed, spat, gulped down three aspirin he found in a truck's glove compartment.* —Louise Erdrich

5.   *A rising sheet of water curved over him, fell down upon him, blinded him, strangled him!* —Ambrose Bierce

P *olysyndeton*

Polysyndeton [pol-e-SIN-di-ton], the opposite of asyndeton, means a generous use of conjunctions in a series of phrases or clauses. Polysyndeton has the opposite effect of asyndeton: it tends to separate the elements, to make each one important and individual, and to slow the pace. It can often create a solemn effect, and the conjunctions separating the elements seem to say about each: "Look at me!"

Polysyndeton: Some Model Passages

Here are some passages containing polysyndeton. Study them all carefully, choose one passage to work with, and copy it, thinking about its structure as you write. Then construct your own passage, trying to imitate the model passage word for word, phrase for phrase, clause for clause.

1.   *He was two years old and at first he cried for the shack and the familiar smell of the wood stove and his mother's lean, hard hands.* —Annie Proulx

The repetition of *and* imitates the way that young children tell stories—by piling detail upon detail and connecting each one with and. This is an appropriate style to describe a two-year-old's response to being without his mother.

2.   *Which of the four is not only the right man for the job but a "real" man (which is the subtle subtext of every presidential election)? By some definitions (war hero or great athlete or Texan or responsible family man), all of them. By other definitions (compassionate and honest and responsible and self-aware and sober and high-minded and battle-tested), none of them.* —Jane Smiley

In this passage, Smiley repeats or and and and to delineate the separateness of each item, as if to tote them up in some sort of reckoning—which is what she is doing: reckoning or figuring who is the right man for the job.

3.   *I will put my law in their inward parts, and write it in their hearts, and will be their God, and they shall be my people.* —Jeremiah 31:33

How would you say the *and*'s function in this sentence? Consider how the sentence would sound without the *and*'s.

Now here are the figures of repetition: assonance, alliteration, anaphora, epistrophe, epanalepsis, anadiplosis, and antimetabole.

A *ssonance*

Assonance [AS-∂-n∂ns] is the repetition of similar vowel sounds in words that are next to or near one another. Although assonance is used primarily in poetry, a prose writer may also use assonance to knit sentences together by repeating sounds. Depending on the repeated sound, other effects may be created: repeated long *O* sounds may emphasize a mournful effect, for instance, and repeated *E's* may create a bright textual atmosphere.

Assonance: Some Model Passages

Here are some sentences containing assonance. Study them carefully, choose one to work with, and copy it, thinking about its structure as you write. Then construct your own sentence, trying to imitate the model closely.

1. *Susskind glanced down at his shabby, baggy knickers.* —Bernard Malamud

Listen to the effect of the short *a* sound in *shabby* and *baggy*. Because the two words sound alike, their effect is increased.

2. *When I'm up to my knees in honeysuckle, I beat a retreat and visit the duck pond.* —Annie Dillard

How do you describe the effect of the *e* sounds? What do the *e* sounds do for the pace of the sentence?

A *lliteration*

Alliteration [∂-lit-∂-RA-sh∂n] is the repetition of initial consonant sounds—that is, consonant sounds occurring at the beginning of adjacent words or words that are next to one another. Like assonance, alliteration occurs frequently in poetry to emphasize particular words or to create a tonal effect. You will also find it often in advertising.

For both assonance and alliteration, moderation is the key. Using either device excessively can create an unintentionally humorous effect.

Alliteration: Some Model Passages

Here are some sentences containing alliteration. Study them, choose one to work with, and copy it, thinking about its structure as you write. Then construct your own sentence, trying to imitate the model sentence closely.

1. *The tide shoves and sucks through the islands and makes the current curl in odd patterns.* —John Hersey

What is the effect of the alliterated s's (shoves, sucks) and c's (current, curl)?

2. *From its tip grew two thin slips of green tissue shaped like two tears; they enclosed, like cupped palms sheltering a flame, a tiny tulip leaf that was curled upon itself and bowed nearly in the middle.* —Annie Dillard

Observe how the repetition of the *t* sound through this sentence knits it together. Underline all the words beginning with *t*. Then read the sentence again, savoring its sounds. What is the effect of the alliteration?

A *naphora*

Anaphora [ə-NAF-ə-rə] is a repetition scheme where a word or group of words occurs at the beginning or front of successive clauses or phrases, phrases or clauses that come one right after the other. Sometimes you find *incremental anaphora*, where the repeated words or phrases change ever so slightly or incrementally with each repetition. Anaphora is quite deliberate, creates a distinct rhythm in the text, and emphasizes a key point or evokes an emotional effect. As more and more words are repeated, the intensity of the passage increases.

Anaphora: Some Model Passages

Here are some passages containing anaphora. Study them all carefully, choose one passage to work with, and copy the passage, thinking about its structure as you write. Then construct your own passage, trying to imitate the model sentence word for word, phrase for phrase, clause for clause.

1. *All that is left upon me is the scent of her perfume and I find, even once I hang the phone up, that I can't get rid of the smell. I can't get it off me. I can't stop thinking of her and I see things. I see her in my deepest thoughts.* —Louise Erdrich

See how *I can't* is repeated at the beginning of three successive clauses. The reader is unable to miss the writer's inability to stop thinking of "her" because the phrase *I can't* is placed repeatedly at places of emphasis.

2. *When I need to relax, I dream of lazy walks along palm-shaded paths, I dream of black swans gliding over tranquil lagoons, I dream of thatched-roof days without telephones, televisions or radios. I dream of Kona Village.* —Advertisement for Kona Village Resort

How do you characterize the effect of the repeated phrase *I dream*?

3. *The reason why I object to Dr. Johnson's style is that there is no discrimination, no selection, no variety in it.* —William Hazlitt

The repeated *no's* emphasize the lack of discrimination, selection, and variety.

4. *The first door lets out drivers. The second door lets out passengers. The third door lets out convention.* —Saturn advertisement

This is an example of incremental repetition; *door* is repeated in each sentence, but with each repetition, the determiner before *door* changes from *first* to *second* to *third*. The final object is especially emphatic not only because it is the last object but also because it is not a physical thing like *drivers* or *passengers*.

E *pistrophe*

Epistrophe [i-PIS-trə-fee] is a repetition scheme where a word or group of words occurs at the end of successive clauses or phrases. Sometimes you find *incremental epistrophe*, where the repeated words or phrases change ever so slightly or incrementally with each repetition. Thus, epistrophe is quite deliberate, creating a distinct rhythm in the text, emphasizing a key point, or evoking an emotional effect.

Epistrophe: Some Model Passages

Here are some passages containing epistrophe. Study them carefully, choose one to work with, and copy it, thinking about its structure as you write. Then construct your own example, trying to imitate the model word for word, phrase for phrase, clause for clause.

1. *The lobbyists don't like you. The voters don't like you. The majority doesn't like you. (Our judges will love you.)* —Advertisement for The John F. Kennedy Library Foundation Profile in Courage Award

The phrase *don't like you* is repeated so many times that when the readers come across the last phrase, *will love you*, they are pleasantly surprised. This sentence also illustrates antithesis in the contrast between *don't like you* and *love you.*

2. *Wherever there is a needy child, there is a great cause. Wherever there is ignorance or want, there is a great cause. Wherever there is violence and hate, there is a great cause.* —John McCain

Besides being an example of epistrophe by virtue of the repeated noun cluster at the end of each sentence, *a great cause*, this passage is also an example of anaphora (*Wherever there is* is repeated at the beginning of each sentence. When both epistrophe and anaphora are present in the same sentence (as they are here), this figure is called symploce.

3. *One cannot think well, love well, sleep well, if one has not dined well.* —Virginia Woolf

The repetition of *well* at the conclusion of the verb phrases links all the verbs together and emphasizes the importance of doing all these things *well.*

E *panalepsis*

Epanalepsis [e-pan-∂h-LEP-sis] is a repetition scheme where a word or group of words from the beginning of a clause or sentence is repeated at the end of that same clause, sentence, or sometimes passage. This scheme lends an air of finality to a sentence, bringing it to a close at near the same place where it began. It has a nice round "feel" to it that satisfies a reader's need for closure. Yet it is an extremely rare scheme because it is so powerful. To overuse it seems extremely self-conscious, so be very discreet with it.

Epanalepsis: Some Model Passages

Here are some passages containing epanalepsis. Study them carefully, choose one passage to work with, and copy it, thinking about its structure as you write. Then construct your own passage, trying to imitate the model word for word, phrase for phrase, clause for clause.

　　1.　*That a famous library has been cursed by a woman is a matter of complete indifference to a famous library.* —Virginia Woolf

　　Famous library is introduced at the beginning of the sentence and reiterated at its end.

　　2.　*Erotic pleasure, derived from the most physical contact, thrives on the paradox that only by keeping alive the strangeness of that other person can eroticism last.* —Siri Hustvedt

　　Erotic, the first word in the sentence, is repeated in its nominal (or noun) form, *eroticism*, at the end of the sentence. Thus this key word is both the first thing the reader "hears" in the sentence as well as its closing note.

　　3.　*The most incomprehensible thing about the world is that it is comprehensible.* —Albert Einstein

　　Notice that *incomprehensible* at the beginning of the sentence is repeated in its opposite form, *comprehensible*, at the close of the sentence. This is a variation of epanalepsis employing contrast via a variant form of the repeated word. Thus, the sentence employs not only epanalepsis but contrast and balance as well.

A *nadiplosis*

Anadiplosis [an-∂-d∂-PLO-sis] is a repetition scheme where a word or group of words is repeated at the *end* of one clause or sentence and then subsequently at the *beginning* of the next clause or sentence. This scheme neatly links sentences or clauses and at the same time repeats important ideas or phrases for emphasis.

Anadiplosis: Some Model Passages

Here are some passages containing anadiplosis. Study them carefully, choose one to work with, and copy it, thinking about its structure as you write. Then construct your own passage, trying to imitate the model word for word, phrase for phrase, clause for clause.

1. *For Chrysler, it's about creating extraordinary cars. Cars born from breakthrough design and brought to life through innovative engineering.* —Chrysler advertisement

Notice how *cars* ends the first sentence and begins the second. This strategy emphasizes *cars* and underscores the identification of *cars* with *Chrysler*.

2. *But Moses is dead, dead without the preparations and failures of old age, dead in the midst of his strength.* —Max Apple

Here *dead* ends the first part of this compound predicate adjective phrase and begins the second. Look how *dead* is repeated anaphorically for a third time in yet another predicate adjective phrase.

3. *If David has had Uriah killed with the sword, the sword will rampage among his sons.* —Lore Segal

Do you see the anadiplosis? Point it out in this sentence and in the examples that follow.

4. *Reading is an activity that makes a difference, and this difference cannot be minimized or foreshortened. . . .* —David Shapiro

5. *How then can higher education escape dogmatism, narrowness, the invasion of academic freedom, and failure in its proper intellectual task and still do its duty by morals and religion? A possible answer lies in the Great Conversation. The Great Conversation began with the Greeks, the Hebrews, the Hindus, and the Chinese and has continued to the present day.* —Robert Maynard Hutchins

A *ntimetabole: A Scheme of Balance and Repetition*

Antimetabole [an-te-mə-TAB-ə-le] is a scheme of balance involving two repeated series. A phrase at the beginning of a passage (usually a sentence) is repeated at the end of the passage—but with its elements reversed. This reversal combined with the elements of balance and repetition creates a very powerful epigrammatic sentence or passage. Use it wisely to drive home a very important point or to make your words especially memorable.

Antimetabole: Some Model Passages

Here are some passages containing antimetabole. Study them carefully, choose one to work with, and copy it, thinking about its structure as you write. Then construct your own sentence or passage, trying to imitate the model word for word, phrase for phrase, clause for clause.

1.   *In fact, Daniel suggests that ideas do not make history but history makes ideas. . . .* —Lore Segal

In this complex sentence with compound noun clauses, you can see the reversal and repetition of the noun clauses' subjects and direct objects, *ideas* and *history*. These are the key ideas in the sentence, and Segal emphasizes them deftly at the end of the sentence so that the reader is left with this epigrammatic twist at the end.

2.   *But though I could not with a crayon get the best out of the landscape, it does not follow that the landscape was not getting the best out of me.* —G. K. Chesterton

Here we have a complex sentence with an introductory adverb clause. The two words that are repeated and reversed in the antimetabole are *I*, subject of the introductory clause (which becomes object of the preposition *me* in the base clause) and *landscape*, which is the object of the preposition in the introductory clause and the subject in the base clause.

And finally, here are two other noteworthy devices of style, onomatopoeia and the virtual sentence.

O *nomatopoeia: A Device of Sound*

Onomatopoeia [on-∂-mat-∂-PE-∂] is a figurative strategy where the sound of words echoes their sense or meaning. Its effect is therefore to create an immediacy, an intimacy, between the reader and the text. Onomatopoeia also makes a passage more memorable, easier to remember because of its musicality.

Onomatopoeia: Some Model Passages

Here are some passages with examples of onomatopoeia. Study them carefully and copy one of them, thinking about its structure as you write. Then construct your own example, trying to imitate the model as closely as you can. Can you hear the onomatopoeia in *lapped, scraped, roaring, slap, clink, clack, creak, thudding*?

1.   *An apron of sound lapped out of each dive. Inside, chairs scraped on the floor, loud music and talk tangled with roaring laughter, there was endless traffic toward and from the back where little rooms lined the hall and young black girls took customers until their flesh was raw, the rap of matches, the slap of cards and the clink of bottles on glass, the clack of glasses on tables, the creak of table legs on the floor, the thudding feet of dancers doing the slow drag, the itch, the squat, the grind.* —Annie Proulx

This noisy passage lives up to the forecast of an apron of sound in the opening sentence. Listen to the sounds: lapped, scraped, tangled, laughter, rap, slap, clink, clack, creak, thudding, grind. The many broad a sounds and the g and p sounds create the effect of knocking and clapping throughout so that the passage resounds with cacophony.

2.   *The Ultra-Blast Key Chain consolidates three tools into one: a compact key chain, a high-intensity flashlight with a 180-degree radius of bright light, and a built-in, shockingly loud whistle.* —from *Levenger: Tools for Serious Readers* catalog

This passage sounds shrill, with its assonance of repeated *e* and *i* sounds. *Whistle* is a good example of onomatopoeia; the word *whistle* itself sounds like a whistle.

3.   *The raindrops plopped and blobbed on the window sill, pooling in a shimmering circle of water.*

Plopped and *blobbed* evoke the sound of soft objects landing noisily; in addition, there is considerable assonance in the repeated broad *o* sounds. In addition, *shimmering* sounds like a motion of soft undulation.

4.   *"What!" Mrs. Holley screeched.* —Alice Walker

Screeched is an excellent imitation and evocation of a high-pitched, scratchy, and altogether unpleasant yell. Thus we get a fine sense of what Mrs. Holley's voice sounded like.

T *he Virtual Sentence*

The **virtual sentence** is a purposeful reduction of any basic sentence pattern. It is not a sentence fragment or an incomplete sentence, for it is used by a writer who is entirely in control and wishes to create a certain effect. Use the virtual sentence to introduce a topic, to describe a scene, to represent conversation, to provide a succinct (even sometimes terse) conclusion, or to emphasize a point or an idea. Most virtual sentences depend a great deal on the reader's understanding the context of the sentence. Be sure, then, to use the virtual sentence when there is a purpose as well as a clear context available to your readers.

The Virtual Sentence: Some Model Passages

Here are some passages with virtual sentences. Study them carefully, choose one passage to work with, and copy it, thinking about its structure as you write. Then construct your own passage, trying to imitate the model word for word, phrase for phrase, clause for clause.

1.   *Early, grainy half-light in an old apartment by the frozen river. Gerry slips into the brown-aired entryway and jiggles the key in the lock, pulling outward the way Dot told him, closing the door after and treading softly up the cat-grey carpeted stairs.* —Louise Erdrich

The first sentence, a virtual one, sets the scene for the action that occurs in the second sentence. The virtual sentence sketches an image for readers and helps them think about the coming action. Because there is no verb in the virtual sentence, the effect of timelessness is created, an effect reinforced by the present tense and present participles of the second (and complete) sentence.

2. *Still, in years to come, I tried to practice all I'd learned, always made the inward cut, took the step forward, always looked where I was hitting. These, I considered, were the crucial aspects of the science. Insider's knowledge. A part of who I was.* —Richard Ford

Here the virtual sentences repeat and underscore those crucial aspects referred to in the second sentence: *insider's knowledge* and *a part of who I was*. Because each idea is in its own virtual sentence, it has more weight and is grammatically more important. Did you notice the compound verbs and the asyndeton in the first part of the passage (*tried to practice, made the cut, took the step forward*, and *always looked*)? The lack of conjunctions is actually echoed in the two short virtual sentences at the end of the passage.

3. *He had been expecting something more definite—chest pains, a stroke, arthritis—but it was only weakness that put a finish to his living alone. A numbness in his head, an airy feeling when he walked. A wateriness in his bones that made it an effort to pick up his coffee cup in the morning.* —Anne Tyler

The virtual sentences articulate the weakness, enumerate examples of it, show us readers what the writer means by *weakness*. The writer sketches the feeling for the reader with strokes of virtual sentences, a different weakness for each virtual sentence. Did you also notice the alliteration of *weakness, when* and *walked*? This repetition helps to link the sentences and lend coherence to the passage. There is further coherence with the alliterative *coffee cup*—and a noun adjunct/noun pattern as well.

4. *The next three years I was probably the happiest I'd ever been outside of Tonic or Molokai. No more frustrations with the ladies at the temple.* —Allegra Goodman

The virtual sentence at the end of this passage explains why the writer was happy in the next three years: *no more frustrations*. As the first word in the virtual sentence that has no verb, *no* is especially emphatic.

After you have written many sentences imitating these figures and stylistic turns, you will have acquired them in your repertoire of stylistic devices, ready to be called up by your mind when your subject matter demands them. It is good to maintain a habit of trying your hand at reproducing the sentence structure of other writers because doing so forces you into another way of seeing and thinking about the writing: it opens your style up to the interesting aspects of others' styles.

In the next chapter, you'll find longer passages for your reading and grammatical analysis. You might try copying some of those too.

8

A Dozen Prose Passages: Reading for Style and Grammatical Understanding

*T*his chapter concentrates on the relationship of grammar to style, specifically on analyzing passages to understand how writers use grammatical and figurative structures to create specific stylistic effects. Here you will find a number of stylistically interesting passages to read, enjoy, analyze, discuss.

As you read and talk about these passages, perhaps with your writing group, be especially aware of your initial response to each passage, to its tone and its subject matter. Your first response to the passage will be important to your analysis of the writer's style: you'll want to ask yourself first, "What am I thinking and feeling about what I just read? and then "How did the writer create this effect or response in me?" and "What grammatical structures are at work here?"

Gerald Early on Muhammad Ali

This passage is from Gerald Early's essay about prizefighter Muhammad Ali, "Ali, the Wonder Boy," one of Philip Lopate's choices of best essays of 1999, collected in *The Art of the Essay*.

> What unnerves us now about Ali and brings out the insipidness of victimology is that he has wound up like an old, broken-down prizefighter. The guilt we feel is that we used him as a commodity and that he used us to create great dramas of his fights, dragon-slaying heroics, extraordinary crises of our social order. It mattered greatly whether he won or lost and we are guilty about having been conned into believing a prizefight means much of anything in this

world, guilty about what our being conned did to the confidence man. But Ali, far from being a victim, is perhaps one of the most remarkable examples of triumph over racism in our century. It is not surprising that so many white people hated him; it is surprising that before his career ended a good many had come to love him. (156)

You might begin thinking about this passage by doing a grammatical/rhetorical/stylistic analysis of the paragraph. Such an analysis involves counting paragraph elements (to find out how the paragraph is constructed) and then analyzing them (to determine what grammatical, rhetorical, and stylistic devices the writer used to create the effect). Here are questions to guide your rhetorical analysis:

1. How many sentences are in the passage?
2. How long is the longest sentence (in words)?
3. How short is the shortest sentence (in words)?
4. What is the type (simple, compound, complex, compound-complex) of each sentence?
5. Does a particular sentence pattern dominate this passage?
6. Are there any examples of transformations? Note them.
7. Who (or in some cases, what) is the agent in the passage? What person or force is driving this prose?
8. What grammatical patterns do you observe? Do you see balance? repetition? pairings?
9. Are there repeated words or repeated concepts? Note them.
10. Do you notice any unusual words? Are certain words strategically placed?
11. Is there any unusual punctuation? Note this.
12. What's going on in places of emphasis in the passage—particularly at the end and at the beginning?
13. Now add up all your responses in about three sentences that describe this writer's style and, for this passage, the effect on the reader. Speculate about the writer's possible aims for the passage and point out specific devices and strategies that lend themselves to the accomplishment of these aims: what does Early make you think and feel about Ali and how does he do it?

O liver Sacks—from "A Leg to Stand On"

In this passage, Oliver Sacks, professor of clinical neurology at Albert Einstein College of Medicine and writer of many brilliantly readable books about life and medicine, describes a scene from *A Leg to Stand On* where he encounters a bull while hiking alone in the wildness of a Norwegian fjord. As you read, be particularly aware of how Sacks describes the bull, which he had been warned about but whose presence he had disbelieved. In the sentences just before this passage, he describes his feelings of physical competence and well-being as well as his energy and exuberance during the climb, characterizing himself as "strong as a bull." As he climbs, he seems to inhabit a mystical landscape, the mists and clouds around him creating a surreal atmosphere where he's not always sure what is real and what is not. (A note: the italicization and punctuation are of course Sacks's.)

> The real Reality was not such a moment, not touched in the least by ambiguity or illusion. I had, indeed, just emerged from the mist, and was walking round a boulder as big as a house, the path curving round it so that I could not see ahead, and it was this inability to see ahead which permitted *the Meeting*. I practically trod on what lay before me—an enormous animal sitting in the path, and indeed totally occupying the path, whose presence had been hidden by the rounded bulk of the rock. It had a huge horned head, a stupendous white body and an enormous mild milk-white face. It sat unmoved by my appearance, exceedingly calm, except that it turned its vast white face up towards me. And in that moment it *changed*, before my eyes, becoming transformed from magnificent to utterly monstrous. The huge white face seemed to swell and swell, and the great bulbous eyes became radiant with malignance. The face grew huger and huger all the time, until I thought it would blot out the Universe. The bull became hideous—hideous beyond belief, hideous in strength, malevolence and cunning. It seemed now to be stamped with the infernal in every feature. It became, first a monster, and now the Devil. —Oliver Sacks

What is Sacks's response to the bull? How does he present the bull? With what words and images does he characterize the bull? What words are repeated? Why are the italics important? How does punctuation help to create the effect or to shape this paragraph? Write a description of Sacks's style in this passage.

R *honda White's Autobiography*

Rhonda White is a native Alabamian with a gift for storytelling. In this excerpt from her autobiography, she recalls her grandfather, Papa Pete:

> Now my Papa Pete (grandfather) was what we call a character. He drank his coffee from the saucer; dipped snuff till the day he died; put his feet on the kitchen table after supper (even if everyone else was still eating); hid his liquor from my Big Mamma (grandmother); cussed politicians, the law, and referees on Saturday Night Wrestling at Boutwell Auditorium via the television; and walked to town every day to catch the local gossip down at the drug store and pick up the latest Cullman *Times*. Now that he is the person described above at the fragile age of around seventy-five, it boggles the mind to think what he was like at around thirty when he married my Big Mamma, but that is another tale altogether best saved for another day. The point is that my Papa Pete was **not** the most responsible man, even at an age when he had nine little responsibilities running around. After being sent to prison during

Prohibition for making moonshine (for the second time), Papa Pete decided with the consensus of all concerned that the time had come for my daddy to obtain gainful employment. After all, he had a seventh-grade education just going to waste.

Look for sentence variation (contrast sentence one with sentence two, for starters) and for patterns of punctuation. Notice the multiple verbs in sentence two and observe how this sentence is punctuated. Listen for alliteration and assonance and consider how the sound of the passage creates coherence. The tone of this piece is decidedly colloquial: how does White create this effect grammatically? Also think about how White makes you feel part of the story, how she creates a comfort zone for readers.

M ary Roach and the Common Cold

England's Common Cold Unit is a research facility where volunteers are exposed to cold viruses and suffer colds so that one day perhaps the common cold can be eliminated. As Roach describes the unit, it is an all-expense paid vacation in the Salisbury countryside—except for the fact that visitors are subjected to deliberate exposure to at least one of the over-200 cold viruses being studied at the Unit. In this section Roach explains how you catch cold—and how you can prevent colds.

> A cold virus is harmless until it gets inside a nose cell—where it takes over and begins replicating itself. Researchers recently discovered how a virus gains entry to our cells: deep openings in the virus particle's surface fit protruding receptors on our nose cells. Researchers are working on two types of drugs, one that plugs the openings on the particle, and one that monopolizes our receptors. Although the main application is prevention—particularly for people with asthma or bronchitis, in whom a cold can trigger a serious attack—these drugs may one day prove useful in treating symptoms.
>
> For now, the only way to prevent colds is to keep the viruses out of our noses. This would be a lot easier if we didn't sneeze. Sneezes—and, to a lesser extent, coughs—launch a mist of virus-laden droplets. (Breathing and talking disperse relatively few virus particles.) The smaller, lighter droplets remain airborne, where they either evaporate or are inhaled by a passing nose. The larger droplets fall to the nearest surface. From there they catch a lift noseward on passing fingertips.
>
> Polite cold sufferers who put hands to face while sneezing or coughing will cut down on airborne transmission; unfortunately, the virus is now all over their hands. If you touch what they've touched before the virus dries up and becomes inactive (several hours with a large droplet), your fingers will pick up the virus.
>
> Bearing all this in mind, there are several ways to minimize your risk, should you find yourself in the company of a cold sufferer.
>
> ■ Wash your hands often (and have your friend with the cold do the same).

- Try your best not to touch your nose and eyes—the primary transfer points from fingertip to nasal cavity. It happens more often than you'd think. According to University of Virginia cold researcher Jack Gwaltney, people pick their noses and touch their eyes about once every three hours. (These astonishing statistics are based on timed observations of adult Sunday school classes and medical students on rounds.)

- Avoid hand contact. Shaking or holding hands is one of the riskiest things you can do with a cold sufferer—far riskier than kissing. Studies have shown that couples are no more likely than platonic roommates to catch one another's colds.

How to think about this passage: first, ask yourself what you believe to be Roach's purpose for writing this piece. Then consider what pronouns she uses to address you, her readers. Think about the kinds of sentence patterns you find here. Notice all the imperative modes (used for the suggestions). Look at the formatting. Find the transitions that make it easy for the reader to bridge ideas. Look for repeated words. Add everything up; then write a paragraph describing how she uses grammar to accomplish her rhetorical purpose(s).

C*harles McGrath: Thinking about Internet Time*

Several years ago, Charles McGrath made some trenchant observations about time in cyberspace and how it differs from "real" time. Although cyberspace now is significantly different than it was five years ago, some things about the Internet don't change much. You could say they are frozen in time. Here's what McGrath says:

> It's customary in Net-speak to make a distinction between "r/t," or real time— the time in which all these delays and jam-ups occur—and "v/t," or virtual time, which is time on the Net: a kind of eternal present in which it is neither day nor night and the clock never ticks. V/t is time without urgency, without priority. One factor contributing to the Internet traffic jams, in fact, is that the system makes no distinction between the electrons carrying your Elle MacPherson photos and those carrying the verification codes for my six-figure stock transaction; it devotes exactly the same amount of attention, and at the same pace, to each. V/t is also time without subjectivity. It affords neither those moments of speeded-up intensity when everything seems to be happening at once nor those moments of deep immersion when you sink so thoroughly into a project or activity that afterward you can't recall where the time went.
>
> V/t is shallow time, surface time—time elongated in such a way that to me it most resembles that skittering, half-suspended state that occurs just before sleep, when random circuits begin firing in your brain, initiating loops of thought that never quite connect and causing your body every now and then to twitch in slow motion. But the main thing that has to be said about v/t is that it is an enormous waster of r/t, which is a problem if, instead of hanging out at the computer mall, you happen to have a full-time job. Most people I

know who have embarked even halfheartedly upon the Net say they have no time any more to read, watch TV, visit with their friends—no time to do all the things they used to like to do.

In this passage, McGrath is all about defining v/t or virtual time. Notice how he does this; observe his use of contrast. Observe repeated words. See how he uses the appositive strategy for defining and notice how he uses dashes. Copy this passage, then when you think you understand his stylistic strategies, write a paragraph explaining them to your friend.

T homas Paine's "The Crisis": Enjoining Patriots

Quitting this class of men, I turn with the warm ardor of a friend to those who have nobly stood and are yet determined to stand the matter out: I call not upon a few, but upon all: not on this state or that state, but on every state: up and help up; lay your shoulders to the wheel; better have too much force than too little, when so great an object is at stake. Let it be told to the future world that in the depth of winter, when nothing but hope and virtue could survive, that the city and the country, alarmed at one common danger, came forth to meet and to repulse it. Say not that thousands are gone, turn out your tens of thousands; throw not the burden of the day upon Providence, but "show your faith by your works" that God may bless you.

The passage begins with a fine transition wherein Paine literally quits one association and *turns* to another one. Find the repeated words, antitheses, and exquisite balances. Explain why the imperative mode (*Let it be told*) is effective and why the adverbial phrase *when nothing but hope and virtue could survive*, is an effective interrupter in its sentence. Copy the passage and then explain Paine's stylistic strategies to one of your classmates.

M olly Ivins on America

Molly Ivins is a Texas writer with a sly sense of humor and a barbed wit. Her columns are syndicated from the Ft. Worth *Telegraph-Standard*. In this piece, "A Nation Undeterred by Reality," she fondly catalogs the "lovable stuff about America." This essay is a celebration of the quirkiness, yes the individuality, of the American character. As you read, consider in particular what Ivins accomplishes with the catalogs or lists.

For some reason, many people believe that England is the great nation for eccentrics; this is because they see nothing peculiar about people who have dedicated their lives to setting a world record for knocking over dominoes in sequence. Or crocheting toilet paper covers. Or collecting Fiesta-ware. Of course, this means that our [U.S.] teenagers have to dye their hair blue, green or orange in order to be considered odd, but what the hell, it adds color to the streets.

We're the country that put Elvis on a stamp! We buy pink lemonade and striped toothpaste! Sixty-seven point two percent of us believe that Alexis de Tocqueville never should have divorced Blake Carrington! Huge numbers of us believe in flying saucers, horoscopes, palm readers, the lottery and pyramid power, that John Kennedy was killed by the CIA and that you can get AIDS off toilet seats. A nation undeterred by reality—no wonder we went to the moon!

Consider American cuisine: pizza, kungpao chicken, sushi, tacos, bratwurst, tofu burgers and corn on the cob. Who wants to live in a place that favors unanimity and uniformity? Consider American music: jazz, blues, pop, country, folk, opera, heavy-metal rock, Cajun, polka, Gershwin, Sousa, bluegrass, Tejano, baroque, Cole Porter, punk, Latino, industrial rock, Three Tenors, reggae. . . . This is not a case of 37 flavors of the same thing, which is more than anyone needs—this is about *possibility.*

In this passage you'll find considerably more than just catalogs of words. Look for parallelism, patterns of repetition. Look at the diction, the words, that Ivins uses. Look for alliteration and assonance. What is the effect of the compound sentence that begins the passage? What do you think of Ivins's use of the exclamation point after *moon?*

K im Hendon on Learning to Read in a Private Religious School

Kim Hendon attended a private religious academy as an elementary student. She was precocious and learned to read very quickly, devouring first all the designated first grade books, second grade books, third grade books, and on through each successive grade. By the time she reached eighth grade, she was close to exhausting Mrs. Rosser's (the librarian's) resources:

> I distinctly remember getting to the eighth grade section and Mrs. Rosser's handing me S.E. Hinton's *The Outsiders.* (Students were not allowed to select any book they wanted in Mrs. Rosser's library. Mrs. Rosser selected books and handed them to students). I was happily reading about Ponyboy when I came to a square hole in the novel. I was aghast that anyone would desecrate a book. I pointed out this atrocity to Mrs. Rosser and was horrified to discover SHE HAD DONE IT! She said there had been a "nasty" word there and she had cut if out of the book. Good Christian children did not read filth and did not question their elders. I thought, "Oh hell!" (That was the only bad word I knew at the time, and that word I had gleaned in chapel service when the older students were called upon to repent for saying or thinking it.)

Did you notice that Hendon uses the possessive case before the gerund *handing*? Notice how Hendon uses interrupters to create effects. What is the effect of the parenthetical comment about book selection? Point out where and how interrupting elements work in this passage. Also, look for specific words that are memorable: consider how you think the diction helps to create a specific emotional effect.

W ilbert Rideau: Why Prisons Don't Work

Wilbert Rideau is a murderer sent in 1962 to the Louisiana State Penitentiary for life. In 1994, his essay, "Why Prisons Don't Work," was published in *Time* magazine. In this excerpt from the piece, see if you can spy what rhetorical strategies and devices, what figures and structures, are at work.

> Crime is a young man's game. Most of the nation's random violence is committed by young urban terrorists. But because of long, mandatory sentences, most prisoners here are much older, having spent 15, 20, 30 or more years behind bars, long past necessity. Rather than pay for new prisons, society would be well served by releasing some of its older prisoners who pose no threat and using the money to catch young street thugs. Warden John Whitley agrees that many older prisoners here could be freed tomorrow with little or no danger to society. Release, however, is governed by law or by politicians, not by penal professionals. Even murderers, those most feared by society, pose little risk. Historically, for example, the domestic staff at Louisiana's Governor's mansion has been made up of murderers, hand-picked to work among the chief-of-state and his family. Penologists have long known that murder is almost always a once-in-a-lifetime act. The most dangerous criminal is the one who has not yet killed but has a history of escalating offenses. He's the one to watch.

A suggestion: look for contrasts, opposites. And notice sentence length, one of the ways that Rideau creates interest. What is the effect of the repeated word, *long*? How does the alliteration of *politicians, penal, professionals*, and *pose* **function**?

J ohn Irving's Personal History: "Slipped Away"

In this excerpt from "Slipped Away," Irving recalls his prep-school days at Exeter, particularly his wrestling experiences. The first quarter of the piece reports his difficulties at Exeter and his anger at nearly everything.

> There was one place at Exeter where I was never angry. I never lost my temper in the wrestling room—possibly because I wasn't embarrassed to be there. It is surprising that I felt so comfortable with wrestling. My athletic skills had never been significant. I had loathed Little League baseball. (By association, I hate all sports with balls.) I more mildly disliked skiing and skating. (I have a limited tolerance for cold weather.) I did have an inexplicable taste for physical contact, for the adrenal stimulation of bumping into people, but I was too small to play football. (Also, there was a ball involved.)
>
> When you love something, you have the capacity to bore everyone about *why*— it doesn't matter why. Wrestling, like boxing, is a weight-class sport; you get to bump into people your own size. You can bump into them very hard, but the

place where you land is reasonably soft. And there are civilized aspects to the sport's combativeness: I've always admired the rule that holds you responsible, *if* you lift your opponent off the mat, for your opponent's "safe return." But the best answer to why I love wrestling is that it was the first thing I was any good at. And what limited success I had in the sport I owe to my first coach, Ted Seabrooke.

What do you notice in this passage? Pay particular attention to the punctuation in the first paragraph. What is the purpose of the parentheses? Do you see a pattern? What is the effect of the repeated *never*, early on?

G *eorge Orwell, "Marrakech"*

This passage describes a funeral procession. After you read it, stop a moment to evaluate the emotional effect it creates in you. Then reread the passage and point to the various rhetorical strategies and devices that work in concert to establish the effect.

> As the corpse went past, the flies left the restaurant table in a cloud and rushed after it, but they came back a few minutes later.

> The little crowd of mourners—all men and boys, no women—threaded their way across the market-place between the piles of pomegranates and the taxis and the camels, wailing a short chant over and over again. What really appeals to the flies is that the corpses here are never put into coffins; they are merely wrapped in a piece of rag and carried on a wooden bier on the shoulders of four friends. When the friends get to the burying-ground, they hack an oblong hole a foot or two deep, dump the body in it, and fling over it a little of the dried-up, lumpy earth, which is like broken brick. No gravestone, no name, no identifying mark of any kind. The burying-ground is merely a huge waste of hummocky earth, like a derelict building-lot. After a month or two no one can even be certain where his own relatives are buried.

Do you see a repeated word or concept? Consider how diction works in the excerpt. Also notice the anaphora near the end of the passage; what is the effect of this device? What is the purpose of the alliterated *corpses* and *coffins*? *Burying, body, broken brick*? *Huge, hummocky*?

A *nne Bradstreet, a Seventeenth Century "Meditation, Divine and Moral"*

Anne Bradstreet was a devoted Puritan who also happened to be a fine American poet and writer. She used her writing as a way to work through knotty problems in her faith and ultimately as an affirmation of her devotion to God. This brief devotion is an example of her prose.

MEDITATION 40

The spring is a lively emblem of the resurrection: after a long winter we see the leafless trees and dry stocks (at the approach of the sun) to resume their former vigor and beauty in a more ample manner than what they lost in the autumn; so shall it be at that great day after a long vacation, when the Sun of righteousness shall appear; those dry bones shall arise in far more glory than that which they lost at their creation, and in this transcends the spring that their leaf shall never fail nor their sap decline.

This passage is one long sentence. Begin by finding all the separate independent and dependent clauses; if Bradstreet intends to keep all her ideas collected in one sentence, then she means to keep it tidy and coherent. You'll want to keep this in mind as you analyze the sentence. Next, observe Bradstreet's play with the seasons: what do you think the seasons might symbolize to her? Notice the repetition of *dry*, *leaf* (or *leafless*), and *sun*. Why do you think Bradstreet wants to emphasize these words for her readers?

9

A Punctuation Gallery

E *xternal Punctuation*

period

The period is the most elemental and definitive mark of punctuation. It is final. It marks the end of the sentence and the conclusion of the thought. In speech, the period requires a full stop at the end of a sentence and is the equivalent of coming to a complete stop at a traffic stop sign. A period draws the boundary between sentences. It is probably the first mark of punctuation you learned as a young writer. You will find the period at the end of declarative sentences or sentences that make a statement, at the end of most virtual sentences, after initials and some abbreviations. Periods are important for reading because they help readers construct text by grouping ideas. Instinctively, readers know to process the text between periods as a complete idea; they expect that the territory between periods to be inhabited by something intelligible and finished. Let's look at some examples.

Periods after Declarative Sentences

A period signals the end of a declarative sentence, as in

   a. At 40,000 feet Yeager began his speed run. —Tom Wolfe

   b. I could see her defeat and helplessness. —Janet Frame

   c. A good many factors contributed to the decline of sport. —E.B. White

   d. Warts are wonderful structures. —Lewis Thomas

   e. I loved to pick through trash piles and collect empty bottles, tin cans with pretty labels, and discarded magazines. —Russell Baker

Periods after Virtual Sentences

Periods also conclude virtual sentences and, because many virtual sentences are short anyway, emphasize their punch. Here are some examples:

   a. Weird. Sleeping in the neuropsych ward at night, I sensed the presence of a very large rabbit under my bunk. A seven-foot rabbit with brown fur and skin sores, who took long, raking breaths. —Thom Jones

Notice how the one-word virtual sentence *Weird* sets the tone for what follows, prepares your mind to accept the oddity of it. And observe too how the final virtual sentence describing the giant rabbit is given additional importance by existing as its own sentence and by not being attached to the previous sentence as an appositive.

   b. I guess I'd resolved the soul and sin thing by lapsing from my heavy-duty Catholic background, giving up my immortal soul for a blues kind of soul. Funky and low-down, the kind inspired by reading too much Carlos Castaneda and Rilke and Robert Bly and dropping acid with a guy who claimed to be my cosmic mate from a past life. —Julia Alvarez

The virtual sentence, which begins with *Funky and low-down*, draws out what Alvarez means by a *blues kind of soul*. That it has its own sentence elevates it to the status of important information. Did you also notice the repetition of *soul*? And the cluster of words that have a metaphysical connotation—*soul, immortal, cosmic*?

   c. She had ten wigs, ten colors, fifty styles. She looked different, the same, and very good. A human theme in which nothing began anything and was gorgeous. To me she was the world's lesson. —Leonard Michaels

A human theme in which nothing began anything and was gorgeous is a virtual sentence because it has no verb cluster. This virtual sentence comments upon the various appearances of the woman, who always looks good regardless of which wig she has on, and it interprets the woman's chameleon-like appearance. Did you also notice the asyndeton in the first sentence: *ten wigs, ten colors, fifty styles*? The asyndeton and the virtual sentence create a clipped, slightly terse tone for this passage.

    d. Here ghosts sat as if already in the World-to-Come, explicating Scripture. Or whatever. —Cynthia Ozick

The *Or whatever* virtual sentence is a blunt, sarcastic comment on the notion of the ghosts in *the World-to-Come, explicating Scripture*. The speaker is not only disbelieving but also dismissive. It is the current equivalent of saying "Not!" after a declarative statement.

    e. Still, Rita suspects, even knowing all there is to know about her, he sees her as his entryway to the land of dreams. His bridge. His American girl. —Lynne Sharon Schwartz

The two virtual sentences at the end of this passage are grammatically parallel: *His bridge, His American girl*. They articulate what the writer means by his entryway to the land of dreams. The virtual sentences would be appositives if they were in the base sentence.

    f. I am Dell Enterprise. PowerEdge servers, storage, infrastructure software, and Premier Enterprise Services. And I am backed by thousands of service and support people: on-site, online and on the phone. —Dell advertisement

At the center of this excerpt is a virtual sentence that defines what Dell Enterprise is by providing a catalogue of its services. Virtual sentences are common in advertisements, where the writer wants to reach the reader with short bits of trenchant information. Notice the other aspects of this selection: the very short opening sentence; the third sentence beginning with the conjunction *and* as if to remind the reader of the connection to the first sentence; the paired and alliterative *service* and *support*; and the anaphoric structure following the colon: *on-site, online and on the phone*. The style of this magazine is to not include the comma after the next-to-last item in a series.

Periods with Abbreviations

Periods also mark abbreviations and initials, as in

M.D. (Medical Doctor)

Ph.D. (Doctor of Philosophy)

etc. (et cetera or *and so on*)

a.m. (ante meridian—before the meridian or noon)

Esq. (Esquire)

L.L.C. (limited liability corporation)

Mr. (mister)

Increasingly, however, periods are disappearing in abbreviations. Abbreviations are being written in capital letters and without the period, particularly acronyms or words created from the initials of each word in a phrase, such as *RAM* (random access memory). This trend may have accelerated with the U.S. Postal Service, which quite a few years ago asked the American public not to put periods after state abbreviations on U.S. mail. Indeed, the Postal Service completely rewrote state abbreviations so that each was only two letters with no periods, all the better to be read by machines scanning envelopes and sorting mail. (Evidently, periods throw glitches in the scanning procedures.) So the abbreviation for *Illinois* (*Ill.*) became *IL* (two capital letters, unpunctuated); the abbreviation for *Oklahoma* (*Okla.*) became *OK*; and the abbreviation for *Indiana* (*Ind.*) became *IN*. The postal service also created new, easily scanned abbreviations for words like *street* (formerly *st.*; now *ST*); *lane* (*LN*); *road* (*RD*); *court* (*CT*). Interestingly, British, Australian, and Canadian convention is not to use periods in abbreviations.

In most acronyms, the periods have totally disappeared, and in many (like *scuba*, which was originally an acronym representing *self-contained underwater breathing apparatus*) the original meanings have been nearly obscured. Do you know what these acronyms represent?

NATO (North Atlantic Treaty Organization)

GRE (Graduate Record Exams)

YWCA (Young Women's Christian Association)

NAACP (National Association for the Advancement of Colored People)

AMA (American Medical Association)

MLA (Modern Language Association)

APA (American Psychological Association)

Periods Indicating Ellipsis

Periods are also used in threes (generally with intervening spaces) to indicate ellipsis or omitted words or a pause in speech. Four periods indicate an ellipsis plus the period at the end of the sentence.

    a. She doesn't even answer me. She says . . . you want to know what she says? —Grace Paley

This ellipsis indicates a pause in the speech.

    b. But though I pined away and talked about it, I knew that I couldn't go; there was no money . . . . —Mary Mebane

Each section of this autobiographical piece concludes with an ellipsis just like this one. Perhaps the ellipsis indicates the omission of certain details or even the passage of time between recorded events.

    c. And there I was, caught up in a mass flight into collective murder, into the fiery furnace. . . . Something had come up from the depths, and it was happening now. —Louis Ferdinand Céline

Something is omitted here between the actual recounted events of fleeing and the reflection or interpretation of those events. The ellipsis functions as a kind of transition between the remembered past and the present.

> **d.** She tries to speak and then stops and takes a shuddering breath, and the tears pour and pour down her face. "I'm . . . resting," she says finally. "Just resting." —Paula Keisler

These ellipses indicate a pause in the conversation.

> **e.** It was one in the morning, and I began to count ahead in my mind . . . two, three, four, five . . . sunrise. —Victor Montejo

Here the ellipsis indicates the omitted numbers intervening between the beginning of the counting and sunrise.

question mark

The **question mark** indicates a question or posits a condition of tentativeness or uncertainty. Even its shape, curving first one way and then another, suggests an insecurity about which direction it should turn. Use the question mark after any of the question transformations or after a declarative sentence or phrase that you want to transform into a question. You can also use the question mark to show the reader that you are unsure about something you are writing. Like the period, the question mark requires a full stop at the end of an utterance or sentence.

Question Mark as Part of a Question Transformation

In all the following sentences, the question mark comes after a question transformation. You can tell because of the inversion of subject and verb and the insertion of the subject between verb and auxiliary: *Was he? How have you been? Do you take? Has a quarter disappeared?*

> **a.** Was he deranged, was he a sex maniac? —Margaret Atwood
>
> **b.** How have you been this week, sweetheart? —Ann Beattie
>
> **c.** When friends dropped over and sat around the kitchen table, my grandma would ask, "Do you take cream and sugar?" —Stuart Dybek

    d. Has a quarter disappeared from Paula Frosty's pocket book?
        —William H. Gass

    e. Do you think anybody will come back on Thursday?
        —Charles Johnson

Question Mark Causing a Question Transformation

In these questions, the question mark itself causes the question transformation because the word order is regulation subject-verb. The only thing that differentiates these questions from their indicative counterparts is, in fact, the question mark.

    a. You don't like the nose? —Thom Jones

    b. You know what I'm thinking? Of all the people in Cedar Falls, you're the one who could understand Vern best.
        —Bharati Mukherjee

    c. You don't know? Typical. Burton's leaving, see?
        —Mary Robison

    d. "You live in a Hetrick and Dewitt?" said Doreen.
        —Michael Chabon

    e. I must be hungry. And not you? —Allen Hoffman

Question Mark Indicating Writer's Uncertainty

In these questions, the question transformation occurs after a declarative sentence: there is no internal transformation in the grammatical structure of the sentence or alteration of syntax. In some of them, a grammatical tag reinforces the writer's uncertainty, but in others, the question mark alone accomplishes this purpose.

    a. Julie's place is that way, right? —Ron Carlson

    b. Sometimes it's hard. You know what I'm saying?
        —Raymond Carver

    c. I gotta ask. You two married, or what? —Jonathan Penner

    d. You believe what you saw—the crown? —Bernard Malamud

A Note about Question Marks

Notice that question marks go with the section of the sentence that actually is the question or the section that actually asks the question. Also observe that question marks may go inside or outside quotation marks, depending on where the question actually concludes. Consider this sentence by Ann Beattie:

> "I've come up against Amy Vanderbilt's timetable for accepting a social invitation at Thanksgiving?" he asked.

In this sentence, the question mark accompanies the actual question—the part about the Thanksgiving invitation timetable—and thus goes inside the quotation marks to identify it as part of what was said. The *he said* is **metalanguage**, language about language, language reporting on the speaker's actions or words.

These sentences illustrate times when you would place the question mark outside the quotation marks:

Do you mean that we're supposed to underline all mentions of "euro"?

and

Who screamed "Fire"?

and

What rhymes with "weaponize"? —Dennis Cass

In all, the quoted material is within the original utterance, a part of it, and the entire utterance is a question. Therefore, the question mark goes after the complete utterance, which includes the quotation mark.

exclamation point

The exclamation point, highly dramatic, wants to jump off the page. It is primed for excitement. Because this mark indicates such intensity, use it sparingly and wisely. One exclamation point is always sufficient. Multiple exclamation points can suggest anything from a writer out of control to one just plain silly or hysterical. Overused, the exclamation point loses its potency, and readers become inured or accustomed to it—therefore rendering it useless. Like the period and the question mark, the exclamation point requires a full stop (although a series of words or short phrases punctuated with exclamation points can create a rush of motion). The exclamation point is a fine indicator of surprise, extreme pleasure, sound effects, threats, or any heightened emotion.

The exclamation point follows a classic exclamation or the **exclamatory transformation**, which denotes surprise or astonishment and requires a transformation of a base sentence. To create an exclamatory transformation of the sentence *You look pretty,*

1. move the complement before the subject: *pretty you look;*
2. insert *what* a or *how* at the front of the sentence: *How pretty you look;*
3. then finish it off with an exclamation mark: *How pretty you look!*

Other examples of exclamatory transformations are *How green is my valley! How delightful you look today! How dreadful! What a big nose you have!* The exclamation mark can also have the effect of converting any indicative utterance to an exclamatory one. Here then is the exclamation point in action.

   a. "I can't believe it!" she cries out, aware of triteness, as Thant hands over the bags to her. —Alice Adams

This exclamation point emphasizes the disbelief. Notice that there is no other end punctuation for the clause and that the exclamation point goes inside the quotation marks because her words, not the entire sentence, are exclamatory.

   b. How dreadful is the state of those that are daily and hourly in the danger of this great wrath and infinite misery! —Jonathan Edwards

This sentence from the famous sermon "Sinners in the Hands of an Angry God" is the result of an exclamatory transformation. Notice the *how* and the inverted syntax.

   c. "You are a shining star!" she says with amazing volume and venom. "Stick to your plan!" —C.S. Godshalk

The exclamation points go inside the quotation marks in both these instances because they apply to the material being quoted only—not to the whole sentences.

   d. Breaking into somebody's place there's a way your heart beats, like a hummingbird's whirring wings, and a sharp taste in your mouth you don't get anywhere anytime else! —Joyce Carol Oates

Here the exclamation point underscores the extremity of the sensation described in the sentence.

   e. Doctors used to be so confident that severed nerves could not transmit pain—they're severed!—that nerve cutting was commonly prescribed as a treatment for pain. —Melanie Thernstrom

In this sentence, the exclamation point applies to the interrupting clause and has the effect of increasing its emphasis, which is already considerable because of the dashes.

   f. But they let you go free! —Ursula K. Le Guin

This exclamation point seems to express amazement and surprise.

   g. This is a country of six million people, and it can mobilize a million in twenty-four to forty-eight hours! —David Remnick

Here the exclamation point seems to reinforce the excitement of the discovery, along with amazement.

   h. Now that's rapid-fire convenience! —Todd Lappin

A strong feeling of affirmation is conveyed by this exclamation point.

**Passages
to
Punctuate:
Terminal
Marks**

Copy the following passages, either by hand or by keying them into your computer. As you copy, find sentence boundaries in the passages and punctuate each passage with terminal punctuation marks only—that is, punctuation at the end of sentences. Internal punctuation (commas, semicolons, and colons) is already here, but capitals signaling the beginnings of sentences have been removed.

From Anthony Bourdain's *Kitchen Confidential*

The last cook to arrive is our French fry guy this is a full-time job at Les Halles, where we are justifiably famous for our frites Miguel, who looks like a direct descendant of some Aztec king, spends his entire day doing nothing but peeling potatoes, cutting potatoes, blanching potatoes, and then during service dropping them into 375-degree peanut oil, tossing them with salt and stacking the sizzling hot spuds onto plates with his bare hands I've had to do this a few times, and it requires *serious* calluses

From Annie Dillard's "An American Childhood"

We children lived and breathed our history—our Pittsburgh history, so crucial to the country's story and so typical of it as well—without knowing or believing any of it for how can anyone know or believe stories she dreamed in her sleep, information for which and to which she feels herself to be in no way responsible a child is asleep her private life unwinds inside her skin and skull; only as she sheds childhood, first one decade and then another, can she locate the actual, historical stream, see the setting of her dreaming private life—the nation, the city, the neighborhood, the house where the family lives—as an actual project under way, a project living people willed, and made well or failed, and are still making, herself among them I breathed the air of history all unaware, and walked oblivious through its littered layers

From Bobbie Ann Mason's *Zigzagging Down a Wild Trail*

Peyton slept beside her, not waking until they crossed the Mississippi River again, at Memphis when he stirred, she turned to peer out the window at plow-scarred fields after Memphis, the delta stretched out flat and blank—old cotton fields waiting to be submerged under something new and transforming billboards planted in the fields like scarecrows marked the way to the casinos in the distance the casinos began to appear, rising out of the fields like ocean vessels on the horizon—a Confederate armada positioned along the Mississippi, protecting the delta from northern invaders

I *nternal Punctuation*

comma

The comma is slight but not insignificant. Probably the most frequently used mark of punctuation, it is also possibly the least well understood. Although there is a fine logic to placing commas, many writers merely sprinkle commas through text where they think the reader should pause, mentally as well as conversationally. Actually, there is some point to this method of punctuation—one use of the comma is to prevent misreading, to keep apart two words or phrases that, if allowed to elide, might confuse. Bottom line: there are some clear instances where a comma is necessary, obligatory (you are obliged to use one), and where you should learn to insert it. But there are other structures where you may choose a comma, no punctuation, or a different mark. Let's look at the uses of commas.

Commas and Coordinators in Compound Sentences

When you join two (or more) independent clauses in a compound sentence and use a coordinator (*and, but, for, or, nor, yet*), you need a comma after each pattern and before the coordinator separating the patterns. A schema for this structure might look like this:

> Pattern 1, *but* pattern 2.

or

> Pattern 1, pattern 2, *and* pattern 3.
>
> It was unbelievable, but here it was. —Louis L'Amour

The first independent clause or complete pattern is *It was unbelievable*. The second complete pattern is *here it was*. Here are more examples:

a. His fingers were stiff, and it took him a long time to twist the lid off the holy water. —Leslie Marmon Silko

b. The market is full of exotic produce, and the prices are being driven up. —Allegra Goodman

c. There is an accident, and Cruise winds up charged with murder and disfigured. —David Denby

d. I smiled, but I feared she was right. —Daphne Merkin

e. At school boys were thinking of college, and girls were thinking of boys. —Nessa Rapoport

f. The edge of the ice sheet lies some ten miles away, and it can be seen—a ghostly white blue in the distance—by climbing just about any hill. —Elizabeth Kolbert

Commas between Very Short Independent Clauses

If the independent clauses in a compound sentence are very short and you want the sentence to move rapidly, it is possible to use only a comma (without its usual coordinator as accompanist) between the two patterns. In addition, in these kinds of sentences, there is typically a very tight relationship between the two clauses, and the two may be structurally quite similar. Be extremely careful when you do this, however: some punctuation purists may consider this a **comma splice** (that is, a compound sentence where two independent clauses are spliced—or held together in a fragile manner—with only a comma, where a comma and coordinator are required). Here are some examples:

a. His mother was half-English, his father was half-French. —Joseph Conrad

b. Certainly there will be work to do, everyone must work here. —Primo Levi

c. We negotiate the steps, we knock over some books. —Anne Enright

Commas Setting off Introductory Clauses and Phrases

Mark introductory adverbial clauses or introductory long phrases with a comma. The comma is the doorstop that gently prevents the introductory clause from slamming into the main clause.

a. As if to take another reading of the girl's plain face, I looked again into the coffin on my way out. —Saul Bellow

b. Since George W. Bush took office, there's been a grand total of zero Alaskan oil spills. —Advertisement for "That's My Bush" on Comedy Central

c. If you only had a few days to spare for a Caribbean vacation, where would you spend it? —Advertisement for Postmark Caribbean

d. In memory of him and out of respect for mankind, I decided to live for love. —Grace Paley

e. Nothing in nature is exhausted in its first use. When a thing has served an end to the uttermost, it is wholly new for an ulterior service. —Ralph Waldo Emerson

But No Commas When the Adverbial Clause Concludes

Adverbial clauses that slide in at the end of a sentence are generally not set off by a comma. If you listen hard to these sentences, you'll be able to detect that there is no pause, oral or mental, when readers get to the adverbial clause. Here are some examples:

a. The night was breaking when they got to the house. —Bruce Jay Friedman

b. When she lifts her foot to take a step, she no longer trusts the ground to be there when she puts it down. —Francine Prose

Note that in Prose's sentence both adverbial clauses begin with the same subordinator, *when*. The first clause introduces the sentence and is followed by a comma; the second clause concludes the sentence and has no punctuation between it and the main clause *she no longer trusts the ground to be there*.

c. After that Thanksgiving, Pop gradually sank as if he had a slow leak. —Saul Bellow

d. I was working under my plastic roof when I heard someone shouting. —Nguyen Quang Sang

e. We stood in the shade of the supply room tent along with the rest while the first sergeant and the supply sergeant filled out forms. —Larry Heinemann

The exception to this rule involves clauses beginning with *even though, although, as though, as if, since* and sometimes *while*. These subordinators introduce such a powerful contrast that they generally (but not always) demand some separation from the main clause.

a. I felt wild and new, as though I could swim the heavens and fly through waves. —Amy Tan

b. There was something almost apologetic in her way of uttering her tender avowal, as if she would beg her listeners not to consider her too bizarre in her taste. —Dorothy Parker

c. His entire frame jerks and twitches, as if he is taken by a fit. —Rebecca Goldstein

    d. The cleanest water in our country flows from our forested landscapes. The national forests produce about fourteen percent of the runoff, even though they account for only eight percent of the acreage of the lower forty-eight states. —Adapted from Chuck Sudetic

Commas, NonRestrictive Clauses and Restrictive Clauses

Remember adjective clauses? They pattern with nouns, typically begin with *who*, *whom*, *that*, *which*, or *where*, and provide information in noun clusters. You will remember that adjective clauses can be either **restrictive** (providing essential information) or **nonrestrictive** (providing interesting but not essential information). Do not separate restrictive clauses from the rest of the sentence with commas; restrictive clauses need to hug their nouns because they are very close to their nouns. Restrictive clauses add essential information; that is, they identify which thing or person is being discussed.

    Nonrestrictive clauses are, however, another matter. Do use a comma to separate a nonrestrictive (or nonessential) adjective clause from the rest of the sentence. A nonrestrictive adjective clause presents interesting and informative material —but not information essential to the reader's comprehension of the sentence. Here are some examples of sentences with restrictive and nonrestrictive clauses for you to study. First, the sentences with nonrestrictive clauses, in bold:

    a. We walked the most part of a mile before we came to a house, **which proved to be a sort of a tavern**. —Elizabeth Ashbridge

    b. I sit in a psychiatrist's office, **where courtesy reigns**, and begin my story once again. —Daphne Merkin

    c. He was one of your wary men, **who never laugh but upon good grounds—when they have reason and the law on their side**. —Washington Irving

    d. This pleasingly observant and intelligent movie was written by Bacri and his partner, Agnes Jaoui, **who directed the movie (plainly but effectively) and also appears in it as a free-living bar girl**. —David Denby

    e. The loud laughs of the musketmen were silenced by the authoritative voice of Richard, **who called to them for attention and obedience to his signals**. —James Fenimore Cooper

    f. Even New York Republicans now admit that it chilled lawmakers from other states, **who smelled pork**. —Frank Bruni

And now the restrictive adjective clauses, which restrict or limit the meaning of the nouns they modify:

    a. Soon after our arrival here, our companions **who passed through Cuscowilla** joined us. —William Bartram

    b. The result was a share price collapse **that hastened the demise of the company**. —Cory Johnson

c. Rickie Lee Jones is a singer and songwriter **who has performed her blend of smoky, finger-popping music for more than two decades**. —Anonymous in *The New Yorker*

d. A thirteen-year-old defensive tackle **whose mother was missing and whose father is dead** was found to be raising himself, his guardian grandpa having grown senile. —Katherine Boo

e. Last August, Dino sent a letter to the town board with a proposal **that, predictably, wasn't well received**. —Mark Singer

f. The first people **who interviewed me in white coats from behind a computer** were only interested in my health-care benefits and proposed method of payment. —Audre Lorde

Commas with Verbals and Absolutes

Use a comma to separate nominative absolutes and long verbal phrases that introduce the sentence (you'll remember that these are called **free modifiers**) from the rest of the sentence. In these sentences the verbal phrases and absolutes are in bold face.

a. There's a softness in the air, **the stench of the river temporarily overwhelmed by the smell of potted chicken wafting from the windows over the shops**. —Steve Stern

In Stern's sentence, a nominative absolute is set apart from the base sentence. Notice how the absolute sketches the details of *softness in the air*.

b. My parents gaze absentmindedly at the ocean, **scarcely interested in its harshness**. —Delmore Schwarz

This modifier, a past participial phrase, modifies and gives us more detail about *parents*.

c. And he laid hands upon Sholem Waldman, **pulling him by his vest and flailing him about the side of the head**. —Wallace Markfield

Two present participial phrases explain what happens when *he* lays hands upon Waldman.

d. But the child, **wholly exhausted**, cried with weariness.
   —Harriet Beecher Stowe

This interrupting past participial phrase explains why the child cries wearily.

e. Auda came swinging up on foot, **his eyes glazed over with the rapture of battle**. —Lawrence of Arabia

This is a nominative absolute that lends more detail to the image of Auda's coming up swinging.

Commas Marking Interrupters

Commas provide one way to separate interrupting phrases from main clauses in which they take up residence. Interrupters may provide transitions (*incidentally, for instance, after that, for example*), or they may present information that the reader needs. You can also use parentheses and dashes to set off interrupters. Of these three ways to punctuate the interruption of a sentence, paired commas (one on either side of the interrupting element, whether it be word, phrase, or clause) is the mildest and least obtrusive way. So if you want to create the rhetorical effect of merely pausing the sentence or slowing it down somewhat or if you want to move the sentence along relatively swiftly and not lend the interrupting element considerable weight, use the commas. The pair of dashes will draw the reader up short, gasping (see the section on em dashes). The pair of parentheses sometimes effectively engages the reader as a co-conspirator in the reading. Here are examples of commas setting off interrupters; notice the kind of information presented by the interrupting phrase.

> **a.** There was no possibility, she decided, of ever working for such a place. —Robin Hemley

The interrupting clause *she decided* is set off by commas to provide a momentary slowing around it.

> **b.** It was a way to make the hours pass, that's for sure, thought Hershleder. —Helen Schulman

This sentence interrupter, *that's for sure*, is a clause. Besides the interrupter, which reiterates the validity of Hershleder's perception, this sentence has an inverted structure. Its normal order without the interrupter would be *Hershleder thought it was a way to make the hours pass.* Schulman inverted the sentence to emphasize the thought itself and then added the interrupter to underscore the importance of the idea of making the hours pass.

> **c.** Hester Prynne, therefore, did not flee. —Nathaniel Hawthorne

Here the interrupter is a conjunctive adverb. By cleaving the sentence precisely between subject and verb, the conjunctive adverb gives the sentence more weight and emphasizes the idea that Hester did not flee.

> **d.** The night's most electric moments, many attendees agreed, came in performances by Solomon Burke and Aerosmith.
> —Jenny Eliscu and Austin Scaggs

The interrupter, *many attendees agreed*, is a clause that provides confirmation of the opinion that is uttered in this same sentence.

> **e.** I was, strangely enough, indifferent to this news. —Nguy Ngu

Strangely enough is an adverbial interrupter explaining the writer's reflection on the indifference. Interestingly, we learn about the fact that the writer finds the emotion strange in the split second before we learn what the emotion is.

Commas Setting off Appositives and Nouns of Address

Use a comma to set off nonrestrictive appositives from their appositional nouns; this is especially important if the appositive phrase is a long one. If the appositive is one noun falling immediately after its partner noun, it is restrictive and does not need to be set off with a comma.

Also, use a comma to set off nouns of address—that is, when you call someone by name or address someone specifically by name (often at the beginning of a sentence).

a.   They describe a surrealistic landscape, a city without lights, a walk without people. —E.M. Broner

City with its cluster and *Walk* with its cluster comprise two appositives in apposition with *landscape*.

b.   Ida, the retired homemaker, is wearing her reading glasses and flipping through Genesis. —Allegra Goodman

In this sentence, *the retired homemaker* explains which *Ida* is referred to.

c.   Do you, my friend, perceive the path I have found out? —St. Jean de Crevecoeur

Friend is in apposition with *you* in this sentence. In addition, there is an element of address in this appositive. The writer is posing a direct question to the *you*.

d.   We had a new colonel now, Colonel Crawshay, who proved to be the best we ever had. —Isaac Rosenberg

The proper noun *Colonel Crawshay* is in apposition with the common noun *colonel*; *Colonel Crawshay* explains which person is the colonel.

e.   I found myself liking these people, Luu, Khanh, Quang, Ngo Minh. —Lynda Van Devanter

Luu, Khanh, Quang, and *Ngo Minh* are all in apposition with *people*. The appositive enumerates and explains *these people*.

f.   Well, I think I'll turn in now, Rainsford. —Richard Connell

In this sentence, *Rainsford* is a noun of address. The other character, General Zaroff, is addressing Rainsford or talking to him. The noun of address, Rainsford, could just as well have occurred at the beginning of the sentence: "Rainsford, I think I'll turn in now."

Commas Separating Items in a List

Use commas to separate a series of anything: a series of compound verbs (as in sentences *a* and *b*, next), a series of nouns, or anything in a simple list (that is, a list of single items without other words clustered about).

a.   Three hundred faces stared, blinked, squinted, and otherwise engaged the camera while recounting the most awful moments of the century. —Melvin Jules Bukiet

b.   All within my breast was tumult, wildness, and delirium! —Olaudah Equiano

    c. Among steam's vocal opponents were the operators of canals, private toll roads and bridges, stagecoach lines, and the network of merchants and taverns that serviced them.
—Wil McCarthy

    d. I only know she's clever, she deserves an education, and she's going to get one. —Vivian Gornick

    e. Uncles, cousins, nephews, brother would have looked, too, had they been home between journeys. —Maxine Hong Kingston

Many magazines follow the style of eliminating the comma before the last item in the series so that Equiano's sentence (c, previous) would in this style read like this:

> All within my breast was tumult, wildness and delirium!

This is an acceptable style, but be careful that the items are indeed separate when you omit that last comma. Compare these two sentences:

> At the grocery store, we bought these items: Doritos, apples, macaroni and cheese.

and

> At the grocery store, we bought these items: Doritos, apples, macaroni, and cheese.

The two sentences have slightly different meanings. The first suggests that macaroni and cheese was purchased as a package, the ingredients to be prepared together in an entree. The second suggests that macaroni was purchased and cheese was purchased, but that they were not necessarily to be prepared together, in a macaroni-and-cheese dish. The comma makes all the difference. Sometimes it is helpful to have the comma simply to prevent misreading.

    Unless you are writing for a journalistic publication that demands otherwise, you will always be correct if you use the comma after each item in the series.

Commas Between Coordinate Adjectives

Separate **coordinate adjectives** not joined by *and* with a comma. When more than two adjectives modify a noun separately and their order can be rearranged, they are coordinate adjectives. But if some of the adjectives modify or pattern with some of the other adjectives, then they are not coordinate; they are cumulative. One way to determine whether adjectives are coordinate adjectives is to ask yourself whether the word *and* can be inserted between the adjectives. If it can, you need a comma. Look at these sentences to see the difference:

> Spicy, full-bodied filler tobacco is wrapped in a darker reddish-brown Connecticut shade leaf. —Georgetown by Post

Two noun clusters here have adjectives piled up before them in a cluster: *spicy, full-bodied filler tobacco* is one, and *darker reddish-brown Connecticut shade leaf* is the other. Let's look at the last cluster first. The adjectives in this cluster are cumulative; they lean on one another. We cannot put *and* between each adjective and have the sentence make sense: we don't say a *darker and reddish-brown and Connecticut shade leaf*. Thus the adjectives are cumulative. In the first cluster, *spicy* and *full-bodied* are coordinate: we can say *spicy and full-bodied filler tobacco*. Thus there is a comma between spicy and full-bodied (where an *and* might go).

Here are some examples where adjectives are coordinate and commas are used (you can insert an *and* for every comma):

a. The New York streets sprawled out, wet, dirty, impenetrably dark. —Isaac Bashevis Singer

b. It had been a scorching, dirty afternoon at a Colorado fairgrounds, the showers dead and dry. —Annie Proulx

c. The lieutenant, who was briskly businesslike, introduced me to the director, a young, tall, vigorous engineer who was more businesslike and who evidently had already been told about me. —Primo Levi

d. A wee drop of pure, cool (but not cold) water brings out the subtleties in a dram of fine whiskey. —Glen Waggoner

e. I passed all the familiar faces and listened to their harsh, dust-choked greetings. —Amy Tan

Commas for Clarification or Contrast

Sometimes you need a comma to separate words just so the reader can process them correctly and understand them. This clarification is especially important when you introduce a contrast. Here are a few examples:

a. I am only a victim, not a perpetrator. —Nguyen Mong Giac

b. Sloth, by bringing on diseases, absolutely shortens life. —Benjamin Franklin

c. Soon after, the mutilated deer started to appear: reminders to Wheeler, evidence of crime. —Wayne Karlin

d. Narrowing her eyes, she spun around, but saw nothing. —Louise Erdrich

e. It was as if our daughters were the adults, with friends all their own, and we were the children, too young to be included. —Tova Mirvis

Commas and Quotations

You often find commas and quotation marks keeping company because they are both associated with quoted material or with transcriptions of what happens. Please note that commas go inside quotation marks when a **metalanguage** tag (*he said*, for instance) follows the quoted material. When, however, the tag introduces the quotation or begins the sentence, the comma remains with the tag and not with the quotation but before it, outside it. Read all the following examples and in your study group explain why the comma goes where it goes.

  a. "Community is the most valuable thing that you have in African-American culture," he explains. —John Lahr

  b. I awoke to my father shaking his head and saying, "That kid's got a glass jaw." —Naton Leslie

  c. "Beyond just the scenics, these amazing locations in the mountains of New Zealand," says Viesturs, who was one of 50 professional climbers on the set, "the actors themselves trained for a month with mountaineers." —Jason Adams

  d. "Leave it be," broke in the marshal. —Max Brand

  e. "Oh, my dear child," whispered Gitl, pulling her close, "thank God that your parents are not alive to see you now." —Jane Yolen

More on When Not to Use a Comma

Sometimes writers are tempted to put commas into a sentence for leavening or perhaps for interest; the sentence looks empty, they think, so they sprinkle in a comma or two. Too often, these commas end up near the word *and*. Perhaps some teacher has instructed them to pair the comma and *and* in a long sentence, not realizing that what matters is the number and kind of patterns, not the repetitions of *and*. So here is something to remember about using commas: *Don't use a comma between separate parts of a compound subject, compound verb, compound adjectives, compound adverbs, or compound objects.*

  a. I went to meetings in an awful frame of mind and endeavoured to be inwardly acquainted with the language of the True Shepherd. —John Woolman

There is no comma between the two verb chunks *went to meetings* and *endeavoured to be inwardly acquainted with the language of the True Shepherd.*

  b. She tosses her blonde hair back and smiles down at everyone. —Yusef Komunyakaa

Observe: no comma between *tosses* and *smiles down.*

  c. Paule Marshall was both surprised and pleased; she made her son pick up the phone and listen.—Hilton Als

  d. His wife and two children are already asleep. —Max Apple

  e. Shy and formal and breathless, my parents are always meeting for the first time. —Le Thi Diem Thuy

A Concluding Comment about Commas

Commas are becoming scarcer. The trend in printed material is to use fewer, not more, commas. So you will see that many editors abjure even the comma after the introductory phrase or clause. Many editors retain the comma chiefly as a guide to reading. Don't be surprised, then, if you find exceptions to the guidelines in this chapter.

semicolon

The semicolon, one of the most misunderstood marks of punctuation, has two primary purposes: separating independent clauses in compound sentences or separating items in a long and grammatically complex list. In both instances, it is a weighty mark that identifies boundaries between major grammatical structures.

Separating Independent Clauses with Semicolons

When you join two (or sometimes more) independent clauses to create a compound sentence and you aren't using any coordinators (conjunctions like *and, or, for, but, nor*), you may use a semicolon. In this case, make sure that you have a complete pattern on both sides of the semicolon, which acts like a fulcrum for the sentence, balancing grammatically equal halves. Here are some examples:

   a.   And meanwhile the dust piled up in corners; the refrigerator
            wheezed and creaked for want of defrosting. —Anne Tyler

Tyler's sentence has two patterns: *dust piled up* (S-V) and *refrigerator wheezed and creaked* (another S-V). No coordinator separates the patterns, so the semicolon is necessary to keep these strong, but related, grammatical elements separate. Did you see the phrasal verb (*piled up*)? And the gerund as object of the preposition (*defrosting*)?

   b.   I can work outside all day, breaking ice to get water for washing;
            I can eat pork liver cooked over the open fire minutes after it
            comes steaming from the hog. —Alice Walker

The first pattern is S-V (*I can work*), and the second one is S-V-O (*I can eat liver*). The semicolon separates them. Note how closely related they are;

both independent clauses testify to the speaker's endurance and toughness. Did you observe the anaphora in the repeated *I can* phrase? And the participial phrase that contains within it an infinitive phrase whose object is a gerund: *breaking ice to get water for washing*? The second pattern has an adverbial clause, *after it comes steaming from the hog*. This is a very rich sentence.

    c.   It smelled of harsh antiseptic; it smelled too clean and hard and metallic. —Ray Bradbury

This sentence also has two complete patterns, thus two independent clauses. *It smelled* is an S-V pattern, where *smell* functions as an intransitive verb (there is no complement or completer, nor is one needed). *It smelled clean and hard and metallic* is an S-LV-PA sentence where *clean*, *hard*, and *metallic* are adjectives describing *it* and *its* smell. The semicolon separates the two patterns and makes the sentence easier to read. Did you notice the anaphora again, the repetition of *smell*? And did you also observe how all the adjectives are themselves filled with hard consonants (*k, d, t* sounds) and dry, hard vowels, particularly the *e* sounds? In this instance, sound definitely echoes sense.

    a.   By most standards of literary worth, DeLillo's jewel-like distillation of a novel is very fine; Rayner's overheated melodrama is rather bad. —Mark Levine

After the introductory *by* phrase, these independent clauses are parallel and antithetical. The first clause

    DeLillo's jewel-like distillation of a novel is very fine

closely matches the grammatical form of

    Rayner's overheated melodrama is rather bad.

The ideas, however, are antithetical; Levine likes DeLillo's book but not Rayner's.

    b.   We wake and find ourselves on a stair; there are stairs below us, which we seem to have ascended; there are stairs above us, many a one, which go upward and out of sight.
        —Ralph Waldo Emerson

This sentence has three independent clauses, separated by semicolons. Notice that each successive clause is longer and more grammatically complicated than the one before it. Did you notice the repetition of *stairs*? What is the effect of the repetition?

Separating Items in a Complex List

Readers can easily get tripped up in long and complicated sentences. That's why we have punctuation: to help them find their ways in and to help them interpret the text. In sentences with grammatically complex lists, especially lists where there is internal punctuation, semicolons can help you keep items separate. Notice how the semicolon works in the following sentences:

    a.   During those years I was picking coffee on the wet highlands of Venezuela on hills so steep your shoulders almost touched the hillside; staying up all night reciting Pablo Neruda in Syria; going to Catholic christenings, Jewish weddings, and Moslem funerals; looking into the faces of The Disappeared on the Plaza de Mayo in Argentina and seeing the tiny portraits of disappeared children; standing on the steps of a mosque in Beirut and staring at the hands of the old women holding tiny photographs of their sons disappeared in the war; feeling the rasp of stone from a hundred monuments commemorating valor and sacrifice in the service of one's country; standing over an acre of freshly turned earth mixed with common garbage where civilian bodies are buried. —Harry Mattison

This rich catalog is a complex list of images, each of which is kept separate by virtue of the semicolon barrier.

    b.   Three tribes dominate: the Jola, from the country's southwest; the Fula, from the east; and the Serer, from the north, whose fierce and sinewy athleticism makes them the most popular and storied of competitors. —Anonymous, "Anybody Want Some of This?"

Besides the use of the semicolons to separate the listing of three Gambian tribes, notice also the parallelism of the items listed and how the sentence is cumulative, that is, how it builds with the longest cluster describing the most famous tribe of wrestlers at the end or at a position of great emphasis.

    c.   It takes two hours to get them undressed; two more hours for bathtub, bath tantrums, and bath mop-up; an hour to get them into their Dr. Denton's; and three hours of reading The House at Pooh Corner to put them to sleep. —P.J. O'Rourke

O'Rourke is writing about the time required to get his two toddler daughters to bed. Of course, he's exaggerating quite a bit, but notice how he repeats the key words *bath* and *hours* to reinforce how long he and his wife spend on their daughters' baths. And note how the semicolons keep the different aspects of bath time separate so that you, the reader, can keep them straight.

    d.   Before establishing the frame design, consider the information you must include: the title of the presentation, of course; perhaps a subtitle; the speaker's name, title, and affiliation; the company name and corporate logo; the name of the organization or meeting and the date; and funding agencies or other attributions. —Margaret Rabb

The items in this straightforward list describe the basic element of the frame design. Each element is composed of more than one aspect or component, thus requiring internal punctuation of commas. The semicolons are necessary for keeping the items straight in the reader's mind.

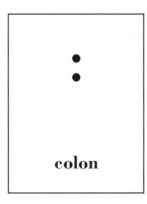

colon

The colon is much like the semicolon, but with even more power. It is more rare and requires more care. The colon is most commonly found in two places. You can find it between two independent clauses that are very closely linked by a cause-effect or call-and-response relationship. You can also find it after an independent clause announcing a word, phrase, or list to come later in the sentence. Here are some examples.

Colon Between Independent Clauses

When you see a colon between two independent clauses, most likely the clauses are extremely closely related. Commonly the first clause sets up the first one or introduces some necessary background or condition for understanding or appreciating the second clause. Sometimes the first clause sets the scene for the second. Often the second clause restates or elucidates the first clause. Here are some examples:

a. First lay aside your black veil: then tell me why you put it on. —Nathaniel Hawthorne

The first clause is the condition for the second: the minister must take off the veil and then explain why he put it on.

b. I have spoken of the learning of Ligeia: it was immense—such as I have never known in woman. —Edgar Allan Poe

In this sentence, the first clause leads us to the revelation in the second clause. The writer uses the whole first independent clause to remind us of the subject and then the whole second independent clause to comment on the subject. This way the idea is weightier than if he had written *The learning of Ligeia was immense.*

c. In every stage of these oppressions we have petitioned for redress in the most humble terms: our repeated petitions have been answered only by repeated injuries. —Thomas Jefferson

In this sentence from *The Declaration of Independence*, the first clause introduces the topic of petitions, which the second clause reiterates with the new information that the petition has been met only with further insults.

    d.   That most of us have found adulthood just as morally ambigu-
         ous as we expected it to be falls perhaps into the category of
         prophecies self-fulfilled: I am simply not sure. —Joan Didion

In this sentence, the long and complex first part of the sentence prepares
us for the punch line after the colon and emphasizes the uncertainty with
which the sentence concludes.

    e.   All of a sudden there was silence: the rain had stopped.
         —Heinrich Boll

The first clause sets the scene for the revelation of the clause beyond the colon.
First the reader "hears" silence; then he realizes that the rain has stopped.

Colon That Introduces

You will also find the colon used as a herald; that is, to announce that
something important or significant is approaching at the end of the sentence. The colon brings the reader nearly to a halt; it is not as full a stop
as a period, but it is close. Thus you can use it to take your reader right
to the brink of something expected, then draw him or her up short and
pop the important idea, word, phrase, or list in right after. You can also
use the colon to introduce a long or extended quotation or a quotation
that you want to make very emphatic. It is important to remember that in
most cases you must have an independent clause or a full and complete
sentence pattern before (or left of) the colon. Look at these sentences for
examples of correct colon use:

    a.   Oh yes, I thought, she was like Paul: cold, beautiful, critical.
         —Lev Raphael

Notice how the colon narrows the reader's attention to those three important words at the conclusion of the sentence.

    b.   A cloudy day: do you know what that is in a town of iron-works?
         —Rebecca Harding Davis

In this sentence the virtual sentence before the colon frames the material after the colon. The reader is meant to think of a town of iron-works in the
context of a cloudy day.

    c.   My brother says: "Thirty years ago, honest to God, I would've been
         with the guys with the bats. In August, I swear to God, I would
         have been with the protestors." —Barbara Grizzuti Harrison

The colon introduces the quotation from the brother. In this context, a colon
is more emphatic than a comma.

    d.   Far away, deep in the tunnel of the past, Anton heard the six shots
         ring: first one, then two, then two more, and finally one last shot.
         —Harry Mulisch

The introductory material prepares the reader for the emphatic hearing of
individual shots in the last half of the sentence. Notice how the many tran-

sitions in the second half of the sentence slow the pace and make each cluster of shots distinct: first there is one; then there are two; then there are two more; and finally there is one more. *First, then, then,* and *finally* effectively underscore the number of shots.

> e.   When Rodrigo Hertas opened his eyes the morning of October 24, he understood in a flash that he had exhausted all of his choices save one: suicide. —Luis Lopez-Nieves

This dramatic use of the colon assembles the whole weight of the sentence to point to one word, one idea, one option for Rodrigo Hertas. The last word is doubly emphatic because of this accumulation.

And don't forget that a colon follows the salutation in a business letter:

Dear Mr. Barney:

Dear Sony Customer:

Honorable Senator Schumer:

**Passages
to
Punctuate:
Internal
Marks**

Copy the following passages, either by hand or by keying them into your computer, then add internal punctuation. Sentences boundaries are already marked with terminal punctuation, but you will need to add commas, semicolons, and colons inside the sentences where they are needed.

From Temple Grandin's *Thinking in Pictures*

> The world of the non-verbal person with autism is chaotic and confusing. A low-functioning adult who is still not toilet-trained may be living in a completely disordered sensory world. It is likely that he has no idea of his body boundaries and that sights sounds and touches are all mixed together. It must be like seeing the world through a kaleidoscope and trying to listen to a radio station that is jammed with static at the same time. Add to that a broken volume control which causes the volume to jump erratically from a loud boom to inaudible. Such a person's problems are further compounded by a nervous system that is often in a greater state of fear and panic than the nervous system of a Kanner-type autistic. Imagine a state of hyper-arousal where you were

being pursued by a dangerous attacker in a world of total chaos. Not surprisingly new environments make low-functioning autistics fearful.

From Alvin D. Hall's *Getting Started with Stocks*

An asset allocation fund is a variation on the balanced fund that invests in stocks bonds and cash equivalents. There are two types of asset allocation funds fixed and flexible. A fixed asset allocation fund maintains a fixed percentage of its assets in each of the three asset classes stocks bonds and cash equivalents. This type is therefore quite similar to a balanced fund except that the fixed percentages differ. A flexible asset allocation fund adjusts the mix of its assets in response to changing market conditions and investment opportunities. This flexibility is this fund's major advantage. The disadvantage however is that its success depends almost entirely upon the fund manager's skill.

From Annie Proulx's *Accordion Crimes*

He came to the funeral home at dusk with men from the Polish Club the good singers. Hieronim soaped and shaved and dressed in a shark-skin suit lay in his walnut case like a polished knife in a silver chest. The singers filed in and stood along the wall. To their left was a small table covered with a white cloth and on it a dish of peppermints and a saucer of cloves. The hymns and the prayers began Hail Marys hymns to the Mother of God to the saints then after an hour the men went out to the parking lot and drank beer and whiskey to intensify their grief while the women said the rosary voices elongating drawing out the ancient words. The men wiled in again with flushed faces belching and hiking at their belts stood once more along the wall.

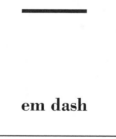

em dash

The em dash—mostly known as just a dash—is emphatic and attention-grabbing. It draws the reader's eye straight to the page and dramatically separates two chunks of text (clause, phrase, word) from one another. It can separate interrupting elements from the main part of the sentence; it can separate examples from generalizations; it can separate a salutation or greeting from the body of a note (but it's breezy, not formal, so be careful). One more thing: when you key in the dash, allow no space between it and the words it butts against.

Take a look at the em dashes in these sentences:

a. It was not desperation—not exactly that—that she heard in this invocation. —Michelle Herman

Notice how the dash interrupts the flow of the sentence to call the reader's attention to the idea that *desperation* is being qualified or clarified.

b. Always the diction is glorious—ready, with only a bit of memorizing, for Shakespeare. —Norma Rosen

This dash separates the generalization (that the diction is glorious) from a specific application of it (it is ready for Shakespeare).

c. He was—it was reduced to this—excited. —Stanley Elkin

In this sentence two dashes separate the interrupter dramatically from the rest of what is a short sentence, emphasizing the idea of his being excited.

d. After the First World War they had stayed in Italy—in Milan as much as necessary, in a house overlooking Lake Varese as much as possible. —Ann Cornelisen

Here the dash separates the assertion (that they had stayed in Italy) and additional detail (in Milan, etc.) to solidify the assertion as if to emphasize where they stayed.

e. And hospitality and generosity—character—were measured by the amount of meat you served your guests. —Barbara Grizzuti Harrison

The dashes in this sentence separate an interrupter that is a definition. Here hospitality and generosity are equated with and defined as character.

f. The world is made up of two classes—the hunters and the hunted. —Richard Connell

In this sentence, Connell uses the dash to separate an idea from the elucidation or development or explanation of that idea. *Hunters and the hunted* explain what the *two classes* are.

hyphen

The hyphen is less weighty than a dash and resides within and between words. Whereas the em dash separates items, the hyphen connects ideas.

Typically, the hyphen connects words too closely related to remain separate words but not intimate enough to become one word: *commander-in-chief*, for instance. After a period of being hyphenated, many hyphenated compounds become one word, as with apple *turn over*, which became apple *turn-over*, which eventually became apple *turnover*. Here are other examples of the use of the hyphen.

a.   The Black newcomer had been recruited on the desiccated farm lands of Georgia and Mississippi by war-plant labor scouts. The chance to live in two- or three-story buildings (which became instant slums), and to earn two- and even three-figured weekly checks, was blinding. —Maya Angelou

Angelou's sentence has many hyphens. Notice in particular the compound determiner-noun hyphenations of *two- and three-story* and *two- and three-figured*: observe that when the hyphenated material is compounded with the same word in the last part of the hyphenation, that last word is not repeated with each iteration. It would be more tiresome for the reader to read *two-story or three-story buildings* than *two- or three-story buildings*.

b.   In a late-summer drizzle, I teeter atop a starting block, my arms swollen as sausages from lactic acid, my head pounding from tension, lack of food, and good old self-loathing. —Jim Thornton

Here *late* is connected to *summer* and qualifies it, and *self* is appended to *loathing*, the object to the verb, to create a complex noun that fits neatly into the prepositional phrase as an object. The hyphenated structure allows the writer to include in a succinct way the idea of self-loathing as one of the causes of the pounding head. A verbal phrase would have made his sentence more cumbersome.

c.   He has ready such a fresh top-of-the-morning salutation as conjures up the spirits of those days. —Henry David Thoreau

Here Thoreau uses the hyphenated words to create a complicated noun adjunct that does, however, pattern smoothly before the noun *salutation*.

d.   The man was game enough, when his blood was up: but he was no favorite in the mill; he had the taint of school-learning on him—not to a dangerous extent, only a quarter or so in the free-school in fact, but enough to ruin him as a good hand in a fight. —Rebecca Harding Davis

Here *school* is attached to *learning* to insinuate that there are other kinds of learning than learning in school, and *free* is attached to *school* to explain the school as a public one in a time when not all schools were public. There are other interesting things about this sentence. Notice the colon that separates two major ideas: that, first, the man was game when he was emotionally ready (when his blood was up); and second, that the man was not a favorite in the mill. The material in the independent clause after the semicolon explains why the man was not popular in the mill: he had had some education. The information after the dash qualifies the extent of his education: he wasn't dangerously educated, but he was spoiled for fighting.

> **e.** This drew rueful laughter from the crowd, which was made up of family-law types and members of the Trollope society. —Rebecca Mead

Family and *law* are hyphenated to describe the kind of law being referred to.

apostrophe

An apostrophe is the sign of something missing; where you see an apostrophe, some part of a word has been omitted. Apostrophes appear in contractions—to indicate that part of a word has been left out—*we're too tired*. The apostrophe also indicates possessive nouns and pronouns—*the boy's coat*. And you'll often find it when writers are writing dialect or approximating speech; they typically spell the word phonetically to indicate how it sounds and use apostrophes to indicate omitted letters. The apostrophe is also used in pairs to indicate quoted material within a quotation. Here are some examples of apostrophes.

> **a.** "She had taken the orientation lecture seriously since the one on God. It has been given by a tiny, handsome Scot, a Presbyterian padre who had begun by saying, 'I'm no' here to talk about games, I'm here to talk about God.'" —Mary Lee Settle

The first apostrophe is part of the contraction of *I* and *am*: *I'm*. The second apostrophe—*no'*—indicates the omitted letter *t* in *not*. This is a representation of a speech dialect; the author is approximating sounds of conversation. And finally, the quotation within the quotation (what the Presbyterian padre actually says) is framed by single quotation marks.

> **b.** "Looka here, Gracie. You don't tell Leandro 'bout this."
> "How come?"
> "He don't like that boy coming 'round here."
> "That's why?"
> "Yeah." —Norton Girault

This excerpt illustrates the popularity of the apostrophe in speech. Two words, *'bout* and *'round*, have apostrophes to indicate omitted *a*'s. The apostrophe in *Don't* signifies an omitted letter *o* from the original *do not*. The style of this conversation is very colloquial.

    c.   She said, "In the retail reality world, it all boils down to one question: 'Did you sell it?' We still don't know." —James Collins

Don't has an apostrophe to signify the missing *o* in *do not*. This signals informal diction.

    d.   The low, serious drugstore voices that accompanied the Park View's weekly decorum were swept away by revolving, laughing crowds—carnival crowds. —Cynthia Ozick

The apostrophe in *Park View's* signals possession. This structure is a nod toward informality even as the sentence refers to the sweeping away of decorum.

    e.   Here's what they don't tell you about Prozac. —Lauren Slater

The apostrophe in *Here's* indicates an omitted *i* in *Here is*. This is also the mark of an informal utterance.

’’

**quotation
marks**

Quotation marks, which come in pairs, embrace a speaker's exact words. They can also be used for emphasis, in effect to underscore a particular word and draw the reader's eye to it. Quotation marks also identify titles of poems, short stories, songs, essays, articles, and brief musical numbers or programs.

    a.   From Herman Melville's "Benito Cereno" here is an example of a conversation between the ship's captain, Captain Delano, and a sailor, Don Benito. Notice how the quotation marks enclose each speaker's exact words and how the combination of either a new line or a new paragraph means a new set of quotation marks and indicates that another speaker has taken the floor:

> Glancing towards the hammock as he entered, Captain Delano said, "You sleep here, Don Benito?"
> "Yes, Senor, since we got into mild weather."
> "This seems a sort of dormitory, sitting-room, sail-loft, chapel, armory, and private close all together. Don Benito," added Captain Delano, looking round.
> "Yes, Senor; events have not been favorable to much order in my arrangements."

b. And here's another conversation, from Vivian Gornick's "Fierce Attachments." Note that the commas remain within the quotation marks and that other end punctuation marks (question marks, exclamation points) are, in this case, also within the quotation marks. These terminal marks are within the quotation marks because they pattern with the quoted material itself, not with the sentence as a whole or with its metalanguage (its language about language)—as in *she says* or *I say*:

> "Can you believe this?" she says. "A nice Jewish boy shaves his head and babbles in the street. A world full of crazies. Divorce everywhere, and if not divorce, this. What a generation you all are!"
> "Don't start, Ma," I say. I don't want to hear that bullshit again.
> "Bullshit here, bullshit there," she says, "it's still true. Whatever else we did, we didn't fall apart in the streets like you're doing. We had order, quiet, dignity. Families stayed together, and people lived decent lives."

c. In the next example, the quotation marks suggest the way that the phrase *side effects* might be read: with an exaggerated irony. The quotation marks call specific attention to the words they enclose.

> For seven years I lived with a hand tremor, diarrhea, the possibility of kidney damage and all the other "side effects" of lithium.
> —Kate Millett

d. How do the quotation marks tell you to read *slave name* in the sentence that follows?

> Bingham met Ali thirty-five years ago in Los Angeles shortly after the fighter had turned professional and before he had discarded his "slave name" (Cassius Marcellus Clay) and joined the Black Muslims.
> —Gay Talese

e. Finally, explain how Joy Williams uses the quotation marks in this sentence:

> While legions of other biological life forms go extinct (or, in the creepy phrase of ecologists, "wink out"), human life bustles self-importantly on.

parentheses

Parentheses set words, phrases, ideas aside: they cradle them. They often suggest the conspiratorial message, whispered behind the cupped hand. They are an effective vehicle for conveying surprise, disdain, amusement, or confusion. Use them to include definitions, afterthoughts, extra information. Here are some examples:

a. The girls could not get telephone calls (calls from our families went through Miss Preston, our principal), so it must have been in one of those letters that he told me when and where to meet him. —Mary McCarthy

Notice that in this compound-complex sentence, the parenthetical material patterns within the first pattern. Therefore, the comma separating the patterns goes properly after the parens.

b. I didn't go to school, nor had my sister (nine years older) done so except briefly, another thing which set our household apart from others. —Denise Levertov

In this sentence the parenthetical material explains how old the sister was, thus presents information that the reader can use to make more sense of the sentence.

c. About half the students were Southerners from Louisiana and Arkansas and Mississippi, as well as the farm country of east Texas (with a few city girls from Houston and Dallas mixed in), but the rest were Texans from the high plains, and they were noticeably different from the rest of us. —Shirley Abbott

The parenthetical material in this sentence provides additional, more specific information about the students.

d. A compromise was reached by sending a kit of parts to the frontline units so that an extra cannon (20-mm MG151) could be bolted under each wing. —Len Deighton

Definition and explanation are the purposes of this parenthetical material, which is more specific than the noun in the text—*extra cannon.*

    e.   I am at once repulsed and fascinated by the bullet, which remains lodged in his spine (having done all the damage it can do, the doctors say). —Debra Dickerson

The parenthetical information in this sentence provides the reader a tidbit of information about the bullet. In this sentence it presents a gossipy effect because of the tag, *the doctors say.*

brackets

You will use brackets rarely. They enclose editorial remarks or comments inserted into quoted text; sometimes the editor comments on the text, and sometimes the reader inserts something that the author may have omitted. They are also used for stage directions. And if you need to use parentheses within parentheses, you should make the internal set brackets rather than use a double set of parens so as not to confuse the reader with double parentheses. Here are some examples of sentences with bracketed information. Explain why you believe the editor put the information in brackets.

    a.   Thus it pleased God to vanquish their enemies and give them deliverance; and by His special providence so to dispose that not any one of them were either hurt or hit, though their arrows came close by them and on every side [of] them; and sundry of their coats, which hung up in the barricado, were shot through and through. —William Bradford

The editor added the *of* to facilitate reading; it had probably been inadvertently omitted in the original version.

    b.   In surveying various responses to plagues in the Middle Ages, Barbara W. Tuchman writes, "Medical thinking [. . .] stressed air as the communicator of disease, ignoring sanitation or visible carriers." —Joseph Gibaldi

Here the brackets enclose an indication of ellipsis and tell the reader that part of the sentence was omitted.

    c.   Graphic artists, multimedia professionals, desktop publishers, and many others use paint software and image editing software to create and modify graphics such as those used in DTP documents and Web pages [Figure 3–29]. —Shelly/Cashman/Gunter

In this sentence, the bracketed material directs the reader to a figure accompanying the text.

d. Sharing everything with everyone [was] very difficult because I am a very private person. —Prince William, describing living conditions on a community-service mission

In this example, the writer changed the tense of the verb, most like originally *is*, in the original quotation so that it would fit with the rest of the article, which was written in past tense.

slash/virgule

The slash or virgule extends from one side to another and is both vertical as well as horizontal. Its character is equally indecisive. Use the slash to separate a series of words indicating choices for the reader, to point out where a line of poetry ends when you quote it, and to substitute for the word *per* as in miles/gallon. The slash also indicates ratios. And you will find it separating elements of Web addresses. Regardless of where it appears, its purpose is to break up text so that readers can understand it more clearly. Here are some examples of the slash in use:

a. We have, however, had some real success with cognitive/behavioral treatments. —Lauren Slater

In this sentence the slash separates *cognitive* and *behavioral*, which both modify *treatments*. Slater could have written *cognitive and behavioral treatments*, but the slash suggests a simultaneity that the *and* does not: that the treatments are at once, immediately, both cognitive and behavioral.

b. But I, for one, can think of a million and one uses for the new hatchback Mini and its folding 50/50 rear seats, against only about 395,000 for the Z3. —Jamie Kitman

Here the virgule separates 50 and 50, to indicate that the rear seat is split and that each half folds.

c. TheNewQ.com/RearViewMonitor—Infiniti advertisement

The slash divides the name of the feature from its description and makes it possible for the reader to perceive almost instantly what TheNewQ.com actually is.

  d. For a free action kit on how to end discrimination in the work-place, go to http://www.aclu.org/gayrights.

Here the slash divides one link—gayrights—from the main Web page—www.aclu.org (doubtlessly on the ACLU's server). You will also see slashes in the entire Web address, separating the *http*: section from the section denoting the server. The entire Web address for the gayrights site would be http://www.aclu.org/gayrights.

  e. To get information on events that happened on a specific day, go to the This Day in History Web site at http://www.historychannel.com/thisday/.

The slashes divide sections of the Internet address and make it easy to readers to identify segments, thus easier to key in or even to remember them.

  f. In a large bowl, toss lettuce, arugula, mint, papaya and/or mango, and green onions with the balsamic vinegar/olive oil dressing.

The slash between *and* and *or* is common, suggesting that the writer finds either coordinator appropriate and the reader may choose. In other words, you may add papaya and mango. Or you may add either papaya or mango: it doesn't matter. The slash between balsamic vinegar and olive oil suggests that both ingredients are combined in the dressing.

  g. This conflict was sometimes overshadowed by the antagonisms of friends and family at home, a situation which understandably gave the soldier poets pause. "Oh hell, he thought," writes Sassoon in "Remorse": "There are things in war one dare not tell / Poor father sitting safe at home who reads / Of dying heroes and their deathless deeds." —anonymous student

Here the slashes mark the lines of poetry. Also notice that the name of the poem is in quotation marks and that the colon introducing the quoted lines goes outside the quotation marks.

**Passages
to
Punctuate**

Copy each of the following passages and add both internal and external punctuation. Some capitalization may be provided to assist you, but you will have to supply some capitals as well as all other punctuation. You will find that there will be several interpretations of how these passages may be punctuated.

From Donald McCabe's "Cheating: Why Students Do It and How We Can Help Them Stop"

Students find teachers' failings real or supposed useful in justifying cheating the relevance and fairness of assessments are issues students often raise the question here is not the difficulty of the tests or the course material Everyone has heard students talk with pride about courses they have taken where despite the difficulty of the course they simply would not cheat however students speak angrily about teachers who give tests that cover material not discussed in class or highlighted in homework assignments and they may find it relatively easy to justify cheating in such cases Whatever the truth in individual student complaints there is no question that cheating can be used to express disrespect for a teacher and defiance of the teacher s authority

From Dr. Race Foster's "Checklist for Visits to Your Veterinarian"

Make sure to ask what the prognosis outcome is is it curable will it come back or can you prevent it e g pancreatitis from too much people food

Is there a special diet your pet has to follow can you get it at any pet store make it at home like a rice ground beef mixture or is it only available at your veterinarians

Is this disease or injury common to your pets breed or size

From Diane Ackerman's *A Natural History of the Senses*

The other senses may be enjoyed in all their beauty when one is alone, but taste is largely social humans rarely choose to dine in solitude and food has a powerful social component the Bantu feel that exchanging food makes a contract between two people who then have a clanship of porridge we usually eat with our families so its easy to see how breaking bread together would symbolically link an outsider to a family group throughout the world the stratagems of business take place over meals weddings end with a feast friends reunite at celebratory dinners children herald their birthdays with ice cream and cake religious ceremonies offer food in fear, homage, and sacrifice wayfarers are welcomed with a meal as Brillat-Savarin says every sociability can be found assembled around the same table love friendship business speculation power importunity patronage ambition intrigue if any event is meant to matter emotionally symbolically or mystically food will be close at hand to sanctify and bind it

Glossary

A

absolute negatives: one of these negative words: *not, no, none,* or *never*. Any absolute negative effects a negative transformation of a declarative sentence: *Jane never smiles at the parrot.*

adjective: a form class most closely related to nouns and clustering with nouns. The function of adjectives is to describe and to limit, to tell us more about nouns. An adjective will fit in the test sentence: A(n) _____ something is something that is _____. Examples are *old, first, weird, sane, joyous.*

adjective clause: a dependent clause that functions as an adjective and clusters around or modifies a noun. Adjective clauses are frequently introduced by subordinators like *who, whom, which,* and *that* and are sometimes called relative clauses. Here is a sentence with an adjective clause: *We moved the car* **that had been wrecked.**

adverb: one of the form classes. Adverbs pattern with verbs to tell how, why, when, or where. A typical adverbial suffix is *–ly*; typical adverbs are *clearly, loudly, sadly.* Adverbs may be single words; in addition, adverbial phrases can explain how, why, when, or where: *in the doorway, around the corner, above the ledge.* One distinguishing feature of adverbs is their movability; they may pattern at the beginning, middle, or end of a phrase or clause.

adverb clause: a dependent clause that functions as an adverb. Adverb clauses cluster around verbs and explain *where, how,* or *when.* They are frequently introduced by words like *if, when, although,* and *because.* An example of a sentence with an adverb clause is **When the rain stops,** *we will leave the building.*

adverbial noun: a noun acting adverbially to explain how, why, when, or where: today, yesterday, home: *Today* we went *home.*

agent: a cognate of the Latin verb *ago, agere,* which means *to do.* In a sentence, an agent is a do-er, someone who does something, who acts. The subject is frequently, but not always, an agent. Here is a sentence with an agent as subject: *The African* **bees** *swarmed noisily and dove viciously at the dark canvas target.* The bees are agents, performing an action.

alliteration: the repetition of initial consonant sounds—that is, consonant sounds occurring at the beginning of adjacent words or words that are next to one another: *the* **b**ig **b**rown **b**ear **b**alanced on the **b**lue **b**all is an exaggerated example of alliteration. Example: *The tide shoves and sucks through the islands and makes the current curl in odd patterns.*

anadiplosis: a repetition scheme where a word or group of words is repeated at the *end* of one clause or sentence and then subsequently at the *beginning* of the next clause or sentence. Example: *If David has had Uriah killed with the sword, the sword will rampage among his sons.*

anaphora: a repetition scheme where a word or group of words occurs at the beginning or front of successive clauses or phrases, that is, phrases or clauses that come one right after the other. Example: *The reason why I object to Dr. Johnson's style is that there is no discrimination, no selection, no variety in it.*

anastrophe: the inversion of the usual or natural word order. Example: *From America letters came.*

antimetabole: a scheme of balance involving two repeated series. A phrase at the beginning of a passage (usually a sentence) is repeated at the end of the passage—but with its elements reversed. Example: *In fact, Daniel suggests that ideas do not make history but history makes ideas.*

antithesis: the placing of contrasting ideas within physical proximity. Example: *United there is little we cannot do in a host of cooperative ventures. Divided, there is little we can do.*

apposition: a relationship that occurs when you place two coordinate nouns (that is, two elements that are grammatically equal) side by side. Typically, the second element (called the **appositive**) then explains or limits the first. Example: *Meet the first in-dash personal assistant, the Clarion AutoPC.*

appositives: nouns patterning with and renaming other nouns. Generally, appositives are **in apposition with** the nouns they relate to—this means that they are literally in position with their nouns, side by side. Here is an example of a sentence with an appositive: *My friend, the championship wrestler, weighs 200 pounds.*

assonance: the repetition of similar vowel sounds in words that are next to or near one another. Although we think of assonance as a device used primarily in poetry, a prose writer may also use assonance to knit sentences together by repeating sounds. Example: *Susskind glanced down at his shabby, baggy knickers.*

asyndeton: a scheme of omission: conjunctions are left out between a series of related words, clauses, or phrases. Example: *Adults have about 10,000 taste buds, grouped by theme (salt, sour, sweet, bitter), at various sites in the mouth.*

auxiliary verb: also known as a **helping verb**. Auxiliary verbs pattern with forms of the main verb to create the perfect (*have grown*) and progressive tenses (*is growing*), the passive voice (*was grown*), and conditionality (*may grow*).

B

base form: the verb form without any endings. The base form is the same as the present tense form for all verbs except *be*. Also called the *infinitive*.

C

casual style: a style marked by informality and an absence of background information. The writer assumes that the reader/listener does not need background and takes public knowledge and information for granted. Two defining features of casual style are ellipsis (omission of words and phrases) and slang (in the strictest sense, a widely current or popular but short-lived expression).

clause: a group of words that contains a sentence pattern, which is a subject and a finite verb. Some clauses are complete sentences, and some are not.

cleft sentence: a sentence that is cut in two, then rearranged with expletives to create emphasis: *Jane bathed Puff* becomes *It was Jane who bathed Puff*. Expletives are place-holding words; they have little meaning, and typically they have no function in a sentence other than to fill a spot so that you can shift the placement of other words. Typical expletives are *it, what, there, here*.

combination sentence: a compound-complex sentence, a sentence containing at least two independent clauses and at least one dependent clause. Also called a **compound-complex sentence**.

comma splice: using a comma to join two independent clauses. This comma is too weak to hold apart the substantial weight of two independent clauses and should be replaced with a semicolon or with the combination of a comma plus coordinator. For instance, the sentence with a comma splice *We saw the woodchucks on the dormitory lawn they were having a party*, should correctly be punctuated *We saw the woodchucks on the dormitory lawn; they were having a party*.

comparative form: a form of adjective or adverb used when you compare two items. When you compare two things, conditions, or states, use the *-er* degree or the word *more* (with most words of more than two syllables). Examples: *This car is slower than a turtle* and *We drove more slowly going home*.

complement: a verb completer. These structures complete the action of the verb, making it sound finished and finite: direct objects, indirect object, predicate nouns, predicate adjectives.

complex sentence: a sentence with one main or base clause (an independent clause) plus one or more dependent or subordinate clauses. Complex sentences express explicit and usually unequal relationships between two or more clauses or patterns. One clause clearly expresses the dominant or main idea, and the other clause or clauses express related but subsidiary ideas or relationships.

compound elements: more than one word occupying a particular slot in a sentence. In this sentence, there are compound subjects: **Nathan** *and* **Emily** *did the homework*. Both subjects pattern with the verb equally. The deep structure of this sentence is two sentences: *Nathan did the homework* and *Emily did the homework*.

compound-complex sentence: a sentence that is at once compound *and* complex. That is, it has at least two independent clauses (like a compound sentence) and at least one dependent clause (like a complex sentence). Also called a **combination sentence**.

compound sentence: a sentence composed of two or more independent clauses. All the clauses must be independent; that is, each clause within the compound sentence can be removed and exist as a sentence all by itself.

conditional verbs: verbs that indicate possibility, wish, or a condition contrary to fact: *may, might, can, could, will, would,* and when it is paired with *if, be.* These sentences have conditional verbs: *We will go if we get tickets, She might want to buy a car, Dad could finish the project tonight.*

conjugation: the recitation of all the parts of a verb through all its tenses and aspects. A conjugation indicates forms appropriate with singular and plural subjects and with first, second, and third person pronouns or nouns. It also indicates the simple tenses, the perfect tenses (or aspect), the progressive tenses; it also demonstrates forms for active or passive voice.

conjunctive adverb: an adverb used as a conjunction, most frequently paired with a semicolon and found in compound sentences. Common conjunctive adverbs are *therefore, moreover, however, henceforth, consequently, nevertheless.* Using conjunctive adverbs slows the pace of your prose and makes it sound more serious.

consultative style: a style marked by the explicit giving of information, background, and explanation. Someone writing consultative style does not assume that she or he will be understood automatically and as a result offers context and definition of what might not be clearly comprehended. Indeed, consultative style presents information as fast as it is needed and sometimes anticipates the need for it.

coordinate adjectives: two paired adjectives coming most typically after a noun, as in Wordsworth's line, "'Tis a beauteous evening, calm and free."

coordinator or **coordinating conjunction**:   a conjunction that joins two equal grammatical structures, like two subjects, two verbs, two direct objects, two predicate adjectives, two objects of prepositions. A coordinator acts like the equal sign in an equation, mediating the two sides that must balance. The coordinators are *and, but, or, not, so, for.*

correlative conjunction: conjunctions that come in pairs, two coordinators that *correlate* or *relate with* one another: *either* and *or; neither* and *nor; both* and *and; not only* and *but also.* Correlative coordinators join compound elements.

D

dependent clause: a clause that is a complete pattern with a finite verb but that does not sound quite right or complete enough to be a sentence. Also called a **subordinate clause**. Example: *because we ate too much peanut butter.*

determiner: a structure word preceding and signaling a noun. This class of words limits the range of a noun and helps the reader determine the nature of the noun. Determiners help to *determine* or specify nouns. Common determiners include *a, an, the; this, that, these, those; his, her, my, our, their; much, many, most; first, second, third,* etc.

diction: word choice. Speakers and writers choose a level of diction appropriate to the formality or informality of their purposes and aims for writing.

direct object: a noun that follows the verb and completes its meaning by answering the question *Whom?* or *What?* Example: *Izzy* (subject) *recited* (verb) a *slam poem* (direct object).

E

ellipsis: deliberate omission of a word or a cluster of words. Example: *His eye was open to beauty, and his ear to music.* The phrase *was open to* is ellipted in the second independent clause.

emphatic transformation: transforming a sentence pattern to shift emphasis. Emphasis can be shifted by changing word order, changing the verb to passive, using an expletive or cleft structure, or by formatting.

epanalepsis: a repetition scheme where a word or group of words from the beginning of a clause or sentence is repeated at the end of that same clause, sentence, or sometimes passage. Example: *That a famous library has been cursed by a woman is a matter of complete indifference to a famous library.*

epistrophe: a repetition scheme where a word or group of words occurs at the end of successive clauses or phrases. Example: *The lobbyists don't like you. The voters don't like you. The majority doesn't like you.*

essential clause: an adjective clause necessary for the clear understanding of the noun with which it patterns; also known as a restrictive clause. Example: *We read the book **that the teacher assigned.***

exclamatory transformation: a transformation that enables the speaker or writer to express surprise, extreme pleasure, or emotion. The exclamatory transformation is punctuated with an exclamation mark, as in *What big teeth you have, Grandma!*

expletive: a word like *there, here,* or *it* that fills a space without contributing any meaning. Expletives are placeholders: they take up space that other words might occupy—and they give the writer a chance to delay using a word, perhaps to gain greater impact by using it later in the sentence: *There is Jamal's car.*

extraction: a situation where the listener or reader extracts some pattern or meaning from a casual sentence spoken by someone very close to him or her. What the speaker says may not be intelligible to anyone else except the person with whom he or she is intimate. Extraction means deriving some meaning from an expression or utterance that appears to have no relationship at all to ordinary words.

F

figure of speech: a generic term for any artful deviation from the ordinary mode of speaking and writing; a construction that uses balance, repetition, unusual devices of sound, or unusual word orders to enhance plain diction or to create appropriate emphasis.

finite verb: a verb that is complete, that has all parts of a tense structure. Example: *placed* or *will have been going*.

first person: refers to the person speaking, *I* or *we*.

form classes: major sentence building blocks that carry most of the meaning of the sentence. The form classes are *noun, verb, adjective*, and *adverb*. Together, form classes and structure words constitute the English vocabulary.

formal style: a style that informs and maintains a distance between the writer/speaker and the reader/hearer (the opposite of intimate style). The speaker or writer typically absents her- or himself from the text itself (no first person, usually) and depends on a strict form or shape, logical links among ideas, and explicitness. Formal text, characterized by detachment and cohesion, inserts background information in depth and with ordered precision; it assumes a captive, nonresponsive audience. It refrains from using ellipsis and contractions. Its sentences tend to be long and complex. It is usually characterized by third person and frequently by words of many syllables derived from Latin.

free modifiers: modifiers and modifying phrases that affix themselves not to any particular word but to the concept expressed in the sentence; also known as sentence modifiers. Example: **Tires deflated, frame bent**, *the bike rested against the wall*.

functional labels: labels that describe the *function* or *job* of each sentence component rather than its appearance or form. *Direct object* is a functional label whereas *noun* is a descriptive label.

G

gerund: a verbal that always ends in the *-ing* suffix: *eating, sleeping, reading, thinking*. Gerunds function as nouns only.

get passive: a passive transformation where *get* substitutes for *be*: Example: *The new wallpaper got shredded by Janie's cat*.

give verbs: a rather small class of verbs like *give* that appear in the indirect object pattern.

grammar: a system of thought that describes what a language does and explains how it works.

H

headword: the word at the head or center of the cluster; the word that the other words and phrases cluster around.

I

incremental anaphora: a repetition pattern where the repeated words or phrases at the beginning of a phrase or clause change ever so slightly or incrementally with each repetition. Example: *She liked the new shoes, the new blue shoes, the new blue patent shoes.*

independent clause: a subject-verb pattern that can stand on its own as a sentence. Example: *The bean plants blossomed overnight.*

indicative mode: the mode of statements, the most common mode. Example: *We washed the dishes.* You can remember the term because *indica*tive mode *indicates* or points something out or makes a comment.

indirect object: elements intervening between the verb and direct object. Indirect objects receive the indirect action of the verb. They answer the question *To whom was something done or given?* or *For whom was something done or given?*

infinitive: a verbal consisting of *to* plus a base verb: *to eat, to sleep, to read, to think.* Infinitives may function as nouns, adjectives, or adverbs and may have their own clusters.

intensifier: one of the classes of function words that pattern with adverbs or adjectives (and sometimes verbs) to intensify their meanings, as in words that pattern like *very*: *quite, hardly, barely, scarcely.*

internal punctuation marks: punctuation marks used within sentences (commas, semicolons, colons, dashes).

interrogative question transformation: a question transformation that uses interrogative words and phrases like *who, where, what, when, why, how,* and *how much.* This kind of question demands answers of more content and substance than do yes/no questions. Example: *Where were you at 8 p.m. on Sunday, July 23?*

intimate style: a level or register of style used between people who know one another extremely well—good friends, family, very close colleagues. Intimate style is characterized by extraction and jargon.

intransitive verb: a verb with no complement whatsoever, no object or predicate complement; also called an **intransive complete** verb because it is complete in itself. Example: *The sun shone brightly.*

introductory clause: a dependent adverb clause that introduces a sentence. This clause is set off from the rest of the sentence with a comma: *When she was good, she was very, very good.*

inversion: a grammatical situation that occurs when major sentence elements, especially the subject and verb or complement and verb, are reversed, thus shifting the emphasis of the sentence. Example: *Afraid we were, certainly.*

imperative mode: the mood or mode of command. In imperative mode, the subject is often omitted: *Clean up that kitchen! Wait! Don't do that. Show me.*

J, K

jargon: certain words or expressions used among people in close or intimate relationships, often professional relationships where a special language set describes the profession or job environment. Jargon acts as a kind of shorthand to refer to a vast set of experiences.

L

linking verbs: verbs that join or link the subject to the complement. The most common linking verbs are *am, is, are, was, be, being, been, looks, tastes, sounds, smells, feels, seem, appear, become, grow, remain.* Example: *The commercials were stupid.*

M

metalanguage: language about language, the language we use to describe language and to talk about grammar. This book is an example of metalanguage because it contains language written about language.

modal verb: verb forms that express conditions applying to main verbs. Modals are never used as main verbs, only as auxiliaries (except in some sentences where the verb is implied). Modals can help the main verb express these conditions: possibility (*can, could*); probability (*may, might*); obligation (*shall, should*); necessity (*must, have to*); anticipation (*will, would*).

multifunction word: a word that can have different grammatical functions depending on its place or task in the sentence. *Turn*, for instance, can be either a noun (*he took a wrong turn*) or a verb (*he turned down the wrong road*).

N

n-group: noun group or another term for noun cluster, a noun plus its immediate modifiers.

negative transformation: a transformation effected by adding *no, not, never,* or another negative word to a sentence or utterance. The purpose of the negative transformation is to negate, deny, correct, or clarify an incorrect or previously held impression. It is also used to counteract what is said or heard or expected, to call into question someone else's positive or affirming statement.

neologism: new word formations (*neo* = new and *logos* = word) like *computerize*.

nominative absolute: a noun-headed phrase that conveys the notion of a sentence absolutely—yet without a finite verb. A nominative absolute evokes the absolute essence of a sentence and looks like a sentence except that it doesn't have a finite verb. It has a subject or a noun (or nominative) at its head. Example: *Head held high, Therese strolled calmly out of the room.*

nonessential or **nonrestrictive clause**: an adjective clause or a subject-verb pattern that modifies a noun and whose information is not required for an understanding of the noun it modifies. Nonessential or nonrestrictive adjective clauses are set off with commas. Example: *Julia Child's new cookbook,* **which has earned rave reviews**, *is sitting on the cabinet.*

nonfinite verb: a verb not complete enough to constitute the entire main (or finite) verb in a sentence. A nonfinite verb is typically a participle missing an auxiliary verb. Example: *going to the store.*

nonrestrictive clause: another name for nonessential clause, an adjective clause whose information is not necessary for identifying the noun it modifies. Example: *The French teacher,* **who spent three years in Paris**, *had a marvelous accent.*

noun: a naming word, one used to label objects, people, and ideas. Examples: *pencil, glass, honesty, friend.*

noun adjunct: a noun functioning in an adjunct position to other nouns (or alongside them in a supporting role). Noun adjuncts function only **before** the noun, not in post-noun or post-verb positions as complements. For instance, we can say *The patient has a* **skin** *disease* but not *The patient has a disease* **skin** or *The disease is* **skin**. Other examples are *attention span; computer expert; snow storm, grocery list.*

noun clause: a subject-verb pattern that functions as a noun. Noun clauses may assume any noun's position in a sentence and may function as subject, object, or complement. Example: **What you left behind** *was valuable.*

noun cluster: a noun plus its attendants, the words and phrases and clauses that pattern with it, modify it, or describe it; also called an n-group. Example: *the gold* **earrings** *with the pearl insets.*

number: whether a noun or verb is singular or plural; literally, whether the word refers to one item or to more than one item. *Friend* is singular in number; *friends* is plural in number.

O

objective complement: a noun or adjective that completes the direct object, as is *Queen of the May* in the sentence *We chose Hermione Queen of the May.* The direct object and the objective complement have the same referent.

onomatopoeia: a figurative strategy where the sound of words echoes their sense or meaning. Its effect is therefore to create an immediacy, an intimacy, between the reader and the text. Example: *The raindrops plopped and blobbed on the window sill, pooling in a shimmering circle of water.*

P

p-group: another name for a prepositional phrase or a preposition plus its noun object.

parallelism: a rhetorical strategy where pairs or series of related words, phrases, or clauses have very grammatically similar structures. The sentence

We took photos of elephants, giraffes, and cats has parallel direct objects; all are plural nouns without adjectives or prepositional phrases.

parenthesis: a figurative structure that occurs when a cluster of words interrupts the normal word order of a sentence. The text within the parentheses is called *parenthetical matter*. Example: *The Park View Pharmacy—the drugstore my parents bought—stood on Colonial Avenue between Continental and Burr.*

participle: the verb form that patterns with the perfect aspect (past participle like *walked* or *eaten*) or with the progressive tense (present participle like *walking* or *eating*).

particle: a preposition that follows a verb and subtly affects the meaning of the verb. If a particle patterns with a noun, we consider it a preposition. Example of a particle: *up, out, down* as in *turn up, turn out, turn down.*

parts of speech: a term associated with traditional grammar, which identified eight kinds of words that compose discourse: noun, verb, adjective, adjective, pronoun, interjection, conjunction, and preposition.

passive voice: a transformation of the direct object pattern characterized by a form of *be* plus the past participle of the verb. In the passive transformation the subject is not an agent; it is acted upon and is passive: *Our team **was beaten** in the playoffs.*

past participle: the form of the verb that patterns with the auxiliary *have* in the perfect tenses (*has eaten, have slept, had read, has thought*) and with *be* to create passive voice (*was torn, is seen*).

past tense: the tense that indicates a time that is immediately past. Past tense typically ends in *–ed*, but it may also end in *–t*, as in *you waited, you dropped the ball, you shot the gun.*

pattern: the basic ways that English sentences fit together. Each of the six patterns has a complete subject and a finite verb.

phrasal preposition: a phrase that functions as a preposition, such as *by way of* or *according to*, and that takes an object.

phrase: a group of related words functioning as a grammatical unit, a cluster that does **not** include a complete sentence pattern or that does not contain a subject plus a finite verb.

polysyndeton: a generous use of conjunctions to link a series of phrases or clauses; the opposite of asyndeton. Example: *He was two years old and at first he cried for the shack and the familiar smell of the wood stove and his mother's lean, hard hands.*

possessive form: the form of a noun that indicates possession of a material object (my *sister's* coat, *Janet's* new briefcase). Possessive form, indicated by an apostrophe plus an *s*, can also simply describe—as in *a day's wages for a day's work.* Also called **possessive case**.

predicate adjective: an adjective occurring in the predicate after a linking verb. A predicate adjective describes or modifies the subject and has the same referent as the subject: *The bag is empty.*

predicate noun: a noun occurring in the predicate after a linking verb. A predicate noun describes or modifies the subject and has the same referent as the subject: *Cindy is a nurse.*

prepositional phrase: a phrase built of a preposition and its object, a noun, and any words that may cluster around the noun object. If the noun object has modifiers of its own, all the modifiers are *constituent*—that is, they *constitute* part of the prepositional phrase and are thus considered part of the prepositional phrase. Example: *of the beans, from the balcony, in the soup, with friends, under the weather.*

present participle: a part of the verb that ends in –*ing* and patterns with the auxiliary *be* in the progressive tenses (*eating, sleeping, reading, and thinking*).

principal parts of verbs: principal parts of the verb that constitute the various tenses. They are the base verb (I *do*); the past tense (I *did*); the past participle, used to create the perfect tense or aspect (I *have done*); and the present participle, used to create the progressive tense (I *am doing*).

pronoun: a word that can stand in or substitute for a noun, like *I, you, it, he, she, they, him, her.*

proper noun: a noun that refers to the name of a very specific or particular person, place, organization, or thing: *Mississippi River, Samuel Langhorne Clemens, Missouri, The Adventures of Huckleberry Finn.*

Q

qualifiers: (also called **intensifiers** by some grammarians) intensify or change the degree of meaning of words with which they pattern. The rhetorical effect of words like *too, very, quite, almost, so*, and *extremely* is to mitigate, increase, or reduce the impact of the words they modify. Intensifiers frequently pattern with adverbs in verb clusters.

question mark: the mark of punctuation used to signal the question transformation: ?

question transformation: a transformation that creates a question from a declarative statement. The question transformation can be effected by reversing the order of subject and verb. Only the *be* verb reverses simply, however. With verbs other than *be*, the question transformation requires the addition of an auxiliary verb, usually *do* or a form of *do* appropriate to the tense of the sentence being transformed. Examples: *Do you know the way to the castle? Why are you late for the jousting?*

R

referent: what a word refers to. Two words have the same referent if they refer to the same entity or object.

register of expression: a level of style from casual to formal.

relative pronoun: a pronoun that acts as a subordinator to introduce adjective clauses. The relative pronouns relate a dependent clause to the main clause because they articulate and define subordinate relationships: *that, who, whom, whose, which, what.*

restrictive or essential clause: an adjective clause essential to the understanding of the noun it modifies. A restrictive clause is not set off by commas. Example: *The boy who ate worms was sent to the hospital.*

retained object: when an S-V-IO-DO or S-V-DO-OC sentence is transformed to passive voice, the direct object is retained or kept in the transformation. Example: *Grandfather gave Freddy his gold watch* becomes *Freddy was given a gold watch by Grandfather*—and *watch*, the direct object, is retained or kept in the transformation.

rhetoric: a discipline that considers the way that grammatical elements (or parts of sentences) work together to create certain effects in the text. Whether you place a clause at the beginning of a sentence instead of at its end, for instance, you send readers a particular message and you emphasize a specific aspect of your message.

S

S-group: a group of words that constitutes a sentence; a subject and a finite verb: *We ate lunch.*

S-LV-PA: the predicate adjective sentence pattern whose main elements are subject, linking verb, and predicate adjective: *The food was free.*

S-LV-PN: the predicate noun sentence pattern whose main elements are subject, linking verb, and predicate noun: *The students are the winners.*

S-V: the intransitive verb sentence pattern whose main elements are subject and verb: *Birds sing in the lilac bushes.*

S-V-DO-OC: the objective complement sentence pattern whose main elements are subject, verb, direct object, and objective complement (which may be either a noun or an adjective): *The painters painted the woodwork green.*

S-V-IO-DO: the indirect object sentence pattern whose main elements are subject, verb, indirect object, and direct object: *Grandfather gave Sammy his gold watch.*

S-V-O: the direct object sentence pattern whose main elements are subject, transitive verb, direct object: *Everyone saw the alien.*

second person: pronouns that refer to the person spoken to, *you* and *yours.*

simple sentence: a sentence with just one independent clause and no dependent clauses.

slang: a widely current but short-lived, informal expression like the recent *way cool,* which is already passé.

structure words: the metaphorical cement that joins form class words to one another and makes their relationships clear. Although structure words definitely have meaning, they function more to link, enhance, and clarify the form class words than to present the concepts of the text. Structure words include these classes of words: *pronouns, prepositions, conjunctions, expletives, intensifiers, auxiliaries, interrogatives.*

subject: a noun that represents what the sentence is about and that is related to the verb in the predicate of the sentence; it is usually found at the first of the sentence. Example: *Geese* (subject) fly south for the winter.

subjective complement: a completer of the subject or a complement that modifies the subject. Predicate adjectives and predicate nouns are subjective complements because they complete the meaning of the subject. In *The nuns were strict, strict* is the subjective complement.

subjunctive mode: the mode or mood used to express situations hypothetical, contrary to fact, or expressing wishes. Example: *If I were you, I'd invest in magic carpets.*

subordinate clause: a clause that is a complete pattern with a subject and a finite verb but which does not sound complete enough to be an independent sentence. Subordinate clauses are introduced by subordinators and also called dependent clauses. Example: *although we had plenty of money.*

subordinating conjunction: conjunctions used to link subordinate or dependent clauses to independent clauses. Subordinating conjunctions introduce adjective clauses, adverb clauses, and noun clauses. Examples are *when, if, as, although, because.*

superlative form of the adjective: represented by the suffix *–est* or the word *most* (used with most words of more than three syllables): *tightest, poorest, smallest, most lovely, most endearing.* Sometimes we also use *more* and *most* with the basic form of the adjective because the sound is more euphonious or pleasing. Example: *The guppy is the **smallest** fish in the tank.*

syntax: the way the words and grammatical parts of a sentence are arranged or put together; the order of the words and the structure of a sentence.

T

terminal punctuation: punctuation at the end of a sentence or question; periods, question marks, exclamation marks.

***then* adverbs**: a class of adverb; adverbs of time, like *when* and *then.*

There V-S transformation: the transformation of the intransitive pattern S-V so that an expletive begins the sentence, followed by a verb and then the subject: *There goes the black poodle.*

***there* adverbs**: a class of adverb; adverbs of place, like *where.*

third person: the pronouns referring to persons spoken about: *he, she, it, they, him, her, it, them* or nouns referring to someone spoken about: *Aunt Ginger, Mr. McGowan, Dr. Malkin, the old lady in the flowery hat.*

***thus* adverbs**: a class of adverb; adverbs of manner, like *slowly.*

transitive verb: a verb that *takes* or requires an object and that *transfers* some kind of action from subject to object. In *Nancy cooked the casserole, cooked* is a transitive verb because it takes a direct object, *casserole*.

U, V

verb: one of the two major form classes, verbs express or refer to action in a sentence, to reveal what is happening. Verbs are identified by the ability to have past tense. Sample verbs are *fry, skip, tease, argue, cajole*.

verb-frontal language: a language where the verb is the first word in the sentence.

verb-medial language: a language, like English, where the verb typically occurs in the medial or middle position in the sentence.

verbal: a verb form that doesn't act or function like a verb. Verbals have all the physical characteristics of verbs, but verbals do not function as verbs. Rather they function as nouns or adjectives. Kinds of verbals include infinitives, gerunds, and participles.

verbatim recoverability: an aspect of ellipsis where the omitted or understood words are grammatically compatible with the part of the sentence actually on the page. *Jan scored 85 on the test; Ian, 60.* What is omitted from the second clause is *scored*, the verb of the first clause, and *on the test*, a prepositional phrase. Thus the sentence has verbatim recoverability.

virtual sentence: a purposeful reduction of any basic sentence pattern. It is not a sentence fragment or an incomplete sentence, for it is used by a writer who is entirely in control and wishes to create a certain effect. Virtual sentences are used to set a scene or to comment on an event or to describe: *Five o'clock. The smell of sizzling sausage penetrated the stairwell.*

W, X, Y, Z

yes/no question: a question that can be answered with *yes* or *no*. This kind of question typically begins with *do* or *did*: *Do you like Cocoa Puffs?*

Index

A

Abbott, Shirley, 202
abbreviations, 173–74
absolute, 184
absolute negatives, 62
Ackerman, Diane, 149, 151, 206
acronyms, 174
Adams, Alice, 178
Adams, Jason, 189
adjective, 30–32
adjective clause, 56, 123–29
adjective pairs, 31
adverb clause, 123, 129–33, 181–82
adverb of time, 129–30
adverbial, 19
agent, 3, 67
agreement, 41
alliteration, 153–54
Als, Hilton, 189
Alvarez, Julia, 172
ambiguity, 60
anadiplosis, 156–57
anaphora, 154–55
anastrophe, 146–47
Angelou, Maya, 198
antimetabole, 157–58
antithesis, 145–46
apostrophe, 28, 29, 199–200
Apple, Max, 104, 157, 189
apposition, 147–48
appositive, 14–15, 185–86
Armstrong, Ami Sue, 403
Armstrong, Emma Beth, 402
Armstrong, Zachary, 300
article adjectives, 53

Ashbridge, Elizabeth, 183
aspect, 42
assonance, 153
asyndeton, 151–52
Atwood, Margaret, 175
auxiliary verb, 48–49, 57, 62

B

Baldwin, James, 120
Barsotti, Charles, 135
Bartram, William, 183
base verb, 40
Beattie, Ann, 175, 176
Bellow, Saul, 104, 181, 182
binary, 39
Boll, Heinrich, 194
Boo, Katherine, 184
Booth, George, 4, 125
Bourdain, Anthony, 179
brackets, 203–04
Bradford, Richard, 107
Bradford, William, 203
Bradstreet, Anne, 169–70
Brand, Max, 189
Broner, E. M., 104, 186
Bruni, Frank, 183
Bukiet, Melvin Jules, 104, 186
Burch, Nathan JPS, 278
Burch, Paul William, 250
Burch, Paul William, Jr., 301

C

capital letters, 27
Carlson, Ron, 176
Carver, Raymond, 176

Cass, Dennis, 176
casual style, 80
Céline, Louis Ferdinand, 174
Chabon, Michael, 176
Chast, Roz, 63
Cheever, John, 120
Chesterton, G. K., 157
clause, 113–14
cleft sentence, 77–79
Collins, James, 200
colon, 120, 193–95
combination sentence, 138–43
comma, 118, 124, 125, 126, 148–49,
    180–90, 201
comma splice, 181
comparative construction, 133
comparative form, 31–32
complement, 3
complex sentence, 123
compound sentence, 116–22, 180
compound sentence elements, 7–8,
    87–89, 186, 189
compound-complex sentence, 138–43
conditional mode, 41
conjugate, 42
conjugations, 42–53
conjunction, 55–57
conjunctive adverb, 57, 119–20, 185
Connell, Richard, 186, 197
Conrad, Joseph, 119, 181
constituent, 34
consultative style, 79
contraction, 199
coordinate adjectives, 187–88
coordinating conjunctions, 55
coordinator, 55, 118, 180
Cooper, James Fenimore, 183
Corbett, Edward P. J., 143
Cornelisen, Ann, 197
correlative conjunctions, 56
Cottle, Michelle, 148
count nouns, 27
de Crevecoeur, St. Jean, 186

D
dash, 149, 185, 196–97
Davis, Rebecca Harding, 194, 198
declarative sentence, 172
Decurtis, Anthony, 104
degree (of adjectives), 31–32

Deighton, Len, 202
demonstrative adjectives, 54
Denby, David, 140, 181, 183
dependent clause, 116
determiner, 25, 33, 53–54
determiner form of pronouns, 55
Dickerson, Debra, 203
Dickey, James, 140
diction, 79–83
Didion, Joan, 194
Dillard, Annie, 153, 154, 179
direct object, 3 ff.
Doctorow, E. L., 104
Dorris, Michael, 107
Dybek, Stuart, 175

E
Early, Gerald, 161–62
Edwards, Jonathan, 178
Einstein, Albert, 156
Eliscu, Jenny, 104, 185
Elkin, Stanley, 197
ellipsis, 80, 150–51, 174–75, 203
Ellis, Benjamin, 141
em dash, 196–97
Emerson, Ralph Waldo, 150, 182, 191
Emma Lee, 291
emphasis, 31, 6
emphatic transformation, 61, 75
Enright, Anne, 181
epanalepsis, 156
epistrophe, 155
Equiano, Olaudah 186
Erdrich, Louise, 154, 159, 189
essential clause, 124–27
exclamation point, 177–79
exclamatory transformation, 178
expletive transformation, 61, 73–75
expletive, 73–74
extraction, 80

F
Faulkner, William, 119
figure of speech, 143
first person, 41
Fitzgerald, F. Scott, 120
Five Clocks, 79
Ford, Richard, 160
form class, 25–26 ff, 60
formal style, 81

formatting, 82
Foster, Race, 206
Franklin, Benjamin, 188
free modifiers, 105, 184
Friedman, Bruce J., 182
Friedman, Devin, 111
Fuchs, Daniel, 104
functional labels, 22

G

Gardner, John, 107
Gass, William, 176
gerund, 89, 94–98, 102–04, 106, 112
get passive, 68
Giac, Nguyen Mong, 188
Gibaldi, Joseph, 203
Girault, Norton, 199
Giuffrida, Meg, 438
give verbs, 10
Glick, Hersh, 141
glossary, 207–220
Godshalk, C. S., 178
Gold, Michael, 104
Goldberger, Paul, 141
Goldstein, Rebecca, 115, 182
Goodman, Allegra, 104, 131, 135, 160,
    181, 186
Gornick, Vivian, 186, 201
grammar, 1–2
grammatical analysis, 162
Grandin, Temple, 195–96
Gray, Francine du Plessix, 141
Grice, Gordon, 124

H

Hall, Alvin D., 196
Handelsmann, J. B., 91
Harrison, Barbara Grizzuti, 194, 197
Hawthorne, Nathaniel, 185, 193
Hazlitt, William, 154
headword, 36
Heinemann, Larry, 182
Hemingway, Ernest, 111, 120
Hemley, Robin, 185
Hendon, Kim, 167
Herman, Michelle, 197
Herr, Michael, 116
Hersey, John, 154
Higgins, Jack, 107
Hoffman, Allen, 176

Hustvedt, Siri, 156
Hutchins, Robert Maynard, 157
hyphen, 197–99

I

imperative mode, 41
indefinite pronominal adjectives, 53
independent clause, 116, 190, 193
indicative mode, 41
indirect object, 8–9
indirect object pattern, 8–11
infinitive, 40, 89, 90–94, 102–04, 112
intensifiers, 50
internal punctuation, 180–206
interrogative, 58
interrogative question transformation,
    65–66
intimate style, 80
intonation in questions, 66
intransitive complete, 19
intransitive pattern, 19–21
intransitive verb, 2
introductory clause, 130, 181
inversion, 75
Irving, John, 168–69
Irving, Washington, 183
Isabeau the Magnificent, 321
Ivins, Molly, 166–67

J

jargon, 80
Jaroff, Leon, 129
Jefferson, Thomas, 193
Jeremiah, 152
Johnson, Charles, 176
Johnson, Cory, 183
Jones, Thom, 172, 176
Joos, Martin, 79

K

Kacher, George, 148
Karlin, Wayne, 188
Kazin, Alfred, 104
Keisler, Paula, 175
Kennedy, John F., 116
Kingsolver, Barbara, 54
Kingston, Maxine Hong, 187
Kitman, Jamie, 148, 205
Klinkenborg, Verlyn, 124
Kohn, Stanislaw, 141

Kolbert, Elizabeth, 141, 181
Komunyakaa, Yusef, 189
Kusz, Natalie, 149

L
Lady Magic, 400
Lahr, John, 189
L' Amour, Louis, 181
Lappin, Todd, 179
Larson, Gary, 69, 106, 127
Lawrence of Arabia, 184
LeGuin, Ursula K., 179
Leslie, Naton, 189
levels of usage, 82
Levertov, Denise, 202
Levi, Primo, 141, 181, 188
Levine, Mark, 190
Lewisohn, Ludwig, 104
Lincoln, Abraham, 115
linking pattern, 15–19
linking verbs, 16, 71
lists, 186–87, 191
Lord, Audre, 184
Lopes-Nieves, Luis, 195
Lorenz, Lee, 121
Lowth, Robert, 90

M
Mailer, Norman, 103
Malamud, Bernard, 103, 153, 176
Manguel, Alberto, 119
Mankoff, Robert, 131
Markfield, Wallace, 53, 184
Mason, Bobbie Ann, 180
Mattison, Harry, 192
Matz, Nena, 352
Mayer, Jane, 103
McCabe, Donald, 206
McCain, John, 155
McCarthy, Mary, 202
McCarthy, Wil, 187
McGrath, Charles, 165–66
McLane, Daisann, 147
McPhee, John, 27
Mead, Rebecca, 199
Mebane, Mary, 174
Melville, Herman, 200–01
Merkin, Daphne, 181, 183
metalanguage, 177
Michaels, Leonard, 172

Miller, Arthur, 103
Millett, Kate, 201
Minco, Marga, 141
Mirvis, Tova, 188
modal verbs, 48–49
mode, 41
Montejo, Victor, 175
movability of adverbs, 49
Mukherjee, Bharati, 176
Mulisch, Harry, 194
multifunction words, 55, 57–58, 90
Munro, Alice, 119

N
negative transformation, 61–64
neologism, 47
N-group, 9
Ngu, Nguy, 185
nominal, 26
nominal style, 59
nominative, 26
nominative absolute, 104–11
non-essential clause, 124–27
nonfinite verb, 96
non-restrictive adjective clause,
    124–27, 183–84
noun, 25–39
noun adjunct, 33
noun clause, 123, 144
noun cluster, 3, 26, 30–38
noun headword, 110
number, 27

O
Oates, Joyce Carol, 178
object, 3
object pronouns, 55
objective complement, 12
objective complement pattern, 11–15
Olsen, Tillie, 104
Ondaatje, Michael, 140
onomatopoeia, 158–59
Oppenheimer, Mark, 120
ordinal adjectives, 54
O'Rourke, P. J., 192
Orwell , George, 169
Ozick, Cynthia, 104, 115, 149, 173, 200

P
Paine, Thomas, 166

pairs of adjectives, 31
Paley, Grace, 103, 174, 182
parallelism, 144–45
parentheses, 149, 202–05
parenthesis, 148–50
Parker, Dorothy, 121, 182
participle, 32, 89, 98–101, 102–04, 112
particle, 47–48
parts of speech, 26
Paskey, Janice, 76
passive transformation, 61, 67
past participle, 40–41, 68
past tense, 40–41
patterns, 2, 21–23
Penner, Jonathan, 176
perfect tense, 42–43, 46
period, 171–75
person of pronouns, 41
personal pronominal adjectives, 54
p-group, 114
phrasal preposition, 5, 35,51
phrasal verb, 47–48
phrase, 113–14
plural, 27–29
Poe, Edgar Allan, 120, 121, 193
Pollan, Michael, 120
polysyndeton, 152
Porter, Katherine Ann, 111
position of adjectives, 30–31
position of noun, 26–27
position of verb, 47
possessive, 199
possessive case, 27–29
possessive form, 27–29
predicate adjective, 16–19
predicate noun, 16–19
prepositional phrase, 5–7, 34–35, 51–53
present participle, 40–41
principal parts of verbs, 40
progressive tense, 42,44–46
pronoun, 54–55
proper nouns, 27
Proulx, Annie, 152, 158, 188, 196
Prose, Francine, 182
punctuation, external, 171
punctuation, internal, 180

Q

qualifier, 50
question mark, 175–77

question transformation, 61, 64–66, 175–76
quotation marks, 188, 200–201

R

Rabb, Margaret, 192
Raphael, Lev, 194
Rappoport, Nessa, 147, 181
Remnick, David, 179
referent, 9–10, 12
registers of expression, 81
relative clause, 56
relative pronoun, 56, 123
restrictive clause, 124–27, 182–83
rhetoric, 2
Rideau, Wilbert, 168
Roach, Mary, 164–65
Roberts, Paul, 30
Robison, Mary, 176
Rosen, Norma, 197
Rosenberg, Isaac, 186
Roth, Henry, 104
Roth, Philip, 104

S

Sacks, Oliver, 162–63
Sang, Nguyen Quang, 182
Scaggs, Austin, 185
Schechter, B. J., 148
Schulman, Helen, 185
Schwarz, Delmore, 184
Schwarz, Lynne Sharon, 173
second person, 41
Segal, Lore, 157, 158
semicolon, 119–20, 190–93
sentence, 25
Settle, Mary Lee, 199
s-group, 114
Sherman, Don, 140
Shanahan, Danny, 12
Shapiro, David, 157
Sharlet, Jeff, 37
Sheehan, Paul, 147
Silko, Leslie Marmon, 181
Simic, Charles, 147
Simon, Kate, 104
simple present tense, 40–41
simple sentence, 113
Singer, Isaac Bashevis, 104, 188
Singer, Mark, 185

slang, 80
slash, 204–05
Slater, Lauren, 123, 200, 205
S-LV-PA, 16–19, 21, 76
S-LV-PN, 16–19, 21
Smiley, Jane, 152
Smith, Betty, 140
Sontag, Susan, 123
Specter, Michael, 116
Spiegel, Isaiah, 141
split infinitive, 90
Stern, Steve 184
Stowe, Harriet Beecher, 184
structure words, 25, 53–59
style, 111–12
Styron, William, 149
subject, 3
subject pronoun, 55
subjective complement, 16
subjunctive mode, 41
subordinating conjunction, 56, 130
subordinator, 56, 130
Sudetic, Chuck, 183
suffixes, adjectives, 32
suffixes, noun, 29–30
suffixes, verb, 47
superlative form, 31–32
S-V, 19-21,74
S-V-DO-OC, 11–15, 21
S-V-IO-DO, 8–11, 21
S-V-O, 3–8, 21, 67
syntax, 25–26, 39, 60

T, U

Talese, Gay, 124, 201
Tan, Amy, 107, 182, 188
tense, 39–41
test sentence for adjective, 32
test sentence for adverb, 50
test sentence for noun, 30
test sentence for verb, 47

there/thus/then, 49
There V-S, 73
Thernstrom, Melanie, 107, 178
third person, 41
Thoreau, Henry David, 198
Thornton, Jim, 107, 198
Thuy, Le Thi Diem, 189
titles, 200–201
transform, 61
transitive verb, 2, 67
Tyler, Anne, 160, 190
Tyler, Royall, 150
Updike, John, 107, 121

V

Van Devanter, Lynda, 107, 186
verb, 3, 39–53
verb cluster, 26, 48–53
verb-frontal, 2
verb headword, 110
verb-medial, 2
verb, phrasal, 47–48
verb stem, 40
verbal, 89–104
verbal style, 59
verbatim recoverability, 151
virgule, 204–05
virtual sentence, 159–60, 172–73

W, X, Y, Z

Waggoner, Glen, 188
Walker, Alice, 159, 190
White, Rhonda, 163–64
Williams, Joy, 201
Winkelman, Carol, 151
Woolf, Virginia, 155
Woodman, Harold, 119
Woolman, John, 189
yes/no question transformation, 65
Yolen, Jane, 189

More praise for *Last Breath*

"Peter Stark tells us to 'step beyond the self.' But not too far beyond, into oblivion. If you've ever wondered just where that edge might be, physically, read *Last Breath*. It's thick with specific information, *and* with vividly rendered, often hair-raising stories—both useful and entertaining, a compelling read for those interested in testing their limits, and a pastime and sport for those of us who sort of aren't."

—WILLIAM KITTREDGE

"You'll read [*Last Breath*] for the fun of it, for the adventure, and you'll remember it for the scares, frights of life on the brink. . . . [Stark] writes beautifully, his prose bursting with life and color, his energy as boundless as his explorers'. He has a winning style that just won't quit, that flows fast and furious all around the reader. He writes with an abiding love of the exotic situations and extreme conditions that fell his victims. With his guidance we experience every heart-pounding moment of these travails."

—*The Missoulian*

"Death comes to us all. *Last Breath* introduces us to the people who tempt fate and experience their final expiration. We witness their intimate encounters with death from multiple angles. Stark's craft as a storyteller blends physiology, ecology, physics, psychology, and metaphysics into a compelling read. *Last Breath* is a page-turner!"

—IRA BYOCK, M.D.
Author of *Dying Well*

Please turn the page for more reviews . . .

"Viscerally engaging . . . Packed with scientific detail, historical anecdotes, medical suspense, and baited with a monster narrative hook, [*Last Breath*] reads from cover to cover like an enchanting, freely roaming malarial dream. . . . Within each chapter, Stark strikes a sublime balance between narrative and character development, with an incredible wealth of medical and scientific data, historical background, and metaphysics."

—*Missoula Independent*

"Those who have read Jack London's chilling short story 'To Build a Fire' will be drawn to *Last Breath*."

—*Pittsburgh Tribune-Review*

"A fascinating, cautionary book that also explores why people engage in risky behavior."

—*The Tampa Tribune*

LAST

BREATH

By Peter Stark

Driving to Greenland
Last Breath
At the Mercy of the River

Edited by Peter Stark

Ring of Ice

LAST

BREATH

THE LIMITS OF ADVENTURE

PETER STARK

BALLANTINE BOOKS / NEW YORK

A Ballantine Book
Published by The Random House Publishing Group

Copyright © 2001 by Peter Stark

All rights reserved.

Published in the United States by Ballantine Books, an imprint of
The Random House Publishing Group, a division of Random House,
Inc., New York, and simultaneously in Canada by Random House
of Canada Limited, Toronto.

Ballantine and colophon are registered trademarks of Random
House, Inc.

www.ballantinebooks.com

A Library of Congress Catalog Card Number is available from the
publisher.

ISBN 0-345-44151-6

Cover design by Carl Galian
Cover photo: Randy Lincks/CORBIS

Manufactured in the United States of America

First Hardcover Edition: October 2001
First Trade Paperback Edition: October 2002

9 8 7 6 5

TO THOSE WHO PUSH TO THE EDGE,

AND TO THOSE WHO HELP BRING THEM BACK

CONTENTS

Acknowledgments   IX

Introduction   *Ars Moriendo:*   1
    The Craft of Dying

Chapter 1   As Freezing Persons Recollect the Snow: 11
    Hypothermia

Chapter 2   A River of One's Own: 25
    Drowning

Chapter 3   Arching Toward the Clear Light: 45
    Mountain Sickness

Chapter 4   The Cold Hug of the White Sphinx: 81
    Avalanche

Chapter 5   Steller's Last Laugh, or Better Living   105
    Through Botany:
    Scurvy

Chapter 6   Warm to the Touch: 135
    Heatstroke

Chapter 7   Pitched from the Vertical Realm: 151
    Falling

Chapter 8   The Sharp Sting of Paradise: 177
    Predators

Chapter 9   Bubbling from the Bottom Up: 203
    The Bends

Chapter 10   In Love's Blood: 229
               Cerebral Malaria

Chapter 11   In a Land Beyond the Shade: 249
               Dehydration

Sources   293

ACKNOWLEDGMENTS

The generosity, patience, expertise, and insight of dozens of individuals both inside and outside the medical field allowed me to write this book. With very few exceptions, everyone I contacted for help gave unstintingly of their time and knowledge; this generosity of spirit came as a great encouragement to me throughout the process of researching and writing.

I'd like to start by thanking Doug Webber, M.D., physician specializing in emergency medicine at St. Patrick's Hospital in Missoula, Montana. A climber, kayaker, scuba diver, and marathoner as well as a doctor on the front lines of the medical field, Doug guided me through many knotty questions of physiology and emergency treatment in addition to lending his outdoors expertise. I would like to thank for his psychological insights Scott Elrod, M.D., also of Missoula. I received help for many of the chapters by attending the 16th Annual Wilderness Medicine gathering in Keystone, Colorado, sponsored by the Office of Continuing Medical Education at the University of California, San Diego, School of Medicine. It was a tremendous resource to have so many experts assembled in one place, and I welcomed the opportunity to attend as a layman. Below I thank the individual physicians from the conference along with others who helped with various chapters. I have tried to render as accurately as possible what I've learned from them; I apologize to them for any lapses.

For the hypothermia chapter, which originally appeared as an article for *Outside* magazine in 1997, I had the advice of several experts on hypothermia, including Daniel Danzl, M.D.; Robert Pozos, M.D.; William Forgey, M.D.; and Cameron Bangs, M.D. Tom Bulger, M.D., also an emergency physician at St. Patrick's Hospital, helped me with details of medical procedure, and Paul Ryan of Pipestone Mountaineering, Missoula, Montana, added his expertise with outdoor equipment. Patrick Gallagher related his own harrowing encounter with hypothermia. Outdoor guide and skiing companion Skip Horner, of Skip Horner Worldwide, gave graphic details of what it's like to sleep in a tent at −48 degrees in Antarctica.

For the drowning chapter, I received help from Jerome Modell, M.D., of the University of Florida, a nationally known expert on drowning and near-drowning. Kayak instructor Kurt Doettger gave an account of his experience of near-drowning during a whitewater rescue operation in North Carolina. John Anderson and John Cox of The Trailhead outdoors store in Missoula, Montana, provided details of kayaking equipment, and Richard Gallun and Mark Wheelis lent their whitewater expertise. Jeff France of Board of Missoula described his experiences as a kayaker who has recirculated in large whitewater holes and dropped over waterfalls.

The mountain sickness chapter benefited greatly from the expertise of Peter Hackett, M.D., one of the participants in the wilderness-medicine conference and a leading researcher on the physiological effects of altitude. Also at the conference, Clifford

Zwillich, M.D., gave a helpful lecture on sleep apnea at high altitude, and Rob Roach, Ph.D., lectured on the physiology of women at high altitude. A former next-door neighbor of mine and backcountry ski partner who has gone on to become one of the Himalaya's most accomplished climbers and guides, Daniel Mazur of Himalaya Incorporated, provided many details of high-altitude climbing and its physiological effects, usually via e-mail from Tibet, Nepal, or Pakistan. Delbert Kilgore, avian physiologist at the University of Montana, helped with the physiology of birds that breathe at high altitude. Noel Ragsdale gave valuable insights on details of character, and climber Chris Brick described her own case of pulmonary edema while climbing in the Andes.

The neurofeedback descriptions and brain wave research that are included in the avalanche chapter would not have been possible without the generous assistance of freelance writer Jim Robbins of Helena, Montana, author of *A Symphony in the Brain: The Evolution of the New Brain Wave Biofeedback*, and Bernadette Pedersen, also of Helena, and her business, Brainworks Neurofeedback Services. Bernadette kindly hooked me up to a machine that read my brain waves and allowed me to try the fascinating practice of neurofeedback as I nudged my brain waves down a kind of video highway. Les Fehmi and Susan Shor-Fehmi gave their neurofeedback expertise. Scott Lewis shared his incredible story of being buried for twenty-seven minutes several feet deep in an avalanche while heli-skiing in British Columbia (he handled it much more calmly than the character described here), and Linda Parker told of her brush with an avalanche. Physical therapist Fred Lerch gave me insights on the interaction between mind and body. Beau Johnson of Board of Missoula helped with snowboarding details, and the National Weather Service office in Salt Lake City filled me in on why it snows so much in the Wasatch Mountains. Neil Beidleman, climber, engineer with Big Air Design, and lecturer at the wilderness-medicine conference, demonstrated the Black

Diamond vest designed for breathing in an avalanche. For an understanding of the physiology of avalanche victims, I am grateful to Colin K. Grissom, M.D., and Martin I. Radwin, M.D., who with their colleagues have been conducting fascinating research in the mountains of Utah by burying volunteers under the snow to simulate an avalanche and monitoring their physiology.

For the scurvy chapter, sailing companion and all-around outdoor expert Tom Duffield provided nautical accuracy about boats and the waters of Puget Sound.

For the heatstroke chapter, bicycle racer Charlie Holbrook gave an insightful account of a racer's strategy and vivid description of the strain on a racer's body when hill climbing, while Len LaBuff, owner of Open Road bicycles in Missoula, provided details of equipment. Peter Felsch, meteorologist with the National Weather Service in Missoula, and Bryan McAvoy, meteorologist with the National Weather Service in Greenville, South Carolina, helped with setting a realistic weather scenario for the chapter. P. Z. Pearce, M.D., a speaker at the wilderness-medicine conference, presented a useful lecture on heat illness.

I heard detailed, thoughtful descriptions of their long falls for the falling chapter from Otto Plattner, of Innsbruck, Austria, who tumbled far down a couloir in the Tyrolean Alps and lay in the snow for hours waiting for a rescue, and Bill Watson of Missoula, who survived, unhurt, a fall from the fourth floor of a building under construction. Climber Jack Tuholske and Susan Duffield suggested mountaineering and climbing literature for me to read, and Ann DiCesare, librarian at *Reader's Digest*, managed with amazing speed to locate the account of the tailgunner falling out of the airplane that I remembered having read in my youth, as well as the article about the Swedish hunter buried for eight days in an avalanche. For technical details of rock climbing, I am grateful to J. R. Plate of Pipestone Mountaineering and to Doug Webber, M.D., for a realistic climbing and trauma scenario. Ebo Uchimoto, professor of physics at the University of Montana, helped with the physics and calculations in the chapter, as did Jennifer Fowler, lab technician in the department. Chuck Leonard of the University of Montana's Department of Physical Therapy clarified some of the motor movements, and Charles Vogel helped with the character's financial background.

The predators chapter and description of the physiology of a box jellyfish sting benefited from the knowledge of Paul Cullen, M.D., emergency physician at Cairns Base Hospital in Cairns, Australia. The fascinating statistics on worldwide and North American land animal attacks were given in a lecture at the wilderness-medicine conference by Michael Callahan, M.D., medical director of rescue medicine at the University of Colorado, Health Sciences. Missoula writer Connie Poten, a former resident of Cairns, provided details of setting, and Nici Holt and Andy Cline told the riveting story of their excruciating entanglement with a swarm of stinging jellyfish while sea kayaking off Hawaii.

Essential details about the life and language of the Caribbean for the bends chapter came from Paul Reneau, a native of Belize who is a school counselor in Missoula. Carl Thomas, scuba instructor and employee of Gull Boats in Missoula, lent a great deal of expertise and patience in explaining details of diving equipment, planning, and techniques. Tom Neuman, M.D., of the University of California, San Diego, helped with expertise on the physiological effects of diving.

Mark Bracker, M.D., of the University of California, San Diego, School of Medicine and codirector of the wilderness-medicine conference, gave me timely and insightful comments on the physiology of malaria. I heard harrowing accounts from Bryan Di Salvatore and Jill Belsky of malaria in their traveling companions.

For the chapter on dehydration and desert survival I had the help of Ronald and Peter Kummerfeldt, instructors at the wilderness-medicine conference and survival instructors at Outdoor Safe of Colorado Springs, Colorado. Jay Christopher provided his story of dehydration while hiking in Utah.

Besides the assistance with individual chapters, I had the experience and insights of companions in recent years on various outdoor adventures of my own, among them Fred Haefele, Steve and Matt Rinella, Christopher Preston, Bill Bevis, Ted Stark, Paul Jensen, and Gray Thompson. Ira Byock, M.D., author of *Dying Well*, and Yvonne Corbeil gave me insights into the process of dying.

Vaughn Stevens and Don Spritzer of the reference desk of the Missoula Public Library always managed to find answers to my hard-to-answer questions, such as "How many stars are there in the universe?" Shawn Lake of the Mansfield Library at the University of Montana provided helpful references for several chapters, and I am grateful also to the staff of the medical library at St. Patrick's Hospital.

The idea for the book itself grew out of an article on hypothermia I wrote for *Outside* magazine. Mark Bryant, then editor of *Outside*, was instrumental in shaping what started out as a vague idea in my mind for an essay on cold and the human body. Laura Hohnhold and Gretchen Reynolds helped edit the piece and bring it to its final form. My agent, Frances Kuffel, kept up the encouragement to expand it into a book and provided a valuable sounding board throughout its conception. Jennifer Weltz of Jean V. Naggar Literary Agency has been helpful throughout. Missoula writers Bryan Di Salvatore, Steve Krauzer, Fred Haefele, and Bill Vaughn all gave me inspiration and advice at crucial moments. My father, William Stark, and my father-in-law, Wilmott Ragsdale, both writers and both great adventurers of the old school, read the chapters as I went and encouraged me by both word and example.

I've felt fortunate from the beginning that the book found a home with Ballantine. I am deeply grateful to my editor, Dan Smetanka, who has been a pleasure to work with and whose contributions to this book are beyond measure, and to his assistant, Allison Dickens, for her help and valuable input. Last, I'd like to thank my wife, Amy Ragsdale, for encouraging me to undertake the book in the first place and her unwavering support and suggestions throughout the writing of it, and my children, Molly and Skyler, who showed their own form of human endurance while waiting for me to come out of my office to play.

ARS MORIENDO:

THE CRAFT

OF DYING

I fear death.

I recall the precise moment that I grasped the utter certainty of my mortality. It didn't occur while clinging to some snowy mountainside or plunging in a kayak through Class IV whitewater— places where several victims in this book grasp the certainty of their own mortality. The moment occurred as I sat at a richly polished reading table in the hushed calm of Sanborn House, the elegant English-literature library at Dartmouth College. I don't recall what book I had open on the table before me. What I do remember is staring for a long time into the deep brown and black swirls of that rich wood grain illuminated by the reading lamp and thinking, *I'm going to die. All this will end.*

The thought was no more nor less complex than what millions— billions—of humans come to realize, sooner or later, during their short lives on earth. What surprised me then and still does was the emotional depth of that realization. I was *grief stricken* by the thought. I already mourned my own death, although I was twenty years old at the time and, barring disease or disaster, I could expect to live at least another fifty years.

I don't know precisely what triggered this realization; in retrospect, however, I find clues. Someone close to me had recently attempted suicide. Several of my friends had recently died of drug overdoses. But, despite the accumulated impact of these, I think an altogether different incident may have finally triggered my sudden realization of the inevitability of death.

I'd spent a recent spring weekend skiing at Tuckerman's Ravine, the famous thousand-foot-high headwall near the summit of New Hampshire's Mount Washington that for decades has been a mecca for snow and ice climbers—and for skiers—in search of the steep. After a few exhilarating runs down the headwall's main section, a friend and I kicked our way up the extremely steep section that is known as the Left Gully. The sun had dropped low by the time we arrived at the top, casting part of the ravine's great bowl in shadow. I proposed to my companion, who happened to be a mountain climber as well as a skier, that we ski some cleft or couloir that dropped off from where we stood. He looked over the edge, tracing with his eye the way the slope fell away into shadow and disappeared from sight, visible again a thousand feet below at the ravine's bottom. "No, we shouldn't go there," he said. "The snow down below is now in the shadow and it's freezing up hard. If we fall, we could slide a long way down into the rocks."

It hadn't occurred to me that snow conditions might change that rapidly—this was before I knew much about wilderness skiing—but what my climbing friend said made good sense. I deferred to his judgment. We skipped the steep, shadowy couloir and instead skied the larger, safer main headwall again, where the snow remained softer and no rock outcrops stood in the path of descent. About an hour later, the day's fun was winding down and people were starting the long trek down the forest trail to their cars when a helicopter suddenly buzzed into the ravine. It landed, then quickly took off again. Not until the next day did I learn what had happened. A young man skiing the steeps just in the area that I'd been eyeing had fallen on the icy, shaded snow and slid far and fast down the slick couloir into the rocks below. He died.

How easily that could have been me. It nearly *was* me but for the mountain wisdom of my friend. This incident, I think, is what triggered my revelation at the Sanborn House reading table—how close death really is, how mortality lies just a step off the curb or a wrong turn of the skis away, and just how irrevocable that ending will be.

That simple revelation occurred nearly thirty years ago. Yet still I go back to the wilderness mountains, still I love to ski the steeps, still something compels—*impassions*—me to be up there when I look out my window on a sunny spring day and see white peaks against the sky. I'm drawn by the beauty and by the silence and by the physical exertion; by the cold wind and warm sun and hot sweat, by the *exhilaration*. But another part of what compels me—a big part of it, and one that accentuates all the others—is the sense of the nearness of my own mortality that I first experienced that spring weekend at Tuckerman's Ravine. That's one premise of this book: that there are countless others who climb or ski or snowboard, who paddle whitewater, who trek in deserts, or who engage in adventures of a milder nature. Like I am, they are drawn by the beauty and silence and weather and exhilaration, and yet beneath these reasons flows an emotional undercurrent that often remains unidentified, or at least unarticulated. That is, these activities bring one nearer to an ineffable something that contains a sense of one's mortality and also reaches beyond it. Paul Bowles, writing of the compelling attraction of the Sahara Desert despite its brutal and sometimes fatal discomforts, described this something as "the absolute."

A century ago death commonly visited the bedroom next door. It was here that a relative or grandparent would die of sickness or old age, in the midst of the household. Death then was a part of everyday life. Today we don't see death in that everyday way—it is whisked away to the sanitized environment of the hospital (although fortunately the hospice movement has begun to change this). We don't talk about death. We carefully deny that death exists so close to us all, as if it has become a kind of obscenity, or, alternatively, a cardboard shoot-'em-up character in the movies. It may be our distance from death that makes us at once afraid of it, fascinated by it, and yet wanting to *understand* it. In contrast to the Western attitude toward death, the Japanese calmly prepare for their demise with a centuries-old tradition of writing in their last days or moments what are known as "death poems." The Christian tradition in medieval times placed more emphasis on familiarity with death, and scholars wrote texts such as *Ars Moriendo*, "The Craft of Dying." Throughout the world, many cultures display more familiarity with death than in the West. *The Tibetan Book of the Dead*, read aloud to the person who is dying, is an intimate portrayal of the process of death and the opportunity it presents for liberation. According to the Tibetan tradition, you must understand death intimately and prepare yourself for it in order to live a full and satisfying life.

My intention with *Last Breath* has been to produce a sort of *Ars Moriendo* for those who engage in adventurous, eminently rewarding, often risky, and sometimes fatal activities such as climbing, whitewater paddling, extreme skiing or snowboarding, and remote travel, although the themes of risk, death, and enlightenment addressed in these chapters should pertain to the many others who don't necessarily pursue these outdoor activities. Every one of us shares an inescapable fate: We are inhabitants of a body that will someday die. Moments in this book intimately follow that process as it occurs to the bodies of those who push the boundaries of outdoor activities. In each chapter I've intertwined a story of a character in a desperate outdoor situation with the physiology—the medical science—of what is happening to his or her body as this occurs. I've also tried to address some of the spiritual aspects of dying—how other cultures regard death—as well as explore, obliquely, where the scientific and the spiritual intersect in the moment of death.

During the course of research, it has never failed to amaze me how ingeniously the human body adapts to the constant changes in its external and internal environment—to changes in air pressure and oxygen, food consumption and water intake, increased physical workload, heat and cold, fear and other emotions, and blood loss. Yet that resiliency can be misleading. The human body, in many ways, is as delicate as a hothouse flower, capable of existing in only an extremely narrow band of conditions. We, as a species, are genetically adapted to a belt of tropical temperatures that prevail only around the equator; without technological innovations such as insulated clothing, furnaces, and campfires, we would quickly perish if we strayed from that narrow belt a few thousand miles north or south. While we can still roam widely within this tropical belt on the *horizontal* plane, on the *vertical* plane we can travel only a very short distance without destroying the proper functioning of our bodies. Humans cannot live on a permanent basis more than about 3.5 miles above sea level. Likewise, humans are extremely sensitive to environments that lack fresh water—deprived of fresh water, they perish within a few days, the exact number (from as few as one day to as many as ten) depending on air temperature, exertion, and other factors.

If you set the small belt that offers the precise conditions necessary for human life against all the rest of the planet—against all of the earth's surface that is desert and ice, rock and ocean—you realize exactly how limited our life-sustaining environment actually is. More important, you realize how simple it is to step beyond it, how easily we can break through the thin web of life that supports the delicate human organism. And if you set that band of life against the enormity of the solar system, or of the Milky Way galaxy, or of the unknown reaches of the universe, we as a species occupy a niche far smaller than a tiny tuft of wildflowers sheltered by a small boulder atop an otherwise barren mountain peak that harbors in that single tuft the only life on an entire planet of barren mountain peaks. This is what, at some level, science and religion both are trying to tell us— how infinitesimally small the scale of human life is against the scale of the cosmos—but at the same time they also tell us that human life forms a part of the vastness. That vastness is known by different names to different people. Some call it the expanding universe, some simply call it emptiness, and some call it God.

Last Breath's subtitle refers to the scenarios rendered in each chapter as "cautionary tales." Explorer Vitus Bering's is the only historical death described in this book. The other ten chapters portray invented characters and invented situations that approximate physiological reality as closely as possible. I've based these chapters on interviews with individuals who have survived avalanche burial, hypothermia, near-drowning, falling, pulmonary edema, and other maladies. In addition, I've interviewed specialists who treat these victims, and I have conducted extensive research in medical databases, journals, and academic as well as anecdotal sources. My major printed sources are listed after the last chapter; the acknowledgments list the many generous individuals who have helped me with the research for this book.

As I've strived to render the physiology and medical science of these deaths and near-deaths as accurately as possible, I have attempted to portray realistically the background settings and risky situations in which the victims find or place themselves. I bring a good bit of personal background to this task as a backcountry skier (and former ski racer), kayaker, and whitewater canoeist. Over the years I have traveled (usually the hard way, and usually for extended periods) to many of the remote regions portrayed here—the Himalaya and Tibet, the Arctic, the Sahara Desert, West Africa, Sumatra, China's Tiger's Leap Gorge—as well as to closer ones such as Cádiz, in the Andalusia region of Spain, where I lived for a time. I've chosen to create composite characters based on my extensive interviews and research because this gives me much greater flexibility to explore the physiological, psychological, and spiritual aspects of death than I could by tying the narrative to the experiences of a single person. My hope is that this choice finally makes for a more dramatic, comprehensive, and insightful book.

Yet these scenarios have been cautionary tales for me, too. Writing this book has, in some respects, formed a part of my ongoing personal explorations. I come from an adventurous family. My grandfather, starting early last century, loved to canoe wilderness rivers, and my father, among many other adventures, crewed in 1949 as one of the sailors on the last commercial windjammer to round Cape Horn. I inherited this legacy of adventure and had it nurtured in me when, at age four, my father and grandfather took me with them on my first overnight canoe trip. The series of adventures that started then continues to this day.

I've always felt a tension, however, about how far to push on these adventures—where, if at all, I should pull back. So many times I've found myself in a place where I feel both compelled and yet scared to go farther—whether staring from a riverbank at a set of big rapids, peering down a steep slope of powder snow that's a potential avalanche zone, or heading up with backpack on my shoulders into some mist-shrouded jungle highlands of Asia or into a small African country on the verge of revolution. I suppose this tension grows in part from the fear that I'm somehow not measuring up, that I'm letting my grandfather and father down by not pushing farther or higher or steeper, as if I'm scared of "being scared," scared of how others might judge me for it. The tension also springs from the fact that I genuinely love to do these things—ski the steeps, or paddle whitewater, or explore new terrain and unfamiliar cultures—and I hate to turn back and miss the opportunity to go on. And another part of the tension—a big part of it—is uncertainty, for uncertainty is a scary place to be.

Staring down at a steep slope or a big set of rapids, one cannot expect a definite answer to the question *What will happen?* There are only probabilities, guesses, approximations, hopes. It is here that you must rely utterly on your own judgment. To step from a daily life that is carefully bounded by laws and safety locks and guardrails into a situation where your life hinges on your own ability to assess a rapid or a slope can be both disconcerting and exhilarating. I think there is a profound desire for this kind of self-reliance among many people who live in an era when, in the Western world anyway, there is very little opportunity for it. In a difficult or risky situation in the wilderness, the total reliance on oneself and trust in one's teammates and the need for total focus—whether climbing a rock face, skiing a steep chute, or paddling a whitewater canyon—brings a crystalline awareness of the world around one and at the same time a kind of obliteration of the separateness of the self. One hears it again and again: that at moments like this the participant feels acutely alive.

There are risks, of course—risks of all sizes—and sometimes the participant pays the ultimate price for them. I've learned while writing this book that there are no sure answers, no solid black lines to demarcate caution from boldness and boldness from foolishness, or rather that those lines constantly shift depending on circumstance and individual, but this book has also helped me answer an even more important question: *Why go in the first place?* The answer, which I've tried to state through the medium of some of the characters in these chapters, has something to do with that sense of being acutely alive; it also has something to do with death.

I see how, over the years, my own attitude toward risk in the outdoors has changed. I envision this change as a progression from the ignorance of my teens, when on occasion I suspected I was skiing on an avalanche slope without being entirely sure what an avalanche slope was. My twenties, especially my early twenties, I characterize as a period of brashness; we liked to do things after late-night parties such as race iceboats at 60 miles per hour over the inky blackness of a frozen lake. As I headed toward my thirties and learned more about the outdoor world as well as about my ambitions in writing about it, brashness gave way to calculation—how large a ski jump can I handle without really hurting myself? As I've moved through my forties and toward my fifties, I find that caution has usurped calculation—or rather, I try to calculate well on the side of caution. I don't know if I'll be any more or any less cautious in the outdoors after having written this book, but I do think, paradoxically, that for all the death described in detail here, I'll fear death less—at least my own.

I fear it less than I did not only because I know more about the physiology and spiritual aspects of it than before I wrote this book, but also because I now find it easier to turn back. I no longer care as much whether I'm somehow "measuring up." Is it the self-confidence that comes with advancing age that gives me the ability to turn around, go home, and come back another day? I have small children now— that's part of it, too. I fear for them and their well-being more than my own. One's scale of adventure changes with children; it broadens and becomes simpler and at the same time infinitely more complex. With our small children, I've had adventures—and frights—in the highlands of Irian Jaya and the Sahara Desert as well as in the park across the street.

Ultimately, each person who ventures out must make his or her own decisions about how far to go and at what point to turn back. There's an old saying among prospectors who comb the hills for gold here in the American West: "Gold is where you find it." You can say the same about adventure. For that matter, you can say it about risk, about death, and about being acutely alive.

CHAPTER ONE

AS FREEZING PERSONS

PERSONS

RECOLLECT

THE SNOW:

HYPOTHERMIA

When your Jeep spins lazily off the mountain road and slams backward into a snowbank, you don't worry immediately about the cold. Your first thought is that you've just dented your bumper. Your second is that you've failed to bring a shovel. Your third is that you'll be late for dinner. Friends are expecting you at their cabin around eight for a moonlight ski, a late dinner, a sauna. Nothing can keep you from that.

Driving out of town, defroster roaring, you barely noted the bank thermometer on the town square: −27 degrees at 6:36. The radio weather report warned of a deep mass of arctic air settling over the region. The man who took your money at the Conoco station shook his head at the register and said he wouldn't be going anywhere tonight if he were you. You smiled. A little chill never hurt anybody with enough fleece and a good four-wheel drive.

But now you're stuck. Jamming the gearshift into low, you try to muscle out of the drift. The tires whine on ice-slicked snow as headlights dance on the curtain of frosted firs across the road. Shoving the lever back into park, you shoulder open the door and step from your heated capsule. Cold slaps your naked face, squeezes tears from your eyes. You check your watch: 7:18. You consult your map: A thin, switchbacking line snakes up the mountain to the penciled square that marks the cabin.

Breath rolls from you in short frosted puffs. The Jeep lies cocked sideways in the snowbank like an empty turtle shell. You think of firelight and saunas and warm food and wine. You look again at the map. It's maybe 5 or 6 miles more to that penciled square. You run that far every day before breakfast. You'll just put on your skis. No problem.

There is no precise core temperature at which the human body perishes from cold. At Dachau's cold-water immersion baths, Nazi doctors calculated death to arrive at around 77 degrees Fahrenheit. The lowest recorded core temperature in a surviving adult is 60.8 degrees. For a child it's lower. In 1994, a two-year-old girl in Saskatchewan wandered out of her house into a −40 night. She was found near her doorstep the next morning, limbs frozen solid, her core temperature 57 degrees. She lived.

Others are less fortunate, even in much milder conditions. One of Europe's worst weather disasters occurred during a 1964 competitive walk on a windy, rainy English moor; three of the racers died from hypothermia, though temperatures never fell below freezing and ranged as high as 45.

But for all scientists and statisticians now know of freezing and its physiology, no one can yet predict exactly how quickly and in whom hypothermia will strike—and whether it will kill when it does. The cold remains a mystery, more prone to fell men than women, more lethal to the thin and well muscled than to those with avoirdupois, and least forgiving to the arrogant and the unaware.

The process begins even before you leave the car, when you remove your gloves to squeeze a loose bail back into one of your ski bindings. The freezing metal bites your flesh. Your skin temperature drops.

Within a few seconds, the palms of your hands are a chilly, painful 60 degrees. Instinctively, the web of surface capillaries on your hands constrict, sending blood coursing away from your skin and deeper into your torso. Your body is allowing your fingers to chill in order to keep its vital organs warm.

You replace your gloves, noticing only that your fingers have numbed slightly. Then you kick boots into bindings and start up the road.

Were you a Norwegian fisherman or Inuit hunter, both of whom frequently work gloveless in the cold, your chilled hands would open their surface capillaries periodically to allow surges of warm blood to pass into them and maintain their flexibility. This phenomenon, known as the hunter's response, can elevate a 35-degree skin temperature to 50 degrees within seven or eight minutes.

Other human adaptations to the cold are more mysterious. Tibetan Buddhist monks can raise the skin temperature of their hands and feet by 15 degrees through meditation. Australian Aborigines, who once slept on the ground, unclothed, on near-freezing nights, would slip into a light hypothermic state, suppressing shivering until the rising sun rewarmed them.

You have no such defenses, having spent your days at a keyboard in a climate-controlled office. Only after about ten minutes of hard climbing, as your body temperature rises, does blood start seeping back into your fingers. Sweat trickles down your sternum and spine.

By now you've left the road and decided to take a shortcut up the forested mountainside to the road's next switchback. Treading slowly through deep, soft snow as the full moon hefts over a spiny ridge top, throwing silvery bands of moonlight and shadow, you think your friends were right: It's a beautiful night for skiing—though you admit, feeling the −30 degree air bite at your face, it's also cold.

After an hour, there's still no sign of the switchback, and you've begun to worry. You pause to check the map. At this moment, your core temperature reaches its high: 100.8. Climbing in deep snow, you've generated nearly ten times as much body heat as you do when you are resting.

As you step around to orient map to forest, you hear a metallic pop. You look down. The loose bail has disappeared from your binding. You lift your foot and your ski falls from your boot.

You twist on your flashlight, and its cold-weakened batteries throw a yellowish circle in the snow. It's right around here somewhere, you think, as you sift the snow through gloved fingers. Focused so intently on finding the bail, you hardly notice the frigid air pressing against your tired body and sweat-soaked clothes.

The exertion that warmed you on the way uphill now works against you: Your exercise-dilated capillaries carry the excess heat of your core to your skin, and your wet clothing dispels it rapidly into the night. The lack of insulating fat over your muscles allows the cold to creep that much closer to your warm blood.

Your temperature begins to plummet. Within seventeen minutes it reaches the normal 98.6. Then it slips below.

At 97 degrees, hunched over in your slow search, the muscles along your neck and shoulders tighten in what's known as pre-shivering muscle tone. Sensors have signaled the temperature control center in your hypothalamus, which in turn has ordered the constriction of the entire web of surface capillaries. Your hands and feet begin to ache with cold. Ignoring the pain, you dig carefully through the snow; another ten minutes pass. You know that without the bail, you're in deep trouble.

Finally, nearly forty-five minutes later, you find the bail. You even manage to pop it back into its socket and clamp your boot into the binding. But the clammy chill that started around your skin has now wrapped deep into your body's core.

At 95, you've entered the zone of mild hypothermia. You're now trembling violently as your body attains its maximum shivering response, an involuntary condition in which your muscles contract rapidly to generate additional body heat.

It was a mistake, you realize, to come out on a night this cold. You should turn back. Fishing into the front pocket of your shell parka, you fumble out the map. You consulted it to get here; it should be able to guide you back to the warm car. Your core temperature starts to slip below 95; it doesn't occur to you in your increasingly clouded and panicky mental state that you could simply follow your tracks down the way you came.

And after this long stop, the skiing itself has become more difficult. By the time you push off downhill, your muscles have cooled and tightened so dramatically that they no longer contract easily, and once contracted, they won't relax. You're locked into an ungainly, spread-armed, weak-kneed snowplow.

Still, you manage to maneuver between stands of fir, swishing down through silvery light and pools of shadow. You're too cold to think of the beautiful night or of the friends you had meant to see. You think only of the warm Jeep that waits for you somewhere at the bottom of the hill. Its gleaming shell is centered in your mind's eye as you come over the crest of a small knoll. You hear the sudden whistle of wind in your ears as you gain speed. Then, before your mind can quite process what the sight means, you notice a lump in the snow ahead.

Recognizing, slowly, the danger that you are in, you try to jam your skis to a stop. But in your panic, your balance and judgment are poor. Moments later, your ski tips plow into the buried log and you sail headfirst through the air and bellyflop into the snow.

You lie still. There's a dead silence in the forest, broken by the pumping of blood in your ears. Your ankle is throbbing with pain, and you've hit your head. You've also lost your hat and a glove. Scratchy snow is packed down your shirt. Meltwater trickles down your neck and spine.

This situation, you realize with an immediate sense of panic, is serious. Scrambling to rise, you collapse in pain, your ankle crumpling beneath you.

As you sink back into the snow, shaken, your heat begins to drain away at an alarming rate, your head alone accounting for 50 percent of the loss. The pain of the cold soon pierces your ears so sharply that you root about in the snow until you find your hat and mash it back onto your head.

But even that little activity has been exhausting. You know you should find your glove as well, and yet you're becoming too weary to feel any urgency. You decide to have a short rest before going on.

An hour passes. At one point, a stray thought says you should start being scared, but fear is a concept that floats somewhere beyond your immediate reach, like that numb hand lying naked in the snow. You've slid into the temperature range at which cold renders the enzymes in your brain less efficient. With every 1-degree drop in body temperature below 95, your cerebral metabolic rate falls off by 3 to 5 percent. When your core temperature reaches 93, amnesia nibbles at your consciousness. You check your watch: 12:58. Maybe someone will come looking for you soon. Moments later, you check again. You can't keep the numbers in your head. You'll remember little of what happens next.

Your head drops back. The snow crunches softly in your ear. In the −35 degree air, your core temperature falls about 1 degree every thirty to forty minutes, your body heat leaching out into the soft, enveloping snow. Apathy at 91 degrees. Stupor at 90.

You've now crossed the boundary into profound hypothermia. By the time your core temperature has fallen to 88 degrees, your body has abandoned the urge to warm itself by shivering. Your blood is thickening like crankcase oil in a cold engine. Your oxygen consumption, a measure of your metabolic rate, has fallen by more than a quarter. Your kidneys, however, work overtime to process the fluid overload that occurred when the blood vessels in your extremities constricted and squeezed fluids toward your center. You feel a powerful urge to urinate, the only thing you feel at all.

By 87 degrees you've lost the ability to recognize a familiar face, should one suddenly appear from the woods.

At 86 degrees, your heart, its electrical impulses hampered by chilled nerve tissues, becomes arrhythmic. It now pumps less than two-thirds the normal amount of blood. The lack of oxygen and the slowing metabolism of your brain, meanwhile, begin to trigger visual and auditory hallucinations.

You hear jingle bells. Lifting your face from your snow pillow, you realize with a surge of gladness that they're not sleigh bells; they're welcoming bells hanging from the door of your friends' cabin. You knew it had to be close by. The jingling is the sound of the cabin door opening, just through the fir trees.

Attempting to stand, you collapse in a tangle of skis and poles. That's okay. You can crawl. It's so close.

Hours later, or maybe it's minutes, you realize the cabin still sits beyond the grove of trees. You've crawled only a few feet. The light on your wristwatch pulses in the darkness: 5:20. Exhausted, you decide to rest your head for a moment.

When you lift it again, you're inside, lying on the floor before the woodstove. The fire throws off a red glow. First it's warm; then it's hot; then it's searing your flesh. Your clothing has caught fire.

At 85 degrees, those freezing to death, in a strange, anguished paroxysm, often rip off their clothes. This phenomenon, known as paradoxical undressing, is common enough that urban hypothermia victims are sometimes initially diagnosed as victims of sexual assault. Though researchers are uncertain of the cause, the most logical explanation is that shortly before loss of consciousness, the constricted blood vessels near the body's surface suddenly dilate and produce a sensation of extreme heat against the skin.

All you know is that you're burning. You claw off your shell and pile sweater and fling them away.

But then, in a final moment of clarity, you realize there's no stove, no cabin, no friends. You're lying alone in the bitter cold, naked from the waist up. You grasp your terrible misunderstanding, a whole series of misunderstandings, like a dream ratcheting into wrongness. You've shed your clothes, your car, your oil-heated house in town. Without this ingenious technology, you're simply a delicate, tropical organism whose range is restricted to a narrow sunlit band that girds the earth at the equator.

And you've now ventured way beyond it.

There's an adage about hypothermia: "You aren't dead until you're warm and dead." This points up the importance of attempting to warm and revive seemingly dead victims, for despite all appearances to the contrary, they might still retain the spark of life.

At about 6:00 the next morning, his friends, having discovered the stalled Jeep, find him, still huddled inches from the buried log, his gloveless hand shoved into his armpit. The flesh of his limbs is waxy and stiff as old putty, his pulse nonexistent, his pupils unresponsive to light. Dead.

But those who understand cold know that even as it deadens, it offers perverse salvation. Heat is a presence: the rapid vibrating of molecules. Cold is an absence: the damping of the vibrations. At absolute zero, −459.67 degrees Fahrenheit, molecular motion ceases altogether. It is this slowing that converts gases to liquids, liquids to solids, and renders solids harder. It slows bacterial growth and chemical reactions. In the human body, cold shuts down metabolism. The lungs take in less oxygen, the heart pumps less blood. Under normal temperatures, this would produce brain damage. But the chilled brain, having slowed its own metabolism, needs far less oxygen-rich blood and can, under the right circumstances, survive intact.

Setting her ear to his chest, one of his rescuers listens intently. Seconds pass. Then, faintly, she hears a tiny sound—a single thump, so slight that it might be the sound of her own blood. She presses her ear harder to the cold flesh. Another faint thump, then another.

The slowing that accompanies freezing is, in its way, so beneficial that it is even induced at times. Cardiac surgeons often use deep chilling to slow a patient's metabolism in preparation for surgical procedures. In this state of near suspension, the patient's blood flows slowly, his heart rarely beats—or, in the case of those on heart-lung machines, doesn't beat at all; death seems near. But carefully monitored, a patient can remain in this cold stasis, undamaged, for hours.

The rescuers quickly wrap their friend's naked torso with a spare parka, his hands with mittens, his entire body with a bivvy sack. They brush snow from his pasty, frozen face. Then one snakes down through the forest to the nearest cabin. The others, left in the predawn darkness, huddle against him as silence closes around them. For a moment, the woman imagines she can hear the scurrying, breathing, snoring of a world of creatures that have taken cover this frigid night beneath the thick quilt of snow.

With a "one, two, three," the doctor and nurses slide the man's stiff, curled form onto a table fitted with a mattress filled with warm water that will be regularly reheated. They'd been warned that they had a profound hypothermia case coming in. Usually such victims can be straightened from their tortured fetal positions. This one can't.

Technicians scissor with stainless-steel shears at the man's urine-soaked long underwear and shell pants, frozen together like corrugated cardboard. They attach heart-monitor electrodes to his chest and insert a low-temperature electronic thermometer into his rectum. Digital readings flash: 24 beats per minute and a core temperature of 79.2 degrees.

The doctor shakes his head. He can't remember seeing numbers so low. He's not quite sure how to revive this man without killing him.

In fact, many hypothermia victims die each year in the process of being rescued. In what's called rewarming shock, the constricted capillaries reopen almost all at once, causing a sudden drop in blood pressure. The slightest movement can send a victim's heart muscle into wild spasms of ventricular fibrillation. In 1980, sixteen shipwrecked Danish fishermen were hauled to safety after an hour and a half in the frigid North Sea. They then walked across the deck of the rescue ship, stepped below for a hot drink, and dropped dead, all sixteen of them.

"Seventy-eight-point-nine," a technician calls out. "That's three-tenths down."

The patient is now experiencing after-drop, in which residual cold close to the body's surface continues to cool the core even after the victim is removed from the outdoors.

The doctor rapidly issues orders to his staff: intravenous administration of warm saline, the bag first heated in the microwave to 110 degrees. Elevating the core temperature of an average-size male 1 degree requires adding about 60 kilocalories of heat. A kilocalorie is the amount of heat needed to raise the temperature of 1 liter of water 1 degree Celsius. Since a quart of hot soup at 140 degrees offers about 30 kilocalories, the patient curled on the table would need to consume 40 quarts of chicken broth to push his core temperature up to normal. Even the warm saline, infused directly into his blood, will add only 30 kilocalories.

Ideally, the doctor would have access to a cardiopulmonary by-pass machine, with which he could pump out the victim's blood, warm and oxygenate it, and pump it back in again, safely raising the core temperature as much as 1 degree every three minutes. But such machines are rarely available outside major urban hospitals. Here, without such equipment, the doctor must rely on other options.

"Get me the peritoneal dialysis setup," he calls out.

Moments later, he's sliding a large catheter into an incision in the man's abdominal cavity. Warm fluid begins to flow from a suspended bag, washing through his abdomen, and draining out through another catheter placed in another incision. Prosaically, this lavage operates much like a car radiator in reverse: The solution warms the internal organs, and the warm blood in the organs is then pumped by the heart throughout the body. A catheter is inserted into his bladder, and warm fluid from another suspended bag flows into it.

The patient's stiff limbs begin to relax. His pulse edges up. But even so, the jagged line of his heartbeat flashing across the EKG screen shows the curious dip known as a J wave, common to hy-pothermia patients.

"Be ready to defibrillate," the doctor warns the EMTs. Yet he is aware how rare it is at such low core temperatures that an electrical shock will restore normal heart rhythm.

For another hour, nurses and EMTs hover around the edges of the table where the patient lies centered in a warm pool of light. They check his heart. They check the heat of the mattress beneath him. They whisper to one another about the foolishness of having gone out alone tonight.

And slowly the patient responds. Another liter of saline is added to the IV. The man's blood pressure remains far too low, brought down by the blood flowing out to the fast-opening capillaries of his limbs. Fluid lost through perspiration and urination has reduced his blood volume. But every fifteen or twenty minutes, his temperature rises another degree. The immediate danger of cardiac fibrillation lessens as the heart and thinning blood warms. Frostbite could still cost him fingers or an earlobe. But he appears to have beaten back the worst of the frigidity.

For the next half hour, an EMT quietly calls the readouts of the thermometer, a mantra that marks the progress of this cold-blooded proto-organism toward a state of warmer, higher consciousness.

From somewhere far away in the immense, cold darkness, you hear a faint, insistent hum. Quickly it mushrooms into a ball of sound, like a planet rushing toward you, and then it becomes a stream of words.

A voice is calling your name.

You don't want to open your eyes. You sense heat and light playing against your eyelids, but beneath their warm dance a chill wells up inside you from the sunless ocean bottoms and the farthest depths of space. You are too tired even to shiver. You want only to sleep.

"Can you hear me?"

You force open your eyes. Lights glare overhead. Around the lights faces hover atop uniformed bodies. You try to think: You've been away a very long time, but where have you been?

"You're at the hospital. You got caught in the cold."

You try to nod. Your neck muscles feel rusted shut, unused for years. They respond to your command with only a slight twitch.

"You'll probably have amnesia," the voice says.

You remember the moon shining over the spiky ridge top and skiing up toward it, toward someplace warm beneath the frozen moon. After that, nothing—only that immense coldness lodged inside you.

"We're trying to get a little warmth back into you," the voice says.

You'd nod if you could. But you can't move. All you can feel is throbbing discomfort everywhere. Glancing down to where the pain is most biting, you notice blisters filled with clear fluid dotting your fingers, once gloveless in the snow. During the long, cold hours the tissue froze and ice crystals formed in the tiny spaces between your cells, sucking water from them, blocking the blood supply. You stare at them absently.

"I think they'll be fine," a voice from overhead says. "The damage looks superficial. We expect that the blisters will break in a week or so, and the tissue should revive after that."

If not, you know that your fingers will eventually turn black, the color of bloodless, dead tissue. And then they will be amputated.

But worry slips from you as another wave of exhaustion sweeps in. Slowly you drift off, dreaming of warmth, of tropical ocean wavelets breaking across your chest, of warm sand beneath you.

Hours later, still logy and numb, you surface, as if from deep under water. A warm tide seems to be flooding your midsection. Focusing your eyes down there with difficulty, you see tubes running into you, their heat mingling with your abdomen's depthless cold like a churned-up river. You follow the tubes to the bag that hangs suspended beneath the electric light.

You begin to understand. The bag contains all that you had so nearly lost. These people huddled around you have brought you sunlight and warmth, things you once so cavalierly dismissed as constant, available, yours, summoned by the simple twisting of a knob or tossing on of a layer.

But in the hours since you last believed that, you've traveled to a place where there is no sun. You've seen that in the infinite reaches of the universe, heat is as glorious and ephemeral as the light of the stars. Heat exists only where matter exists, where particles can vibrate and jump. In the infinite winter of space, heat is tiny; it is the cold that is huge.

Someone speaks. Your eyes move from bright lights to shadowy forms in the dim outer reaches of the room. You recognize the voice of one of the friends you set out to visit, so long ago now. She's smiling down at you crookedly.

"It's cold out there," she says. "Isn't it?"

CHAPTER TWO

A RIVER OF ONE'S OWN:

DROWNING

Under heaven nothing is more soft and yielding than water
Yet for attacking the solid and strong, nothing is better.

TAO TE CHING, SIXTH CENTURY B.C.

Matt knew in the first instant that he'd entered rapids far more powerful than any he'd paddled before. From the calm eddy near the shore he gave three quick strokes to drive his kayak into the mainstream. His boat's bow was seized and jerked downstream by the river that roller-coastered through the canyon, the sudden acceleration snapping back his head and torso in the cockpit as if he'd stomped the gas pedal of a race car. Instinctively he pressed his paddle blade facedown in the water to brace his boat upright. Leaning on the blade as he crested the first great, rolling wave, a single thought whisked through Matt's mind: *Holy shit!*

To Matt's kayaker friends on the shore, the river's cascade of foam and noise and spray resembled a freight train, flying by so close and fast and loud you couldn't make out the rail company's name on an individual car without quickly swinging your eyes and head to follow its motion. The entire volume of the Yangtze River cascaded over the edge of the Tibetan Plateau, the "Roof of the World," and spilled down a 500-mile-long series of gorges like a cloudburst down a giant drainpipe. Halfway down, this giant drainpipe was blocked by the Jade Dragon Mountains, a steep, beautiful, snow-capped range that formed an 18,000-foot-high dam. Eons ago, an earthquake had snapped the mountains' spine with a 2-mile-deep fracture—so narrow and so deep that the Chinese knew it as Tiger's Leap Gorge, for the hunted tiger that once had supposedly leapt across it. Here the world's fourth-longest river literally tipped sideways to squeeze through this crack in the mountains in a roaring chaos of water seeking the quickest path to the sea.

No one had ever run the gorge in a kayak. No one had even *tried*, so daunting and remote was this stretch of river. At great expense and effort, Matt and his friends had traveled to Yunnan Province to attempt the gorge's first kayak descent—a feat that, if successful, would claim a small but significant place in kayaking history. For three days they'd camped on a broad shelf of rock carved from the gorge's wall to scout the rapids, scanning the river through binoculars and scrambling over the boulders along the shore. The power and noise and size of the water was far larger in real life than anything they'd imagined from the warm safety of home, and Matt, finally, was the only one willing to attempt it.

"I don't know, Matt," one of the group had cautioned around the campfire. "You're the best paddler here, but did you see the *size* of those holes? They could swallow an entire cargo raft, not to mention your little kayak."

Matt stared into the flames. He could hear the distant roar of the water from deep in the canyon, ululating on the night breeze like the ebb and flow of far-off surf. In his mind's eye, he saw the holes, where enormous boulders had fallen from the gorge's walls into midstream and now stood as obstacles to the river's flow. As the current flowed up and over a boulder, it fell down the far side and formed a depression in the river's surface—a "hole"—always on the downstream side. Rivers constantly tried to "fill" their holes by pouring in water from just downstream of the hole or from the sides, creating a foaming, spinning drain in the river's smooth flow.

You could find tiny holes in the smallest brooks, their little mustaches of whitewater just downstream of pebbles. On a big, steep river, the water thundered into a hole with such force that, should you inadvertently tip your craft into one, it could pull you, your life jacket, and your kayak down into it. It could bring you up to the surface again, pull you down again, bring you up—endlessly recirculating you as the water spins through the hole. This was known as a "keeper." From a keeper, there is only one exit: straight down. You would let the water pull you deep, and then—against all instinct, and while the oxygen disappears from your burning lungs—you swim even deeper, until finally the force of the down-pouring water spends itself on the river bottom and discharges you downstream. Then you swim to the surface. Assuming, of course, you're still alive.

The flames bent in the breeze, and the distant roar of the rapids sounded as if it had gone underground, then emerged again. Matt had missed his line and dumped his kayak into holes before, lots of times, although the holes he'd seen the last three days were bigger—*much* bigger—than any he'd encountered in all his years kayaking. He'd started paddling with his friends the summer after their freshman year in college. When fall had come that year, he just couldn't walk away, as they managed to do, from the searing intensity and delicate finesse of a ride through whitewater and settle back into a classroom.

"What am I *doing* here?" he asked himself after the first twenty minutes of the first class, as the professor droned on about the fundamentals of accounting. When the bell rang at the end of the hour he walked to the bookstore and returned the fat accounting textbook for cash. He never looked back.

Since then, he'd scraped by with whatever decent seasonal job he could find—laying asphalt, pouring concrete, building swimming pools—and spent all his spare time seeking out whitewater rivers. He organized a big trip once a year with his old kayaking buddies, and it had been his suggestion that they try Tiger's Leap Gorge. He was surprised at first that they'd agreed to his proposal; either they didn't comprehend quite what a fearsome stretch of water it was, or they knew they could always bow out of the paddling. For Matt, however, it was much more complicated. They would go home and make their marks in their professional fields—their software designing and their company managing—and simply chalk up a failed expedition as a nice trip to an exotic place. But kayaking was what he *did*. It was how he thought of himself. He wasn't a company manager or a software designer or a securities trader, he was a kayaker. This, right here—this gorge, this first descent, this moment—was his.

Matt looked up. The firelight reflected in their eyes as they watched him. "I've worked for two years framing houses to make enough money for this trip," he said. "I'm not going home without at least trying. Besides, I'm not planning on dumping into one of those big holes. And if I do—well, I guess I'll just have to hang on, go deep, and wait till it kicks me out below."

No one spoke. They looked down into the hissing coals and up at each other, silently asking, *Should we try to stop him?*

"Have you ever read Lao Tzu—the Tao Te Ching?" Matt asked suddenly, looking around at the silent, firelit faces. After he quit college, he'd made a point of continuing to read, as if to compensate for his lack of studies, and tightly gripped his discoveries with the passionate single-mindedness of the self-educated. "It's a lot about water," he told them. "The way it moves and how it flows around obstacles like rocks and a lot about how this is the way you should live your life. That you have to yield to something in order to overcome it. That's how a paddler has to think. Especially in a big hole. You can't fight the hydraulics. You have to give yourself over to it in order to be let go."

His friends looked at each other again across the flames. "You're talking Class Six rapids in that gorge, Matt," said one. "Wanting to run it as badly as you do doesn't sound like 'yielding' to me."

"Well, I'm going to do it anyway," Matt said abruptly. "You can either help me, or I'll do it alone."

After a breakfast the next morning of green tea and Chinese noodles, Matt and his friends hauled his equipment down to a slab of rock near the water. Though the kayakers each usually looked after his or her own equipment and preparations, they all now helped Matt dress for the run, attending to him like squires preparing a knight for battle. They held open the back of his full-length Gore-Tex dry suit as he climbed into it, zipped it up the back, and fussed with the rubber gaskets around his wrists, ankles, and neck, designed to seal the water out, tightening down each with a Velcro overlay strap. They knelt before him and helped him slip on his river shoes, designed with mesh uppers to drain water, and rubber soles stiff enough to push away from submerged boulders should he have to swim from his kayak, but sticky enough to scale a canyon wall if that was his only escape from the gorge.

As his friends cinched straps and sealed Velcro and zipped zippers, Matt's body was already shifting into battle mode. Triggered by the fearsome pounding of the river and the task at hand, his brain signaled his adrenal glands, perched atop each kidney, to release. He felt a fluttery quickness spread in his torso as they poured adrenaline and noradrenaline into his heart, which pumped it to his muscles and organs, where the volatile molecules contracted the fibers to prepare him for either fight or flight when he met his foe. His 35 feet of small intestine shut down, his anus snapped closed, his liver dumped out sugar into his bloodstream to fuel his muscles, and his heartbeat suddenly doubled, jumping from its resting rate of 60 beats per minute to 120. The adrenaline hit the muscles around his chest and diaphragm, and his breathing surged and deepened from 12 shallow breaths per minute to 20 deep ones. His body was taking on oxygen as if it knew, more than he, just how badly he'd be needing it.

His friends helped strap on his high-flotation, bright yellow life vest, easy to spot should he be trapped underwater, and equipped with a built-in harness to which they could clip a carabiner and rescue rope, attaching it to a pulley system rigged on shore to hoist him out if he or his kayak was pinned by the current against a log or boulder. Finally, like squires lowering a battle helmet over the knight's head, they fitted his Kevlar paddling helmet and strapped it beneath his chin. This would protect his skull from collisions with underwater rocks if his kayak tipped and he floated along upside-down underwater attempting to right it with that quick flick of his paddle and hips known as an Eskimo roll.

"Do you want your face guard?" one of his friends asked, holding up a meshwork of metal that fitted to the front of his helmet to protect his face from contact with submerged rocks.

Matt brushed it away. "I'd rather be able to see where I'm going."

Carrying his bright red polyethylene kayak and carbon-fiber paddle with the translucent yellow Kevlar blades, the group shuffled over the ancient rock of the gorge to the slab's edge, where it dropped abruptly 5 or 6 feet to the river's surface. Just upstream from where they stood, a point of rock projected from the shore into the roaring current and formed a back eddy—a quieter, sheltered piece of water where the current actually travels upstream like the air swirling in behind a windbreak. Matt snuggled his legs down inside his kayak's fat, stubby hull, padded exactly to fit his body, and stretched his spray squirt around the cockpit to prevent water from leaking in. The kayak's design was known as a "creek boat"—preferred by expert kayakers for running steep and very technical whitewater, stable yet quick-turning, and its hull designed to cushion the impact of kayakers free-falling over waterfalls and landing their boats with the boat bottoms flat to the river in the maneuver known as a "boof."

Matt loved the rhythm of whitewater kayaking: first the mist-soaked concentration as he clambered along the shore scouting for a perfect, clean line through the puzzle of rocks and crosscurrents and holes that formed a rapid; then assembling in his mind a series of moves like a choreographed dance. The run as he wished it to happen etched and rehearsed and rerehearsed in his memory, there followed the preparations of dressing while the tension built inside him; then the incredible intensity and focus and exertion of the run itself, and, if it went well, the final release in a gentle pool below the rapids when serenity and warmth and relief wrapped his whole being. If big-water kayaking resembled some high-speed, high-stakes game of chess, where the moves were memorized beforehand, running a section as powerful and untried as Tiger's Leap Gorge was like playing against a grand master who had never lost a game.

Matt's friends strapped on their own life vests and spread out along the ledges and rocks along the shore, each carrying a bag that contained a floating polypropylene throw rope that they could fling to Matt in case he needed help. Sealed into the cockpit, Matt used his hands like a seal uses flippers to maneuver his kayak to the very lip of the rock shelf, took up his paddle, waved to his friends, and gave a final jerk of his hips. The kayak tilted off the ledge and boofed down into the eddy with a splash.

With three quick strokes, he launched out into the roller-coastering surge of the main current, vaguely sensing his friends' presence sweeping past him on shore, blue and red smudges of rain parkas and life vests in the corner of his eye, hearing shouts growing faint in the roar: "Go, Matt! Go!"

Matt held his brace, leaning on his paddle, over the first big rolling wave, down into the trough, and up the second, ready to make his move. Some of the toughest maneuvering came at the beginning of the run—an S-curve between three big boulders, and then a hard pull to the left to avoid where the river cascaded over a chunk of rock as large as a house that sat to the right of the river's center. Just downstream of the rock loomed a hole as big as a five-car garage. That's what he had to avoid.

Spotting the first boulder of the S-turn, Matt paddled hard right, back left, then right again, weaving his way through the obstacles. To his friends onshore it appeared his red helmet and whirling yellow paddle blades were some child's toy bouncing down an enormous foaming set of stairs.

Then the House Rock. *Left! Left! Left!* When he'd scouted it from shore, Matt hadn't noticed how profoundly the current shifted here to the right—the opposite of the direction he needed to go. He pulled with all his strength, feeling the flex of his paddle shaft, the clench and release of his biceps, the wheeze of his lungs, the dig of the blades. He was fighting the entire force of the current that slid sideways in a bubbling, swirling sheet like a glacier that had come to life, shoving him inexorably across the channel toward the wrong shore, toward House Rock. Matt's cardiovascular system was now in overdrive. His breathing rate jumped to 35 breaths a minute, near the maximum for efficient breathing, taking in 130 liters of air—about 35 gallons—each minute. His heart beat at 190 beats per minute and pumped nearly 30 liters of blood, or over 7 gallons each minute, enough to fill a bathtub up to the overflow drain in four minutes. This river of blood, the amount a trained athlete's heart puts out near maximum performance, is what it took to supply Matt's muscles with enough oxygen to paddle Tiger's Leap Gorge.

His paddle blades whirled and pulled against the flow, straining left, and his little cork of a craft was still being swept to the right. Thirty yards away he could see how the moving sheet of water arched in a huge glassy bulge over House Rock, like a crystal dome. *Pull. Pull. Pull.* He could feel the sharp cut of the breeze on his wet face as the current accelerated toward the rock. He had to pull harder. His kayak was spinning sideways. He was being whisked up that glassy bulge. He could hear the thundering roar of the hole beyond the bulge. He braced his paddle to try to straighten his kayak. He saw a maelstrom of white and noise far below him. He was being tossed into the air. Then he was falling upside down, vainly paddling through the empty air, with the kayak still attached to his legs trailing behind him like some molded-polyethylene kite tail, as he plunged down into the hole's spinning eye.

His friends on shore couldn't see what happened. They watched Matt shoot up on top of an enormous rooster tail of water as if launching from a ski jump, his blades windmilling in the air, and then he was gone.

One of the sea's most exceptional diving mammals, the white whale *Delphinapterus leucas* (or beluga), can hold its breath for seventeen minutes and plunge to depths of half a mile under the ocean's surface. The elephant seal can remain submerged for up to two hours. Other seals can dive nearly a mile deep. These deep-diving marine mammals manage their stunning feats by storing oxygen in tissues and blood while breathing on the surface, and drawing on their reserves underwater. Some have respiratory systems that allow their lungs to collapse under the pressure of extreme depths, and some drop their heart and metabolic rates on extended dives to curb oxygen use. It is believed that deep-diving penguins rely on anaerobic metabolism—metabolism without oxygen—to power their swimming muscles while underwater, while ducks allow their brains to cool to temperatures low enough to prevent brain damage from lack of oxygen.

Humans, however, are very different. Unlike the marine mammals, one unfortunate side effect of our evolution as a species is that as our human progenitors climbed from the warm seas and began to walk about on dry land, they retained almost zero capacity to warehouse oxygen. We as a species possess very little capacity to hold our breath. For precisely this reason, drowning is the third most common cause of death from accidental injury in the United States, at 8,000 deaths per year. In Europe, 35,000 people drown annually, and worldwide nearly half a million people perish, placing drowning in fourth place in deaths from injuries—just ahead of falls and just behind murder and violence.*

More than many forms of death, drowning retains a literary quality, as if the act of submersion itself connotes surrender, submission to something greater, or, among the despairing, the abandoning of all hope. Having used water imagery in much of her fiction, Virginia Woolf, fearing another bout of madness in the spring of 1941 as German bombs dropped on England, loaded the pockets of her heavy fur coat with stones and waded out into a favorite stretch of the River Ouse. The first wife of the romantic poet Percy Bysshe Shelley drowned herself after Shelley took up with a sixteen-year-old girl, and Shelley himself drowned a few years later when his small yacht, *Ariel,* capsized off the coast of Tuscany in 1822.

For centuries, drowning has loomed in the popular imagination as a gruesome but often-preventable form of death. Europe and America's original humane societies, founded in the late 1700s, were chartered not for the humane treatment of animals but for reviving nearly drowned humans—such as London's Society for the Recovery of Persons Apparently Drowned. It was later renamed the Royal Humane Society for the Apparently Dead, to include other types of what was called "sudden death," such as falls and lightning strikes. The London and Amsterdam societies alone were said to have saved over a thousand lives in a twenty-year period.

Their detailed case reports describe how to perform CPR techniques developed in the late eighteenth century that appear

---

* *World Health Report 2000: Annex Table 3: Deaths by cause, sex and mortality stratum in WHO Regions, estimates for 1999.* Geneva, Switzerland: World Health Organization, 2000. Traffic accidents and suicides are the world's leading causes of death from injuries.

startlingly modern: mouth-to-mouth resuscitation ("the medium of a handkerchief or cloth may be used to render the operation less indelicate"), the use of tubes to keep the breathing passages clear, and the use of bellows, which all resuscitation teams were recommended to carry, to assist the ventilation of the lungs. Rescuers discovered that electric shock could stimulate a stopped heart back into action. In 1819 Giovanni Aldini, nephew of the famed researcher of electricity Luigi Galvani, wrote a book titled *The Application of Galvanism for Medical Purposes, Particularly in Cases of Suspended Animation*. The Humane Society of New York concurred that electricity was indeed a "most powerful agent, a very proper remedy," recommending that "strong sparks . . . should be drawn from the left side over the heart." It appears from her own introduction to the book that this use of electricity to revive the near-dead was inspiration for Mary Wollstonecraft Shelley, wife of the soon-to-be-drowned poet, for her 1818 novel of terror where the monster comes to life with the application of a bolt of lightning, *Frankenstein*.

Dr. Frankenstein's fame notwithstanding, many of these techniques were abandoned or lost and not rediscovered and refined by researchers until the 1950s. Today they are used routinely. One difference, however, is that those eighteenth-century victims succumbed in lakes, rivers, and the sea, while in the United States about half of today's victims (and many in Australia) drown in swimming pools—especially toddlers who fall into private pools. Unlike a few centuries ago, drownings in the sea are comparatively rare except in cold-water fishing communities. Drownings among whitewater boaters—kayakers, canoeists, or rafters who are paddling in rapids—also make up only a small fraction of all drowning deaths, under fifty annually in the United States according to whitewater accident reports, the number having climbed as more paddlers pursue ever steeper and bigger descents.

Whatever the specific circumstances—a sinking ship, a swimming pool, a rock-laden fur coat, a kayak in Class V rapids—drowning is the archetype for all human deaths. At the very end almost everyone—heart patient, cancer victim, the very aged—perishes from the very cause so dramatically embodied in drowning: lack of oxygen to the brain. In the case of these illnesses, it can take days or weeks or years to reach that final moment. But drowning accelerates the process to a horrifying pace: the average person can hold his or her breath for about a minute and a half before inhaling or blacking out. In a victim on dry land whose breathing has stopped, brain damage starts to occur after about four minutes, and doctors consider the chances of brain recovery virtually nil after ten minutes. Underwater, however, especially cold water, these times can attenuate. One study of fifty-seven near-drowning survivors showed they were totally immersed for an estimated average of eleven and a half minutes. This is still a very short time.

O minutes, 03 seconds: *Get a few big breaths!* That's Matt's only thought as he wheels upside down through the air over House Rock. He has no time to think, no time to be scared, no time except for the most instinctive reactions. He manages to suck in just short of 5 liters—a little over 5 quarts—of air in his last breath. This is nearly his vital capacity, or the maximum amount his lungs can take in with a single breath, which ranges among individuals from 2 to 6 liters. The air Matt pulls in, just like every other breath of the earth's atmosphere, is composed of four-fifths nitrogen and one-fifth oxygen. This gives him 1 liter of precious oxygen trapped in his lungs—about a quart—to keep the spark of life burning for his journey beneath the surface.

He plunges into the hole headfirst. He is instantly ripped out of his kayak. The water snaps his paddle shaft in two and tears it from his grip, strips the contact lenses from his corneas, pulls the helmet off his head, and yanks at the straps of his life vest as if some great animal were shaking him in its teeth. He feels himself plunging down through layers of water as if slicing through some giant layer cake: first whitish foam, then foam churned with green water, then invisible clouds of dark-green water buffeting him silently as he's pulled toward the river bottom. Far above him he can hear the deep bass rumble of the water thundering over the rock.

Profound changes in his physiology occur even in these first few seconds. All humans, to a greater or lesser degree, retain a ghostly genetic inheritance of the marine mammals' diving response, which flips one's metabolic switch from fast to slow in order to conserve oxygen while underwater. Simply by dipping your face in ice water, you can drop your heart rate from 70 to 45 beats per minute, and some athletes can lower their pulse rate with ice-water facials to under 6 beats per minute. As his heart rate drops, Matt's veins and arteries in his arms and legs constrict to channel his remaining oxygenated blood to his brain, heart, and other vital organs. Like a seal or whale, his body strains to conserve that single liter—that 1,000 milliliters—of oxygen.

0 minutes, 12 seconds (825 milliliters of oxygen remaining): Matt stays down, holding his breath. Already he can feel the strain in his lungs. Carbon dioxide—what his cells expel as a waste product after they've burned fuel—is building in his muscles and organs and is taken away by his bloodstream to his lungs. Extremely precise sensors in his brain "taste" the slight acidic content of his blood from the buildup of carbon dioxide, and signal his lungs—urgently—to exhale it. It's this carbon dioxide buildup, and not lack of oxygen, that largely triggers his urge to breathe. For this reason, underwater distance swimmers sometimes hyperventilate beforehand to partially cleanse their blood of carbon dioxide, helping them short-circuit the body's urge to breathe. "I felt like I could swim forever without a breath," is how some of them have described their state shortly before they blacked out and had to be dragged from the bottom of the pool. Matt managed a good breath before going under, but he didn't hyperventilate and hasn't totally overridden his breathing urge. He feels an intensifying pressure inside his chest, almost like an inflating

balloon. *Breathe out!* his body is telling him. *Expel that carbon dioxide! Breathe out!*

Hang on, he's telling himself, marshaling all his will to fight that expanding pain in his chest. *Don't panic,* he tells himself. *You've been here before.* It's a giant Maytag, as the kayakers say—a hole that endlessly recirculates whatever it's caught. He can feel himself being lifted toward the surface by the billows of black current welling up from down deep and, as he rises, slammed back down toward the bottom by sledgehammer blasts of whitewater that have cascaded over the rock. His lungs scream for him to break to the surface, to struggle wildly to the top. *Stay down!* he tells himself. *Don't fight the water! Go deeper!* Overcoming every human instinct to go up, he kicks and strokes downward, bumping and scraping down along the submerged face of House Rock, which slides past him like the wall of an elevator shaft.

0 minutes, 22 seconds (640 milliliters of oxygen remaining): He can't hear the profound thunder above him anymore, and the water stays consistently dark. He senses he's been flushed out of the hole's Maytag cycle and sent downstream. But still-powerful underwater crosscurrents flail him about, his arms and legs whipped around like lengths of wet tissue paper as he tries to relax and let the water take him until it slows a bit and he can surface. Under the buffeting of the currents, his life jacket feels as if it has all the buoyancy of a soaked sweatshirt. It's as if he's swum into a herd of huge underwater animals whose fins brush and knock him about.

Meanwhile, remarkable events unfold inside his lungs. Matt's precious liter of oxygen fills three hundred million tiny sacs in each lung called alveoli, which, if spread out, would cover an area half the size of a tennis court. These sacs are enmeshed with blood-filled capillaries so fine and extensive that one physiologist likens them to spreading a single glassful of blood so thinly, it covers the entire surface of that half-court. What's more, this blood is squeegeed up from the tennis court and a new glassful spread over its surface more than once each second as his heart pumps blood through his lungs.

In that fraction of a second each glassful of blood unloads its waste carbon dioxide and dumps it into his lungs and at the same time loads up with a fresh cargo of oxygen in the process known as gas exchange.

0 minutes, 28 seconds (490 milliliters of oxygen remaining): The buffeting along the river bottom gentles for a moment. He's entered a calmer pool, a slack spot in the current's flow. *This is it*, he thinks. *Make your move.* He kicks and strokes upward, trying not to flail, conserving his body's resources. As he slices upward, the water color lightens—dark green to pale green to swirling foam. The bubbles spin around his head and in his ears—the crackling, breathy sound of the surface, of air, of life. He's about to break the surface. This is it. He'll suck in a huge lungful of fresh air. But the current abruptly lifts his body, tosses it down. He tumbles over a submerged boulder. Another hole. Down, down, down he goes again through the layers of light. It's black. He can't breathe. He's tumbling over and over. He has to get out, to fight, claw, scratch his way out. *No!* he tells himself. *Yield to it! Yield, and overcome!*

0 minutes, 37 seconds (415 milliliters of oxygen remaining): Already his consciousness has begun to shrink from lack of oxygen, like a globe of light that slowly contracts and dims. His oxygen delivery and carbon dioxide monitoring systems are on red alert. Instead of a rich, oxygenated red, his blood has begun to turn bluish. His heart thumps and his ears ring loudly with its thumping. His thoughts turn slower and slower beneath the water: *You're going to die if you stay here any longer*.

Part of him wants to panic, but he can't quite manage it, as if the panic itself occurs in slow motion. He kicks and pulls for the surface. His actions seem strangely ineffective, dreamlike. He is suffering the symptoms of hypoxia—lack of oxygen reaching the body's tissues. Distantly he can feel his arm and leg muscles burn, like the far-off pain of a dentist's drill faintly penetrating the anesthetic. Without adequate oxygen to metabolize his body's fuels, lactic acid has built up in his muscles to painful levels. Still the black gusts of current hold him down. He looks up through the green blackness toward the direction he thinks is the surface. His friends are up there waiting for him. They are reaching out for him. He can't disappoint them. They didn't want him to go down here. Now they want him to surface. He can't stay down.

He summons his whole concentration, like scooping up an armload of fallen leaves that want to waft away on the wind. *Up, up, up.* He strains up through the dark water to see the silvery surface. *Up is life. Down is death.*

More than actually seeing it, he senses the light again. He feels his body tossed upward. He hears swirling bubbles. White foam surrounds him. Cold air strikes his face. The roar of water fills his ears. Reflexively he exhales a great sigh of carbon dioxide. His mammalian instincts take over, and he pushes up his head like a seal pushing its nose through a hole in the ice. He breathes in. As he does, his body is tossed over into another hole. Matt's last breath is a breathful of foam.

o minutes, 54 seconds (325 milliliters of oxygen remaining): Matt gags on the foam as he goes down again. His larynx is in spasms, reflexively closing on the water and foam. No more water can enter his lungs. Many drowning victims inhale only a glassful or so of water, and in "dry" drownings—about 10 to 15 percent of all victims—the larynx closes before inhaling and the lungs contain no water at all.

Matt doesn't know quite what's happening to him. He has a vague sense of tumbling, as if he's in a giant, warm whirlpool and helping hands are massaging and lifting him.

1 minute, 23 seconds (220 milliliters of oxygen remaining): Drowning doesn't happen all at once. It happens gradually. Matt's consciousness shrinks to a smaller and smaller spot, then blackens. He's tumbling along the dark and turbulent bottom. The water he inhaled has filled some of the alveoli sacs and "washed out" their surfactant, or protein coating. Without it, the lungs' inflatable sacs can stiffen and collapse, as in the case of premature infants who are

born with a surfactant deficiency and whose lungs are treated with substitutes made from cow or human amniotic fluid. Even if Matt were now brought to the surface and revived, he could perish a few hours later of "secondary drowning"—when the damaged lungs fill with fluid from the victim's own body, causing pulmonary edema and drowning the victim from within.

By now, however, there is little chance that someone will rescue Matt. Immersed in the crashing river sounds and brilliant daylight that bathes their ledge of rock, Matt's friends scan the river, straining to see where he's gone. They begin to worry. He should have popped up by now in a calm pool along the riverbank. They see nothing, not even his kayak. They don't realize that Matt—or what is becoming less and less Matt—is 8 feet below the river's surface and already a quarter mile downstream from the hole he tumbled into at House Rock.

2 minutes, 16 seconds (98 milliliters of oxygen remaining): Matt is like a rag doll. Concentrating his blood in heart and brain, his body makes its last stand against the approach of death. That last stand can be miraculously long in certain cases, especially among young children drowning in frigid water, when the diving reflex, for unknown reasons, responds profoundly and hypothermia slows the victim's metabolism nearly to a standstill, preserving a faint hint of life.

On February 6, 1974, at 11:30 A.M., in a classic and well-documented incident, a four-year-old Norwegian boy was seen to fall through river ice. By the time divers arrived from 15 miles away and located his body in 10 feet of water, the boy had been submerged for exactly forty minutes. His body was gray and lifeless, his pupils fixed and dilated, his pulse absent. Given immediate CPR, he was rushed to the hospital, arriving ten minutes later. Doctors ventilated his lungs with pure oxygen, rewarmed him on a water-filled mattress, and injected his blood with a solution of baking soda to correct its high acid content caused by so much carbon dioxide and metabolism without oxygen. The doctors kept up chest compressions for an hour after his arrival, when his heart kicked in strongly on its own. By that evening, the boy moved his eyes and stirred his limbs, and the next night he understood verbal commands. The day after that he was fully conscious. He left the hospital eight days after his admission in order to celebrate his fifth birthday at home. That spring—having fully recovered mentally and physically—he learned to ride a bicycle.

4 minutes, 21 seconds (37 milliliters of oxygen remaining): Matt is slowly ceasing to exist. He's not young enough and the water isn't cold enough for him to experience a diving reflex as profound as that of the Norwegian boy. His feeble heartbeat still pushes a residual amount of oxygen to his brain.

7 minutes, 55 seconds (trace amounts of oxygen remaining): Now alarmed, Matt's teammates scramble downriver along the rocky banks, searching for his kayak, his paddle, him. They see nothing. Matt's body is already half a mile down the rapids, tumbling at a depth of 12 feet.

19 minutes, 36 seconds: Matt's brain function has ceased but for the faintest flickers of electrical pulses. Two of Matt's friends begin to hike—run, really—up the steep, rocky trail out of Tiger's Leap Gorge to summon help. His other friends continue to comb the riverbank. Maybe he's dragging himself to shore somewhere downstream, out of sight. They hope against hope.

1 hour, 6 minutes: The searchers reconvene half a mile downstream from where they started on the ledge of rock. Even here, the whitewater is frightening in its violence, its tossing, foaming mounds of water shaped like haystacks and its sucking holes. Over the roar of the rapids, they shout back and forth to each other, waving their arms at various holes and pools of the river where Matt should be but isn't, their panic climbing, then subsiding like the ululating roar, until it's finally overcome by resignation and surrender to the obvious: Matt has drowned.

5 hours, 23 minutes: The two who went for help reach a small

Chinese village terraced into a mountainside. Inside the mud-brick government office is a single old black telephone. The Chinese official in charge picks it up to alert the authorities in the county seat. When he hangs up he looks at them for a few moments in silence, then speaks quietly in broken English. He tells them that the Chinese have no resources to spend on an elaborate search with helicopters or rescue divers, even if there were any around, which there are not. Chinese people fall into the rivers every day and drown, the official tells Matt's friends. You'll see them in the Yangtze, downstream, if you ride a passenger boat. Their bodies fill up with gases and rise to the surface and bob along like logs. No one has rescued them. Your friend has chosen to put himself in dangerous water. Now the dangerous water will carry him away to the sea.

Matt's friends rage against the official. They pound his desk with their fists and kick his office walls. But they know that their anger and frustration have nothing to do with the official or any attempts at rescue. Matt, they are sure, is long dead.

Finally they leave the office. They walk through the village back toward the gorge, cursing the official, cursing China, wishing they had never come. The mud-brick village with its red-tiled roofs and mountain backdrop that looked so charming when they first arrived now looks impoverished, callous, mean-spirited. At the far end of the village, they walk past the Taoist temple. They cannot read Chinese characters, but if they could they might note the inscription whitewashed onto its ochre mud wall:

> *The highest good is like water.*
> *Water . . . does not strive.*
> *It flows in places men reject and so is like the Tao.*

CHAPTER THREE

ARCHING TOWARD THE CLEAR LIGHT:

MOUNTAIN SICKNESS

"Adrian's stumbling," Mara called out.

Beneath the rush of wind across the snow Mara heard her own breath—one, two, three, four times her chest heaved before she could take the next step up the slope. Just above, the three women of the first summit team waited. At her shout they turned their heads in unison down the slope. Mara could see the sharp flash of high-altitude sunlight off their dark glacier glasses as their eyes traced the 150-foot rope from Mara, who led the second team, down to Adrian, who was its middle climber.

Adrian's head was down. She lifted each foot excruciatingly slowly up the steps that the first team had kicked into the snow slope. It looked as if the sharp metal points of the crampons, strapped to the soles of her thick plastic climbing boots to prevent her from slipping, were adhering to the snow with half-cured epoxy resin. As the women watched, she inexplicably lurched to her left, dropped to one knee, and tried to catch herself from falling forward onto her face by leaning on her ice axe as if it were a cane, but it slipped from her grip and she sprawled in the snow.

She lay facedown, her arms making slow swimming motions as

if absently exploring a way to push herself up out of a pool of water. From the lower end of the rope, Linda, the last climber on Mara's team, shouted encouragement.

"Come on, Adrian, get up, you can do it! Just up to the others! Get up to the others and we'll rest!"

Slowly Adrian pushed herself to her knees, maneuvered one foot under her, then the other, and started up again.

The two were just an hour or so short of the summit. To get this far had taken them three weeks of hard labor, climbing without bottled oxygen and pioneering a difficult new route up the north face of the Himalayan giant—or rather giantess. This mountain was known to the natives as Annapurna, or "Goddess of the Harvest." At 26,504 feet, it was the world's tenth highest mountain, thrusting up out of the lush green rice fields in the center of Nepal in an enormous massif of a central peak surrounded by dozens of subsidiary peaks. Not as high as Everest nor as technically difficult as K2, the world's second highest peak at 28,251 feet in Pakistan's Karakoram Range, it was still a very formidable mountain. It was known for its beautiful surroundings and its remoteness, as well as for the enormous avalanches that swept down from its broad upper slopes and tumbled over the icefalls and glaciers thousands of feet to the valleys below. Its snow was abundant, its storms frequent and fierce, and its weather and avalanche risk could easily trap the unwary in places far higher than they wanted to be.

Mara reached the three women waiting above. "We've got to let Adrian rest," she gasped between breaths. "She's getting clumsier with every step."

"We can't rest too long or we're not going to make it," said Becca, the lead climber on the first-team rope. Becca was also the organizer of this all-women expedition, the one who had planned the summit attempt and kept everyone moving on schedule, delicately balancing their ambitions to make the top, their physical condition and need to acclimatize, and the fact that the monsoon was due to arrive any day, bringing with it storms that would prevent any further climbing.

Adrian finally kicked her way up the last steps to the little group. She sat down abruptly in the snow, head between her knees, back heaving.

"How are you feeling?" asked Becca. "Do you think you can keep going, or do you want to rest here for a few minutes?"

"I'm having a hard time today," was all Adrian said, her head still between her knees.

"What's going on?" Linda asked as she came up the last steps and completed the two teams gathered in a little clump on the vast white slope that rose to Annapurna's summit.

"We're resting," replied Becca, the way one might use the collective *we* when referring to a child.

Linda looked again at Adrian, head on knees, back and shoulders heaving for air. "Then what?"

"I don't know," said Becca. "Let's wait and see how she's feeling."

"Not up, I hope," Linda said. "Not when she's like this."

"Well," spoke up Gayle, one of the first-team climbers, "I'm not planning on going down, if that's what you mean."

The silk caravans of the ancient Chinese crossed two passes in the Karakoram Range named Little Headache and Big Headache, as recorded two thousand years ago by the Chinese official Too Kin. No one understood at the time that the earth's thinning atmosphere at high altitude triggered the symptoms of headache, nausea, fatigue, and a host of other problems that characterize mountain sickness. High-altitude travelers and residents offered many other explanations for the malady. The Tibetans, inhabitants of earth's highest plateau just to the east of the Karakoram, believed that travelers became sick when crossing high passes from inhaling the poisonous gases that swirled about the tallest peaks. On the opposite side of the globe, inhabitants of the Andes called the malady *mareo de punas*—seasickness of the high deserts—or *soroche*, a term also referring to antimony ore, as it was believed that noxious vapors from the ore sickened the laborers who worked the high-altitude mines. José de Acosta, a sixteenth-century Jesuit priest who traveled with the Spanish conquistadores over the Andes, wrote: "I was surprised with such pangs of straining and casting as I thought to cast up my heart too."

If you could weigh a column of air 1 inch square that reaches many miles up into the sky until the earth's atmosphere altogether vanishes, it would weigh at its base at sea level 14.7 pounds (thus the air pressure at sea level is 14.7 pounds per square inch). At 18,000 feet, however, it would weigh only about half of that, or a little more than 7 pounds, containing one-half the oxygen of the air at sea level. Nowhere in the world do humans live permanently above about 17,000 feet, the altitude of Peruvian mine sleeping quarters; above 19,000 feet the body can no longer acclimatize and slowly but progressively deteriorates, weakening and losing weight. An unacclimatized human suddenly placed without an oxygen mask atop the summit of 29,035-foot Mount Everest, where that 1-inch-square column of air weighs only about 5 pounds and contains one-third the oxygen, would lose consciousness in about a minute and a half and probably soon die. This is what befell the two companions of the balloonist Tissandier, who in 1875 made a rapid, three-hour ascent to 26,000 feet. He then passed out, and the balloon sank into an hour-long descent to the earth, whereupon Tissandier regained consciousness surrounded by his dead companions.

This is in stark contrast to birds, whose many adaptations allow them to tolerate extreme altitudes easily. Their lungs are something like a jet engine, in that they absorb oxygen continuously on both inhale and exhale, using a series of air chambers to maintain the continuous flow. The special hemoglobin in their blood snaps up oxygen even at very low pressures. In some birds, such as the bar-headed goose, the muscle tissue appears almost black due to the concentration of myoglobin, which helps store and deliver oxygen to the muscle cells' mitochondria, permitting the members of this species to follow their regular migratory route flying nonstop over the top of Mount Everest and the Himalaya between the plains of India and the highlands of Tibet. The highest-flying bird ever recorded was a Ruppell's griffon that whapped into an airliner while soaring on a warm updraft of air at 37,000 feet over the African plains. Like Hemingway's leopard lying in the snows of Kilimanjaro, no one could explain what it was doing up there. Even the common house sparrow pecking at the bird feeder in one's backyard can breathe the air at 30,000 feet, or 6 miles high, without any problem.

While it can't manage nearly as well as the sparrow, in its remarkable adaptability the human body is capable of adjusting to short stays at extreme altitudes (defined as those over 18,000 feet). A few powerful and well-acclimatized climbers such as Reinhold Messner and Peter Habler have even attained Everest's summit without breathing bottled oxygen, so close to the margins of the earth's thin atmosphere and of human endurance that for the last thousand feet of altitude they collapsed in the snow to rest every ten or fifteen steps. Over time—measured in days or even weeks—the body calls on a complex array of compensatory mechanisms to counter the lack of oxygen at high altitudes, adjusting its blood chemistry, fluid balance, and heart and breathing rates the way that a computer chip adjusts the fuel and air mix in the engine of a car to compensate for altitude. One study dramatically showed this adaptability to altitude by placing Peruvian highlanders in a special chamber and removing the air until the chamber's interior reached a simulated altitude of 30,000 feet. Eight of the sixteen highlanders remained conscious indefinitely, while the two sea-level dwellers, used as control subjects, blacked out in a minute and a half.

Like the computerized fuel-injection system, however, the acclimatization mechanisms in the human body sometimes go askew, especially when a visitor to high altitude doesn't take the time to adjust slowly and pushes too high too fast. The result is mountain sickness, whose symptoms are well known but whose exact workings are poorly understood. In its mildest form it consists of headache, tiredness, nausea, and a feeling of malaise. These symptoms are very common to visitors even at altitudes as low as 8,000 feet—the same as many Colorado ski resorts. Even a lowlander's visit to Denver, at only 5,000 feet, will cause some loss of night vision as the lack of oxygen affects the vision centers of the brain. In most cases, visitors to up to 8,000 feet become acclimatized after a day or two of rest, the headaches disappear, and they go on with their vacations. Only a very small percentage develop more severe forms of mountain sickness and must be hospitalized.

Rapid ascents above 8,000 feet boost the likelihood of both the less severe forms of mountain sickness as well as the two potentially fatal forms: high-altitude pulmonary edema (HAPE) and high-altitude cerebral edema (HACE). Roughly 3 to 5 percent of trekkers ascending to 14,000 feet in the Everest region were afflicted with mountain sickness and about 1 percent suffered pulmonary edema, according to one study. Pulmonary edema's incidence among climbers on Mount McKinley, where climbers ascend quickly with heavy loads in very cold temperatures, has been estimated at one in fifty. The low oxygen pressure and heavy exertion strain the lungs in such a way to fill their sacs with fluid, which, if left unchecked, drowns the victim from within. For many decades its symptoms were mistaken for those of pneumonia: extreme shortness of breath, fatigue, coughing, sometimes blood in the sputum. The symptoms of the less-frequent high-altitude cerebral edema, when the brain swells with fluid, imitate those of an evening spent at a bar: stumbling, lack of coordination, hearing or seeing things, drowsiness. The difference is that one may never wake from the coma that follows.

Treatment for both HAPE and HACE is really very simple and, if undertaken promptly, usually very effective. One high-altitude physician, with succinct urgency, describes the first three choices for treatment this way: "Descend! Descend! Descend!"

The problem is, it's not always possible to descend quickly. And in the places where one is most likely to suffer high-altitude pulmonary or cerebral edema—at 26,000 feet on a Himalayan mountainside—one is not likely to find a hospital.

"I don't think she's getting any better," Linda said after they'd been resting five minutes or so.

Becca placed her hand gently on Adrian's back. "Do you want a few more minutes?"

Without looking up, Adrian nodded.

"I think we should take her down right now," Linda said. "It might be exhaustion, or it might be something more serious. Either way, she can't go another hour like this."

Becca stood and looked up toward the summit ridge, silhouetted against the dark blue sky, a plume of snow spinning off it, and then the first-team climbers. No one spoke. Mara sensed the tension, the unspoken pressure on Becca, who had to make the decision. It would have been an easy decision if they weren't so close, if they knew they had more time, if the monsoon weren't due to arrive . . .

"Look, I'll stay with her if no one else will," Linda finally said. "Everyone else can go all the way up. Adrian and I will wait here until you get back."

"Are you sure you want to do that?" asked Becca. "This is probably going to be your only shot."

"She's my ropemate and my tentmate and my friend," Linda said. "I care more about her than I care about the summit."

Mara felt the group's attention shift to her, now that her two ropemates would stay behind.

"What about you, Mara?" Becca asked. "You can come with us, and we'll just rope together in two teams of two."

Mara tried to think it over. *Go or stay.* Her mind seemed to spin so slowly in the thin air, like a cloud gently tumbling over a peak. She'd climbed since high school, when she'd gone camping with a friend whose parents guided her up a small peak. She'd attended mountaineering camps during the following summers, eventually becoming an instructor, then went to college in a mountain town and studied environmental education with the hope that teaching about wild places could keep her close to the mountains. There were a thousand reasons she loved the mountains, and each mountain offered its own pull on her affections. Sometimes it was the sight of that pure white snow against the deep blue sky that compelled her, the sharp white edge between heaven and earth, or the tiny blue and pink wildflowers poking up so cheerfully among the weather-blasted barren rock, or the cold wind scrubbing her face and whipping tears from her eyes, or the satisfaction of solving a difficult problem—how to find a graceful and safe route to the top, cleverly using the ridges and couloirs and snowfields to help her toward her goal. Sometimes it was standing on top of a peak and feeling so tiny against the huge, indomitable mountain and the vast world spread out below. Sometimes it was the sense of teamwork when roped together and working as a single unit, and other times it was the independence and confidence it gave her. In a world that didn't easily recognize women's achievements and often tried to undermine them, climbing a peak was an undeniable and tangible attainment. No one could say she hadn't done it.

When Becca, whom she'd known along with Linda from their days instructing together at a mountaineering camp, told her she was organizing a major Himalayan climb for women, Mara jumped at the chance. All the compelling reasons she knew for climbing lesser peaks, she figured, would be magnified enormously by the sheer scale of the Himalaya. In addition, there was the nearness to Tibet. Annapurna's summit lay only about 30 miles—as the bar-headed goose flew—from the high ridge that marked the Tibetan border. She liked the notion that she could peer down from one of the earth's highest peaks onto its highest plateau, one of the strong-holds of Buddhism, a religion she'd been drawn to out of its respect for living things.

She wanted to attain that summit in a manner she felt good about. Leaving her two ropemates behind while she made the final climb seemed an act that she'd end up regretting. Instead of grace, it felt like selfishness. But maybe there was still a way she could catch a view of Tibet without going all the way to the top.

"I'll stay," she finally said.

"Mara, you should feel free to go," Linda urged. "We can man-age here without you."

"That's all right," Mara replied. "I'll stick with you two."

Adrian, head still down between her knees, raised her right hand slightly to acknowledge Mara's decision, a gesture of thanks.

Adrian's problem had started several weeks earlier, on the two-week trek from the low Nepalese valleys to Annapurna's base. With hired porters hauling the heavy loads of tents, climbing gear, and food, the women walked up the mountain trails, sleeping at some-what higher camps each night in order to acclimatize slowly as they ascended from the rice fields up to the hill farms. By the time they reached the higher villages at about 10,000 feet, their bodies had be-gun to respond to the thinning air—but, at first, in two curiously contradictory ways. Two sensors in their bodies, each adjusting to the new altitude, were working against each other. As they climbed into the thinning air, the oxygen sensors in their carotid arteries noted the dropping level of oxygen in their bloodstreams and sent out mes-sages telling their lungs to suck in more air with each breath. But the more deeply the lungs breathed in, the more carbon dioxide they ex-pelled with each outbreath. The carbon dioxide sensors residing in the brain noted the falling carbon dioxide levels in the women's bloodstream. They told the lungs to slow down—the women were altering their blood chemistry by breathing so hard.

They needed to acclimatize. Slowly they made their way beyond the last of the trees to Base Camp at 15,000 feet, where they pitched their tents among the heaps of broken, tumbled rock, known as moraines, pushed down the mountain by glaciers. After nearly a week at high altitude, their bodies had engineered a peace pact between the warring mechanisms. Their kidneys, serving as mediator, cleverly tricked their carbon dioxide sensors into thinking their blood contained more carbon dioxide than it actually did by removing some of the blood's alkaline substances, thus making the blood more acidic, as if it contained carbon dioxide that needed to be expelled. Now, instead of contradictory messages, both the oxygen and the carbon dioxide sensors were sending the same urgent signal to the lungs: *Breathe, and deeply!*

This physiological urge to breathe deeply at high altitude is a good thing—an adaptive mechanism—but varies widely among individuals. A strong hypoxic ventilatory response (HVR), as this urge is known, helps one adjust more easily to altitude, while a weak one, it is suspected, makes one more susceptible to mountain sickness. Contrary to what one might expect, there is evidence that training for long-distance sports may actually weaken rather than strengthen one's HVR. It has been proven over and over again that climbers who are in top physical shape are just as prone to mountain sickness as those who are not. Perhaps also contrary to expectations, men have a weaker HVR than women; female hormones such as progesterone and estrogen help stimulate breathing. In one study conducted atop Colorado's 14,000-foot Pike's Peak, the extra oxygen in women's blood, probably due to this increased breathing, was the equivalent of knocking 540 to 1,640 feet off the summit for the women in the group compared to the men. Researchers speculate that this may be why women have a substantially lower incidence of high-altitude pulmonary edema than men.

But they are not immune to it.

As the group trekked to Base Camp, Adrian had suffered head-aches and nausea. After they'd spent a few days quietly in camp, these had subsided, aided by twice-daily doses of acetazolamide, or Diamox, a drug that increases the respiratory rate by reducing the alkaline content of the blood. The team then slowly began to estab-lish higher camps up Annapurna's north face, ferrying the loads from one camp up to the next. They'd been careful to observe a gen-eral rule of thumb, not sleeping more than 1,000 to 2,000 feet higher each night and taking frequent days off to rest. It is the sleeping altitude and not the maximum height one reaches during a day's climb that largely determines how profoundly one is affected by alti-tude. Thus the climbers' adage, "Carry high, sleep low."

Once on the mountain Adrian felt better. From Base Camp, they climbed the glacier at the mountain's foot, marking a winding route through the crevasses with wands, and established Camp I. Above it came some of the most difficult climbing. They ascended nearly sheer ice faces on the mountain's lower ramparts, kicking the spiky front points of their crampons into the ice and planting the picks of their two ice axes with solid thunks so they were clinging to the faces like spiders on a windowpane. Finally, they screwed into the ice threaded alloy tubes—ice screws—and to these the women fastened permanent ropes for safety and assistance as they ferried loads up the walls to establish the higher camps on the less-steep slopes above, like rungs on a ladder.

By the time the women established Camp V, just under 25,000 feet, their physiologies were undergoing other odd transformations. Their bodies were busily producing extra red blood cells to carry more oxygen. Their heart rates when lying in their tents rose from a normal pulse of about 50 to about 90 beats per minute, and their maximum heart rates when carrying heavy loads dropped from about 180 per minute down to 140, until, if they'd gone as high as the summit of Everest, their resting and maximum rates would nearly equalize, as one climber's did, around 115. At these altitudes, there was simply no longer enough oxygen to keep the heart and all the organs fully supplied, and more and more of the oxygen was siphoned off by the hard-working muscles that pumped their panting lungs. By Camp V, their climbing rate had dropped way down, to about 500 vertical feet per hour, compared to over 2,000 feet an hour at sea level. (Near the summit of Everest at 29,000 feet, the rate would probably bog to 100 or fewer feet per hour. Even the great Messner, who near sea level could climb in one hour the equivalent of five World Trade Centers stacked on top of each other, or more than a vertical mile, took an hour to drag himself, without supplemental oxygen, up Everest's last 300 feet.) Had they been Sherpas, Tibetans, or Peruvian highlanders, the womens' bodies may also have compensated for the lack of oxygen in still more subtle ways, down inside the mitochondrial furnaces of the cells, where high-altitude rabbits and other mountain animals appear to metabolize their bodies' fuels at a faster rate than their lowland counterparts.

After three weeks and their long, slow acclimatization, everything was in place for the summit attempt. As the weather cleared to perfection and Becca gave the go-ahead for the summit, the first team happened to be up at Camp IV and the second team down at Camp III. This meant that for the second team to catch up while the good weather lasted, they had to climb long and hard in one day all the way from Camp III to Camp V, the jumping-off point, gaining over 4,000 vertical feet in one day and thereby violating their rule of thumb.

When she woke on summit day at Camp V, Adrian complained of feeling nauseous and tired but said she'd try for the summit anyway. They'd climbed through the pink dawn without problem, ascending above the sun-touched, ice-capped lesser peaks that surrounded Annapurna, until about midmorning, when Linda and Mara noticed her stumbling and weakening. Finally they'd called out to the first team to stop.

"Are you ready to try descending?" asked Mara.

Adrian, still sitting in the snow, nodded, as if too tired even to speak, and clumsily moved her boots beneath her in an attempt to stand.

Mara and Linda each took an arm and helped her to her feet. While Mara belayed them from above, Linda wrapped her arm around Adrian's waist and propped her up as they descended. They'd been climbing together for years, and Adrian was the godmother to Linda's daughter. But even with Linda's help, Adrian frequently stumbled. Sometimes Mara would have to climb down to help.

Once, as they were pulling her back up, Adrian suddenly turned to Mara. "I know what you two are trying to do. You're trying to cut me out of this climb."

Mara looked closely to see if Adrian was joking, but her jaw was thrust forward, and behind the dark glacier goggles her eyes appeared wide with anger. Irrational behavior was one symptom of high-altitude cerebral edema.

"Adrian, you're not well," said Mara. "We're taking you down so you'll be better."

"You want the summit for yourselves," Adrian countered. "I'm on to your scheme."

"There is no scheme, Adrian."

"I thought you were my friends, and now you're betraying me."

"Adrian, we're trying to help you," Linda said soothingly.

"I don't want any help from you backstabbers," Adrian fired back, and sat down abruptly in the snow.

Mara turned to Linda, speaking quietly over Adrian's head. "Let me try something." She then bent down and spoke clearly. "Adrian, I'm going to walk to that knoll over there. I'll be right back."

Adrian said nothing and slumped further in the snow, as if now too fatigued to respond.

Mara untied from the rope and set off alone, traversing across the slope. She hoped that from the knoll she could finally see down into Tibet, and that her brief absence might jog Adrian from her angry paranoia. Working carefully, planting the pointed shaft of her ice axe into the snow to serve as a self-belay to hold her if she slipped, Mara steadily made her way across the slope. But the knoll lay farther off than it looked, and it took Mara nearly half an hour to reach it. Kicking a few steps into the snow to its small summit, she realized the view of Tibet was still blocked by a section of ridge line. All she could see were a few black specks that might have been birds winging past. Looking down from the knoll, Mara also noticed the first misty clouds of what looked like an oncoming storm, billowing upward from the valleys below like a cottony quilt. The sky still shone blue above.

With a rising sense of worry, Mara hurried back across the snow slope, or hurried insofar as she could, hyperventilating at just under 26,000 feet. They'd have to move quickly to descend to Camp V before the clouds rose and engulfed the upper mountain. She looked up, hoping to spot the first team. High above on the snow slope, against the blue sky, three black dots were making their way down, tiny orderly points on the vast luminous ceiling of white and blue. They must have made the summit.

The wind was rising when she reached Adrian and Linda.

"She's been talking to you while you were gone," Linda said, speaking just loudly enough to be heard over the hiss of snow blowing at boot level across the slope. "She thought you were sitting right beside her, even when I pointed you out over there."

Known as the "phantom companion," this hallucination is not uncommon among those suffering mountain sickness, especially cerebral edema, at extreme altitudes. Climbers have spotted highway crews working at 20,000 feet on an Andean peak when the nearest road was many days away, and offered pieces of candy to climbers who weren't really there beside them on Everest. One recovering victim of high-altitude cerebral edema kept seeing Marilyn Monroe moving about in his hospital room. In one epic incident in 1981, a Swiss climber lingered a few extra minutes late in the afternoon after his friends had started down from the 23,191-foot summit of

Glacier Dome, just east of Annapurna. He soon found himself accompanied by a German-speaking man who pointed out a shortcut down to the party's highest camp. Following the advice of the stranger, who soon disappeared, and descending into the darkness, the climber spent a forced night in an icefall at temperatures of around −40 degrees Fahrenheit. He suffered severe frostbite and nearly died in an avalanche, hallucinating at one point that his friends had constructed a cable car up to him but wouldn't let him board it. They did finally show up—on foot and not in a cable car—and rescued him.

Mara and Linda pulled Adrian, now nearly limp, to her feet and slowly moved down the mountain again, taking turns propping her and at times belaying each other. Adrian's feet bumped into each other and her crampon points caught in the fabric of her gaiters, the protective sheath that covered her climbing boots and boot tops to keep the snow out, tripping her, so that she stumbled drunkenly until Mara or Linda dragged her upright again. It was excruciatingly tiring. Mara felt she was carrying a sack of cement through deep snow as she and Linda took turns struggling under the additional weight. Adrian was of no help at all. She didn't seem to care if she went up or down, if her mittens were on or off, if she was helped or not. Mara focused on one thing: getting them all safely down to Camp V.

The stumbling and lack of coordination—known as ataxia— the lassitude, and the inability to care for oneself all are classic symptoms of high-altitude cerebral edema. No one knows exactly why it would have afflicted only Adrian and not the others. Some researchers believe that everyone's brain swells during rapid ascent to high altitude but some individuals tolerate the swelling better than others. The precise cause of the swelling is also a mystery. Blood flow to the brain jumps as much as 25 percent when someone—anyone— first ascends to high altitude, but as acclimatization occurs over several days it drops back down. This initial high flow, however, might rupture brain capillaries and leak fluid and blood into brain tissues, causing the swelling. Or perhaps the leaks in the capillaries are microscopic holes opened by the sprouting of tiny new branch capillaries—known as angiogenesis—which is one of the many ways the body attempts to deliver more blood to oxygen-starved tissues.

In either case, the brain swells. Floating in its bath of cerebrospinal fluid, the brain is totally enclosed in the tight space of the skull. As it swells, something has to give. If not, the pressure inside the skull builds enormously. There is, however, a kind of overflow valve for the fluid, and this valve may work better in some people than in others. As the brain expands, it squeezes excess cerebrospinal fluid from the skull down into the hollow centers of the uppermost vertebrae. Depending on individual physiology, some people have more space in their vertebrae for the excess fluid and more space inside their skulls to handle the swelling, perhaps making them less susceptible to high-altitude cerebral edema. Perhaps Adrian was the only one who suffered because she had an unusually tight fit between her brain and skull and little space in her upper vertebrae.

By the time the first team approached Mara and Linda and Adrian slowly making their way down the slope, windblown wisps of cloud, luminous at first with sunlight like brilliant shards of fog, were whipping past the mountain and coloring the deep blue of the sky with shades of pastel and sending patches of sun and shadow scudding across the broad white face of Annapurna's upper slopes.

"You made it?" Mara called out as they neared.

Becca raised her hand in a quiet gesture of success. Mara noticed that she and the other first-team climbers said no more about their victory, as if self-conscious about the price at which it might have come. Instead, the first words Becca spoke when the two groups finally joined on the slope were "How is she?"

"Very bad," Linda replied.

Everyone knew there was no time to be lost. The weather was shifting fast. The first team quickly moved ahead to break trail through the snow on gentler slopes where they didn't need belays, while Mara and Linda walked on either side of Adrian, propping her up. The ragged shards of flying cloud thickened into a featureless white mist whipped by the wind until Mara could barely see the members of the first team ahead of her. With the white clouds and white snow, she could no longer tell which was upslope and which downslope. It made her head feel like it was spinning. Spots danced before her eyes. It soon became obvious that they weren't going to make it down to Camp V that night. Adrian was falling continually, the other women were exhausted, daylight was dimming, and they were having trouble staying on route. They'd carried neither tents nor sleeping bags that morning in order to be as light as possible for the summit attempt.

"I think we should dig a snow cave while we still have some light," said Becca at a halt.

Exhausted as they were, no one spoke against it. They kicked back and forth across the slope with their boots to find the proper snow in which to build a cave. They needed a deep, windblown drift of snow that had compacted into a firm consistency, so the cave would hold its shape, but still soft enough so they could dig easily in it. Finally, stumbling through the whiteout to the left of their route down, they plowed into a deep drift. As the light dimmed and clouds swirled, they took turns with the two lightweight shovels they packed and bored a tunnel sloping upward into the drift, scooping the snow behind them and shoving it out the tunnel, laboriously hollowing out a cavern. The tunnel had to slope upward so that the warm air from their bodies, which rises, would be trapped in a kind of bubble inside the drift. Inside the cavern, they left a raised platform of snow across the rear half of the cave on which to sit, as the Inuit did in their igloos, so they'd be elevated above any cold air that pooled on the floor. Poking upward with the shaft of an ice axe, they bored a small air vent through the roof, and fashioned a block of snow to seal the doorway. Snow, consisting of mostly air, has very formidable insulating properties. With subzero temperatures prevailing outside, Inuit families used to lounge topless inside the comfort of their snow igloos in the light and warmth of their seal-oil lamps.

Pulling Adrian inside, the women propped her on the bench, first laying down empty packs to insulate her from the snow, and pushed the snow block in place over the tunnel entrance. Becca produced a candle from her emergency kit. The cave took on a cheery yellow glow from the candle light reflecting from the sparkling walls, and slowly began to warm up.

Situating themselves in the candlelit cavern, the climbers drank from their water bottles and ate a few pieces of candy. Wedged on the snow bench between Linda and Mara, Adrian appeared a little livelier. How was she feeling? Okay. Did she want water? Yes. It appeared that even the drop in altitude of only 1,200 feet or so had helped relieve her symptoms. Plus, at Becca's urging, Adrian had tried hyperventilating, which infuses oxygen into tissues and brain and can help relieve symptoms. Still, if they asked her to subtract one number from the next or if she knew where she was, she'd only shake her head. Mara wondered if Adrian knew she was in a snow cave at 25,000 feet on a Himalayan mountainside.

Becca took out a small stove that she'd packed for just such a situation, plus a little pot, and heated some instant soup that the women passed among themselves. Mara could feel the warmth trickling into her. In early evening at their regular appointed time, Becca moved to the tunnel entrance and called by handheld radio down to Base Camp to explain the situation. Base Camp radioed back medical advice. From the high-altitude medical kit that Becca carried, they should give Adrian an injection of dexamethasone—a steroid that acts as an anti-inflammatory agent and has been shown helpful in treating mountain sickness and cerebral edema—and give her tablets of it every six hours thereafter. Base Camp also told them to try to keep her in a sitting position.

Using her headlamp, Becca carefully gave the injection in Adrian's buttock. Everyone now knew there was nothing to be done except wait for first light.

After about an hour in the cave, eating and drinking and situating themselves, Gayle, of the first team, spoke up.

"We should blow out the candle."

"Why should we blow out the candle?" Linda replied testily. "The light's doing Adrian good."

"Because we might need it later."

"I think we need it more now," Linda said.

"Who knows what the weather will be tomorrow," Gayle replied evenly but coldly.

"Let's not think about tomorrow's weather," Linda shot back. "Let's think about now."

"Okay," Becca interjected. "Let's burn the candle another fifteen minutes or so and then blow it out and try to sleep. We can still use our headlamps."

With the candle out, utter blackness filled the cave. There was no sound of the windstorm outside, its scream muffled by walls of snow several feet thick. Mara heard only the small scrapes and crinkles of the cold-stiffened fabric of their climbing suits as the women made small adjustments to their positions on the bench, and beside her she heard the quick panting of Adrian's breath.

Adrian's breathing seemed to grow faster the longer they stayed in the cave, instead of slowing down with rest, as Mara's own breathing had, and was punctuated by fits of coughing. This fast breathing—or dyspnea—while at rest is one of the warning signs of HAPE, or high-altitude pulmonary edema, which often accompanies and may in some cases trigger high-altitude cerebral edema. Like HACE, no one knows exactly why or how HAPE occurs. It appears that the lack of oxygen at high altitude causes the blood vessels to constrict in certain parts of the lungs but not in others, at least in those who are susceptible to the illness. Large volumes of blood are forced through the vessels that remain open, the theory goes, forcing open tiny holes in their walls and spilling fluid and red blood cells out into the lungs' air sacs and passages. With a stethoscope, or even by placing her ear under Adrian's clothes and against the bare skin of her back, Mara would have heard a rasp or bubbling sound with each of Adrian's breaths, a condition known as rales or crackles, as the fluid, slowly beginning to suffocate her, moved in her air passages.

Mara feared that what she was hearing might be a case of pulmonary edema in the making. She was sure Becca suspected it also, and perhaps the other women, too. No one said anything, not wishing to alarm Adrian and thinking there was nothing they could do until morning anyway. Mara tried to ignore the panting breaths of Adrian beside her and the crinklings of the fabric, tried to ignore her own uncomfortably slouched position against the back wall, the crunch of the snow against her head. She tried to lie down, but the bench was too narrow and her legs projected over the floor. She shifted back to slouching.

Sleep seemed impossible. She tried to meditate, following her daily practice at home, when she would sit cross-legged on the soft, carpeted floor of her hushed bedroom, but here it was so much harder, with the crinklings and rustlings and pantings, with the cold scrape of snow on her back, with the raspy *hacckk . . . hacckk . . . hacckk . . .* of Adrian's cough. It was like trying to meditate inside a darkened refrigerator full of breathing, rustling living things. Mara gave it up. Instead, she attempted to sleep, trying to snuggle into the snow wall at her back. All around her, she could hear tiny, impatient noises.

"Okay, who brought the chips?" someone finally said in the darkness.

"And the Diet Pepsi," said another voice.

"And the beer and the music," said a third.

They started to laugh, the giddy, black-humored, semihysterical, tension-breaking laughter of people in an impossibly difficult place, abetted by the scant oxygen making its way to their brain tissues.

"Don't forget the men," someone said.

"Don't you remember? We left them three vertical miles below us."

"They're down there doing the housework while we're up here enjoying ourselves."

More giddy laughter. Even Adrian seemed to be laughing; Mara felt the rhythmic jostling against her shoulder, although it wasn't clear if Adrian caught the jokes, her clarity of mind sharpened somewhat by the injection of dexamethasone, or whether, in her frail, oxygen-starved state, she was simply carried along by the others.

And so it went through the night in the snow cave. After the giddiness subsided, they told stories about their first climbs, their first loves, their favorite music, their idea of what, at this very moment, would make a perfect dinner menu, whether dessert should be hot apple pie, or cake, or a stack of pancakes dripping maple syrup.

They periodically dozed, and when someone was asleep Mara could hear the peculiar disturbed breathing of extreme-altitude sleep, when climbers inadvertently wake themselves up to 150 times per hour as the body falls victim to its own vicious respiratory cycle. The lack of oxygen in the blood triggers the oxygen sensor, which tells the lungs to hyperventilate. The hyperventilating expels carbon dioxide from the blood, triggering the carbon dioxide sensor, which tell the lungs that there's no hurry to take another breath. The lungs stop breathing. The oxygen level in the blood suddenly plummets, waking the sleeper with the sense that he or she is suffocating, and triggering another bout of hyperventilating and the cycle begins again, over and over. Even acclimatization can't break the periodic-breathing cycle that occurs at extreme altitudes, and some researchers believe that the reason humans can't live permanently above 19,000 feet is that they get so little sleep, their bodies simply fall apart.

Though she slept fitfully, Adrian's cough worsened throughout the night. Toward dawn, she fell into long hacking bouts that brought up fluid from her lungs; bent over at the waist, she let the fluid fall from her mouth into the snow between her feet. When Becca momentarily shone her headlamp on the thin, pinkish sputum, bloody streaks were visible.

"This is not a good sign," she said. "Not a good sign at all."

Becca took her pulse, timing it with her wristwatch, and calculated it at about 130, her respirations about 35 per minute compared to a normal 12 or so at sea level. Both heart and lungs were working furiously to bring oxygen to her tissues, but the oxygen from the air simply wasn't being absorbed by her saturated lungs. Now they could all hear in the periods of silence the gurgling sound inside her lungs with each inhalation and exhalation, and imagine in the darkness the foam around her mouth.

Her condition was now progressing to severe high-altitude pulmonary edema. Meanwhile, her brain was still swollen with cerebral edema.

They decided to wait until 6 A.M., when they'd have enough light to descend, to unplug the snow block from the cave's entrance. If things went well and Adrian could walk, they could reach Camp III by afternoon, where at 21,000 feet the air was noticeably thicker and could help her greatly. A descent of even only 1,000 or 2,000 feet can bring about substantial improvement from pulmonary edema; the early Spanish accounts from Peru used to describe this as recovery *por encanto*—as if by magic. The women stowed their bits of gear in their packs, tightened the straps of their crampons, zipped shut their clothing. Every few minutes they checked their watches. At exactly 6 A.M. Gayle crawled down the tunnel and pushed aside the block of snow. Mara saw the dim gray light filter into the tunnel, followed by a cold rush of air, then the muffled shriek of the wind.

"What's it like out there, Gayle?" Becca called out.

"It's a whiteout," she called back. "It's a frigging blizzard."

"Can we descend?" Becca said.

Gayle pushed herself farther out the tunnel, then slid back in.

"Not a chance. We'd be totally lost within the first hundred feet."

She shoved the block of snow back into position, casting them into darkness again, and crawled backward into the cave, the beam of her headlamp glancing about as she maneuvered back onto the bench.

"I hope this isn't the start of the monsoon," she said.

"If you hadn't insisted on summiting," Linda said out of the darkness, "we wouldn't be sitting here worrying about monsoons. We'd have Adrian down at Camp Three by now, and she'd be recovering, and we'd all be in our sleeping bags drinking hot tea."

Gayle's headbeam swung through the darkness to fall on Linda.

"Didn't you want to summit?" Gayle said, her presence in the darkened cave only an angry voice and a cloud of vapor rising into the beam. "If you didn't want to summit, what did you happen to be doing hurrying up to twenty-six thousand feet on Annapurna? Looking for a decent café?"

"I wanted to summit," Linda said, switching on her own headbeam. "But I also know when to back off. No summit to me is worth putting someone's life in serious jeopardy."

"Don't go blaming me for where you find yourself," countered Jill, the other member of the first team, her voice rising. "You can claim you're climbing for the beauty or the camaraderie or whatever, but every time you set foot on a mountain, you're putting your own life in danger, plus the life of whoever's at the other end of the rope. If you didn't want the risk, you should have stayed home and watched TV."

"All right! Enough!" shouted Becca. "Instead of arguing, why don't we figure out what we're going to do."

But there really wasn't much to do except wait for the weather to clear. Sitting there, Mara felt her own sense of guilt rising. If she hadn't been so eager to traverse over to the knoll and see Tibet, she and Linda might have had enough time to bring Adrian down to Camp V before the storm hit. And now here they were.

Becca, always thinking of logistics, moved down the entrance tunnel, opened it partway, and made another radio call to Base Camp, telling them the weather was too socked in to move. One of the climbers in Base Camp had heard of a team trapped by weather relieving pulmonary edema by physically squeezing the fluid out of their teammate's lungs. Linda and Mara, following the instructions conveyed by Becca, took turns crouching behind Adrian, who was bending over with her head between her knees, wrapped their arms around her torso, and squeezed hard whenever she coughed, forcing the fluid from her lungs.

It gave some relief for a while, but then they'd have to do it again. And again.

Water was now a serious issue, for they'd long ago drained their bottles. Although their sense of thirst was blunted by the extreme altitude, their bodies also needed far more water—4 to 6 liters per day, compared to less than 3 when resting at sea level. Once above 22,000 feet they, like all climbers, inevitably became dehydrated. The cold, dry air at extreme altitude evaporated the moisture from their throat and lungs at a ferocious rate. It was difficult, up where there was no free-running water but only snow and ice, to melt enough each day to drink. Stoves didn't work efficiently. Water boiled at such a low temperature in the thin air that the ice was slow to melt, in water that might be boiling but not very hot.

Mara helped Becca set up the little stove, carefully balancing it on the packed snow of the floor and igniting it. Each act demanded long and careful forethought, as if the mind couldn't sprint but only place one foot ploddingly in front of the other. Memory and conceptual reasoning both drop off sharply above 14,000 feet. Cognitive performance tasks—the equivalent of assembling some mechanical device—could still be performed at extreme altitudes but at a considerably slower pace. Despite these short-term mental deficiencies brought on by hypoxia, there has never been any conclusive scientific proof—contrary to what many climbers believe—that long stays at extreme altitudes cause permanent intellectual impairment. Take the case of eminent Danish physicist Niels Bohr. As he was spirited from Sweden to England on a high-altitude flight to escape the Nazis during World War II, Bohr didn't understand the pilot's instructions to turn on his oxygen. Bohr endured altitudes up to an estimated 30,000 feet and several hours above 15,000 feet. Lifeless when he landed, Bohr recovered fully and went on to a distinguished career in atomic research.

The women scraped bits of snow and ice from the walls of the cave and laboriously fed them, a few chips at a time, into the little pot. Slowly they managed to fill three empty bottles. A fourth they'd already employed for a "pee bottle," used when it's too difficult to relieve oneself outside the tent, which they emptied in a corner of the entrance tunnel.

They sat silently much of the time, trying to doze, turning inward to their thoughts. Adrian's cough worsened as the day went on, becoming wetter, and her panting grew harder as fluid slowly filled the sacs and passages of her lungs.

"I can't get enough air," she said, one of the few times she spoke all day. "It feels like someone's sitting on my chest."

These few words sent her into spasms of hyperventilation and coughing. If they were standing outside the cave in daylight, the women would have noticed the bluish tinge—known as cyanosis—that the lack of oxygen had given to her fingernails and lips, to her nose, tongue, and ears. Her symptoms would begin to clear in just a few minutes and she'd recover completely in twenty-four hours if she were breathing high-flow oxygen through a face mask—6 to 12 liters per minute, compared to the much lower flows of 2 to 3 liters per minute that a climber attempting a summit would use. But carrying enough oxygen to treat a pulmonary edema victim would be extremely burdensome. A lightweight alternative, weighing about

15 pounds when folded up, is the hyperbaric bag. The victim is zipped into this large, airtight fabric sack like some giant frozen burrito sealed inside its plastic pouch while the victim's teammates, working a foot pump outside, inflate and pressurize the bag, giving the effect of 5,000 to 6,000 feet of descent.

But the women had neither supplemental oxygen nor a hyperbaric bag. Descent was their only option. Every hour, one of the women crawled down the entrance tunnel, shoved the snow block open a crack, and reported: "The same."

By midafternoon, Adrian could no longer sit upright. She slumped over first on Linda and then on Mara. Semiconscious, she seemed to be drifting in and out of sleep and couldn't coherently answer their questions. It was difficult for them to go on performing the squeezing maneuver, and it was now clear that, with the storm still raging, they would have to spend another night in the snow cave. Helpless to do anything else to assist her, frustrated at their helplessness, the five women went to work to enlarge the snow cave so Adrian could rest more comfortably. Taking turns with ice axes and shovels, they hollowed out a side chamber, shoving the excavated snow down the entrance tunnel. When it was Mara's turn with an ice axe, she kneeled in the side chamber with her headbeam bouncing over its back wall as she chipped away at belly level. Suddenly her axe broke through the wall. Gray daylight and a rush of snow swirled into the chamber. She carefully leaned forward and peered out.

"Oh my God!" said Mara.

"What do you see?" asked Becca.

Mara was kneeling on the brink of an enormous cliff of rock and ice that dropped away and disappeared into the swirling mist. Without realizing it in the previous afternoon's whiteout, they had dug their snow cave into a cornice—the sculpted wave of windblown snow that forms at the top of cliffs. During the night in their snug snow cave, their backs had rested on the other side of the snow wall on the edge of a thousand-foot drop.

Mara plugged the hole with a block of icy, semitransparent snow that kept out the wind but allowed a faint light to enter the cavern. On the bench they'd carved for Adrian on the side opposite the window, the women carefully laid down an insulating layer of backpacks and carried her into the side chamber.

But by evening, Adrian had slid into a coma.

Outside, the wind still raged, but they no longer bothered to check. The women took turns in the side chamber watching over Adrian. They were very quiet. Becca's stove was almost out of fuel. Their bits of food were mostly gone. If the storm didn't relent by to-morrow, their bodies, badly dehydrated and weak from a lack of food and the extreme altitude, wouldn't have the resources to ward off the cold. Nor would their legs have the strength and balance to carry them down the mountain. The saliva had dried on the roof of Mara's mouth into a thick coating. She could feel the cold seeping up through her feet and hands like a palpable force, stiffening her fingers and toes, sending sudden chills through her body in twitches and shivers, reminding her of the dissected frog's legs that twitched when a certain nerve was touched by a scalpel.

No one mentioned it directly, but their own survival now had come into question.

"This storm has to let up before too much longer," was all that they said to each other.

Sitting through the long hours, each woman reacted in her own way to the growing desperation of their situation, as if their own mortality and their fears about it were mirrored in Adrian. Linda spent long stretches kneeling beside her old friend massaging her legs and arms, whispering to her, "Hang on, hang on," telling her to keep fighting, that the weather would clear and they'd take her down soon. But then Linda would start sobbing—sobbing for the loss of her friend, sobbing, perhaps, in fear of her own death. Becca, at least outwardly, kept up a stoic front. When it was her turn, Becca sat beside Adrian and constantly fussed with Adrian's clothing and insulation, trying to make her more comfortable, as if simple efficiency and a sense of order—putting everything in its exact proper place—could restore Adrian to consciousness. Gayle, in contrast, refused even to enter the side chamber, huddled alone along the farthest wall of the main chamber, turning inward to escape the inescapable end.

"Couldn't you at least spend a few minutes with her?" Linda finally said. "You're supposed to be her teammate, after all."

"I'd really rather stay here," Gayle replied.

Mara, in her turn, held Adrian's mittened hand and tried to remember what she'd read from *The Tibetan Book of the Dead.* It is the belief of Tibetan Buddhists that the art of dying is as important as the art of living. While Westerners tend to fear death, Tibetan Buddhists welcome it as an opportunity to break free of the endless cycle of rebirth and suffering. But the mind of the dying person must be trained properly to seize the moment of death and ride it to liberation. To this end, *The Tibetan Book of the Dead,* as it's known in English—or to Tibetans, *The Great Book of Natural Liberation Through Understanding in the Between*—is read aloud by a lama into the ear of the dying or dead person. It serves as a kind of guidebook or road map through the labyrinths that one negotiates between death and rebirth—the period they call the Between—and includes chapters such as "The Out-of-Body Reality Clear Light," "Encountering the Lord of Death," and "Choosing a Good Womb."*

One practice Mara had studied that could be used to help a dying person is called Tonglen, or giving and receiving. It is an exercise in compassion—the greatest gift, the Tibetan Buddhists believe, that you can give to a dying person. Sitting in the darkness on the snow bench, Mara imagined all of Adrian's suffering as a hot, black, grimy cloud of smoke. She inhaled that cloud of black smoke on her in-breath. She took the hot, black cloud into her own heart and

---

* *The Tibetan Book of the Dead: Liberation Through Understanding in the Between,* translated by Robert A. F. Thurman (New York: Bantam Books, 1994). For the practice of Tonglen meditation, see *The Tibetan Book of Living and Dying,* by Sogyal Rinpoche (New York: HarperCollins Publishers, 1993).

drew it into the worst part of herself, the grasping, selfish part. Mara used that hot black cloud to destroy the part of her own being that was selfish and grasping, purifying her own heart. Then she breathed out, exhaling to Adrian a cool, white, soothing light of peace and joy, compassion and love, that purified Adrian's negative karma, too. Even if Adrian wasn't conscious, her karma benefited from the practice, as did Mara's, the Tibetans believe. "For me," writes one Tibetan lama, "every dying person is a teacher, giving all those who help them a chance to transform themselves through developing their compassion."

Adrian's own breathing now had grown shallower. Becca lit the remaining stub of the candle, bathing the walls of the snow chamber with its warm yellow glow. Spontaneously, the other women crowded into Adrian's chamber, one after the other. Even Gayle squatted in the doorway. To Mara, it felt as if Adrian were surrounded by midwives who, instead of helping her give birth, were trying to ease her passage into death, back into the time before life.

The Tibetan Buddhists believe each dying person "dissolves" in the same manner, even someone undergoing a violent death, although the stages may pass extremely quickly and not always in the same order. First the outer senses dissolve, and the dying person cannot recognize the acquaintances at her bedside. Then the four elements withdraw from the body. The dying person cannot sit upright after the earth element withdraws. The bodily fluids leak out when the water element withdraws. As the fire element withdraws, the person's warmth seeps away. Finally, the air element withdraws. The dying person pants and rasps, hallucinates, and has visions—frightening visions if he or she has led a negative life, and pleasant visions of old friends or heavenly places after a life of kindness and compassion. The in-breaths become shallower, the out-breaths longer, and the dying person gives three long out-breaths. Breathing suddenly stops, and all vital signs vanish. At this point, the inner dissolution has just begun.

Just before 3 A.M., with Linda hugging her on the snow bench, Adrian exhaled her last rasping breaths. Linda remained there, hugging her. The others sat and squatted and knelt silently in the chamber while the steady yellow flame of the candle burned near her head.

After a few minutes, Linda moved away. Becca came forward and removed Adrian's heavy mitten and felt for a pulse.

"She's gone."

They sat there for a long time, each in her own thoughts, while the candle slowly burned down.

In Western medicine, the generally accepted legal time of death is when the entire brain, including the brain stem, which controls breathing and other basic processes, ceases to function. In Scandinavian countries, as well as Germany and Austria, legal standards demand that tests prove no blood is flowing into the brain. Tibetan Buddhists, however, believe that after the dying person's breathing stops, "inner respiration" continues for "the length of time it takes to eat a meal"—about another twenty minutes. It's during this period that the process of conception reverses itself. The father's "white and blissful essence" migrates from the dying person's head toward the heart, dissolving anger as it goes, giving the person a clarity of awareness and the experience of "whiteness." At the same time, the mother's "red and hot" essence migrates upward from the abdomen, where it has resided; this dissolves desire, giving the dying person the experience of bliss and of "redness." Meeting at the heart, the male and female essences enclose consciousness between them. The dying person experiences blackness. The mind is freed from all thought, as well as from delusion and ignorance. The dying person then experiences the great state of insight known as Ground Luminosity or Clear Light.

To the Tibetan Buddhists, death does not abnegate consciousness. By dissolving the roadblocks erected by anger, desire, and ignorance, death instead carries one to ever more subtle levels of consciousness until one reaches Buddha nature—what other religions call the self, or the essence of mind, or God—the subtlest level of all.

Mara slept fitfully, half slouched, half lying on her spot on the snow bench, Adrian no longer beside her. She dreamt, as many climbers do when afflicted with the periodic breathing of extreme altitude, of swimming underwater. As dawn arrived and the first dim light appeared through the snow window, she saw that Linda was curled up on the floor of Adrian's chamber, as if to keep her friend company. There was the sound of rustling in the main chamber as someone stirred; a dark form that looked like Becca crawled down the entrance tunnel to the door.

She carefully pushed back the snow block a crack. Suddenly she pushed it back more.

"It's clear!" she shouted. "The wind's stopped! The sun's rising!"

The women, one by one, crawled from the entrance tunnel and stood up in the still dawn. They staggered slightly, unused to being upright, weakened by lack of water and food. They could almost feel the warmth of the sun about to touch them. The sky glowed pink and orange over the glacier-draped peaks of the high Himalaya to the east, while below them Annapurna's slopes, tinged pink, rolled and humped and fell off toward the 2-mile-deep valley where Base Camp waited in the lingering pool of night's shadow. To their left, just past the entrance of the snow cave, the sculpted wavelike form of the cornice rose slightly and then dropped the thousand feet to the crevassed surface of the glacier. It was as if their vision now had suddenly cleared of the frigid, wind-driven mists of two days and two nights of snowy dreaming.

"If we leave now, we can be back at Camp Three by early afternoon," Becca said, "and Base Camp by tomorrow."

No one spoke. Everyone knew what everyone else was thinking.

"What about Adrian?" Linda finally said.

"I don't know what else we can do," Becca said quietly. "There's no way we can get her down the ice faces, and even if we could, it would take days of work, and the monsoon-season storms will surely be here by then." She swept her hand past the ice-capped peaks and pink sky before them. "Look at this incredible place. I think she'd be happy here. I know I would be."

And so it was agreed to leave her in the snow cave. They crawled back in—already to Mara it seemed impossibly small and claustrophobic—and packed up their gear, anxious to get moving before another storm arrived and yet anxious not to seem as if they were abandoning Adrian. Becca then summoned the team to crowd into Adrian's chamber. Mara could see Adrian's face in the dim light. It appeared grayish white and dull, as if there were no vital forces inside her to reflect the natural light.

Looking at her lying on the snow bench, Mara thought how this peaceful resting spot was preferable to what would have happened to Adrian had she died at home. An autopsy of her brain would have showed edema and hemorrhaging of the tissues, followed by a trip to the funeral home, and perhaps the care of a mortician who would inject formaldehyde or wood alcohol into her veins to preserve the flesh. She'd probably end up in a steel box buried in the earth, with the mistaken notion that it would isolate her from tiny living creatures that might consume her flesh. In fact, there are plenty of bacteria already in the box to do the job.

Instead of trying to shield her body from the earth's natural process of decay by closing up her remains in a box, the Tibetan Buddhists would have cast her body as widely as they could through the world. After death, they'd leave her carefully undisturbed for three days, until her consciousness had the chance to fully leave her body, and then her body would be carried to a special spot in the mountains where monks would chop it into pieces, mix it with barley flour, and let the great soaring birds of the Himalaya descend to feast on it—what the Tibetans call a "sky burial."

Only the most highly trained and prepared individuals are not overwhelmed by the Ground Luminosity when it arrives at the moment of death and are able to use it as the great opportunity for liberation. The majority of dying people return to this endless cycle of death and rebirth and suffering called samsara. The Tibetans believe that Adrian's consciousness, having left her body and not attaining liberation, would linger for forty-nine days in the "bardo of becoming"—the Between, a kind of airport transit lounge for consciousnesses en route to their next lives, as one well-traveled Tibetan master has described it. Her past habits and acts have had consequences—known as her karma—that would buffet her this way and that, finally pushing her toward her next mother and father and the womb of her next life: anything from a cockroach to a bird to a human, who can continue to work toward liberation, to a demigod.

Mara studied her lying cold and lifeless in the dim light of the snow cave and wondered where Adrian might be now. Or maybe she was nowhere and would never be anywhere again. Who knew? Who would ever know? But it was nice to think that even now Adrian was somewhere out there finding her way to another womb. It made Mara feel that Adrian wasn't lost to her. That she would meet her again.

Becca said a short prayer, a kind of nondenominational hope that Adrian's spirit and love for life and for the mountains would inspire others. She had died in the mountains—a place that she loved—and here her body would remain.

"Does anyone have anything else to add?" asked Becca when she'd finished.

"Just a moment," Linda said.

Mara heard the sharp crackle of cold paper.

"I'd like to leave these fig bars and tea bags with Adrian to give her sustenance wherever her next journey takes her," Linda said. She leaned forward and placed the food beside the bench.

Mara felt herself choking up. She remembered the half of a fruit-and-nut chocolate bar, wrapped in golden foil, that she'd tucked away in her parka pocket, saving it for the descent—the last that remained of her food. She pulled it from her climbing suit's inside pocket and gently placed it on the little pile of food Linda had made. Becca then offered up to Adrian her lip balm and sunscreen. Finally, when it came to Gayle's turn, she reached inside her turtleneck shirt and lifted over her head a gold chain with a stone on it.

"I have no food left to offer, but I'd like to give Adrian this—a ruby that my grandmother gave me when I was a little girl. It's been my good-luck charm all these years, and I'd like Adrian to have it."

She gently placed the loop over Adrian's head, resting the stone on the breast of her climbing suit, and turned to crawl from the chamber. Mara lingered, wanting to be the last out. She gave Adrian a long hug—her friend's body stiff and cold and small beneath her—and then rose to her knees and with her ice axe smashed out the snow window she had built. Bright daylight flooded into the chamber. Kneeling closer, she looked out. Through the opening—the view that Adrian had from her snow bench—Mara could see the deep blue sky and the cliff falling away. The other white peaks of the high Himalayan crest lay below her, and beyond them she saw at last the dry barren hills of the enormous Tibetan Plateau: colors in shades of gray, green, blue, brown, of dry earth and rock, peaks capped here and there with snow. It looked as mysterious and alien as the surface of a separate planet. From this height she could see the luminous layer of air that hugged the hills—the thin veil of atmosphere that wrapped the earth. Here and there a spirelike peak projected up through it, poking through the veil toward the sunlit, blue-black depths of space. She was amazed how thin this layer was that sustained life. She could see from this perch that the Tibetans lived just below the margin between earth and space. No wonder they cherished the existence of even the smallest living thing that managed to survive.

She pulled herself away from the view and considered the dimensions of the window. If any bird wanted to enter the chamber, griffon or kite or vulture or sparrow, there was ample room to fit through the opening. Satisfied with her work, she crawled out the entrance tunnel into the bright sunlight. With the others' panting help, she pushed the snow block in front of the entrance and packed snow into the cracks to seal it. Then the women tied into their ropes, shouldered their packs, and, breathing hard, slowly started down the mountain.

CHAPTER FOUR

THE COLD HUG OF THE WHITE SPHINX:

AVALANCHE

All morning, under a cobalt blue sky, the three of them had been snowshoeing with their snowboards slung across their backs up a high ridge in Utah's Wasatch Mountains, a range that offers some of the world's deepest, lightest, and therefore best powder snow. Moist air from the Pacific Northwest churns over the warm Great Salt Lake, then climbs a vertical mile up the Wasatch's wall of 11,000-foot stony peaks into the cold, thin air, releasing its moisture on the slopes below in a thick blanket of feathery flakes. These peculiarities of geography and weather make the Wasatch a mecca for snowboarders and skiers, who travel from throughout the world to the range's winter resorts. Others seek the vast, wild, unregulated expanses of federally owned lands that lie beyond the boundaries of the patrolled ski areas. This is the beyond-the-bounds mountain terrain that its aficionados—like the three snowboarders— know as the backcountry.

Leaving the trailhead at the highway just after dawn, they had slogged up through the aspen groves of the range's gentler lower slopes and entered the shady fir forests of the middle slopes. It was a little past midmorning when they'd run into a Forest Service ranger snowshoeing his way down the trail.

"You kids headed up to the bowl?" he'd asked.

"That's where we're headed," said Jeremy, who was in the lead.

"Be careful up there," the ranger said, eyeing the seven silver earrings that ran like rivets up Jeremy's left ear. "I was just taking a snow survey, and it doesn't look very stable."

"We'll check it out," said Jeremy.

He started snowshoeing past the ranger. But the ranger remained standing in the narrow snow-packed trough of the trail and didn't move to let him pass.

"You better know what you're doing," he said.

Jeremy kept walking forward, kicking three quick steps into the snowy wall of the trail's trough, past the ranger.

"You're blocking the trail, man," Jeremy said, and kept kicking his way up it. Liz and Dougie followed. The ranger glared at them but said nothing. Then he adjusted the straps on his pack and slowly started down again.

They did in fact know what they were doing. They'd attended seminars on avalanche avoidance and wilderness survival, logged countless trips into the backcountry, spent days at a time camping and boarding in high-mountain bowls similar to the one that hovered above the treeline, over their heads, like a great white rising moon. Still, it seemed that they were always tangling with the authorities—the authorities at ski areas who denied them use of the lifts or told them to slow down or get lost, the authorities in the Forest Service who wanted to regulate the use of the backcountry, the parental figures at home. One of the great joys of boarding the backcountry, usually, was that out there lay a whole world free from authority. It didn't discriminate against people simply because they had spiked hair or a pierced tongue or an attitude. The backcountry distributed its joys and its hardships equally, without discrimination.

By late morning, sweating in the bright high-altitude sun, the trio finally arrived at the ridge top. The folded white peaks of the

Wasatch Range stood all around them, some slightly higher, some slightly lower. The great bowl opened at their feet, treeless and white like a giant amphitheater, its rim capped by a 10-foot-high snowdrift called a cornice. Standing back from the cornice's dropoff, they removed their snowshoes from their feet, plunging thigh-deep into the soft snow. They pulled their portable shovels from their packs and dug a pit deep into the snow to study its walls for weak layers in the snowpack. Near the bottom of the pit, they spotted a layer of crumbly snow with a sugary texture.

Jeremy squatted in the pit and picked up a fistful of the snow in his gloved hand. He squeezed his fingers closed. Then he opened it again. The sugary particles of snow refused to stick to each other, pouring from his palm like a fistful of sand.

"It looks kind of loose," said Jeremy, "but on the way up I didn't see any evidence of recent slides in the other bowls around here, so I think we're okay."

He was referring to the telltale scars on steep, snowy slopes and the heaps of churned-up snow at their bases that marked the path of a recent avalanche. Jeremy had more experience in the backcountry than Liz and Dougie, and they deferred to his judgment. The threesome replaced their shovels, strapped their snowshoes to the backs of their packs, and buckled their soft, calf-high boarding boots into the stiff plastic cuffs of their snowboard bindings. The boards themselves resembled short, very fat skis bent up on both ends—a kind of hybrid between a ski and surfboard. They double-checked their avalanche beacons—small radio transmitter-receivers strapped to chest harnesses beneath their parkas. These devices emitted a signal on an internationally set frequency, 457 kHz, that, like the emergency locator beacon of a downed airplane, could be picked up by the radios of others in the group or of other rescuers if an avalanche buried someone. The trio hopped awkwardly toward the lip like frogs nailed to surfboards. The bowl spread out below them, dropping over a thousand feet in elevation—a great symmetrical scoop that an ancient glacier had chewed and ripped from the solid rock of the ridge's bulk that was now blanketed with a thick, white, luscious coat of powder snow.

It was Dougie's turn to make first tracks. The bowl was so big and so steep and filled with so much empty space, it almost made him dizzy to look down into it.

"Well, do you plan to stare at it all day or are you going to board it?" asked Jeremy, reaching down to tighten a buckle on his binding.

"Give me a minute, will you?" Dougie replied.

"When it's his turn for first tracks, he can think about it all day if he wants," said Liz, standing up for Dougie. "That's the way we've always done it."

Jeremy backed off. "I know, I know. It's just that this bowl looks so *sweet*, I can hardly *stand* it!"

"I wish Cat were with us," said Liz, looking at the surrounding peaks, the pinnacles of sharp black rock protruding from the wind-sculpted waves of snow. "She'd love this place."

"I don't know," said Dougie distractedly, still peering down into the long, sweeping open slopes of the bowl. He could feel his heart pumping in his chest, his breathing coming faster. "She really hasn't been that into boarding since Kayla was born."

For three years, Dougie and Cat had been living together in a small rental cabin down in the canyon, waiting tables or working as lift attendants at the ski area as the season and their wallets demanded. With Liz and Jeremy and two or three other boarders, they'd hung out as a group, defying their parents' entreaties to go to college or get real jobs or do something besides snowboard all winter and mountain-bike all summer. Then Cat got pregnant. Kayla was now ten months old—just walking. Dougie loved her—loved to play with her, make faces and watch her laugh, teach her to walk. But some days he had to get out of the little house with its smell of dirty diapers, its crusted puddles of baby food on the kitchen counter, the bouts of crying, the attention that Cat gave to the baby with little left over for him or for the things they used to like to do together. Without boarding, he'd go crazy with claustrophobia. Until he'd discovered boarding, he *had* been crazy. He'd hated his parents—both sets of them. He had been tossed out of school, dispatched to a series of psychologists and counselors and, finally, probation officers. It was boarding that finally gave him a place in the world that felt like his own.

"Whaddaya think, Jer, straight down the middle, or lean a little to the right?" Dougie asked, still studying the bowl.

"I'd say stick to the right," Jeremy answered. "There's a kind of hump in the middle that could really drop off on the other side."

"You think it'll hold?" Dougie asked, more to himself than to the others.

"We'd sure as shit better hope so," said Jeremy. "Look, if you don't want first tracks, I don't mind going ahead."

Dougie looked down into the bowl again. The smooth slope revealed nothing, yet somehow contained all the complexity and random chance of the cosmos. The trillions of snow crystals, each with their own design, were stacked on the slope in an infinite number of possible combinations, adhering to each other—or not—depending on temperature and humidity at their countless points of contact. The slightest extra weight on their surface—the weight of a snowboarder, for instance—could send them tumbling down. Or the slope could hold. Would it avalanche or would it not? You could pose the question, but the slope—smooth, blank, white—would keep its mysterious silence. It was like the Sphinx, the precise alignment of its trillions of snow crystals holding the answer to the riddle. It was like gazing up at the infinite stars of the night sky. Dougie could ask what it intended—what it *meant* for him—but though he could make an educated guess, he wouldn't ultimately know for sure until he tried it.

Dougie pulled his red-lensed goggles from his purple pile hat down over his eyes and cinched up the snow cuffs of his gloves. Certainty wasn't what he valued most in life. If it was, he would have stayed down in the valley and punched a time clock five days a week at a normal job.

"I'll do it," he said.

"Yeah, Dougie!" called out Liz.

"Nail it, dude!" shouted Jeremy.

For a long moment he stared over the edge of the cornice, visualizing his landing and the turns he'd make after it. He breathed slowly and deeply, calming himself. If there happened to have been an EEG machine sitting on top of the cornice and its electrodes were adhered to his skull, the computer screen would show a sudden surge from his left hemisphere in alpha brain waves—the waves, of about 8 to 13 cycles per second (8 to 13 Hz), that correspond to a calm, meditative state. This same surge in alpha waves has been recorded by researchers in archers who are about to deliver an arrow accurately to the bull's-eye, and some athletes are now learning to train their brain waves to put themselves in the "zone" of peak athletic performance. Dougie made three big exhalations and jumped his board so that it pointed straight at the edge. He gave two little hops, then a big one that launched him, plummeting, over the brink.

"Yaaahoooo!"

Dougie heard the quick whistle of wind in his ears as he dropped off the cornice. In the air, he concentrated on keeping a balanced poise—arms out, knees slightly bent, eyes focused on his rapidly approaching landing zone on the snowy slope below the cornice . . .

Whump!

He landed perfectly—"stomped" the landing, as the boarders said. He absorbed the tremendous force of the impact—165 pounds of body weight dropping from the equivalent of a second-story window—by doubling over at the torso and deeply bending his knees. The board punched a divot into the soft layer of powder snow, and an instant later Dougie sprang from his crouch and popped the board up to the surface. Suddenly he was shooting downhill.

He banked into a swooping right turn—his toe side, meaning the toes of his bindings were aligned toward the right side of the board. The board was skinnier in the middle than at the ends; as

Dougie leaned it up on edge to make his turn, it flexed like a bow and carved a graceful arc. Clots of the soft snow flew up and splattered against his red parka and black pants and his face like a cold, wet, delicious brush.

"Yeah, carve it!" he could hear Liz yell from above.

"Make those pow-turns!" Jeremy shouted.

He rocketed out of the first turn, almost airborne, and leaned left—his heel side—and the board sliced down through the second turn, surfacing again as he finished the arc, the steep slope of the bowl falling away beneath him, and he was soaring and plummeting all at once. The feeling was one of utter freedom, the wind sharp on his face, the powdery snow whipping up, the sky a deep winter blue, the bowl huge and untracked below him. He loved it. His body and board played with the implacable pull of gravity, back and forth like a violin bow playing the giant resonating board of the mountain. His brain waves agilely shifted back and forth between frequencies as circumstances demanded, jumping from the quiet alpha up to the normal waking frequency called midrange beta, and above it to states of higher alertness as tricky bits of terrain demanded, and back again to quieter alpha, with the quick and easy shifting up and down that has been measured in the brain waves of B-2 test pilots as they move from easy to difficult tasks and back again while flying their jets.

Three turns. The wind whistling in his ears.

Four turns. He'd found the rhythm.

Five turns. Into long, ripping arcs with a screaming plume of powder trailing behind him like some alpine comet.

Six turns. There was the hump . . . lean right to avoid it.

Seven turns. Not far enough . . . he was headed for it . . . no panic . . . he could see below . . . an easy drop, though the slope steepened below . . . a little air time, was all.

And suddenly Dougie was airborne. He grabbed the heel side of the board with his left hand in the stylish maneuver known as "method air." There was a moment of suspension, a fleeting sense of soaring—birdlike, poised, confident—out over the great expanse of the bowl.

He landed, stomping it again, another perfect landing.

"*Yooooowww!*" he shouted, hoping Liz and Jeremy could hear him on the cornice above and know what a great run he was having.

Eight turns. Something odd out of the right corner of his eye . . . a long, blue-tinged crack in the snow.

Then a sound and the snow reverberated with a hollow noise like a giant hand knocking on a giant pumpkin.

Nine turns. The snow all around him was moving, breaking into thick slabs.

Another shout, his own, one only he could hear.

Already he was instinctively dropping into a low crouch, arms extended for balance—the instantaneous response to a sudden sound or light or surprise known as the "startle reflex." His eyeballs spun, reflexively searching for the source of the danger. The adrenaline pumped into his system. His brain waves screamed up to the high-alert, high-anxiety zone—known as high beta—over 30 cycles per second. The danger was all around him: a slab avalanche, big, soft plates of the new snow fracturing into chunks and falling away down the slope like an old building dynamited for demolition that drops to earth in a sudden cloud of dust.

Dougie swung his board to the right, toward the far edge of the crumbling mass, riding the churning snow like a surfer in the foam . . . for one second . . . two seconds . . . three seconds . . .

A 3-foot-thick slab of snow slammed him from behind, knocking him off his feet.

Onto his back . . . he could feel the avalanche gaining speed, churning snow all around him . . . 40, 50, 60 miles per hour . . . tumbled over . . . submerging . . . swimming with his arms to stay on top . . . feet pinned by his board . . . tumbled over again . . . a breath of air mixed with powder snow . . . like swimming in the foam of a breaking wave . . . wondering when it will stop . . . wondering if it will slam into trees or rocks . . . it was slowing . . . swim hard for the surface . . . one hand over the mouth to create an air pocket . . . shove the other to the top to signal the others . . . the snow suddenly turning heavy and dense and dark . . .

. . . and then it stopped.

There was a famous holy man in Pondicherry, India, by the name of Yogiraja Vaidyaraja, also known as the Burying Yogi. As proof of his devotion, the yogi routinely climbed into a small box and let himself be buried in the earth, remaining there for several days. In 1973, a team led by U.S. biofeedback researcher Elmer Green traveled to Pondicherry, constructed a box 3.5 feet by 3.5 feet by 5 feet, equipped it with a glass observation window, and sealed the box with wax and polyurethane foam. The box was so airtight that a candle placed inside died out for lack of air after an hour and a half. After the researchers had hooked him up to a battery of electrodes to measure his vital signs and brain waves, the yogi climbed in the box and it was sealed. As Vaidyaraja assumed the lotus position, Green's observations began. The equipment measured that the yogi's brain waves immediately switched from high-frequency beta waves, corresponding to a state of alertness and wakefulness, to the long, slow alpha waves corresponding to calmness and a meditative state. His heart rate dropped by half, and his breathing slowed to a mere one-third the normal waking rate—4 breaths per minute. The yogi remained in this suspended state for a full eight hours before he asked to be removed from the airtight box, complaining of electric shocks received from the equipment.

The yogi would have made a good avalanche victim—or rather, a good avalanche survivor. Snow is mostly air—anywhere from over 95 percent in fresh, fluffy, undisturbed snow to 60 percent or less in the compacted snow of avalanche debris. The buried victim can suck in the air trapped between tiny snow particles—at least for a short while. This assumes, of course, that he or she has not been killed by the violent tumbling of the avalanche or slammed into trees or rocks or tossed over a cliff, that the churning snow has not clogged his or her air passages, and that the weight now piled on top of the victim has not constricted the chest too much to take in a breath. Even if the victim has survived all this and is breathing beneath the snow, asphyxiation is likely to come soon. Carbon dioxide from the lungs' exhalations will saturate the area around the victim's face, and he or she will begin to suffer from hypercapnia—excess carbon dioxide in the blood—as well as the lack of oxygen in the blood known as hypoxemia. Meanwhile, a thin mask of ice—a kind of alpine death mask—freezes near the mouth and nose due to the victim's warm, moist exhalations, and blocks the airflow from the snow to the victim's lungs.

The statistics of avalanche survival are daunting and precipitous: After fifteen minutes' burial under the snow, the victim has a 92 percent probability of survival. Only twenty minutes later—after thirty-five minutes' burial—that probability has plunged to 30 percent, and after a little more than two hours, the chances for survival are very slim, only 3 percent.* Some very fortunate victims, however, have stretched the odds to incredible lengths. In 1955, a twenty-five-year-old Swedish hunter named Evert Stenmark survived burial in a small avalanche for eight days, having melted and carved out an air pocket, and subsisting on a diet of raw ptarmigan, ski wax, meltwater, and dwindling hope while search parties looked for him in vain. A big fan of movies, Stenmark had saved in his wallet every ticket stub of every movie he had ever attended. His brother finally spotted the red stub of a ticket from Stockholm's Black Cat theater

---

* Figures from "Avalanche Survival Chances," letter by M. Falk, et al., in *Nature*, 1994, 368:21. Also from "Respiration During Snow Burial Using an Artificial Air Pocket," by Colin K. Grissom, M.D., et al., *Journal of the American Medical Association*, May 3, 2000.

that Stenmark had extracted from his wallet, wired to a tree branch he'd discovered beneath the snow, and poked above the surface.

Such are the strange vagaries of avalanche survival. Most people's chances of being caught in an avalanche are extremely remote—unless one happens to be in the wrong place at the wrong time. By one estimate, a hundred thousand avalanches tumble down U.S. mountains each year—the vast majority of them in the remote ranges of the West such as the Rockies, Sierras, and Cascades—and tens of thousands more fall each winter in Canada and Europe. Together they kill only about forty people annually in North America and about one hundred in Europe. While U.S. avalanches mostly claim recreationists as victims—the numbers climbing in recent years as more skiers, snowboarders, snowshoers, and snowmobilers explore the wintry backcountry—it's the villagers in high valleys of the Alps who have lived for centuries under the constant threat of avalanches. They've developed countless strategies to defend themselves: They maintain forests and build fencelike barriers to anchor the snow on steep slopes, place their buildings with a close eye to avalanche run-out chutes, cover roads with shedlike roofs, and even construct their churches and houses with heavy, prowlike walls to deflect the onrush of snow like a ship plowing through the sea.

Unlike the sea, an avalanche's power is instantaneous, the more stunning for its suddenness, reminding us that the ground we live on and the mountains themselves—those very symbols of stability—are not static but in their own way alive and ever-changing, as is the snow that covers them. When it does release, the thundering rush of snow can flatten houses, buildings, and forests; it can rush over the top of smaller mountains like a great white wave or bury an entire valley floor. Avalanches have been clocked in Japan's mountains at speeds of 230 miles per hour, have been measured in Alaska as traveling a distance of eight miles, and have killed—in the case of a Peruvian ice, snow, and mud avalanche that in 1970 broke off an Andean mountaintop and dropped thousands of feet, tumbling miles through a populated valley—twenty thousand people.

Some of the most famous victims of avalanches include Hannibal's soldiers and battle elephants, decimated in 218 B.C. by avalanches as the battalions crossed the Alps from the north on their way overland from Spain to attack Rome. "Snow falling from the high summits engulfs the living squadrons," wrote the epic poet Silius Italicus. Not far from that spot, two German hikers in 1991 discovered the five-thousand-year-old body of a hunter thawing from the ice of a glacier, soon to be world famous as the Ice Man, or Otzi (after the Otztal Alps), and possibly the victim of a prehistoric avalanche. Prince Charles narrowly escaped burial in an avalanche during a 1988 ski outing in the Alps when he and his party, including a Swiss mountain guide, ventured into high terrain that had been deemed hazardous, and one of his closest friends, Major Hugh Lindsay, a former equerry for the queen, perished in the slide. Hundreds of climbers have died in avalanches in ranges all over the world, including Alex Lowe, considered by many to be America's best alpinist, who was buried by an enormous avalanche in 1999 while attempting to ski a mountain in Tibet.

It is not difficult to understand how some of the world's most knowledgeable mountaineers have been caught or killed by avalanches. For all the research that has been conducted into their causes and the physics of snow, avalanches remain one of the most frightening phenomena of the mountains. The lure and beauty of the high mountains in winter is almost irresistible for some, and yet it is nearly impossible to go there without encountering some degree of avalanche risk. Each year, hundreds of thousands of skiers, climbers, and snowboarders willingly take that risk and set off into the wintry backcountry. And if they do decide to ski or board a steep slope of untracked deep powder—that blank and tempting mystery— it is truly a leap of faith. It can either reward them with an ecstatic and heart-thumping run or finish them with a slow suffocation beneath thousands of pounds of snow.

There was a faint dawnlike light. There was no sound. The weight of the snow pressed on him. He tried to take a breath; his chest expanded slightly and was squeezed by the settled snow around him that already felt as hard as a concrete shell.

He smelled wet leather. The palm of his glove was pressed close to his face. It formed a small air pocket. Dougie tried a smaller breath . . . and then another . . . and another . . .

He sensed he was lying on his side, his face turned partially up. He squirmed, trying to move his arms to dig a bigger air pocket in front of his face. They were pinned, utterly, as if in plaster casts bolted to a steel table. He tried to move his legs. Nothing. Only his toes moved inside his boots. He tried to twist his torso. Nothing. It was like being locked inside a cold, dark trunk with his hands and feet bound.

He wanted to scream.

Struggling, he frantically twisted his head from side to side as if to drill and butt his way out. His head moved slightly, the snow crunching in his ears. He'd lost his hat somewhere. He knew it was cold, but he wasn't thinking about cold; hypothermia wouldn't set in for a good deal longer. He wiggled his hand. His fingers moved inside his glove. With his fingers he clawed at the snow in front of his face. The pocket grew an inch or two in diameter. But then a chunk of snow that he dislodged with his fingers dropped into his mouth. He was choking on the snow, a cold cottony mass in his mouth. He tried to spit it out, but it was too big. With his gloved index finger, he managed to snag the chunk and extract it.

He could breathe again, but already his breath was coming harder, the air moist and dense. He felt panic rise up in him, his childhood fear of small, dark rooms, of waking in his bed and choking on the blackness, the night like a pillow held over his face, smother-ing him, stopping him from screaming out for his mother and father.

"Help!" he shouted, banging his head back and forth. "Help! Get me out of here!"

The snow muffled his shout. The effort made him pant. Some-one pushed the pillow harder against his face.

I'm going to die, he thought. *If they don't find me, I'm going to die.*

The panic surged up in him again. He smashed his head harder against the walls of snow, clawing with his fingers at the same time. Now his breath came in short pants, his chest squeezing against the hard shell of snow, his heart pounding at over 100 beats per minute.

He'd been buried for two minutes. The oxygen in his blood-stream had dropped only slightly, from 92 percent saturation—the level a twenty-year-old male would have while breathing normally at about 9,000 feet—to a little under 91 percent. But the carbon dioxide in his exhalations had jumped, and, worse, the carbon diox-ide in his *inhalations* had soared by a factor of 100, climbing from about .035 percent of the air in each breath—just a trace amount for someone walking around breathing normal air—to 4 percent car-bon dioxide in each breath. This level was still too low to affect Dougie's central nervous system—the limit of human consciousness occurs when breathing air with a 15 to 20 percent carbon dioxide concentration—but it was enough to trigger the carbon dioxide sen-sors in his brain to tell his lungs to work harder, to breathe more deeply and faster to try to clear his bloodstream of the carbon diox-ide. Meanwhile, his brain waves were bouncing around in the 30- to 35-cycles-per-second range of high beta—anxiety, fear, hyperactivity.

He screamed again.

Again the snow muffled his plea, as if the huge mass on top of him remained utterly indifferent to his desperation. He thought of Cat and Kayla sitting on the old frayed sofa down in their cabin in the valley, waiting for him to walk in the door. He'd never see them again. He smashed his head back and forth in a frenzy, as if by butting his skull against the hardened snow he could obliterate the actuality of his entrapment.

He stopped. He was panting hard now but still remained breathless. He wanted to yell and twist again, trying to slam his way out. But if he did, he realized, he'd run out of air much more quickly.

He'd now been buried for four minutes. His blood oxygen saturation had dropped to 89 percent, still not low enough to cause major discomfort, as people can survive with blood oxygen saturations as low as 50 percent. The carbon dioxide he exhaled had filled the air pocket immediately in front of his face and saturated the tiny air pockets between the snow crystals. From that same stale pocket he was now inhaling air that contained 6 percent carbon dioxide, and the concentration was climbing quickly, into the range that impairs mental capabilities. He was beginning to show the symptoms of acute hypercapnia—excessive carbon dioxide in the blood—which range from faster and deeper breathing, anxiety, and some impairment of mental function at levels of 4 to 10 percent to severely impaired brain function at levels of 10 to 15 percent, followed by unconsciousness at 15 to 20 percent and convulsions at levels over 20 percent. Monkeys and dogs breathing an extremely high level—30 to 40 percent carbon dioxide—have showed an elevated heart rate and other cardiac irregularities but were able to survive breathing the carbon dioxide–air mixture for many hours, although if they were returned too abruptly to normal air, their hearts tended to go into ventricular fibrillation— severely abnormal rhythms—and they abruptly died.

Had Dougie been wearing a new type of vest that recently appeared on the outdoor-equipment market, he might have avoided some of these problems. Instead, he would have inhaled through a tube in the vest's collar that connected to a mesh-fabric area embedded in the vest. This mesh acts as an artificial air pocket for avalanche victims. He could suck the pure air straight from the snow that lay against his vest front while the carbon dioxide from his exhalations would be vented by a separate tube into the snow at his back. The amount of carbon dioxide he inhaled would not have climbed nearly so high or so quickly as it did breathing from the pocket in front of his face.

But he wasn't wearing a vest like this. The high concentration of carbon dioxide in his bloodstream kicked up his respiratory rate and caused him to pant, but the panting did no good. With every quick, deep breath he simply took in more carbon dioxide. There was only so much room for gases in the tiny sacs of his lungs called alveoli; as the carbon dioxide level rose in them, the amount of oxygen they contained dropped. Dougie was beginning to suffer from what is known as displacement asphyxia.

Liz and Jeremy hooted as Dougie made his great carving arcs down the bowl followed by a contrail of powder. They saw him launch over the hump, grabbing his board in a graceful method air. They heard his "yooowww" of delight as he stomped the landing. Then they saw him suddenly drop into a crouch. His arms shot out for balance. They could see the slope around him fracturing into slabs and fall away, slowly at first, and then with amazing speed. Standing on the cornice several hundred yards above the avalanche's starting zone, they were not themselves in any danger from the slide.

"Get out of it, Dougie, man," Jeremy shouted, "get out of it!"

"To the side, Dougie, to the side!" Liz cried.

But Dougie was down, a black and red speck, and then he was gone, swallowed up in the churning, descending cloud of white.

There was no noise at first; it took a second or two for the sound to travel up to where they stood on the cornice. Then they heard the thunking cracks of the snow, a whoosh, and an enormous roar that reverberated around the bowl.

"Don't lose the spot where you last saw him!" Jeremy shouted to Liz. "I'll watch for him down in the run-out."

Within a few seconds, the plume of snow had swept the 400 or so yards to the bottom of the bowl, spilled out onto the flats in a broad rubbly fan at least the size of a football field, and abruptly come to a stop. The roar continued to echo for a moment after the snow stopped moving. Then it was silent. Jeremy squinted at it. No red. No black. Nothing.

"I have it marked," said Liz.

She pointed to the spot where they'd last seen him—about 50 yards downhill from the hump's right side. They each marked it in their minds.

"We have to be really careful," said Jeremy, "or we'll be buried, too. I'll go first, and when I'm below the hump, you follow."

Jeremy hopped his board over the edge of the cornice, dropped into the bowl, and made long fast swoops down to the hump, sheltering himself below its bulk in case Liz knocked down another avalanche from above. In a minute she had joined him, just above the avalanche's fracture line—a 3-foot-high escarpment in the snow where the slabs had split away. Underneath lay a smooth and even surface that was exposed when the thick outer scalp of snow peeled away.

Within the snowpack, stacked in layers like the leaves of a book, lay an entire history of the winter as it occurred in the bowl. Two months earlier, winter's first big snowfalls had been followed by a cold snap. The warm earth below the snowpack and the frigid air above it caused the snow particles near the bottom to vaporize. The water vapor migrated upward and recrystallized on the underside of the uppermost, colder particles that lay near the frigid air, like frost coating a windowpane. Eventually the entire layer had recrystallized into tiny ribbed pyramids and cups known as "depth hoar" or "sugar snow." No bonds held these loose particles. Then more snowstorms fell on top of this depth hoar, but these newer layers didn't undergo the big temperature difference between warm earth and frigid air, and the particles bonded with each other. First the little arms of the individual snowflakes broke off or receded until there was a roundish particle of ice, and then tiny necks of ice called sinters formed from one particle to the next, like the little knobs holding together a string of fake pearls. This loosely bonded mass of trillions of snow particles and thousands of tons of snow, however, rested on the weak, shaky foundation of the unbonded depth hoar. Dougie's landing— *whump!*—was enough of a shock to send a fracture through the upper layers and set them sliding over the weak underlayer, rapidly accelerating in the great, crumbling plates of a slab avalanche.

Liz and Jeremy side-slipped on their boards quickly down the scalped surface of the depth hoar, straight downhill from the spot where they'd last seen Dougie. The avalanche rubble at the slope's base was like the snow piled up at road's edge by a plow—big chunks interspersed with looser snow, the whole of it already bonded into a solid mass. As they reached the rubble, they flipped open the buckles of their bindings and jumped out of their boards.

There was no sign of Dougie.

"Let's switch to receive," Jeremy said. He, too, was hyperventilating with anxiety. His heart was hammering at 135 beats per minute. Liz and Jeremy yanked off their gloves, reached into their parkas, and pulled their transceivers out of their harnesses. They pushed the buttons that allowed them to receive the signals emitted by Dougie's. As they did they heard a steady *beep . . . beep . . . beep.* His signal was here somewhere. The question was exactly where. Their transceivers had directional antennas built into them, and a glowing red arrow would light up when the transceiver was pointed in the direction of Dougie's signal. Standing in the avalanche debris, they rotated their transceivers back and forth to find the direction of his signal while listening to the steady beep.

It had now been seven minutes. Dougie was climbing a high peak with a heavy pack through deep snow—panting, panting, panting— but didn't have enough air to take in. He dreamt that he'd been caught in an avalanche while climbing the mountain. But he must still be climbing the mountain because he was panting so hard. The carbon dioxide in each inhalation had risen over 7 percent—closer to the range of severe mental impairment. His blood oxygen saturation had dropped to 83 percent. His breathing rate, due to the carbon dioxide he was inspiring, had jumped to nearly 30 breaths a minute—heavy, difficult panting—but he was taking in less and less oxygen. What finally kills avalanche victims, it appears, is severe hypoxemia—lack of oxygen in the blood that sends the body into a kind of downward, self-perpetuating spiral. The lack of oxygen in the blood eventually causes brain function and heart rate to slow. With the slowing heart rate, blood pressure drops. The victim blacks out under the snow. The dropping blood pressure causes even less oxygen to reach the tissues of the heart. The oxygen-deprived heart slows even further. Blood pressure drops more, and still less oxygen reaches the heart. Finally, between 15 and 35 minutes after burial, the heart usually stops beating altogether.

Dougie thought of Cat and Kayla on the sofa again, realized where he was, and felt the panic rise in him again. He woke up, wanting to scream. Then he thought that if he screamed, he would die. He would use up even more oxygen. No, he couldn't scream. He had to do the opposite of scream. He had to be very, very quiet. He had to believe the others were out there, somewhere, looking for him. He began by slowly moving the fingers of his gloved hand. He managed to scrape his air pocket an inch or two larger. Instantly, he felt some relief as fresher air leached from the snow into the pocket. Now he had to find the calm spot inside himself. *Just go with it*, he told himself, like a mantra. *Just go with it. Just go with it.*

Seven years earlier, after he'd been suspended from junior high school, after he'd been arrested for shoplifting, after his parents and teachers had sent him to a long series of meetings with counselors and he'd been diagnosed as hyperactive, an innovative juvenile-court judge had sentenced Dougie to neurofeedback therapy. The therapist, a gentle, middle-aged woman, pulled aside tufts of his unkempt hair, dabbed a bit of conductive adhesive on several places of his scalp, and fixed electrodes to them. He reclined in a soft armchair and watched a computer screen across the small office. A broad highway unfurled toward a pastel desert horizon dotted with distant buttes that reminded him of Arizona. The therapist told him to try to prevent the highway from widening as it unfurled, although she didn't tell him how.

"You'll discover for yourself how to do it," she said.

The highway's width was actually a measure of the frequency of Dougie's brain waves—the electrical pulses that constantly move through our brains and shift frequency for reasons that are still not clear but which correspond to different levels of mental activity or agitation. Neurofeedback researchers have found that those suffering from attention deficit disorder are more or less stuck down in the slow, low-level alpha and theta frequencies near daydreaming and sleep, while those who suffer from hyperactivity spend too much time in the high-level, agitated beta frequencies. The theory of neurofeedback is simply to train the mind to shift more easily between frequencies; it has also been shown to be highly effective in treating epileptics, though the practice is still not widely accepted by mainstream medicine.

Dougie discovered that with a certain, indescribable kind of soft focus, he could quite easily keep the unfurling highway narrow. When he did, the computer made a soft binging sound that indicated he was scoring points—a kind of game—and when he scored enough points the buttes on the horizon erupted in a glorious display of color. After finishing each forty-minute session, Dougie felt relaxed and the world seemed remarkably vivid and clear. After six months of the sessions, his concentration had improved vastly, and he was calmer and doing much better in school.

Now, pinned under the thousands of tons of snow in the semi-darkness, panting, wanting to scream, he thought of those sessions. He remembered that soft focus. He remembered trying not to concentrate on any particular object or thought but on a kind of empty space. Now he imagined that space—all the space inside this cast of snow, the spaces between the trillions of snow crystals, all the space of the universe. He couldn't let himself think of Cat and Kayla playing on the sofa, waiting for him to walk in the door. Instead he had to think of a vast empty space.

In a way, what Dougie was doing was not all that different from the basic meditation techniques of Eastern yogis, who instruct the aspirant to attempt to empty the mind of all thoughts while meditating, and find serenity within that emptiness. If there were an EEG machine and electrodes hooked to Dougie's scalp, they would now have shown his brain waves move out of the high-beta frequencies of extreme agitation. They slowly slackened from around 30 cycles per second down through the lower beta ranges and into the alpha frequency at 8 to 13 cycles per second. There were a hundred billion nerve cells in Dougie's brain. Like snowflakes, each one had a different structure as well as a different function. Unlike the billions of snowflakes that surrounded him, each of which was in contact only with those snowflakes immediately beside it, a single brain cell can potentially communicate by tiny electrical impulse with several million other brain cells. All the scientists in the world could not at this point tell exactly what was going on in Dougie's brain, or in anyone's brain; it has been calculated that the number of possible combination of connections—one definition of the number of possible brain states or "thoughts"—in a single human brain exceeds the number of atoms in the universe. So complex that it makes a supercomputer look as simple as an abacus, the human brain may never truly be able to understand itself.

Dougie's brain was now sending out what are known as synchronous alpha waves, which can be triggered by the imagining of space. In the normal waking beta range, the brain emits somewhat different frequencies from different parts of the brain. But in a state of synchronous alpha, the waves originate everywhere synchronously— "like a smooth hum over all the brain," as one description puts it. It is a deeply relaxed state, one where the entire body seems to let go of its stresses. In this state, Dougie's heart rate now slowed from 120 to 70 beats a minute. His respiratory rate, though still fast, became steadier. He'd entered the realm of the Burying Yogi. He had imagined calmness and empty space, and then he was in it. He was surrounded by space. The snow crystals touched one to the next; his neurons touched one to many, sending up the pulsing electric waves of synchronous alpha, a cycle spinning out into the spaces between the snow crystals, between the stars. He imagined his synchronous alpha waves pulsing out into space, toward unknown receivers thousands of light-years distant, like the mysterious electromagnetic signals received by earth's astronomers from far-off stars and the deepest reaches of the universe.

For the first time since he'd triggered the avalanche, he was not struggling and stirring. He could hear the slow, powerful thump of his heart. For the first time, the snow was not scratching in his ears as he banged his head about in his encasement. He now heard down near his chest the transceiver sending out its signal, a tiny beep each time it launched an electromagnetic pulse out through the densely packed snow.

On the surface, Liz and Jeremy were working their way through the chunks of snow in the bright morning sunlight, watching and listening to their transceivers. There was always the danger of another avalanche coming down on top of them. Stumbling often in the rubble, they moved quickly, knowing that these were the most crucial minutes in an avalanche rescue. Rotating their beacons back and forth, they picked up the direction of Dougie's signal, indicated by the red illuminated arrow. They started walking toward it, spread slightly apart from each other. From a grove of subalpine fir trees at the bottom of the bowl, Liz could hear a crow protesting their presence in the sunny morning calm. Then she spotted something purple 30 feet ahead of her.

"Dougie's hat!" she shouted out to Jeremy. "Here's his hat!"

He ran across the rubble to where she stood, holding the hat.

"Check your beacon!" he said, panting.

They looked down at the small readout on her beacon. It read 12 meters. That was the distance from them at which, according to her beacon's interpretation of it, Dougie's signal originated.

They stumbled across the snow again, following the directional arrow on their compact yellow boxes, the handles of their rescue shovels protruding from the backs of their packs.

The crow flew through the still winter air to another tree.

The numbers on the readout on Liz's beacon dropped: 12 . . . 7 . . . 4 . . . 1 . . .

She stopped.

"Here!" she shouted to Jeremy. "He has to be right here!"

He had already peeled off his pack, stripped off the shovel, and started to dig in the hard snow.

A calmness had overtaken Dougie. He was dreamy again. *If this is dying,* he thought vaguely, *it isn't hard.* He was using only a small amount of oxygen. There was only a small amount of oxygen left to use.

In his left ear, Dougie heard a peculiar crunch. It sounded very close and harsh—not something pulsing vaguely between the stars. Something hard hit his left shoulder, then his head. It might have hurt if he'd cared. It was as if he'd been sleeping. Now somebody was shaking him. He opened his eyes. A black-gloved hand was moving back and forth over his face, brushing away the clumps of tiny crystals of snow.

CHAPTER FIVE

STELLER'S LAST LAUGH, OR

BETTER LIVING THROUGH BOTANY:

SCURVY

Gusts whistled through the rigging and rain thumped on the deck planking just overhead, but down below in his sailboat's small salon, Phil was warm and dry. On the teakwood table in front of him lay an open book, and beside it stood a glass of the red Bordeaux that his local Seattle wine merchant claimed would be highly drinkable on a long sea voyage, although Phil—whose tastes usually ran more to highly caffeinated soda—was the first to admit he wouldn't have known the difference if the stuff were swill. Still, a glass of claret seemed in the spirit of his undertaking—the beverage that British Royal Navy officers were always knocking back before jamming their ships into the icepack for another doomed attempt at the Northwest Passage over the top of North America. Likewise, Phil could have switched on the salon's 12-volt electric lights but preferred the soft glow of the reproduction brass oil lamp that he'd purchased for $199 at the ship's chandlers before he'd left

Seattle three days earlier. His first discovery on this voyage of self-discovery had been that nautical atmosphere did not come cheap.

With its electronic beep, the marine radio signaled the start of another cycle of the weather report. Phil looked up from his book.

"Small-craft warning in the Strait of Juan de Fuca for tomorrow, with southwesterly winds of twenty-five to thirty knots and swells six to eight feet. . . ."

It was the same forecast he'd heard all afternoon. This storm system would be followed immediately by another, lingering at least until Sunday. The question for Phil was whether to chance a crossing of the Straits in the morning or wait two, three, or even four days for the wind and waves to drop. Three or four days! That was an eternity in the world where he'd been operating—long enough to start up a company and then sell it.

He went back to his book. He was finding it hard to put down, despite his anxiety about the weather. Georg Wilhelm Steller's *Journal of a Voyage with Bering, 1741–1742.* Vitus Bering was the aging Danish navigator commissioned by Russia's Peter and Catherine the Great to sail east from Siberia and locate the unknown northwestern coast of the North American continent. He is now memorialized in the names of the Bering Sea and the Bering Strait, the latter separating Asia from America. The journal's author, Steller—who served as the physician, mineralogist, and naturalist on the voyage, as well as Bering's cabinmate—was a young, rigorous German scientist who held nothing but contempt for the ship's officers and crew. The feeling was mutual. Unlike so many gilded explorers' chronicles, Steller, embittered by the treatment he received, pulled no punches—especially when it came to describing the officers' incompetence and misjudgments and the astounding series of disasters that these shortcomings helped trigger.

Phil's girlfriend, Myrna, had given him Steller's journal just before he set sail. Or rather, his ex-girlfriend. Several months earlier, when he began planning the voyage, he'd asked her to accompany him. She'd thought about it for a while; in the end, she'd turned it down—and turned down Phil, more or less, along with it. Things just weren't going to work between them, she'd said. She wanted a settled, predictable life. She wanted a nice house, a vegetable garden, a regular job with regular hours, and children. He was too restless for that—or so she'd said. He had protested, claiming that he wanted that life, too—someday, although in truth he wasn't sure. But first he had to make this sea voyage. He had to do this before he did anything else. Couldn't she understand that?

"Yes, I can understand that," she'd said. "Just don't expect me to be waiting for you when you return."

That had been the last they'd seen of each other. But as Phil made his last-minute supply runs, from the chandler's to the grocery store to the bank, with stops in between, he returned to his boat at its downtown mooring to find Steller's journal placed carefully on the deck, along with a small package wrapped in brown paper that bore Myrna's return address. He dropped the book through the hatchway onto his berth and angrily stowed the package below without opening it. He then hauled down the boat's gangway his bags of groceries and cases of Bordeaux, his new foul-weather gear and the spare fittings for the deck, the other sea journals that he'd collected to read on his journey, charts, spare batteries, and dozens of other items.

His plan—admittedly vague—was to sail off somewhere and read the journals and drink the wine until he figured out what to do next with his life. The Seattle software company where Phil had worked had seen its stock climb in value at an astounding rate over the last year; Phil realized it had to stop somewhere, so he bailed out before it did, quitting work and selling the stock. With a chunk of the money, he'd purchased his sailboat—not a huge yacht, but a nice 35-foot sloop that had a fiberglass hull and handsome wood trim. Below deck, a fore cabin in its bow contained a V-berth double bed; moving aft, one encountered a closet-sized space containing a small shower and toilet—or head, as it was known at sea—and still farther aft, in the widest and deepest part of the boat's hull, sat the salon, offering plenty of headroom and a teak dining table that converted to an extra bunk, plus the sailboat's small galley. The boat was also equipped with automatic sail-furling devices that allowed him to man it single-handedly, plus a good radio as well as a GPS device that located his position on the globe via satellite.

He knew something about sailing, having handled small boats at his family's summer cabin on a lake on the east side of the Cascades, although this kind of big-water sailing by comparison was the difference between operating a pocket calculator and a computer equipped with the latest high-speed processors. The yacht broker had assured him that the boat was fully capable of crossing the Pacific to Hawaii and beyond—assuming Phil was bold and skilled enough to handle her. He'd proudly christened her the *Myrna Loy*, after the actress and after his girlfriend, who at that point he'd still hoped would accompany him. His chances of seeing her again, however, hadn't been helped when the shipyard painters misspelled it the *Myrna Lay*.

North, he'd finally figured. He'd sail north. He'd much more quickly find the wilder shores where he could think things over by sailing north than south. If he really wanted, he could sail the Inside Passage all the way to Alaska—staying in the shelter of islands most of the way except for a few big gaps where he'd be exposed to the open ocean. Only three days out from Seattle, he'd reached the first of those gaps—the 25 miles of the Strait of Juan de Fuca, between the southern edge of the San Juan Islands and Victoria, British Columbia. Daunted by the wind and rain that swept down on him, the big swells hammering against the *Myrna Lay*'s bow, the cold rain trickling down his neck, the seesawlike heaving of the deck, he'd sought shelter late that afternoon and anchored off an island in a small cove rimmed by a forest of fir trees.

He was hoping to find the courage in the Steller journal to

weigh anchor in the morning. Phil admitted that, whatever else the Bering expedition's problems, it must have taken a lot of heart to sail a small ship across a stormy, unknown northern ocean to an unexplored coast. Phil's was in part a journey to the unexplored coasts within his own mind—the farther shores of possibility—which were looking a lot farther than he anticipated now that he'd stalled out a mere three days into his voyage.

He leaned over the journal again in the soft yellow light from the brass lamp. At least on board the *Myrna Lay* he didn't have to deal with any warring personalities, unlike on Bering's *St. Peter*. The conflict was apparent almost from the moment she and her sister ship, the *St. Paul*, sailed from Siberia's Kamchatka Peninsula on June 4, 1741. Steller, son of a music teacher, was a self-motivated student who had worked his way as part-time preacher through courses in theology, philosophy, medicine, and the natural sciences at Halle, one of Germany's most progressive universities. After his university education, he'd moved to Russia to try his prospects there and became captivated by the idea of joining the explorations then under way in the Russian Far East and North Pacific. Only thirty-two years old when Bering hired him on and the expedition got started, Steller immediately began dispensing unsolicited advice based on his learned scientific observations to the *St. Peter*'s roughly educated, and mostly Russian, officers and crew.

Sailing across the North Pacific toward America, Steller urged a more northerly heading because floating seaweed and other flora and fauna indicated to him that land lay nearby in that direction. The officers brushed him off.

"You are, after all, no seaman," they told him.

"They, of course," confided Steller to his journal, with a pen he never hesitated to dip in acid, "have been in God's council chamber!"

He noted that by ignoring his advice, it took the *St. Peter*—which soon became separated from the *St. Paul*—an extra six weeks to find land. When they finally did reach the coast of what is today

Alaska, Steller, observing the local water salinity and currents, pointed out to the officers what he deduced was a good anchorage at a river mouth. They told him to forget it.

"Have you already been there and made sure?" they asked him.

When they did drop anchor in a spot of their own choosing, the officers wanted to stay only long enough in America to replenish their water barrels and immediately turn back toward Siberia, not even allowing Steller off the *St. Peter* and onto the American shore with the water carriers to fulfill his naturalist's duties. They finally did concede to his ten-hour frenzy of botanizing and collecting on the new land, then sent him a message. "I was to get my butt on board pronto, or, without waiting, they would leave me stranded."*

These conflicts, however, were only differences of opinion over nautical matters; the real problems commenced on the voyage back to Siberia, when scurvy took hold. A few weeks into their return trip across the North Pacific, the crew began to weaken. Bering was bedridden with the disease by the time the *St. Peter* anchored at an island off today's Alaska Peninsula for more water. Steller asked the officers to assign him a few men to help gather plants that he knew would help cure the disease, and he pointed out a spring that offered fresher water than the brackish pond the ship's crew had chosen to refill the barrels. By then, however, the officers—to their own great detriment, it would turn out—had altogether ceased to listen to Steller's unsolicited advice. Steller, equally disgusted with them, on the spot made a vow.

"Although I had already built a hut because of the evening's rain and had wished to spend the night ashore, I decided to go on the ship to bring up, emphatically and with the greatest modesty once

---

* Steller's quotations here and elsewhere in this chapter are from *Journal of a Voyage with Bering, 1741–1742*, by Georg Wilhelm Steller, edited by O. W. Frost and translated by Margritt A. Engel and O. W. Frost (Stanford, California: Stanford University Press, 1988). The actual German of this pithy quote in Steller's manuscript reads: *"ich sollte mich nur geschwinde nach dem Fahrzeuge paken."*

more, my opinion about the unhealthy water and the gathering of plants. But when, concerning the water, I saw myself spurned and rudely contradicted and heard myself ordered to gather the plants as if I were a surgeon's apprentice subject to their command, and the matter that I recommended affecting their own interest, health, and lives was not deemed worthy of the work of one or two persons, I regretted my good opinion and resolved, in the future, to look after the saving of myself alone, without the loss of one word more."

Phil heard the beep of the weather radio, starting its cycle again. He looked up from the journal and listened. Still the same report. Still the heavy winds, rain, and 6-to-8-foot swells. He could feel the gusts through the rigging sway the *Myrna Lay* and shift her bow about on the anchor line. He hoped the anchor would hold in the cove's rocky bottom. He didn't have much experience with anchors. In fact, as he'd motored into the cove, he'd had to pull out his sailing manual and frantically skim over the section on anchors and anchoring before he ran to the bow, heaved his anchor over the side, and paid out what the manual said was the proper amount of line.

He poured himself another glass of the Haut-Médoc. He looked about the salon—the brass lamp, the wood paneling, the shelf of books with the wooden bar across to hold them in place when the boat heeled over, the little galley, the food lockers. All Steller's talk of food made him hungry. He stood up and went to the food lockers. He unlatched the uppermost one and surveyed its contents: two large bags of barbeque potato chips, five cans of ravioli, eight packets of creamy chicken ramen, three 2-liter bottles of diet cola, an 8-ounce bag of Gummi Bears. He unlatched the bottom locker: a jar of peanut butter, a jar of jelly, two loaves of white bread, tortilla chips, a 2-pound bag of Seattle's finest coffee, a 5-pound bag of sugar . . .

It was then that Phil realized he hadn't stowed aboard the *Myrna Lay* a single piece of fresh fruit or a stalk or leaf of vegetables.

In the late 1400s, with the advent of new ship designs and navigation techniques, and much longer voyages in search of sea routes to the Orient, scurvy—"the explorer's sickness"—suddenly became epidemic among ships' crews. Typically it struck after ten to twelve weeks at sea. "Many of our men fell ill here," the Portuguese explorer Vasco da Gama wrote in 1497 as his expedition rounded the southern tip of Africa en route to the Orient, "their hands and feet swelling, and their gums growing over their teeth so that they could not eat." The men were saved by the timely appearance off Mombasa of a boatload of Moorish traders carrying oranges—"better than those of Portugal"—that quickly firmed up their gums.

This pattern was repeated in countless expeditions that followed. After three or so months at sea, the crew succumbed to scurvy and rapidly started to die unless they made landfall, where a few days' worth of fresh food "miraculously" rehabilitated them. One sharp-penciled Portuguese paymaster calculated in 1634 that in the previous five years, less than half of five thousand soldiers making the outbound voyage between Lisbon and India survived the twin catastrophes of shipwreck and scurvy—known to them as *amalati de la boccha*, or "the curse of the mouth." One leading theory was that bad air caused scurvy, especially the bad air belowdecks, although the Spaniards on transpacific voyages believed they fell victim to a foul and subtle wind blowing off California's Cape Mendocino that triggered—and perhaps still does—"some corruption of the bad humors."

Though individual sea captains and ship's physicians apparently understood that fresh fruits and vegetables prevented or cured scurvy, a remarkable amount of confusion persisted about it for nearly three centuries. It is almost inexplicable why a sure cure, so readily available in nature and so well known to many native peoples, was not widely prescribed by the European sea powers hundreds of years sooner. Because there was no standard prescription for scurvy for so long, some two million sailors lost their lives between 1500 and 1800, according to calculations made from nautical records.

There were ample clues to scurvy's causes and cures. In the 1530s, a French expedition under Jacques Cartier searching for a sea route across North America wintered in the icebound St. Lawrence River, and by mid-February scurvy had laid low the crew. Finally only three or four men—including Cartier, who must have nourished himself from a private food cache—possessed the strength to move from their bunks. Twenty-five of a party of 110 had died. Cartier ordered an autopsy on one of the victims, twenty-two-year-old Phillip Rougemont of Amboise, in the hopes of finding a hint about how to stop the disease from killing the entire crew.

"It was discovered," wrote the expedition's chronicler, "that his heart was completely white and shrivelled up, with more than a jugful of red date-coloured water about it. His liver was in good condition but his lungs were very black and gangrened. . . . His spleen for some two finger breadths near the backbone was also slightly affected, as if it had been rubbed on a rough stone. After seeing this much, we made an incision and cut open one of his thighs, which on the outside was very black, but within the flesh was found fairly healthy. Thereupon we buried him as well as we could."

Cartier wouldn't let the local Indians near his ship for fear they'd see the expedition's vulnerability to attack, but it was those same Indians who had a cure. Outside the ship one day, Cartier ran into Dom Agaya, an Indian who, when Cartier had first met him some days earlier, was suffering from his own case of scurvy. When Cartier asked how he had been cured, Dom Agaya and two women from his tribe showed the captain how to cut branches from the "annedda" tree, grind up its bark and foliage, boil it in water, and drink the infusion every two days, applying the dregs to scurvy-swollen legs.

"The Captain at once ordered a drink to be prepared for the sick men," wrote the chronicler, "but none of them would taste it. At length one or two thought they would risk a trial. As soon as they had drunk it, they felt better which must clearly be ascribed to miraculous causes; for after drinking it two or three times, they recovered health and strength and were cured of all the diseases they ever had. And some of the sailors who had been suffering for five or six years from the French pox [syphilis] were by this medicine cured completely. There was then such a press for the medicine that in less than eight days a whole tree as large and as tall as any I ever saw was used up."

One modern investigator concluded that the mysterious and potent "annedda" tree probably was the white cedar. An expedition a few years after Cartier's journey carried samples of the white cedar back to France, where it received the name *arborvitae*—"tree of life"—that is so familiar to gardeners these four and a half centuries later. Its powers to cure scurvy, however, apparently were soon forgotten. Not ten years after the Cartier expedition, another French party wintering in nearly the same spot on the St. Lawrence lost fifty out of two hundred to scurvy. A few decades later, wintering on the St. Croix River in today's Maine, Monsieur de Monts' party lost thirty-six out of eighty to *mal de terre*—"land disease." In a mix of wild speculation and accurate guesswork, the expedition's chronicler, Monsieur Lescarbot, attributed the disease to the "great rottenness in the woods during the rains of Autumn and Winter," to "rude, gross, cold and melancholy meats," and—cutting through Lescarbot's rhetoric—to unrelieved lust.

Only his citing of the "melancholy meats" was close to the mark, for scurvy is above all a nutrition-deficiency disease. Whatever the weak spots of his analysis, Monsieur Lescarbot did note the curious connection between scurvy and stress—one that's been cited by modern researchers as well. The disease "found out" sailors who

were "grudging, repining, never content, idle." As for a cure, Lescarbot's prescription might be called the French school of scurvy reme-
dies: rich butter sauces to be served with capon and fresh game, plus
tender springtime herbs, a happy spirit, and plenty of sex, although
this last element was allowed only within the confines of a Church-
approved union. "It resteth necessary . . . for every one to have the
honest company of his lawfull wife: for without that, ones minde is
always upon that which one loves and desireth; the body becomes
full of ill humours, and so the sickness doth breed."

With some exceptions—such as Sir Francis Drake's circum-
navigation of the globe in the 1570s in the *Golden Hind*, when his crew
"refreshed" themselves with South America's wild herbs, the crayfish
of the Celebes, and West Africa's lemons and fresh oysters—the
British fared no better on long voyages than the Portuguese, Spanish, and French had before them.* The Plymouth colony itself lost
half of its original group of English settlers to scurvy, while the
colony's later settlers treated themselves with lemon juice brought by
ship. "This is a wonderful secret of the power and wisdom of God,
that hath hidden so great and unknown virtue in this fruit," wrote
Sir Richard Hawkins of the British navy after his scurvy-ridden
crew had been saved by lemons and oranges upon landing in southern Brazil in 1593. Despite the strength of many testimonials like
Hawkins' for the curative powers of citrus fruits, and his observation
that in twenty years at sea he'd seen probably ten thousand men consumed by scurvy, English authorities went on debating the efficacy
of treatments such as drinking seawater, gargling with sulfuric acid,
and—here's the British school of scurvy cures—chugging pints of
wort made from soaking malted barley in water. The theory was that

---

* A British seaman's typical daily diet in 1740 consisted of the following:
1 pound of biscuit, 1 gallon of beer or a ration of liquor, 1 pound of salt beef or
pork, 2 ounces of cheese, 1 ounce of butter, 7 ounces of oatmeal, and 4.5 ounces
of dried beans or peas. From *The History of Scurvy and Vitamin C* by Kenneth J.
Carpenter (Cambridge: Cambridge University Press, 1986).

the wort would ferment inside the patient as it did inside the beer-brewing vats back in England and work some unknown therapeutic effect.

It wasn't for another two centuries after Hawkins' voyage and testimonial that Gilbert Blane, a socially prominent physician who had served with the British fleet in the West Indies and treated dozens of scurvy cases, finally persuaded the Office for Sick and Hurt Seamen and the Lords of the Admiralty to approve the now-famous daily issue of .75 ounce of lemon juice per man. The edict went into effect in 1795; over the next twenty years, the British navy issued 1.6 million gallons of lemon juice (later changed to lime juice, although the terms back then were often used interchangeably). The allowance dramatically cut the incidence of scurvy, helped the British navy defeat the French and Spanish fleets at the Battle of Trafalgar in 1805, and dubbed British citizens at outposts around the globe with the name "limeys." "The British Empire," one medical authority has written, "blossomed from the seeds of citrus fruits."

Scurvy, however, by no means had been eradicated. It still cropped up during Europe's Great Potato Famine and the California Gold Rush of the late 1840s, during polar expeditions, and during the American Civil War when it caused a quarter of the twelve thousand deaths at the Confederacy's infamous Andersonville Prison. In the late 1800s, doctors in both Europe and the United States saw growing numbers of cases of "infantile scurvy" as babies' diets shifted to more processed foods and cow's milk and away from highly nutritious breast milk.

Though it was now relatively easy to cure, no one knew exactly what caused scurvy. A big breakthrough occurred in 1907 when two Norwegian scientists attempted to induce beriberi—another nutrition-deficiency disease afflicting Norwegian sailors at the time—in guinea pigs by feeding them nothing but bread. Instead they induced scurvy, discovering that guinea pigs are, like humans, subject to the disease. The guinea pig discovery made possible widespread scurvy experiments on animal subjects, and research progressed rapidly. Four years later, in 1911, a young Polish chemist by the name of Casimir Funk floated a radical theory that scurvy and several other diseases resulted from diets that were each deficient in different substances that he called "vital amines." Other researchers worked with rats and searched for unidentified dietary substances they called "fat-soluble factor A" and "water-soluble factor B"; scientists hunting the active element in foods that prevented scurvy logically called it "accessory food factor C." Though these unknown substances weren't necessarily amines—a type of base compound—Casimir Funk's term "vital amines" was soon adopted in shortened form. We thus take our daily allowance of vitamins A, B-complex, and C instead of, as was apparently proposed, a dose of "funkians."

Credit for the actual isolation of vitamin C finally went to a scientist from Hungary, biochemist Albert Szent-Györgyi, who was working on an altogether different chemical problem when he isolated a crystalline substance from the adrenal glands of oxen and later from cabbage, oranges, and paprika. The crystals' molecular composition resembled that of common sugars such as glucose and fructose, known chemically as the hexoses, and, unsure of his crystals' exact molecular structure, Szent-Györgyi wanted to call it "ignose" or "godnose." The editor of a scientific journal made him change it to "hexuronic acid"—later known as ascorbic acid or vitamin C. Although he hadn't set out to find vitamin C, his work won him the Nobel prize for physiology and medicine in 1937. "The whole problem," he wrote thirty years later, "was, for me too glamorous, and vitamins were, to my mind, theoretically uninteresting. 'Vitamin' means that one has to eat it. What one has to eat is the first concern of the chef, not the scientist."

Phil swayed slightly from the Bordeaux and the wind-driven rock of the *Myrna Lay* as he stood in the salon and gazed into the open food lockers. He'd skipped the oranges at the supermarket—too much trouble to peel. He'd passed up the apples—too mushy. He hadn't even considered the lettuce or red and green peppers because he preferred to avoid all the mouth-crunching effort a salad demanded of its eater. No, he preferred concentrated foods. And, like the sailors of two and three centuries ago, he had them aboard—in abundance. *Lack* of food wasn't the problem. It was *quality* of food. He rummaged around behind the bags of chips and canned ravioli and diet cola and Gummi Bears. He found a tin of processed cheese, a stick of plastic-wrapped garlic salami, a box of saltine crackers.

This wasn't going to do—not at all. He unconsciously let go of the locker door and moved his right hand to his upper incisors. He tried to wiggle them with his fingers. Already they felt a little loose. The thought of eating the sticky gummi bears with scurvy-loosened teeth made him want to heave the bag of candy overboard. Or was he just imagining the teeth? He was only three days' sail out of Seattle, after all, not three months'. But maybe his body's stores of vitamin C had been well depleted before he left; scurvy might strike him far sooner than the usual two or three months. He did feel a little weak. That was the first sign. Weakness could set in days or weeks before the loose teeth and other really gruesome symptoms appeared. How low had his body's stores of vitamin C been before he embarked? That was the key question. *Really* low, probably. He tried to remember the last time he had eaten a salad. Or a piece of fruit. Or any green vegetable at all. He wondered if he could count the green olives on the double-mozzarella pizza he'd stuffed into his face while arguing with Myrna during their final date.

Phil plunged his hands back into the upper locker, digging for something to eat that might contain vitamin C.

It's not clear exactly how much Steller knew about scurvy cures when the *St. Peter* put in at the island off the Alaska Peninsula. He was familiar with the scurvy grass—*Cochlearia*—that some European physicians and navigators had been prescribing to treat the disease for more than a century and possibly much earlier.* With his insatiable botanical curiosity, Steller apparently had also noted what plants were eaten for their health by the natives of Kamchatka, where he'd spent several months prior to the expedition's departure. Although he was brusquely denied help at the island stop, Steller nevertheless went ashore on the island and gathered what medicinal plants he could. In addition to a native variety of scurvy grass, these plants included a species of dock (a member of the buckwheat family) that was eaten raw by Siberian Eskimos, as well as gentian and "other cresslike plants that I gathered only for my use and the Captain-Commander's."

As Steller gathered plants, one of the sickest sailors, Nikita Shumagin, was brought ashore by the water carriers in the hope that simply being on land would do him good. (One scurvy theory of the time had it that humans needed exposure to certain mysterious "earthy

---

* William Shakespeare's son-in-law, the Stratford-on-Avon physician John Hall, left detailed notes of successfully treating on-land scurvy patients with scurvy grass. These included his wife—Shakespeare's eldest daughter—the forty-seven-year-old Susanna, whose nasty 1630 scurvy case was accompanied by "Pain of the Loins, Corruption of the Gums, Stinking Breath, Melancholy, Wind, Cardiac Passion, Laziness, difficulty of breathing, fear of the Mother, binding of the Belly, and torment there, and all of a long continuance, with restlessness and weakness." Quoted in *The History of Scurvy and Vitamin C* by Kenneth J. Carpenter (Cambridge: Cambridge University Press, 1986).

particles.") Soon after he arrived ashore, Shumagin died. Named by the men of the *St. Peter,* the Shumagin Islands off the Alaskan Peninsula still commemorate their first fallen crewmate.

Predictably, the other ill sailors in the crew of the *St. Peter* at first wouldn't touch the plants Steller had gathered on the Shumagin Islands. But their tune soon changed. "Ungrateful and coarse men though they were, my ministrations, under divine grace, very clearly caught their attention when, simply by giving him raw scurvy grass, I managed to bring the Captain-Commander—so bedridden with scurvy that he had already lost the use of his limbs—so far within eight days that he was able to get out of bed and on deck and to feel as vigorous as he had been at the beginning of the voyage. Likewise, the *Lapathum* [dock] I prescribed to be eaten raw for three days firmed up again the teeth of most seamen."

Apparently the supply didn't last—through their own neglect at refusing to help Steller gather it. The ship weighed anchor on September 6 and inched its way again across the North Pacific into an onslaught of autumn storms that greatly hindered its progress and allowed the scurvy to take hold again. The wind screamed and whistled through the rigging. Waves battered the *St. Peter*'s hull like the concussion of a cannon shot. The veteran steersman of fifty years' experience, Andreas Hesselberg, had never witnessed storms so violent. "Every moment we expected the shattering of our ship and no one could sit, lie down, or stand," Steller recorded. "No one could remain at his station, but we were drifting under God's terrible power wherever the enraged heavens wanted to take us. Half our men lay sick and weak, and the other half was healthy out of necessity but thoroughly crazed and maddened by the terrifying movement of the sea and ship."

On October 2, during a lull between storms, Steller took stock: twenty-four men sick and two dead. The gales had blown the ship backward toward America some 230 miles. The supply of brandy ran out. But the storms continued, and so did the scurvy. By October 20,

a man was dying nearly every day. Only ten men, including Steller—
who pointed out that it wasn't in his job description but who helped
sail the ship nonetheless—had enough strength to work the *St. Peter*
at all. Even they were so weak that the *St. Peter* didn't put in for fresh
water at a small island they spotted because the decimated crew
couldn't have hauled up the anchor from the bottom.

It was then that the two highest-ranking officers below the ail-
ing Bering, Master Khitrov and Lieutenant Waxell, issued a strange
and sudden order—strange and sudden, according to Steller, anyway—
to change course and head more northward, thus "criminally deviat-
ing" from the agreed-on plan to aim straight for the *St. Peter*'s home
harbor at Avacha on the Kamchatka Peninsula. Soon after, the officers announced with "mathematical certainty" that the *St. Peter* was
about to make landfall on the Kamchatka Peninsula. The crew, at
least those who could still walk, gathered on the *St. Peter*'s deck early
on the morning of November 5, 1741, to witness the truth of this pre-
diction. "To the astonishment of all," reported Steller, "it came to
pass that at nine o'clock land was sighted."

After joyous celebration and prayers of thanks, the officers and
men examined sketches of Avacha and compared them to the features of the coast ahead of them, and the two were found to agree
completely. They even thought they spotted the mouth of Avacha's
harbor and its lighthouse. The *St. Peter* sailed in closer. The sun appeared, and the officers took a noon bearing with the sextant. But
something was amiss. The observation located them between 55 and
56 degrees north latitude instead of down near 52 degrees, where
Avacha lay and where they believed they were from the look of the
coast. They attempted to work the ship back to the south, near to
the point they'd identified as Cape Isopa, but strong headwinds hindered them. Another gale rose, and the crew no longer possessed the
strength to climb aloft and furl the sails. During the night, the raging wind and the unfurled sails whipping about shredded the ropes
that supported the mainmast.

The next morning, November 6, the ship's officers and commander argued about how to proceed. Bering insisted they keep sailing south until they reached the certain safe haven of Avacha, although the mainmast was now too weak to carry much sail and the crew even weaker. However, Master Khitrov—"professing if this were not Kamchatka he would let his head be chopped off"—went about convincing the sailors that the *St. Peter* should put into land immediately on the unknown coast. The crew sided with Master Khitrov, and when one lower officer objected to Khitrov's plan, Khitrov and Waxell tossed him out of the meeting. "Out!" they shouted, according to Steller. "Shut up you dog, you son of a bitch!"

That night, as the *St. Peter* put into a cove of the unknown shore, high seas suddenly rolled in, tossing the ship up and down "like a ball." The superstitious among the sailors unceremoniously pitched the recent dead, who had been saved for a land burial, head over heels overboard in hopes of calming the tempestuous sea. The next morning Steller—still healthy, presumably due to his regimen of raw herbs, and no doubt eager to get off the ship—was the first ashore along with the surveyor Pleniser, Steller's cossack servant, and a few of the sick. He carried with him as much of his luggage as he could; given the poor anchorage and lack of healthy crew, he knew that the first storm would blow the *St. Peter* out to sea or smash her on the beach. He spent that first day, November 7, exploring, noting particularly how little fear of humans the sea otters showed—an animal that was heavily hunted on the mainland for its pelt—in the way they scampered down the beach and into the water to greet their rowboat as it landed. Later, returning to the landing spot, he found Lieutenant Waxell, weak with scurvy, taking the air on shore.

"God knows if this is Kamchatka," Steller said.

"What else would it be?" Waxell replied. "We will soon send for posthorses."

Over the next two days, Steller and his two companions—his cossack hunter and servant, Thoma, and his friend and fellow German, the surveyor Pleniser—further explored the unknown shore. Steller found more clues—blue foxes that were extraordinarily cheeky, the total absence of trees or shrubs on the mountainous land, the "sea cows" lying on the beach that Thoma said he'd never seen before on Kamchatcka, and the presence of sea clouds in the distance that indicated water all around.*

Perhaps, Steller thought, they'd beached on a large island.

No doubt the trio mulled over this prospect—or rather, Steller expounded on it to the other two—as they sat around their campfire the first night on shore. As they sat there, Steller reported, a blue fox strolled into their camp and before their eyes walked out with two of the ptarmigan—a type of grouse—they'd hunted. In what proved to be a pivotal moment of the voyage, Thoma, who was also suffering from scurvy, suddenly turned to Steller and angrily blamed Steller and his curiosity for all of his troubles.

Steller reported his reply: " 'Cheer up!' I said. 'God will help. Even if this is not our country, we still have hope of getting there. You will not die of hunger. If you cannot work and wait on me, I will wait on you. I know your honest heart and what you have done for me. Everything I have is yours also. Just ask and I will share with you half of all I have until God helps.' "

The conversation started Steller thinking about preparations for winter, should the unknown shore turn out to be an island. At his urging, Pleniser agreed to help him build a hut, and they entered a pact to help each other as friends. With makeshift shovels the threesome soon began to excavate a pit house with a roof supported by driftwood similar to those built for winter dwellings by Kamchadal natives. Three other German crew members of the *St. Peter* joined

---

* Also called Steller's sea cow, this marine mammal grew as long as 25 feet, propelling itself through the water with a fluked tail to feed on seaweed. It was hunted to extinction for food by Russian sealers within thirty years of the time it was first described by Steller, who also first described hundreds of other plants and animals in Siberia and America and for whom the Steller's jay and Steller's sea eagle are also named.

their household, plus two more cossacks, and Bering's two servants, all of them pledging to "enter into a community of goods."

Within a day or two, the other members of the *St. Peter's* crew who still had strength enough to row to shore began digging out their own underground huts in imitation of Steller and organizing their own households. Steller, no longer the scorned physician and botanist, had suddenly become by example a leader. Master Khitrov's star, meanwhile, was sinking fast. The ill sailors blamed him for their misery and isolation. He begged and wheedled the Germans for a corner in their hut so he wouldn't have to sleep with the ordinary seamen, who were uttering threats against him day and night. Steller and his housemates, however, were "offended by him, and we refused him all hope, because he was healthy and lazy, and he alone had plunged us into this misfortune."

Work continued on the huts on November 12, a week after land had first been sighted, and was completed the following day. But their shelter proved too late for many of the crew.

"That day many sick were brought from the ship," Steller wrote, "among them some who, like the cannoneer, died as soon as they came into the air, others in the boat on the crossing over like the soldier Savin Stepanov, others once on shore like the sailor Sylvester. . . . Even before they could be buried, the dead were mutilated by foxes that sniffed at and even dared to attack the sick—still alive and helpless—who were lying on the beach everywhere without cover under the open sky. One screamed because he was cold, another from hunger and thirst, as the mouths of many were in such a wretched state from scurvy that they could not eat anything on account of the great pain because the gums were swollen up like a sponge, brown-black and grown high over the teeth and covering them. . . . The barracks was finished, and during the afternoon we carried in a lot of the sick. But because of the narrowness of the space, they were lying about everywhere on the ground, covered with rags and clothes."

Though he did not give a precise description of the men dying on the beach, Steller probably saw all the classic symptoms of scurvy. Typically, the sailor would first start to weaken before any outward physical marks appeared. The first of these was small purple spots on the sailor's buttocks and the back of legs as small hemorrhages formed around the hair follicles. His skin turned dry and rough. He sometimes couldn't catch his breath. His joints ached deeply, especially his knees, hips, and ankles, because his weight alone caused trauma inside the joints that led to swelling. His legs swelled and hurt from hemorrhaging within the muscles and tissues beneath the skin. He bruised with the slightest touch. Old scars reopened as the tissues pulled apart. Scratches and wounds didn't heal. He became so weak he couldn't lift his own limbs. As their capillaries ruptured, those most famous symptoms of scurvy appeared—his gums swelled into black and purplish masses that were too tender to chew food and which bled with the slightest scrape. His teeth loosened in his skull. If he'd had any strength at all, he could have plucked out his own teeth with his fingers alone.

"If the situation continues," as one scurvy description puts it, "the body will degenerate into a bleeding pulp for which death is a blessing."

What finally happened to the sailor—moaning on the cold beach in pain and cursing his officers and his gods for bringing him there—was that he overexerted himself by, for instance, trying to crawl into the shelter of the newly built underground barracks. This sudden exertion burst scurvy-weakened major blood vessels near his heart. He dropped dead, facedown into the frozen sand.

Phil had now torn most of the food packages out of the upper and lower lockers and flung them to the salon floor in his effort to find something fresh, something that might contain some vitamin C. Rolling out on the floor went the cans of chili and refried beans. Between the crashing of the cans he could hear the rain thumping on the deck overhead with renewed vigor. How long might he be pinned in this cove? Down went a box of taco shells, a can of anchovies, an extra tube of toothpaste. At least he'd remembered his toothbrush; he hadn't totally neglected his health. But last night hadn't he spotted a streak of blood when he spit out the toothpaste into the little stainless-steel sink in the *Myrna Lay*'s head? Or was that just the detritus from a red Gummi Bear? Or the dregs of the bottle of Haut-Médoc? He imagined the gums that belonged to Bering's sailors dying on the beach. How long would it be before his own gums looked like that? The thought of scraping the extra-stiff bristles of his toothbrush over those pulpy, purplish black masses of dying tissue—the brushing action tearing off strips of flesh—made him want to gag.

Phil momentarily abandoned his search to run to the head and check his mouth in the mirror.

There is a brief but fascinating history of researchers who have induced scurvy in themselves, intentionally or not. It started in the mid-eighteenth century when one William Stark—a young, eccentric English physician who'd met Benjamin Franklin and who may have taken a little too seriously the ever-practical Franklin's commendation of a simple diet—managed to kill himself by eating mostly bread and water.

In 1939, a surgeon at Harvard Medical School, John Crandon, intentionally induced scurvy in himself, developing the first signs of it after twelve weeks on a diet that, in the eyes of some undergraduates, no doubt contains all the key food groups—bread, crackers, cheese, eggs, sugar, chocolate, and beer. A few years later, during

World War II, a small group of conscientious objectors in Sheffield, England, volunteered for an experiment in which the vitamin C had been boiled, aerated, or otherwise destroyed in milk, potatoes, and other foods they were fed, after the volunteers had initially boosted their vitamin C levels with large doses. After four to eleven weeks on the diet, however, the vitamin C level in their blood plasma had dropped to almost undetectable levels. By twenty weeks, all of them showed little plugs forming in the hair follicles of their buttocks and backs of their legs, and six of ten had hemorrhages beneath the skin. After the twenty-sixth week, wounds that had been intentionally inflicted on the volunteers—who by this point might have wished they'd chosen the war front instead—no longer healed.

By the thirty-sixth week, the gums of nine of ten had become "purplish, swollen and spongy" and "special incidents" occurred. One of the volunteers, a twenty-two-year-old student, after heavy exercise suffered what was diagnosed as a heart attack. Another awoke in the night with chest pains and a systolic murmur. A chest X ray in another had revealed the sudden growth of a small, preexisting tubercular lesion. Immediate, massive injections of vitamin C cured all the special problems. Researchers then reined in the experiment, giving each of the remaining volunteers 10 milligrams of vitamin C each day—only about one-sixth of today's recommended 60-milligram daily intake in the United States for healthy adults and about one-fourth of the 25- to 40-milligram daily intake recommended by Canada. Even with this minimal dose of vitamin C, within two weeks the volunteers had showed marked improvements and after ten to fourteen weeks had fully recovered.

Using sophisticated biochemical analysis, researchers have since understood that vitamin C serves as a kind of atomic welder in the body's protein-making factories. Humans constantly produce protein in order to grow bigger or to replace worn-out parts—a half a ton of it during a child's first few years alone and over a lifetime some five tons of it, which would halfway fill a dump truck. This is forged inside the cells' tiny ribosomes, which select an array of the body's twenty amino acids and fasten them together in different combinations. One of the most important of these proteins is collagen—an extremely tough but flexible material that forms the basis of the body's connective tissues such as ligaments and tendons as well as bones, and forms layers within blood vessel walls and skin. (Leather, for instance, is preserved animal collagen.) In essence, vitamin C, or ascorbic acid, tacks an extra group of oxygen and hydrogen atoms onto some of the amino acids that form collagen, causing them to bond extremely tightly together and giving the collagen its tough, flexible quality. It plays a similar but less clear role in the production of elastin, a protein in the body's elastic fibers, including those in veins and arteries.

As the crew of the *St. Peter* lay moaning on the beach, their tissues and blood vessels containing these proteins, without the bonding influence of vitamin C, were literally coming unraveled like the shredded rigging aboard the *St. Peter*. Captain-Commander Bering was among the very sick. He had been carried to shore and placed in a sailcloth tent on the sand, whereupon he asked Steller what he thought of this new land.

"It does not look like Kamchatka to me," Steller said.

"The ship probably cannot be saved," Bering replied. "May God spare us our longboat!"

Steller frequently checked in on Bering; the captain's two servants now mostly looked after their own survival. He gave Bering drinks of water and brought food, such as a baby sea otter still nursing on its mother that Steller knew contained plenty of nourishment. "But he declared a very great aversion to it," wrote Steller, "and wondered at my taste, which was adapted to the circumstances and place."

Once again the officers of the *St. Peter*, to their great detriment, had shown rigidity where Steller showed flexibility and improvisation. Though he "refreshed" himself with ptarmigan, Bering sunk deeper into illness and despair. His body teemed with lice. He had himself buried in the sand from the waist down.

"The deeper in the ground I lie," he said, "the warmer I am."

Two hours before daybreak on December 8, 1741, Captain-Commander Vitus Bering died. "He would undoubtedly still be alive," Steller wrote, "if we had reached Kamchatka and he could have had the benefit of a warm room and fresh food. As it was, he died more from hunger, cold, thirst, vermin, and grief than from a disease." Still, Bering's body showed abundant signs of scurvy: swelling of the feet and joints, as well as decay—"mortification"—of the tissues. Composed and even "blissful" as he died, Bering retained his reason and speech until the end. "He wished nothing more than our deliverance from this land," Steller wrote, "and from the bottom of his heart, his own complete deliverance from this misery. He might well not have found a better place to prepare himself for eternity than this deathbed under the open sky."

Phil stared at his gums in the head's mirror over the little sink, illuminated by the 12-volt lightbulb. They looked normal—kind of. Maybe they appeared a bit darker than usual. And his teeth had a reddish tinge. Was that the Bordeaux, or the first sign of hemorrhaging capillaries? But purple spots on the backs of his legs and buttocks should have showed up first. Phil quickly unzipped his jeans and peeled them and his boxer shorts down to his knees. He pulled up his shirttails and twisted his head around. He couldn't see. He ran his right hand over the skin of his buttocks. He felt small bumps. *Damn!* He twisted farther. On the back of his thighs and his buttocks *there were at least four or five small purple spots!* Were they just pimples? Or was it the onset of perifollicular hemorrhage?

Pulling up his pants with one hand, Phil hurried back into the salon, kicking with his bare feet through the dozens of scattered packages and cans of food. There had to be some vitamin C *somewhere* in this mess.

Bering's death marked the end of the rapid die-off of the crew. By Christmas, the survivors had recovered their health if not their full strength. A storm, meanwhile, drove the *St. Peter* ashore and buried her hull in sand, and she was deemed no longer seaworthy. Search parties returned to report that they were, as Steller had predicted, on a large island—one that showed absolutely no signs of human habitation. Whatever attempts the marooned party would make at rescuing itself would have to wait for spring.

Hunting sea mammals for their basic food, the castaways settled in for the winter. Like the Eskimos, who traditionally have lived scurvy-free, the sailors found that an all-meat diet could provide them with the nutrients they needed—especially the organ meat, eaten raw or lightly cooked. A 3.5-ounce chunk of raw seal liver alone can contain enough vitamin C to meet the Canadian daily recommendation, as do two or three pounds—not an unusual amount on an all-meat diet—of lightly cooked seal flesh, as exposure to oxygen and excessive heat destroys the vitamin. The Yukon Indians ate the raw, vitamin C–rich adrenal glands of field mice to cure scurvy. Even today, native hunters in Manchuria, Greenland, and other northern climates extract the still-warm kidneys and liver of deer, seal, and other animals they have just killed and hungrily swallow them on the spot like giant, raw, dripping capsules of vitamin C. They also love to chew on vitamin C–laden whaleskin. These mammals—like all other mammals—need vitamin C as badly as humans but have their own mechanisms for manufacturing it from simple glucose. The only known land mammals that cannot make their own vitamin C are the guinea pig, the fruit bat, primates (including humans), and a bird called the red-vented bulbul—all lacking a key enzyme for the final conversion from glucose to ascorbic acid.

With the fresh meat, the ascorbic acid level in the sailors' bloodstream began to rise, and their organs absorbed it. Their adrenal glands took in large amounts in order to manufacture norepinephrine and epinephrine, which are secreted when the body is under stress to kick up the heart rate, dilate blood vessels, and release extra fuels into the bloodstream to prepare for fight or flight. Thus people under stress—like the sailors on the Bering expedition—may need more vitamin C and are more susceptible to scurvy.

Assuming they were consuming at least 10 milligrams of it per day in their sea-mammal diet, the vitamin C would have started to restore the crew's health within two weeks. Their strength returned, their teeth firmed up. Within eight weeks their skin would have resumed its normal coloring, except for brownish patches where the hemorrhages had occurred. After ten to fourteen weeks their gums would have totally recovered, judging by the results of the World War II experiments with the conscientious objectors. Still, on the island complete recovery may have been slower.

During the long winter, the party suffered a severe outbreak of gambling accompanied by quarrels and strife. All gambling was finally banned by the petty officers. In spring, work commenced on the construction of a new, smaller boat out of the salvaged timbers of the *St. Peter*. From chaos—a "state of nature," as Steller called it—the renourished survivors organized themselves into a functioning society. Everyone signed a pact: the twelve men who knew how to wield axes would work full time as carpenters on the new boat, and the remainder would divide into two hunting shifts to ensure a constant supply of meat. Under this common purpose—their deliverance from the island—work proceeded quickly as the snow melted. Their emaciated bodies were nourished by runs of fish so abundant that a single haul of their old nets caught enough to last them eight days. Aided by Steller's keen botanical eye, they savored Kamchatkan sweet grass, bulbs of sarana lily, roots of wild celery, oyster-leaf, shoots of fireweed, and salads of scurvy grass, brooklime, and bitter cress, all washed down with tealike infusions of lingonberry and wintergreen. Lieutenant Waxell reported that he didn't recover his full strength until eating these greens with the coming of spring.

By mid-July, they'd built the new hull. For the next month they fashioned the rigging, spars, and mast, forged the hardware, baked ship's biscuit from their salvaged flour supplies, and put up barrels of salted sea cow. On August 13, the castaways boarded the 42-foot-long boat, a one-masted hooker also named the *St. Peter*. Out of the original crew of 78, only 46 had survived. There was nevertheless barely room to jam themselves in to sleep between the supplies in the hold and the deck planking—the supplies including nine hundred valuable otter pelts they'd hunted on the island. A fair wind and sunny skies propelled them past the southern tip of Bering Island, as they christened it. They looked one last time at the mountains and valleys they'd come to know so well. "God's grace and mercy became manifested to all," wrote Steller, "the more brightly considering how miserably we had arrived there on November 6, had miraculously nourished ourselves on this barren island, and with amazing labor had become ever more healthy, hardened, and strengthened; and the more we gazed at the island on our farewell, the clearer appeared to us, as in a mirror, God's wonderful and loving guidance."

Barefoot in the salon, his pants hitched halfway up his hips, Phil plucked from the floor the most nutritious-sounding items and, holding the packages toward the light of the brass lamp, read the nutritional labels printed on the back.

A can of chili—zero vitamin C.

He tossed it back to the floor and snagged the can of refried beans. Zero.

Down it went again. There was the toothpaste—*no way*—and

the sugar and coffee—*forget it*. A box of macaroni and cheese, a bag of powdered-sugar doughnuts, a package of spaghetti. All 0 percent.

Phil then inadvertently stepped on a bag of barbeque potato chips. It made a loud crunch. He wasn't even going to bother to pick it up. But if the Great Potato Famine had triggered a widespread epidemic of scurvy, potatoes must contain some vitamin C that had kept it at bay.

He reached down. He held the bag's silvery back to the lamp-light. He couldn't believe it. A single serving—about fifteen chips—contained 10 percent of the 60 milligrams that was the U.S. recommended value of vitamin C, in other words about 6 milligrams. If the conscientious objectors during World War II recovered from their experimental scurvy on a mere 10 milligrams daily, this meant that two big handfuls of potato chips daily would be enough to stave off or eventually recover from a case of scurvy. If the Bering expedition had only carried enough potato chips, Phil realized, they would have survived just fine.

Phil ripped open the bag and stuffed a fistful of the spicy, salty chips into his mouth, chewing them as he kicked through the remaining cans and packages and jars, the orangish crumbs falling from his lips. A jar of salsa bumped his toe. That was about as close to a fresh vegetable as anything he'd stowed aboard the *Myrna Lay*. He checked the label. *Another score!* Two tablespoons of the salsa—one serving—contained 8 percent of the daily RV. It must be in the vitamin-rich peppers. He twisted open the lid and jammed another fistful of chips into it, pushing the dripping chips into his mouth. The salsa trickled down his chin and splattered to the floor.

He looked down. At his feet lay a package of grape Kool-Aid. He picked it up and read the label. Each serving contained 10 percent of the daily value of vitamin C. He dug through the galley cupboards, and found a plastic pitcher and mixed up a quart of the Kool-Aid. He took a long swig straight from the pitcher. It was delicious. He could almost feel the vitamin C flowing out through his

limbs like the sap that rises in a tree with the spring sun. Those perifollicular hemorrhages—or pimples, whichever they were—wouldn't
stand a chance.

It was then, on the little shelf above the galley sink, that he
spotted the package wrapped in brown paper Myrna had left on
board along with the Steller journal. In his anger at her, he'd stashed
the package there before he'd cast off. Now it occurred to him that
maybe it contained food. Maybe even fresh fruit.

He snatched the package off the shelf and tore it open. Inside
was a small cardboard box. He ripped apart the box. There was tissue paper stuffed inside it. He could hear something rattling inside
the tissue paper. He shredded the tissue and found a small plastic
bottle. He held it up to the lamplight. The plastic was dark-colored—
strong light could destroy the potency of its contents—and the label
was marked "Vitamin C Supplement, 500 mg."

Taped to the bottle was a note. Phil read it. "To keep you safe.
Love, Myrna."

Smiling, he opened the bottle, tossed two of the pills into his
mouth, and washed them down with Kool-Aid.

CHAPTER SIX

WARM TO

THE TOUCH:

HEATSTROKE

The top of the pass and she's won. The rest will be downhill, fast, the wind whistling through her helmet and whirring through her spokes. They'll never catch her then. The top of the pass and the prize money is hers. Hers and her family's—her mother and father, younger sister and brother, her wild-haired, curse-spewing grandmother, still shouting at imaginary Nazi invaders fifty years after they left—a family who shares an apartment in a crumbling concrete building in an Eastern European city. The top of the pass and she'll escape this brutal heat, dive down the far side into a cool breeze, into a stream of those green American dollars.

She must be close. From the early-morning start at the chamber of commerce, which sponsored the race hoping to spur the region's economic development, the course funneled the competitors along a strip of fast-food restaurants and car lots, and then up, up, up the winding, narrow road into the Appalachian Mountains. She made her breakaway on the first big hill. Her coach has always said, "Attack on the climbs, defend on the downhills. It's on the climbs where races are won."

She looks back. No one in sight.

She's always been a good climber but has never made a break-away half so bold as this. Back there, somewhere, is the rest of the pack, and somewhere in the pack are the three best hill climbers in the world—the Italian girl and the French girl and the Colombian girl, famous riders all. She is a nothing to them, a nobody. She knows it, and they know it, but this is exactly what she plans to work to her advantage. For now, they let her go sprinting away by herself in front of the pack, figuring they could easily reel her in once she'd exhausted herself. She'll surprise them. That's her strategy: to get so far ahead on this climb that they never catch her.

How many more switchbacks on the road? she wonders. It can't be far. It's so hot. Her thighs burn with the strain of pumping uphill, and her neck and arms and shoulders and back join in the pain, the muscle groups working in tandem to shove her entire body down like a piston to power each stroke of the pedals. Did she break away too soon? If she'd waited much longer, they wouldn't have let her get away. It's so hot. Short, quick breaths exhaust rather than revive her—like inhaling steam. *Breathe deeply,* she reminds herself. It's so hot that the pace car overheated on the first steep hill, spewing a column of steam beside the road as the pack whisked past. Then she stood on her pedals and sprinted away from the others as they rode in a stately bunch, and she was in front, by herself, with only open road ahead that wound ever upward into the leafy hardwood forest.

Push, push, push, she tells herself.

It's so hot. The sweat rolls down her neck, her back, her arms, her legs. It's so hot—it's predicted to reach 95 degrees today, they said at the start—that a bluish haze of moisture saturates the air. The beech trees along the shoulder look as if they were painted by an Impressionist who blurred their green edges and laid in thick splotches of dark oil to render the shadows within the forest. Her coach warned her about the Appalachian humidity—nothing she's ever experienced in Europe. She should have come two weeks early to acclimatize herself, as he suggested, instead of staying with her family, where it was cheaper, and training each day in the cool Baltic air. She should have listened more closely to her coach. Now he's not here, either—there's no longer enough money back home to send him abroad. For this race, her strategy is her own. She's decided that this is her moment to put it all on the line.

To lie down in those dark, thick Impressionist shadows. But first the prize money. Just the top of the pass, and the prize money is hers. The rest is downhill, easy to defend. *Concentrate!* she tells herself. She focuses on the smooth, circular stroke of her pedals and the rhythm of her breathing, ignoring the burning pain in her thighs. Just the top of the pass, that's all she needs, and then the cool breeze, and the money, is hers.

But it's so hot.

Jesus Christ possibly was a heat victim. According to one medical theory, crucifixion, an execution method favored by the kings of ancient Persia and the Mediterranean, relied on the sun's rays to do the job cheaply and effectively. (Another theory attributes death by crucifixion to difficulty working the breathing muscles.) With the victim—often a pirate or political agitator—nailed or tied upright to a wooden cross and exposed to the full heat of the sun, the veins in the legs and other extremities dilated as part of the body's cooling mechanism. But if the legs remained motionless long enough, and there was no muscular contraction to help squeeze the blood from the lower extremities upward, large volumes of blood collected in the legs' swollen veins and arteries, and not enough was pumped up to the brain. For this reason military guards standing at attention in the heat are instructed to contract and release their toes, to keep the leg muscles working. If not, they can suddenly collapse, regaining consciousness once they're stretched out on the ground and blood can flow again easily from the legs to the brain.

Propped upright on a cross for hours without relief, however, the crucifixion victim's state of unconsciousness deepened, his face grew cold and white, heartbeat and breathing faded, and eventually he died, a process that was sometimes hastened by shattering the transgressor's legs with a metal bar, which undoubtedly ruptured veins and arteries and caused further loss of blood. One historical curiosity of this medical condition brought on by crucifixion—known as orthostatic hypotension (upright-standing low blood pressure)—is that the victim can appear dead before actually dying and, laid horizontal in a cool place for a few hours, can recover fully. Some commentators have raised the question whether this is how Jesus, laid out in his tomb after he was removed from the cross, might have "risen from the dead."

An Old Testament mystique surrounds the notion of death by heat, not the least of it the concept of hell as a burning pit. Judaism, Christianity, and Islam all were born amid burning desert sands, where unbearable heat and thirst provided a fitting punishment for sinners—temperatures that meant paradise to the Vikings, who imagined hell as an underworld of cold and dark. References to heatstroke are sprinkled throughout the Bible, such as Manasses who died after harvesting barley in the hot fields. The Arabians called heatstroke "siriasis"—after Sirius, the Dog Star, which in the hot summer months chases through the sky behind the sun. Roman legions that marched into Arabia in 24 B.C. were wiped out by a much more deadly enemy than opposing armies, discovering that heatstroke, according to ancient historians, "attacked the head and caused it to become parched, killing forthwith most of those who were attacked." Early European adventurers returned from the tropics fearing the sunlight itself, believing it contained deadly "actinic rays" that could penetrate the skull. Up until 1940, the British army issued its tropical units spinal pads and headgear to deflect the fatal rays, creating that symbol of Britannia's colonial potency as well as her bodily frailty in the face of tropical disease and heat—the pith helmet.

On average, about 200 people are reported to die in the United States each year from heat-related causes, although the actual number is probably higher; heat-wave summers can raise the number close to 1,000 and even higher if heat is counted as a contributing factor in other deaths. The 1995 Chicago heat wave alone killed an estimated 700 people in a week's time. During the 1977 New York City power blackout and heat wave, deaths jumped from 197—the city's usual daily average for that season—to 237 and climbed again to 298 when the temperature hit 104 degrees.

Heatstroke can strike anyone. However, it especially seeks out the elderly, the overweight, those with chronic illnesses such as cardiovascular disease, and those who have taken certain medications or consumed too much alcohol. People living alone who have few family members or close friends to check up on them, people living on the top floors of buildings (where hot air accumulates), and people who don't have air-conditioning all are more likely victims of heatstroke. A fan can help, but once the temperature tops 90 degrees, a fan does not offer protection.

Classic heatstroke—the slow rise of body temperature among sedentary people in hot environments—accounts for most heat-related deaths. The other heat killer, exertional heatstroke, attacks the young and the healthy. These are the foot soldiers and field laborers and gold miners, marathon runners and bicycle racers, high-school wrestlers and football players. They are the people who drive their bodies— or whose bodies are driven by taskmasters, real or imagined—too hard in hot or humid conditions, and they are especially vulnerable if they have not drunk adequate water or lack proper acclimatization to heat, a process that takes the human body about two weeks. Heatstroke ranks third behind head and neck injuries and cardiac disorders as a cause of death among U.S. high-school athletes. "Probably no greater strain is put on the human body," writes one medical expert on the subject, "than heavy physical exertion in the heat."

Strangely, the human body can tolerate large drops in its internal temperature, when metabolism slows to a crawl (hypothermia), but can survive only very small rises when metabolism shifts into high gear (hyperthermia). Women resist cold better than men, due to their insulating layer of fat, but heat strikes them harder. When it does occur, heat illness can take many forms, a complex continuum of maladies that traces the curve of the body's rising temperature. First is the mildest of the heat illnesses, heat edema, when feet and legs swell due to the dilation of the veins and arteries after long periods of sitting or standing. Then heat syncope—fainting or dizziness—and heat cramps, painful spasms in the muscles of the legs, arms, and abdomen that can be exacerbated by lack of salt or diuretic medications. Heat exhaustion—a term often confused with heatstroke but a less serious condition—results from sweating excessively in the heat and humidity and is marked by body temperatures over 100 degrees but less than 105, as well as headache, dizziness, nausea and vomiting, chills, weakness, rapid heartbeat, and low blood pressure.

Untreated by cooling, rest, and rehydration, heat exhaustion can rapidly develop into the very dangerous condition known as heatstroke, when the core temperature of the human body soars to 105 degrees and above. Survival depends on just how long the victim has remained overheated, and the condition demands immediate and rapid cooling. Some victims who receive prompt treatment have survived very high internal temperatures, such as Willie Jones, dubbed by the press "the Human Torch," whom doctors rapidly cooled with ice water from an estimated body temperature of 120 degrees after he was found unconscious in 1980 in his Atlanta apartment. Another victim survived a body temperature of 113 degrees after he had a minor accident with a police cruiser, swallowed a gram of methamphetamine he was apparently trying to hide, and, chased by police, fled on foot as his core temperature soared to catastrophic levels. Prompt cooling and rehydration at the hospital brought his temperature down to 100.6 degrees within ninety minutes, he recovered from a coma after twenty-six hours, and he was discharged from the hospital in stable condition after five days. Due in part to its many physiological complications—heatstroke can affect virtually every organ in the human body—estimates of mortality from heatstroke vary wildly, from 10 percent to as high as 80 percent, but whatever the exact number, doctors are unanimous in calling heatstroke one of the few true medical emergencies.

Complicated equations exist to describe the body's heat gain, but they reduce to a simple physiological truth: If your body generates more heat than it's capable of dispersing, you will become hotter.* And if you don't stop generating heat—seek shade, lie down, cease your muscular contractions—you will eventually overwhelm your internal thermostat. Your body's temperature then will go haywire. Your cellular metabolism will accelerate wildly, generating even more heat. A fairly predictable sequence of events follows: unconsciousness, convulsions, and death, as the body essentially cooks its own flesh from within.

P*ush . . . push . . . push* . . . Push the pace as hard as she can, beyond what the other riders can handle, push until the distance between her and the pack stretches like a rubber band, tighter and tighter, longer and longer, until it snaps and they'll never catch her.

Her muscled thighs pump up and down in a smooth, circular motion. Her breathing keeps a half-time beat to the rhythm of her legs, a counterpoint played by the precise click of the bike chain as she downshifts and it hops to a larger sprocket of her rear hub. More power, less speed. The road steepens as she swings around a switchback, twisting and tunneling upward through the beeches and maples and oaks. The lush Appalachian scenery for her provides only a passing sensation of light and shadow, of hot and cool, as an animal might perceive the forest when moving quickly through

---

* S = M − E +/− (R + C) − (+/− W), where S = heat storage in the body; M = rate of energy metabolism; E = rate of evaporative loss of heat; R + C = rate of radiant and convective loss, when the sign is positive; W = work rate, where +W represents work energy done on an external system and −W represents work energy absorbed by the body. Values of W are usually small with respect to M. From *Sports Medicine and Physiology*, ed. R. H. Strauss, M.D. (Philadelphia: W. B. Saunders Co., 1979), p. 137.

it. Her whole focus is instead on the rhythms of her legs, the fine-tuning of her gears to subtle shifts in gradient, the huffing depth of her breathing. *Click*—again she downshifts, her legs still whirling steadily, but now the bicycle moves more slowly, her whole being straining to push it up the steep incline.

Trickles of sweat swell to rivulets. Every nine seconds, each of her two million sweat glands—tightly coiled tubes just beneath her skin that would reach 4 feet if stretched out—suddenly contracts and squirts a few drops of moisture through her pores and then recharges, each hour spilling out over half a gallon of sweat, composed of 99.5 percent water plus dissolved salts. She periodically drinks from the water bottle mounted to her bike frame, but the human body can't absorb water from the stomach—no matter how much one pours in it—any more rapidly than a little over a quart an hour. Even while drinking copiously, she's slowly becoming dehydrated.

In chillier weather, her body's extra heat would be wafted away by cool air moving over her skin—the term for this is *convection*—but at an air temperature of over 95 degrees, sweating is the body's only means of cooling itself. Simply sitting at rest, she would grow hotter, due to her own metabolism, by 2 degrees hourly without some means of cooling down. (The human brain alone, awake or asleep, sharp or dull, puts out as much heat as a 15- to 20-watt lightbulb.) Straining up the switchbacks, she'd reach heatstroke temperatures within 10 to 12 minutes without the sweat that evaporates from her skin surface and carries off much of her body's excess heat. That's assuming, of course, that her sweat evaporates easily, which on this day is a problem.

She pedals upward. Her core temperature still lies within the "fever of exercise" zone—the elevated temperatures that the human body can reach without damage under long and heavy exertion. In a trained athlete, the zone extends from about 100 to 104 degrees, as first measured in runners finishing the 1903 Boston Marathon. There is a very fine line, however, where "fever of exercise" ends and heatstroke begins.

With each powerful downstroke her temperature climbs a tiny fraction of a degree and her physiology adjusts to cool it. Her entire body now operates just like the radiator of a car. She feels a tightness around her wrist as her watchband cuts into her flesh. Just beneath her skin surface her blood vessels swell to carry the hot blood from her contracting muscles and overheated organs to her sweat-cooled exterior. The blood flow to her fingertips alone now is one hundred times what it would be in cold weather. In the heat, the capillaries of her entire skin surface can expand so far that to fill them completely would require a gushing flow of up to eight liters of blood per minute. Her heart, meanwhile, must pump furiously in its attempt to keep them running full.

The road switchbacks left, then right up the mountainside, growing steeper as it makes each bend. *Click* go her gears as she downshifts further, into her lowest gear. It's still not low enough. Her thighs burn. Her pedal strokes drop—from 80 to 60 to 50 revolutions per minute. *Keep it going,* she tells herself, *keep it going.* She stands up on her pedals to throw her full body weight into each downstroke. Heat shimmers off the pavement as her bike crawls up the mountainside, shiny puddles of heat. She longs to hear the zipping splash of her tires through the puddles, the flicking drops of road moisture tossed from the tires into her face, but it never comes.

Instead, sweat rolls down off her body and drops in dark, spidery splashes on the cracked, dry asphalt. When the atmosphere's relative humidity climbs over 75 percent and into the 90th percentile, very little sweat can evaporate into the moisture-laden air, especially without a breeze that whisks a large volume of air past the skin surface. This lack of evaporation was what killed three American high-school and college wrestlers who, in three separate incidents in the fall of 1997, wore water-impermeable suits during heavy workouts in an attempt to sweat off pounds rapidly so that they could compete in lower weight classes. Likewise, once she shifts into her lowest gear and is barely moving up the mountainside, the breeze generated by her forward motion has all but ceased. Her sweat glands are firing wildly, but her cooling system has been rendered nearly useless by the high humidity and heat and lack of moving air.

She feels enveloped in heat, inside and out. Even the patches of shade on the black asphalt are hot. If she had followed her coach's advice and come to the sweltering Appalachians two weeks ago, her body would have learned to dilate its blood vessels and kick its sweat glands into action at a lower core temperature, turning on its refrigeration unit sooner rather than waiting for her temperature to climb too high. After several weeks' exposure to a hot climate, when the body has become fully acclimatized to the heat, a person can pour out two and a half times more sweat than before.

She pumps through a hamlet of four or five dilapidated houses: weather-beaten clapboard, crumbling asphalt shingles, wrecked cars propped in the yards. Families sit on sagging porches in greasy dungarees and T-shirts as she strokes past in midnight-blue-and-black Lycra shorts and skintight jersey, mounted on a streamlined titanium-alloy racing frame. They stare at her, unblinking lizards taking refuge from the midday heat beneath the shade of a rock.

She passes a sign that says 25 miles per hour. It's rusty and shot full of bullet holes. She passes an abandoned mobile home beside the road. Its door swings ajar, on broken hinges. Her temperature now begins to push toward 105 degrees, beyond the "fever of exercise" zone, into the twilight realm where concentration falters, emotions swing, hyperirritability sets in. It angers her to see the abandoned mobile home. There is such waste in this land of abundance, she thinks, unlike her country, where everything is used, and then reused, and reused again. The trailer's faded metallic skin gleams dully in the sunlight.

She keeps going. Yes, she'll take the money from this country, and then she'll leave it. Light filters through the forest around her, as if the trees are thinning. The Impressionist painter has lightened his palette into brighter, airy shades of yellow and green. She feels the terrain begin to break, to roll over, like the rolling back of a dolphin surfacing and then diving deep into the cool water. One more switchback, two more switchbacks—it can't be far. Her whole body hurts. She's hyperventilating now, great gulps of air that seem to give her no oxygen. The road bends into a gully, swings out again. She breaks out of the Impressionist-painted forest. But it's not the top— not by a mile, maybe two. It is as if a giant palette knife has scraped and gouged away the lush green pigments. Underneath is a waste-land of red dirt and brown tree stumps climbing in a vast broad slope to the barren ridge line. Waves of heat from the sun boil up-ward from the baking red dirt. The shimmering black asphalt road runs in a sinuous curve up toward the summit. Reddish water spills down a ditch beside the road like a trickle of the earth's blood. Why have they done this? How could they do this to *her*? She's come so far, and she was almost finished, and now they've put this naked patch of heat and effort and pain ahead of her. She wants to collapse off her bike, lie down in the dirt, and curl up in a ball as if she were two years old.

Concentrate! she tells herself. *Keep going! You can make it!* She imagines her wild-haired grandmother careening from room to room in their little apartment. She peers back over her shoulder down the mountain. Two turns back, she spots a flash of sunlight glinting off polished alloy. Four riders slice up the road in a tight line. She recognizes them by their jerseys: the Italian and the French and the Colombian girls, plus a German rider who's barely tagging along. Even from up here she sees how hot their pace is, how strong the pumping of their thighs—they're still sitting in their saddles— the churning, unrelenting determination of their counterattack.

Push . . . push . . . push . . . Just to the top. She can hear her coach: "Get there first and the race is yours, but if they catch you now, they'll blow right past and you'll never catch up. You'll have *nothing*."

She leans hard into her pedals, the bike swaying under her,

as the road traverses up the barren slope of red earth. The moist heat nearly chokes her. She strains past a sign promoting the wood-products corporation that logged the mountaintop: "Putting Your Nation's Forests to Their Best Use." Dozens of bullet holes riddle its thick metal, as do the dented clusters of shotgun blasts, like punches thrown from the depths of an inexpressible rage.

She's not sure she's going to make it. She feels weak all over. Painful knots are forming in her biceps and calves and the muscles of her abdomen—heat cramps, perhaps the result of sweating out so much of the sodium from her body. Her heart pounds with great, powerful, athlete's contractions but still can't pump quite enough blood to keep all her dilated veins and arteries filled and still supply the oxygen demands of her muscles. It's as if her arteries were so many water balloons attached to a single tap that lacked the pressure to fill them all at once. Blood flow to the upper reaches of her body, and to her brain, slackens. Her vision blackens and turns fuzzy at the edges, sparking like swarms of fireflies looping through the night. A chill runs through her body; the hairs on her arms stand erect in goose bumps. Her bike begins to weave dizzily back and forth across the pavement, her body lunging awkwardly down on the pedals, her stroke square instead of rounded. Her head pounds and she feels nauseous—the symptoms of heat exhaustion.

She has no freewheel left—her gears are maxed out. She tries to weave her bike back and forth across the road to make the last steep pitch easier, as a child does when biking uphill, but she totters drunkenly and can barely keep it upright. She doesn't dare look back; she doesn't have enough strength to spare to look back. In a blur of heat and pain and sweat she crests the top, her hyperventilat-ing breaths flinging out of her body like animal groans. The road crowns. The pain in her thighs, her arms, her back, her neck sud-denly eases. Groves of shady hardwood trees cascade down the far side of the mountain, like a waterfall of shade and coolness. The road plunges through switchbacks underneath the cool flow of shade. She knows she should shift gears for the downhill, but she can't remember which way to move the lever. Her wild-haired grandmother is standing in the road beckoning her forward, pointing her downhill toward that cool waterfall of shade, toward the finish line, toward that stream of American money, just down that hill. She aims her bike straight ahead where her grandmother has pointed. Oddly, there's no one at the finish line, but she knows she has crossed it. The victory and the money are hers—yes, *hers*—but the road itself has turned, and now her bike is tumbling down an embankment, and then it is black.

It might have been different if she'd landed in the shade. Instead, the sun bores down on her exposed arms and legs and head, its heat absorbed by her midnight-blue-and-black shorts and jersey and her black sports bra as she lies sprawled beside a rhododendron bush with her bike frame on top of her.

Her heat-generating muscular contractions have ceased, but her body continues to swelter from both within and without. Hot sunlight beating on the skin of a seminude human body can add up to the same amount of heat as the exertion of walking, about 250 kilocalories per hour. Simply sitting produces about 100 kilocalories per hour. This means that if a 150-pound, seminude person were sitting in the hot sun—whether sprawled on a beach or on an Appalachian hillside—and there is no mechanism to disperse the heat either through sweating, a cooling breeze, a jump in the ocean, or whatever, that person's body temperature would rise more than one degree every ten minutes and reach heatstroke range—over 105 degrees—within the hour.

But the bike racer's furnace is burning much hotter than if she were simply sitting. Her cellular metabolism speeds up at higher temperatures, so that when her core temperature reaches 105 degrees, her cellular metabolism—her cells breaking down fuel into energy—is occurring 50 percent faster than it does at a normal temperature of 98.6. This activity adds to the heat building inside her body.

Though her skin glistens with sweat, the high humidity prevents it from evaporating and cooling her. As she lies comatose in the hot sun, her temperature soars beyond heat exhaustion, far into the realm of heatstroke. Her systems now fail so profoundly and in so many ways that the damage is difficult even to track.

105 . . . 106 degrees . . . Seizures ripple through the muscles of her arms and legs and torso.

107 . . . 108 . . . 109 degrees . . . She vomits repeatedly, and her sphincter releases.

110 . . . 111 . . . The heat begins to destroy her cells. Proteins melt and distort, and the mitochondria, a cell's powerhouse, degenerate. Her muscle tissues deteriorate. The heat sears the fine tubes inside her kidneys and kills liver cells. It swells the dendrites of her cerebellum, the part of the brain that coordinates muscular contractions, and annihilates the Purkinje cells in her cerebral cortex, the thinking part of her brain. It causes hemorrhaging throughout her body, including heart and lungs, and damages the thin sheathing inside her blood vessels. Her circulatory system responds as if her blood vessels had been cut, triggering their clotting mechanisms and causing what's known medically as a clotting cascade. Her blood begins to coagulate inside her veins and arteries.

She vomits again, the vomitus now bloody. Perforations open in her intestinal wall, and toxins emitted by spent digestive bacteria escape into her bloodstream, which may trigger septic shock in some heatstroke victims. Others die of heart failure, presumably from heat damage to the cardiac muscle.

The list of bodily destruction from heatstroke goes on—and on. Autopsies of heatstroke victims show damage to virtually every major organ. As she lies comatose and vomiting blood, her arms and legs flailing with seizures, purple hemorrhagic spots appearing on her shoulders, what is happening inside her body is not unlike the meltdown of a nuclear power plant. There is one fortunate protective mechanism her body has granted her in the face of this massive assault of heat: She's unconscious and has no idea what is happening to her. If she were now revived, she'd remember nothing.

A little more than three minutes after her collapse, the Italian and French and Colombian riders crest the pass in a disciplined line, having shaken the German. The three of them are wondering where she is, pushing hard together to catch her, although once they do, it's every rider for herself.

The derailleurs *click, click, click* in precise succession as the three nose over the top of the pass and plunge down the other side, their spokes whirring and ball bearings singing, leaning so deeply into the curves in pursuit of the Eastern European that their derailleurs almost scrape the pavement. Their passing *whoosh* stirs the bushes that line the road, the cooling breeze rushing over their sweaty bodies.

They don't notice her lying sprawled off in the bushes. The only hope for her now would be immediate and dramatic cooling. Usually this is done with ice packs, immersion in cold water, or, best of all, a cool mist of water blown over the skin. Military heatstroke victims have been treated successfully in the field with the cooling rotor wash from a helicopter that hovered over them. With prompt treatment and hospitalization, many heatstroke victims now survive, although statistics vary wildly as to just how many, and of those, how many will suffer permanent damage to the brain or other organs. One sobering study tracked fifty-eight victims of classic heatstroke who were hospitalized during the 1995 Chicago heat wave, and found that half developed kidney failure, 21 percent died in the hospital, 33 percent were "moderately to severely disabled" at the time of discharge, and a year later 28 percent more had died. Most of the survivors had not improved.

Seventeen minutes after cresting the pass, the Italian rider wins the final sprint to the finish. She flashes under a sagging banner to some desultory clapping and brakes to a stop in the village that's wedged into a tight mountain valley. She collapses off her bike under a tree. Her coaches run up to her with wet towels and thermoses of ice water. She doesn't realize at first that she's won the race, believing that the Eastern European, through some superhuman effort, has crossed the line first.

No one misses her until the awards ceremony, an hour later, after the last stragglers finish, and the racers ask each other questions: *Wasn't she in the lead? Where has she gone?* The director of the regional chamber of commerce hands the award check to the Italian. A clutch of local politicians each say a few words, but by now the locals have retired to their porches and air-conditioned trailers and the politicians don't get much exposure. The economic benefit for the region has been virtually nil except for the money spent at a few motels and restaurants back in the county seat, plus the economic benefit for the Italian racer, who plans to spend the prize money on a new sports car.

By late afternoon, the sheriff has rounded up some locals who keep coonhounds, and disperses them in pickup trucks along the road, starting at the point where she was last seen. The packs set off, sniffing up and down the pavement. Toward evening, the air temperature has dropped to a relatively cool 87 degrees. The hazy orange ball of the sun is sinking beneath the distant purple ridges when they find her lying beside the rhododendron bush. Her body is still warm to the touch of the deputy who searches for a pulse as the nuclear furnaces of the burning sun finally disappear behind the earth's shadow.

CHAPTER SEVEN

PITCHED FROM THE VERTICAL REALM:

FALLING

His limbs splay out to reach for holds on the rock face like a daddy longlegs: fingers of his left hand extending up and wrapping their tips in a cling grip over a nubbin of rock, left leg spread wide to edge with the instep of his climbing shoe on a projecting flake, or tiny ledge, his right foot toe-jammed for purchase into a vertical crack. All of these are secure holds. The problem is his right hand. He's trying to touch a hold shaped like a mushroom cap that hovers to the right about two feet above his head. Get past this one move—the crux of the climb—and he's got it. The top, no problem.

He has no rope. Besides his daypack, and a small bag of chalk dangling from his hip in which he dips his fingers to absorb the sweat, he wears only a yellow T-shirt and baggy black Lycra-and-cotton stretch pants, riding up high on the calf like Tom Sawyer's raggedy trousers. On his feet he wears his most essential piece of equipment: climbing shoes as delicate and closely fitted as Cinderella's slippers, thinly shod with special sticky rubber engineered to adhere to the rock.

Holding fast with his three points of contact—his two feet and his left hand—he stretches with his right hand above his head for the mushroom hold. Splayed to their maximum reach, his fingertips fall 5, maybe 6 inches short of it. He needs a bit more stretch, a little more body length. If he releases his left foot from his edging hold and brings it directly beneath his torso instead of off to the side, his body will shift into a more vertical stance. This alone might give him the few extra inches of reach with his hand.

He carefully removes his left foot from the edging hold. He swings it beneath him, letting it dangle over the void. Taking a deep breath, he extends up again with his right hand. Still short. He didn't anticipate so hard a move; he must have strayed from the regular climbers' route up the face. He regathers himself, still dangling his left foot. He's panting now. The fingertips of his left hand are tiring. His right quad, with his climbing shoe toe-jammed in the crack, bears most of his body weight. It's beginning to burn. He's going to have to do something. Soon.

He assesses his options. What he really needs to do is a dynamic move, known to climbers as a "dyno"—a move that demands full commitment. The climber releases all his holds and, with nothing at all supporting him, makes a controlled lunge like a flying squirrel for the next hold. This dyno is not far. He has to lunge only a few inches. And the handhold is big, simple to grip as he lunges at it. He knows he can make it easily. Or he could on the artificial climbing wall in the health-club gymnasium, where if he missed he would risk a drop of only a few feet to the floor. Or if he had protection—if he were tethered to another climber who was securely anchored to the rock face and could arrest a fall instantly by tightening the safety rope in a move known as a belay. But he's not at the climbing gym. There is nobody here belaying him. He looks down to the alpine meadow on the valley floor—the green tufts of shrubs, the yellow and blue splashes of wildflowers. Only two narrow ledges and 150 feet of air time between up here and down there. He's not that high, really. But he's plenty high if he misses the move.

He'll *probably* make it. He guesses he has a 60-40 chance of

success. In business he has his 60-40 rule: If he estimates that he has
a 60 percent or better chance of succeeding, he goes for it, and screw
the consequences. He's in the takeover business, and he is hired—for
a very hefty sum, of course—by investors who want to snap up huge
blocks of stock and seize control of a weak and vulnerable company
with the idea of restructuring it, firing employees and downsizing it,
breaking it into pieces and selling it off, somehow squeezing more
money out of it. In his line of work, the odds of 60-40 are daring
and buccaneering—but reasonable enough. After all, it's not *his*
money or his job that might be lost in the attempt. But this is different. This is his life.

He looks up again at the handhold. A dyno 150 feet off the deck
with no protection. This is a loser's move. He feels it in his gut.
There are two types of people in the world: the winners, like him,
and the losers, a group who make up the other 95 percent of the
population. Winners know when to push ahead and when to hang
back, and sometimes to remain a winner you have to stay back. He
tells that to his clients all the time. As for the losers, they usually get
what they deserve for making stupid moves. For making moves like
this one.

Back off. That's the right plan. Downclimb to a ledge or the valley floor and scout another route. Or forget the climbing this weekend. On Monday he'll return to the office and tell the guys about his
close brush on the wall. They know how hard he is—physically,
mentally, in every way that counts. They've seen how he has put the
screws to a target company's management team when no one else
had the balls to do it. They know damn well he wouldn't back off
from this wall without very good reason. He's free-soloing a 5.9 climb,
after all. He'll make sure they know free-soloing is the most high-
stakes climbing of all.

There are no safety nets in free-soloing. In aid climbing, the
most equipment-heavy type of climbing, you wedge various types of
anchors into cracks in the rock or otherwise attach them to the
face—items called nuts and cams, pitons and bolts—and fit them

with ropes and slings that you use as hand- and footholds, building a kind of artificial ladder up the face. Then there's free climbing: You and a partner climb by clinging to the natural holds on the rock and can easily enough slip from them but have a backup safety system of anchors and belay ropes. You climb one person at a time so you can arrest each other in case of a fall. But in free-soloing there are no backup safety systems—no ropes, no anchors, no belays—nothing except you, and the face of the rock, and your own skill and judgment. It is by far the riskiest type of rock climbing, and the rarest, and those who pursue it are considered a breed apart.

He'll make sure at the office they understand all that, and he'll explain to them, in his knowing and expert way, the system of rating climbs, just so they fully grasp what he was up against. A flat trail receives a rating of 1.0. A 2.0 route might be a rough trail going uphill. On a 3.0 route, the terrain has become steep enough so you might have to pull yourself up with your hands in a few places. When you're on a 4.0 route, you've entered the climbing realm, and you're using handholds and footholds, although the surface may be short of vertical. You're into the true vertical realm—the realm of the spider, the sheer faces of cliffs—with climbs rated 5.0 and above, sliced into many precise gradations of difficulty from 5.1, the easiest of the truly vertical climbs, on up to 5.8, 5.9, 5.10. All of the climbs in the 5.0 and above range resemble scaling the sheer wall of a building; the difference lies in the texture of that building's facade—how large and far apart the hand- and footholds are spaced, how much they demand of one's reach and limberness and strength and innovation.

In recent decades, however, as the precise and competitive world of serious rock climbing has blossomed into international events, climbers' skills have outpaced the old rating system. More numbers added to the scale now designate excruciatingly difficult climbs where climbers lock only the very tips of their powerful fingers over the tiniest bumps of rock for handholds and "smear" their sticky shoe soles on the slightest bulges in the wall that constitute footholds. They often dangle like monkeys from beneath overhangs hundreds of feet above the ground. Now there are 5.10 climbs rated into a, b, c, and d grades of difficulty, and minuses and pluses within each one of those letter grades, and beyond those are the 5.11 climbs. The system and the skill levels currently reach up to 5.14d, the most difficult rock climb that anyone in the world has "red-pointed"— completed without falling or without resting on an artificial piece of equipment. "Climbing it clean," they call it.

He's doing a 5.9 climb—not all that difficult for a decent climber under most conditions. But he's not doing it under most conditions, no, not at all, he's free-soloing it, and a 5.9 free-soloing— without a rope, without any protection, with nothing between you and the hard, hard ground except your own technique and your iron-fast confidence—that's getting to be heady stuff. That he even attempted it is surely enough to enhance rumors of his legendary *cojones*, a reputation that has served him so well in the business of intimidating the opposition. But there are other reasons he likes to climb beyond the sheer gutsiness of it. He likes the immovable feel of the rock under his hands and feet, the different textures and structures—rough rock and smooth, the ledges and flakes and elegant systems of vertical cracks. He likes solving the complex intellectual puzzle of finding a route to the top, mentally arranging the handholds and footholds into a precise, choreographed sequence of moves, and he likes the sinuous animal strength of his arms and legs as he works up the face, through his own power and grace and brains overcoming this massive obstacle thrust up by unspeakably profound forces from deep within the earth. At moments like that he is master of the rock.

Yes, he'd tell the story of his climb to the guys at the office on Monday, especially to Antoni. He'd rub it in. That shithead Antoni had promised to go climbing with him this weekend. If Antoni were belaying him on the other end of a rope, he wouldn't be here with fingertips going numb clinging to the face of the rock, worrying about making a lunge move. He'd simply lunge, and if he didn't make it and peeled off the wall, he'd yell, "Falling," and the harness would suddenly tug tight around his waist as Antoni clamped down on the rope and caught him after a fall of only a few feet. Assuming Antoni was paying attention. He'd never really trusted the guy. Then he calls up on Friday night and cancels out in order to spend the weekend with his wife and daughter. Well, fuck him. Antoni's not going anywhere. Staying home with his wife and daughter! Antoni has just joined the ranks of the losers.

To start the climb down, he probes the wall with his dangling foot. Retreat—yes, he can live with it. He's still as hard as he ever was. He can hear the thin rubber sole of his left climbing shoe scraping about on the rough, naked granite like a dog pawing at the locked back door. *Where's that left foothold?* He tilts his head down to look. *There*—slightly higher and farther away than he remembers. He reaches with his left leg, stretching his baggy black climbing pants tightly around his ropy left quadriceps. He can't quite put his left toe on the hold. In all his maneuverings, his right toe has slid a few inches down the crack where he'd jammed it. He's now slightly lower on the wall and can't reach that left foothold. He suddenly realizes that he is stuck. He can't go up. He can't go down. He's attached by only two points of contact—left hand and right foot—like a barn door swinging on two hinges from a rock face 150 vertical feet above the valley floor. "Fuck!" he whispers, stretching again for the foothold.

The first blast of panic washes through his body. His heart suddenly leaps to its maximum rate, about 160 beats per minute. His right knee, bearing most of his weight, begins to tremble, bouncing quickly up and down. "Sewing machine leg," the climbers call it, or "Elvis leg." Tense with fear, he pushed down and stood on his toe harder than he needed to, tightly contracting the muscles of his right calf. When he tries to relax them now, however, the muscles stretch. This stretching places additional tension on them, triggering the muscular reflex to contract again, then relax, then contract, over and over in a staccato cycle known as clonus. *Clickety, clickety, clickety,*

clickety goes his right knee, like an old Singer stitching its way through a long hemline or like Elvis rocking and rolling up on his toes in his black boots. His fingertips go numb. Through their battered tips, he senses them losing purchase on the tiny nubbin of rock. He'll come off the wall unless he does something fast. No rope, no protection. A second wave of panic blasts through him. His breathing, about 24 breaths per minute when he was climbing smoothly, jumps to 40 breaths per minute in quick, sharp pants of fear. He kicks and scrapes with his free foot, scrabbling for a hold on the sheer granite. Nothing. He has to do something—*fast*. He pulls hard with his left arm on his single handhold, attempting to elevate his body in order to reach the foothold.

It is in that moment, there, that his fingertips slip from the rock.

The longest fall a human has survived without a parachute is 6 miles and 551 yards—the equivalent of a three-thousand-story building—when flight attendant Vesna Vulovic tumbled to earth inside the broken-off tail section of a DC-9 that blew up on January 26, 1972, over what is now the Czech Republic. Not far behind her in epic plummets is Nicholas Stephen Alkemade, a Royal Air Force tail-gunner who bailed out, sans parachute, from the flaming inferno of a crippled British bomber over Germany on the wintry night of March 24, 1944, and fell 18,000 feet. What he recalled from his long drop through the cold, starry night sky was a sense of resting comfortably on a cushion of air and a great relief at having escaped the heat and flames. His only regret was that he couldn't say goodbye to his sweetheart, Pearl, waiting for him back in Loughborough. Alkemade's vertical idyll ended abruptly when he tore through a canopy of fir branches at a terminal velocity estimated at 122 miles per hour—the maximum velocity a falling body attains, no matter how

great the height of the fall, due to the increasing wind resistance—
and thudded into thick, snowy underbrush. When he regained consciousness three hours later, burned and very sore and unable to
walk, he lit a cigarette from his flattened pack and eagerly began to
blow his rescue whistle, more than happy to be taken a prisoner of
war by a German *Kommandant* and his officers. The Germans found
his parachute in the plane wreckage a few days later and verified
Alkemade's incredible account, jubilantly offering him their con-
gratulatory handshakes, slaps on the back, and good wishes for this
story he could tell his grandchildren.

Overcoming the pull of gravity is our universal metaphor to describe achievement. We speak of the rise of civilizations, of royal
houses, of great talents; we speak of soaring happiness. And just as
universally we speak of falling to signify unhappiness and failure—
failure that often results from excess pride and presumptuous meddling in the ways of the gods. Satan fell from heaven. Adam and Eve
fell from God's grace. Icarus flew too close to the sun—the realm of
the gods—and melted the wax on his wings. "It is the gods' custom,"
wrote Herodotus, "to bring low all things of surpassing greatness."

That our perception of the world is so profoundly shaped by
gravity and the prospect of falling surely springs from our physiology. Humans learn at a very young age to balance precariously on
two points—their feet. The danger of a fall never leaves us from the
moment we tumble from the womb until the day we topple into the
grave. We can fall from trees, roofs, buildings, ladders, bridges, mountains, stairs; we can slip on ice, in the bathtub, on wet floors; we can
tumble from bicycles, cars, horses, carts, chariots, airplanes; we can land
on earth, stone, wood, concrete, water, and—for the fortunate—a
net, a mattress, straw.

Gravity follows us everywhere we travel on the face of the
earth, although it's about 0.5 percent stronger at the North and
South Poles than it is at the equator, where one is standing at the
metaphorical rim of the merry-go-round instead of its center, and

there is a slight outward-pulling centrifugal force to offset gravity's downward tug. Galileo, contrary to legend, didn't drop weights from the Leaning Tower of Pisa, but he did measure gravity's acceleration of an object falling to the earth's surface: 32 feet per second per second. This means that after each second, the falling object is traveling 32 feet per second (or some 22 miles per hour) faster than after the previous second. It didn't matter if the object was a feather or a lead ball, Galileo understood. Assuming there was no air resistance—if they were in a vacuum—they would plummet at exactly the same rate.

Isaac Newton, lingering in his mother's Lincolnshire garden after the plague had shut down his studies at Cambridge in 1665–66, speculated whether the same force that caused an apple to fall to earth extended out into space as far as the moon. Studying the orbits of the moon and planets, he arrived at the classical formula that describes the universal force of gravity: Every particle of matter in the universe exerts a force of attraction on every other; larger masses exert larger forces of attraction than smaller ones; and this force of attraction, opposite of that between lovers, weakens greatly as distance separates the objects.*

Galileo spent the last eight years of his life under house arrest for his meddling with gravity and the heavenly bodies, as if proving Herodotus' dictum. The brilliant Newton fared poorly, too, simmering with rage and jealousy and paranoia at his rivals' successes, punctuated by frequent nervous breakdowns. His father had died in Newton's infancy, his mother remarried a wealthy man and moved away to a nearby village, leaving him with grandparents until he was eleven while young Isaac threatened to burn down his mother and stepfather's house with them in it.

Surely Newton had a visceral understanding of the hazards as

---

* Newton's formula is $F = G(m_1 m_2)/d^2$, where F is the force of attraction, G is the universal constant for gravitation, m_1 and m_2 are the masses, and d is the distance between them.

well as the benefits of the gravitational attraction between bodies. Without gravity, we'd all launch off the face of the earth into space; at other times—all too often—gravity hugs us far too closely for our own health. Falls are so prevalent and so universal, they rate their own listing in the World Health Organization's mortality report: about 300,000 deaths annually. Falls, like heart disease, are an afflic-tion of the wealthy nations, killing twice as many people proportion-ately from rich countries (1 percent of all deaths) than poor ones (0.5 percent of deaths), presumably because the inhabitants of wealthy nations have more buildings, power lines, and bridges from which to tumble, as well as the luxury of living beyond infancy long enough to climb them.

Mountain-climbing accidents account for only a tiny percent-age of falling deaths—about thirty-five fatalities annually in North America. But what they lack in numbers they make up for in meta-phorical richness. Like Icarus, climbers venture close to the lofty and rarefied realm of the gods. What you make of this depends on where you stand. For those who remain below, it's easy—perhaps too easy—to interpret a climbing fall as the gods' retribution for the hubris of the climber. For the climber, the very possibility of a fall may be part of climbing's subliminal attraction. It is not an attrac-tion to death, but the opposite—a passion for that sense of acute aliveness and total focus and full sensory alert when danger is near. Rock climbing demands one's total attention. There is no past and no future when climbing, no distant hopes for what might be or lin-gering regrets for what could have been. There is only the present, this moment, this movement up the rock—at times beautiful and graceful, at times awkward and difficult, but always utterly encom-passing. A fall—whether a tumble quickly stopped by an alert climb-ing partner on the other end of the rope or an uncontrolled and fatal plummet to the earth—is the price one pays for that sense of being so acutely in the present, so acutely alive.

If for a poet a fall is metaphor and for a climber it's a kind of in-tensifier, from a physicist's point of view, a fall might represent the gravitational attraction of one mass for another. For a doctor a fall most likely means a broad and variable medical condition captured in two words as harsh and abrupt as the event itself: blunt trauma. Caused when some blunt object strikes the human body, or the human body strikes it, blunt-force trauma is distinct from penetrating-force trauma. The latter would include knife and gunshot wounds, while the former might occur when a tractor rolls over on its driver, or someone is thrown onto the pavement from a car that's rolled over, or, in this case, when a climber falls to the ground. In this event, the medical terminology becomes more specific—"deceleration injury." This includes the array of damage that can occur when the human body comes to a stop. A sudden stop.

There is no time to feel fear as he topples backward. Within a few hundredths of a second, his sudden release from the rock triggers his startle reflex—a response demonstrated by even the smallest infants if suddenly lowered a few inches. His arms fly outward as if to grab something, his eyeballs spin to seek the danger's source, his torso curls forward to protect his organs. The implacable tug of earth's gravity, meanwhile, accelerates his body at Galileo's 32 feet per second per second. Translated, this means he'd be falling about 22 miles per hour at the end of the first second, 44 miles per hour at the end of the next, and about 66 miles per hour at the end of the third. He wouldn't speed up as quickly, however, as he fell faster and wind resistance increased. By about the ninth second, he would have reached a terminal velocity of about 110 miles per hour in the spread-eagle position that skydivers use. In a headfirst dive, he'd reach a terminal velocity of about 190 miles per hour.

Few falling climbers hit terminal velocity, even in a long fatal fall, for they'd need to drop down a sheer face for nearly a thousand feet before reaching that speed, assuming the climber is in the spread-eagle position. What climbers have witnessed—and what a few very lucky ones have survived—is an awful kind of bouncing fall. The unroped climber slips on a steep, icy slope, or rappels off the end of a rope, or the rope's anchors pull out during what should be an arrested fall. Climbers below report how the victim's body starts to tumble, bouncing down the slope or face, perhaps coiled up in a nest of rope, bounding along like a tumbling rock in ever greater leaps, ice axes, gloves, hats spinning off, "rag-dolling"—that's the word they use—until the climber is no longer a person but an object whooshing down the mountain, and sails off some lip into the void, sometimes into an entirely different country—from Nepal into Tibet, for instance—probably dead of massive head injuries long before impact. It is, as they say, a very short story.

But this fall, climbing alone up the rock face and cursing at Antoni, is really quite prosaic. He drops 30 feet in 1.4 seconds, or the equivalent of a three-story building in the time it takes to say "How are you this morning?" He has no chance to sort out the tumbling confusion of the fall, much less watch his life flash before his eyes. There is a moment's blur of rock and sky, an instant of suspended silence. *Crack!* His right leg strikes a ledge. The blow somersaults him head over heels backward. He hears a sudden rush of wind in his ears, a rattle of falling stone, senses a churning whirl of blue sky and gray rock as though they were being beaten together in a bowl . . .

Suddenly it's very quiet and he's nowhere. He floats in the dark, suspended, indefinitely. After what seems an eternity, he hears a slowly gathering rush of sound, a clattering, like a horse and rider galloping over cobblestones toward him. He feels peppering little hits over his body, and a *plonk* onto his forehead. That was something real—falling stones. He's not dead, after all. He tries to breathe. Nothing happens, as if all the air has been squeezed from his body like a spent balloon, and it requires more effort and pressure than he possesses to reinflate it. Is it worth it? So much easier not to breathe. But if he doesn't breathe, this is the end. He will die.

He wills his chest and diaphragm again, forcing a spasm of a breath, then another and another. He becomes aware of an intense pain far in the back of his chest, between his shoulder blades, as if a hand were reaching through his chest and tearing at the flesh along his spine. Just as suddenly it subsides. Panting raggedly, he opens his eyes. He's lying on his side. He's looking out across the valley to the rock face on the opposite side and, still well below him, the alpine meadow of the valley floor.

An intense wave of nausea wells up from his gut. He leans his head over the edge, gags once, spews a slurry of maple-flavored oatmeal and $18-per-pound Kona coffee in a long arc out into the void, pants three times hard, then projectile-vomits over the edge again. After so severe a blow to the torso, his body instinctively rids itself of its burdensome abdominal contents, preparing itself for fight or flight. The human body doesn't want to be worrying about digesting breakfast when a battle is at hand.

He settles back, panting, feeling slightly better, and slowly pieces together what must have happened. After he peeled off the wall, he fell 20 or 30 feet, struck a ledge, bounced off, which helped slow the fall, fell another 20 feet or so, and landed on this ledge. It's about the size of his condo balcony, maybe 10 feet wide and 20 feet long, a few tufts of dried grass growing from the crevices at the far end. It's solid granite. He's fortunate; he landed on his backpack, which helped cushion his fall. It's a law of physics that the shorter the distance of deceleration, the greater the force of impact. With his backpack offering about 1 foot's worth of cushioning, and his body weight of 170 pounds and a fall of 20 feet, he hit the granite ledge with the equivalent of about 3,400 pounds of force. If, instead of landing on the backpack, he'd landed on, say, a thin sleeping pad that offered only one-tenth that amount of cushioning, and assuming his body didn't compress at all on impact, he'd pile onto the granite ledge after a 20-foot fall with around 34,000 pounds worth of force, or about 17 tons.

After he vomits again, gasps for breath, and regains some of his equilibrium, he slowly squirms back from the edge. Something feels odd about his right leg. He looks down. It appears that a thick, broken stick has somehow lodged itself in his climbing pants. Did he hit a tree limb during his fall? He looks more closely and discovers that it's not a chunk of wood at all but a chunk of his right femur—his thigh bone—protruding from the stretchy black fabric. He tears the fabric of his pants into a larger hole and peers inside. The end of the fractured bone sticks from an ugly red rent in his skin that exposes the shredded muscle tissue and a sticky film of blood.

Oddly, it doesn't hurt much—at least for now. What else could he have broken during the fall? A dull pain throbs from his lower left ribs. He mentally runs a check over his whole body—head, arms, back. Everything else seems okay—it's just the ribs and the leg. The pain's not even that bad. He'll be all right. He might even be back climbing in a couple of months. He guesses it's an 80-20 chance—probably even better than that—that he'll heal up like nothing happened. He definitely made the right choice up there on the crux. Yeah, he fell, but he's still alive, isn't he? That's a lot better than being dead, isn't it?

He leans his head over the edge. Pillars of granite drop to the valley floor. At least 100 vertical feet of 5.9 downclimbing, like working his way down the outside of a ten-story building. There's no fucking way. It would be hard enough with two good legs, jamming his way back down the cracks the way he came up, wedging feet and hands in crevices. If only he had a rope, he could anchor it up here, wrap it around his torso, and rappel off the ledge. He'd be standing down there among the wildflowers in ten minutes. But he hadn't bothered to put a rope in his climbing pack. What good's a rope if you don't have a climbing partner who can tie into the other end and belay you?

The cell phone! *Yes!* He'd forgotten about that! Angrily packing on Friday night after talking to Antoni, he'd tossed his spare cell phone into his climbing pack instead of his rope. Ounce per ounce, he'd figured that in the unlikely event he needed a rescue, an 8-ounce cell phone carried a lot more punch than an 8-pound rope. *Yes!* That was the kind of thinking ahead of the curve that had served him so well in the business world. He shucks off his pack, leans back against the wall with his feet toward the void, and probes into his pack, feeling for the phone's calfskin sheath. His chance of success has just jumped well up into the nineties.

Emergency-room physicians know how to calculate odds, too. They frequently refer to something called "the golden hour." Unless a trauma injury is catastrophic, for about an hour afterward the human body can more or less hold itself together and maintain blood pressure despite internal bleeding from a ruptured organ. Once the hour is past, the odds of survival start dropping precipitously. An hour, of course, is a long time if you've had a traffic accident in a major city and an ambulance whisks you to an operating room and within thirty minutes of impact you're under the surgeon's knife. An hour in the wilderness, however, is hardly the beginning of an evacuation that, especially if helicopter rescues are ruled out by bad weather or impossibly steep terrain, might take many hours or even days until the victim—if still alive—is brought to some rural outpost.

As he digs into his climbing pack, past his water bottles, his lunch, his emergency kit, his rain parka, he dimly notes the dull pain from his lower left rib cage. Blaming it on the fractured ribs, he's unaware that the impact of his fall not only broke the ninth through twelfth ribs on his left side but, just beneath them, momentarily squashed his spleen, the fist-sized organ on the left side of his abdomen that filters his blood. When the soft, blood-filled mass hit the ledge, it split open like a ripe cantaloupe dropped on the sidewalk—not a huge split, but one large enough that his spleen is now leaking his blood supply out of his circulatory system and into his abdominal cavity. There are few nerves in the spleen, however, and he feels no severe pain from the injury. He has no idea that he's slowly bleeding.

He finds the cell phone at the bottom of his pack, slides it from its elegant sheath, flips open the mouthpiece, clicks the power button, punches in 911 and hits send. He hears a click, and then a rapid *beep beep beep*. No connection with a tower; he must be too deep in the canyon. *Fuck!* He clicks the power off, clicks it on again, tries 911 again. *Beep beep beep.* He punches buttons faster: o for the operator. The number of his office. His old home phone number, now the number of his ex-wife. Still only the *beep beep beep* of a failed connection, as if all of cyberspace were filled to capacity with more-powerful devices and no place could be found for his lone, weak signal from the ledge.

He can still see the pimply face of the smarmy clerk at the electronics store who sold him the phone. The lying little shithead said it was the most powerful model going and guaranteed it for life. The only reason he'd bought the thing was that he'd made a pile of money buying up a piece of the company that manufactured them. He'd known that half their products were pieces of shit, but it didn't matter what *he* thought, it only mattered what the chumps out there who bought the stock on the open market thought, and you couldn't go wrong betting on the lemminglike instinct of the chumps. Sure enough, the stock began to climb. He'd figured that deal at 75-25, and he'd turned up a winner. Again.

But now he wants to fling the cell phone over the edge and watch it shatter into its shoddily made silicon components on the rocks below. No . . . he'll hang on to it and try again later. The radio signals might strengthen at night, and he can make a connection. If he does, the first number he'll call is 911 and the second will be Antoni's, to tell him what an asshole he is for doing this to him.

He looks over the edge, assessing his situation once more. No rope. No cell phone. A badly broken leg. But he'll turn up a winner again. He's sure of it. If he had to put down money, he would *defi-*

nitely, definitely place it on himself. That's what he'd honestly tell a client. No bullshit. We're talking 96, 97, maybe even 98 percent chance of success. You'd have to be an idiot to bet against him. Here's what's going to happen, he'd tell the client: On Monday morning—that's only the day after tomorrow, forty-eight hours—they'll miss him at the office. Antoni will know he went climbing this weekend and sound the alarm. A few hours later a rock climber from SAR—search and rescue—will rappel down onto the ledge from above, lower down a litter, and he'll be plucked by rescue helicopter *outta here*. That's the scenario. He's sure of it. And by Monday evening he'll be resting comfortably in a hospital bed with his leg in a cast and clean sheets and some young-babe nurse massaging oil into his chafed and bruised winner's body, admiring his finely sculpted winner's pecs.

He can make it to Monday, no problem. It's just a broken leg and a few fractured ribs. He has a liter of water, plus the cheese, apple, bread, and candy bars in his lunch. It won't be that cold tonight. Yeah, *at least* 98 percent chance of success. Probably more like 99. Antoni had better show up at the office on Monday morning . . . that's the only thing. He'd better not skip out of work like he bailed out of this climbing trip. Did Antoni say he was taking a long weekend with his family, a few extra days off? He can't remember. He was too pissed off at the time to listen. He'd jammed his thumb on the phone's off button while Antoni was still blathering away about his commitments to his family. Antoni had better be at work *early* and notice the empty office, the lack of a commanding presence in the halls, the vacuum left by his take-no-prisoners, balls-to-the-walls drive that has been a powerful engine in the firm's success. He'd *better* notice. Antoni's the key. If Antoni doesn't realize he's in trouble, then he really is in trouble. Goddamn you, Antoni, look around. Open your fucking eyes for once.

The golden hour slips away in his chattering mental monologue of calculated odds, a statistical shield of denial to keep the fear at bay. But soon he has much more to think about than odds. Once the golden hour ends, the real pain begins. His brain has been so busy dealing with the immediate aftermath of the fall—maintaining his vital functions, assessing his physical situation, bolstering his will to survive—that it's blocked out the pain signals trying to force their way up his nerves from his broken leg. It does this by releasing the body's natural painkilling substances called endorphins ("morphine within") and the extremely potent form of it known as enkephalin. Just like morphine manufactured from poppies, which it closely resembles in chemical structure, these molecules attach themselves to the nerve endings that are receiving pain signals from the broken leg. Thus they prevent the nerves from emitting substance P, the chemical that transmits the pain signal to the next set of nerves farther up his body and to the brain.

Past the golden hour, however, his brain lifts the blockade, wanting him to know exactly how badly injured he is, and telling him of the urgent need to do something about it. Shifting his back, which is propped against the rock wall, into a more comfortable position, he accidentally jars his leg. The two shattered ends of bone grate against each other. Pain impulses race through his nerves, now unplugged by endorphins, toward his brain at speeds up to 300 miles per hour—twice as fast as a jet on takeoff.

"*Shit!*" he groans.

His fingers clench into fists. He holds himself there, his whole body tensed. When the wave of pain subsides momentarily, he pulls out his emergency kit from his pack—a small plastic box containing matches, compass, bandages and gauze, and whistle—pops open the canister of ibuprofen, tosses three of them onto his tongue, and washes them down with a gulp of water. They'll block the production of prostaglandin by his damaged tissues, a chemical that helps clot the blood but also sensitizes the nerve endings to pain. But for a compound fracture of the femur, the three ibuprofen will do about as much good for the pain as a Band-Aid.

The pain rises in waves, like ocean swells before a storm. Across the valley, the golden band of afternoon sunlight slowly climbs the opposite cliff, the warm ochre hues it throws on the granite gradually replaced by gray shadow. A chill wash of air tumbles down the cliff. The rock beneath his body turns cold and hard; he looks for something softer. He has his pack, his rain jacket, and then he spots the tufts of grass sprouting from crevices on the far end of the ledge. Dragging himself slowly on his elbows, he maneuvers to the far end and lies on the vegetation. With his backpack as a pillow and rain jacket as a blanket, the thin, organic mattress provides some insulation and padding from the cold rock. But still the leg sends up throbbing waves of pain, causing him to twist facedown on the bed of grasses, digging his fingers through the bed of vegetation, scraping his nails against the rough granite until they bleed, and he crests the wave, surfing down the far side, until the swell starts to rise again.

He can't stand this. Not for forty-eight hours. He knows the angulated femur should be set—the bones aligned in their proper position—but how? He's seen old movies where the wounded hero lies in a sweaty grimace while his buddy jerks his leg straight. But how to do it alone? The thought of yanking on his leg, even if he could, makes him want to vomit. But he has to do something.

As he catches his breath during one of the troughs, he spots a rabbit skull wedged in a crevice in the rock. Perhaps an eagle deposited it there, or maybe it somehow tumbled from the top. The skull stares at him with empty eye sockets.

"Stop looking at me," he hisses at it, panting.

It stares back vacantly.

He stretches his arm over to the crevice, grabs the skull, and flings it over the ledge.

"Get outta here, you nasty little fucker."

The effort costs him another nauseating wave of pain but reveals his opportunity. He slowly wheels himself on his back, like a turtle spinning, until his feet lie near the rabbit-skull crevice. He tears the thin fabric of his climbing pants open further, assessing the angle of the bone jutting out. The lower shaft of the femur overlays the upper shaft by about two inches. As he watches, his powerful thigh muscles involuntarily spasm into contractions, and he can see the shattered bone ends shift and subtly grate against each other, triggering another overwhelming wave of pain.

Clenching his teeth, he hoists the leg and wedges the gummy sole of its climbing shoe into the crevice. Bracing his left foot against the rock, he lies back on his elbows, takes three deep breaths, and, as if he were stomping his foot in anger, shoves hard off the rock with his good leg.

"*Uuuuuuunnnngggghhh,*" he exhales, a guttural string of consonants of effort and pain. He can feel the thigh muscles stretching.

There's a grating and a click. The projecting end of bone suddenly disappears back into the ragged, red aperture of the wound. The pain eases, as if the pounding of the surf suddenly flattened into calm gentle seas. He lies back, exhausted from the effort, his foot still wedged in the rock. It feels so much better here. He decides to leave it wedged, pulls over a small boulder that's lying on the ledge, and props it carefully under the back of his knee to hold his leg in the raised, stretched position. Without really knowing it, he has put his leg in traction—the correct treatment for a broken femur. The steady pull of traction stretches the spasmodic, contracted thigh muscles back to normal length and closes the veins and arteries, stopping further bleeding. Relieved of the torment, and not eager to jar the leg, he searches in his pack for something with which to splint it. Finally, with his pocket knife he slices a piece from the foam backboard of the pack itself, carefully wraps it around his leg and fixes it with the pack's cannibalized straps.

He lies back, panting slightly, pleased with himself. Making it to Monday's no problem now. He's back up in the 97th, 98th, even 99th percentile. Just stay calm, ration the food and water, get some sleep, and before he knows it some young search-and-rescue guy—who knows, maybe it will be a babe—will be rappeling down and landing on his ledge with a cheery "How ya doin'?"

He'll act nonchalant, like it was nothing to be out here two nights with a broken leg. "Got stiffed by my climbing partner," he'll say. "So I'm just sitting here enjoying the view."

That ought to impress them. Yeah, things are looking good. The leg feels so much better. Now it's only the ribs and the odd pain—a kind of pressure from inside, really—just beneath them. He runs his fingers over the tender area. Probably bruises, he tells himself. Still okay. Still up there in the high nineties. Still a winner.

He lies back again on his grass bed, very tired, still panting slightly, hearing the pounding of his heart in his ears. It's now well into the third hour since his fall. The blood slowly leaking from his spleen has formed a pool so large—as large as a grapefruit—that it presses out against his peritoneum, the membrane sack that surrounds his internal organs, causing him to feel the odd pressure. He's lost about two quarts of blood out of his total of about five quarts. His heart must pound faster to speed the diminished supply through veins and arteries in an attempt to maintain blood pressure. His heart rate jumps, more than doubling from his resting runner's pulse of 55 beats per minute to 130 beats, but his heart is losing the battle and can't keep the blood vessels adequately supplied. His blood pressure sinks from its normal of 120/80 to 80/50—the first number in the pairing, his systolic blood pressure, referring to the pressure of the blood his heart squeezes out into the arteries during its contraction, while the second number, the diastolic pressure, measures the arterial pressure during the heart's relaxation phase. Like barometric pressure, both are calibrated in millimeters of mercury that this amount of pressure would force up a glass tube containing a vacuum.

He slides into a state of shock. Not the layman's version—that emotional daze in the immediate aftermath of a trauma—but the medical version, hypovolemic shock, or low-blood-pressure shock. In someone who has a heart condition or is elderly, this drastic fall in blood pressure could trigger a heart attack or stroke, but he is relatively young and healthy and the drop alone is not life-threatening. Without adequate blood pressure, however, his muscles and organs don't receive the oxygen they need. He begins to hyperventilate like the wounded cowboy hero in the Hollywood shootout. His oxygen-starved muscles ache all over his body. He craves water as his thirst sensors tell him to replace the fluid lost through internal bleeding. From lack of oxygen, his thinking blurs into a timeless drift, floating on the slowly fading ochre light, hovering beneath the stars that appear in the purple sky. A sense of anxiety and doom—a physiological response to very low blood pressure—comes over him.

He might die here. The thought is an abstraction to him. He tries to calculate the odds but comes up with double zeros, the numbers pushed aside by the simple thought that he might die here, alone on a ledge suspended above a green alpine meadow. What does it mean? He doesn't know. Why in this way, on this ledge, of all ways? It doesn't really matter. Has he lived a good life? He clumsily tries to wrap his mind around the sum total of his actions, but he can't seem to manage it. He still possesses the bluntness to ask the question but not the mental agility to answer it. He drifts in a vacuum, as if his supply of ready justifications has deserted him, suddenly leaving him without anchor points to the world that he knew, without a rope, without a belay, hovering above the surface of his own life, his head spinning with vertigo. He can't think what he would or would not do differently. He can't think at all.

By the fifth hour, his ruptured spleen stops bleeding. Enough blood has leaked out into the surrounding tissues that the growing lump of blood-infused tissue, known as a hematoma, presses against the puncture and essentially plugs the leak. It's helped in this by his low blood pressure—the body's last line of defense against a major wound—as if it slows all systems in order to repair itself or to simply buy time. His condition begins to stabilize, although at an impaired

level. His heart and breathing rates remain high, but his consciousness slowly clears, especially when he lies quietly, burning little oxygen. He sits up briefly, dizzy and light-headed, craving water. He
forces himself to eat one of his candy bars, masticating as if it were a
mouthful of dry leaves, carefully drinks a few mouthfuls from his
precious liter of water, then lies back again beneath the black sky.

He wakes only once during the night, hyperventilating slightly,
heart still pounding, and lies quietly on his back, his head somewhat
clearer, and stares up at the icy bright stars. If he dies on this ledge,
only the stars will watch him vanish. Who will miss him? His parents are dead. His wife has divorced him. He has no children. Would
there be a funeral? They'd do something for him at work. All the
money he made for the firm. Or would they just shuck his memory
aside like it was another asset they'd acquired and no longer needed?

The warm tears gather at the corner of his eyes and trickle
down his temples. The stars of Orion, sword dangling from his belt,
spin slowly overhead, until he finally lapses again into sleep.

He wakes at dawn, under a pinkish sky. Slowly, methodically, he
pulls himself to his elbows and checks his condition. He feels as
though he could drink a gallon of water in one, long gulp, but other
than that, he seems better. He moves his good leg. He examines his
bad one. No blood from the break. He feels his pulse—it's slower,
and he's breathing easier, as if the quiet rest of the night helped restore oxygen to his system. The odd pressure still pushes from beneath his ribs, but he seems otherwise stable.

He feels pretty good, all things considered. Back up there in the 95th percentile, even higher. One more night and he's home free. The night wasn't bad at all, except when he woke up, thirsty again, and started thinking too much. *Shit!* He's getting soft on himself. Survival of the fittest—that's the way the world works, the way it always did, and he's one of the very fittest. He's made sure of it. Damned sure of it.

The sun now cracks over the top of the opposite cliff, a brilliant white disk shooting the warm rays of life down onto his ledge. Yes, he made it. We're talking 99.9 percent certainty. At least. Yes, still a winner.

"I'm still here, you sons of bitches!" he screams out into the void. "I'm still here and I'm alive!"

It would have been far better at that moment, for his sake, if he'd simply kept quiet. Fifteen hours earlier, when he landed on his side on the granite ledge, his torso suddenly stopped falling on impact, but his heart continued its momentum for a short distance inside his chest. The heart moved freely except for one part—the aortic arch, the thick blood vessel running upward out of the heart to supply the upper body. It is anchored both to the heart and to the spine. If the heart moves inside the chest too far and too fast, the aortic arch can tear or sever where it connects to the spine—one of the deceleration injuries that strikes drivers in severe auto accidents who are thrown very hard into the steering wheel, dying almost instantly.

This was the severe pain he felt far in the back of his chest on impact. The trauma of his fall didn't sever the arch's walls entirely, however, but split the middle of the wall's three layers, like the delamination in the sandwiched layers of a piece of plywood or cardboard. The fall "dissected the media" of the aortic arch, in medical terminology. For the last fifteen hours, blood continued to flow through the aortic arch in a "false channel" between the layers of the wall, all the while forming a growing bulge called an aneurysm. As the aneurysm grew, which they tend to do over time, the walls weakened. It was good for his aneurysm that he'd had a quiet night. It was very bad for his aneurysm that he now started screaming victoriously, angrily, defiantly, into the void.

Adrenaline pumps through his circulatory system. His heart rate, which had been down around 90 beats per minute, climbs to 120. Worse, his blood pressure jumps from 100/60 to 140/100.

"Wake up, Antoni, goddamn you!" he screams, the words echoing between the cliff faces. "Here I am!"

When he screams, he superinflates his lungs, bringing up his diaphragm to generate the air pressure for his shout, which increases pressure on the large blood vessels in his chest, which backs up the blood in his veins. This causes the jugular vein to stand out boldly in his neck in the manner of angry, red-faced bosses in the midst of a screaming fit. It also, unfortunately for him, forces his blood pressure higher still.

It's then that the aneurysm ruptures. He feels an odd blow deep between his shoulder blades. The aortic arch splits open. A pulsating river of blood gushes with every powerful pump of his heart not to his upper body and brain but directly into his chest cavity.

He doesn't even have time to get off one more shout at the sons of bitches out there. Within ten seconds he loses consciousness. He crumples backward onto his grass bedding. His heart gives a last hundred beats, emptying his blood supply into his chest cavity. Then it stops.

It was just as well for his sake that it happened as it did. Antoni didn't come back to the office that Monday morning, away with his family for a few days' vacation. When the search did finally start for him, the firm called in his sister from a thousand miles away, and Antoni told the police and the search-and-rescue team where they'd planned to climb. The searchers quickly found his new SUV parked at the trailhead. But then the trail went cold. He wasn't on any of the climbing routes that he and Antoni had discussed, nor on the ones nearby, and he hadn't told anyone else just where he was headed. People speculated whether he was a victim of murder, or was a suicide, or had perpetrated an embezzlement scheme. The firm checked and double-checked its accounts, but found no funds missing.

He was finally discovered by a hunter who was glassing the cliffs from above for mountain goats and saw something strange. He's found in the exact position in which he collapsed with his last shout, leg still wedged in the rocks, but it's six years later now, and of course all that's left is a skeleton picked over by the birds but for a few unappetizing tatters of Lycra and cotton, plus a cell phone, its black plastic weathered gray by sun and rain and snow, lying on the ledge beside the bones of the outstretched hand.

CHAPTER EIGHT

THE SHARP STING

OF PARADISE:

PREDATORS

"Smell this!" Mary said, pressing the flower toward Gil's nose. "I wish we'd had some of these at the wedding."

He sniffed cursorily and turned his face away. "Let's go find a beach."

"Why don't we stay here awhile first?" Mary said. "We can find beaches anytime. But this"—she waved the flower up toward the leafy, cathedral-like ceiling of the rain forest's canopy, the thick vines dangling from the arching branches, the orchids sprouting from tree trunks, the tangled profusion of life—"this place is *extraordinary*! This looks like the land before time!"

"I'm heading back to the car," Gil said, shifting his sandaled feet over the forest floor as the ants crawled up between his toes.

"How can you expect to appreciate the beauty of a place if you refuse to spend some time in it?"

"I don't consider this place beautiful," Gil said. "I think it's malevolent. And besides, there are ants. Let's go."

She dropped the hand holding the flower down to the hip of

her khaki shorts. Her hand just missed brushing the leaves of gimpi-gimpi or stinger plant, whose hollow hairs inject poison into the skin that can itch and burn for up to six months after contact. Meanwhile, a taipan, one of the world's deadliest snakes, had curled up to sleep a few hundred steps away.

"You always want to be somewhere else, Gil," Mary said. "Why can't you just enjoy where you are?"

"As if you're never in a hurry," Gil said. "I seem to remember you were in quite a rush to get married."

"And you certainly didn't waste any time walking out on your ex."

But he'd already started to walk back along the overgrown path toward the car, angrily shaking his feet as he went to dislodge the ants.

They drove in silence north up the coastal highway. Dark clouds had bunched over the coastal range on their left and rain began to spit against the windshield of the rental Jeep. To the right, through breaks in the low forest that fringed the beach, they caught glimpses of the sea—calm and blackish green as the rain peppered the surface. The rainy season—"the wet," as people called it here in northern Australia—was almost over. They knew the shower would last only a few minutes before the sun broke through again. They'd planned their honeymoon to take advantage of exactly this month, April, on the cusp between the wet and the dry, having flown halfway around the world to spend two weeks amid the exotic flora and fauna of Queensland's Cape York Peninsula and the area nearby. The peninsula was a lush and beautiful spit of land that projected from the north coast of Australia into the tropical waters of the Coral Sea like a sharp spine about to puncture the underbelly of the great bird-shaped island of New Guinea.

Gil held the wheel steady as the car planed through a large puddle, the water thunking up against the floor boards. They didn't see the saltwater crocodile lounging in a wet spot—a billabong—near the road.

"When do you want to go out to the reef?" Gil asked.

It was his way of offering to make up.

"How about tomorrow?" Mary replied. "We could go to the beach today and head out to the reef tomorrow. We can ask the hotel desk clerk tonight to arrange a boat."

It was her way of accepting his offer. They both knew that later in the day, back in their room overlooking the sea at the big resort, their lovemaking would be particularly ardent.

Still, the honeymoon had been rough. They seemed to fight at least once every day, followed by long, dripping silences. It hadn't been like this back in the States. They'd met at a bird-watching camp on the New England coast when her first marriage had just ended and his was about to end, a victim of too much time devoted to his law practice. They'd each, in their own way, repaired to the seashore to sit on the dunes and watch the birds wheel about on the sea breezes as a means to restore some balance and harmony to their own lives. By the camp's end, they'd arranged their first "date": a four-day snorkeling expedition to the Bahamas. It only seemed appropriate, when he proposed to her at sunset on the beach at the end of the fourth Bahamian day, caught up in the headiness of it all, that for their honeymoon they should choose one of the world's most beautiful wild places: the Cape York Peninsula.

"How about here?" Gil said, slowing the car where a sandy track led from the highway toward the beach.

"It looks fine," said Mary.

Gil swung the Jeep onto the rutted track and they bounced along for a few hundred yards until it ended in deeper sand and an open forest of palms and eucalyptus. They climbed out of the Jeep, picking up their daypacks laden with cameras, sunscreen, water bottles, and towels, and walked to the beach, watching where they placed their feet. They'd been warned that, basking in the sun or hidden in the undergrowth, the death adders looked like driftwood.

"Oh, Gil, it's spectacular!" Mary said as they stepped out on the beach.

The sun was just breaking through the wet clouds that clung to the headland—richly textured with its green mat of tropical foliage—at the beach's far end. The curving strip of yellow sand glistened, and the water radiated a vivid aquamarine. They couldn't see another sign of human life along the 3-mile crescent. Gil wrapped his arms around Mary and hugged her.

"I'm so happy to be here with you," she whispered into the soft blue fabric of his T-shirt. She was quite sure she meant it.

"And I with you," he said into her sweet-smelling, honey-blonde hair. They'd get used to each other eventually, he figured. It would probably work out all right.

They dropped their packs, pulled out their towels, and spread them on the warm sand. They unfastened their shorts, slipping them down tanned legs. Underneath he wore a fashionably baggy, fashionably faded blue bathing suit, and she a small black bikini bottom. She was proud of her body and, as she moved into early middle age, worked diligently to keep it in shape.

"The water looks lovely," she said. "Let's go for a swim."

"I don't know about swimming here," Gil replied, sitting down abruptly on his towel. "There aren't any enclosures."

Back at the popular beaches near the resort town he'd seen people swimming inside what the locals called "stinger nets." These were floating, corral-like enclosures made of fine netting designed to keep out jellyfish. As he'd strolled along the beach, he'd read the sign posted at one enclosure: "Warning: Marine stingers are dangerous October to May." The sign had then listed the emergency treatment procedures for a severe box jellyfish sting.

"I saw people swimming outside the enclosures," Mary said. "They say the worst of the jellyfish season is over."

"I still don't think it's a good idea," Gil said.

"Gil, how can you let this incredible blue water go to waste? Here we are in paradise, and you're sounding like a lawyer."

"I'm just trying to be prudent in a place where we don't know the score."

She stripped off her white T-shirt and let it drop to the sand.

Underneath she wore a strapless black bikini top. She started walking toward the water, as much propelled by her defiance of his oppressive caution—of his whole being—than drawn by the tempting blue sea.

"You're being foolish, Mary."

"Whatever it is I'm being," she called back over her bare shoulder, "it's better than what you are."

H*omo sapiens* is, by far, the most lethal predatory species on the face of the earth. Instead of sharp teeth, lacerating claws, or death-inducing venom, the species is equipped with powerful brains and nimble fingers with which they have learned to fashion clubs, spears, knives, axes, pit traps, blow darts, M-16 rifles, land mines, napalm, nerve gas, supersonic fighter jets, cruise missiles, and neutron bombs. *Homo sapiens* preys on and kills over 1 million humans annually—about 940,000 through war and another 200,000 through violent crime. The next most lethal animal, snakes, by comparison kills 100,000 humans per year, about only 10 percent of the number *Homo sapiens* kills. The third most lethal animal, the crocodile, dispatches only about 960 humans annually, and the fourth, the tiger, claims roughly 740 human victims each year. The much-feared shark falls far down the list—only about 9 human victims annually worldwide—making it a lightweight compared to the ostrich, which can kick viciously with hammerlike feet and sharp talons when cornered and kills about 14 people every year. As for the ferocious grizzly bear, it ranks slightly below the puny, ratlike mustelids (weasels, badgers, skunks, ferrets, etc.), which kill about 4 humans a year, primarily pet ferrets attacking unattended human babies.*

---

* "Human Death from Animal Attack 1978–1995," by S. A. Baily, S. A. Ishiakara, and M. V. Callahan, data gathered by Remote Care Management. War and homicide statistics vary depending on year and source. World Health Organization

Who would guess that in the United States and Canada you have more to fear from the moose—that seemingly benign creature immortalized in affable cartoon characters—than any other creature, except snakes? When Bullwinkle, who can weigh nearly a ton, has sex on his mind, he likes to mix it up with his love rivals, for whom he might mistake you, using his antlers for weapons. Even gentle Bambi claims about one human each year in the United States and Canada. And here are a few more reassuring statistics: The most likely place in the United States to be attacked by an alligator (three deaths between 1992 and 1998) is not deep in some swamp but on a golf course. Your chances of being attacked by a shark while swimming along the coast of North America are approximately one in five million, although there is an area off the coast of northern California known as the "red triangle" where great white sharks occasionally mistake wet-suit-clad surfers who are paddling their boards for basking elephant seals, which happen to be one of their favorite foods.

Very few animals stalk humans as prey, and those that do, such as the infamous man-eating tigers of India or lions of Africa, tend to be individual animals that for some reason lose a fear of humans and develop a taste for their flesh. Animals, for the most part, attack humans when they are surprised by them and feel threatened, when their territory is invaded, or when defending their offspring. Snakes kill far more humans worldwide than any other animal, but, as one authority emphatically states, snakes *have never been shown to attack without provocation despite lengthy historic commentary to the contrary.* Most bites occur when rural villagers unwittingly disturb a snake, often by stepping on it in the darkness; in the United States, by way of contrast, many victims know the snake is venomous, are under the

---

statistics for 1998 show 736,000 deaths from homicide and violence, and 588,000 from war; for 1999 they show 527,000 deaths from homicide and violence, and 269,000 from war. *World Health Report 1999* and *World Health Report 2000.* Geneva, Switzerland: World Health Organization, 1999, 2000.

influence of alcohol or drugs, and, in the words of one expert, are "messing with it." Researchers in Alabama have noted a statistical drop in venomous snakebites among adult males when University of Alabama or Auburn University football games are televised locally, presumably because instead of being out somewhere looking for wild snakes or messing with pet ones, the would-be victims are ensconced safely on the couch with a cold beer in hand.*

Humans have long been fascinated with creatures more powerful than they, although for equally long they have remained undecided whether to worship the beasts or destroy them, as if the very idea of a being on this earth more powerful than they offends the reach of ego and lies beyond comprehension. The Egyptians worshiped a crocodile god, Sebek; the native peoples of the northern forests honored the bear, offering elaborate apologies to its relatives before killing it; Amazonian tribes elevate the jaguar as a mythical beast. In mythology, powerful beasts can create the world or they can destroy it. Like the gods themselves, the beasts possess the sacred power to breathe life into humans and to take it away. They can—in the form of monsters such as Beowulf's Grendel, emerging from the swamp in the night to attack King Hrothgar's great mead hall—represent chaos and darkness lying just beyond the edge of the known world. They can embody sin, such as the serpent in the Garden of Eden. They can pose a crucial barrier one must overcome to earn one's manhood, such as the slaying of a Masai's first lion or an Inuit's first polar bear. What they almost never represent in the human imagination is what they almost always are: creatures not looking for trouble but, like everyone else, simply trying to survive in the world.

There are no statistics showing that one region of the world is

---

* Unpublished observations, M .V. Callahan and R. M. Pitts cited in "Field Recognition and Management of Exotic Snake Envenomation," lecture by Michael V. Callahan, M.D., Wilderness Medicine Conference, Keystone, Colorado, July 2000.

more dangerous than another for animal attacks. Still, one can speculate. It would seem that parts of Africa inhabited by big-game animals—tiger, lion, elephant (an unpredictable herbivore that's been known to stalk humans), hippo, and Cape buffalo—would make the list, as would the snake-infested Amazon basin and parts of Southeast Asia such as Vietnam's Mekong Delta, where, in a rice-farming region hardly larger than Rhode Island, researchers have found that cobras, kraits, and vipers kill over 2,700 adults and children each year.

On the list, too, one expects, would be the northern coast of Australia and the region around the Cape York Peninsula. Besides its assortment of venomous snakes such as the death adder and tai-pan, its viciously stinging plants, and its poisonous fish and sharks, it is also home to the estuarine or saltwater crocodile, *Crocodilus porosus*—locally known as a "salty" to distinguish it from the more innocuous "freshie." Salties and their cousins throughout tropical Asia account for more human deaths annually than the African crocodiles who wrestled their way to fame in Tarzan movies. Salties can grow to be over 20 feet long and can keep pace with a speedboat in the water and with a horse on land. Their jaws are powerful enough to snap the propeller off an outboard motor. Hiding at water's edge, a salty knocks its victim—kangaroo, cow, human—into the water with its powerful tail, seizes a limb, and performs a "kill spin," revolving over and over underwater and mangling the limb until the victim dies of bleeding or simple drowning. One saltwater croc, according to re-ports, when cut open was found with the remains of an Aborigine in its stomach as well as a four-gallon canister containing two blankets.

But of all the crocs, snakes, and other faunal hazards of north-ern Australia, one creature, despite its diminutive size, towers above the rest. This is a small, graceful-looking jellyfish not much larger than a grapefruit, known by the scientific name of *Chironex fleckeri*—sometimes generically called a box jellyfish or sea wasp. Venomolo-gists regard *C. fleckeri* as perhaps the venomous creature most lethal to humans on the face of the earth. The venom itself—still largely a mystery to researchers—may prove to be among the most toxic substances known. At least sixty-three people have died along the coast of northern Australia from *C. fleckeri* or similar stings in cases documented since about 1900. *C. fleckeri* or related species also probably cause many unrecorded deaths in Southeast Asia and especially in the Philippines. Compared to the Atlantic Ocean's Portuguese man-of-war—not a true jellyfish—whose sting is painful but rarely fatal, *C. fleckeri*'s sting is in a class of its own. By some estimates, it can kill a human in less than a minute.

Years ago, no one knew what invisible presence along these coasts caused its victims to suddenly scream and thrash in the water with the instant and excruciating pain of a sting and sometimes die. The species itself wasn't identified until a boy's death by jellyfish sting in 1955. A Queensland radiologist and amateur naturalist, Dr. Hugo Flecker, urged police to net the beach in order to find the offending creature that eventually was named after him. For a time it was known as a sea wasp, but tourists from other parts of Australia began to show up on northern Queensland's beaches wearing hats and umbrellas to repel what they thought were flying insects, and so the name was discouraged. Now, during the wet season, when *C. fleckeri* congregates near shore, swimmers at popular beaches stay inside netted enclosures designed to keep it out. Researchers have developed Lycra suits to guard swimmers against the stings and a box jellyfish antivenin by injecting sheep with nonfatal doses of the creature's venom and extracting their blood products. Quickly administered, the antivenin does much to ameliorate the jellyfish's sting. Resuscitation using CPR has also proved effective in reviving victims. *C. fleckeri* stings are now relatively rare compared to stings of other, less potent jellyfish, though they still occur. The effectiveness of all the measures and education put into place to prevent box jellyfish stings depends, of course, on the measures being followed and obeyed.

"Come on in," Mary shouted, up to her knees in the clear water, waving to Gil. "See, there's nothing to be scared of."

"I'm not scared," he called out to her. "I'm prudent."

He was lying back, propped on his elbows on the beach towel that he'd spread on the warm sand, and watching her through his tortoiseshell sunglasses.

"You're going to let your new bride swim all alone?" Mary said.

"I'm admiring my new bride from afar," he called back.

Mary turned and waded deeper. The rippled sand deliciously massaged the bottoms of her feet, and the warm tropical water soothed her skin like a mineral bath. She now stood as deep as the middle of her thighs. Calm and blue-green, the sea extended like a huge placid lagoon toward the Great Barrier Reef, some 30 miles offshore. She badly wanted to see its beautiful coral and spectacular fish. It was hard enough to convince Gil simply to go for a swim; how difficult would it be to drag him out there? He'd become so un-adventurous since the honeymoon began, as if this profusion of life—the tropical rain forest with its spectacular butterflies, birds, and wildflowers, and the coral reefs, with their rich sea life—that filled her with elation unnerved him, and he took refuge from it in their air-conditioned hotel room with its satellite television and minibar and on the local eighteen-hole golf course. She waded a lit-tle deeper. The water nearly ringed her hips. She knew she wasn't being prudent, but the water looked fine, and his annoying, persis-tent caution made her want to wade deeper, away from him. Would this be their life together, she wondered—she ready to explore, meet new people, while he dragged behind, unwilling to let go of the safe and the familiar? Was this a mistake, this marriage? Already the fights she had with Gil resembled the same shopworn arguments she'd had with Tom, her ex-husband. He would have loved the resort, too, and found few reasons to venture beyond its manicured grounds that kept the forest and its creatures at bay. A real estate developer, he would have seen beauty—and a lot of risk—in the boldness it took to carve a resort from this remote reach of Australia. To her, no matter how pleasant its amenities, it was a desecration of the primordial landscape. If Gil turned out like Tom, cautious and unimaginative, interested mainly in money, she'd leave him. Maybe first have the child she wanted, and then leave him.

"Is that all I can expect from my new husband, admiration from *afar*?" she called out, twisting halfway around toward him. "The water's delicious."

He waved her off. "I'm perfectly happy sitting right here," Gil said.

But he wasn't perfectly happy. How could he be happy with someone who was pushing him all the time? A constant, tiny *shove shove shove*. This was supposed to be vacation, wasn't it? He pushed himself hard enough at work. Every day he went out and laid his reputation on the line. It wasn't glamorous, doing corporate tax work, but it was demanding and extremely exacting, and you couldn't afford mistakes. The government regulators could smell the faintest trace of blood in the water—the tiniest vulnerability that might be hiding much deeper problems—and they'd come charging in for a feeding frenzy. Yes, it was a hostile world out there, and he didn't need someone pushing and telling him to loosen up. Mary now reminded him of his ex-wife, Betsy, who for five years had chided him to work less, travel more, go for hikes and picnics and visits to galleries, invite near-strangers to their house for dinner. He told her he wasn't *opposed* to these things; he just had to concentrate on the task at hand, namely, his career. She wouldn't let up. He'd finally moved out. Then, strangely, he found himself taking up some of the activities he'd resisted for so long, as if to prove to her that he wasn't the stodgy person she thought. It had been a great relief to meet Mary at the bird-watching camp—she was so patient and understanding when he told her about his failed marriage—but now it seemed he was reliving those five bad years all over again. Couldn't she just give it a rest? Relax a bit instead of charging from rain forest to reef to outback? He didn't want to think about how it would be when they got back home. He'd already made the mistake. A stupid mistake—the kind he always chided himself to avoid in his corporate tax work. How long would a divorce take? And, more important, what would it cost him?

He looked out over the blue-green water where she stood hip deep, her black bikini bottom low on her hips, the curve of her back sinuous, a crescent of the roundness of each breast just visible along her sides when she raised her arms. He had to admit, she had a great body.

"Last chance!" she called, twisting her head halfway around toward him.

"Hurry up and swim if you're going to swim," he called back, his irritation rising. "Otherwise let's go back to the hotel."

She brought her arms over her head and sprang gently off the sand with her toes. As she dove underwater, sliding in with a gentle splash, she made her decision: *That's it. We're finished.*

About a year earlier, late in the wet season, two spawning *Chironex fleckeri* released sperm and egg into a river estuary not far from Gil and Mary's isolated beach. Joining in the warm water, they soon grew into a minute ball of cells—the planula, as this stage is known—and dropped to the river bottom, attaching to the underside of a rock. There, through the dry season, the planula sprouted the beginnings of a crown of tentacles and grew into a tiny polyp—a kind of protojellyfish—that by the end of the dry season had metamorphosed into a small medusa, or what's commonly known as a jellyfish. Just ahead of the monsoon rains, the *C. fleckeri* propelled itself out of the estuary and into the Coral Sea.

For the next few months it gently pulsed through calm waters along the coast, avoiding violent currents and waves that could tear its delicate tissues, feeding and growing. Its body, an almost transparent milky white that consisted of 95 percent water, developed into a graceful bell shape with a squarish, four-cornered bottom rim—thus the name "box jellyfish" to designate *C. fleckeri* and about fifty related species in the order Cubomedusa. By filling its bell with water and squeezing it out like an umbrella opening and closing, the jelly could jet along at speeds up to 4 miles per hour. A chicken-foot-shaped projection called a pedalium sprouted from each of the four corners of the bell's rim, and from these grew the jelly's tentacles—up to fifteen tentacles from each foot. Only a ¼ inch in diameter, and on a large adult jelly stretching over 10 feet long when fully extended, the tentacles formed ringlike segments and resembled twisted lengths of skinny—and highly charged—electrical conduit.

Using primitive eyes to help it avoid bumping into large objects, the jelly followed schools of shrimp that congregated just off the sandy beaches. Sensitive to strong sunlight, the jelly lingered near the shallow bottoms of the sea during the height of the day, rising toward the surface as the sunlight weakened in late afternoon, dangling its long tentacles behind it, trolling for its prey, often moving into the shallower water near the beach on an incoming tide. As it waited, a shrimp came past, extending and fanning its tail, swimming backward. Inadvertently brushing one of the jelly's tentacles, it died almost instantly. Like some mariner cowboy roping a calf, the *C. fleckeri* reeled in the shrimp with its tentacles, finally feeding the meaty morsel into wide, grasping lips.

The sea was calm, the tide rising, the sun settling down into the latter part of the afternoon as Mary put her hands over her head to make her dive. Virtually invisible to her, the jelly was swimming along 12 feet seaward of her in water 5 feet deep, its tentacles trailing behind for shrimp.

Mary never saw it.

Plunging beneath the smooth surface, she glided underwater, savoring the trickling sound in her ears and the smooth, wet warmth of the tropical sea flowing over her bare skin, extending her glide, kicking along underwater, enjoying it, relieved that she'd made the decision to leave Gil. Then something brushed against her arms. She flinched, startled. Was it seaweed? Then it brushed against her shoulders, her midriff, her back.

Reflexively, the jelly's tentacles contracted, piling themselves in loops and S-shapes onto her skin in its instinctive attempt to apply maximum tentacle surface area—and thus maximum venom—to its victim. Each tentacle was embedded with millions of tiny sacs of venom called nematocysts, the entire jellyfish armed with an estimated four billion of them. The touch of Mary's skin—indistinguishable, as far as the jellyfish was concerned, from a shrimp or a fish—bent down a triggerlike spike known as a cnidocil that projected from the top of each sac, springing open the nematocyst's lid like a jack-in-the-box. Instead of a clown, however, inside was the equivalent of a hypodermic needle—a tiny coiled tube with a sharp pointed tip. The tubes now launched out—thousands of them—extending about .03 of an inch, and jabbed their tips into Mary's skin, injecting venom from the sacs into the tissue and capillaries of the dermis just beneath the outer skin surface. Meanwhile, a wrap of tiny spikes around each tube's base snagged her skin like a coil of barbed wire to fasten the tentacles securely to her body.

Mary gasped underwater. A stream of bubbles escaped from her mouth. The stinging swelled into an incredible mounting surge of pain, burning over her bare arms, her shoulders, back, torso. No, she thought, not seaweed. A thousand hornets had embedded their stingers in long, pulsating strips across her skin.

She kicked and arched toward the surface, tearing at the stinging things adhering to her skin. She held in a scream of pain, the bubbles spurting from her nose and mouth. *Get your head up first*, she thought. *Get your head up.*

Gil, leaning back on his elbows and staring with irritation through his tortoiseshells, watched her graceful dive and then the long, suspended moment of her underwater glide. The surface erupted in a bubble of thrashing foam. He sat up. It was Mary's head, her sun-streaked hair wet and sleek, her arms flailing wildly at the water around her, clawing at her chest and back and shoulders at something that he couldn't see. Her screams and grunts of pain carried across the calm surface, short and gutteral at first as she plucked and tore at her skin, then sustained and high-pitched as she tried to twist toward shore for his help.

He knew immediately what had happened. *Why hadn't she listened?*

"I'm coming!" he shouted, launching himself off his beach towel and onto his feet

He would be the heroic husband, vindicating himself for the caution that she had so derided. He sprinted to the water's edge where the Coral Sea lapped weakly against the wet sand, stripped off his $375 pair of sunglasses, and manfully flung them aside. He charged into the water, splashing up great heroic sprays from his feet as he raced through the shallows. He advanced as deep as his knees. Then he suddenly stopped.

Would it sting him, too?

She was about 50 feet away, in water that was probably just over her head. He could see her struggling to put her feet down to the sandy bottom. He stared hard at the water around her. He couldn't see anything unusual. How long were its tentacles? He had no idea. Where was it? It could be anywhere. She was looking up at him with the wide, panicked eyes of a wounded, trapped animal that knows it doesn't have much time. She was trying to call out to him, but her words were garbled with the seawater splashing into her mouth as she clawed and thrashed, as if pushing away invisible tentacles in the water around her.

"Where is it?" he shouted. "Where is it?"

It was as if Gil, standing paralyzed in knee-deep water near shore, had also been injected with the jellyfish's powerful, stunning venom. He looked up and down the beach for something, anything, that might help—a person, a boat, a long stick, a board, a rope. Nothing. They'd chosen this beach precisely because no one was here. What did he have in the car? Nothing useful. He looked back to her, thrashing in the water.

"Can you swim?" he shouted. "Swim to me!"

She raised an arm helplessly toward him, and he could see the red weals already spiraling along it in raw whiplashlike marks as she gasped and gagged on the seawater.

He realized that she was going to die unless he did something. But what? He could run to the car and drive for help. How long could she last? Five minutes? It would take at least an hour to get to town and back. He could see them charging down the beach, and there'd she be, washed up on shore, dead. And what would happen then? Would there be a coroner's inquest, or the Australian equivalent? Would he be exonerated if she died? Could he somehow be held as an accessory in her death?

No one knows exactly what's in the venom of *Chironex fleckeri* that makes it so potent. Research has been stymied partly because *C. fleckeri*'s venom is thermolabile—meaning it becomes unstable when warmed to 131 degrees or above, making it difficult to handle or analyze without chemically altering it. Researchers believe the venom, made up of proteinlike substances, contains three major components: one toxin that causes dermatonecrotic damage (damage and death to the skin), another that affects the blood, and a third that works, potentially fatally, on the heart and other organs. The incredible skin pain, some have speculated, may be due in part to a compound called 5-hydroxytryptamine, a pain producer that is found in the tentacles of many types of jellyfish. This compound triggers the release of histamine from the victim's body. While it is also one of the irritating chemicals in bee stings and nettles, histamine plays a helpful role in the body's immune system by opening blood vessels—thus causing inflammation around a wound—in order to speed immune agents to the injury.

But the pain caused by histamine inflammation is relatively mild compared to the incredible agony a *C. fleckeri* victim experiences. There is some other substance at work as well. Not much is known about how the venom affects blood cells; what is becoming clearer, however, is how the venom can affect the heart.

It has been estimated that *C. fleckeri* venom enters the circulatory system of a healthy person within twenty seconds of the sting, as the tiny tubules inject thousands of tiny doses of venom directly into the capillaries just beneath the skin. This is unlike snakebite, where the fangs leave a few large deposits of venom in the tissue, and this venom is slowly absorbed through the body, the full effects taking hours. In both cases, the fight-or-flight response—which might be useful if one were being attacked by a saltwater crocodile and needed the response's physiological boost to extract one's leg from the croc's mouth, as one near-victim managed to do—can work against the victim of jellyfish stings or snakebite.

Mary's fight-or-flight panic had sent surges of adrenaline through her body, boosting her heart rate from 80 beats per minute to its maximum of 170 beats. Her struggling contracted her muscle tissues, which demanded oxygen, triggering a flood of blood from her heart and lungs to her thrashing muscles and back again. The effect is what physiologists call the "muscle pump," and it helped carry the venom from the capillaries beneath her skin to her heart.

The venom quickly concentrated in her heart. Something in the venom—a cardiotoxin, researchers call it—began to wreak havoc with the heart's electrical system. In its normal resting state, a muscle cell of the heart holds a negative electrical charge inside it. This is because it contains negative ions—certain types of atoms that are missing electrons. When an electrical message passes from one muscle cell to another, channels open in the cell membranes, allowing negative ions to flow out of the cell and positive ions from outside the cell to flow into it. For an instant the charge inside the cell becomes slightly positive. This impulse is passed on to the next cell and the next, like a wave traveling along the muscle fiber, causing it to contract, and as it passes the positive ions move back outside the cell again, and the cell's charge returns to its original negative state.

But the cardiotoxin in *C. fleckeri* venom, according to experiments conducted on the heart tissues of rats, apparently triggers a big upsurge in the number of calcium ions with a positive charge entering the heart's muscle cells. An excess of calcium ions inside these cells is well known to cause spasms in the carefully timed sequential contractions of the heart muscle, a bit like throwing a bucket of water onto the circuitry of a spinning electrical motor.

Suddenly Mary's heart lost its rhythm and jumped with irregular, spasmodic contractions. The ventricles, the heart's two main chambers, normally start their contraction from the bottom point of the chambers and work smoothly up the powerful muscle walls to the top of the chamber, squeezing out the blood. But the jelly's venom triggered chaotic contractions that began somewhere in the middle of the muscle, and at an extremely rapid pace—240 beats per minute. Instead of a powerful, coordinated stroke pushing out 3 ounces of blood with every beat, it dribbled out less than one-twentieth that amount per beat. Her blood pressure plummeted. The blood flowing to her brain slowed to a trickle. The bright thrashing circle of sunlight and seawater and raw pain faded to a dim, lazy pool of twilight. *Keep your head up,* came the message from somewhere deep in that pool. *Keep your arms moving.*

It seemed to Gil she was losing consciousness. Her head dropped facedown in the water, bobbed up, dropped down again.

She wasn't screaming now. She floated facedown in the water, but the back of her head still protruded above the surface. Her lesioned arms still waved vaguely keeping her afloat.

"Mary! Mary!" he shouted, shuffling his feet a foot or two closer across the sandy bottom.

She gave no indication that she heard him.

Gil had never seen anyone die before, but it was perfectly clear to him that she was almost dead. He knew he'd replay this moment for the rest of his life, carrying this image of her, floating facedown, her arms still stirring dully, her hair gently fanning out on the surface, while he stood paralyzed, his feet fixed to the sandy bottom in knee-deep water and simply . . . watched. It wasn't a charging lion he was confronting, or a marauding bear, or even a hungry saltwater crocodile. It was a lowly jellyfish! One that just happened to be swimming by! People would laugh—the man who watched his wife die because he couldn't take on a jellyfish. He felt his lungs hyperventilating and his heart pounding. In Gil's panicked state—torn between fighting the jellyfish and fleeing from it—his heart rate had jumped nearly to its maximum of 150 beats per minute. He couldn't bear it—the idea of living the rest of his life thinking of himself as an inch-at-a-time, always-weigh-the-consequences tax lawyer who watched his wife die because he was afraid to help. Because he'd been so cautious, so afraid to die, he'd also been afraid to live. And now, because of his caution, his wife was about to die, too.

He moved one foot forward across the sandy bottom. Then he moved the other. Then the first again. Suddenly he was thrashing into the water toward her, no longer caring what happened to him, what happened to either of them, as long as he *acted*, churning his way out, swinging his arms back and forth for balance. Thigh deep . . . waist deep . . . chest deep. She lay floating only 10 feet away. . . . 6 feet. He stopped. He shuffled two steps closer. He stretched out his right arm, reaching up over the surface of the water, above any stray tentacles. He touched her left hand, feeling the sticky softness of the tentacles that were wrapped around it. He pulled away. Oddly, he felt no stinging. Were they somehow spent?

They were not spent; he felt no sting because the tiny venom-filled tubes launched by the nematocysts didn't have enough power to penetrate the thick skin of his palm. The hair on the back of his hand also acted as a barrier to their penetration. Women and children, who have more hairless, tender skin and a smaller body mass than men, are for this reason more susceptible to *C. fleckeri* stings. Even a layer of panty hose can repel jellyfish stings, as discovered by surfers and Australian life guards, who pull pantyhose over their legs and other pairs over their torsos, cutting holes in the seats to poke their heads out, when swimming in jellyfish-infested waters. Sea turtles are equipped with some sort of cast-iron gullet that allows them to chase down and gobble up with great relish large quantities of these jellyfish.

Gil reached out again. He took a grip on her left wrist, between tentacles. Adrenalin pumping, he dragged her 122 pounds splashing through the shallow water and pulled her up onto the dry sand.

He dropped to his knees beside her. His total focus was on how to revive her, an intensity of concentration he'd never before experienced, a kind of crystalline clarity unobstructed by ceaseless whispers of caution. She lay facedown. Loops and S-shapes of tentacle torn by her thrashing from the jelly's delicate body adhered to her torso, etching the spiraling purplish brown lesions on her skin. If she survived, the tissue could die, and she might be scarred for life with the whorled markings of *C. fleckeri* tentacles, as if tattooed by a heap of rope.

Gil remembered the sign posted at the beach near town. "Flood sting with vinegar" was the first instruction for treating severe box jellyfish stings. Gil had noticed the jugs of vinegar placed at regular intervals along that beach. Dousing the adhering tentacles with vinegar prevents the nematocysts from firing further. But Gil had no vinegar. Instead, he ran to his beach towel that bore the resort logo in big blue letters, snatched it up, and, running back to her, wrapped it around his right hand. Working his fingers through the fabric like a surgical glove, he quickly plucked the tentacle fragments from her skin, flinging them to the warm sand behind him.

About 12 feet of tentacle had made contact with her skin. The severity of a *C. fleckeri* sting depends largely on how much tentacle has made close contact with the victim; about 6 feet is considered roughly the minimum for a lethal dose in an adult human. By some estimates, a full-grown *C. fleckeri* contains enough venom in all its tentacles combined to kill between ten and twenty adult humans.

Gil rolled her over and quickly pulled the tentacle fragments from her midriff. As a precaution, he had taken a course in cardio-pulmonary resuscitation years earlier and a refresher course before their trip to the Caribbean, nervous about the medical facilities—or lack of them—in the islands. He placed one hand under her neck and tilted back her head to make sure her breathing passages were open, then watched her sand-covered abdomen and chest for a faint rise and fall of respiration. Nothing. He put his face close to her mouth and nose to feel a flow of air. None.

The sign had instructed: "If breathing stops, give artificial respiration. Give closed-chest massage if heart stops."

He could feel his own heart pounding, his hands trembling, his breath coming in short gasps. *Concentrate,* he told himself. *Remember the CPR sequence.*

He leaned down over her, opened her mouth with one hand, pinched closed her nostrils with the other, placed his open mouth over hers, exhaled once, turned aside, took a breath, and exhaled into her mouth again. He watched her chest. It rose slightly as the air went in, then fell. This meant that, although she needed artificial respiration, her air passages weren't blocked. But what about her heart? He placed his index and middle finger on her throat and slid them to the side, slipping them into the slot between trachea and neck muscles to feel for the pulse in the carotid artery that supplies blood to the brain. He held his sand-gritted, trembling fingers as still as he could. Nothing. Her heart was still in wild and chaotic spasms at over 200 beats per minute. But it is not possible to feel a pulse in the carotid artery with one's fingers if the victim's systolic blood pressure—the pressure during the heart's contraction phase—is less than 80, compared to a normal of about 120. With her heart in spastic contractions from the *C. fleckeri* venom, Mary's systolic blood pressure now stood at a mere 40. And her diastolic pressure—the pressure during the heart's expansion phase, usually the weaker of the two—was zero.

Gil had to become both her heart and her lungs, at least long enough for her own physiology to recover from the venom's shock and regain some of its equilibrium, and he knew this was not a simple task for one person alone to perform. He'd have to work extremely quickly. Already the anxious sweat spilled down his forehead, from his armpits, along his forearms. Kneeling beside her sprawled form, he laid his right hand on top of his left and placed them on her breastbone (careful to avoid its lower tip, or xiphoid, which could snap off under too much pressure), stiffened his elbows, and shoved down hard, compressing her sternum about 2 inches, then released and shoved again. He tried to keep a quick, steady rhythm of 80 thrusts per minute, although he would have aimed for a slower pace of 60 thrusts per minute if he'd had help and didn't have to stop periodically to ventilate her lungs himself. With his tax lawyer's mind for numbers, he easily recalled the key ratio for a person performing CPR alone—15:2. After the first 15 thrusts he leaned down, pinched closed her nostrils again, and gave her two quick breaths, then resumed another set of 15 compressions. *One-and-two-and-three-and-four* . . .

Though the air he breathed into her was expired from his own lungs, it still contained plenty of oxygen. With each downward thrust of her sternum, Gil squeezed her heart's right and left ventricles, one pushing blood to her lungs, where it could absorb the oxygen, the other sending the oxygenated blood coursing throughout her body. His rapid, steady compressions kept blood moving up her carotid arteries and into her brain at one-third its normal rate of flow—not a lot, but enough to deliver the crucial supply of oxygen to the brain's starving tissues.

Thirty seconds passed. Gil leaned into his chest compressions, forcing the blood through her heart's chambers. He didn't dare look up, didn't dare speak to her, didn't dare urge her back to life, didn't dare utter a prayer, so intent was he on maintaining the quick, steady *compressing, compressing, compressing . . . breathe . . . breathe . . . compressing, compressing . . .*

A minute passed. He paused for an instant, panting to catch his breath, to feel with his shaking fingertips for a pulse in her carotid artery again. Still nothing. He went back to his intense, steady rhythm.

Another forty seconds passed. Sweat flying from Gil's face and arms fell onto Mary's sand-crusted face. He didn't know how long he could keep up this pace.

Inside the roof of the right atrium, one of the two small chambers that sit above the ventricles, is embedded the heart's own pacemaker—a bundle of special muscle fibers called the sino-atrial node that, like a metronome, generates its own impulses. As it fired, it sent electrical impulses traveling through her heart muscle like a wave, ordering the firings of the exact proper muscle tissue in the exact proper sequence. But the tiny holes in her cell membranes remained open from the venom's effects, and the calcium ions passed too easily into the cells, leaving the muscle still in spasms.

The second minute passed—he'd now done eight sets of 15 thrusts. Gil stopped again to probe for a pulse in her carotid artery. He felt . . . something. But what? Was it his own thumping heart, pushing blood out into his fingertips? Sand coated his fingers, their tips half numbed from the pressure of giving the compressions, and he was panting and trembling and couldn't see through the sweat dripping in his eyes. He swiped it away with a forearm, felt again. Was it his pulse, or hers, or his imagination? Whatever it was, he had to do something—fast. He needed someone to help him— someone with calm, clean, steady fingers.

He placed his hands on her sternum again and resumed the frenzied pace of the chest compressions, punctuated by the breathing. Another four sets of 15 thrusts—another minute. He was panting so hard now, he had to pause to catch his breath. It seemed that he'd been working over her frantically for a very long time. Was this futile? Had he got to her too late? Had he stood in the shallows too long while her life slid away? He felt again for her carotid artery. He held himself over her as quietly as he could, trying to understand what he sensed in his fingertips. It was then that he first heard a small gasp. He looked at her chest. There was another small gasp. He saw her rib cage fall slightly.

He let go of her neck and thrust his ear to her chest. He could hear something. He pressed his ear closer against the gritty skin. Was it the *lub-dub* sound of her heart's valves opening and closing as they should, the rushing blood vibrating in the heart's walls and vessels? Or was it his?

"Keep going, Mary!" he shouted. "Keep going!"

He lifted his head from her chest. Now her breath came in small gasps—the half breaths known as agonal breathing.

"That's right, breathe, Mary, breathe!"

He watched closely as her chest moved up and down more firmly. Had it actually worked? That he'd breathed life back into her?

Her limbs began to stir, brushing against the dry sand as if she remembered, deep in her subconscious, that she was supposed to swim. Her head started to loll back and forth on the sand. Gil quickly brushed the crust of sand from her face. Her eyes were still closed. He needed a plan—and quickly. He decided that the moment her eyelids opened, he'd pick her up in his arms and haul her over the soft, boggy sand to the Jeep under the palms, prop her in the passenger seat, jounce over the rutted beach road to the highway, and race into town. They'd arrive in twenty minutes, maybe a little more, and the hospital in town would surely have a ready supply of the box jellyfish antivenin. They'd put her on a respirator if she still needed it, and give her medicine for the pain that would surely return.

What would happen then? he wondered. What would they say to each other? Would she in some way be a different person, not pushing him all the time? And would he be different, not hanging back? Could a brush against this odd, drifting, tentacled creature that had no brain—no sense of good nor evil, of right nor wrong, but simply was—change a life, two lives, a marriage?

He jumped up. He ran to the pile of clothes they'd shed on the beach and grabbed his daypack with the car keys in it. He knelt again beside her.

"Come on, Mary, come on!"

He allowed himself to wish now, to hope. She could relapse— *Chironex fleckeri* victims sometimes show a brief improvement and rising blood pressure before suddenly expiring—but Gil knew that he'd done for her everything that was humanly possible for him to do, far more than he would have ever guessed he could. As Mary's chest rose and fell, tears began to sting his eyes.

CHAPTER NINE

BUBBLING FROM THE BOTTOM UP:

THE BENDS

Slightly out of breath from racing through the cobblestone streets to arrive at the appointed hour, Robert—or Roberto, as he'd been known for these past nine months in Spain—strode up broad stone steps to the massive black door of an old merchant's house at 49 Calle San Jose in the ancient port city of Cádiz. Robert knew the seaport's history well. Claiming to be the oldest continuously occupied city in Western Europe, Cádiz's heavily fortified harbor was first constructed thirty centuries ago by Phoenician traders on a rock-and-sand spit just outside the Straits of Gibraltar. Cádiz had served as the first port of call in the Old World for many of the treasure fleets arriving from Spain's vast American colonies. It was this last fact that interested Robert most.

Wiping his sweaty cheeks and forehead with a handkerchief, he composed his face into what he thought was a dignified but friendly expression. He then pressed the buzzer mounted on the stone jamb.

"*Qué?*" a voice said through the speaker.

He gave his name. There was no response, only the harsh buzz of the electronic lock pulling back.

He pushed open the heavy door. He'd been in old Cádiz merchant houses before—many had been cut up into apartments—but he'd never seen one so beautifully preserved. He followed the tunnel of a barrel-vaulted stone foyer until it suddenly jumped open in an atrium that reached up a full five stories to the sky. A tall palm stood in its center, and its marble floor—black and white squares like a chessboard—had been hollowed in places by centuries of boot traffic striding across it to the in-house merchant offices that once occupied the ground floor and mezzanine.

"*Aquí!*" a voice called, echoing through the atrium. "*Venga!*"

Robert looked up. A young woman in a black skirt and white blouse stood on the third-floor balcony, its filigreed wrought-iron railing encircling the atrium like the balconies above and below it, each leading off into several doors.

Robert started up the marble stairs. On the landings he passed antique Mudejar chests inlaid with ivory arabesques created by Moorish craftsmen who lingered in Spain after the Christians had reconquered it starting in the eleventh century. There were chairs upholstered in embroidered leather dating from the sixteenth century. Everywhere Robert looked he saw expensive relics from Spain's distant and glorious past. *This has got to be the place,* he thought.

At the top of the stairs, the young woman led him along the balcony into a sitting room. There, in a straight-backed armchair with her hands carefully resting on the arms, sat an elegant old woman. A white Andalusian shawl, laced like the web of a spider, was draped over the shoulders of her black dress. Her white hair was pulled back so tightly, it stretched the skin against her skull.

She lifted a hand to gesture to another straight-backed chair, this one upholstered in red velvet with spiraling Moorish-style legs. Robert sat down. The chair creaked and popped under his weight. He felt the sweat trickle down his cheeks.

"You're not the first, you know," the woman abruptly began.

"Someone has been here before me?"

"Not since my time, " she replied slowly, her lips moving carefully. "I only know what my grandmother told me when I was a girl. She heard it from her mother. Someone went to look for the ship.

They say that no one will ever reach it because the ship lies *muy hondo*. Very deep."

"But that was many, many years ago," Robert said. "Now maybe it is easier to find with modern diving equipment. It's possible to go very deep."

"*Quizá,*" was all the woman said in reply. Perhaps.

As they sat, Robert sweating in the creaking, straight-backed chair, the young woman who had led him in carried in a tray bearing a silver coffeepot. Robert instantly noticed the dented heaviness of the silver and the rich design, an encircling band of squared, intertwined frogs, almost Mesoamerican in spirit, of the type Aztec craftsmen made under Spanish rule. The two of them watched as she poured out with slender white hands a thick, black stream of coffee into two cups.

"This is my granddaughter," said the old woman.

For the first time, Robert, so transfixed by the house's furnishings, closely noticed the young woman's face. In a quiet way, she was beautiful. She had a finely sculpted nose, a strong but delicate jaw line, and jet black hair piled on her head that accentuated her white skin. Her eyes were dark and deep and wide when she looked up shyly at Robert to ask him if he'd like anything in his coffee, and her lips were carefully painted a blush of red.

"A little sugar, if you have it, *gracias,*" Robert said.

He watched her dextrous fingers, the long nails painted red, measure out a spoonful and a half of sugar, mix it into his coffee, and hand him the cup and saucer with a slight bow of the head. Then she straightened up and left the room.

"Why do you think I can help you?" the old woman asked.

"Please, *señora,*" Robert began. "I've been to the archives in Sevilla. For months I've been reading the old manuscripts and the merchant bills of lading. I know about the storm in 1605 and the loss of the ships of that year's fleet. As I explained in my letter to you, I know how much your ancestor lost. I know the ships and his lost wealth have never been recovered."

"Why do you want to search for *oro y plata*?" she said. "Gold and silver have given blood and trouble enough to the world."

"I collect things, " Robert replied, suddenly aware that this was not much of an explanation.

The ancient Scandinavians believed that a malevolent giant by the name of Aegir lived under the sea, married to a lascivious and greedy wife named Ran. To satisfy her lusts, Ran stirred up the sea with tempests, capsized the Scandinavian ships, and caught the drowning sailors in her nets as they disappeared beneath the waves. If the sailors gave her a tribute of gold, she rewarded them with an eternal place at her undersea banquet table and in her watery bed.

Ran, however, was only one of many potential lovers for a drowning sailor. Seductive and treacherous "women of the sea" occur in the myths of maritime cultures around the world. In the ancient Mediterranean, the Sirens, beautiful but deadly nymphs, used their sweet, hypnotic songs to lure sailors toward the rocks where their ships would founder. For the Irish and Scottish, the White Ladies made their home beneath the waves, and the Slavs believed the sea hid the beautiful drowned girls known as Rousalki. The Eskimos tell the story of the luscious but handless Nerrivik—whose name translates literally as "Food Dish"—who lives at the bottom of the sea and whose long hair must be combed by shamans to release the bountiful fish and sea creatures that are tangled in her locks.

These female myths represent the two faces of the sea—calm and alluring, tempestuous and deadly—with which sailors have lived and died for centuries. Deep beneath the waves the sea does not show its tempestuous side. It offers instead a peacefulness and aquamarine beauty and silent mystery that are just as seductive as the sparkling blue surface and perhaps even more deadly. Divers, like ancient and modern sailors, have many terms, medical and other-

wise, to describe the physiological consequences of this undersea se-
ductiveness. Perhaps the most apt was coined by the pioneering—
and poetic—French divers describing what happens to those breathing
compressed air who descend too far into the serene depths: "rapture
of the deep."

The human body is surprisingly adaptable to the depths, at
least on the way down. All humans, in different ways, thrive on pressure. Not just pressure from work or money or romance, but actual
pounds-per-square-inch pressure. As a species, humans have adapted,
more or less, to live contentedly with 14.7 pounds per square inch,
the air pressure at sea level. The 14.7 pounds—the equivalent of an
average frozen turkey perched on every square inch of one's body—
represents the weight of a very tall 1-inch-by-1-inch column of air
that extends from sea level many miles up to the farthest edge of the
earth's atmosphere. This pressure pushes on us equally from outside
as well as from inside—inside our lungs, our throats, and elsewhere—
and is the key reason why we don't notice the groaning weight of all
those frozen turkeys piled on top and pressing around us.

Water, however, weighs vastly more than air. A 1-inch-by-
1-inch column of seawater would only need to be 33 feet tall to weigh
the same amount—14.7 pounds—as that miles-tall column of air.
This difference in weight has profound consequences for humans
who leave the relative comfort of sea level and dive under the sea. If
a person sitting in a boat were to jump over the gunnel and swim
down to a depth of 33 feet, the pressure on his or her body would
double from the standard 14.7 pounds at the surface to 29.4 pounds
per square inch, or two frozen turkeys. This is known as two atmospheres of pressure. At 66 feet in depth, the pressure would triple to
three atmospheres, or 44.1 pounds per square inch (psi); at 99 feet, it
would quadruple to four atmospheres or 58.8 psi; and at 132 feet,
about the recommended limit for recreational divers using scuba
gear, the pressure would be five atmospheres or 73.5 psi. At this
depth the average-sized human male experiences a total of about
100 tons or 13,400 frozen turkeys pressing over his body surface.

Along with the obvious need to breathe, divers for thousands of years have struggled with these tremendous pressures of the deep. Greek sponge divers of Aristotle's time knotted ropes around their waists, packed their ear canals with oil-soaked sponges to help equalize the pressure stabbing at their eardrums, took a curved knife in one hand and a heavy stone in the other, and plummeted to the bottom, relying on their compatriots above to pull them—sometimes dead—to the surface after they'd gathered the harvest. The ancient Arab pearl divers pierced their eardrums to relieve the pressure of the depths. Today's breath-holding pearl divers of the Tuamotu Archipelago, northeast of Tahiti, dive to over 100 feet many times a day; as a result, they frequently suffer from the sickness they call *taravana*—"fall crazily"—whose symptoms include dizziness and nausea and, in severe cases, paralysis and death.

The perfection of the diving suit in the mid-nineteenth century, while allowing divers to go deeper and stay down longer than those who simply held their breath, only aggravated these pressure-related maladies. In the perfected design, compressed air was pumped from the surface down through a hose to the hard-helmeted diver. (Common sense says a diver only needs to poke a tube up to the surface and suck ordinary air through it, but the water pressure on the diver's chest makes it impossible to inhale using this method in water any deeper than snorkeling depth—about 1 to 2 feet.) Those Aegean Sea sponge divers abandoned the methods Aristotle had described and in 1867 adopted this new diving suit, trying to maximize their profits by staying at the bottom for long periods of time, then ascending quickly. Of twenty-four divers using the new suits, ten of them died.

As the Industrial Age surged forward, other inventions allowed workers to breathe deep beneath the surface. French engineers devised a new method to build bridge pilings by placing large metal cylinders on the river bottoms, pumping these "caissons" full of compressed air, and placing workers inside to construct the bridge footings. Strange new maladies, however, began to appear. During construction of the Brooklyn Bridge in the late nineteenth century, workers emerging from the caissons walked about bent stiffly forward at the hips due to the sudden onset of joint pain. Their fellow workers thought the gait resembled the fashionable "Grecian bend" of the tightly corseted New York society women. The name "the bends" stuck. During World War II, French gas engineer Emile Gagnan and a soon-to-be-famous diver named Jacques-Yves Cousteau invented the self-contained underwater breathing apparatus, or scuba—a system that allowed divers to dispense with the cumbersome suit and hose and carry their air supply in tanks on their backs. The genius of the Gagnan-Cousteau equipment was a small disklike device on the mouthpiece called a demand regulator that, using a diaphragm to sense the water pressure, fed compressed air from the tanks to the diver at the exact same pressure as the water pushing on his lungs from outside. With the pressure exactly equalized inside and outside the chest walls, breathing far beneath the surface was effortless. But divers using the gear, it turned out, were subject to the same "bends" that caisson workers suffered. And there were still other maladies that divers came to know as "the chokes," "the itches," "the staggers," "the narcs," "the niggles," and "the creeps," having to do, variously, with uncontrollable coughing upon surfacing, itching of the skin, dizziness and nausea, and odd but fleeting aches.

Starting with autopsies on Greek sponge divers, researchers continued to try to understand what great pressure does to the human body, especially divers breathing compressed air. They discovered that the pressures of the depths drive nitrogen contained in the compressed air into the diver's blood and tissues. A breath of air is, after all, four-fifths nitrogen and only one-fifth oxygen. At depths over 100 feet, the nitrogen absorbed by brain tissues can anesthetize the diver like laughing gas. This is the French "rapture of the deep"—also known as nitrogen narcosis or "the narcs." If the diver ascends slowly from these depths, the nitrogen seeps out of the blood and tissues on the way to the surface and is harmlessly expelled by the lungs. A too-rapid ascent, however, causes the pressurized nitrogen to fizz inside the tissues and blood like the gas bubbles in a just-opened soda bottle. These bubbles cause the bends. Its most common symptom consists of pain in the knees, shoulders, and elbows—"limb bends" or "joint bends." But the bubbles or related symptoms can also occur in many other places such as the skin, and, much more seriously, in the spinal cord and brain. When this occurs, the bends can result in paralysis or death.

At the turn of the century the eminent British physiologist J. S. Haldane, who worked with bends-afflicted divers and depressurized goats, concluded that the human body generally can tolerate a two-to-one reduction in pressure without suffering the symptoms of decompression illness. This would allow a diver to ascend from two atmospheres to one (33 feet to the surface) or from four atmospheres to two atmospheres (99 feet to 33 feet) without fear of the bends. But, at least according to Haldane's original model, ascending above the depths specified by this ratio without pausing to "decompress" would place the diver in danger. Based on this work, Haldane developed a set of schedules—much refined by later generations of divers—that they could use to plan their dives and avoid the bends.

If the diver does suffer from a case of the bends, he or she must be recompressed—recapping the soda pop bottle, so to speak—by returning below the surface and resuming the ascent in stages to let the nitrogen reabsorb in the tissues and then slowly seep out. This treatment is a long and difficult process to accomplish underwater. A better alternative is to place the diver in a recompression chamber and pump it full of compressed air to mimic the high water pressures undersea. This act accomplishes the same thing—allowing the nitrogen to seep out by slowly decreasing the pressure. One problem with this treatment, however, is that recompression chambers are often located far from the remote reefs and islands that divers seek out, and that flying in an airplane to reach a chamber can create more bubbles in the stricken diver's body as the plane ascends and cabin air pressure drops. The evacuation plane must fly low—below 1,000 feet.

The bends, however, is not the most fatal of the pressure-related maladies grouped under the term *dysbarism.* Drowning still remains the leading cause of death among divers. The second most common death is a form of dysbarism that occurs when, due to panic or haste, the diver doesn't breathe out regularly as he or she swims to the surface. The compressed air in the lungs expands with the lessening of the water pressure like an inflating balloon. If the diver keeps holding his or her breath, the lung tissues will rupture. Through the ruptured lung tissues, the air in the lungs then enters directly into the bloodstream, and coarse bubbles foam through the heart and into the brain. The result is cataclysmic.

To dysbarism researchers and doctors, this syndrome goes by the acronyms POPS and AGE—pulmonary overpressurization syndrome accompanied by arterial gas embolism. Divers, however, partial to their own nomenclature, know it by a term that much more graphically illustrates its pathology: "burst lung."

"Nothing down there for you to see, mon. All the pretty fish are over there."

The small wooden boat rocked on the blue swells just off the Caribbean reef, its outboard motor idling with a rhythmic gurgling sound. Robert was pointing out to the fisherman, Felix, the exact spot he wanted to dive, a deep channel that cut through the reef's paler greenish waters like a deep, thick vein of the sea's dark-blue blood. Felix, however, was gesturing in the other direction, half a mile distant, to the better place where the pretty reef fish lived. Ignoring him, Robert again consulted his chart and then the digital readout on his handheld GPS—the global positioning device that read satellite signals to give his exact position on the face of the globe. He jabbed his finger to where the deep blue channel cut through the foaming white crest of the reef.

"Right there."

"Nothing but sand down there."

"That's the place."

"Why do you want to go to that place?"

"Because that's where I want to go," Robert insisted. "Because I'm paying you to go there."

"Okay, mon. I'll take you there if you want to go, but I tell you for certain you see only naked sand down there in the deep water."

Two days earlier, Robert had claimed a window seat on the wide-bodied jet flying over the Atlantic Ocean between Madrid and Mexico City. He'd left back in Cádiz the old woman in the straight-backed chair and her granddaughter with the beautiful dark eyes and quiet manner. Robert remained motionless with his forehead pressed against the cold, clear plastic and felt the high hum of the engines in his skull while each of his slow, steady exhales lightly fogged a patch of window near his mouth. From 33,000 feet up, the Atlantic appeared so deep a shade of blue, it looked almost black. Focusing hard with his tired eyes, Robert could just make out the tiny corrugations of the swells and the chalky white flecks where the biggest swells had crested and tumbled into long streaks of foam. It must be rough as hell down there, Robert thought. He wondered how long it would be before he was bobbing among those same swells, or rather, diving under them. His ears suddenly popped with the decreased cabin pressure, finally clearing.

Robert had always been a collector of things. As a boy, he dug through small dark spaces—closets, basements, into the earth itself—seeking marbles or pennies, beetles or worms, old bottles or square nails. He assembled his treasures into collections, neatly gluing or pinning the objects to pieces of labeled cardboard, then carefully locking them away in a special plywood box in his bedroom. The collections were his secret world, and Robert protected them fiercely, guarding the relics he so eagerly sought out.

Staring out the window at the midnight blue Atlantic 6 miles below, wondering what might lie under its opaque surface, it occurred to Robert that all humans were genetically wired for the hunt, the perpetual search for bigger game to kill or fatter roots to dig or sweeter fruit to pick, but that some had chosen—by chance or by personality or by necessity—to refine and develop that innate skill to its fullest potential. Robert realized that he would soon put that highly developed skill of his to its most difficult test ever.

Now, two days later, Robert was eager for the dive to begin. Felix reached back, flipped the outboard's gear lever into forward, and twisted the throttle. The heavy wooden boat heaved over the swells toward the broad, deep blue stripe of the channel. Just short of it, still over the reef's submerged shelf in about 40 feet of aquamarine water, Felix cut the engine and flung the anchor overboard.

"Now you go," Felix said. "Over the side and swim to the deep spot." In silence but for the sloshing of the swells up the sides of the boat's hull and the clanking of his air tanks, Robert began to prepare his equipment. He'd hired Felix in a fishing village on a small island off the coast, surprised at the fisherman's willingness to take him out on the water as soon as he wanted.

"Wherever you want to go," he'd told Robert, "I'll take you there."

Felix now watched Robert's careful preparations. Robert knew how to dive from his days as a collector, combing lake bottoms to hunt for old bottles that had been discarded there decades before. Robert strapped his air tanks to his BC, or buoyancy control—a vestlike device into which the diver could inject or release air to maintain neutral buoyancy while underwater. Robert spun his tank valve full open, then closed the knob back a quarter turn. The air pressure gauge jumped to 3,000 pounds per square inch, indicating the air pressure inside the tanks. Each of the two tanks contained 80 cubic feet of air squeezed to a fraction of that volume, which would sustain him beneath the surface. He punched in the diaphragm of the regulator mounted to the mouthpiece and checked the loud hiss of escaping air. He then released it, inserted the mouthpiece, and inhaled—once, twice, three times. The air flowed easily into his lungs. He examined his spare regulator, or "octopus," attached to its own hose should his main regulator fail. He consulted the all-important dive-planning tables. At a depth of 90 feet—as deep as the bottom of the channel, according to the charts—he could spend a maximum of twenty-one minutes. Any deeper or any longer and he would have to make stops on the ascent, spending several minutes at various depths while the nitrogen slowly seeped out of his tissues.

Though Robert now dove less than he once did, he intimately knew the safety checks. He meticulously followed all of them except one: *Never dive alone.*

"Okay, are you ready, mon?" Felix asked once Robert had slipped into the shoulder straps of the tanks, fastened its belts, and pulled on gloves, fins, and face mask. Propping himself on the gunnel of the dory, Robert fitted in the mouthpiece and sucked on the regulator, one hand holding his mask tightly against his face. He nodded to Felix.

"Okay, one, two, three, over you go."

With a little nudge from Felix, Robert tumbled backward off the gunnel into the swells in a gentle splash.

5 feet (1.2 atmospheres of pressure or 17.6 psi): A swirl of bubbles swept across his mask, and warm tropical water trickled into his ears and wetsuit. The vigorous rocking of the boat softened to the gentle up-and-down motion of the sea just beneath the swells, comforting and familiar, as if the gentle watery lifting and sinking awakened some primordial memory of the womb. The harsh sound of wind and waves suddenly ceased, replaced by the underwater clicking and scraping of unseen fish along the reef.

Robert righted himself from his tumble. He hovered for a few moments, belly down, to orient himself. In his left hand he held a small instrument console connected by a slim hose to his tanks. One dial was his air pressure gauge, another his depth gauge, and a third his compass. He took a compass bearing to the northwest, flipped his fins, and slanted down toward the bottom.

Robert knew exactly the direction he wanted to go, thanks to the old woman and her granddaughter back in Cádiz.

"Look at this room," the old woman said as she waved a thin arm at the ivory-inlaid *vargueño* cabinet, the thick walnut table with the wrought-iron stays, the high-backed armchairs in which they sat, the wooden chests with the star-shaped patterns, even the heavy beams of the ceiling that Robert knew had been hewn from Cuba's forests and shipped to Cádiz centuries before. "What am I to do with all these old things now?"

"They are very beautiful," Robert said politely.

"They belonged to my family for generations," she said, "back to those who lost their precious belongings when the ships went down in the year 1605."

From the bills of lading preserved so carefully in the Sevilla archives, Robert knew exactly what her ancestor's cargo had included: gold rods in various sizes and weights that merchants such as he had ordered smelted to ship home their wealth; an emerald-studded gold crucifix, gold rosaries, and other items of jewelry fashioned by the skilled New World gold- and silversmiths; plus hundreds of in- gots of silver that had been laid like brick ballast in the bottom of the hull.

"The loss was a very difficult one for our *negocios*—our busi- ness," the old woman went on. "So I was told as a small girl by my mother and grandmother. But you can see"—here she gestured again at the room, at herself—"my family survived the loss."

Robert noticed that between the fingers of her left hand she worked a rosary. It made a tiny clicking sound as its alternating beads of polished red coral bumped its well-worn beads of gold. She now appeared lost in thought, staring out the window. Beyond the wrought-iron balcony and over the rooftops across the street rose the dome of Cádiz's cathedral. It looked like a great yellow ceramic bowl—almost a dome that belonged on a Moorish mosque. Robert knew that the cathedral occupied the same site as the mosque from the Moorish occupation that had begun in A.D. 711 and that the mosque had sat atop the site of Cádiz's original Roman temple. This probably had been built over its three-thousand-year-old Phoenician temple, where the ancient traders had no doubt practiced their ritual sacrifices of animals and human infants to the god of storms, Baal, to the fertility goddess, Ishtar, and to others. Since Robert had arrived, archaeologists working in the bishop's patio had unearthed a gold ring embossed with a swimming dolphin—a fertility symbol—that dated from Phoenician times. The old woman stared silently at the dome, clicking her beads through her wrinkled fingers. It was as if that particular spot were the repository for the ancient gods as well as for her family memories.

Robert leaned slightly forward in his chair toward her. He wanted to appear interested but not too eager. As he leaned, his shirt hung loosely in front and he felt a runnel of sweat trickle over his belly.

"Did your ancestors know where the ship went down?" he asked carefully.

"There are many letters describing the disaster," she replied. "Descriptions of reefs near where the ship sunk. But as I have told you, it is down too deep."

Robert leaned farther forward in the Moorish chair.

"Do you know what happened to the letters?" he asked. "Do they still survive?"

"*Claro,*" she said, with another click of the rosary beads.

"Where are they?"

"I have them here," she said, picking up a small brass bell that sat on an end table beside her chair and shaking it, the tingling sound echoing out in the old house's marble atrium. "They are under my bed. My granddaughter will show you."

Robert then leaned forward in his chair so far that it swayed on the verge of collapse.

As he descended, Robert paused every few feet to check his instruments and clear his ears. He did this by thrusting his jaw forward and by swallowing, opening the 1.5-inch long eustachian tubes that served as air passages from his throat to the air-filled chamber of his middle ear. If the tubes, inflamed or blocked by a cold, remained closed, the increasing water pressure on the outside of his ears as he dove deeper would collapse the tympanic membrane—his eardrum—inward, finally rupturing it. But by opening his eustachian tubes, Robert allowed the compressed air in his throat to fill the middle-ear chamber at a pressure equal to that of the outside water, thus keeping the eardrum intact. Middle-ear barotrauma is diving's most common medical problem, but even in its most serious form—a rupture—the damage usually heals in a week or two.

33 feet (2 atmospheres or 29.4 psi): A few feet below him, Robert spotted Felix's anchor lying amid patches of coral and sand. A large grouper drifted off to his right, where the reef sloped gently toward the deeper sea. The pressure on his body had now doubled since leaving Felix's boat. A balloon full of air—12 liters, for example—blown up in Felix's boat and brought to this depth would have now been compressed to half its size, or 6 liters, according to Boyle's law of gases. Likewise, each breath of air Robert's regulator fed him from his tanks was twice as compressed as a breath of air at the surface, meaning, all things being equal, that his air supply would last only half as long at this depth, and would last even less than that the deeper he dove.

Leaving the anchor, Robert followed his compass bearing of 340 degrees northwest across the reef's shelf toward the deeper blue cut of the channel. The swimming was easy. He stayed focused straight ahead. After a few minutes, the coral suddenly plunged steeply down-ward in an underwater wall.

55 feet (2.7 atmospheres or 39.7 psi): He paused at the dropoff, just able to make out the bluish, sandy floor of the channel far below. Brightly colored fish flitted past—black-and-white spotted drums, damselfish, indigo hamlets. Robert ignored them; he was focused on a far bigger catch. He checked his pressure gauge: There were 2,750 pounds per square inch of air remaining in his tanks. He checked his watch: seven minutes had elapsed since he left the surface. He felt good. His breathing came easily, although quickly. He felt a warm flush of excitement even under his wet suit. He loved the dramatic arc of the hunt: the first clues triggering that sense of excitement, followed by the patient reconnaissance of the terrain, then the anx-ious fever of closing in and finally the euphoria of discovery. As he angled down the reef's wall, his pulsing fins propelling him deeper, he was no longer a paunchy, lonely, middle-aged schoolteacher but a sleek, black-clad undersea creature. He was a shark that used his in-tellect instead of his sense of smell and movement to locate his prey.

72 feet (3.2 atmospheres or 47 psi): The reef's wall resembled a tropical flower garden tilted to the vertical and submerged beneath the sea. Robert swam down past the boulder coral, wire coral, black coral, and yellow tube sponges reaching out like fingers to strain tiny creatures from the seawater. His body now was experiencing a pres-sure of nearly 50 pounds per square inch. But he noticed physiologi-cal changes more subtle than profound: a pressing on his sinuses, the need to keep opening his eustachian tubes, and a slightly greater ef-fort to breathe as the air he inhaled became more dense. According to Pascal's law, pressure applied to one part of a liquid is distributed evenly throughout that liquid. Robert, like all humans, was made up mostly of water; he felt no extra pressure on particular tissues be-cause each cell in his body was pressed equally from all sides.

80 feet (3.4 atmospheres or 50 psi): Robert glanced again at his depth gauge, then down the reef wall to the bottom. He'd nearly reached the planned limit of his dive—90 feet—but the bottom, still

lying well below him, was farther than he'd thought. "Plan your dive," was one of the diver's mantras, "and dive your plan." He knew he should dive no deeper. But he was so close. He could feel the presence of the wrecked ship. He could sense the precious metals—the gold rods stamped with their purity, the silver ingots bound for the merchants and the royal treasury, the golden chains and scepters and emerald crucifixes. He knew he was in the right place. He couldn't bear the thought of leaving that collection, of wasting the dive, wasting the air in his tanks, wasting the time at the surface to let the nitrogen seep out of his system. Not when he was this close. No, this was his chance.

He'd stick to his plan, but he'd modify it slightly: he'd descend to 90 feet, maybe a bit farther, and swim along at that depth and try to scan the bottom.

99 feet (4 atmospheres or 59 psi): He now could see the bottom clearly, although he was still well above it. Flat and sandy, it was bathed in deep bluish hues—only the blues and greens of the light spectrum penetrated this deeply into the sea—and it was littered with broken pieces of coral. Hovering above it, he calculated his strategy: He'd remain at 99 feet only 15 minutes instead of the twenty-one minutes that, according to the dive-planning tables, he was allowed at 90 feet, and he'd make a brief "safety stop" on the way up. At this depth—four atmospheres—the pressure would squeeze a balloon to only one-fourth the volume it had been on the surface; his air supply would last only one-quarter the length of time. He'd have to watch closely the gauge that measured the air remaining in his tanks.

110 feet (4.3 atmospheres or 63.2 psi): Robert continued swimming on his 340-degree heading, rocking his head from side to side to scan the bottom, angling slightly deeper as if working along a line of tension between the upward pull of his dive plan and the downward pull of the wreck. He'd now dived so deep that a third law of the depths besides Boyle's law and Pascal's law came into play. Some divers call it Martini's law: Every additional 50 feet a diver descends

from the surface is the rough equivalent of consuming one martini on an empty stomach.

Nitrogen is one of several inert gases that dissolve easily in the body's fatty substances but become potent narcotics under high pressures, possibly by interfering with the signals jumping across the brain's nerve junctions. Divers who go too deep breathing compressed air risk the hallucinations, fantasies, and euphoria of nitrogen narcosis or "rapture of the deep." This state is famously illustrated by the apocryphal diver who offered his mouthpiece to a passing fish, or, in a confirmed case, the French diver who at 160 feet patted his nonexistent pockets looking for his cigarettes. The first subtle signs of nitrogen narcosis, depending on the individual, begin at about 100 feet. By 180 feet, experts agree that "no trust should be placed in human performance." By 300 feet, a special mixture of helium, oxygen, hydrogen, and nitrogen must be used to prevent nitrogen narcosis, as divers inhaling simple compressed air can black out and, of course, drown.

115 feet (4.5 atmospheres or 66.2 psi): Robert felt like laughing, joyous over this wild pursuit of his, this search for the lost wealth of the Indies. Like a childhood fantasy it seemed, this treasure hoard so nearby. How clever he'd been to track down the old merchant family in Spain! And once he'd finally found the old woman, it had been so easy! And her granddaughter was so beautiful!

The granddaughter had led Robert out of the sitting room and along the balcony circling the atrium. The heels of her slim, knee-high suede boots echoed on the black and white marble squares. Her black silk skirt fell in pleats nearly to the tops of the boots, but fitted snugly around her graceful hips, which flicked ever so slightly as she moved, as if keeping rhythm with the sway of her silver pendant earrings. Robert could feel his breathing grow shallow with anticipation. The granddaughter led him into a large bedchamber, a room filled with still more antique furniture. The late-afternoon sunlight was falling through gauzy aquamarine curtains that hung in windows set in thick white walls, the light bathing the room in watery, shifting hues of blue. A tall four-poster bed was draped with a thick quilt of midnight blue.

She leaned down, pulled a small wooden trunk from beneath the bed, opened it, and extracted a packet wrapped in old, stiff paper and bound with a faded pink ribbon. She stood before him, holding the old packet in both her hands, as if unsure what to do next.

"I'd like to make a proposal to you," he said, filling in the awkward silence. "If you and your grandmother share these letters with me, I will share with the two of you whatever I find."

As he spoke, she stood with her brown eyes cast aside in shyness. When he had finished, she looked out the window and over the rooftops at the yellow-tiled dome of the cathedral that sheltered the figure of Christ and all the gods of the earth and the sky, and especially of the sea, that had come before Him in this ancient port at the gates to the Mediterranean.

She looked from the window back to Robert. He could feel the sweat forming on his hands again. He subtly wiped them on the thighs of his corduroy pants.

"My grandmother is an old woman and cares little for treasure," she said, finally fixing him with her deep brown eyes. "She will tell you to give her share of it there, to *la catedral*." She gestured toward the dome out the window. "So if you find it, you may do with the treasure what you wish. But if you do find it, I ask that you set aside a small share for me without telling my grandmother. Use that share to take me away from here."

With that she stepped toward him and, peering into his eyes, lifted up the package with both her hands, as if making an offering to him.

Robert surveyed the bottom, kicking along, holding his instrument console in his left hand, keeping closely to 340 degrees. It couldn't be far now, he thought. And then he saw it. A spiky rod protruding from the sandy bottom. It lay below him by 15 or 20 feet. He glanced at his air pressure gauge—still 1,700 pounds left in his tanks—and without another instant's hesitation he put his head down, fins up, and dove for it. He was the predator coming to the glorious climax of the hunt, powerfully pumping through the water and closing in on his prey.

135 feet (5.1 atmospheres or 75 psi): He tried to shake it. It was wedged solidly in the sandy bottom. It felt like iron, he thought, encrusted with coral and tiny shells. Maybe the anchor shaft. Yes, it had to be the anchor shaft. Only the metal would remain. The ship's wooden parts couldn't survive four centuries of tiny marine animals feasting on them, unless buried in the sand. He looked around in the drab light. The objects looked clear and sharp, but their colors were washed out into bluish grays like an old black-and-white film shown late at night on a bad television set. About 50 feet away he spotted a low, sandy mound from which long tubes protruded like giant porcupine spikes. They were too uniform in shape for sponges. He swam quickly to the tubes. A fine sediment covered them. He brushed one with his neoprene glove. Small puffs of sediment floated up. He saw the dull glint of metal. Bronze. A cannon. An old Spanish cannon! He was in the right place! He looked past the mound. A deeper shelf dropped down another 30 feet or so. On it, below him, he spotted another mound. More wreckage!

165 feet (6 atmospheres or 88.2 psi): He kicked down along the incline. The pile was lumpy, sand-covered, unnatural-looking. His gloved hand penetrated easily into the sediment. Wriggling and work-

ing his fingers deeper, nearly to his elbow, he felt something solid. He moved his fingers over the object. It was heavy and rectangular, about the size of a brick. A silver ingot! He tugged at it. The accretions of sand and marine life had cemented it to the surrounding objects. It didn't move. He felt about. More rectangular shapes. More ingots! He tugged harder. Still he couldn't budge it. He extracted his hand and began brushing the layers of sand from the pile, sending up clouds of silt, along with great bursts of bubbles from his labored, excited breathing.

Digging away with gloved hands toward the silver ingots, Robert thought of the Mayans and Aztecs and Incas whose sweat, blood, gods were distilled here, in this mound of precious metal. Empires rose and fell, and gold followed the shift in power, or was it the power that followed the gold? Inevitably the two finally moved on— from the Andes and the Yucatán to Spain, then to northern Europe, then eventually to North America. This pile had been diverted from the flow of power for four centuries, and now he'd claimed it. He would ride it into that great historic flow of empire. His hunter's instincts had led him here, and now the treasure would change his life. He wouldn't make the selfish mistakes that others had made over it. He'd do good things with it. He'd share it, starting with the beautiful granddaughter, who had asked him to take her away.

He'd now excavated a 2-foot-wide hole in the sand that covered the pile. He let the sediment settle for a moment. As the water cleared, he could see the black rectangles piled atop each other— surely covered with the black tarnish of the silver.

He reached in to give another hard tug at one of the ingots, sucking in a big breath of air and bracing himself for the effort. But the breath only half filled his lungs. Suddenly there was no more air coming through his mouthpiece.

He released his grip on the ingot and grabbed the instrument console dangling at the end of its slender hose. At this depth he'd been using up air six times faster than at surface pressures. The needle was pegged all the way to zero, having crossed through the red warning zone that started just under 1,000 pounds per square inch of air in his tanks. It was very clear. There was no air left in the cylinders.

Looking up, he saw the last of his exhaled bubbles jiggling up toward the silvery surface far above. There were now sixteen stories of water above Robert. He was hovering at the very bottom of the channel, beside the collection of treasure.

It was the custom in Cádiz to kiss acquaintances of the opposite sex—even near-strangers—on both cheeks in departure. After she had given him the packet of old letters in the bedchamber, the grand-daughter had reached up and kissed him on both cheeks. Then, in a grip that was surprisingly strong, she had pulled him toward her and pressed his bulky body against her slenderness.

"Buena suerte," she had whispered into his ear.

Now, with the panic hitting his chest moments after the lack of air, he realized that he was trapped in the embrace of the young woman.

165 feet (6 atmospheres), 2 liters of air in his lungs: Fingers of his gloves working madly over his chest, Robert unclipped the fasteners on his BC and wrestled his cumbersome tanks off his shoulders, as if fighting his way out of her arms, so the tanks' bulk wouldn't drastically slow him on the ascent. Lungs already straining for breath, he furiously kicked for the surface with a single, panic-infused thought: to get away from here, from her, and get up there.

132 feet (5 atmospheres): With the lessening water pressure, the air in his lungs expanded to 2.4 liters. Robert didn't notice. Fins flipping like some baitfish under a predator's pursuit, the tables of hunter and hunted having turned, he raced upward past the shower of tiny bubbles that danced toward the surface from his last breath. A diver's rule of thumb is not to ascend faster than those tiny bubbles, about 30 feet per minute, to allow the nitrogen to seep from the tissues. Worse, he violated another essential scuba-diving rule: to keep breathing regularly on the ascent. These abstract rules were

overridden by a single basic instinct: to hold on to his air until he reached the top.

99 feet (4 atmospheres): The air in his lungs expanded to 3 liters, slightly easing his need to breathe. It also gave him extra buoyancy for his ascent, as did the expanding air pores in his wet suit. He shot toward the surface.

Scuba divers in advanced training practice emergency ascents from 60 feet on a single breath, and submariners in training ascend inside dive towers—tall tubes filled with water, with recompression chambers near at hand—on a single breath. Ironically, the problem is not lack of air but too much air. A single breath of compressed air inhaled from a scuba tank at 60 feet will expand in the lungs with the lessening pressure to the equivalent of three breaths by the time the diver reaches the surface. The trick is to allow the expanding air to escape the lungs in a controlled manner while not exhaling the entire lungful at once, leaving nothing but seawater to breathe.

66 feet (3 atmospheres): The shimmering underside of the swells grew more distinct, their foaming crests visible as bubbly streaks that Robert had seen as chalky specks from the airplane at 33,000 feet. The surface suddenly looked possible for him to reach. The air in his lungs doubled from the original half breath to 4 liters, or nearly a full breath. But he had also kicked his way straight up through Haldane's ratio and the decompression stops he should have made to let the nitrogen exit his tissues. Instead, as he shot upward, he fizzed inside like a just-opened bottle of soda. Some bubbles formed in his joints, which, in a matter of minutes or hours after their formation, would cause the characteristic joint pain of the bends. Others formed in his skin—soon to cause the itching and rash known as the "skin bends." Other nitrogen bubbles forming in his tissues damaged his capillary walls, entered his veins, and grew in size as they were pumped through his circulatory system.

For reasons still unknown, the nitrogen bubbles also have an affinity for the white matter of the spine, which contains nerve fibers that carry messages between body and brain. The victim often feels a tingling or sense of constriction around the chest or abdomen upon surfacing. This is followed over the next thirty to ninety minutes by numbness, weakness, loss of bladder and bowel control, and sometimes pain in the back and chest. In severe cases of this neurologic decompression sickness, the victim sometimes loses consciousness and then awakens to discover that his or her legs are permanently paralyzed.

33 feet (2 atmospheres): The silver underside of the surface pulled Robert upward. The air in his lungs had expanded to 6 liters—as much as a very large breath—filling his lungs to maximum capacity. But this last 33 feet to the beckoning surface was in some ways the most dangerous underwater zone of all. Air doubles in volume as it expands from two atmospheres of pressure at 33 feet to one atmosphere at the surface. A diver holding his or her breath with full lungs needs only to ascend between 4 to 8 feet to damage them.

25 feet (1.8 atmospheres): There was no pain. If he hadn't been so panicked to reach the surface, Robert would have noticed the expanding fullness in his lungs. But he kept kicking hard, shooting up like an undersea missile with the buoyancy of the expanding air. In the last 25 feet to the surface, the air sacs in his lungs, called alveoli, ruptured without pain. By the time he reached the surface, the air in his lungs would have ballooned to 12 liters, double the size of his largest breath, if he could contain it. He couldn't. As he fought the last few feet to the top, a stream of bubbles forced its way up his air passages and out his mouth.

0 feet (sea level, 1 atmosphere): Robert broke the surface in a flurry of bubbles, his upper body shooting above the water before toppling back down like a surfacing whale. The wind and waves and bright tropical sunlight slapped suddenly against his face. It had been less than a minute since he left the bottom. He exhaled, gulped for air in a great gasp; as he did, he spotted Felix's boat about 300 feet away, rising and sinking on the swells. He managed to raise his arm to signal Felix to come pluck him out. Limp with exhaustion, Robert

slowly treaded water and tried to catch his breath. Inside his lungs, however, the broken capillaries of the ruptured alveoli were now exposed to the air he was sucking in with every fresh, eager breath. Besides the nitrogen bubbles already lodged in his tissues, air from his lungs entered the broken capillaries in small bubbles, pumped through the left side of his heart, then raced up toward his brain. The bubbles lodged in the tiny capillaries of his brain. They prevented the flow of blood, rich with oxygen borne in its hemoglobin, from delivering its vital load to his brain tissues. More and more air bubbles raced from his lungs toward his heart until it beat only on bloody foam. There was nothing but foam to pump up his aorta toward his brain. Within seconds of surfacing Robert lost consciousness.

By the time Felix sighted Robert, pulled the cord of the outboard motor, hauled up the anchor, and motored through the swells to the deep blue channel, Robert was no longer waving. He was facedown, rising and sinking with the motion of the swells, his wet suit keeping him afloat.

Felix, grunting and straining and with the help of the swells' lifting motion, managed to haul Robert's neoprene-clad bulk over the gunnel. Robert tumbled heavily into the boat's bilge like some great black fish.

Felix pulled off Robert's mask, peeled back his hood, and tugged down the zipper of the sleek black wet suit to expose his fleshy white chest, no longer moving. He scanned the surface for any gear that might have risen with Robert. Nothing. He checked again for vital signs. Nothing. The only thing of any interest that Felix knew of down in the deep cut of the reef was an old cargo barge that had struck the reef and sunk years earlier. Occasionally he or one of the other fishermen would inadvertently haul up a brick in one of the nets from its ballast scattered all across the bottom.

Felix then assessed the direction of the wind and swells, scanned the horizon for storm clouds, and checked the level of the gas tank, which sat in the bilge of the boat. The satchel of photocopied letters from the old woman and her beautiful granddaughter in Cádiz still lay in the bottom of the boat beside Robert's body. Felix flipped the gearshift into forward and swung the bow of the wooden boat south toward the island, running at half speed to avoid the pounding from the swells.

There was no reason to hurry.

CHAPTER TEN

IN LOVE'S

BLOOD:

CEREBRAL MALARIA

Their first night on the beach, Zach and Jason pitch their tent near some other travelers and walk beneath the coconut palms toward the only light. This is a little restaurant that an enterprising local family has set up to cater to the beach-loving foreigners. As they enter, dim orange bulbs under the thatched roof throb unsteadily to the beat of the local generator. A boom box puts out a steely, cascading music that sounds like a fusion of reggae and gamelan. Clumps of young Western travelers sit at benches around bamboo tables laden with bottles of Indonesian beer and plates of food, talking and laughing.

"Over there," says Zach quietly, gesturing with his chin toward an empty table.

Jason picks up the cue. Beside the empty table is one surrounded by three women, their hair sun- and salt-streaked, their skin tanned, their arms sinewy and muscular from stroking through the warm sea. After two weeks up in the highland jungle climbing volcanos, the closest thing approaching a social life that Jason and Zach have had has been a persistent band of monkeys hanging around their camp. Jason heads eagerly toward the table, thinking, *What luck!*

"Let's stay cool for a minute," whispers Zach as they sit down. They've been traveling through the tropics for nearly six months now, living on the cheap out of their backpacks in Fiji, Irian Jaya, and now an island off the coast of Sumatra. They'd heard about this spot all the way back in Fiji: a great beach, some good smoke, a small colony of Western surfers and snorkelers and backpackers looking for a laid-back time.

The teenage daughter of the proprietor comes around to their table and takes their order of beer and fried noodles. As she speaks her halting English, just behind her head, on a dried leaf of palm that's woven into the underside of the eaves, sits a small brown speck. Even if they were looking, Zach and Jason probably wouldn't notice it, and they certainly wouldn't know that it is a female anopheles mosquito—the carrier of the malaria parasite. Instead, they are working hard to appear casual in front of the three women. When the waitress returns with the beer, they each take a few quick slugs from their bottles, and Zach casually leans over to the closest woman.

"How's the snorkeling here?" he asks.

Fifteen days earlier, that small brown speck hatched from a pupa lying atop a rainwater puddle near the village temple. Letting her wings dry for a few hours in the daylight, she set out at dusk to find a mate. Near the village meeting hall she heard the irresistible buzzing wingbeats of a swarm of male anopheles. She and a male threw themselves at each other and copulated, he injecting his sperm into her followed by a secretion that seals her entrance to any other male's sperm. She now carried all the sperm she needed to fertilize her entire lifetime's egg production—a few weeks, a month, maybe more. Separating, the spent male anopheles flew off in search of a refreshing drink of fruit juices; the female, in contrast, took to the air to sniff out a meal of human or animal blood proteins to nourish her eggs.

"The snorkeling's great, mate," the woman at the next table is telling Zach. "Come on out on the reef tomorrow and see for yourself."

"I'll do that," says Zach. "I'll be there."

She's Australian, it's plain from her accent, and seems very friendly. Her blue sarong matches her lively blue eyes. Her feet are bare in the powdery sand. Zach gives a little knowing look to Jason that conveys, *This situation could be good for both of us, but let me handle it to start.* Jason gives a little nod of acknowledgment.

Zach leans closer. His skin has begun to flush with beer and tropical heat and restrained eagerness. "What's your name?"

"Chloe," she replies.

The two other women are talking about the embroidered Sumatran fabrics that they saw that morning in the market town a 6-mile motorcycle ride away.

"Have you been here a long time?" Zach asks Chloe.

"Not long enough," she says. "Two months. I came here from Perth with my boyfriend, but he's so particular about his little domestic comforts that he couldn't stand living on the beach and went home. I said to him, 'Rack off, then,' and decided to stay."

What an idiot! Jason is thinking about the boyfriend.

Abandoning their trysting spot at the village temple, the female mosquito flew off to a nearby family compound and found a teenage boy curled up on a sleeping platform. From the exposed skin behind his knee she sucked up a stomachful of his blood. His blood happened to be carrying *Plasmodium falciparum*, the tiny parasite that is responsible for the deadliest strain of malaria. Like many dwellers in endemic malaria zones, he had been exposed to it repeatedly since childhood and, though other village children died of it at an early age, he, like other survivors, developed a partial resistance to it known as "premunition." The malaria manifested itself in the boy in intermittent fevers, weight loss, and an enlarged liver and spleen. If this village were in sub-Saharan Africa instead of Asia, however, some of the village children would be protected from *P. falciparum* malaria by an abnormality in their blood hemoglobin, known as the sickle-cell trait.

As the village boy's blood was sucked up into the mosquito's proboscis and slid down into her stomach, his red blood cells burst open to release *P. falciparum* parasites in their sexual form. Inside the mosquito's tiny stomach, the male *P. falciparum* sperm, their whip-ping tails propelling them relentlessly forward, drove at the female eggs, connected, then merged. These fertilized *P. falciparum* eggs, in one of the infinitesimally tiny but profound engineering marvels of the malarial world, shaped themselves into little augurs and drilled their way out of the mosquito's stomach. There they attached themselves to the gut's outer wall and swelled up like water balloons filled with hundreds of tiny eel-like creatures called sporozoites. The cysts burst, and thousands of *P. falciparum* sporozoites flooded out, swimming directly for the mosquito's salivary glands.

This all took at least two weeks from the time the mosquito first ingested the parasite in the village boy's blood. During those two weeks, she'd laid a batch of her own eggs, replenished herself with human blood, and laid more. But these earlier bites to humans were not infectious; the *P. falciparum* parasites, in their various forms, were contained in her stomach or encased in cysts on her stomach's outer wall. But now, as Jason and Zach sit at the table beneath her perch in the palm-thatch roof, the *P. falciparum* sporozoites have burst forth from their cysts and are swarming through her salivary tubes.

"Do you mind if I join you?" Zach says to Chloe, sliding toward her along the bench, while sliding along the table his tall bottle of Bintang beer.

"Please do," she says to Zach, and then nods toward Jason. "And tell your friend he's welcome to join us, too."

As Zach slides onto Chloe's bench, his billowing exhalations of carbon dioxide and the waves of body heat from both their elevated skin temperatures rise toward the palm-thatch eaves. The glowing body heat and clouds of carbon dioxide catch the attention of the small brown speck perched on the dried palm leaf. Instinct tells the anopheles female that human blood is rising close to the skin surface somewhere nearby. She craves the blood to nourish yet another batch of her eggs.

She springs from her perch and flitters down toward the table, unobtrusive and unseen in the dim light. She circles above their heads, first the two women, who emit the least heat and carbon dioxide, then to Jason, who she senses is warmer, and to Chloe, warmer still, and finally to Zach, wrapped in a rich cloud of carbon dioxide and emitting intense infrared rays from an exposed V-shaped patch of skin on the side of his neck outlined by two stiff ropes of his Rasta braids. She lands lightly on her six legs—too lightly for him to notice. Zach is animatedly telling Chloe about his adventures climbing the volcano with Jason, and how an explosive hail of lava rock nearly struck them down at the summit. He makes an explosive gesture with his hands to show the dire danger they were in from the lava bombs, and just then the anopheles mosquito thrusts her tiny proboscis into his neck.

Malaria has something of a romantic reputation, at least here in the temperate regions of the globe. Eradicated in the United States nearly a century ago, it remains in many of our minds the disease of explorers and adventurers, Amazonian missionaries and African ivory merchants. How many Hollywood jungle dramas have we seen where the hero is lying by lamplight in a thatched hut, delirious with fever and face shiny with sweat while his faithful retainers look on anxiously? After all, it was a jungle fever—no doubt malaria—that finally felled that most magnificent specimen of these adventurers, the ivory-trader-gone-native Kurtz in Joseph Conrad's *Heart of Darkness*.

The Congo River setting for Kurtz's malarial demise couldn't have been more appropriate, because it is believed that the malaria parasite *Plasmodium* (the name refers to a genus that contains several species) first adapted to human hosts during the Neolithic period in this very region—the same exotic-disease hothouse that much more recently spawned the AIDS and Ebola viruses—as humans encroached on jungle lands for farming. From there, migrating peoples unwittingly carried the parasite to Europe, Asia, and the Americas, where the anopheles mosquito already lived. Malaria is thought to have arrived in the Americas, somehow, several centuries before Columbus. During periods of human history, malaria has been a great scourge, not unlike the Black Plague or the AIDS epidemic, and its outbreaks have altered the course of history. Malarial fever decimated the cream of the Athenian army in 413 B.C. when its soldiers camped in a swamp while attempting to lay siege to Syracuse, and Athens never fully recovered its power or prominence. Likewise, it was probably cerebral malaria that killed the otherwise indomitable Alexander the Great in 323 B.C. at age thirty-three in the city of Babylon on the Euphrates River, and with his death the enormous empire he had assembled through conquest all the way to India quickly came unraveled. The great Italian poet Dante Alighieri died of malaria, Holy Roman Emperor Charles V succumbed to it in Spain in 1558, and the American colonial settlers in Jamestown struggled against several different strains of malaria brought by English ships and African slaves.

For centuries, malaria's actual cause and means of transmission remained a mystery, but humans always associated it with damp, low places. Shakespeare, whose contemporaries knew the periodic malarial fevers as "agues," has his Caliban wish on Prospero "all the infections that the sun sucks up / From bogs, fens, flats . . ." Surrounded by swamps, it was the citizens of Rome who gave the disease its current name—*mal aria*, or "bad air." Up until the end of the nineteenth century it spread far beyond the tropics, summer epidemics sweeping up into temperate regions as far north as Holland, to the Russian city of Archangel, just below the Arctic Circle, and throughout the more moist regions of the United States and southern Canada.

In 1880, Alphonse Lavaran, a French army doctor living in Algeria, spotted through his microscope tiny parasites in the blood of his malaria patients. Seventeen years later, Ronald Ross, a surgeon-major in the Indian army, discovered that the parasite was transmitted by a very specific type of mosquito—the small, unobtrusive members of the genus *Anopheles*. Western doctors had known since the early seventeenth century of a treatment for malaria—quinine, derived from the bark of Peru's cinchona tree, a secret known by Inca herbalists who conveyed it to Jesuit missionaries. But with the discovery of the mosquito transmission of malaria—for which Ronald Ross won the Nobel prize in 1902—hopes soared that it might be eradicated from the face of the earth.

Swamps were drained, insecticides sprayed, villagers educated, and new drugs invented that mimicked, with greater potency, quinine's effects. This battle wiped out malaria in almost all of Europe, the United States, and other temperate regions. But the disease not only lingered on stubbornly in the tropics, but continued to thrive and at times explode as the stubborn mosquito and clever parasite developed resistance to new insecticides and drugs. In India, 100 million people suffered from malaria in 1952; ten years later, with the spraying of DDT on mosquito-breeding areas, this plummeted to 60,000, only to rebound into the millions soon after. Today, some 3 billion of the world's people—roughly half—live in malarial areas. The infection rate among children in some parts of Africa exceeds 50 percent, many of whom will die. The World Health Organization estimates that 300 million cases of malaria appear each year, and 1.1 million people die of it. In terms of mortality, malaria reigns as the world's third-leading infectious and parasitic disease behind tuberculosis (1.6 million deaths annually) and AIDS (2.7 million deaths).

To temperate-region dwellers, malaria may be a disease tinged with the romance of exotic jungles but to those who live in the tropics it is an everyday fact of life. Most strains of malaria cause a form of fever and illness no more dangerous, at least according to some authorities, than a case of influenza. But one strain of the disease is deadly among the native populations, especially in small children ages one to five who have not yet developed a tolerance to it, as well as in travelers from the temperate regions. This strain of the malaria parasite, called *Plasmodium falciparum*, can be treated easily in its early stages, though its symptoms are difficult to read and often mimic other diseases. If they are prudent and know of the danger, travelers can take preventive antimalarial drugs before entering the tropics. Left untreated, it can develop into severe or cerebral malaria, however, and it fully merits the mysterious last utterance of Conrad's Kurtz. Instead of referring to the fallen state of his soul or the unmitigated rapacity of European civilization in the Congo, his words "The horror! The horror!" could just as easily have been describing the rampages of *Plasmodium falciparum* throughout his bloodstream and brain.

As Zach talks animatedly to Chloe in the palm-thatch restaurant, special cutting tools on the proboscis that are designed for human skin slice down through Zach's epidermis, into his underlying dermis layer and the thin layer of subcutaneous fat beneath. Here, a network of tiny capillaries branch out like the limbs of a tree toward the skin surface. They have dilated with Zach's flushing and are pumped full by the excited beat of his heart. The proboscis penetrates a capillary and strikes Zach's blood. The mosquito contracts her glands to squirt saliva into his blood to prevent it from coagulating as she sucks it into her gut. With her saliva, scores of the tiny *P. falciparum* sporozoites swim into Zach's blood vessels.

"We thought we were dead." Zach is telling Chloe about their volcano-climbing adventure. "Lava bombs dropping everywhere—*whump, whump, whump!*"

He makes splattering gestures with his hands on the table. Chloe laughs appreciatively.

"We ran for our lives," he says. "We started at ten thousand feet on the summit and we didn't stop running until we were down to five."

The women laugh at the image of Zach and Jason sprinting downhill through the jungle-covered mountain flanks with lava bombs chasing them. Had they stayed up near the summit, however, and taken their chances with the lava bombs, there would be no sporozoites now swimming in Zach's blood vessels. Malaria's delicate and complicated transmission cycle requires a steady, warm temperature averaging at least 60 degrees for a solid month to keep the mosquito alive long enough for the parasite to grow fully within her. Even on the equator, malaria can't be transmitted above 10,000 feet because it's too cold there.

Zach hardly feels the bite. He unconsciously scratches at the side of his neck between his Rasta braids. By then, the anopheles mosquito, heavily laden with his blood in her gut, has hefted into the air and returned to her perch on the underside of the thatched eaves.

"Hey, I have an idea," says Zach. He's feeling itchy and hot in the tropical night. "Let's all go for a swim in the lagoon."

"Let's do!" says Chloe. "The phosphorescence is phenomenal!"

The others assent, and they pay their bill and spill forth from the thatched restaurant into the warm, buzzing night, leaving the female anopheles slowly and contentedly digesting Zach's proteins under the eaves. Here she will remain for three days, shaded from the sun and close to her feasting site, as she digests Zach's blood proteins and her eggs grow. Then she will fly off to lay them on a nearby pool of fresh water to complete her reproductive cycle.

The swimmers strip off their clothes in the dark and pile them on the sand. Zach is thinking that this night he might have the chance to complete a reproductive act of his own. They plunge into the sandy lagoon in shallow dives, watching each other underwater as the phosphorescence streaking off their bubbling bodies leaves glowing streaks like comets. Fish scatter, leaving their own quick flicks of phosphorescence as swirling fins agitate the light-emitting microorganisms.

As they frolic in the dark lagoon, diving under each other, over each other, between each other's legs—just another clump of sexually charged organisms in the wide, fecund, life pool of the tropical sea—the *P. falciparum* parasites are doing the same in Zach's blood, with even greater single-mindedness and without the immediate need for a partner. They'll carry their traveling party to various destinations in Zach's body over the next nine days. The first hot spot to which they head is his liver, which they need to reach immediately or they perish, and they spend some time there to let the party gather steam. Upon arrival, each sporozoite drills its way into one of Zach's liver cells. Cloaked within the cell walls, the sporozoite changes form and undergoes an orgy of reproduction, dividing again and again—the party suddenly gone mad—until finally the liver cells burst open. Each ruptured cell releases 10,000 to 30,000 tiny swarming creatures with the frightening name of invasive merozoites.

The hordes of merozoites now spill out of Zach's liver into his bloodstream. They are marching to a mission: to colonize as many of Zach's red blood cells as possible so that if some hungry female anopheles mosquito should again land on him for a blood meal, she'll be sure to suck up enough of Zach's parasitized blood cells to kick off *P. falciparum*'s reproduction cycle in her stomach and spread it to another human. This is how *P. falciparum* keeps itself alive as a species, although sometimes in its zealousness to survive it kills the human host that feeds it.

Once they've escaped from his liver and are afloat in his blood, the pear-shaped invasive merozoites work with bluntness and efficiency, shoving with their conical noses through the walls of Zach's red blood cells in the remarkably short time of twenty to thirty seconds after initial contact. Shedding their outer cloak roughly upon entry like an uninvited guest, they change form, feast on a groaning banquet of cytoplasm and hemoglobin, then divide into eight to sixteen new merozoites that crowd the blood cell to the bursting point and heartily earn the name parasites. Finally the red blood cell, or what's left of it after its been eaten away from inside, bursts open and releases this new family of invasive merozoites. They each invade other red blood cells, produce more offspring, and the cycle continues, as the numbers of invaded cells and *P. falciparum* parasites in Zach's blood rise astronomically.

Jason hardly sees Zach during the next nine days. The midnight skinny-dipping party breaks up when Zach and Chloe climb dripping and naked out of the water, gather up their clothes, and walk alone together down the beach. The frolicking spirit suddenly drained from the party by this private liaison, Jason and the two other women dress awkwardly and disperse to their separate tents, Jason all the while recriminating himself for not being more aggressive like Zach. Another missed chance, he thinks. He always misses his chance. Zach is always the chosen one.

Zach doesn't return to their tent that night, nor the next nor the next. By day, Jason sees him with Chloe on the beach or snorkeling on the reef, while he's left glumly to entertain himself. The invasive merozoites, meanwhile, are furiously busy beating the streets of Zach's circulatory system, taking it over cell by cell. On the ninth day, Jason is lying under the shade of a palm tree reading—for the second time—a collection of Somerset Maugham stories about British colonists washed up in the tropics that he purchased at a bookstore back in Singapore. He notices Zach's shadow fall across the page.

"So where's Chloe?" Jason says without looking up.

"She left," Zach replies.

Jason puts down the book in the sand. "She *left*? You're joking, aren't you? Why did she leave? I thought she wanted to stay here forever. Especially since she met *you*."

Zach flops down on the sand beside him, lies on his back with his Rasta braids splayed, and stares up into the palms. His fingers absently work the grains of sand clinging to his browned chest.

"She said she misses her boyfriend back in Australia," he says absently.

"Bummer, man," says Jason. "After all this, she wants to go back to her boyfriend? I was getting ready to pack up and go on without you. Well, I'm glad that's over. At least now maybe we can have some fun."

"Yeah, whatever," replies Zach, closing his eyes. "But, man, I'm *really* tired."

In the night, Zach becomes chilled in his green nylon bag. Jason, holding the flashlight in his mouth, pries a small yellow pill from its cardboard casing and hands it to Zach lying beside him. Zach's hand emerges from the green cocoon. He tries to grasp the pill, but his hand trembles violently and he drops it. Jason picks it up, drops it on Zach's tongue, gives him a sip from his water bottle.

The pills, antihistamines, have worked every other time when they couldn't sleep, tossing uncomfortably in the tropical nights with insect bites or sunburn or coral cuts on their feet. Instead of antihistamines, however, what they should have been taking was a preventive dose, weekly or daily depending on the type, of one of the antimalarial drugs.

Zach curls up on his side, hugging himself with his arms inside his bag to stay warm. Paradoxically, this feeling of chill and shivers is the body's response to a rapidly rising internal temperature—the onset of fever—which will play a therapeutic role: to try to cook the invading parasites to death.

When confronted by bacteria, viruses, or other foreign invaders, the white blood cells in the human circulatory system release proteins, known as pyrogens, which cause a series of chemical reactions that trigger the body's thermostat, located in the hypothalamus portion of the brain, to dial its temperature up to a higher setting. The malaria parasite floating about in the blood is so effective at inducing these fevers that in the 1920s, before the advent of penicillin, blood infected with *Plasmodium falciparum* parasites was injected straight into the frontal lobes of syphilis patients. The resulting "therapeutic malaria" fever proved effective in killing off the syphilis bacteria in 80 percent of the cases, though the malaria parasite itself survived the fevers intact and had to be treated separately.

Jason switches off the flashlight and lies back on top of his bag. As he falls asleep, he can hear the rustle of nylon as Zach twists and curls about in his bag with the chills and shivers. These help generate muscular heat to elevate his temperature to the new setting.

With each 1-degree rise in his temperature above 98.6, Zach's metabolic rate—his respiration rate, heart rate, blood flow—jumps by 7 percent.

101 degrees: mild fever . . .

102 degrees: the body's metabolism is hopped up some 30 percent higher than its normal rate, causing extreme nervousness and irritability . . .

An hour after falling asleep, Jason is woken by a thrashing of arms and legs in the sleeping bag beside him.

"Give me some air," Zach cries out. "I'm really hot."

Jason, sitting up in alarm, unzips the flap of the tent.

"Do you want to go for a swim?" he asks.

"Not a swim," says Zach, recoiling. "Fuck the swim!" The idea of the seawater on his burning skin makes him think that he might explode like a hot rock tossed into cold water. His head is pounding with pain and his neck is stiff. He twists about on top of his bag, trying to find a cooler spot, and finally drags himself on elbows and knees out onto the cool, powdery sand like a lizard regulating its body temperature by lying in sun or shade.

103 degrees: confusion . . .

104 degrees: delirium . . .

Zach's internal temperature hits 105.2 degrees Fahrenheit, enough to kill syphilis and many other bacteria by starving them of the blood iron they need, but not the malaria parasite itself. Jason makes a bed for him under the stars, then drags out his own bag and falls asleep beside him. Zach neither wakes nor sleeps but tosses in the netherworld of fever dreams, not knowing where he is, only that he's beneath the night sky and the stars, an overheated lizard writhing on the earth, tail lashing about, until, toward dawn, sweat suddenly pours out over his skin, bathing him, cooling him. Zach dimly begins to remember that he is on an island off the coast of Sumatra and that the lump beside him isn't a rock or another lizard but his friend Jason. He then falls into a deep, exhausted sleep.

Zach's first fever bout has run the typical course noted by physicians since ancient times: chills, a quickly soaring temperature, a feeling of crippling heat for one to two hours, and then a pouring sweat that indicates a falling temperature and is so familiar from the tense bedside vigils of the Hollywood jungle dramas—"Tell the natives! Bwana's fever has broken!"—until the body's temperature drops back to normal five to eight hours after the attack began and the victim lapses into exhaustion.

They awaken late, with the sun filtering through the palm leaves onto the white sand. Zach's fever has totally disappeared. He feels fine, although tired.

Jason sits up, rubbing his eyes against the sunlight. "Maybe it's something you ate," he says helpfully.

"Yeah," says Zach. "Tonight, remind me to stay away from those Sumatran chili peppers."

They both laugh. It'll make another good story when they get home.

That day they spend quietly, with Zach resting near the tent and reading Jason's copy of the Somerset Maugham stories. They'll go to the caves tomorrow, they decide. Zach's fever hasn't really ended at all, however; it's only that the *Plasmodium falciparum* parasites in his red blood cells have taken a short breather. The *P. falciparum* parasite splits on a forty-eight-hour cycle, from the time a merozoite invades a red blood cell to the time the eight or sixteen new merozoites burst from the cell to invade new cells. Because the merozoites manage this in coordinated fashion, Zach's fever thus will attack him at forty-eight-hour intervals—a bout of fever on the first day, a break on the second day, fever on the third day, a break on the fourth, fever on the fifth day, and so on. This every-other-day fever cycle is what's known as tertian malaria. It is characteristic of three of the four strains of the malaria parasite that infect humans, though the clocklike cycles often blur in the case of *P. falciparum*, and in the case of *P. vivax* they can appear years after the initial infection.

That night Zach sleeps soundly beside Jason in the tent and experiences no fever. The next morning he feels well enough. He is still weak, however, because so many of his red blood cells have burst that he is becoming anemic. Trembling slightly, he walks with Jason along a sandy path into the village, and they find two young men with motorcycles willing, for a price, to transport them into the hills and guide them to the caves. For much of the day, trailing the village youths, Jason and Zach slip and slide along muddy paths. At the base of white limestone cliffs overhung with curtains of vines, dark apertures suddenly appear in the earth. With their camping headlamps and a couple of candles, the foursome poke a short distance into the caves, marveling at the stalactites hanging from the ceiling that glisten in the light of their headlamps and the thousands of inverted bats that cling to the cave roof, their wings folded in sleep, awaiting the wakening of the tropical night.

In similar fashion, Zach's parasitized red blood cells have begun to adhere to the ceilings of the tiny capillaries in his brain. This is the beginning of the highly dangerous condition known as cerebral malaria. The *P. falciparum* parasite is unique in that the red blood cells invaded by the parasites develop tiny knobs on their surface containing a protein that causes them to stick to the cells of the blood vessels. They have a particular tendency to migrate to the blood vessels in the brain and stick there. Of the many bizarre properties of malaria, one is that this process of sequestration appears suppressed among inhabitants of malarial regions who have developed a tolerance to the disease, and—no one knows quite why this is so—also among individuals who are missing their spleens.

Likewise, the sickle-cell trait fights sequestration because the abnormal hemoglobin inside the red blood cell that is invaded by parasites bundles up into a stiff mass and destroys the cell. Thus the sickle-cell trait is thought by geneticists to be a preventive adaptation to malaria among sub-Saharan Africans, where the deadly *P. falciparum* form accounts for the majority of the disease.

But Zach is from the temperate north; he possesses a spleen and normal hemoglobin, and he hasn't been taking malaria pills. Toward late afternoon he starts shivering again. At first he thinks it's only the cave's cold and damp, but the chills and shakes don't stop when he crawls out into the muggy, leafy daylight. "Fuck!" he whispers to himself, his lips trembling, as he sits on the ground and hugs his knees to his chest. After a shaky ride back to the beach, Jason and the village youths help him from the motorcycle saddle and lower him gently onto the sand near the tent. Once again, the chills give way to the unbearable heat, until midnight, when Zach's tossing fever finally breaks into sweat, and then he sleeps. Jason, keeping a vigil, is truly alarmed; this is something far more serious than an overdose of Sumatran chili peppers.

After his own restless night, Jason is already awake and squatting on the sand near their camp stove brewing tea when he notices Zach open his eyes the next morning.

"What do you want to do?" Jason says quietly. He stirs sugar into the pot, trying to hide his alarm.

"I don't know," says Zach without raising his head, staring out toward the breakers crashing on the reef. "I don't know how many more nights like that I can take."

"Where do you want to go?" asks Jason, trying to sound neutral. He wants Zach to come to the decision that he already has.

"Wherever there's a decent hospital, I guess. Back to Singapore."

"Good," says Jason, turning off the little knob of the stove. "Let's do it."

The ferry takes twelve hours back to the main island of Sumatra, then they must ride six hours by bus to the opposite shore and board another ferry to Malaysia, followed by a train south to Singapore. By now Zach's fever is not arriving at forty-eight-hour intervals but seems to rise and fall in wild, erratic swings. He's fainted twice upon standing, once getting off the bus and again getting on the train, because the blood supply to his brain is slowly being choked off by knobby red blood cells packed with *P. falciparum* parasites sticking to the walls of the capillaries. As his brain loses oxygen, odd personality changes occur. He becomes inexplicably irritable toward Jason, who's hauling both their backpacks and propping up Zach at the same time.

"Take it easy, dude," Jason says gently. "I'm only trying to help you."

On the final train run into Singapore, Zach's head lolls against the back of the compartment seat, eyes half open and unseeing, and his arms and legs twitch and spasm sporadically. Jason must hire a porter to help carry Zach from the train. He looks like a drunk, staggering half conscious under their support through the station; in regions where it is not common, cerebral malaria is sometimes mistaken for other afflictions such as epilepsy and meningitis, or for alcohol intoxication. But here they know about malaria. When their taxi reaches the hospital, Zach is totally unconscious. He's rushed into the emergency room, and the nurses and orderlies and doctors who examine him and question Jason immediately suspect the cause. They draw blood, it's dispatched to the lab, and the slide is quickly examined by microscope. The iron from the hemoglobin digested by the *P. falciparum* parasite has left malaria's characteristic dark pigment.

A short time later, a doctor hurries into the waiting room. She's a tall middle-aged German woman who speaks English with a thick accent.

"Why have you waited so long to bring him here?" she barks out at Jason. "His blood is *black* with malaria!"

She then turns and rushes back.

Zach lies in the intensive care unit. An oxygen mask is over his face to increase the oxygen flow to his choked brain. The doctor has ordered an IV in his arm and a large loading dose of quinine pumped into his circulatory system over a thirty-minute span, to be followed by a maintenance dose at eight-hour intervals. The doctors could have chosen from other, more modern, synthetic antimalarial drugs, but quinine still remains one of the most effective, nearly four centuries after missionaries learned of it from the Incas and many decades since the British in India discovered they could disguise its bitter taste by mixing it with gin, thus giving birth to the gin and tonic. The first widely used modern antimalarial drug, chloroquine, was discovered by German scientists in the 1930s and helped protect Allied forces in Asia during World War II. During that war and in the years that followed, in an enormous battle to combat malaria, some half million substances were tested as antimalarial drugs, but only a few were found to work. In some regions the always inventive *P. falciparum* parasite developed a resistance to chloroquine. In these areas, doctors must rely on newer drugs such as mefloquine or fall back on the old standby, quinine. Derivatives from a traditional Chinese medicinal herb—*qing hao*—have also been shown in clinical trials to clear the parasites rapidly.

As he breathes slowly through the oxygen mask, thick wads of parasitized red blood cells clog in the tiny capillaries of Zach's brain like fallen leaves plugging a rainspout. The quinine coursing into his circulatory system from the IV attacks the parasite's nucleus and cytoplasm, but the *P. falciparum* parasite now infects over 30 percent of his total red blood cells.

Zach is in a deep coma. Jason sits in the waiting room, trying to read his Somerset Maugham stories. Across the room, Singaporean children tumble about their parents' legs. Jason can't concentrate on the story, wondering if he could have done more to help. How stupid of them, he thinks. Malaria. Why didn't they think of that days ago? Or would days ago have mattered?

The German doctor now pushes slowly out the door to the waiting room. She sits down beside Jason, and Jason already knows what she is going to say.

CHAPTER ELEVEN

IN A LAND BEYOND THE SHADE:

DEHYDRATION

You don't know why they're doing this to you. You don't even know exactly what it is that they've done. All you know—here in the middle of the Sahara Desert—is this:

In early evening the caravan stopped. They dismounted from their camels and walked barefoot in their flowing blue robes to your mount. You couldn't guess what they were thinking; their traditional turbans and blue veils—*tagilmusts*—wrapped across their faces revealed only keen, dark eyes. They forced your camel to sit. Silently, they removed your wristwatch and with rough, hand-plaited grass rope lashed your wrists to the tall pommel, then knotted a *tagilmust* as a blindfold around your eyes. You could hear the mutters and protests of the camels as they remounted. Then, taking your camel by its halter, they led you deep into the desert night.

You guess it's now past midnight. Other nights when the caravan has traveled so late, you felt this same cooling of the Saharan air and the aching soreness of your back from the hours of rocking on the camel's back. It's been two weeks since you've joined their caravan, five days since you left the last oasis with them, when they summoned you from the interview you were conducting under the palms with the marabout—the holy man—and told you the caravan was moving again. They're supposed to be taking you to the nomad guerrilla fighters out in the desert who have been conducting the raids on government outposts. Why are they doing this to you? And why now? Are they trying to scare you into keeping their secrets? Or prevent you from seeing how to get to the guerrilla strongholds? Or is it that they think you already know too much and plan to kill you? They know you're sympathetic to their struggle against a government far more powerful than they, one that wants to settle them, rule them, steal their freedom. That's the name they've always called themselves as a people—Imazighen, which means "free." To their sedentary neighbors at the Sahara's edge, however, they are known by another name, one meaning "those who are cast out by God."

A fashionable New York magazine has dispatched you here. The editor, leaning conspiratorially over the table during lunch at a trendy downtown trattoria, told you that the assignment could make your career as a freelance writer.

"And let's face it," he'd said, forking up with a deft spin another ample bite of spaghettini with black truffle sauce and washing it down with a sip of Barolo wine, "you've been struggling. Your career could use the help."

You couldn't argue with that. You *had* been struggling. The magazines no longer wanted to buy your lengthy, insightful articles about hard travel to remote places. They all clamored for upscale travel pieces—preferably involving Mediterranean countries and celebrity sunbathers (especially those sans tops) on large yachts, plus plentiful shopping opportunities. But when you'd called up the editor and proposed writing a piece about the nomads' guerrilla war in the southern Sahara Desert—a place you'd always wanted to experience—it caught his attention. He invited you to lunch, and you pitched it to him and he thought it over as he chewed his spaghettini and swilled his Barolo. Finally he told you the piece could forgo the shopping opportunities and celebrities as long as it promised the threat of violence. That's when he'd leaned conspiratorially over the table and said the piece not only would add a bit of *faux dangereux* thrill to the magazine's well-heeled image but could truly *make* your career.

And so in late April you flew to Paris and then boarded another flight full of tall men in elegant embroidered robes down to Ouagadougou, near desert's edge. It took over a week riding in hot buses and on the backs of trucks to get to the dusty provincial town where you first made clandestine contact with a representative of the nomad guerrillas. You explained what the guerrillas stood to gain by taking you into their confidence and out into the desert where they operated. Maybe your piece in the fashionable magazine would sway public opinion back at home. Maybe the nomad guerrillas would get help—foreign aid, perhaps even weapons, the small, potent, sophisticated handheld missile launchers that could knock a helicopter or even a fighter jet right out of the sky. The guerrilla nodded thoughtfully. He seemed to understand. One night he took you to the edge of town, where the mud walls gave way to sand, and introduced you to the nomads in the blue veils who were taking a caravan out into the desert. There were eight nomads, each mounted on his own camel and each leading a string of two or three other camels that carried loads draped over each side. The loads were small and heavy and wrapped in woven-straw matting. You didn't know what was inside them. You didn't want to ask.

"Go with them," he said. "They will take you to the people you wish to meet."

You immediately liked the nomads—their competence in the desert, their grace, their quick humor—and you thought they liked you. You could communicate with them, barely, in your broken French and the few words of their native Tamachek that you'd picked up. It had been a long, hard two weeks of travel in the desert, broken twice by stops at palmy, cool oases. All along, both in the oases and in the caravan, the people you'd met had showed you hospitality, and you sat with them late into the starry desert nights and drunk small glasses of sweetened green tea. You laughed and joked and tried to learn their songs. You shared their food. You passed goatskins full of lunch back and forth as you walked across the sands so as not to let the camels stop and lie down, each of you taking long gulps of the *aragira*—a slurry of pounded millet, dry goat cheese, dates, and water. But even then they never showed you their faces, drinking their tea or *aragira* from underneath the scarflike wrap. It is the men, not the women, who wear veils in this nomad culture; it is considered impolite for a man even to show so much as his nose. Instead there are their gaits and their eyes to distinguish them—eyes that are sometimes laughing, sometimes angry, always bright and acute.

"What are you doing to me?" you now call out from behind your blindfold.

But in reply you hear only the creak of their heavy loads as the camels plod slowly onward over the night-cooled sands.

They stop only once, to open a *gerba*—a goatskin bag that looks like a large football with a leather spout—dangling from a camel. You hear the sloshing of the water as it pours into a wooden bowl. They offer the bowl to you first, holding it to your lips.

"Drink," one says.

Swallowing gulp after gulp, you drain the entire contents of the bowl to slake the desert thirst that never leaves, only lessens. The water is wonderfully cool and refreshing despite the goat hair from the *gerba* and flecks of camel shit from the pool of water back at the oasis. Drinking the cool, refreshing water from the wooden bowl held to your lips is the last thing you remember.

You don't know where you are. You're lying on your side. First you see a rose-colored sky. Then, at eye level, an expanse of dull orange sand whose grains are as fine and unadulterated by pebbles, rocks, or anything else as a vast pile of table salt. You begin to remember: You're in the desert. You lie still. You listen for familiar sounds—the murmur of sleepy voices, the clank of a cooking pot, the mutter of a camel. Nothing. Not a chirp of a bird. Not a whisper of wind. Not a drip of water. There is only silence. Utter, absolute, stone-dry silence.

Alarmed, you sit up. Someone has draped a blue robe over you to serve as a blanket and placed beneath your head a mounded *tagilmust* for a pillow. But where are the people who brought you here? Surely they are nearby. You look around. Nothing but the fine orange sand cresting in low dunes. Overhead, the scraggly branches of a single acacia tree under which you've been placed. Then you notice the camel tracks. They lead off in seven or eight different directions where the nomads of the caravan apparently split up, each heading his own way purposefully over the naked dunes, as if to confuse you should you try to follow them.

It's then that you have a single, all-powerful thought: *Where's the* gerba?

At dawn on August 23, 1905, a bellow echoing up the canyon awakened naturalist W. J. McGee from his camp alongside some pools in a gorge in Arizona's remote Gila Desert, where he'd been studying the effects of light on desert life. McGee and the Papago Indian he'd hired as a tracker, Jose, sprang from their bedrolls to investigate. A quarter mile down the trail, they came upon Pablo Valencia—a formerly robust forty-year-old, 155-pound prospector who had passed through their camp eight days earlier in search of a "lost mine." Or rather, they came upon what McGee later described as "the wreck of Pablo."

"Pablo," wrote McGee with the precise observation of the naturalist in what has become a classic account in the literature of thirst, "was stark naked; his formerly full-muscled legs and arms were shrunken and scrawny; his ribs ridged out like those of a starveling horse; his habitually plethoric abdomen was drawn in almost against his vertebral column; his lips had disappeared as if amputated, leaving low edges of blackened tissue; his teeth and gums projected like those of a skinned animal, but the flesh was black and dry as a hank of jerky; his nose was withered and shrunken to half its length, the nostril-lining showing black; his eyes were set in a winkless stare, with surrounding skin so contracted as to expose the conjunctiva, itself black as the gums; his face was dark ... and his skin generally turned a ghastly purplish yet ashen gray, with great livid blotches and streaks; his lower legs and feet, with forearms and hands, were torn and scratched by contact with thorns and sharp rocks, yet even the freshest cuts were as so many scratches in dry leather, without trace of blood or serum; his joints and bones stood out like those of a wasted sickling, though the skin clung to them in a way suggesting shrunken rawhide used in repairing a broken wheel. From inspection and handling, I estimated his weight at 115 to 120 pounds. We soon found him deaf to all but loud sounds, and so blind as to distinguish nothing save light and dark. The mucus membrane lining mouth and throat was shriveled, cracked, and blackened, and his tongue shrunken to a mere bunch of black integument. His respiration was slow, spasmodic, and accompanied by a deep guttural moaning or roaring—the sound that had awakened us a quarter of a mile away. His extremities were cold as the surrounding air; no pulsation could be detected at the wrists, and there was apparently little if any circulation beyond the knees and elbows; the heartbeat was slow, irregular, fluttering, and almost ceasing in the longer intervals between the stertorous breathings."*

Although he was at first unable to speak or even swallow, Pablo was slowly brought back to life over several days by the ministering of McGee and Jose, improving immensely several days later in Yuma after an all-day watermelon-eating and sleeping binge. Like many

---

* W. J. McGee, as quoted in *Thirst: Physiology of the Urge to Drink and Problems of Water Lack* by A. V. Wolf (Springfield, Illinois: Charles C. Thomas Publisher, 1958).

victims of what's known as "desert thirst," Pablo had thrown away every possession he carried during his waterless 100- to 150-mile ordeal, the result of a missed rendezvous with a partner who was supposed to bring full canteens. First he'd tossed away his gold nuggets, followed by his food, his coat, then his trousers, whose pockets contained his money, his tobacco, and his knife—even though it was the thought of stabbing his partner that helped propel him onward. Then he left behind his hat until he carried only a canteen in which to collect and drink his dwindling drops of urine. On the morning before McGee and Jose found him, Pablo had knelt down in the shade of a bush as the sun rose, said a final prayer, laid down facing east, and, regretting his lack of consecrated water, made the sign of the cross. Then, as far as he knew, he died. His body lay on the baking desert floor while some innermost part of him hovered nearby watching the buzzards inspect his corpse. That night, however, the desert mercifully cooled to the low 80s. Something stirred in Pablo. Naked, unable to see but feeling with his hands along the old settlers' trail near the Mexican border known as El Camino del Diablo—"Road of the Devil"—he struggled through the night toward McGee's camp and water, where he collapsed in the dust at dawn.

There is something mystical about the desert itself and the profound thirst that can so easily claim one there. Desert thirst is a hallucinatory experience. Not only does one encounter the stereotypical mirages—the shimmering "lakes" of water caused by sunlight reflecting off layers of air of different temperatures near the desert surface—but the victim deep in its throes sees visions, hears things, undergoes out-of-body experiences. Like Pablo, the victim often sheds all clothing and belongings and—having stripped oneself of all that one has acquired on this earth—crawls naked through the naked desert beneath the naked sky. Surely it is no coincidence that the desert has long been visited by mystics, prophets, and seekers. Its nakedness distilled and shaped some of the world's great religions. Moses and the Israelites traversed desert realms in their forty years wandering in the wilderness. Before he founded his own faith, Jesus probably was a follower of the desert ascetic and wanderer John the Baptist. Muhammad's parents sent him as an infant away from the unhealthy climate of Mecca to live with a nomadic desert tribe. It is as if the desert strips away all superfluous layers—not only the rich, green layer of life that blankets so much of the planet, but also the superfluous layers of humans, of material acquisitions, of personality, even of ego itself.

The French, those great colonizers of the Sahara, have a term for the way in which the desert transforms a person: *baptême de la solitude*—"baptism of solitude." "It is a unique sensation," writes the novelist, musician, and Saharan wanderer Paul Bowles about standing alone in the desert night, "and it has nothing to do with loneliness, for loneliness presupposes memory. Here, in this wholly mineral landscape lighted by stars like flares, even memory disappears; nothing is left but your own breathing and the sound of your heart beating. A strange, and by no means pleasant, process of reintegration begins inside you, and [you] have the choice of fighting against it, and insisting on remaining the person you have always been, or letting it take its course. For no one who has stayed in the Sahara for a while is quite the same as when he came."

But the desert not only can profoundly transform the human spirit; it can also profoundly transform the human physiology. Humans are, by weight, nearly two-thirds water. Not only does the human body serve as an aquarium that bathes its living cells, as one French aquatic philosopher mused, but each cell itself is a tiny aquarium. One of the many remarkable properties of water is that it is a highly effective solvent—it easily dissolves many other substances. Thus in the form of aqueous bodily fluids such as blood plasma, which in humans is made up of over 90 percent water and transports nutrients, wastes, and heat through the body, water plays a role in almost every biological process of both plants and animals.

The aquarium or reservoir that is the human body is equipped with a precise system of valves to maintain its water level with extreme accuracy—within about .22 percent of one's body weight over a twenty-four-hour period, which in a 155-pound male translates to about half a cup. If too much water is taken in the reservoir's inlet—the mouth—the body's outlet valve, the kidney, will excrete the excess in the form of dilute urine. If too little water enters the body through the mouth or too much water dissipates from the reservoir—in the form of evaporating sweat, for instance—the level drops and the reservoir will close its outlet valve, allowing little urine to run out. But if the reservoir level continues to drop due to continued evaporation and lack of inflow—as can so easily happen in the desert heat and aridity—the reservoir's most distant, shallowest, and least important bays and arms start to dry up. Soon those distant arms and bays begin to expose their muddy, cracked bottoms. If the reservoir continues to shrink, all that remains is a muddy pool of sludge at its center that cannot support life.

Dipsologists—those who study thirst—measure a human's lack of water by calculating the loss as a percentage of body weight. An adult male weighing 155 pounds who is 60 percent water contains about 42 liters' worth. Under the most gentle of circumstances, he loses a minimum of about 1.5 liters of water each day—or about the contents of five big tumblers. Most disappears through urination, while about a third to half dissipates via sweat or the humid air from one's exhalations. Hot climates and hard work can boost water losses enormously to 1.5 liters or more *per hour*, mostly in the form of sweat to cool the body. A loss of 1.5 liters—whether it occurs over the course of an entire day or merely one very sweaty hour—represents about 2 percent of that male's body weight. The body can tolerate with only moderate problems a deficit of 3 to 4 percent of body weight, though one may suffer a powerful thirst, which kicks in at about a 0.8 percent deficit, or about a pint. At a 5 to 8 percent deficit—down about 3 to 5 liters—the victim becomes exhausted, complaining, prone to collapse, and at a 10 percent deficit—a very serious loss—physical and mental deterioration begins. By 12 percent—down about 8.5 liters—the victim can no longer swallow and is likely going into shock. Death occurs somewhere in the range of a 15 to 25 percent deficit. Or, put another way, death, in a previously healthy male weighing 155 pounds, occurs at a loss of 10 to 17 liters. Walking in the desert sun and sweating hard at 1.5 liters per hour, that moment could arrive in as little as seven hours.

"How long could I go without water, if by any chance I were left without it?" wrote J. S. Chase, a veteran traveler of the California deserts in the early twentieth century. "In that fierce heat, and struggling with that terrible country, a few minutes was as long as one could go without drinking. In a flash I saw what would be my condition *in a single hour*—torture: two hours—delirium: after that raving madness, till agony passed into insensibility, and that into death."

The classic studies of thirst conducted by E. F. Adolph and other U.S. military researchers in the deserts of southern California during World War II concluded that a person walking in 80-degree heat can travel 45 miles without water. A person walking in 100-degree heat can travel 15 miles without water. And a person walking in 120-degree heat—a temperature that is entirely possible in the Sahara and other deserts—will collapse after a mere 7 miles. Adolph's studies recommended as a general rule that the traveler on foot in the desert carry 1 gallon, or about 4 liters, for every 20 miles walked at night. To cover 20 miles on foot during the heat of the day, the desert traveler should carry 2 gallons. By this rule of thumb, to walk by day for 100 miles through the desert—an inconsequential distance in the vast Sahara, which, at 3.3 million square miles, could just about contain the entire United States—a traveler would have to haul on his or her back a staggering load of about 80 pounds of water. It is for precisely these reasons that it wasn't until the camel—a desert animal capable of walking for three weeks without water in winter desert conditions, tolerating huge swings in body temperature (and thus needing less water to cool itself than other mammals), and drinking 33 gallons at a time—was introduced by the Romans that humans could travel deep into the Sahara.

The experiments of dipsologists such as Adolph, thorough

though they may have been, did not measure the effects of water loss on humans beyond about 10 percent body weight, where serious physiological complications begin. Instead, for descriptions of what happens beyond that point, they had to turn to the observations of desert travelers such as McGee and people such as Pablo. In McGee's day, the old desert rats of the Southwest and Mexico had defined, in their own laymen's terms, precise stages of "desert thirst," each of which roughly corresponds, according to more modern researchers, to a 5 percent water loss by body weight. The names themselves provide a graphic progression of the stages of thirst. They run in order like this:

Clamorous
Cotton-mouth
Swollen-tongue
Shriveled-tongue
Blood sweat
Living death

And yet, risking all this, still wanderers and travelers head out into the deserts of Africa, Asia, the Americas, Australia, and still they die of thirst, or a dozen other ways. Each wayfarer has his or her own reason for heading out into the vast emptiness, whether it's gold, the renown of exploration, or a spiritual quest. But, at least at some level, all those reasons finally intersect the one given by Paul Bowles when he rhetorically asked himself, despite the ever-rising level of discomfort one faces in the Sahara, "Why go?":

"The answer is that when a man has been there and undergone the baptism of solitude he can't help himself. Once he has been under the spell of the vast, luminous, silent country, no other place is quite strong enough for him, no other surroundings can provide the supremely satisfying sensation of existing in the midst of something that is absolute. He will go back, whatever the cost in comfort and money, for the absolute has no price."

No *gerba* lies on the ground nearby. There is only the silence, and the camel tracks dispersing in seven or eight different directions. The first brush of morning sun skips across the tops of the orange dunes. Already you feel the air heating, although the sand on which you sit remains chilled from the night air. You dig your fingers in as if to grasp its coolness. Beside your right hand you notice a dark splotch. You look up. A *gerba* hangs from a low branch of the acacia tree. It drips one slow drop after another, and those drops are drunk, as the nomads say, by the desert.

You jump up and seize the *gerba* in your arms; then, like lifting an infant from a basket, you carefully hoist it and its leather strap from the branch. The tiny pores in the goatskin are leaking, like all *gerbas* do at times. You've watched the nomads plug the leaks with tufts of camel hair. Ignoring the pain in order to save the precious water, you yank out a few strands of your own hair, twist them, and wedge them into the hole.

The leak stops. Cradling the *gerba*, you look around again. Where have they gone? Merely off on some brief errand or another? Or do they plan to stay away a long time? You haven't a clue. What are you supposed to do? Wait here under the weak shade of the acacia tree hoping they will return and take you to safety? Or are you supposed to start walking? No matter what else happens, if you don't find them or they don't find you, your water is going to run out—sooner rather than later. Maybe they really do want you to die. Why else would they tie your hands and blindfold you? Maybe it's as simple as that. Maybe you knew too much about their guerrilla activities. Or maybe you didn't know enough. But if they really wanted to kill you, why didn't they just do it when they had the chance?

The silence gives no answers. You sink back to the sand,

cradling the precious goatskin bag on your lap. The ball of the sun has lifted a notch higher, intensifying from orange toward yellow. You shake the *gerba*, listening to its heavy contents sloshing back and forth. You guess it contains about 10 liters. As you sit there pondering the contents of the goatskin and your course of action, complex changes are already occurring in your physiology. During the night and early-morning hours since you last had a drink, your body lost about half a liter of water through its usual routes—respiration, sweat, urine. As you slowly become dehydrated, the concentration of salts and other substances in your blood plasma rises, increasing what is known as its osmolality—in essence, the amount of other substances that are dissolved in a fluid. The normal osmolality of your blood plasma ranges between 275 and 295 milliosmoles per kilogram of water. It's this varying level of osmolality that determines whether your body should open the floodgates and spill out water through your kidneys or close them down.

As you slowly lost water through the night and into the morning, your osmolality climbed above 280 and toward 290 mOsm/kg, triggering the osmoreceptors in the hypothalamus of your brain to tell your pituitary gland to release the substance that acts as the reservoir's floodgate closer—arginine vasopressin, or AVP. This signals your kidneys, which constantly filter the water content of your blood and extract urine from it, to reabsorb more of the water that they might otherwise excrete with the urine. The volume of urine your kidneys constantly produces drops as your blood plasma osmolality climbs and the pituitary releases AVP. By the time you first become aware of your thirst—which varies from person to person but occurs somewhere around an osmolality of 295 mOsm/kg—your urine flow has already fallen to 10 percent or less of its normal amount. In other words, your brain is telling your kidneys to hold onto your body's water long before you consciously sense thirst.

Sitting with the *gerba* on your lap, you've already crossed the 295 mOsm/kg threshold. You feel thirsty, but for the moment you hold off from drinking, wanting to save your water. Instead, you get up to pee. Your urine—concentrated because your kidneys are holding back water—already looks a darker yellow.

Beyond the scraggly acacia tree, the sunlight has shifted higher up the spectrum from yellow toward hot white, shifting the sand's hue along with it, and the sky has transformed from pinkish dawn to the luminous blue of full day. You search for clues the nomads may have left. You pick up the blue robe that lies on the sand. You shake it out. Nothing. You pluck up the end of the 12-foot-long blue *tagilmust*. Your spiral reporter's notebook comes tumbling out and, neatly clipped to its cardboard cover, your pen. You quickly leaf through the pages looking for a message they may have left you. The scrawled pages of handwriting it contains are all your own—interviews, landscape descriptions, odd facts. No clue from them. You slump again under the tree. Then you realize—*you have your notebook!* The notebook contains a story that will be like a sheaf of thousand-dollar bills when you finally get home! It will make your career and make you a lot of money besides. The important thing now is to keep a careful ongoing journal in it so that you can write a vivid, brilliant account of your experience on your return. The notebook, you realize, is just as important as the *gerba* full of water.

The sun has climbed another notch. You squirm closer to the acacia's trunk, where shade lingers. The sun forces you to think— hard. So what are your options? Stay here under the shade of the acacia tree and hope. Follow the camel tracks back to the last oasis and its mud village, date palms, cool ponds, and irrigation channels. Or follow one of the seven or eight tracks that lead away from the acacia tree with the hope that it will soon bring you to water, or at least to help.

Three options—that's all. Stay here . . . or go back . . . or go forward. You shake the goatskin again. Ten liters. That's worth roughly two nights of walking, or one day. The last oasis is five days' walk back. No way can you make it that far on the contents of the *gerba* alone. That leaves two options: stay put or go forward. What should you do?

Whatever you decide, you're not going anywhere until the heat of the day has passed.

Curled up against the trunk of the acacia with the *tagilmust* under your head and the *gerba* and notebook beside you, you doze on and off through the morning. The caravan, when traveling, usually didn't stop until late in the nights, and you, like the nomads, managed only a few hours of sleep before breaking camp in the mornings. You need to sleep. Each time you rouse from your slumber the air feels hotter. You must squiggle your body each time a few inches through the sand to keep in the depth of the single patch of weak shade. You know that you're saving water, in effect, simply by staying quietly in the shade. Adolph's experiments with soldiers during World War II showed that a man walking at 3.5 miles per hour in the desert sun at 100 degrees lost each hour through sweating about 1 quart of water—roughly 1 liter. Sitting quietly in the shade at 100 degrees, he lost only a quarter of that—about a cup each hour. This is one of the fundamental facts of the desert.

It is now May, and the summer daytime temperatures hit 100 degrees. You remember how at the last oasis no one moved around outside during the heat of the day. Instead the inhabitants retreated into the cool labyrinth of the *casbah*—a sort of thirteenth-century fortresslike apartment complex constructed of thick mud walls and covered passages that blocked out all sun but for small patches that entered through open skylights. Dozens of related families lived in the *casbah*, two or three hundred people, their thick wooden doors opening off the low, cavelike passages into cool, windowless rooms. It was there, while sharing heavily sugared green tea with one of the endlessly hospitable families, that you met a bright boy who spoke decent English. In late afternoon, as the sun lowered and the heat weakened, he guided you around the oasis, along the trickling and gurgling irrigation ditches, the carefully kept patches of grain, the groves of palms with their thick clusters of dates.

Under the palms, you came to a man sitting cross-legged in front of a simple mud hut who appeared to be chanting in poetic rhythms. Instead of the blue of the nomads, he wore a white turban and a patched, multicolored robe. He was thin and handsome in face and in limb, neither young nor old, neither quite dark-skinned nor quite light-skinned, and he stopped chanting when he saw you—a Westerner—walking on the path through the grove.

"Who is that man?" you asked the boy.

"He is a marabout, a holy man," the boy replied. "Sometimes he comes from far away and stays here for a time."

"May we talk with him?" you asked the boy.

"Of course," he replied. "That is why he comes here. So people may talk to him."

The marabout welcomed you with a gentle smile and gestured to a place facing him on the ground. You sat down cross-legged. With the boy translating, you explained to the marabout that you have come to the Sahara to write an article for an important magazine in America about the nomads and their struggle. He nodded and again smiled gently and noncommittally, as if the concepts of "magazine" and "America" are about as near to this particular spot as the planet Jupiter. You asked the boy to ask him if he minded telling you something about what he does.

"What would you like to know?" he asked.

You quickly tried to think up questions that would elicit information from him as well as a colorful response, snippets of quotes that you could use to give authenticity and texture to your magazine piece. Who knew? Maybe he'd even pull out a hookah and smoke a bowl of hashish with you—if these marabouts did that sort of thing. It would make a great anecdote for the article. Your editor would love it—exotic drug use in foreign cultures was almost as good for a travel piece as a few topless celebrities around the pool. Wherever the interview might lead you, you decided to approach the marabout slowly, by casting your net wide.

"What do you teach the people?" you asked.

"I am a Sufi," he replied with his quiet smile. "I teach the traveler—the *salik*—to follow the *tariqat*, the path. I teach he who would be a traveler on that path the seven stages of the Sufi way."

"Can you teach me about the Sufi way and its seven stages?" you asked, now pulling your reporter's notebook from the back pocket of your khakis. You hadn't wanted to bring it out earlier for fear of frightening him into silence.

He didn't seem at all put off by the notebook and pen as you quickly and as surreptitiously as possible scribbled down the Sufi words for "traveler" and "path." You knew you could weave them somewhere into your piece.

"You would like to learn the Sufi path?" he asked, again with his quiet smile.

"I am very eager to learn," you said.

"You would like to learn to be a traveler?"

"Yes, I would," you said as sincerely as you could.

It was partly true, anyway. You'd long been attracted to Eastern mysticism, and you'd always thought that someday you'd follow that path. Not that you knew that Sufism was at all the same path. Nor was this the time and place to follow it. What you were really here for was to learn all you could from the Sufi that would make good material for your article.

It was at this point that the Sufi asked if you knew of the great Sufi poet Hafiz, who lived in Persia in the fourteenth-century.

"I don't," you said, your blue felt-tipped pen at the ready over the open page of your notebook. "But could you tell me how to spell his name?"

It was then that the Sufi reached over gently and took the notebook from your lap. Laughing, he looked up at the palm-fringed desert sky, whirling the notebook in one hand over his head, and in a loud, rich, melodious voice chanted out a verse of Hafiz:

> Oh thou who are trying to learn the marvel of love from the copybook of reason,
> I am very much afraid that you will never really see the point.*

Under the reddish sky of sunset you pour another long drink from the *gerba* down your dry throat. Through the hot afternoon, dozing under the acacia tree, you managed to hold yourself to one long drink. Adolph and fellow researchers determined that rationing one's water does not help in the desert—that whether you drink quickly or drink slowly, your body finally needs the same quantity of water. In some ways it's better to drink sooner rather than later, they found, because without drinking—no matter how hardened you think you are to deprivation—you cannot maintain the strength to march. Still, as you sit under the acacia, you feel better practicing some restraint.

Each long drink amounted to about 0.5 liter, now leaving you 9 liters in the *gerba*. But during the heat of the day you lost one cup—about 0.25 liter—each hour in sweat to cool your body in the 100-degree heat even in the shade of the acacia. So in the course of the day you've drunk 1 liter but sweated out 2, on top of the 0.5 liter you already were down on waking at dawn. That leaves you now down a total of 1.5 liters, or just over 2 percent of your body weight—still not quite enough to impair your efficiency, but certainly enough to make your body want water.

Paradoxically, if you had all the water in the world to drink, you

---

* Quotations and translation from *The Persian Sufis* by Cyprian Rice (London: George Allen and Unwin, 1964).

could kill yourself with that, too. Over the years, some fifteen marathon runners have died by drinking too much water during races—a condition known as water intoxication. The gut, with its blood diverted to the muscles, cannot absorb the excess water until the race's end, when it floods the bloodstream, upsetting the body's sodium balance. The same upset of the sodium balance can occur to workers in the desert heat, even if they drink water copiously and regularly. The body can sweat out its sodium—known as an electrolyte, due to its role in transmitting electrical impulses in the body—that normally is contained in the blood plasma and other fluids. Although the water lost from sweating is replaced by drinking, the sodium, normally ingested by humans in the form of salt in their food, is not. This loss causes the osmolality—the amount of a substance dissolved in a fluid—of the blood plasma to drop in relation to the osmolality of the water inside the body's cells, and the body tries to equalize this difference in osmotic pressure by sending water from the blood plasma through the cell membranes into the cells. This can cause the brain cells to swell, resulting in seizures and, if untreated, death. For these reasons, "sports drinks" advertise that they contain electrolytes to replace those the athlete loses in sweating.

But the water in your *gerba* contains small amounts of salt from the wells of the oasis and from the goatskin in which it rides. Sodium depletion is not a problem. Furthermore, in the cool of the evening, desert wanderers lacking water often find that their sense of thirst diminishes. You now feel more clear-headed than you did during the heat of the day. All afternoon you've been reviewing the possibilities. It's now become obvious that the nomads didn't go off on some brief errand with the intent to return. You begin to think maybe you should move on. You *know* you're supposed to stay put. That's what the wilderness manuals and camping handbooks say. The first rule about being lost is, don't get any more lost. Stay put and wait for your rescuers. But who's going to rescue you? The only people aware that you're sitting under this lone acacia tree in the middle of the Sahara Desert are the nomad guerrillas, and their entire intention might be to make sure you *stay* lost. Of course, there's your editor. You dropped him a postcard two weeks ago telling him about your plan to head out with the caravan, but it will be weeks more before he receives it and still weeks more before he misses you. Besides, what's he going to do then? Cancel a month of luncheon dates, buy a designer safari suit, and come to the Sahara to search for you? Not likely. Or maybe he'd consider it if he thought there might be some publicity in it for the magazine and his own editorial savoir-faire. But by then the supposed object of his dashing mission—you—would be long dead.

Yes, maybe you should move on. Choose one set of camel tracks, follow them, and hope for the best. Maybe wait another hour or two to see if they return this evening, and then move on. It's a big, scary thought—especially the thought of the desert by day, of leaving the safety of the acacia's tiny patch of shade and walking alone into that huge burning emptiness with zero idea of where you are heading. But if you don't walk into it—if you don't face it—that huge burning emptiness will just as surely kill you where you sit.

There is a brilliant half-moon high in the black desert sky as you prepare to set out. The air temperature has dropped to a soothing, almost chilly 70 degrees. On the dry skin of your face, however, you can still feel the invisible infrared rays of the day's heat radiating from the sand beyond the acacia tree like the sudden heat from the orange coils of a broiler oven that's been opened on the far side of a kitchen.

You gather up the robe and slip it over your head, pushing your arms into its flowing sleeves. You attempt to wrap the *tagilmust* around your head in the nomad fashion, but it unravels each time. Finally you simply give it several turns around your waist and knot it. You slip your reporter's notebook into the back pocket of your khakis. At times during the day you made notes about your situation and your thoughts. It is all more material for your article.

You sling the *gerba* over your shoulder by its leather strap; it and the notebook are the twin safeholds of your future. The high half-moon illuminates the sands around you like wide, silvery swells. In the moonlight, the camel tracks radiate outward from your lone acacia tree in dark lines like the threads of a spider's web. Each set of tracks seems to mark where one of the eight nomads and the two or three camels he lead headed in a different direction. You've been pondering this problem since sunset and finally decided to follow the set of two tracks intertwined together that are heading east. That's deeper into the heart of the desert, but it's also the direction in which the caravan had been bearing before they abandoned you. Since the last oasis where you'd met the marabout they've traveled five days without water. In the next two or three days, the camels will need to drink and the nomads will need to refill their empty *gerbas*. They'll have to find a water source soon. So runs your logic.

You step out from the acacia's small patch of moon shadow and set one sandaled foot and then the other on the open desert, like stepping gingerly out of the controlled comfort of a space capsule onto the waterless, airless surface of the moon. You are leaving behind your only tie to the fertile, green world into which you were born. A sudden tremor of anxiety jumps up to your chest. The nomads might be returning any hour. You will be gone. You will have missed them. But then you realize that if they wish to find you, they'll track you easily. They are born trackers. They can squat down beside a set of camel tracks and, like a fingerprint expert, identify by the particular marks it leaves in the sand an individual animal they haven't seen for years. They can read by a person's footprints how fast he is traveling, what condition he is in, whether he is in a hurry due to some suspicious activity. "A man's conscience," the nomads say, "is reflected in his tracks."

"The desert and the track cannot lie," they say.

And they have another saying—one on which you're about to stake your life: "The track brings the man."

You don't care if their track brings you to them or to someone else, or your track brings them or someone else to you, as long as the meeting results in copious draughts of water to pour down your throat.

At first the walking is easy, with the broad, thin desert sandals you purchased back in the last oasis staying atop the soft surface. The dunes roll gently up and down, like great ripples in the shallows of a beach. These great seas of sand cover only a portion of the Sahara and are known in Arabic as *erg* or *areg* ("sand deserts") or in Tamachek as *edeyen* where the dunes are flat and *iguidi* where they are steep. Much of the rest of the Sahara is covered by gravelly or stony plains known as *reg* or *serir* and by very rugged rocky ones called *hammada*—which means, with very good reason, "to die off."

Fortunately for you, in the dunes of the *erg*, it is easy to follow tracks. You trace the dark intertwined thread of the camel tracks over their silvery swells. Your thirst seems to have diminished. You feel strong. You like the cool watery heft of the fat *gerba* under your arm and the thick notebook full of possibility stuffed in your back pocket.

After waving it over his head and quoting the Persian Sufi poet Hafiz on the futility of learning love from books, the Sufi handed your notebook back to you.

"You may keep writing in your small book if you like," he said.

As the sun moved down through the desert sky above the shading palms, you slowly learned the precepts of the Sufi way by asking him your careful questions, through lines of poetry the Sufi quoted with his chanting, melodious voice, through his pithy bits of explanation. You understood how, founded in Persia in the ninth century A.D., Sufism is part of Islam but also a reaction to Islam's austerity and how, through poetry and music, dancing and chanting, it aimed at abandoning the self for a mystical, ecstatic union with God.

"To be a Sufi," he said, quoting Abu Said of Mihneh, who lived in the eleventh century, "is to give up all worries, and there is no worse worry than your you-ness. When occupied with self, you are separated from God. The way to God is but one step: the step out of yourself."

You scribbled as quickly as you could in your notebook to take down all the quote. Yes, you thought, this brief encounter with the Sufi would make rich color for your magazine article. Your editor had never minded a little Eastern mysticism thrown into a travel piece, especially if it contained the suggestion of ritualized sex, as long as he didn't have to think too hard about the concepts. While it didn't appear that ritualized sex was up the Sufi line, trials and trances certainly were, and those weren't bad for color, either.

"The seven stages," the Sufi went on in his own words, "come not through *mushahada*, contemplation, but from *mujahada*, striving. The traveler must transcend the self by constantly training the purity of his intentions and eliminating all *gharad*, ulterior motives."

The Sufi paused. You kept writing.

"Do you understand?" he asked.

"I do," you replied, looking up quickly from your notes.

"And you are still wishing to know the Sufi way?" he asked.

"I am," you said. You still needed more material for the piece. Maybe he'd eventually bring out the hashish or go into a trance. "Let's continue."

"The traveler on the Sufi path must know that God Himself will help him reach his goal of abandoning the self by sending the traveler mysterious afflictions," the Sufi said. "This will help the traveler attain *maut i ikhtiari*—voluntary death."

You are awakened by heat. Burning desert heat. On your head, your arms, your legs, inside your mouth and throat, even in your lungs. You struggle to sit up. You're at the apex of a small dune. This is the spot where you laid down in the predawn darkness to rest. You'd followed the intertwined camel tracks for seven hours or so, covering—you guessed—between 15 and 20 miles across the *erg*. As Adolph's calculations predicted, the effort to cover that distance— 20 miles per gallon in the cool of a night march—has sucked 3 liters of water from your body. Wisely, you stopped to drink four times, about 0.5 liter each, even though you didn't feel you were that thirsty. Humans working in the heat, physiologists have found, never have the urge to drink as much fluid as they've lost until hours later. Your periodic water breaks replaced 2 of those 3 sweated-out liters. But overall you lost 1 liter during your night's trek on top of the 1.5-liter deficit you had before you even started walking. So, as you laid down in the predawn darkness to rest atop the sand dune, you were experiencing a 2.5-liter deficit, and lost another 0.5 liter in the four hours you've been asleep in the early sun. As you awaken in the burning heat, you're down 3 liters, or (figuring the weight of 1 liter of water at 1 kilogram and your normal body weight at 70 kilograms or 155 pounds) a total water deficit of 4.3 percent of your body weight. This is still close enough to that 3 to 4 percent range where your body experiences only moderate impairment of efficiency, but you're well into that first phase of desert thirst that the old desert rats and prospectors called "clamorous."

You're extremely thirsty, especially in the late-morning sun. Your mouth feels dry. Each breath seems like a hot wind has entered your lungs, leaching the moisture from them. The sunlight strikes your naked forearms, protruding from the sleeves of your robe, with an almost visceral sense of pressure, as if brushed by the breath of a steaming teapot. In the cool of the night you have forgotten the sun's absolute power during the day. It now charges the air and sand around you with its force, as if the molecules themselves begin to vibrate.

You grab the *gerba*. Before you can stop yourself, you've drained an entire gurgling liter of its contents down your burning throat. The cool, dung-flecked water instantaneously gives you some relief. You carefully retie the thong around the goatskin's neck. It now feels noticeably smaller and lighter than when you began—6 liters sloshing around instead of 10. You cradle the goatskin in your lap. You want to drink more, but you don't dare. You have no idea how far you must walk to find a well, or an oasis, or even another person, and the contents of the goatskin is the only thing that will get you there.

Looking out from the top of the dune, you realize that every square inch of barren sand as far as you can see is seared by the same intense focus of the sun's rays. It's like you've opened the door and stepped into a sauna as large as a continent. How far must you walk even to find a simple spot of shade? Pulling yourself to your feet, you stagger slightly—already the lack of water has affected your balance—and try to wrap the *tagilmust* around your head for protection from the sun. You manage to tie a kind of topknot and wrap a dangling end around your nose and mouth with only your eyes showing. The arrangement seems to insulate your head from the sun and cool the air slightly as you breathe it through the veil. Now you understand why the nomads adopted this dress to cover as much surface area of their body as possible from the desert sun. Adolph's studies found repeatedly and surprisingly that a man wearing a uniform and sitting in the desert sun saved over 0.25 liter of water *per hour* in sweat compared to a man sitting in the sun nearly nude even though he might feel more comfortable without the clothing.

You set out again, slowly, wrapped but for your eyes, along the camel tracks. Summer is coming to the Sahara; this, by far, is the hottest day you've experienced since the caravan entered the desert two weeks before. You have read that on a summer day the Sahara's air temperature can reach 120 degrees in places, and the sands heat up much hotter than that; the air has a bone-dry humidity of 5 percent. As you walk, the sun's rays drum down like a pounding rain. The air shimmers and snaps with them. The heat is a viscous substance you must push your body through. The blue robe helps shield you, but you feel the heat rising through the thin leather soles of your sandals. The surface of your corneas feels dry and hot, as if you stand before a fire. The water has helped, but not for long.

On foot, in the hot desert sun, the human body sweats out water to cool itself at an incredible rate—a liter or more per hour. After an hour's struggle through the dunes, you've lost another 1.5 liters, bringing your total water deficit to 3.5 liters, or a deficit of 5 percent of your body weight. You're down only about a gallon out of the 10 or so gallons your body normally holds, but already you're entering the old desert rats' "cotton-mouth" stage of thirst. You become increasingly weary and start to stumble. Your pulse rate climbs from 70 beats per minute to 100; as you dehydrate your blood volume shrinks, and your heart must beat faster to keep enough blood flowing to body and brain. Your skin feels flushed, and you sense the beginning of a tingling sensation beneath your robe, the first sign of the numbness that afflicts victims of thirst. Dehydration can cause a sense of restlessness that may be related to low blood pressure. A victim of dehydration often feels less discomfort by keeping moving. You push on.

You begin to think more and more about water. You fantasize about water—water sloshing around in the *gerba*, water trickling in cool rivulets under palm trees, water in blue swimming pools, water arcing up from chilled drinking fountains, the glasses of water you've spilled down a bathroom sink after brushing your teeth and rinsing your mouth. If you could only take them all back now! By force of will you don't drink from the *gerba*. You don't know how much longer you can hold back. You keep pushing yourself forward into the hot desert sun. The saliva in your mouth feels sticky and your tongue sometimes sticks to the roof of your mouth, taking a conscious muscular effort to pry it loose. Your breath comes in shorter gasps, and the air you suck in feels hot. The lining of your drying throat can no longer provide the moisture to humidify and cool each inhalation. A lump rises in your throat that you cannot swallow away; the sides of your trachea feel as if they stick together. Your face feels full as your facial tissues shrink and stretch across your cheeks and jawbone. Periodically you hear a drumming and snapping sound—the drying of tissues in your ears.

Your pace slows. Over the second hour you lose another liter of water, for a total deficit of 4.5 liters, or 6.4 percent of your body weight. The dunes look white-hot in the midday sun. Each footstep demands greater effort than the last, each a conscious act of will—*lift . . . place . . . lift . . . place.* If you were traveling with a partner, this is about the point where you would start to argue, become suspicious of each other, even separate as you trudge over the desert sands, then rejoin simply for the sheer satisfaction of arguing again in your cracked, husky voices. But you have no partner. Instead your mind targets your editor. He's ensconced in a leather booth in some Manhattan bistro with the waiter pouring out a bubbling, clinking stream of ice water into his glass. He glances at the menu just long enough to order a poached filet of wild Copper River salmon bathed in a pool of dill-cream sauce and a chilled bottle of Vouvray, then goes back to lamenting across the table to his lunch partner about the sorry state of the magazine industry. When he commissioned the piece, did he have any idea what you would face? Did he care? Did he actually want the story, or only want to have a look at what you came back with? And if it didn't appear all that compelling a story, would he toss you the standard 25 percent kill fee and be done with it? And if you didn't come back *at all*, you now think as you slog through the burning sands, feverishly cogitating on your editor's demonic logic, *he'd even save himself the 25 percent!*

In a hollow between dunes you see a heap of dung. The two camels stopped here. Their tracks move about in ambling circles. You see footprints here, too. You squat down and study the state of the dung's dryness, crumbling it between your fingers. A nomad could tell precisely when the camel had been here—the dung is totally dry after two days. The best you can do, however, is guess that it's less than two days but more than a few hours old.

You stand up, staggering dizzily. You try to make out the intertwined camel tracks again. But the two camel tracks split. One veers south across the next dune. The other keeps to the east. There must have been a rider on each of these camels. Which should you follow? The wall of an insurmountable problem now looms before you. You decide to sit on the hot sand to think it over. Your legs suddenly crumple underneath you, and you realize right then that you're not going to walk any farther this day.

You set out again in the evening. You've survived the blazing heat of the afternoon by scraping away the hot surface of sand to the cooler layer underneath and sitting on it, using your robe as a kind of tent around your body. Adolph's studies revealed—as nomads and old desert rats surely knew intuitively—that the best means of saving your body water in desert heat of 100 degrees was to sit quietly in one's clothes in good shade or under a night sky, both acts using 0.3 liter of water per hour in sweat. Sitting clothed in the sun jumped the sweat loss to 0.5 liter per hour, and lying clothed in the sun, which exposes more of your body's surface to heat gain from the sun's rays, pushed it to around 0.7 liter per hour sweat loss. Walking nude in the sun was the worst thing the desert wanderer could do—a whopping 1.2 liters loss per hour.

Even in your tent of shade your body had to cool itself, squeezing another liter of water from its sweat glands that instantly evaporated in the 5 percent humidity. You had to drink—a lot. Two liters. This doesn't nearly make up for your deficit. You're still down a total of 3.5 liters—5 percent of your body weight—but you're feeling much stronger than you did in the daytime. The goatskin hangs flaccidly in your arms when you pick it up. You shake it. Only 4 of its original 10 liters still slosh about. You have no idea how far those 4 liters will have to take you. You realize how deeply you depleted your water reserves—both in your *gerba* and in your body—by trying to walk in the heat of the day. When you pee, the small stream of urine looks a dark orange. Your kidneys hold back all the water they can.

The half-moon, tonight closer to a three-quarters moon, is high overhead and very bright in the clear desert air. You follow the camel track that bears east instead of the one heading south. That's the way the caravan was headed to start, and you stick to your conviction that that is where the next water must lie. Or are they testing you somehow? Is the split in the path a trick? But you know they'll need water in the next day or so. If you can do another 15 or so miles tonight, and another 10 or 15 tomorrow or tomorrow night, you're bound to reach the watering spot. But can you walk that far on 4 liters?

The dunes roll on unchanging in the sand sea of the *erg*. You carry on, *gerba* securely tucked under arm and notebook stuffed in back pocket. During the heat of the afternoon you even managed to make some notes on the Sufi belief that they are travelers on a quest. In the bright moonlight you trace with your eye the dark thread of camel tracks rolling over the dune tops and down into their shadowy hollows, on and on, until they disappear where the black sky rests on the desert horizon. To your mind, it's no accident that Sufism was founded in and around deserts. In the barrenmost heart of the desert, the central human metaphor is the journey—the journey to come out on the other side, alive, but somehow transformed.

Sitting with the Sufi back at the oasis, the blue of the late afternoon sky turned to the pinkish orange of evening. You pulled a few faded, threadbare bills of the local currency from your pocket, and asked the boy who served as your translator to bring some green tea and palm sugar for the Sufi as a gift. He returned a few minutes later with two bundles wrapped in dried straw and a fat melon. When you offered them to the Sufi, however, he declined them.

"No, they are for you," the Sufi said. "You eat the melon and drink the tea. The Sufi traveling along the path to love must pass through the stage of poverty. When the self that once desired riches no longer exists, the stage of poverty is transcended, and the beloved is all that matters. That is why we say *idha tamima'l faqr, fahwallah* 'where poverty is complete, there is God.' "

Now you understood the Sufi's patched robe and simple hut. Their original outfit centuries ago had been a coarse robe of undyed wool called a *suf*—hence the name Sufi.

The boy ran with the gifts to a mud hut nearby, and a woman there prepared the tea in a pot on a small brazier full of glowing coals and sliced the melon. When the glasses of tea and slices of melon were brought to you on a small wooden tray, the Sufi, with his quiet smile, gestured for you to eat and drink.

You did, gratefully. It wasn't as if you'd taken the vow of poverty yourself. The melon was sweet and juicy and the tea sweet and hot, and though it was thick with tea leaves and bits of fiber from the brown palm sugar, it was curiously refreshing, as ever, in the desert air.

"What are the other six stages?" you asked the Sufi as you sipped tea and ate melon, trying to keep your notebook and pen at the ready. This presented some logistical problems, because by tradition in this part of the world you could use only your right hand to eat, never your left, and your right was also your note-taking hand.

"We Sufis have no single doctrine," said the Sufi. "Each *murshid*—guide—might have his own set of stages, but many of the stages are the same."

He listed the most common ones:

1. *Tawba*—repentance or conversion
2. *Wara*—fear of the Lord

3. *Zuhd*—detachment
4. *Faqr*—poverty
5. *Sabr*—patience or endurance
6. *Tawakkul*—trust or self-surrender to God
7. *Rida*—contentment

Then, in his melodious, chanting voice, the Sufi looked toward the sky and quoted the Sheikh Attar ("the Druggist," for that had formerly been his profession in thirteenth-century Persia), one of the greatest writers and poets of the Sufi mystics, who had expressed his version of the stages this way:

> There are seven valleys on the way. . . . The first valley is questing and seeking. Next to it is the vale of Love; then the vale of Knowledge. The fourth is detachment and liberty of heart. The fifth pure unification. The sixth grievous bewilderment. The seventh, Poverty and utter loss of self. After that valley there is no more deliberate advance: going is forgone, henceforth one is drawn.

You sit and rest for a few hours before dawn, dozing fitfully with head on knees. As the eastern sky brightens, you stand up stiffly and move on. Your plan is to travel as far as possible today before the sun heats the desert sand. You figured during the night's march you logged nearly 15 miles again. But the *gerba* now feels like an empty sack. You shake it. You're down to a mere 2 liters. You walked slowly, breathing easily, to avoid sweating or losing extra moisture through too-fast respiration, but even in the cool night air, you had to drink 2 liters to replace what you were losing and simply to keep up your strength to walk. You've maintained your level of dehydration where it was when you started the night's walk—a 5 percent water deficit by body weight. But now you have the heat of a desert day ahead of you, a mere 2 liters left in the *gerba*, and no idea how far you must walk.

After the first hour, the terrain begins to change. In the hollows between the rolling soft dunes you walk over a gravelly, claylike hardpan. Then the dunes suddenly end—you must have left the *erg*, at least for a while. You take this to be a good sign. Instead you're on a rolling, gravelly plain—the *reg*—although it's still soft enough to show the camel tracks. Half an hour later you reach what appears to be an old, dried-up streambed. A few tufts of vegetation cling to its gravelly crease. The tracks keep going. Another half hour across the plain you reach another shallow, dried-up channel. Here grow two stunted acacia trees. There must be water deep underneath the surface. The sun has now climbed high in the morning sky, and the desert floor has begun to bake. You know you should stay under the shade of the acacia until the heat of the day has passed. But you have only 2 liters of water left—the thinnest of cushions against the intensity of the desert heat. You don't know if you can last another whole day waiting here plus another night's march on the sloshing puddle of water that remains in the *gerba*. You sense that water lies close ahead. You know this will be a fateful decision.

You decide to keep walking.

By noon you know you are in trouble. It doesn't matter anymore whether the decision to keep walking was right or wrong. What matters to you now is simply to keep going. Walking through the hot morning sun, you've drained the last two liters. The *gerba* dangles empty from your shoulder. But the water you drank through the morning hasn't replaced the 1.5 liters of water you sweated out during the morning's hike. Added to your previous 3.5-liter deficit at dawn, this puts you down 5 liters, or 7.1 percent of your body weight, back into the cotton-mouth range. With every effortful step over the gentle rises of the gravelly plain of the *reg* you expect to see a caravan stopped around a well, or the deep green palm fronds of an oasis tracing along some watercourse. You see neither of these things. What you do see is a bluish haze in the distance that looks like mountains.

You can only think about following the camel tracks—their slow, purposeful plod—and about the visions of water you'll find at the end: the oasis, the swimming pool, the drinking fountain, the glass of drinking water at your editor's lunch table. You force yourself to keep walking. You are now in a sprinting race—a hobbled, stumbling sprint—between the rapidly dwindling moisture in your body and the distance that lies to relief. In an hour of plodding in the desert sun you've lost another liter. Your body starts moving more quickly through the phases of dehydration. You're now down 6 liters—8.6 percent of your body weight. At an 8 percent deficit, as Adolph's experiments found with soldiers, your heart is pounding 40 beats per minute faster than normal—or 110 beats instead of 70— but it's putting out considerably less blood volume with each beat than normal. As the water in your blood plasma leaches away to cool your body in the form of sweat, your blood is thickening like oil. Your pulse rises and stroke volume drops, apparently because it takes your heart more and more energy to pump that ever-thickening blood.

If you looked back at your own tracks, you'd see them weaving and stumbling across the *reg*. Still you keep following the camel tracks toward the bluish mountains, past 10 percent deficit, 7 liters down, and you stumble onward into the "shriveled-tongue" phase. As your blood thickens, the process of osmosis causes water from in- side your body's cells to pass through the cell walls and help thin your blood plasma. In effect, your body sucks the moisture out of its living cells to keep its blood liquid enough to flow.

With each beat you hear a crackling in your desiccated ears and see stars jump before your eyes. At times the noise sounds like music coming from just over the next rise. You try to walk faster to reach it, but your feet drag as if the dry white stones themselves were tied to your sandals, and then you realize once again it's only noise in your ears. Your skin turns numb and tingly. The khaki pants you wear beneath the robe grate annoyingly on your skin. You have the robe; you don't need the pants. You lift your robe, unfasten your belt, drop your khakis down your legs, followed by your boxer shorts, and kick them off on the gravelly plain. The freeness around your legs gives some relief from the grating of your leathery skin. But you see you've left your notebook in your pants pocket. You pick it up. You have no pocket for it in your T-shirt beneath the robe. It's too much to carry both the *gerba* and the notebook. You don't need the empty *gerba*. You slip it from your shoulder, drop it to the sand, and stumble onward.

Your head now throbs as if an iron band tightened across your skull. You scratch and tug beneath the turban at your pounding head. You want to unwind it, throw it away. But some deep instinct tells you to keep it on. You're now breathing heavily through desiccated airways. Your eyelids have stiffened from the dryness and don't close properly over your eyeballs. You're developing the desert-thirst victim's characteristic "winkless stare." Your numbed limbs no longer seem attached to your own body; the hand holding the notebook drifts oddly out in front of you, as if carried by someone else. Late in the "shriveled-tongue" stage, reported McGee, one desert prospector, "seeing a luscious-looking arm near by, . . . seized it and mumbled it with his mouth, and greedily sought to suck the blood; he had a vague sense of protest by the owner of the arm, who seemed a long way off, and was astounded two days later to find that the wounds were inflicted on himself."

Your moist tissues exposed to the air dessicate first—mouth, nose, lips. Your body has literally begun to mummify from the outside in while you are still alive. The saliva now has entirely ceased to flow in your mouth, and the mucus has dried into a thick film over your tongue, deadening it. The gums of your teeth and the linings of your nostrils, ordinarily containing much moisture, shrink as the water leaves them. Your nose is literally growing smaller. The lump in your dried-out throat feels like a solid, immovable rock, despite your constant and involuntary reflex to swallow. Finally your tongue hardens into a dead weight. You notice an odd clunking sound in your mouth. Then you realize that with each of your slogging foot-steps across the baking *reg*, your hardened tongue swings like a pendulum on the still-moist tissues of its root and clunks against your teeth. It is this that gives the "shriveled-tongue" phase its dis-tinctive name.

In this phase—if not before—thirst victims often will drink al-most anything to wet their mouths. *Mariposia* is the name given to the drinking of seawater, *hemoposia* to the drinking of blood, and *uriposia* to the drinking of urine—either their own or an animal's. Uriposia is done commonly by those in a bad state of dehydration and was a well-accepted practice in the Southwest and Mexican deserts during McGee's day, at least to wet one's mouth with urine. Even when dehydrated by 7 or 8 percent of body weight, the human body, which normally produces about 1.5 liters of urine per day, con-tinues to produce urine at a reduced rate, although it is believed that the flow ceases altogether as one approaches lethal water deficits. Whether drinking urine helps is not entirely clear, and may depend on many factors; drinking seawater does not slake thirst due to its high salt content. Animal fluids apparently are a different matter. Desert nomads sometimes sacrifice their camels when in desperate circumstances and, piercing the abdomen with knife or sword, drink the bloody, yellowish green liquid—vegetal pap—that pours forth from the incision. One U.S. calvary detachment chasing a band of Indians in 1877 in Texas promptly ran out of water, and members re-ported that they survived only by sucking on the coagulated blood of their dying horses as the party staggered back across the plains to the lake where they'd begun their intemperate pursuit.

Your tongue clunking against your teeth, you stop. You feel a distant need to pee. If you could just moisten your tongue enough, you think, you could keep going farther across the plain, toward the bluish mountains. You lift your robe. Swaying in the desert heat, you try to pee. It takes a long, long time to will up the urine from deep inside you. Your eyes seem to dry further as you stand there, trying to concentrate. It's difficult to see the camel tracks except as a blurry line heading toward the bluish mountains of the horizon. Finally, stinging, the urine trickles out—the color of rusty water. You catch an ounce or two in your cupped hand. You bring it up to your mouth. There is no sense of disgust, only a desire for its liquid. You suck it between your thin, dried lips and hold it in your mouth to moisten your tongue—it tastes salty and wet—and swallow it down your throat, momentarily alleviating the lump. You hold out your hand for more, but nothing comes, no matter how hard you try.

The first blast of wind strikes you from behind, knocking you forward as if you'd tripped on a large stone. The second gust knocks you off your feet. You're on hands and knees on the baked sand and stones, your reporter's notebook still clutched in your right hand, as the sandstorm sweeps over you in a hot, tannish yellow cloud of dust and fine particles of sand. Crouched on the desert floor, the wind whipping your robe, the sand stinging your skin, you try to wrap your *tagilmust* tightly around your face, but the wind rips its end from your hands so that it flutters like a flag in a strong wind. Instead, you pull your head down into the robe, out of the stinging sand and hot wind, and sit there, unsteadily, feverish, only wanting to go on.

You remember the first time you saw the Sahara; it gave you the idea and the desire to come back to follow the nomads. You'd been in southern Spain on an assignment, and you'd taken a ferry to Morocco, rented a car in Tangier, and drove it south, over the mountain range known as the High Atlas, until you reached the edge of the desert. As you crested the mountain pass on the narrow paved road, you could see far out across the great expanse of the Sahara. Far down below you a sandstorm was blowing, filling the great basin of the desert with a luminous yellow haze like an ocean, the sky still a crystalline blue above. As you drove down into it toward an oasis on the desert's edge, the storm and its blowing sand literally blasted the paint off the front of the car.

You are now at the bottom of that blasting yellow ocean, huddled beneath your robe, arms wrapped around you, cradling your life.

The storm ends just as suddenly as it arose. You push your head up through the robe. It takes you three tries to get to your feet. You try to get your bearings. Something is missing: your reporter's notebook. You were holding it in your hand, but you had to set it down to create a shelter out of your robe. It is now no doubt blowing at 40 to 50 miles per hour somewhere to the southeast.

For the moment, you're too dehydrated to understand what you've lost. You stagger forward, following the dim line that remains of the camel tracks.

At a 12 percent water deficit, you've crossed the divide. You can no longer swallow on your own, and if you do find water, you will need someone's help to rehydrate. The potential death zone of dehydration begins soon—at about a 15 percent deficit. No one knows exactly where the boundaries lie that mark the last two phases of thirst described by McGee. The lips and gums and tongue and other tissues crack open with festering wounds, and the tongue swells and forces its way between the teeth and out of the mouth. Flies gather on the tongue and other tissues and drink the blood and fluids that weep from the cracks and the tears of blood that fall from around the eyes. Carrion-eating birds congregate around the victim. A friend of McGee's, an old hand in Mexico's Seri Desert, rescued a vaquero who had been thrown by his horse three days earlier, and graphically described the victim when he found him as "sweating blood and fighting buzzards." For this stage of thirst, McGee used the term "blood sweat."

The final phase—"living death," in McGee's parlance—is a continuation of the previous stage. If the trails the victims leave in the sand and dust are followed, he wrote, one can see that they rip at their scalps and tear out clumps of their hair to lessen the sense of a band tightening around their skulls. They hallucinate that rocks or shrubs or sharp-thorned cacti are pools and carafes of water in which they dig their fingers or onto which they skewer their faces in the attempt to take a drink. Even to more modern researchers, it is not clear what finally kills a victim of dehydration. In cases of desert thirst in hot temperatures, heatstroke may be what kills the victim, as a severely dehydrated victim cannot effectively dispel body heat.

But even in the latter stages, victims of thirst are able to follow a trail to water even though they can barely move or see. Something tells you to keep moving forward. Now you're stumbling badly. You constantly hear noises and music and the harsh rasping sound of your own breathing through desiccated lungs. The desert periodically blurs to a luminous hemisphere above and a darker hemisphere below bisected by the camel track. The robe grates against your parched skin, and you feel a painful tightening around your chest. You don't need the robe. It's too hot. You pull the robe over your head, strip off your T-shirt, tug off your *tagilmust* with its iron bands that have tightened around your skull. The naked legs and arms, drying and cracking in the sun, are not yours. They were left here in the desert to turn to leather by some passing animal. There's a person here, too. You watch him from a distance. He's very tired and thirsty. You leave him behind, too, along with the pile of clothing and the arms and legs.

You stumble onward, following the thin line that leads between the blurry hemispheres of light and dark.

Late that afternoon, a young nomad boy is rounding up his family's camels and goats that have been grazing on a few tufts of grass in a *wadi*—a seasonal riverbed—when he sees a strange naked form crawling along the dry stones. At first he thinks it is some unknown animal—perhaps one of the crocodiles he has heard about that live in the lakes far to the south—but as he approaches cautiously, he sees it resembles a man. Not Imazaghen but a French—the nomad name for all Europeans. His skin is a peculiar gray, his lips have shrunken and turned black, his nose looks like two round holes in his skull, and his eyes, set deep in their sockets, stare at the boy unblinking while the strange man-animal's chest heaves in and out with a bellowing sound. The boy nears the man-animal, his staff at the ready to beat him away if necessary, but the man-animal seems to recognize a living form; his forearms crumple, and he collapses face first into the sand and rocks.

The boy leaves him there. He runs in sandals and robe back to the nomad encampment in the small oasis at the foot of the blue mountains and tells his father what he has seen. Soon a group of nomad men ride camels quickly to the spot, led by the boy riding in front of his father. They know it is not a crocodile or a man-beast but a desiccated French. They pick him up—he is not very heavy, like a dried-out goatskin—prop him into a saddle, where he is held securely by the nomad sitting behind him, and ride him back to their camp.

They lay him on the sandy earth, and the nomad women—some of them bare-breasted—come from their low, goat-hair tents to look at the dried-out French as he is lifted down from the camel. His skin is shrunken around his bones, his belly a deep hollow.

"Like a baby goat that has lost its mother," one of the women says.

If this were the emergency room of a Western hospital instead of a remote Saharan oasis, medical personnel would immediately fix intravenous drips to the victim that contain mostly water, adjusting their exact content once an imbalance of sodium or other substances in his blood was determined. But the nearest medical care—a single village nurse—lies on the other side of hundreds of naked miles of *reg* and *erg*. Together, the men and women make preparations for the traditional method to revive desiccated victims of desert thirst, the method that Saharan dwellers have developed over centuries of experience, as recorded in detail in the 1930s by a French military doctor among the Goranes of the Central Sahara. Some victims can no longer swallow, and if the victim is still able to drink when he or she is found, the desire is to pour water down the throat without stopping until vomiting occurs.

The women now fetch goatskins of water and a robe. The men squat around his naked form and would have stripped away any clothing had he still worn it. The victim is semiconscious, stirring vaguely, mouth moving as if trying to talk. They very carefully pour drops of water onto certain areas of his skin—into the hollows formed atop the shoulder by the clavicle, the armpits, the bend of the elbows, the hollow of the stomach, the folds of the groin. The nomads pat the moistened areas lightly with their hands. They slowly pour out water—drop by drop—over the victim's head and face and pat them lightly, and then repeat the sprinkling and patting on the victim's legs. They take the robe, sprinkle it with water, and cover the moistened victim with it. He falls into a light sleep. A short while later, he wakes. He makes noises with his mouth. Splashing the contents from a *gerba* into a wooden bowl, the nomads give him a little water to drink. He swallows with great difficulty. They then remove the robe and again drip water on all the sensitive areas of his skin, pat it, cover him again, and give him a small drink, repeating the process over and over. Finally the victim falls into a deep sleep.

What you first hear as you come to consciousness is music—a slow, rhythmic beat of drums and what sounds like tambourines. There are voices, too—chanting voices. You open your eyes. You are lying on your back on the ground. The sky vaults overhead in the cool purples of dusk. Palm fronds fringe the purple sky, and orange firelight flickers up their trunks, illuminating their fat bunches of dates. Blue-turbaned heads pulse rhythmically over you, a circle of heads that constricts around you in a ring, rhythmically withdraws to the clanging, thumping beat, then constricts again, slowly turning around you like a wheel around its axle. The nomads are dancing.

You're aware of your weakness and your thirst. Your mouth is no longer dry, but you feel a thirst that stems from your core, outward through your limbs, and beyond them into the desert night, a thirst as broad as the Sahara itself. A veiled man now squats beside you and, his eyes glittering in the firelight over his veil, puts his hand behind your head to lift it slightly to a wooden bowl of water at your lips. You drink. It is the sweetest, coolest water you have ever tasted— artesian water that fell as rain far away on the Sahara in Paleolithic times and slowly migrated beneath the sands to seep from a break between the barren sandy hills and feed the palms of the oasis and their bunches of succulent, sun-sweetened dates. The water flowing between your lips seems a kind of miracle to you. This single bowl of water somehow survived amid the sucking dryness of the desert sands, the superheated, waterless atmosphere that hovers above it, and the desiccated vacuum of the heavens above that arches over both. All the gold and all the books in the world mean nothing beside this one bowl of water. Without this single bowl of water, you are simply dust drifting through those heavens.

You drift off to sleep again to the sound of the drums and the tambourines and the chanting, the veiled faces and glittering eyes and swaying robes and bare breasts slowly wheeling in the firelight against the now black sky. Are they doing all this chanting and moving on your behalf? You don't know. You don't really care at this point. You lapse into dreams of valleys—dry, barren, sandy moonlit valleys—one after the other that you are struggling across. Something good awaits you on the other side. You don't know why and you don't know what, only that you must keep moving through the valleys, down one sandy side, across the hard flat bottom, up the other soft, bogging slope. You had in your hand a wooden bowl that's extremely important, but somehow you've lost it. You miss it, but you know you must leave it behind and keep going.

In your dream, you remember bits of the Rumi poem the Sufi quoted for you:

> In whatever state you may be, keep on the search!
> Thou dry-lipped one, ever be on the search for water!
> Thou dry lip is a sure token
> That in the end it will find the source.
>
> This seeking is a blessed restlessness,
> It overcomes every obstacle and is the key to thy desires.
> Though thou have no vessel, fail not to seek . . .
> Sooner or later he who seeks become he who finds.

When you awaken again, the circle of faces has widened and is moving faster, the drums and tambourines are louder, there is a frenzy to the dance. A pair of dusty, bare, cracked, and callused feet spin in the sand beside your head. You follow them upward to a whirling patched robe, and then, illuminated by the flickering orange light, to a face that you recognize. It's the Sufi. He is spinning rapidly in the center of the circle of nomads with his arms extended, like a top. Now you understand what they are doing. He described to you the Sufi practice of *sama*—a ritual of chanted poetry, much of it love poetry, and music and dance that transports its participants into a trancelike state of ecstasy. In the center of the circle, the spinning Sufi represents the sun, and the dancers are the planets revolving around him.

But what is the Sufi doing here? He should be back at the last oasis, nearly two hundred miles across *reg* and *erg*.

One of the veiled nomad men from beyond the circle sees that you are awake again, and comes forward with a wooden bowl of water. He crouches beside you and once more puts it to your lips.

When you have drunk a few more sips, you try to address him through the drums and tambourines and chanting, using your few words of Tamachek.

"From where does this Sufi come?" you ask.

"From far away," says the nomad.

"But how did he get here?" you ask.

"Do you not know?" says the nomad. "It was he who brought you here. It was he who sent you out into the desert, and he who left his tracks for you to follow."

You will slowly come to understand other things, too, from your experience in the desert. The desert indeed is a place of nakedness that strips away the superfluous layers of the self as it peels away the fertile green layer of life that covers so much of the planet. Like the oxygenless summit of a Himalayan peak or the silent, motionless cold of a 40-below-zero Arctic night, the desert teaches you just how thin that layer of life is, and how fragile your own hold on it. Stepping beyond that fragile layer is no more difficult than shedding your clothes on a cold winter night or walking for a few hours without water in the hot sun. And when you finally do step beyond it, the ego, the vanity, the insignificance, and—often—the pettiness of so much of what passes for human endeavor and striving become abundantly clear. This is what the great religions and the shamans and the Sufi all are trying to tell you—to step beyond the self that blinds you, as the Sufi knows, having stripped away material wealth and worldly ambitions in his pursuit of union, spinning with ecstasy under the stars in the naked desert night.

This is why you climb mountains, and paddle whitewater rivers, and trek into the desert, and seek out remote places; to strip away the superfluous, to remove the protective boundaries between that thing you call a self and something larger. Your body still lies weakened and half shriveled, slowly taking on water to restore itself fully to life, but already as you lie in the sand with the flames of the fire jumping into the night, the desert tempts you back to it. The mountains tempt you to climb them. The rivers tempt you to run them. The remote places beckon.

It is not a question of whether you will go again.

The question for you is: where next?

And the other question is: how far?

SOURCES

Wilderness Medicine Instruction and Reference Books

Auerbach, Paul S., M.D., Howard J. Donner, M.D., and Eric A. Weiss, M.D. *Field Guide to Wilderness Medicine*. St. Louis: Mosby, 1999.

Auerbach, Paul S., M.D. (ed.). *Wilderness Medicine: Management of Wilderness and Environmental Emergencies*. St. Louis: Mosby, 1995.

Forgey, William, M.D. *Wilderness Medicine: Beyond First Aid*. Guilford, CT: Globe Pequot Press, 1999.

Wilkerson, James, M.D. *Medicine for Mountaineering and Other Wilderness Activities*. Seattle: The Mountaineers, 1992.

General

Bodanis, David. *The Body Book*. Boston: Little, Brown and Company, 1984.

Byock, Ira, M.D. *Dying Well: The Prospect for Growth at the End of Life*. New York: Riverhead Books, 1997.

Edholm, Dr. O. G., and A. L. Bacharach. *The Physiology of Human Survival*. London: Academic Press, 1975.

Editors of the National Geographic Society. *The Incredible Machine*. Washington, DC: National Geographic Society, 1986.

Hoffmann, Yoel (ed.). *Japanese Death Poems*. Rutland, VT: Charles E. Tuttle Company, 1986.

Isselbacher, Kurt J., M.D., et al. (eds.). *Harrison's Principles of Internal Medicine*. New York: McGraw-Hill, 1994.

Kübler-Ross, Elisabeth, M.D. *On Death and Dying*. New York: Simon and Schuster, 1969.

———. *Death: The Final Stage of Growth*. New York: Simon and Schuster, 1975.

Nuland, Sherwin B., M.D. *How We Die: Reflections on Life's Final Chapter*. New York: Alfred A. Knopf, 1994.

Pandolf, Kent B., Michael N. Sawka, and Richard R. Gonzalez (eds.). *Human Performance Physiology and Environmental Medicine at Terrestrial Extremes*. Carmel, IN: Cooper Publishing Group, n.d.

Schwartz, George R., M.D. *Principles and Practice of Emergency Medicine*. Philadelphia: Lippincott Williams and Wilkins, 1999.

Stein, Jay H., M.D. (ed.). *Internal Medicine*. St. Louis: Mosby, 1994.

Takahashi, Takeo. *Atlas of the Human Body*. New York: HarperCollins, 1994.

Avalanche

Armstrong, Betsy, and Knox Williams. *The Avalanche Book*, Golden, CO: Fulcrum, 1986.

Carter, Rita. *Mapping the Mind*. Berkeley: University of California Press, 1998.

Kotulak, Ronald. *Inside the Brain*. Kansas City: Andrews and McMeel, 1996.

Ornstein, Robert, and Richard F. Thompson. *The Amazing Brain*. Boston: Houghton Mifflin, 1984.

Ramachandran, V. S., M.D., and Sandra Blakeslee. *Phantoms in the Brain: Probing the Mysteries of the Human Mind*. New York: William Morrow, 1998.

Robbins, Jim. *A Symphony in the Brain: The Evolution of the New Brain Wave Biofeedback*. New York: Atlantic Monthly Press, 2000.

Bends

Berger, Karen. *Scuba Diving*. New York: W. W. Norton, 2000.

Bove, Alfred A., M.D. (ed.). *Diving Medicine*. Philadelphia: Harcourt Brace, 1997.

De Latil, Pierre, and Jean Rivoire. *Man and the Underwater World*. New York: G. P. Putnam's Sons, 1956.

Lyon, Eugene. *The Search for the Atocha*. New York: Harper and Row, 1979.

Mathewson, R. Duncan III. *Treasure of the Atocha*. New York: E. P. Dutton, 1986.

Meyer, Franz O. *Diving and Snorkeling Guide to Belize*. Houston, TX: Gulf Publishing, 1990.

Middleton, Ned. *Diving Belize*. Locust Valley, NY: Aqua Quest Publications, 1994.

Dehydration

Adolph, E. F., and Associates. *Physiology of Man in the Desert*. New York: Interscience Publishers, 1947.

Bowles, Paul. *Their Heads Are Green and Their Hands Are Blue*. New York: Ecco Press, 1984.

Christopher, Robert, with Erik James Martin. *Ocean of Fire: From the Garden of Allah to Timbuktu*. New York: Rand McNally, 1956.

Englebert, Victor. *Wind, Sand and Silence: Travels with Africa's Last Nomads*. San Francisco: Chronicle Books, 1992.

Ernst, Carl W. *The Shambhala Guide to Sufism*. Boston: Shambhala Publications, 1997.

Gardi, René. *Sahara*. Bern, Switzerland: Kümmerly and Frey Geographical Publishers, 1970.

Gautier, E. F. *Sahara: The Great Desert*. New York: Columbia University Press, 1935.

Kruger, Christoph (ed.). *Sahara*. New York: G. P. Putnam's Sons, 1969.

Rice, Cyprian. *The Persian Sufis*. London: George Allen and Unwin, 1964.

Smith, Margaret. *Readings from the Mystics of Islam*. London: Luzac, 1972.

Von Dumreicher, André. *Trackers and Smugglers in the Deserts of Egypt*. New York: Dial Press, 1931.

Wolf, A. V. *Thirst: Physiology of the Urge to Drink and Problems of Water Lack*. Springfield, IL: Charles C. Thomas, 1958.

Drowning

Lao Tzu. *Tao Te Ching*. Trans. by Gia-Fu Feng and Jane English. New York: Random House, 1989.

Modell, Jerome H. *The Pathophysiology and Treatment of Drowning and Near-Drowning*. Springfield, IL: Charles C. Thomas, 1971.

Shepard, Roy J., M.D. *Exercise Physiology*. Toronto: B. C. Decker, 1987.

Strauss, Richard H., M.D. (ed.). *Sports Medicine and Physiology*. Philadelphia: W. B. Saunders, 1979.

Falling

Gardiner, Steve. *Why I Climb: Personal Insights of Top Climbers*. Harrisburg, PA: Stackpole Books, 1990.

Long, John. *How to Rock Climb*. Evergreen, CO: Chockstone Press, 1989.

Potterfield, Peter. *In the Zone: Epic Survival Stories from the Mountaineering World*. Seattle: The Mountaineers, 1996.

Poynter, Dan. *Parachuting: The Skydiver's Handbook*. Santa Barbara, CA: Para Publishing, 1992.

Roberts, David. *Moments of Doubt*. Seattle: The Mountaineers, 1986.

Simpson, Joe. *Touching the Void*. New York: Harper and Row, 1988.

Heatstroke

Edholm, Otto G. *Man—Hot and Cold*. London: Edward Arnold, 1978.

Ingram, D. L., and L. E. Mount. *Man and Animals in Hot Environments*. New York: Springer-Verlag, 1975.

Kavaler, Lucy. *A Matter of Degree: Heat, Life and Death*. New York: Harper and Row, 1981.

Hypothermia

Burton, Alan C., and Otto G. Edholm. *Man in a Cold Environment: Physiological and Pathological Effects of Exposure to Low Temperatures*. London: Arnold, 1955.

Collins, K. J. *Hypothermia: The Facts*. New York: Oxford University Press, 1983.

Forgey, William W., M.D. *Basic Essentials: Hypothermia*. Guilford, CT: Globe Pequot Press, 1999.

Kavaler, Lucy. *Freezing Point: Cold as a Matter of Life and Death*. John Day, 1970.

Jellyfish and Predators

Caras, Roger A. *Dangerous to Man*. Philadelphia: Chilton Books, 1964.

Halstead, Bruce W., M.D. *Poisonous and Venomous Marine Animals of the World*. Princeton, NJ: Darwin Press, 1978.

Ricciuti, Edward R. *Killer Animals*. New York: Walker, 1976.

Williamson, John A., et al. (eds.). *Venomous and Poisonous Marine Animals: A Medical and Biological Handbook*. Sydney: University of New South Wales Press, 1996.

Malaria

Knell, A. J. (ed.). *Malaria: Publication of the Tropical Programme of the Wellcome Trust*. Oxford: Oxford University Press, 1991.

Kreier, Julius P. (ed.). *Malaria*. 3 vols. New York: Academic Press, 1980.

Oakes, Stanley C. Jr. (ed.). *Malaria: Obstacles and Opportunities: A Report of the Committee for the Study of Malaria Prevention and Control*. Washington, DC: National Academy Press, 1991.

Mountain Sickness

Blum, Arlene. *Annapurna: A Woman's Place*. San Francisco: Sierra Club Books, 1980.

Curran, Jim. *K2: Triumph and Tragedy*. Boston: Houghton Mifflin, 1987.

Davidson, Art. *Minus 148°: First Winter Ascent of Mt. McKinley*. Seattle: The Mountaineers, 1969.

Evans-Wentz, W. Y. *The Tibetan Book of the Dead*. New York: Oxford University Press, 1960.

Herzog, Maurice. *Annapurna.* New York: Lyons Press, 1997. (Originally published: New York: Dutton, 1952.)

Houston, Charles S., M.D. *Going High: The Story of Man and Altitude.* Burlington, VT: Charles S. Houston, M.D., and American Alpine Club, 1980.

Hultgren, Herbert N., M.D. *High Altitude Medicine.* Stanford, CA: Hultgren Publications, 1997.

Iserson, Kenneth V., M.D. *Death to Dust: What Happens to Dead Bodies?* Tucson, AZ: Galen Press, 1994.

Krakauer, Jon. *Into Thin Air.* New York: Villard, 1997.

Sogyal, Rinpoche. *The Tibetan Book of Living and Dying.* New York: HarperCollins, 1993.

Sutton, John R., Charles S. Houston, and Geoffrey Coates (eds.). *Hypoxia and Cold.* New York: Praeger Publishers, 1980.

Thurman, Robert A. F. (trans.). *The Tibetan Book of the Dead: Liberation Through Understanding in the Between.* New York: Bantam Books, 1994.

Tullis, Julie. *Clouds from Both Sides: An Autobiography.* San Francisco: Sierra Club Books, 1987.

Scurvy

Brody, Tom. *Nutritional Biochemistry.* San Diego: Academic Press, 1999.

Carpenter, Kenneth J. *The History of Scurvy and Vitamin C.* Cambridge: Cambridge University Press, 1986.

Cuppage, Francis E. *James Cook and the Conquest of Scurvy.* Westport, CT: Greenwood Press, 1994.

Deutsch, Ronald M. *Realities of Nutrition.* Palo Alto, CA: Bull Publishing, 1976.

Kutsky, Roman J. *Handbook of Vitamins, Minerals and Hormones.* New York: Van Nostrand Reinhold, 1981.

Merck Service Bulletin. *Vitamin C.* Rahway, NJ: Merck, 1956.

Steller, Georg Wilhelm. *Journal of a Voyage with Bering, 1741–1742.* O. W. Frost (ed.) and trans. by Margritt A. Engel and O. W. Frost. Stanford: Stanford University Press, 1988.

Wentzler, Rich. *The Vitamin Book.* New York: St. Martin's Press, 1978.

Join Peter Stark as he embarks on the adventure of a lifetime . . .
AT THE MERCY OF THE RIVER

Even in this age of extreme sports and made-for-TV survival games, there still exist places on earth where the most intrepid among us can plunge into truly unknown territory. The acclaimed adventure writer Peter Stark had waited all his life for just such an opportunity. But when he was invited to Africa to join a small expedition kayaking down Mozambique's Lugenda River, he balked. The 750-kilometer river-course was largely uncharted—dotted with rapids, waterfalls, and home to deadly crocodiles and hippos; two of his four travel companions were not skilled kayakers; and he had a family to think of (not to mention that at forty-eight, he himself was feeling a bit old for the life untamed). Suppressing inner doubts and driven by that most human of urges—to see what lies beyond the next bend—Stark signed on for the adventure of a lifetime.

At the Mercy of the River is at times inspiring, heart-thumping, and even amusing. But most of all, it is a riveting adventure story for a time when adventure is in danger of losing its meaning.

 A Ballantine Book • www.ballantinebooks.com

ABOUT THE AUTHOR

PETER STARK is a longtime contributor to *Outside* whose work has also appeared in *Smithsonian*, *The New Yorker*, and many other publications. His article for *Outside*, "As Freezing Persons Recollect the Snow"—the inspiration for this book—was cited as a notable essay in *Best American Essays* (1997). He has been nominated for a National Magazine Award and has published a collection of essays, *Driving to Greenland*. He is also the editor of an anthology of writings about the Arctic, *Ring of Ice*. His assignments and travels have taken him to the Arctic, Tibet, Manchuria, West Africa, Irian Jaya, Iceland, and the Sahara Desert. He lives in Missoula, Montana, with his wife and two young children.